READINGS IN WILDLIFE CONSERVATION

READINGS IN
WILDLIFE
CONSERVATION

EDITORS:
James A. Bailey
  Colorado State University
William Elder
  University of Missouri
Ted D. McKinney
  Oklahoma State University

THE WILDLIFE SOCIETY
Washington, D.C.
1974

The Wildlife Society, Inc.
5410 Grosvenor Lane
Bethesda, MD 20814

Library of Congress Catalog Card Number:

Bailey, James Allen, 1934-   comp.
    Readings in Wildlife Conservation.

    Includes bibliographies.
    1. Wildlife   Conservation—Addresses, esssays,   lectures.

I. Elder, William, 1913-   joint comp. II. McKinney,
Ted D., joint comp. III.Wildlife Society. IV. Title.
QL82.B34   639 '.9 '08   74-28405

ISBN 0-933564-02-3
Reprinted 1983

Editors: James A. Bailey, William Elder, Ted D. McKinney
Technical Editor: H.S. Bruce Linn

Printed in the United States of America for The Wildlife Society
by Valley Offset, Inc., Deposit, N.Y. 13754

ABOUT THE WILDLIFE SOCIETY

The Wildlife Society, founded in 1937, is a professional, nonprofit organization dedicated to the wise management and conservation of the wildlife resources of the world. Ecology is the primary scientific discipline of the wildlife profession. The interests of the Society, therefore, embrace the interactions of all organisms with their natural environments. The Society recognizes that humans, as other organisms, have a total dependency upon the environment. It is the Society's belief also that wildlife, in its myriad forms, is basic to the maintenance of a human culture that provides quality living.

The principal objectives of the Society are: to develop and promote sound stewardship of wildlife resources and of the environments upon which wildlife and humans depend; to undertake an active role in preventing human-induced environmental degradation; to increase awareness and appreciation of wildlife values; and to seek the highest standards in all activities of the wildlife profession.

The Society's membership of nearly 8,000 is comprised of research scientists, educators, communications specialists, conservation law enforcement officers, resource managers, and administrators from more than 40 countries of the world. Its purposes are served through chapter, sectional, national and international meetings, and by publication of the serials, *The Journal of Wildlife Management, Wildlife Monographs, Wildlife Society Bulletin,* and *The Wildlifer* newsletter. Selected books on scientific and professional subjects are used as textbooks, such as the 722-page *Wildlife Management Techniques Manual*, 4th Edition, the 1,344-page *Waterfowl Ecology and Management: Selected Readings*, and the 280-page *Wildlife Conservation Principles and Practices*, a basic work-book.

The Society's unique emblem features Egyptian hieroglyphics. The literal translation of the hieroglyphics, from top to bottom, is: beasts (mammals), birds, fishes, and flowering plants (vegetation).

DEDICATION

This book is dedicated to undergraduate students in wildlife conservation. The future of the wildlife resource depends upon their knowledge and skills and upon how they view their obligations as professionals.

This book is also dedicated to Professor Ralph T. King, whose teaching influenced the personal and professional lives of many young men in the profession.

Professor King was an organizer and first president of The Society of Wildlife Specialists in 1936. This Society became The Wildlife Society in 1937. He was awarded honorary membership in The Wildlife Society in 1964.

Professor King received an M. A. degree from Utah State Agricultural College, Logan in 1925. He served as instructor of zoology at Utah State Agricultural College, instructor of zoology at the University of Minnesota, Head of the Department of Biology at the College of St. Thomas, St. Paul, Minnesota, and chairman of the Department of Forest Zoology at the State University College of Forestry, Syracuse, New York. Retiring in 1965 after forty-two years of full-time teaching, he continued to lecture at many schools across the United States. Throughout his career he did more than teach facts and ideas. He encouraged in his students a philosophically-based dedication to their profession that was exemplified by his own unselfish devotion to their education.

FOREWORD

The Wildlife Society is a professionally oriented international organization with members in more than 70 countries. The Society believes that wildlife and other natural resources are interrelated and that they have a permanent place in our culture. To this end the Society membership is dedicated to sound management and preservation of wildlife resources of the world.

Since its inception in 1937, one of the principal goals of The Wildlife Society has been to increase awareness and appreciation of wildlife values. In line with this goal the Society has published or sponsored several major books to provide a better understanding of both wildlife resources and the environment upon which wildlife and man depend.

Although wildlife conservation is only about forty years old as a scientific profession, much has been written about this diverse subject. Unfortunately, many of the classical articles by the founders of the wildlife profession are out-of-print and more recent scientific contributions are difficult to obtain. To perpetuate these important works and stimulate the professional and layman alike, The Wildlife Society is pleased to sponsor Readings in Wildlife Conservation.

By bringing many of the early works together with more recent writings, the editors hope to establish a broader perspective in wildlife conservation. While the book is primarily directed at strengthening the interests of undergraduate students, it can also serve as a refresher course for both the seasoned conservationist and layman. It should instill and renew in every reader a philosophically based dedication to the wildlife profession. As a repository of selected professional papers, I hope Readings in Wildlife Conservation will be counted among the best sellers.

C. D. Besadny
President
The Wildlife Society

INTRODUCTION

These papers have been selected to present a broad perspective of wildlife conservation.

Wildlife conservation is the social process, including both professional and lay activities, which defines and seeks to attain wise use and perpetuation of wild animals and the biotic communities to which they belong.

Conservation is a social process because it includes the continuous melding of personal values and requires selections between salmon and electricity, elk and plywood, soybeans and prairie chickens. These value judgements are influenced by attitudes and practices of the past. Thus history provides insight for understanding today's conservation process. Public interest and participation in these value judgements may be stimulated by educational programs of public agencies and by activities of conservation organizations such as the Sierra Club and the great variety of sportsmen's clubs. Public agencies responsible for wildlife must seek awareness of the changing desires of people—for in the United States they own the wildlife.

The conservation process includes interactions among many kinds of people—trained professionals, politicians, and citizens, including agencies and organizations having a diversity of biases and interests. The wisdom of goals selected by this socio-political process will be debated as long as people differ in their backgrounds and interests. Thus, conservation remains a social process.

In addition, conservation is a social process because successful programs require communication and cooperation among professionals from many agencies—the State Division of Wildlife, the Forest Service, the Soil Conservation Service, the Bureau of Reclamation and many others. These professionals work in six activities—research, management, public relations, education, law enforcement and administration. Performance in all these activities and several agencies may be critical to success. Failure in one section of an agency often limits possibilities for achievement in others and affects morale and performance throughout the agency and even in other agencies.

Wildlife conservation is based upon knowledge from many sciences—ecology, chemistry, physics, mathematics, statistics, genetics, zoology, botany, economics and sociology. It employs the tools of many professions—agriculture, forestry, engineering, medicine, law, administration, public relations, accounting and planning. Wildlife conservation therefore has need for the specialist and the generalist. The specialist should have knowledge broad enough to comprehend the interrelated roles of the six conservation activities mentioned above. He should be aware of historical influences upon today's conservation and should have a sensitivity toward human values and the philosophical question of what constitutes *wise* use. The generalist should be adequately trained in the sciences so that he can communicate with specialists and can use scientific information to establish realistic goals for solving conservation problems.

Papers in this book either present important ideas or philosophies or are good examples of activities in wildlife conservation. We hope they contribute to the education of those who will, as professionals or as laymen, participate in the conservation process. We believe an increased awareness of all aspects of conservation will help participants to relate their wildlife interests or problems to the whole conservation process, and will provide incentive to each participant and encourage teamwork among them.

This book has been a cooperative effort of The Wildlife Society. More than forty members suggested over 250 titles for consideration. Others reviewed our selections, edited our introductory remarks and offered helpful suggestions. Our sincere thanks go to these, our advisors and critics. However, responsibility for any errors in reproducing selected papers is ours. Thanks are also due our respective departments at Colorado State University, the University of Missouri, and Oklahoma State University for funding our efforts and providing clerical assistance.

James A. Bailey
William Elder
Ted McKinney

TABLE OF CONTENTS

READINGS IN
WILDLIFE
CONSERVATION

PERSPECTIVES

To the sportsman the value of wildlife is self-evident; it provides the very stuff of his game and the place in which to play it. For the farmer, wildlife is a covey of quail he may pursue on a day off—a rabbit or squirrel seen on the way to the barn. It livens his daily chores and shares the products of his toil. It is usually tolerated if not encouraged. To the absentee owner whose farm is run by mechanized mass production techniques, wildlife is simply weeds or mice to be poisoned. The value of wildlife may be strictly economic to the man leasing his land for hunting or charging a fee for daily use. To the urbanite, wildlife is something he may hope to find on a weekend in the country, and includes the setting in which a bird or mammal may be seen. To a rapidly-swelling minority, wildlife includes any observable species of plant or animal, furred, feathered or scaled. To them wildlife value is a personal observation of nature or even anticipation of such a memorable emotional experience. The following papers have been selected to show some of the variety of these attitudes and the philosophic questions which remain as modern man's dilemma.

1

WILDLIFE IN AMERICAN CULTURE (1943)
Aldo Leopold

Perhaps no man so eloquently stated the esthetic value of wildlife as did Aldo Leopold. The two brief essays that follow present some of his thoughts. They are as pertinent today as when written 30 years ago.

The culture of primitive peoples is often based on wildlife. Thus, the plains Indian not only ate buffalo, but buffalo largely determined his architecture, dress, language, arts, and religion.

In civilized peoples the economic base shifts to tame animals and plants, but the culture nevertheless retains part of its wild roots. This paper deals with the value of this wild rootage.

No one can weigh or measure culture, hence I will waste no time trying to do so. Suffice it to say that by common consent of thinking people, there are cultural values in the sports, customs, and experiences which renew contacts with wild things. I venture the opinion that these values are of three kinds.

First, there is value in any experience which reminds us of our distinctive national origins and evolution, i.e., which stimulates awareness of American history. Such awareness is "nationalism" in its best sense. For lack of any other short name, I will call this the "split-rail value." For example: a boy scout has tanned a coonskin cap, and goes Daniel-Booneing in the willow thicket below the tracks. He is re-enacting American history. He is, to that extent, culturally prepared to face the dark and bloody realities of 1943. Again: a farmer boy arrives in the schoolroom reeking of muskrat; he has tended his traps before breakfast. He is re-enacting the romance of the fur trade. Ontogeny repeats phylogeny in society as well as in the individual.

Second, there is value in any experience which reminds us of our dependency on the soil-plant-animal-man food chain. Civilization has so cluttered this elemental man-earth relation with gadgets and middle-men that awareness of it is growing dim. We fancy that industry supports us, forgetting what supports industry. Time was when education moved toward soil, not away from it. The nursery jingle about bringing home a rabbit skin to wrap the baby bunting in is one of many reminders in folklore that man once hunted to feed and clothe his family.

Third, the conquest of nature by machines has led to much unnecessary destruction of resources. Our tools improve faster than we do. It is unlikely that economic motives alone will ever teach us to use our new tools gently. The only remedy is to extend our system of ethics from the man-man relation to the man-earth relation (1). We shall achieve conservation when and only when the destructive use of land becomes unethical—punishable by social ostracism. Any experience that stimulates this extension of ethics is culturally valuable. Any that has the opposite effect is culturally damaging. For example, we have many bad hunters with good guns. Such

Reprinted from: J. Wildl. Mgmt. 7(1):1-6.

a hunter shoots a woodduck, and then tramples the bejeweled carcass into the mud, lest he fall foul of the law. Such an experience is not only devoid of cultural value, it is actually damaging to all concerned. It does physical damage to woodduck, and moral damage to the hunter, and to all fellow-hunters who condone him. No sane person could find anything but minus value in such "sport."

It seems, then, that split-rail and man-earth experiences have zero or plus values, but that ethical experiences may have minus values as well.

This, then, defines roughly three kinds of cultural nutriment available to our outdoor roots. It does not follow that culture is fed. The extraction of value is never automatic; only a healthy culture can feed and grow. Is culture fed by our present forms of outdoor recreation?

The pioneer period gave birth to two ideas which are the very essence of split-rail value in outdoor sports. One is the "go-light" idea, the other the "one-bullet-one-buck" idea. The pioneer went light of necessity. He shot with economy and precision because he lacked the transport, the cash, and the weapons requisite for machine-gun tactics. Let it be clear, then, that in their inception, both of these ideas were forced on us; we made a virtue of necessity.

In their later evolution, however, they became a code of sportsman-ship, a self-imposed limitation on sport. On them is based a distinctively American tradition of self-reliance, hardihood, woodcraft, and marksman-ship. These are intangibles, but they are not abstractions. Theodore Roose-velt was a great sportsman, not because he hung up many trophies, but because he expressed (2) this intangible American tradition in words any schoolboy could understand. A more subtle and accurate expression is found in the early writings of Stewart Edward White (3). It is not far amiss to say that such men created cultural value by being aware of it, and by creating a pattern for its growth.

Then came the gadgeteer, otherwise known as the sporting-goods dealer. He has draped the American outdoorsman with an infinity of con-traptions, all offered as aids to self-reliance, hardihood, woodcraft, or marksmanship, but too often functioning as substitutes for them. Gadgets fill the pockets, they dangle from neck and belt. The overflow fills the auto-trunk, and also the trailer. Each item of outdoor equipment grows lighter and often better, but the aggregate poundage becomes tonnage. The traffic in gadgets adds up to astronomical sums, which are soberly published as representing "the economic value of wildlife." But what of cultural values?

As an end-case consider the duck hunter, sitting in a steel boat behind composition decoys. A put-put has brought him to the blind without exer-tion. Canned heat stands by to warm him in case of a chilling wind. He talks to the passing flocks on a factory caller, in what he hopes are seductive tones; home lessons from a phonograph record have taught him how. The decoys work, despite the caller; a flock circles in. It must be shot at before it circles twice, for the marsh bristles with other sportsmen, similarly accoutred, who might shoot first. He opens up at 70 yards, for his polychoke is set for infinity, and the ads have told him that Super-Z shells, and plenty of them, have a long reach. The flock flares. A couple of cripples scale off to die elsewhere. Is this sportsman absorbing cultural value? Or is he just

4

feeding minks? The next blind opens up at 75 yards; how else is a fellow to get some shooting? This is duck-shooting, model 1943. It is typical of all public grounds, and of many clubs. Where is the go-light idea, the one-bullet tradition?

The answer is not a simple one. Roosevelt did not disdain the modern rifle; White used freely the aluminum pot, the silk tent, dehydrated foods. Somehow they used mechanical aids, in moderation, without being used by them.

I do not pretend to know what is moderation, or where the line is between legitimate and illegitimate gadgets. It seems clear, though, that the origin of gadgets has much to do with their cultural effects. Homemade aids to sport or outdoor life often enhance, rather than destroy, the man-earth drama; he who kills a trout with his own fly has scored two coups, not one. I use many factory-made gadgets myself. Yet there must be some limit beyond which money-bought aids to sport destroy the cultural value of sport.

Not all sports have degenerated to the same extent as duck hunting. Defenders of the American tradition still exist. Perhaps the bow-and-arrow movement and the revival of falconry mark the beginnings of a reaction. The net trend, however, is clearly toward more and more mechanization, with a corresponding shrinkage in cultural values, especially split-rail values and ethical restraints.

I have the impression that the American sportsman is puzzled; he doesn't understand what is happening to him. Bigger and better gadgets are good for industry, so why not for outdoor recreation? It has not dawned on him that outdoor recreations are essentially primitive, atavistic; that their value is a contrast-value; that excessive mechanization destroys contrasts by moving the factory to the woods or to the marsh.

The sportsman has no leaders to tell him what is wrong. The sporting press no longer represents sport, it has turned billboard for the gadgeteer. Wildlife administrators are too busy producing something to shoot at to worry much about the cultural value of the shooting. Because everybody from Xenophon to Teddy Roosevelt said sport has value, it is assumed that this value must be indestructible.

Among non-gunpowder sports, the impact of mechanization has had diverse effects. The modern field glass, camera, and aluminum bird-band have certainly *not* deteriorated the cultural value of ornithology. Fishing, but for motorized transport, seems less severely mechanized than hunting. On the other hand, motorized transport has nearly destroyed the sport of wilderness travel by leaving only fly-specks of wilderness to travel in.

Fox-hunting with hounds, backwoods style, presents a dramatic instance of partial and perhaps harmless mechanized invasion. This is one of the purest of sports; it has real split-rail flavor; it has man-earth drama of the first water. The fox is deliberately left unshot, hence ethical restraint is also present. But we now follow the chase in Fords! The voice of Bugle-Anne mingles with the honk of the flivver! However, no one is likely to invent a mechanical foxhound, nor to screw a polychoke on the hound's nose. No one is likely to teach dog-training by phonograph, or by other painless shortcuts. I think the gadgeteer has reached the end of his tether in dogdom.

It is not quite accurate to ascribe all the ills of sport to the inventor of physical aids-to-sport. The advertiser invents ideas, and ideas are seldom as honest as physical objects, even though they may be equally useless. One such deserves special mention: the "where-to-go" department. Knowledge of the whereabouts of good hunting or fishing is a very personal form of property. Perhaps it is like rod, dog, or gun: a thing to be loaned or given as a personal courtesy, or even to be sold man-to-man, as in the guide-sportsman relation. But to hawk it in the marketplace of the sports column as an aid-to-circulation seems to me another matter. To hand it to all and sundry as free public "service" seems to me distinctly another matter. Both tend to depersonalize one of the essentially personal elements in hunting skill. I do not know where the line lies between legitimate and illegitimate practice; I am convinced, though, that "where-to-go" service has broken all bounds of reason.

If the hunting or fishing is good, the where-to-go service suffices to attract the desired excess of sportsmen. But if it is no good, the advertiser must resort to more forcible means. One such is the fishing lottery, in which a few hatchery fish are tagged, and a prize is offered for the fisherman catching the winning number. This curious hybrid between the techniques of science and of the pool hall insures the overfishing of many an already exhausted lake, and brings a glow of civic pride to many a village Chamber of Commerce.

It is idle for the profession of wildlife management to consider itself aloof from these affairs. The production engineer and the salesman belong to the same company; both are tarred with the same stick.

Wildlife management is trying to convert hunting from exploitation to cropping. If the conversion takes place, how will it affect cultural values? It must be admitted that split-rail flavor and free-for-all exploitation are historically associated. Daniel Boone had scant patience with agricultural cropping, let alone wildlife cropping. Perhaps the stubborn reluctance of the one-gallus sportsman to be converted to the cropping idea is an expression of his split-rail inheritance. Probably cropping is resisted because it is incompatible with one component of the split-rail tradition, free hunting.

Mechanization offers no cultural substitute for the split-rail values it destroys; at least none visible to me. Cropping or management does offer a substitute, which to me has at least equal value, wild husbandry (4). The experience of managing land for wildlife crops has the same value as any other form of farming; it is a reminder of the man-earth relation. Moreover ethical restraints are involved; thus managing game without resorting to predator-control calls for ethical restraint of a high order. It may be concluded, then, that game cropping shrinks one value (split-rail) but enhances both others.

If we regard outdoor sports as a field of conflict between an immensely vigorous process of mechanization and a wholly static tradition, then the outlook for cultural values is indeed dark. But why can not our concept of sport grow with the same vigor as our list of gadgets? Perhaps the salvation of cultural value lies in seizing the offensive. I, for one, believe that the time is ripe. Sportsmen can determine for themselves the shape of things to come.

The last decade, for example, has disclosed a totally new form of sport which does not destroy wildlife, which uses gadgets without being used by them, which outflanks the problem of posted land, and which greatly increases the human carrying capacity of a unit area. This sport knows no bag limit, no closed season. It needs teachers, but not wardens. It calls for a new woodcraft of the highest cultural value. The sport I refer to is wildlife research.

Wildlife research started as a professional priestcraft. The more difficult or laborious problems must remain in professional hands, but there are plenty of problems suitable for all grades of amateurs. In the mechanical field, research has long since spread to amateurs. In the biological field the sport-value of amateur work is just beginning to be realized. When amateurs like Margaret Nice outstrip their professional colleagues, a very important new element is added: the element of high stakes open to all comers, the possibility of really outstanding amateur performance.

Ornithology, mammalogy, and botany, as now known to most amateurs, are but kindergarten games compared with researches in these fields. The real game is decoding the messages written on the face of the land. By learning how some small part of the biota ticks, we can guess how the whole mechanism ticks.

Few people can become enthusiastic about research as a sport because the whole structure of biological education is aimed to perpetuate the professional research monopoly. To the amateur is allotted only make-believe voyages of discovery, the chance to verify what professional authority already knows. This is false; the case of Margaret Nice proves what a really enterprising amateur can do. What the youth needs to be told is that a ship is a-building in his own mental dry-dock, a ship with freedom of the seas. If you are a pessimist, you can say this ship is "on order"; if an optimist, you can see the keel.

In my opinion, the promotion of wildlife research sports is the most important job confronting our profession.

Wildlife has still another value, now visible only to a few ecologists, but of potential importance to the whole human enterprise.

We now know that animal populations have behavior patterns of which the individual animal is unaware, but which he nevertheless helps to execute. Thus the rabbit is unaware of cycles, but he is the vehicle for cycles.

We cannot discern these behavior patterns in the individual, or in short periods of time. The most intense scrutiny of an individual rabbit tells us nothing of cycles. The cycle concept springs from a scrutiny of the mass through decades of history.

This raises the disquieting question: do human populations have behavior patterns of which we are unaware, but which we help to execute? Are mobs and wars, unrests and revolutions, cut of such cloth?

Many historians and philosophers persist in interpreting our mass behaviors as the collective result of individual acts of volition. The whole subject-matter of diplomacy assumes that the political group has the properties of an honorable person. On the other hand, some economists (5) see the whole of society as a plaything for processes, our knowledge of which is largely ex-post-facto.

It is reasonable to suppose that our social processes have a higher volitional content than those of the rabbit, but it is also reasonable to suppose that we contain patterns of which nothing is known because circumstance has never evoked them. We may have others the meaning of which we have misread.

This state of doubt about the fundamentals of human population behavior lends exceptional interest, and exceptional value, to the only available analogue: the higher animals. Errington (6), among others, has pointed out the cultural value of these animal analogues. For centuries this rich library of knowledge has been inaccessible to us because we did not know where or how to look for it. Ecology is now teaching us to search in animal populations for analogies to our own problems. The ability to perceive these, and to appraise them critically, is the woodcraft of the future.

To sum up, wildlife once fed us and shaped our culture. It still yields us pleasure for leisure hours, but we try to reap that pleasure by modern machinery and thus destroy part of its value. Reaping it by modern mentality would yield not only pleasure, but wisdom as well.

LITERATURE CITED

1. LEOPOLD, ALDO. 1933. The Conservation Ethic. Journ. Forestry, 31:634-643.
2. ROOSEVELT, THEODORE, T. S. VAN DYKE, D. G. ELLIOTT, and A. J. STONE. 1902. The Deer Family. New York, Grosset and Dunlap. (See especially the introduction by Roosevelt.)
3. WHITE, STEWART EDWARD. 1903. The Forest. New York, The Outlook Company.
4. LEOPOLD, ALDO. 1938. Conservation Esthetic. Bird Lore, 40: 101-109.
5. BURNHAM, JAMES. 1941. The Managerial Revolution. New York, John Day Publishing Co.
6. ERRINGTON, PAUL L. 1940. On the Social Potentialities of Wildlife Management. Journ. Wildl. Mgt., 4: 451-452.

THINKING LIKE A MOUNTAIN (1949)
Aldo Leopold

A deep chesty bawl echoes from rimrock to rimrock, rolls down the mountain, and fades into the far blackness of the night. It is an outburst of wild defiant sorrow, and of contempt for all the adversities of the world.

Every living thing (and perhaps many a dead one as well) pays heed to that call. To the deer it is a reminder of the way of all flesh, to the pine a forecast of midnight scuffles and of blood upon the snow, to the coyote a promise of gleanings to come, to the cowman a threat of red ink at the bank, to the hunter a challenge of fang against bullet. Yet behind these obvious and immediate hopes and fears there lies a deeper meaning, known only to the mountain itself. Only the mountain has lived long enough to listen objectively to the howl of a wolf.

Those unable to decipher the hidden meaning know nevertheless that it is there, for it is felt in all wolf country, and distinguishes that country from all other land. It tingles in the spine of all who hear wolves by night, or who scan their tracks by day. Even without sight or sound of wolf, it is implicit in a hundred small events: the midnight whinny of a pack horse, the rattle of rolling rocks, the bound of a fleeing deer, the way shadows lie under the spruces. Only the ineducable tyro can fail to sense the presence or absence of wolves, or the fact that mountains have a secret opinion about them.

My own conviction on this score dates from the day I saw a wolf die. We were eating lunch on a high rimrock, at the foot of which a turbulent river elbowed its way. We saw what we thought was a doe fording the torrent, her breast awash in white water. When she climbed the bank toward us and shook out her tail, we realized our error: it was a wolf. A half-dozen others, evidently grown pups, sprang from the willows and all joined in a welcoming mêlée of wagging tails and playful maulings. What was literally a pile of wolves writhed and tumbled in the center of an open flat at the foot of our rimrock.

In those days we had never heard of passing up a chance to kill a wolf. In a second we were pumping lead into the pack, but with more excitement than accuracy: how to aim a steep downhill shot is always confusing. When our rifles were empty, the old wolf was down, and a pup was dragging a leg into impassable slide-rocks.

We reached the old wolf in time to watch a fierce green fire dying in her eyes. I realized then, and have known ever since, that there was something new to me in those eyes— something known only to her and to the mountain. I was young then, and full of trigger-itch; I thought that because fewer wolves meant more deer, that no wolves would mean hunters' paradise. But after seeing the green fire die, I sensed that neither the wolf nor the mountain agreed with such a view.

Since then I have lived to see state after state extirpate its wolves. I have watched the face of many a newly wolfless mountain, and seen the south-facing slopes wrinkle with a maze of new deer trails. I have seen every edible bush and seedling browsed, first to anaemic desuetude, and then to death. I have seen every edible tree defoliated to the height of a saddlehorn. Such a mountain looks as if someone had given God a new pruning shears, and forbidden Him all other exercise. In the end the starved bones of the hoped-for deer herd, dead of its own too-much, bleach with the bones of the dead sage, or molder under the high-lined junipers.

I now suspect that just as a deer herd lives in mortal fear of its wolves, so does a mountain live in mortal fear of its deer. And perhaps with better cause, for while a buck pulled down by wolves can be replaced in two or three years, a range pulled down by too many deer may fail of replacement in as many decades.

So also with cows. The cowman who cleans his range of wolves does not realize that he is taking over the wolf's job of trimming the herd to fit the range. He has not learned to think like a mountain. Hence we have dustbowls, and rivers washing the future into the sea.

We all strive for safety, prosperity, comfort, long life, and dullness. The deer strives with his supple legs, the cowman with trap and poison, the statesman with pen, the most of us with machines, votes, and dollars, but it all comes to the same thing: peace in our time. A measure of success in this is all well enough, and perhaps is a requisite to objective thinking, but too much safety seems to yield only danger in the long run. Perhaps this is behind Thoreau's dictum: In wildness is the salvation of the world. Perhaps this is the hidden meaning in the howl of the wolf, long known among mountains, but seldom perceived among men.

OF MEN AND MARSHES (1957)
Paul L. Errington

The lure of marshes for their special esthetic values and the significance of these marshes to our ecological understanding have been the basic subject for three books which Paul Errington has written, mostly about muskrats. For him this species provided the very framework of wetlands and their values.

We may now consider a view that is held by many thoughtful people. It is not exclusively a view of professional ecologists and teachers, though ecologists and teachers are among those I have heard expressing it most frequently. A single sentence that paraphrases it might be that civilized man could show some civilization by preserving in as natural condition as possible representative types of the different plant and animal communities before they are lost.

Such would mean going farther than preserving the mountain tops that no one would find exploitable, the lands too rocky or otherwise unsuitable for cultivation, the forested lands too inaccessible for lumbering, and the odd pieces of land having slight economic value that "practical" man might not want. It would mean preservation of some places with the best timber or soils or building sites, some that could easily be plowed and kept plowed, some marshes that could be turned into cornfields. It would entail recognition of values other than the monetary.

Apart from any esthetic appreciation that ecologists may feel toward undespoiled wilderness preserves, including marshes, one of their chief motivations in preservation of wilderness is to safeguard areas where ancient interrelationships of plants, animals, soils, and climates may be studied. It is to safeguard areas where comparisons may be made between plants and animals subject to all degrees of human land use and those that live undisturbed (or relatively undisturbed) by man and man's. Their thesis is that important things may be learned about laws of life from wild populations living on wild areas.

At least some of us feel that an understanding of these laws is essential to human welfare, if for no other reason than to help man avoid the more basic of mistakes toward which he always seems to be heading. Enlightene[d] peoples should ultimately learn what may be expected when human affai[rs] and resources are mismanaged and learn something about the gene[ral] landmarks to overwhelming situations without going all of the way.

The laws of life can, most assuredly, catch up with man. We need[n't] restrict our comparisons to the cataclysmic, though it may be a tempt[ation] to compare a botulism outbreak among massed water birds or an epi[demic] in a dense muskrat population with human plagues in the cities of me[dieval] Europe, or to compare other sweeping tragedies among wild popu[lations] with the impacts upon human populations of Asiatic famines, v[olcanic] action, earthquakes, or even the new-style cataclysm introduced a[t Hiro]shima. The less spectacular day-by-day parallels would seem to be th[e] informative concerning the fundamental principles that Life lives by.

In my own professional studies of animal populations, I have never felt more aware of parallels between human and nonhuman responses to natural crises than when working on marshes. No species has taught me more about parallels that I think man should be familiar with than has the muskrat, a living entity that, like man, has problems of living with what endowments it possesses, of meeting vicissitudes, and of getting along with its fellows.

Let us say that we have a marsh and that on it live many muskrats. The muskrats of our marsh are not so numerous that they occupy every square yard or consume the entire food supply. Seldom do we find that sort of thing in mammal populations even at times of acute crowding. Let us say that the muskrats of our marsh are not anywhere nearly as numerous in terms of animals per acre as muskrats could be on marshes and that, on our marsh, they are not as numerous as on some other marshes in their neighborhood.

Nevertheless, matters are not as they once were on our marsh. Human society in like circumstances could find cause to deplore the prevalence of unrest and crime, the lack of opportunity for youth, and the race suicide implied by the falling birth rate.

Patriarchal muskrats do not talk of the prosperous days when their fellows had better dispositions and when families of fifteen or twenty go-getting youngsters were raised in a season instead of a trifling half-dozen that are afraid of their own shadows. They do not ask what the marsh is coming to, within a life-span of its development from the jungle of cattails and bulrushes the settlers went forth to conquer. They do not advocate economic systems operating on the principle of eternal acceleration. Nor do they warn that, unless the community regains the initiative and virtues of its founders, the marsh might as well be left to the minks.

Nor do they invest their racial enemies, the minks, with demoniacal attributes and blame them for all of the trouble of muskratdom. They do not like minks, and no one should expect them to, muskrats being muskrats and minks being minks; but the muskrats at least cannot fairly be charged with the greater follies of scapegoat philosophies.

Insofar as the muskrats are what man calls lower animals, they simply live as their forebears lived, with what they have, for themselves.

The population does not share alike either its resources or its troubles. Some families live in relative security, their young and the young of their neighbors growing up together in the cattails that stretch out beyond the lodges. Some families live in rush and reed clumps of the open-water center, and these families are favorably situated except during storms. Elsewhere, some families get along passably well, and others do not.

Covering the shallows at one side of the marsh, the richest stand of food plants for miles attracts muskrats that wedge in their breeding territories wherever space can be had. It is a busy but not a happy place, and most muskrats do little moving far from what they claim and can hold for themselves.

About the edges of the crowded territories, what a muskrat does is conditioned by what its neighbors permit. Even when acquaintances permit close approach, or when there is some common sharing of marshy tracts or habitations, stranger sooner or later meets stranger if a muskrat ventures on past its neighbors' territories.

When the cattails of the crowded shallows begin to give out, whether because of overuse or for reasons for which the muskrats are not responsible, the residents do not actually starve. They merely grow more irritable and inflict more drastic penalties for trespassing and do more trespassing, themselves.

Strangers appear, battered and furtive or out-and-out predatory. They fight and die of their wounds or go on to wander and fight and die somewhere else. Mostly, they withdraw to the abandoned lodges that fringe the dry edge of the marsh and feed upon their dead and upon the coarse weeds nearby. Old and young they are, the luckless, the footloose.

Life is cheapest among the young. In the more roomy areas, the weaned that are driven from lodges containing suckling young may find a measure of safety in empty lodges, coot nests, or dense vegetation, but, where small territory abuts small territory, the teeth of adults are readier to slash as well as harder to keep away from. Back and forth, from home lodges to neighbors' lodges, wary young slip ahead of and around the adults. Victims crawl upon rushy mats with their entrails hanging out or float with bodies softening in the heat. Four of five are dead before they are a third grown, some whole litters a fortnight after weaning; and the surviving young that live in odd corners or cluster around the more tolerant of the adults include animals that are both stunted and ailing.

The larger young eat of the fresher bodies, especially of the bodies of the very young and not always of bodies of young that are dead when found. Helpless litters in nests are also bitten to death by adults, and parents sometimes care for their own helpless young in the nests of other muskrat litters that they kill. Desertions of the new-born increase with the uneasiness and disturbances of crowding, as do losses from moving litter members from nest to nest. Breeding slackens and stops by mid-summer, though continuing for weeks on less populated areas.

Out toward deep water, a food-rich frontier draws in the young that can reach it and a few of the old that live in the vicinity. It has dangers of its own, and some of the newcomers drown, but the vacant spaces where muskrats can live become filled to the rough and barren water of the center. Yet, most of the marsh-dwellers stay or try to stay where they are as long as that is the most comfortable thing to do—which is throughout the breeding season, or into late summer.

As might be expected, the breeding season is a period of pronounce tensions in our muskrat population. Reproduction of its kind is alwa among the most fundamental of responses of a living creature, with int plays of breeding-season intolerances. Hence, the behavior patterns of muskrats become modified as late summer brings relief from the jealo and frictions associated with mating and care of young. Food is th plentiful as at any time of year, and the muskrats enjoy a freedom of ment that would not be tolerated during the main breeding seaso quarrelsome may still fight if they try, though transients are nea young animals that are neither formidable nor disposed to make tr

If our muskrat population is at all lucky from late summer on to the next spring's breeding season, it may live in relatively uneventful peace for several months—the earlier shaking down of the over-produced young having left the population in a position of some security. If the fall and winter weather remains favorable, if neither insufficient nor too much water covers the cattail and bulrush rootstocks, if the sinking frost-line does not encompass the food supply, the population may get along fairly well. There may be some chewed-up misfits wandering on the new ice of November or December or coming out later to be picked off by minks or foxes. In the spring, of course, a new breeding season and the birth of more young would again accentuate tensions in a crowded population.

Let us say that the muskrats of our marsh are *not* lucky, that, like some human populations, they have to meet a great emergency—an emergency aggravated by their already high densities and the limited alternatives open to them.

When the normal dryness of late summer or fall turns into drought on our muskrat marsh, there is still resilience in social relationships. The first young muskrats that drift into the marsh from surrounding potholes are tolerated the same as the local young that move inward from the drying shores after the breeding season. The big pinch does not come until the hard frosts bring in more wandering strangers and impress the residents with what they, themselves, are up against. One need not indulge in any anthropomorphizing to see that the muskrats recognize a change in their lives when they work to deepen their burrows beneath the frosted mud or travel back and forth between feeding grounds and ice-glazed waterholes or gnaw at exposed and frozen plant parts or sit by themselves with blood oozing from their fight wounds.

As winter approaches, strange muskrats meet with more and more hostility, whether they come from the borders of the marsh or from far outside. They gather in the weedy growths of low ground or spread along the shore. Wanderers are still mainly young ones, easily harassed into staying out of where they are not wanted, but among them are adults. Later, more adults—the last muskrats to abandon some of the long-dry, food-poor environment of the shore zone and outlying sloughs—work toward the deeper parts.

Some of these adults disregard established property rights. Some even kill and eat the less dangerous of the residents, moving from lodge to lodge until they die of their own wounds or from hunger and freezing, or the minks get them. They have raw or healing wounds on face or forelegs (perhaps a hamstrung foreleg, held on by the joint), two-inch gashes across rump, or hind feet or tails bitten through and swollen out of shape. They have abscesses the size of a golf ball under an armpit or bulging out a side, or a string of smaller abscesses running through the liver and the other organs of the body cavity, but, as long as their tough old bodies have life, they hang on to it.

A congested area on a drought-exposed marsh bottom need not be close to any main route of travel of evicted muskrats to be the scene of bloody crises. It need not suffer much invasion by muskrats coming from far outside. Where every stranger is a prospective enemy, taking or trying to take what it wants where it can find it, where viciously defended home ranges confront animals that want to go elsewhere or can find no real refuge anywhere, there we may not expect to find much peace in our muskrat population.

Let us consider our muskrat marsh during another year. We have about a quarter as many adult muskrats in early summer and a total number of adults and young after the breeding season that is perhaps only half as great as after the other breeding season. Food and water are much as before. The center is still rough and shelterless in stormy weather. The shallows still go dry in the fall. Minks range the borders, ready as ever to prey when they can. Things are about as before in all ways except for the fewer muskrats.

Our muskrats may still be said to have the attributes of muskrats in endeavoring to stay alive individually, to multiply, to exploit the marshes, to be more or less peaceable of temperament when comfortable and not aroused, and to be savage when uncomfortable and aroused.

In their own way, they may be called unimaginative, practical creatures, meeting slowly developing problems by default or by improvisions forced by patent crises. An alarming danger typically brings forth action, sometimes appropriate, sometimes inappropriate. The mental processes of the muskrats still function best when required to do but one thing at a time. The animals having the advantage in survival and competition are still the mature ones living in places where they have valid property rights. The psychology of dominant individuals is still of outstanding importance in the social order of the muskrat marsh.

Our marsh now still has muskrats that do not belong, troublemakers, wanderers, the ailing, the unlucky, the desperate. For all of that, there is little serious friction in the muskrat population, even at the height of a drought exposure. Many mothers give birth to three or four litters during the breeding season, and the young thrive in the cattails and bulrushes.

The big difference is in the degree of crowding to which the muskrats are subject and in the resilience with which those muskrats adjust both to population stresses and to emergencies. A population density half as great as a top-heavy one does not have its troubles reduced merely by half. in direct proportion to the numbers of muskrats present. Its gains, in social tranquility, are far out of proportion to the actual lowering of the population numerically.

Most important is the existence of shock-absorbing frontiers for the muskrats of the marsh and routes by which adjusting muskrats might reach them unimpeded, but greater day-by-day *Lebensraum* and comfortable conditions in the regularly maintained breeding territories also have their influence on the dispositions of the animals. Although modern evidence indicates that the psychological tolerances of the muskrats toward crowding may vary with the year as well as with circumstances, a safe generalization would appear to be that little peace can be expected in any population that acts as if it *feels* crowded.

The lives of muskrats cannot be thought to reflect more of human experience than man shares with other vertebrates rather generally. It would be absurd to expect the lives of muskrats and human experience to show parallels in great detail. Man, regardless of what else may be said of him, has demonstrated that he can complicate much of his living beyond comparison with much else, far beyond the complicating abilities of such simple eaters, breeders, fighters, and seekers after greener marshes as our muskrats.

Man seldom goes to such extremes as to rip open his progeny when they get annoyingly under foot. Outright cannibalism is not fashionable among civilized peoples. But the harshness of man toward man can equal anything to be seen on the marshes. It is not the way of muskrats to rationalize their cruder practices in terms of survival of the fittest or of manifest destiny or of chosen peoples or of utopian visions, but the common propensity of man and muskrats for growing savage under stress appears to be basic.

To me, overcrowding is so much the supreme factor underlying stress in the muskrat populations that its lessons may scarcely be overemphasized. It does function as a biological mechanism to reduce, in part, its own evils. Despite the rapidity with which the muskrats can multiply—even as rodents, they are among the more fecund—they are most productive of young at population densities that are neither extremely low nor extremely high for the environment occupied. This is a rule that seems to hold broadly true for other animal life. Moreover, populations of many species of animals show different degrees of self-limitation long before food competition reaches what are conventionally thought of as Malthusian stages. Without crediting to abstract reasoning these adjustments between reproductive potentials and problems of overpopulation, or ascribing to them more uniformity and effectiveness than exist, man should find it of interest that automatic, self-limiting adjustments occur.

Man should also find it of interest that the adjustments almost inevitably mean suffering in species capable of suffering. There is naturalness in them, whether the populations be of men or mice or muskrats, but the naturalness is that of life responding to harassment and frustration and necessity. What I have seen of Nature's way, in this respect, is the ruthless way, little resembling any mysteriously benign process of falling birth rates. Breeding may terminate painlessly with physiological changes at the end of a reproductive cycle, but, when a real self-limiting retrenchment in the normal reproductive pattern of a species possessed of a nervous system occurs, it is very apt indeed to be *forced* by something uncomfortable, if not ominous.

Being only lower animals, the muskrats may not be expected to teach man much about population behavior that is not elementary, but it is surprising—and frightening—how unaware influential people may be of the simpler biological backgrounds of sociology and economics during periods of crisis and political upheavals.

I have here attempted to sketch what should be regarded as a composite picture based upon factual evidence, based all the way through on known case histories of muskrat populations, every last bit of it. I have attempted to present a realistic portrayal of small scenes in the drama of life that may be conducive to more realistic human appraisals of some of the fundamentals underlying social relationships. In this, I recognize that

16

I am coming close to the edge of controversial subjects that I am neither inclined nor competent to discuss. There remains for our thought the fidelity with which muskrats respond to inherent patterns, to resources, to the presence of other muskrats, to the presence of ancient enemies and to the interrelationships that may be observed in a natural society.

The principal moral that the lives of muskrats may have for us may be that the biological foundation of peace is that of moderation. This is admittedly a homely concept and not at all new. It is a concept having its own implications of unsolved problems when applied to human populations, not only of reconciling religious, political, and social differences, but also of actually defining the most enlightened and practical aims. It is a concept that man has a tendency to forget when he loses sight of the fact that he is an animal or when he imagines himself to be a higher, wiser, or more special animal than he is. I cannot see that man has any prospect of more than the uneasiest of temporary peace until he manages to keep his own numbers in sound balance with resources, including a minimum of the things that make human life worth living.

I feel neither sufficiently wise nor brave to say exactly how the problems inherent in human populations should be met. As long as they remain on earth, man and muskrat alike must be subject to some extent to blind forces which no amount of good judgment can completely offset. But man should be able to recognize the menace for his own kind that can build up with his own continued irresponsible increase in numbers, especially in our "atomic age" when what is precious in civilization cannot afford unnecessary risks of mass dislocations, mass agony, and mass desperation, with puppetry and puppet masters, and loss of human dignity, perhaps waiting just beyond.

At the very least, man should cease his obeisance to mere numbers. The merriment in the old saying, "the more the merrier," can become false as extremes are reached, even in such gregarious a species of animal as man can be.

Whether a person thinks of the inconceivable millions of stars, each so much greater than our whole earth, or of only muskrats, or of anything else in Nature that is either greater or lesser than he is, a feeling of humility before the Order that exists in the universe is always appropriate. If disturbed at the parallels between mankind and nonhuman societies, he may be reminded that no man invented life's rules of behavior. They have been in operation for a long time. They will continue to be operative.

The philosophy that man should "work with and not against Nature" may have interpretations differing with the individual or the group, but, in its broader senses, it seems acceptable to enlightened people just about everywhere. Whatever may be the emotional hazards of differing metaphysical and political beliefs, "working with Nature" implies avoidance of misconceptions as to the nature of Nature and, going further, some faculty for choice between wise and unwise alternatives. The lessons as well as the beauties of marshes await the perceptive, as do the lessons and beauties of the skies, of the seas, of the mountains, and of the other places remaining where man can still reflect upon lessons and beauties that are not of human making.

Courtesy of Outdoor Publications, Inc.

LOST MARGINS IN THE ABANDONED FARM (1964)
Eugene M. Poirot

Few farmers see their landholdings as ecosystems; still fewer write of them. One such practical dirt farmer somehow early acquired an ecological understanding, and some thoughts from his book about his farm are recorded below.

The moon hurries me along as I tell the story. She has already quartered her arch in the sky. When I look at her she appears motionless; but looking again I see she has moved. She moves with the same complacent deception that good soil and lifetimes move unnoticed into poor soils and death. I wish she would hold her place tonight so that this part of my story could be told from beginning to end in this month of May, a month long enough to give promises and short enough to keep them. But she moves on, synchronized with the tick of a celestial pulse to record more world hunger and starvation on unproductive soils. Standing by, I count the seconds with her, hoping to reach the one where we shift our course so as to hold the promises of May and avoid the disaster of December.

Tonight big plans are being made in the prairie. The grass grows anew, flowers push away the sod, and the late-booming prairie cock has arranged for his nest. Its creatures dream of wide margins without failure or disaster. They disregard the wolf howling to the moon from the fields of an abandoned farm.

Eighty years ago it was prairie sod too. It held all the hopes and promises of each May, but many Augusts and Decembers have been added to its history. I do not know who plowed it first. His name is not important so let us call him Mr. A. Just why he left his home in Illinois, Kentucky or Tennessee to endure the privations of a pioneer, is a secret he plowed under with sod. Perhaps he was running away from something worse, or perhaps he was seeking something better. He may have had the spirit of adventure, the desire to own something regardless of how humble it might be or, perhaps too, he had the same sort of force within him which now drives some people who work in science, art or commerce to seek out the unknown and to find the new. Regardless of the reason, from plowings by him and by those who plowed like him, there grew the power and the greatness of America. To him our gratitude for a job well done!

Gratitude is all we can give Mr. A and, though quite useless, it is comparable perhaps to other rewards he received for being the first to farm our fields. He lived his life and reared his family without roads, without schools, without the services of a doctor and without the comfort of neighbors. He had a few horses and a cow or two. He lived in a sod house or possibly one made of logs hauled from a great distance. He went to a trading post some twenty miles away once a year to sell his hogs or cattle for any price offered. At another time during the year he went to a mill, more than forty miles away, to have corn and wheat ground into meal

Reprinted by permission from: Our Margin of Life. Vantage Press, Inc., N.Y.

and flour. If he became prosperous he probably spent money on the purchase of a kerosene lamp. If he was extremely prosperous he could send his children to a boarding school some twelve miles away where, as the yellowed and crumbling advertising still reads, they could get "Room and Board, 50 cents a week, candles furnished." If he still had money left he could buy additional land at $1.50 per acre and plow more prairie.

Why did he leave his community, farm and neighbors to come out here and endure all these privations? The answer to this question has been handed down in part by others who did the same thing about the same time, and may be answered by saying they were solving their farm problem. The farm they left in Illinois, Kentucky or Tennessee was worn out. They could no longer make a living on it as their parents and grandparents had done for generations before. They could not grow enough food for their families and have money left for buying candles, shoes and clothing.

At that time there were no government farm programs to offer either advice or money. The scientific approach to farm problems was unheard of. The merchant, banker, school teacher and preacher could not help. They too depended on farm production for their own income. When land became unproductive they were poor. Mr. A had a real farm problem just like many farmers have today—and for the same reason. He knew what it was. He also knew there was richer land in the West. His neighbors could not help him, so he would be better off without them *if* he could find land which would grow enough to feed his family. Many other farmers followed him for the same reason.

After they had plowed new wealth from new prairie soils, the merchant, banker, railroad and industry followed to share in it with them. America grew into a great, strong, prosperous nation of free people on rich soil where a few farmers could supply the food for others. Does this well-known continuous movement from poor to richer land suggest a solution to our present farm problem? We have dismissed it because there is no more new land.

What Mr. A did for himself was one thing, but what he did to the soil of the prairie was quite another. Here was the human factor that, with the aid of the plow, had upset the well-integrated relationship of our soils to plants and animals which had served to conserve the prairies for centuries. It was like shifting Mother Nature's factory into reverse gear.

Bluestem sod fights the plow and harness traces squeak like a new pair of shoes. Horse sweat becomes a soapy lather. A steel plow designed to break up the soil can do little more than turn it in a long black furrow that hangs together like a belt. The sound of turning sod is a strong, cracking, tearing noise protesting the destruction of its age-old function of holding the soil together. Mr. A, of course, did not know that when he killed the grass with his plow he increased the energy food for cellulose-decaying bacteria. These would multiply by billions upon billions to rot it more quickly. Nor did he know that the bacterial increase in numbers was now limited by the available minerals and nitrogen necessary to supply the protein needs or their multiplying bodies. They took these from the soil, held them in their living bodies and thereby made them unavailable to the first crop he planted. He observed these effects and, along with others like him, gave us this conclusion, "For one year after the prairie is plowed it will not grow a good crop. The soil has a 'wild nature' in it which must disappear before a tame crop can be grown."

In unspoken words Mother Nature was giving her first warning that this practice was out of harmony with her simple law of conservation which commands that we "hold the soil in place and return to it that which is taken." The roots of the grass had been holding the soil. They were dead now and bacteria were changing them into large quantities of available plant food as rapidly as microbial growth would permit.

The following year and for years to come Mr. A grew large yields of grain and hay. He prospered. So also did the people who consumed those products. Once eighty per cent of our population had to be farmers to grow enough food for all the people. But, with the plowing of the rich prairies, fewer people were needed to farm the land and more were released to work in the industries of our country. This same reduction in farm population continues with our increased efficiency in agriculture, until now only five per cent or less of our population produce ninety per cent of our farm products.

Other owners and tenants followed Mr. A and profited for a period of roughly thirty years. But during this time Mother Nature was giving her warnings that the margin of fertility was being narrowed. Muddy water carrying soil with it began running from the fields; small gullies became troublesome ditches. Rocks appeared in the fields where none had been seen before; farmers thought they had grown there like a crop. They were exposed now because the original covering soil had been washed away. Another unnoticed depleting process was going on which occurred each time a tenant hauled grain or livestock to the market. In this grain and live-stock were valuable plant foods and minerals which were not being replaced, so the soil became poorer by that amount. The natural process of accumulation of fertility which made prairie soil rich was now reversed.

The crops appeared normal as long as the soil had an abundance of plant food elements, but as the supply went down, the corn began to show purple leaves, oats had a yellow color and wheat was winter-killed. These were symptoms of dire starvation for phosphorus, nitrogen and potassium which showed up first under adverse weather conditions.

Tenants D and E saw these symptoms too but the only way they could interpret them was to believe that the seed was "running out." By now the soil organisms had digested a large part of the organic matter in the soil. The large masses of prairie-grass roots and stems had been reduced long years before, while other growing crops had produced organic matter only in proportion to their yields. Each year they went through the same process of decay and of releasing the plant food they contained so that later crops could get it. There was, however, less and less of it with each successive crop. The destructive process was slow and deceptive like the motion of the moon as she crosses the sky tonight. Look at her and she does not seem to move; then look again and she *has* moved. Slowly, fertility was moving away from the farm. The amount remaining became less and less each year, resulting in smaller crops.

It was during the time that Tenant F came to the farm that plants began to show retarded early growth, disease and insect damages of various kinds. The margins were being narrowed for animal life too. The farmer accepted the lower yields because he never knew the farm had once produced higher ones. He concluded that the answer to this must be found in disease-resistant crops of various kinds and he tried them. These were logical conclusions for him because he had no way of knowing that the microorganism activity in the soil had gone down with the low supply of organic matter. They were now producing fewer and fewer of the growth factors and hormones necessary for rapid growth of the young plants. Nor did he know that these organisms, when well-supplied with energy foods (organic matter), produce such substances in the soil as, or similar to, antibiotics which prevent various diseases in growing plants. Nor did he know that a well-fed plant, like a well-fed animal, has a better chance to survive.

It was perhaps Tenant G—they were moving on and off the farm in rapid succession by this time—who first noticed that his cattle grazed the fence rows and left what appeared to be better grass in the pasture. Some of the more courageous cows actually stretched the wires enough to crawl through and graze the road ditch where the grass grew on soil which had never been cultivated. The grass there tasted better, but Tenant G thought the cows were just of an ornery race so he put yokes around their necks and forced them to stay inside the fence and eat the less nutritious grass in the pasture. He did not know that the grass in his pasture had little calcium or phosphorus in it and that the cow, desperately attempting to produce her calf, was doing her best to get these elements from the grass instead of removing them from her backbone.

The tenant hoped to supply a good calf to his consumers in the city; the calf looked to its mother; the mother looked to the grass; the grass looked to the soil—but the soil was found wanting. The promises of May were now the disappointments of August.

Other tenants tried their art in farming the land. The landlord would not buy lime and other fertilizers for the fields. He had an investment in a farm. It was his. He could do with it as he pleased. It owed him rent and he expected to collect that in full. The banker had loaned the tenant money for seed and equipment. He was standing by to collect in full—with interest.

No one seemed to know that Mother Nature too was standing by, giving warnings which were not heard and pointing directions which were not followed. Patiently she was expecting a return of the fertility which had been taken away. She had entrusted the margin-creating power in her soil to a new group of creatures—those who farm the land and those who would eat its products, creatures who perhaps did not know that she always collects in full and punishes with misery and death if unpaid. She was willing to wait as new tenants were being foreclosed on for failure to pay their mortgages, and being replaced by the landlord because the payment on the rent was too low.

Each in his turn tried different crops which are generally known as "poor land" crops. *Redtop* is one of these. When it grows on soil no longer containing the valuable bone-building element of calcium, it can use sand instead of calcium, but the cows cannot make the same substitution when they eat the grass. Sorghum is another "poor land" crop. Through the process of evolution it has learned how to protect its own reproduction. In order to save itself from being eaten by an animal, when its growth is restricted due to drought or poor land, it will develop deadly prussic acid. Animals either avoid it or die. Other crops surviving on poor soil lack essential trace elements and animals consuming them die of malnutrition.

The soil of the farm had degenerated to this state when Tenant X took over, and that year Mother Nature moved in to collect and write off this creature, Man, as out of harmony with her processes. Mr. X had a wife and four children, six cows and four horses. Half of his livestock died during the summer from eating poisonous plants that grew in the infertile fields. The rest of them died in the winter of malnutrition. The disaster of December was at hand, but the neighbors, occupied with their own troubles, did not observe the desperate circumstances of Mr. X until his children no longer went to school. Upon investigation they found an hysterical wife, four fear-stricken children and Mr. X who, pointing to a five-pound sack of corn meal, told the story by saying, "That is all that we have left."

Weeks before, other students at the school had reported that Mr. X's children seemed to be avoiding their classmates. They did not want to play games, would eat their dinner in the far corner of the schoolyard and when the teacher insisted that they join the group of other children they put away their dinner and said they were not hungry. The reason for such actions was later discovered to be due to their embarrassment and shame at having only corn bread sandwiches—with mashed potatoes as a filler instead of meat. Later, when they had only corn bread, they did not come to school at all.

This family was poor but proud. Failure in farming hurt them as it does any farmer. They had heard others say that the loss of cattle and horses is caused by carelessness. Low yields of crops are due to laziness and poor timing. Any farmer worthy of the name should be able to grow enough food for winter if he tried, even when prices are too low to buy clothes and the like. None seemed to know that a combination of poor soil and low prices, such as corn at fifteen cents per bushel, wheat at forty cents and fat hogs at three cents per pound, could not go together in the early thirties.

The charity of neighbors, federal relief agencies and farm programs of that time eventually provided a living for Mr. X and his family of four children, who later grew up to be an excellent group of citizens. One might conclude that the charity was effective, but one might also add that Mr. X paid a high price for the privilege of growing food for his fellow man on worn-out soil. He did not want charity; he wanted a chance to use his labor to grow a living.

Such a chance was given to Tenant A when he moved west to homestead new land. This land was sold to him by the government. The government had not made it new and fertile. Mother Nature had done that. The land was used for growing crops for people, not only for the farmer. The same chance could have been given to Tenant X if the money given him in relief had been offered to him as a market for restoring his land to its original state of fertility!

He could have solved his problem by again having land as rich as Mr. A's when he first plowed it. He could have produced wealth for merchants, bankers, etc., just as Mr. A did for those following him west. He could have avoided producing a surplus, because soil restoration would have been more profitable on the unproductive part of his land. Relief money as such could not solve his problem because the margins in this land were lost. The thread of life had been cut at a low level. The penalty of death was prevented by the mercy of others, but the violation remained.

Mother Nature had written off the creatures who could not hold their place on the ladder of creation by living in harmony with her laws. She had taken over the long job of rebuilding the abandoned land by her own process of returning what is taken. Her wind tore away the shingles so the rain could rot down the buildings. The same wind brought in the seeds of weeds and sedge to hold the soil and begin all over again to replace organic matter, gather nitrogen from the air and reduce the insoluble rock to soluble plant food—a long, long process but a sure one, to prepare the land again for a wiser set of creatures. Tonight, from gullied fields, the wolf baying at the moon sounds like a dirge tuned to the tragic loneliness that desertion brings. Here man has failed. Little does it matter how much in taxes the politicians have saved or added by allowing it to be destroyed. Nor does it matter to whom the finger of investigation points and blames, because here man lost his basic struggle for survival, a task at which he must first succeed before he can go on to another.

So, Mr. Sharp-shin, my six hundred people who depend upon my soil for their food should hear this story of soil destruction, part of which I have witnessed in its tragic details. They should know that in the record Mother Nature keeps, not just one man has failed here but all those who farmed the land, all those who depended on it for that which they expected to eat and wear, have failed. Some of those eighty people who depend on this farm might have been very rich, some might have been presidents of banks and railroads, yet they were written off in her book as creatures who could not meet the test of survival. It is sad to think of a faraway banker well-supplied with a hoard of indigestible gold, living now by the charity of those who would share with him the margin of fertility still remaining in their farms. Perhaps the thought becomes more understandable if we think of the tenant as the captain of a ship and his eighty people, its passengers. The captain makes a mistake, strikes an iceberg, and his ship goes down. If any of them are to survive, it will be through the mercy and charity of a more skillful captain of another ship who makes the rescue and shares his space with them.

I would then, Mr. Sharp-shin, call attention to the futility of building industrial greatness without also building a soil potential to feed the people it represents. I would then tell my people that as a nation we are rapidly approaching a point (if we haven't already reached it) where two lines cross and begin to diverge. One line is our capacity to produce agricultural products; the other, our increasing demand for them. As the lines separate farther the diets of people change from animal proteins such as meat, milk and eggs to vegetable proteins and oils like those in legumes. The diets then change to cereal proteins and starches like wheat, rice, rye, and root crops. When the lines have separated to reach this last stage, famine becomes a real threat as it is now in many countries in the world.

I would then caution them that, as their farmer, I have my choice of two paths to follow. One is that of restoration; the other leads to the abandonment of land. It is marked by signs emblazoned with such noble words as "free enterprise," "unrestricted agriculture," "unregimented production." Such words come from my six hundred people who urge me on. Perhaps they announce them in a selfish interest to gain cheaper food, perhaps in a blind interpretation of "freedom", or perhaps, choked with abundance, they have accepted the philosophy of a grasshopper. I am tempted to follow such a road; it would serve me well. I could take from the soil all it has to offer and then—like a strip miner—abandon it and pass the problems I have created on to another generation. All this I could do but as their farmer I must point out two failures, theirs and mine. Noble words, power and national greatness cannot turn them into success.

For that reason, the abandoned farm represents still more. It is more than ravaged soil. It is more than gullied fields and distintegrating buildings. It is more than a sample of Mother Nature revealing the long process of restoration. It is more than a history of the misery caused those who last tried to live on it. It is more than the failure of man in his use of land. It is more than all this because it is an indictment by Mother Nature of man's intelligence. Her side of it is very simple. She has a natural process in which only those things live which have a margin. For man the margin came quite recently, and it is in lands rich enough to support both his body and mind. Of him she made the same demands she made of all creatures that went before him. The demand was simply this: "Keep the soil in place and return to it that which has been taken." This demand has been violated on the abandoned farm, and there, man should have the right to defend himself against this indictment. Let us, therefore, play a make-believe game giving man—with all his accomplishments, a chance to show that he can live on the abandoned farm without returning that which is taken. If he can, the indictment is withdrawn. If he can't, Mother Nature gives the punishment.

First, in our make-believe game, we must supply the farm with the human population that represents its part of the total. We will then declare that it shall have a fence around it over which no one can leave or enter. The farm is now ready for the people who may bring with thcm their ideas, tools and any equipment necessary for their demonstration of survival on this proving ground which has been violated.

Let us first give admittance to that farmer who is most capable of removing the last speck of fertility from the soil without replacing it. He may bring in his equipment and livestock—but no fertilizer, since doing so would satisfy one of the demands of Mother Nature which is to "return that which has been taken." Any equipment with which to build terraces would no longer be important since there is little chance to hold the soil which has already gone down the river.

We must have a sample of the workingman both with and without a union card. Perhaps his demand for a living wage, social justice, a pay increase attached to the cost of living, and an effective strike against Mother Nature could solve his problem of survival on the abandoned farm!

The merchant should be there, too. His cost of doing business must be more than twenty per cent or there just isn't any chance for him to live. To live by a twenty per cent margin is so important to him that to consider anything less can generate indignation to intimidate Mother Nature so that she will withdraw the indictment.

The gate will swing wide for the banker. His command over people and their activities cannot be taken lightly. Nothing can happen without money, not even birth and death. I wouldn't be surprised if the banker might threaten to cut off Mother Nature's credit or even to run her out of the margin business!

Professional men have a right to defend themselves against the indictment. The doctor has a point because he extends the margin for humans. The lawyer could perhaps find a flaw in the natural law and win the case without a speck of fertilizer. The engineer and the scientist would figure out the answer quite rapidly. They would be willing to pay up and rush out and get some fertilizer but the gate is locked against that sort of action.

The captain of industry just could not follow such a course because doing so would increase the price of food and that would result in a strike for higher wages. If Mother Nature does not give in, he will close down his plant!

At least two kinds of economists must have their chance. One is the fellow who believes that the law of supply and demand is the answer to all problems, so it must be the answer to this one. He will probably try to accuse Mother Nature of not supplying enough soil-plant food in the beginning. This would defeat his argument that a low supply of a commodity is good because it brings a higher price. Perhaps he is correct, but will Mother Nature listen to him, change her laws and supply the food to feed him from a soil that is short in its capacity to supply it?

The other economist believes that only more efficiency can give the answer. When land becomes inefficient it should be abandoned so that the efficient land can make the other farmers richer. The way we are headed now, someday *all* land will have to be abandoned, so the economist should learn a good lesson as to what will happen as more and more lands become inefficient—the inescapable result of "taking more than that which is returned."

Our make-believe game would not be complete unless we have the housewife who demands that all the food she buys be wrapped in cellophane and then delivered! It just is not good any other way, so to please her we will also let the cellophane maker come in. Perhaps when the food supply gets short he can solve the objections by just passing around the empty package in which it should have been wrapped. Processing and handling costs are more than sixty per cent of the price of food, so the package should have more than half the nutritional value to those who are sure it does not taste good without this extra service.

The educator must have a place in this group too. One with his learning just cannot be accused of having a lack of intelligence, even by

Mother Nature. There must be a mistake somewhere. Doctors' degrees go in droves to all those who have an intimate acquaintance with the liberal arts and sciences. Their culture is supreme as soon as they have mastered the century-old literature and philosophies of those foreign people who have in recent times embraced such ideologies as Communism, Socialism and Fascism. Perhaps the doctors' degrees and all lesser education down to the grades would be worth a bit more to our well-being if they required a lesson or two in what it takes to make America tick. It will be the privilege of him with the doctorate to try, however, to use the classics in their role of feeding the mind as a substitute for the minerals which have not been returned to the abandoned farm.

The politician must go in too. He cannot submit to such an outrage against his honesty and integrity. This calls for at least a Congressional investigation! It calls for laws to limit the powers of Mother Nature and make flow again the bountiful harvest from the abandoned fields. Parity prices will be tried from fifty to one hundred per cent; food will be given away; the budget will be balanced. Stand back, please open the gate and let him in, for he is full of answers. Send the army and air force to protect him and the abandoned farm. There is not enough water for the navy just now but if the admiral thinks he has the answer, the senator will build a pond for him.

Perhaps we have forgotten some, so open the gate and let them in. There are some who believe that prayer will change Mother Nature's demand and they should have their chance. There are others who are sure recreation holds the answer, so let in the crooner, resort owner, the comedian, the musician and the fan-dancer. Before the gate is closed and locked, however, give each one that for which he has worked hardest, that which gives him pride in his accomplishments, that which brands him a success by all who know him. Money seems to be that which he wants most of all. Give him money and lots of it. All the gold buried in Kentucky would be an amount large enough to make each a millionaire many times. Also add some food. Give him his part of the agricultural surplus. It will be about enough to last until he can produce his first crop. Now lock the gate for a year so that each can do his job undisturbed and give his answer to the indictment of Mother Nature. He will have proven Mother Nature wrong in her accusation if he can produce enough to eat on the abandoned land. He will then have proven that man can live by laws of his own creation and that he is the master he believes he is of the world and all of its creatures.

It will be necessary for him to get some quick answers to a few details. The soil no longer can produce carbohydrates and proteins in sufficient amounts for animals or people, which fact Tenant X discovered when he and his family were at the point of starvation. The scientist, however, may find a quick way to make the carbohydrates out of air, water and some atomic energy he brought along. It will be difficult to make a nourishing protein carrying calcium, phosphate, magnesium and the other elements that are necessary to human nutrition, but missing in the soil of the farm. He might try using sand, aluminum and iron. There is still a good supply of these materials, but no food has ever been discovered which could grow out of them alone. If he succeeded, perhaps he could find a way for the human body to digest the new food and thereby grow bones and teeth out of sand instead of calcium and phosphorus and the others. Such bones would be strong and perhaps eliminate all the breakage in the human body except that of the heart. I feel confident that Mother Nature would stand by patiently with considerable interest observing this process she had never thought of using before. If it worked she perhaps would withdraw in shame and give up.

The course that human behavior could take would be a guess for anyone to make. All people there should be happy because now they would be very rich. The banker would not collect any interest since no one would need more money than he already had. Perhaps some might sell their food supply and get all the money for themselves. If then, the chemist could not come through with food from sand and rocks, the rich might die first and there would be a natural redistribution of wealth!

Who would get the blame when the goods could not be produced? It could not be the chemist because he was never in the food business. It should not be the farmer because he is the champion "strip miner" of agriculture. He got that way by following the political philosophy of cheap food for the consumer which included no money for replacing the raw materials taken away. He interpreted the thought of "freedom for agriculture" as meaning "farm it, take all you can get and move on." He believed that when farm prices went down the only way to obtain more dollars was by plowing deeper and growing his crop out of the soil faster. No one thought of telling him that the next generation as well as the present one would like to eat from that soil. On the abandoned farm all these things had already been done, so he was too late to do them again. But who can blame him for following the thinking of well-meaning people?

If the chemist succeeded in supplying the kind of food that changes human bones to rocks using sand for protein, would anyone permit him to produce a surplus so that he could shut down his plant for repairs when that time came along? If he did produce a surplus, would his parity price (a price judged at a living wage level) be reduced so low that he could not afford to reopen his plant again? Would he be punished by low prices if he succeeded too well at producing more than people could eat and then be rewarded by high prices if he only produced half enough? Would people buy his surplus, store it and be willing to pay for the storage? Would they call it a waste of their money? Farmers would be interested in the answers to such questions since they experience their lowest prices when they do their job too well!

If man succeeded here, food would be different from any before. The human body, too, would be different from that of any creature ever to live on the earth. If man failed, the story would be a repetition of what has happened innumerable times before to those who have experienced starvation. Man would lose his reason; his instincts for basic survival would take over. He might even turn cannibalistic. The philosophy of "love thy neighbor" would take wing and the thought of destroying his neighbor would take its place so as to extend life a few days more. All the while, Mother Nature is standing by in silence, waiting for the moment in which she might again take over the endless task of rebuilding, in a slow method-ical way, that which man had destroyed. In the end, all that is man and all he brought to the farm would rust and fall apart except his gold. It would remain untarnished—perhaps because it is gold or perhaps as a monument to that which betrayed him.

The story of this game is not a nice one, nor do I enjoy telling it on this night in May. But I must tell it because even now one-third of our land and one-third of the farmers are at or near that level. The damp air from the pond still carries the breath of winter, and it is chilling to the soul that harbors such thought. The destruction of life is quick and easy, but the destruction of that by which it lives is morbid and sickening. So, too, would be my story if it had nothing more to offer than this ironic tale. Tonight we can rise above the thinking of Malthus and his followers. We can follow the age-old path of the prairie made straight by the skill of scientific research as it teaches us how to obey the laws of creation.

Not far away are restored fields of once desolate acres, now pounding with the throb of life, ready to explode into the best of food for both man and animals. From them, a breeze carrying the perfumed freshness of new life warms our hearts with hope as we begin to understand that human bodies and brains are made of three and one-half per cent well-refined clay, placed in combination with air, water and sunshine in Mother Nature's factory according to her laws, not ours. There, Mother Nature gives her blessing. It is the environment she declared suitable for the survival of man at the moment of his creation. There, abundance of higher quality food has stripped away the farm problem for farmer and consumer alike. Men of science have wondered how high crop yields can come from so low a quality soil. They wonder why once disease-infected animals and their offspring are healthy now, why wildlife can increase under intensive farming, why insects and drought seem to be less destructive than else-where. These are Mother Nature's rewards for obedience.

Government money had no part in buying these results, yet, relief money rewards are often paid to those who unknowingly destroyed the same values on other farms.

THE VALUE OF DIVERSITY (1969)
Douglas H. Pimlott

We live in a world where diversity is declining daily. Agriculture hastens to increase field and farm size to achieve greater efficiency; fertilizers enable farmers to ignore crop rotation; pesticides provide temporary relief from the epidemic spread of disease and insects inherent in one-crop farming; forestry is ignoring the experience of centuries in Europe and is now returning to clear-cut, even-aged, one-species woodlands.

Some of the hazards and fallacies of our times are revealed in Pimlott's timely and thoughtful message.

"When on board H.M.S. Beagle as naturalist, I was much struck with certain facts in the distribution of the organic beings inhabiting South America, and in the geological relations of the present to the past inhabitants of that continent. These facts . . . , seemed to throw some light on the origin of species—that mystery of mysteries, as it has been called by one of our greatest philosophers." (Darwin, 1859)

"Man has always been fascinated by the great diversity of organisms which live in the world around him. Many attempts have been made to understand the meaning of this diversity and the causes that bring it about. To many minds this problem possesses an irresistible aesthetic appeal. Inasmuch as scientific inquiry is a form of aesthetic endeavour, biology owes its existence in part to this appeal." (Dobzhansky, 1951).

"This book is a plea for diversity—for the preservation of natural diversity and for the creation of man-made diversity—in the hope that the prevailing trend toward uniformity can be arrested and the world kept a fit place for the greatest possible human variety." (Dasmann, 1968).

The quotations from Darwin, Dobzhansky and Dasmann serve to indicate that the current upsurge of interest in ecological diversity is just that—an upsurge of interest—not the development of a new concept. Prior to the publication of *The Origin of Species* fascination in the diversity of species was largely an act of marvelling at the remarkable ingenuity of a Creator who had seen fit to put so many different creatures on the earth.

However, in the post-Darwinian era the marvelling changed to questioning—questioning which sought, as Dobzhansky stated it, " . . . to understand the meaning of this diversity and the causes that bring it about." But not until this decade did the word diversity, as an ecological and genetical concept, begin to enter the vocabulary of the wildlife manager or land-use planner. The sudden stirring of interest in diversity among practical people has developed as a result of the realization that technological "progress" is rapidly changing the world and in the process of changing, simplifying and giving both urban and rural environments a similar appearance wherever they occur (Elton, 1958; Dasmann, 1968).

Reprinted from: Trans. N. Amer. Wildl. and Natural Resources Conf. 34:265-280.

Some dread the process of simplification because they fear the sociological and cultural consequences of a world that produces a profound sense of boredom through the monotony of its appearance and through the limited variety of experiences that can be achieved. Dasmann (1968) seeks to stir world thinking on this side of the question in his recent book, *A Different Kind of Country,* which provided one of the introductory quotations. But although ecologists, along with artists and architects may deplore the influence of simplification of the environment on the aesthetic, cultural and spiritual quality of living, their concern goes much deeper and results from understanding of fundamental ecological processes; the very processes which gave rise to the diversity of nature which stirred Darwin's thoughts and resulted in "the conclusion that man is the codescendant with other species of some ancient, lower, and extinct form, is not in any degree new." The fear about the simplification of environments is rooted in the understanding of diversity because innumerable studies have demonstrated that ecosystems which have a simple fauna contain conditions which result in violent oscillations in animal numbers or in the rapid increase in simple plants (e.g. fungi).

The ecological complications that develop when complex, diverse environments have been replaced with simple, unstructured ones are well illustrated by the problems that have resulted from the establishment of monocultures in the form of conifer plantations, vast acreage planted for wheat, market crops or in fruit orchards. These ecological anomalies have frequently been subject to severe damage as the results of the build-up of insect populations or the spread of fungal diseases.

The fears of ecologists have increased as society has become more and more dependent on this form of land use to meet the increasing demand for food; they have increased as the use of chemicals has intensified the processes of simplifications and, in spilling over, have contributed to the degradation of ecosystems which were far removed from those on which the chemicals were originally placed.

The objectives of this paper are twofold: to discuss the concept of ecological diversity in a way that will highlight some of the conclusions that have been drawn by fundamental ecologists on "the meaning of diversity and the causes which bring it about." Such a discussion is, I consider, necessary to the elucidation of the second objective, to discuss the value of ecological diversity. It should be understood at the outset that this paper is primarily a review paper, for neither my education nor my research have particularly equipped me to add much original thinking to the concept of diversity.

THE CONCEPT OF DIVERSITY

Darwin's conclusions about the descent of man resulted from his understanding of the fundamental truth that the variety that occurred in nature was not fortuitous but had resulted from the response of individual organisms to the varied nature of the environments which exist in the world.

It has, however, become evident that the evolutionary response of all animals, for example, has not been of exactly the same nature. Some animals have made a go of things by being generalists and occupying a wide variety of environments; others have specialized and as a result require very specific conditions before they can exist in an area. In eastern North America, the crow and the pileated woodpecker are examples of birds that evolved along wide and narrow lines respectively. As habitats have been changed by human uses it has also become evident that the animals which have taken the narrow road of specialization are those which have been most subject to extinction while the generalists have been prone to increase in numbers, sometimes to very high levels of abundance.

Factors Which Influence Species Diversity:

The observed phenomenon that some areas of the world contain many more species of organisms than others has led to a great deal of speculation about why there is so much variation in the diversity of species. The most common of the hypotheses that have been advanced were discussed in papers by Connell and Orias (1964) and Dunbar (1968).

A popular hypothesis is that the number of species is a direct reflection of the number of niches that are available to be colonized. Since there has been quite intensive study of bird communities it is possible to "document" the point by comparing the large number of species that exist, say, in tropical rain forests as compared with the relatively small number that exist in the simpler (hence fewer niches) community of the boreal forest. It is, however, difficult to argue effectively for this hypothesis without losing the thread of logic. The birds in a tropical rain forest certainly live in a more complex community than those in the boreal forest, but if the number of species of birds depends entirely on the complexity of the forest vegetation, what causes the variation in the complexity of the flora? The soil, or at least the parent material, on which the two floral communities developed does not have nearly the same degree of variability as do the two communities; yet in one area (the tropics) it supports several thousand species of plants while in the other (boreal forest) it supports no more than a few hundred.

A closely related hypothesis suggests that the difference in diversity is a measure of the ecological maturity of environments and that the recurrence of climatic catastrophies (e.g. glaciation) has maintained the northern biota in an immature state (Wallace, 1968; Dunbar, 1960, 1963; Fischer, 1960). Connell and Orias (1964) argued against this hypothesis on the basis of evidence from paleontological studies by Newell (1962) which indicated that although the geographic area occupied by the temperate zone shifted, the shifts did not necessarily result in extinction of species. However, Dunbar (1968) believes that the primary effect to be considered in the ecological-maturity hypothesis is the denudation of large land areas and the setting up of new environmental conditions and not Pleistocene glaciations that caused wide-spread extinctions. He argued that in Arctic situations the evolutionary trend toward complex stable ecosystems works "... contrary to ecological adaptation to the highly oscillating environment, which tends to keep the number of species small." However, he accepts the theory that there is a development in all ecosystems toward stability, but he suggested that in polar zones it is ameliorated by the necessity organisms face to make immediate adjustment to the severe environmental oscillations which occur. He summed up the "effects of selection toward two different environmental objectives" as follows:

Environmental oscillation favors selection toward	Stability of ecosystems favors selection toward
1 / High fecundity given by	1 / Low specific fecundity, given partly by
2 / Large body size with many eggs. This is given by	2 / Small body size with small eggs, or large size with large eggs
3 / Slow growth to maturity (slow energy turnover)	3 / Fast growth to maturity (small eggs) or slow growth (large eggs).
4 / Small number of species giving	4 / Large numbers of species giving
5 / Simple ecosystems	5 / Complex ecosystem

Both objectives are favored by
6 / Increased energy capital.

A discussion of fluctuations by Margalef (1968) suggests that he is in agreement with Dunbar on many of the points listed above.

A third hypothesis is based on variation in the ability of plants and animals to withstand the rigors of severe (e.g. polar) environments (Wynne-Edwards, 1952). However, Connell and Orias (1964) argue that rigorness *per se* cannot be the primary factor because if some animals were capable of adapting then others could also have made the adjustment. At this point it would seem valid to question if it is entirely logical to consider hypotheses one after another as if factors of environment and time were not capable of interacting. In considering environments as diverse as those of tropical and polar regions it is possible that climatic stress (rigor) and time (a factor of maturity) are interacting factors.

Dunbar (1968), in fact, suggests the interaction of factors (time and size of niche) in discussing the fourth hypothesis proposed by Klopfer and MacArthur (1960). This hypothesis suggests that ecological niches in the tropics are narrower than those in northern latitudes and result in greater diversity of species in tropical zones. However, there is a feedback mechanism in that the lack of plasticity limits the ability of many tropical species to colonize temperate zones. In a later paper MacArthur (1965) develops the hypothesis in more detail and in his summary states that " . . . total species diversities, from areas composed of many types of habitats, are usually but not always, much greater in the tropics than in temperate regions. This is accomplished by a finer subdivision of habitats (habitat selection) more than by a marked increase in diversity within habitats."

In a very interesting paper, which has been reprinted in several places, Hutchinson (1959) discussed a number of factors which he considered promoted or limited the diversity of species. One paragraph in his paper summed up his conclusion:

We may, therefore, conclude that the reason there are so many species of animals is at least partly because a complex trophic organization of a community is more stable than a simple one, but that limits are set by the tendency of food chains to shorten or become blurred, by unfavourable physical factors, by space, by the fineness of possible subdivisions of niches, and by those characters of the environmental mosaic which permit a greater diversity of small than of large allied species.

Connell and Orias (1964) described the development of diversity from a model based on Hutchinson's hypothesis that diversity is based on the flow of energy through the food webs that exist in communities (Fig. 1). The model suggests that ". . . positive feedback mechanisms would operate in the early stages of the evolution of a community, ever-increasing its stability, production and diversity. Later, the negative feed-back mechanism would regulate the amount of diversity being maintained, through the instability which is the price of increased specialization and efficiency."

Elton (1946) discussed the relationships which existed within 55 animal and 27 plant communities which he had studied and pointed out that both types contained a high proportion of genera which were represented by only one species. He stated that the difference in species/genus

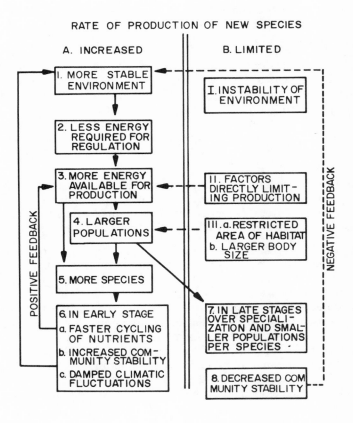

Fig. 5-1.—A model for the production and regulation of species diversity in an ecological system. Solid lines indicate an increase, dashed lines a decrease in the diversity of species. Detailed explanation of model in paper by Connell and Orias (1964).

frequencies of small portions of a major habitat and those covering large regions was attributable to the historical effects of competition between species of the same genus. He suggested also that the relatively small number of species represented in community surveys indicates that there is a limit to the numbers of primary consumers that can exist in any given area and that it may represent a state of population competition. Elton's hypothesis that diversity of species is limited by competition was not included in the reviews by Connell and Orias (1964) or Dunbar (1968) that were previously mentioned.

Diversity and Stability of Populations:

It has been recognized for a long time that in the arctic and boreal forest zones some of the animals such as lemmings, arctic foxes, snowy owls, varying hare and lynx, undergo very marked fluctuations in numbers. The periodicity of the fluctuations is predictable for at least some species. Keith (1962) gives a comprehensive review of the information available for those that appear to have a 10-year cycle of abundance. A number of authors (e.g., Dymond, 1947, MacArthur, 1965) suggested that the fluctuations result from the simplicity of the environment and of trophic links in the existing food webs. In an earlier section I reviewed an hypothesis by Dunbar (1968) which suggests that unstable ecosystems are the consequence of selection toward immediate adjustment to severe oscillation in environmental conditions.

The fact that balance in simple communities is difficult to maintain has also been demonstrated many times by studies of insect populations in monocultures of trees, orchards and food plants. A number of examples are reported in the reviews by Elton (1958) and Pimentel (1961).

Elton (1958) ". . . set out some of the evidence that the balance of relatively simple communities of plants and animals is more easily upset than that of richer ones: that is, more subject to destructive oscillations in populations, especially of animals, and more vulnerable to invasions." He then stated six arguments to show that the complexity of an ecosystem results in greater stability of its constituent populations. His arguments were based on evidence produced by mathematical formulations, laboratory experiments, the historic fact of the invasion of relatively simple island communities, the relative stability of insects in natural communities, and in particular in tropical forests, and finally on the evidence of insect problems that have developed in orchards where pesticides were used indiscriminately.

Pimentel (1961) showed that insect outbreaks are less likely to occur in mixed stands than in those comprised of a single species. In addition to drawing examples from the literature he gave the results of experiments that he had conducted using cabbage and other varieties of *Brassica oleracea* and several species of Cruciferae. He suggested that diversity relates to community stability in at least three ways:

"First, diversity of host and prey species provides alternate food for parasites and predators and this provides greater stability in these population systems.

"Second, diversity in types of parasitic and predaceous species feeding on one species of herbivore may result in greater stability in these population interactions.

"Third, increased diversity of feeding habits of the species members of a community results in more stability of the organizations."

To sum up, the evidence appears to bear out the general conclusion that the greater the degree of diversity in communities the greater the degree of stability inherent in their constituent populations. Stability appears to be one of the most important values of diversity.

Having drawn a conclusion that is at least close to that stated above, both Elton (1958) and Pimentel (1961) argued against clean cultural practices and for the maintenance of as diverse habitats as possible. They suggested that hedge rows and interspersed habitats provide shelter for parasites and predators which may add to the stability of the populations of insects on nearby crop lands.

Although the general conclusion that diversity results in stability appears to be warranted, there is evidence that in some cases competition among predators may cause interactions which allow prey species to escape from their predators (Turnbull and Chant, 1961; Watt, 1965). The complexities of the question are reviewed in some detail by Watt (1968). It is evident from the case he has developed that much more experimental evidence is needed to clarify the question. Connell and Orias (1964) may have glimpsed some of the truth in suggesting that overspecialization results in decreased stability of the community (Fig. 1).

Diversity and Energy Flow:

Theories of succession and diversity are generally in agreement that the natural trend from immaturity to maturity in ecosystems is toward (i) a stable state in which productivity and respiration are equal ($P/R = 1$) (ii) increased diversity and (iii) a more complete utilization of the energy which enters the system.

In his recent book Watt (1968) points out that data which document that the productivity of diverse natural systems is greater than simpler ones are very sparse. He uses two examples, one which suggests that the biomass of big-game animals in primitive North America and of domestic livestock in 1959-60 were similar (I consider this example as invalid since it draws on estimates made by Seton which were certainly no more than the crudest of guesses) and a second one which compares the production of cattle and wild game on a ranch in Southern Rhodesia (Dasmann, 1964; Matthews, 1962). These studies showed that the maximum production of cattle yielded only 78 percent of the profit that was capable of being produced by a sustained cropping of the 13 game species that were present. Watt (1968) suggested that there were at least four basic reasons why this was the case:

"1. Native wild game have been selected by nature for eons to withstand extreme conditions and endemic hazards in their native habitats.

"2. Native wild game make better use of incident solar energy because of their extreme diversification and specialization.

"3. The great variety of wildlife in Africa make for great community stability.

"4. The habitat is ecologically very 'brittle'."

Watt (1968:71-73) discussed each point in some detail and ended the discussion with the conclusion, "No ecosystem should be altered from its natural state by man in the interests of higher productivity unless it can be conclusively demonstrated by experiments that the alteration really does lead to higher productivity."

It is difficult at least for North America, to discuss terrestrial ecosystems, where a similar situation exists and where value in terms of net profit can be so related. There are many instances where productivity, even if greater, does not necessarily have a direct relationship to yield since a considerable part of the productivity may not have an economic value or at best be of low value. To sum up, it is difficult to present a general argument that diversity has economic value because of better utilization of solar energy, for the energy often becomes fixed in forms which are not utilized by humans.

It is possible that the situation may be quite different in the case of aquatic systems such as some of the Great Lakes, but I am not familiar enough with the literature to draw on it for examples. I do, however, recall a simple case presented by Odum (1959) who pointed out that to maximize the yield of fish ponds the diversity of the flora and fauna must be reduced. The example emphasizes again that since productivity and yield are not always synonymous, questions that pertain to the economic values of diversity are not simple ones.

DIVERSITY, WILDLIFE AND AESTHETICS

Habitat Diversity:

The values of habitat diversity as it refers to wildlife management were summed up in a dynamic way by Aldo Leopold in *Game Management* in a chapter entitled "Game Range" (Leopold, 1933). I know of no discussion of the subject that gives a more concise discussion of the values of diversity of habitats to the production and maintenance of wild species. The three paragraphs which introduce the subject and the final one bear quoting directly because of the way Leopold's words set the stage and bring out for the wildlife manager the complexity, and the intellectual challenge of habitat management to produce ecological diversity:

What Is Game Range? When the game manager asks himself whether a given piece of land is suitable for a given species of game, he must realize that he is asking no simple question, but rather he is facing one of the great enigmas of animate nature. An answer good enough for practical purposes is usually easy to get by the simple process of noting whether the species is there already, or whether it occurs on "similar" range nearby. But let him not be cocksure about what is "similar," for this involves the deeper questions of *why* a species occurs in one place and not in another, which is probably the same as why it persists at all. No living man can answer the question fully in even one single instance.

It should be realized, first of all, that the present boundaries of the ranges of our present species constitute a great maze of diversities. If all species boundaries were plotted on a great map of the world, it would look like a wide pavement on a wet morning, after thousands of earthworms had been crawling over it all night, inscribing their irregular tracks.

Secondly, although the boundaries of these present ranges seem so stable to us that we record them in books and maps as fixed facts of nature, they have as a matter of fact undergone continuous change through the ages, each change constituting the response of the species to some change in its environment or in itself.

Then in the final paragraph of the section:

If the assortment of environmental types in any one locality falls short of being adequate to maintain thrift and welfare, the species shrinks in numbers to what the locality will support. When such shrinkage approaches zero, the locality is lost altogether, and the species withdraws. When such withdrawals become too prevalent, the species becomes extinct.

The message is clear that diversity of habitat is the life blood of the majority of species and the ramifications extend from the subsistence of an individual to the viability of a population and to the survival of species. Using the bobwhite quail and white-tailed deer as primary reference animals, Leopold went on to discuss the need that the majority of species have for an assortment of environmental types during the course of the four seasons. He pointed out that ". . . the service rendered by any environmental type not only varies by species and season but is likely to be contained within a very small fraction of the type." The validity of this statement has been documented many times but in no more relevant way than by the work of the Hammerstrom's (1957) which has been converted into an action plan to maintain a small population of prairie chicken in Wisconsin which is close to being extirpated. The program to maintain prairie chicken in Wisconsin relates the interspersion of habitat types to the mobility of the species and considers the tolerance of the species to variation in composition and interspersion of habitat, all matters which Leopold discussed nearly 40 years ago.

Leopold referred to the need for diversity of habitat in terms of *edge-effect* and stated that since most species require three or four environmental types on each unit of habitable range ". . . game is a phenomenon of edges." He stated as a law of dispersion that: "The potential density of game of low radius requiring two or more types is, within ordinary limits, proportional to the sum of type peripheries."

The importance of maintaining diversity of habitat types as perhaps the most vital aspect of management for many species, has been discussed in many publications since Leopold wrote *Game Management*. It is referred to both as a general principle in discussing ways and means of modifying the influence of environmental factors and as it specifically relates to the management of species. Because of the difficulty of making a selection which does not simply reflect the contents of one's own library I will refer only to a few of the more commonly known books, for example, *The Deer of North America* (Taylor, 1956); *Our Wildlife Legacy* (Allen, 1954); *Wildlife Biology* (Dasmann, 1964); *Wildlife Management* (Trippensee, 1948; 1953).

I believe that well before the end of this century a great deal of attention will be paid in wildlife programs to the maintenance of habitat diversity for non-game species. Bird watching, for example, is receiving increasing recognition as one of the most interesting avocations and, if it ever was, is certainly no longer limited to "little old ladies in tennis shoes." Interest in the ecological side of natural history, rather than the pursuit of it as a sort of numbers game, has been promoted by publications such as *A Guide to Bird Watching* (Hickey, 1943). The avocation is being recognized as a way in which an understanding of complex environmental interrelationship can be gained in a relatively small area of land. In this respect land-use practises on many areas of public land, which are being managed for timber production or as public hunting areas, will be modified slightly to improve their attractiveness to naturalists. Many managed areas will not require additional modification but will be good just as they are. In *Game Management,* Leopold has a figure (9) which suggests how the interspersion of habitat types could improve an area so that it could support 6 coveys of quail instead of one. The interspersion of types, he proposed, would add considerably to the interest that the area would have for naturalists as well as hunters, because of the number of species that could be found within a limited portion of the area.

The value of diversity to a species extends beyond the admixture of habitat types to the characteristics of the individual habitat type itself. I have thought of this often in recent years as I have strolled through Queen's Park, a small park in the heart of Toronto which is adjacent both to the provincial seat of government and to the University of Toronto where I work.

The northern section of the park consists of approximately 10 acres and contains an admixture of indigenous and exotic species. The oldest trees in the park are white and red oak; most of the latter are hollow and misshapen and, as they die or are declared a hazard, they are being cut down and replaced by exotic species which are more tolerant of carbon monoxide and sulphur dioxide. The park is a manicured place of asphalt walks, a fountain, benches, strategically placed flower beds and closely mowed lawns. One of the things that makes the park an enjoyable place for the people who use it is the animals that inhabit it. They too are a mixture of native and exotic species. The ones that are likely to be found there at any time of year are gray squirrels, pigeons, starlings and English sparrows.

To the squirrels (the fall population is usually between 25 and 40) the most important element is the oak trees. They provide a very considerable crop of mast and most important of all the "decadent" red oaks are the den trees. Without them, or a substitute, the squirrels would not survive in Queen's Park. One day I talked to a group of landscape architects and tried to draw them out on what they saw in the park, what they would do if they were responsible for its management. I was disappointed to find that they thought only of the land form and of the trees; not one remembered the squirrels in voicing thoughts about what they would do with the park. I urged them to think of the animals as the third dimension, and I argued that the red oak should be maintained as an important component of the park even if it is not as tolerant to an urban environment as some of its exotic counterparts. I argued that the old oaks should be retained as long as they are alive and that perhaps ways might be found to treat the dead stubs so that they could be maintained for use by the squirrels long after the trees have died.

The squirrels add an important element of diversity to Queen's Park and have real value to many of the people who visit it regularly even though their value does not show up in GNP of the country. In other cases, however, where squirrels or other animals are hunted or viewed by naturalists the values are being measured in tangible ways, and some day it will be possible to equate them against the cost of leaving a wolf tree or an overmature red oak in a wood lot because of its importance to wild things.

Diversity and Aesthetics:

It is in terms of values which are most often intangible that the strongest case for the value of diversity can be made. It is on this theme that Dasmann (1968) concentrates in *A Different Kind of Country.* Because it is so thoroughly discussed there, and because in terms of this paper both time and space are limited, I will not talk much about the topic here. However, I would like to state a simple case which suggests that ecological diversity, even that which results from the presence of a single additional organism, can add an important dimension, and hence value, to our lives. I think that the squirrels and pigeons of Queen's Park play such a part in the lives of many people. The Park is not as wild a place as I would prefer it to be, but it is a place many people enjoy; from the first warm days in spring young lovers and old-age pensioners alike make good use of it. Many of those who lunch there, share their food with the animals, and there is one old lady, who buys peanuts by the hundred-weight and comes each day to feed the squirrels or to leave little piles of them at the base of den trees on days when the squirrels are not active.

On several fall mornings I have watched an attractive young lady feeding pigeons as she walked briskly through the park. It is obvious that she does it regularly and enjoys it, for the pigeons swarm around her as she walks and take food directly from her hands; she talks animatedly to them as they flap and fly around her.

A young man who owns a white Alsatian regularly visits the park to give him exercise. The dog delights in chasing the squirrels; I have never seen him catch one, however, it is evident that the activity makes his day, and it is apparent that as long as he is a visitor no squirrel is going to be permitted to lose his affinity for trees or to slow up too much.

Teaching ecology in the heart of a large metropolis can be a textbook type of operation so on a number of occasions I have made a study of *The ecology of the squirrels of Queen's Park* a class assignment. One could say that it is a rather artificial environment for the squirrels. But if so, it really is not important, for they are reproducing, living and dying in Queen's Park; in one way or another all the factors that influenced the squirrels that were living there 300 years ago can be found to apply in the Park today. The diversity added by the squirrels is valuable to us too. We want thought given to maintaining the squirrel population because we think they add a lot to the quality of the Park.

Algonquin Provincial Park in Ontario is 200 miles north of Toronto and is inhabited by deer which are living very close to the northern limit of their range. Because of the stresses that the environment impose they are not nearly as numerous as they are in New York, Pennsylvania or points south. The energy that the deer transfer from plant to animal biomass is often transferred to another trophic level by wolves who prey primarily on deer. Many people go to Algonquin simply because the wolves are there. Those who work at it are sometimes rewarded by hearing a pack howling, by finding a family at a rendezvous site or, in winter, by a day spent tracking a pack which has written a story of its way of doing things on the snow.

Throughout the world people who hunt or who, in other ways, seek to maximize the direct return of the energy of ecosystems to people, kill wolves. In many areas they have succeeded in eliminating them and have achieved their goal at the cost of an important element of the diversity of holarctic environments. But the sense of values change and people who visit Algonquin and other wolf woods of the world are raising more and more questions about the validity of settling a question of tangible versus intangible values in such a final way.

Wolves, coyotes, foxes, goshawks and horned owls are all elements of ecological diversity which will be of greater value to people in the future. I think they, the predators, will be valuable in helping us to come to terms with the total value of diversity in the ecosystems of the world, because their presence causes us to consider the comparative value of tangible and intangible aspects of things that make up our lives.

LITERATURE CITED

Allen, D. L.
　　1954.　Our wildlife legacy. Funk and Wagnalls, New York.
Connell, J. H. and E. Orias
　　1964.　The ecological regulation of species diversity. Am. Nat. 98:399-414.
Darwin, C.
　　1859.　On the origin of species by the means of natural selection. John Murray, London.
Dasmann, R. F.
　　1964.　African game ranching. Macmillan, New York.
Dasmann, R. F.
　　1968.　A different kind of country. Macmillan, New York.
Dobzhansky, T.
　　1951.　Genetics and the origin of species. Columbia Univ. Press, New York.
Dunbar, M. J.
　　1960.　The evolution of stability in marine environments: natural selection at the level of the ecosystem. Amer. Nat. 94:129-136.
Dunbar, M. J.
　　1963.　Ecological adaptation to the glacial climate. Trans. Roy. Soc. Canada. I (Ser. 4):433-440.

Dunbar, M.J.
    1968.   Ecological development in polar regions. Prentice-Hall, Englewood Cliffs, N.J.

Dymond, J. R.
    1947.   Fluctuations in animal populations with special reference to those of Canada. Trans. Roy. Soc., Canada. XLI: 1-34.

Elton, C.
    1946.   Competition and the structure of ecological communities. J. Anim. Ecol. 15: 54-68.

Elton, C.
    1958.   The ecology of invasions by animals and plants. Methuen, London.

Fischer, A. G.
    1960.   Latitudinal variations in organic diversity. Evolution 14:64-81.

Hammerstrom, F. N., Mattson, O. E. and F. Hammerstrom.
    1957.   A guide to prairie chicken management. Tech. Bull. No. 15, Wis. Cons. Dept., Madison, Wis.

Hickey, J. J.
    1943.   A guide to bird watching. Garden City Books. New York.

Hutchinson, G. E.
    1959.   Homage to Santa Rosalia, or, Why are there so many kinds of animals. Am. Nat. 93:145-59.

Klopfer, P. H. and R. H. MacArthur
    1960.   Niche size and faunal diversity. Am. Nat. 94:293-300.

Leopold, A.
    1933.   Game management. Scribner's. New York.

MacArthur, R. H.
    1965.   Patterns of species diversity. Biol. Rev. 40:510-33.

Margalef, R.
    1968.   Perspectives in ecological theory. Univ. Chicago Press, Chicago.

Matthews, L. H.
    1962.   A new development in the conservation of African animals. Advan. Sci. 18: 581-585. (Quoted in Watt, 1968).

Newell, N. D.
    1962.   Paleontological gaps and geochronology. J. Paleontol. 36:592-610.

Odum, E. P.
    1959.   Fundamentals of Ecology. Saunders. Philadelphia.

Pimentel, D.
    1961.   Species diversity and insect population outbreaks. Ann. Entomol. Soc. Am., 54:76-86.

Taylor, W. P.
    1956.   The deer of North America. Stockpole and The Wildl. Mgmt. Inst. Harrisburg Washington.

Trippensee, R. E.
    1958.   Wildlife management Vols. 1 & 2. McGraw-Hill, New York.

Turnbull, A. L. and D. A. Chant
    1961.   The practice and theory of biological control. Can. J. Zool. 39:697-753.

Wallace, A. R.
    1878.   Tropical nature and other essays. MacMillan, London. (Quoted in Dunbar, 1968).

Watt, K. E. F.
    1965.   Community stability and the strategy of biological control. Can. Entomol., 97: 887-895.

Watt, K. E. F.
    1968.   Ecology and resource management. McGraw-Hill, New York.

Wynne-Edwards, V. C.
    1952.   Zoology of the Baird Expedition (1950). I. The birds observed in central and southeast Baffin Island. Auk, 69:353-391.

Courtesy of Cornell Laboratory of Ornithology

THE ORNITHOLOGIST'S RESPONSIBILITY TO THE FUTURE (1958)
Thomas G. Scott

The universal problem of increase in human numbers necessitates looking ahead in a search for solutions and compromises. How often we have heard the axiom that the biggest problem in wildlife management is the management of man. Scott has made an urgent plea for serious projections of the demand for outdoor recreation in the future.

An effort to anticipate and prepare for the future seems desirable, because our generation bears a responsibility for passing on to the next a potential for continued well-being, particularly in the area of bird conservation. Any estimate of the future must be based on projections of past experience and cannot possibly be much more than an assessment of relative probabilities. Such estimates, however, provide the only reasonable basis for long-range planning and have become standard practice in the world of business and government. Inasmuch as we must attempt to ensure the protection of birds and the well-being of man, there appears to be little merit in a policy of deliberate conservatism in our estimate of the future.

The trend in growth of the human population constitutes the key element in long-range planning. Continued rapid growth of our population in the United States appears to be accepted generally by demographers. The possibility of acceptance of population control seems remote. The human birth rate tends to reflect the nation's economic status, and it is certain that government will do everything within its power to maintain prosperity. A major atomic war appears to be the only event which might check the current explosive trend in numbers of people in the foreseeable future.

Projections of the total United States population, based on high fertility and low mortality assumptions characteristic of the period since the end of World War II, have been estimated to be: 202,910,000 in 1965; 237,580,000 in 1975; 342,673,000 in 2000; and 501,825,000 in 2050 (Greville, 1957:27). Luck (1957:903) considered a population of 600 million by 2050 almost inevitable. In the event that these estimates seem excessive, we may be reminded that as recently as 1941 a study of recreational needs anticipated a population of only 158 million by about *1980* (U.S. Natl. Park Serv., 1941:5).

The demand for outdoor recreation promises to grow at a faster rate than the population. The amount of leisure available to the average person has been increasing steadily. The 5-day work week is almost universal, and vacations with pay are an established custom. Old-age insurance and pension plans provide for increasing retirement of the aged. Raushenbush (1955:92) predicted a 37.5-hour work week or its equivalent in annual working time by 1960 and a 35-hour week by 1965. Despite a shorter work week and a heavy tax burden, the trend in disposable income has been

Reprinted from: Wilson Bull. 70 (4):385-393.

upward (Dewhurst and Assoc., 1955:90). The mobility of this population is increasing at a logarithmic or percentage rate. Automobile ownership is increasing more rapidly than population, and the movement of traffic is being facilitated by extension and improvement of the highway system. Clay *et al.* (1955:8-9) reported that almost 58 million motor vehicles were registered in 1954, one for "every 700 feet of every lane in both directions on all streets and highways in the Nation." They predicted that vehicle registrations would reach 81 million by 1965. Also, extensive use of inexpensive aircraft as a future mode of family transportation does not place excessive stress on the imagination.

That the public has been using its increased leisure, income, and mobility to utilize outdoor recreation is in abundant evidence. Statistics reveal that outdoor recreation has been increasing more rapidly than the population. The use of national parks almost doubled in the decade 1947-1956 (Clawson, 1958:23). The very rapid increase in the recreational use of national wildlife refuges is of particular significance to the ornithologist. Clawson (1958:49) showed that the recreational use of national wildlife refuges more than doubled from 1951 to 1956. He compared this "with an increase of 48 per cent for the national park system, and of 75 per cent for the national forests, in the same period." Clawson classified use of national wildlife refuges in 1956 as: hunting, 6 per cent; fishing, 37 per cent; and other, including picnicking, swimming, and wildlife observation, 57 per cent, and he observed that "It would be interesting to know how much of the use was solely or primarily for the . . ." purpose of wildlife observation. Interesting indeed. A survey in 1955 determined that 21 per cent of all people 12 years of age and older hunted, fished, or did both and expended approximately $2,850,979,000 in these activities (U.S. Fish and Wildlife Serv., 1956:7, 17). Outdoor recreation is big business and promises to get bigger.

Projections of the future use of national parks and forests for recreation have been attempted. From 53 million visits recorded in national forests in 1956, it is anticipated that an increase to 65 million in 1960 and to 360 million in 1980 may be expected; from 55 million visits in the national park system in 1956, it is estimated that 60 to 80 million visits may be anticipated in 1960 and 135 to 440 million visits in 1980 (Clawson and Held, 1957:342). This forecast of demand for recreation in the national forest and park systems probably reflects that which may be contemplated for private lands and state, county, and municipal facilities. Thus, we are in the somewhat strange business of struggling to increase facilities to accommodate a rapidly increasing horde seeking outdoor recreation and at the same time using every means within our power to encourage greater interest in Nature as a means of insuring support for its preservation and wise use.

Baker (1952:20) believes that "The greatest progress made in conservation in our generation has been growing recognition of its basic relation to human welfare . . ." There are more private and government agencies encouraging interest in outdoor recreation and the conservation of natural resources than ever before. The business world recognizes that it has a major stake in outdoor recreation. That these agencies together with the public are making their interests known with increasing power is evident in legislation of all kinds. The biologist has a responsibility here which will grow in importance, the responsibility of guiding this power in a realistic direction. And, certainly, the biologist's role in the task of improving upon the perceptive capacity and proper conduct of the public in the out-of-doors will also take on increased importance. Pierce (1957:284) has pointed out some of the responsibilities which we bear as ornithologists.

The well-being of birds will be most vitally affected where the task of meeting the requirements of an exploding human population necessitates permanent change in habitat. The problem resolves itself into whether upwards of 220 million people can live in the continental United States without causing a major adjustment in bird populations. Birds, and people for that matter, must eventually come to terms with the limitations of their environment. An appraisal of this problem and the knowledge needed for its solution or understanding requires projection of trends in land and water use, especially as relates to change in habitat.

Of the total rural land area of the continental United States (1,903,706, 000 acres), approximately 24 per cent is federally owned and federally administered. Of the federal lands, excluding Indian lands (which are not federally owned) and military reservations, it is believed that at least 95 per cent of the remaining 377 million acres will remain in federal ownership (Clawson and Held, 1957:3, 5). In a discussion of major changes in land use to 1975, Wooten and Anderson (1955:1) believed that "the total forest area may be maintained at about the present level. . ." Except for isolated problems, it seems likely that little change will take place on federal lands in the foreseeable future which would result in catastrophic adjustment of bird life. The most important considerations here will be an increasingly intensive forest management program, delay in acquisition of strategic lands to complete the national waterfowl refuge system, management of visitors to insure protection of the bird species in critical status, and excessive exploitation of nonrenewable resources.

The effect of intensive forest management on bird life should be kept under observation. Inasmuch as pines can be grown more quickly than hardwoods, it seems likely that they will be used to an increasing extent for meeting the timber needs of the future. The currently expanding application of herbicides from airplanes to relieve pines of competition from hardwoods has a great potential for producing permanent change in bird populations. Because pure stands of pine support but little wildlife, Lay (1958:5) considered that the problem resolved itself into saving a sufficient proportion of hardwoods to meet the needs of wildlife while removing enough to permit production of a satisfactory stand of pine.

Bellrose and Scott (1955:311) have pointed out the need for stepping up the acquisition of land to complete the national waterfowl refuge system. Competition for land is becoming increasingly severe. Land prices and conflict of interest may reach a point where purchase of land for wildlife refuges will become prohibitive. The encroachment of human activities on wetlands is evident in the remarks of Farley (1955:16): "Today and for years past we have watched marshes and ponds disappear as agriculture has expanded. In the black prairie—pothole region of western and southern

Minnesota and eastern North and South Dakota, agricultural drainage removed, in each of the years 1949 and 1950, about 22,000 potholes, amounting to some 63,000 acres. These areas were the most productive waterfowl lands in the United States, fully equal to the best producing areas in Canada. Similar drainage is occurring in many coastal sections, which are most important to the birds as wintering grounds. Most of the great natural marshes of the Gulf are being ruined or seriously damaged for waterfowl use by salt-water intrusion as a result of the Intracoastal and connecting canals, and by exploration for sulfur and oil. Waterfowl of the Pacific Flyway are rapidly approaching a crisis because the lush marshes which once supported myriads of birds wintering in California and northern Mexico are being turned into cotton and rice fields, orchards, and urban developments."

In 1934 it was estimated that the federal government should own and develop 7,500,000 acres of wetland for the protection of our waterfowl resource (Farley, 1955:17). In 1956, Shaw and Fredine (1956:32) reported that there were 3,270,000 acres in federal waterfowl refuges, thus leaving over 4,000,000 acres to be acquired. In addition, it was estimated that the states should acquire 5 million acres primarily for waterfowl. In 1956, Shaw and Fredine (1956:31) reported that "at least 1,500,000 acres in waterfowl areas are now administered by the States." Judged by present-day tempo, it does not seem likely that we can gamble with delay much longer in acquiring the additional lands. It is most encouraging to learn that the recent amendment to the Duck Stamp Act provides that, beginning July 1, 1960, virtually all receipts from the new $3 duck stamp will be used to acquire wetland areas needed to complete the refuge system. I am doubtful as to whether even this will provide for the necessary acceleration. Another 20 years and we may well be spending our effort trying to keep what we have rather than acquiring new lands. In addition to drainage for the purpose of increasing the area in cropland, such activities as waterway construction, drainage for mosquito control, industrial and urban expansion, highway construction, and disposal of human waste will compete for wetlands with increasing severity. Our concern with waterfowl refuges, great as it is, should not cause us to lose sight of the importance of the neighborhood marsh which provides a center of interest for bird watchers close to home.

Undoubtedly, the most marked adjustments to bird populations will take place on those lands used for agriculture, and by far the majority of our birds live on these lands. Wooten and Anderson (1957:32) estimated that "Roughly, three-fifths of the total area of land in the continental United States, or 1,158 million acres, is in farms, and two-fifths, or 746 million acres, is not in farms. Nearly half the land not in farms, or 353 million acres, is used for grazing. But much of this large area is publicly owned and is used jointly for other purposes, including forests, wild game preserves, watersheds to supply water for irrigation, power, and other uses." Land inventories indicate the following distribution of cropland and pasture on farms: cropland, 465 million acres; and grassland, pasture, and range, 633 million acres (Wooten and Anderson, 1957:33).

Higher crop yields must be achieved in the not too distant future if our population continues to increase at the present rate. Fortunately, the outstanding feature of modern agriculture has been the steady increase in productivity per acre. Leonard (1957:117), however, reported that "In spite of current food surpluses, there is concern in the United States about how to achieve food production that will be adequate to maintain the present diet for the anticipated population of 1975." Wooten and Anderson (1957:33) counseled that "If recent trends continue in the next 25 years, some 20 to 30 million acres of permanent grassland suitable for cultivation likely will be brought into the cropland-pasture rotation. In addition, possibly 10 million acres of fertile farm woodland and brushland likely will be cleared for cropland and rotation pasture, chiefly to improve the layout and add to the tillable acreages of existing farms in the farm-forest regions." The trend is toward larger areas in individual farms (Dewhurst and Assoc., 1955:809). Using the rate of production for 1953 as a base, Wooten and Anderson (1957:35) estimated that livestock products must be increased by more than 40 per cent and crop production by about 25 per cent by 1975. "The greatest increase needed in crop production would be in field crops, feed grains, hay, soybeans, and especially pasture. Crops for which little or no increase in production would be needed to meet requirements include major food grains, potatoes, and cotton." (Wooten and Anderson, 1957:36).

The reduction of crop losses through more effective protection against insects and diseases will take on added importance as our need for food increases. More general use of chemicals for this purpose may be expected unless greater progress is made in the direction of biological control. Unless chemical poisons are found which are more specific for the problem at which aimed and less toxic to birds, losses may be expected and over greater areas than is the case today. The ornithologist bears a responsibility for adding to his knowledge of the long-range effect of modern insecticides on birds. He should at least be prepared to advise the entomologist and the public of probable consequences to bird life which may be expected from the use of particular insecticides in particular areas.

Cultivated fields undoubtedly support greater total numbers of birds now than they did prior to cultivation. Sharp reduction or elimination of waste in cultivated grains and weed plants, however, could result in food shortages for birds which could well become a major limiting factor. The intensive effort to obtain chemical control of weeds seems to be succeeding, and inefficient harvest methods are receiving increased attention. Waste grain from cultivated crops constitutes the greatest volume of food consumed by many birds. Losses in cleanly harvested crops of wheat, oats, barley and rye, even with the best combine adjustment, will vary from 1 to 4 per cent of the yield (Huber and White, 1953:4). It has been estimated that an amount equivalent to 10 per cent of the yield of corn remains in the fields as a result of inefficient harvesting methods (Bateman, Pickard, and Bowers, 1952:3). A marked reduction of waste in corn has already been achieved by a harvesting technique in which the corn is shelled in the field. Even if harvesting techniques did not improve, more corn will be gleaned by livestock in the future. As the demand for livestock production increases it seems likely that more green corn will be cut and chopped in the field to be fed as ensilage, thereby utilizing the whole corn plant.

Wildlife depredations in unharvested grain promise to become of progressively greater concern. Following a study of depredations on cultivated grains by waterfowl in southwestern Manitoba, Bossenmaier and Marshall (1958:31) recommended "The initiation of a long-range program for the development of feasible cultural methods of control . . ." This would seem to constitute an intelligent long-range objective wherever bird depredations constitute a threat.

It is apparent that our agricultural lands are particularly subject to change, and the majority of our birds live on these lands during all, or at least critical periods, of their lives. Our knowledge of the relationship of agricultural land use practices to bird populations is incomplete except for certain game birds and even here our knowledge can be improved upon. Without such knowledge we cannot forecast and prepare for likely changes in bird populations coming out of a more intensive agricultural program. Many changes on farm land are of a subtle nature from the standpoint of their effect on birds. While the trend is all in one direction, the amount of change in any one year is too small to attract much attention. During the past 10 years many miles of osage orange hedge have been bulldozed out in the midwestern United States. This must certainly have had a marked effect on the populations of those species regularly found nesting and rearing young in these hedges. Fencerows, ditchbanks, and roadsides grown to heavy herbaceous or woody cover have been "cleaned up" and many odd, unproductive bits of land have been cleared of brush or drained to improve efficiency of operations and to extend tillable lands. These activities undoubtedly have brought about changes in bird populations which have gone unrecorded. Some species have lost out, others have been favored. But who really knows very much about the adjustment demands being made on continental bird populations as a result of the gradual change taking place on farm land?

An effort also needs to be made in the direction of evaluating agricultural practices which might prove advantageous to future farm needs and to birds. Wide-row corn seems to be one such practice (Vohs, 1958MS).

What the necessary increase in future livestock production may mean to birds also constitutes a problem. The development of improved pasture in the southeastern United States has resulted in marked changes in bird life. Attention, however, has been centered primarily on the local reduction of quail populations (Scott and Klimstra, 1954:6). The demand for grazing privileges on federal lands may well become a problem of increasing difficulty for administrators.

The importance of wildlife as a reservoir of diseases and parasites affecting livestock and man will certainly be cause for progressively greater concern as the human population and its need for food grows. Our knowledge in this field is so incomplete that intelligent action is impossible in many cases. A thoroughgoing knowledge of this subject is needed, if for no other reason than to insure against unwarranted wildlife control or eradiction programs.

50

I have not seen estimates on the total area of land devoted to urban and industrial use or to highways, airports, rights-of-way, and other high value purposes. It is certain that the area devoted to such use will tend to parallel population growth. Wider dispersal of such key areas as a defense measure against atomic attack is being encouraged. The recently approved national highway program involves construction of a 41,000-mile network of interstate highways on an average 300-foot right-of-way which will place over 1 million acres of land along the pavement (Zuckel and Eddy, 1957: 38). Egler (1958:576) estimated that there are now 50 million acres of rights-of-way land. He (1958:573) defined rights-of-way land as "those narrow threads of land which serve for transportation and communication of man and materials. They include highways, railroads, electric power and telephone lines, and pipe lines for gas, oil, and coal." He pointed out that the rights-of-way of utility corporations comprised an acreage greater than all six of the New England states combined.

Management of these vast rights-of-way holdings should be investigated from the standpoint of effect on bird populations. It seems likely that lands devoted to such use will increase in area and, with increasingly intensive use of surrounding lands, may virtually constitute refuge areas for certain species of birds if properly managed. Egler (1958:574) wrote of the use of 2,4-D, 2,3,5-T, and ammonium sulfamate in the control of brush on rights-of-way land as follows: "It must be understood that these chemicals have no known adverse effects on any animals. If used unwisely, they do have an extremely detrimental effect on wildlife habitat, and this, in its way, is far more disastrous than any killing of the animals themselves." Egler (1958:577) also pointed out that "In most cases shrub communities retard reforestation more successfully than do grasslands."

Urban and suburban residential areas are expanding at a rapid rate. Perhaps the average family of the future will tend to satisfy more of its needs for pleasure in the out-of-doors and for escape from the pressures of civilization in its own back yard. The ornithologist should prepare to offer advice on neighborhood management of birds as a part of this scheme of things.

Zahniser (Callison, 1957:150-151) reported that according to available records in 1953 there were 2,030 state parks comprising 5,077,331 acres and a report for 1951 showed 17,142 county and city parks totaling 644,067 acres. Additional parks will undoubtedly be established, especially small parks in urban areas. However, it seems likely that the addition of parks will not parallel population growth. Such parks will receive increasing use and unless managed properly may serve more as a refuge for nuisance species of birds than desirable forms.

While the total water area will be very small by comparison to the land area, it can be of great strategic importance to birds. Impoundments for purposes of hydroelectric power will probably be installed wherever feasible, for they have the advantage of being based on a nonexhaustible source of energy. Impoundments for public water supplies and industry will probably tend to parallel population growth, and their location will reflect the dispersal of industry. The average daily quantity of water consumed "for all purposes increased from 600 gallons per capita in 1900 to

1,100 gallons in 1950 and 1,300 gallons in 1955. By 1975 the country will be using 1,800 gallons of water a day for every man, woman, and child" (U.S. Soil Conservation Serv., 1957:5). The added water areas will undoubtedly enhance the well-being of some birds, if they can be managed for multiple purposes. Water pollution is closely associated with the density of population and with industry; hence, unless protective measures are rigidly enforced, the aquatic foods, especially of animal origin, of birds may undergo undesirable alteration. Industrial pollution may cause direct loss as in the case at Lake Calumet, Illinois, where severe loses among migrating shore birds in fall have been traced to soluble lead.

A reliable basis for appraising long-range adjustments in the numbers and species of birds is needed. Perhaps a running inventory of bird populations, classified to land use or habitat category, in winter and during the breeding season would provide such an index. Excellent information is available for waterfowl, and our knowledge of upland game birds is good and is improving rapidly. The nesting season data published annually in *Audubon Field Notes* are helpful. Nevertheless, objective data of this nature are generally deficient for other species. Ornithologists are either underestimating the importance of this need, are shunning it as a personally unprofitable chore, or are living with the false hope that someone else will do it. The job needs doing in representative habitat categories throughout the country, and responsible leaders must take the initiative in filling the gaps in these censuses of birds. In Illinois, we were fortunate enough to have benefited from the foresight of Stephen A. Forbes who encouraged extensive, systematic censuses of birds throughout Illinois in 1906-09. The data obtained (Forbes and Gross, 1922, 1923) were classified by land-use category. These censuses are being repeated now, some 50 years later, as a means of interpreting the adjustments which have taken place.

Another matter of general concern is the need for early acquisition of land for wildlife management areas. Shepard (1957:9-10) has emphasized the need for "immediate action . . . to preserve specific areas of land before they are overrun and lost forever" and recommended that industry might do well to participate in the acquisition of such lands. He points out that even now "The preservation of even small bits of marshlands or woods representing the last stands of irreplaceable biotic communities is interwoven with the red tape of law, conflicting local interest, the overlapping jurisdiction of governmental and private conservation bodies, and an intricate tangle of economic and social considerations." Along these lines, it is my personal belief that wildlife conservation agencies are gambling with their future well-being when they concentrate all of their land purchasing resources in the so-called waste lands and fail to obtain small, evenly dispersed parcels of land throughout intensively cultivated areas.

Another matter which will attract special consideration will be an increasing demand for birds to hunt. A part of this demand will be met by commercial, controlled shooting areas where the hunter may buy pen-reared game birds for hunting. The search for exotic game birds to occupy those areas where game birds are absent or scarce is likely to receive greater emphasis.

This analysis constitutes an effort to examine problems of bird conservation in the light of human progress. Glass (1957:11) has observed that "Few biologists, outside of an occasional leisure thought, seem to think very frequently or deeply about human progress." While the material presented here barely outlines the problem, it is sincerely hoped that it will serve to stimulate ornithologists to make a careful, critical, and imaginative examination of what the future holds for bird conservation.

LITERATURE CITED

BAKER, J. H.
  1952 The citizen's part in conservation. *Ann. Amer. Acad. Pol. and Soc. Sci.,* 281:20-24.
BATEMAN, H. P., G. E. PICKARD, AND W. BOWERS
  1952 Corn picker operation to save corn and hands. *Illinois Agric. Ext. Serv. Circ.* 697. 12 pp.
BELLROSE, F. C., AND T. G. SCOTT
  1955 Waterfowl conservation in the decade following. World War II. *Wilson Bull.,* 67:310-312.
BOSSENMAIER, E. F., AND W. H. MARSHALL
  1958 Field-feeding by waterfowl in southwestern Manitoba. *Wildlife Monogr.* no. 1. 32 pp.
CALLISON, C. H.
  1957 America's natural resources. Ronald Press Co., New York. 211 pp.
CLAWSON, M.
  1958 Statistics on outdoor recreation. Resources for the Future, Inc., Washington, D.C. 165 pp.
CLAWSON, M., AND B. HELD
  1957 The federal lands: their use and management. Johns Hopkins Press, Baltimore. 501 pp.
CLAY, L. D., S. D. BECHTEL, D. BECK, S. S. COLT, AND W. A. ROBERTS
  1955 A ten-year national highway program, a report to the President. U.S. Government. 57 pp.
DEWHURST, J. F., AND ASSOCIATES
  1955 America's needs and resources. Twentieth Century Fund, Inc. New York. 1148 pp.
EGLER, F. E.
  1958 Science, industry, and the abuse of rights of way. *Science,* 127 (3298):573-580.
  1955 Duck stamps and wildlife refuges. *U.S. Fish and Wildl. Serv. Circ.* no. 37. 22 pp.
FORBES, S. A., AND A. O. GROSS
  1922 The numbers and local distribution in summer of Illinois land birds of the open country. *Illinois Nat. Hist. Surv. Bull.,* 14(6):187-218.
  1923 On the numbers and local distribution of Illinois land birds of the open country in winter, spring, and fall. *Illinois Nat. Hist. Surv. Bull.,* 14(10):397-453.
GLASS, H. B.
  1957 The responsibilities of biologists. *Amer. Inst. Biol. Sci. Bull.,* 7(5):9-13.
GREVILLE, T. D. E.
  1957 Illustrative United States population projections. Actuarial Study no. 46. U.S. Dept. Health, Educ., and Welfare. 53 pp.
HUBER, S. G., AND R. G. WHITE
  1953 Harvesting with combines. Ohio State Univ. Agric. Ext. Serv. 8 pp.
LAY, D. W.
  1958 Pines, profits with problems. *Texas Game and Fish,* 16(4):5-6, 27.
LEONARD, W. H.
  1957 World population in relation to potential food supply. *Sci. Monthly,* 85(3): 113-125.
LUCK, J. M.
  1957 Man against his environment: the next hundred years. *Science,* 126 (3279): 903-908.
PIERCE, R. A.
  1957 [Report of] Conservation Committee. *Wilson Bull.,* 69(3):284-285.
RAUSHENBUSH, S.
  1955 Do resource programs meet people's needs. *Trans. N. Amer. Wildl. Conf.,* 20: 91-99.

SCOTT, T. G., AND W. D. KLIMSTRA
  1954   Report on a visit to quail management areas in southeastern United States. *Illinois Wildlife*, 9(3):5-9.
SHAW, S. P., AND C. G. FREDINE
  1956   Wetlands of the United States: their extent and their value to waterfowl and other wildlife. *U.S. Fish and Wildl. Serv. Circ.* no. 39. 67 pp.
SHEPARD, D. A.
  1957   The wise use of natural resources. *Atlantic Monthly, 200 (4) :3-10.*
U.S. FISH AND WILDLIFE SERVICE
  1956   National survey of fishing and hunting. U.S. Dept. Int. Circ. no. 44. 50 pp.
U.S. NATIONAL PARK SERVICE
  1941   A study of the park and recreation problem of the United States. U.S. Dept. Int. 279 pp.
U.S. SOIL CONSERVATION SERVICE
  1957   Water facts. U.S. Dept. Agric., PA-337. 12 pp.
VOHS, P. A., JR.
  1958MS   Wide-row corn as wildlife habitat. Unpublished Master's Thesis, Southern Illinois Univ.
WOOTEN, H. H., AND J. R. ANDERSON
  1955   Agricultural land resources in the United States, with special reference to present and potential cropland and pasture. *U.S. Dept. Agric. Inf. Bull.* no. 140. 107 pp.
  1957   Land inventory and land requirements in the United States. *Jour. Soil and Water Cons.,* 12 (1) :32-37.
ZUKEL, J. W., AND C. O. EDDY
  1957   Pesticide use on highway areas. *Agric. Chem.,* 12 (7) :38-39.

CONSERVATION (1953)
Aldo Leopold

As a final statement on the philosophy of wildlife values we turn again to the evidence of Aldo Leopold, written a quarter century ago, and find it as fresh and as relevant today. Perhaps it may provide some guiding thoughts for tomorrow.

Conservation is a bird that flies faster than the shot we aim at it.

I can remember the day when I was sure that reforming the Game Commission would give us conservation. A group of us worked like Trojans cleaning house at the Capitol. When we got through we found we had just started. We learned that you can't conserve game by itself; to rebuild the game resource you must first rebuild the game range, and this means rebuilding the people who use it, and all of the things they use it for. The job we aspired to perform with a dozen volunteers is now baffling a hundred professionals. The job we thought would take five years will barely be started in fifty.

Our target, then, is a receding one. The task grows greater year by year, but so does its importance. We begin by seeking a few trees or birds; to get them we must build a new relationship between men and land.

Conservation is a state of harmony between men and land. By land is meant all of the things on, over, or in the earth. Harmony with land is like harmony with a friend; you cannot cherish his right hand and chop off his left. That is to say, you cannot love game and hate predators; you cannot conserve the waters and waste the ranges; you cannot build the forest and mine the farm. The land is one organism. Its parts, like our own parts, compete with each other and co-operate with each other. The competitions are as much a part of the inner workings as the co-operations. You can regulate them—cautiously—but not abolish them.

The outstanding scientific discovery of the twentieth century is not television, or radio, but rather the complexity of the land organism. Only those who know the most about it can appreciate how little we know about it. The last word in ignorance is the man who says of an animal or plant: 'What good is it?' If the land mechanism as a whole is good, then every part is good, whether we understand it or not. If the biota, in the course of aeons, has built something we like but do not understand, then who but a fool would discard seemingly useless parts? To keep every cog and wheel is the first precaution of intelligent tinkering.

Have we learned this first principle of conservation: to preserve all the parts of the land mechanism? No, because even the scientist does not yet recognize all of them.

In Germany there is a mountain called the Spessart. Its south slope bears the most magnificent oaks in the world. American cabinetmakers, when they want the last word in quality, use Spessart oak. The north slope, which should be the better, bears an indifferent stand of Scotch pine.

Why? Both slopes are part of the same state forest; both have been managed with equally scrupulous care for two centuries. Why the difference?

Kick up the litter under the oaks and you will see that the leaves rot almost as fast as they fall. Under the pines, though, the needles pile up as a thick duff; decay is much slower. Why? Because in the Middle Ages the south slope was preserved as a deer forest by a hunting bishop; the north slope was pastured, plowed, and cut by settlers, just as we do with our woodlots in Wisconsin and Iowa today. Only after this period of abuse was the north slope replanted to pines. During this period of abuse something happened to the microscopic flora and fauna of the soil. The number of species was greatly reduced, i.e. the digestive apparatus of the soil lost some of its parts. Two centuries of conservation have not sufficed to restore these losses. It required the modern microscope, and a century of research in soil science, to discover the existence of these 'small cogs and wheels' which determine harmony or disharmony between men and land in the Spessart.

American conservation is, I fear, still concerned for the most part with show pieces. We have not yet learned to think in terms of small cogs and wheels. Look at our own back yard: at the prairies of Iowa and southern Wisconsin. What is the most valuable part of the prairie? The fat black soil, the chernozem. Who built the chernozem? The black prairie was built by the prairie plants, a hundred distinctive species of grasses, herbs, and shrubs; by the prairie fungi, insects, and bacteria; by the prairie mammals and birds, all interlocked in one humming community of co-operations and competitions, one biota. This biota, through ten thousand years of living and dying, burning and growing, preying and fleeing, freezing and thawing, built that dark and bloody ground we call prairie.

Our grandfathers did not, could not, know the origin of their prairie empire. They killed off the prairie fauna and they drove the flora to a last refuge on railroad embankments and roadsides. To our engineers this flora is merely weeds and brush; they ply it with grader and mower. Through processes of plant succession predictable by any botanist, the prairie garden becomes a refuge for quack grass. After the garden is gone, the highway department employs landscapers to dot the quack with elms, and with artistic clumps of Scotch pine, Japanese barberry, and Spiraea. Conservation Committees, en route to some important convention, whiz by and applaud this zeal for roadside beauty.

Some day we may need this prairie flora not only to look at but to rebuild the wasting soil of prairie farms. Many species may then be missing. We have our hearts in the right place, but we do not yet recognize the small cogs and wheels.

In our attempts to save the bigger cogs and wheels, we are still pretty naïve. A little repentance just before a species goes over the brink is enough to make us feel virtuous. When the species is gone we have a good cry and repeat the performance.

The recent extermination of the grizzly from most of the western stock-raising states is a case in point. Yes, we still have grizzlies in the Yellowstone. But the species is ridden by imported parasites; the rifles wait on every refuge boundary: new dude ranches and new roads constantly shrink the remaining range; every year sees fewer grizzlies on fewer ranges in fewer states. We console ourselves with the comfortable fallacy that a single museum-piece will do, ignoring the clear dictum of history that a species must be saved *in many places* if it is to be saved at all.

The ivory-billed woodpecker, the California condor, and the desert sheep are the next candidates for rescue. The rescues will not be effective until we discard the idea that one sample will do; until we insist on living with our flora and fauna in as many places as possible.

We need knowledge—public awareness—of the small cogs and wheels, but sometimes I think there is something we need even more. It is the thing that *Forest and Stream,* on its editorial masthead, once called 'a refined taste in natural objects. Have we made any headway in developing a refined taste in natural objects'?

In the northern parts of the lake states we have a few wolves left. Each state offers a bounty on wolves. In addition, it may invoke the expert services of the U.S. Fish and Wildlife Service in wolf-control. Yet both this agency and the several conservation commissions complain of an increasing number of localities where there are too many deer for the available feed. Foresters complain of periodic damage from too many rabbits. Why, then, continue the public policy of wolf-extermination? We debate such questions in terms of economics and biology. The mammalogists assert the wolf is the natural check on too many deer. The sportsmen reply they will take care of excess deer. Another decade of argument and there will be no wolves to argue about. One conservation inkpot cancels another until the resource is gone. Why? Because the basic question has not been debated at all. The basic question hinges on 'a refined taste in natural objects'. Is a wolfless north woods any north woods at all?

The hawk and owl question seems to me a parallel one. When you band a hundred hawks in fall, twenty are shot and the bands returned during the subsequent year. No four-egged bird on earth can withstand such a kill. Our raptors are on the toboggan.

Science has been trying for a generation to classify hawks and owls into 'good' and 'bad' species, the 'good' being those that do more economic good than harm. It seems to me a mistake to call the issue on economic grounds, even sound ones. The basic issue transcends economics. The basic question is whether a hawkless, owl-less countryside is a livable countryside for Americans with eyes to see and ears to hear. Hawks and owls are a part of the land mechanism. Shall we discard them because they compete with game and poultry? Can we assume that these competitions which we perceive are more important than the co-operations which we do not perceive?

The fish-predator question is likewise parallel. I worked one summer for a club that owns (and cherishes) a delectable trout stream, set in a matrix of virgin forest. There are 30,000 acres of the stuff that dreams are made on. But look more closely and you fail to see what 'a refined taste in natural objects' demands of such a setting. Only once in a great while does a kingfisher rattle his praise of rushing water. Only here and there does an otter-slide on the bank tell the story of pups rollicking in the night. At sunset you may or may not see a heron; the rookery has been shot out. This club is in the throes of a genuine educational process. One faction wants simply more trout; another wants trout plus all the trimmings, and has employed a fish ecologist to find ways and means. Superficially the issue again is 'good' and 'bad' predators, but basically the issue is deeper. Any club privileged to own such a piece of land is morally obligated to keep all its parts, even though it means a few less trout in the creel.

In the lake states we are proud of our forest nurseries, and of the progress we are making in replanting what was once the north woods. But look in these nurseries and you will find no white cedar, no tamarack. Why no cedar? It grows too slowly, the deer eat it, the alders choke it. The prospect of a cedarless north woods does not depress our foresters; cedar has, in effect, been purged on grounds of economic inefficiency. For the same reason beech has been purged from the future forests of the Southeast. To these voluntary expungements of species from our future flora, we must add the involuntary ones arising from the importation of diseases: chestnut, persimmon, white pine. Is it sound economics to regard any plant as a separate entity, to proscribe or encourage it on the grounds of its individual performance? What will be the effect on animal life, on the soil, and on the health of the forest as an organism? Is there not an aesthetic as well as an economic issue? Is there, at bottom, any real distinction between aesthetics and economics? I do not know the answers, but I can see in each of these questions another receding target for conservation.

I had a bird dog named Gus. When Gus couldn't find pheasants he worked up an enthusiasm for Sora rails and meadowlarks. This whipped-up zeal for unsatisfactory substitutes masked his failure to find the real thing. It assuaged his inner frustration.

We conservationists are like that. We set out a generation ago to convince the American landowner to control fire, to grow forests, to manage wildlife. He did not respond very well. We have virtually no forestry, and mighty little range management, game management, wildflower management, pollution control, or erosion control being practiced voluntarily by private landowners. In many instances the abuse of private land is worse than it was before we started. If you don't believe that, watch the straw-stacks burn on the Canadian prairies; watch the fertile mud flowing down the Rio Grande; watch the gullies climb the hillsides in the Palouse, in the Ozarks, in the riverbreaks of southern Iowa and western Wisconsin.

To assuage our inner frustration over this failure, we have found us a meadowlark. I don't know which dog first caught the scent; I do know that every dog on the field whipped into an enthusiastic backing-point. I did myself. The meadowlark was the idea that if the private landowner won't practice conservation, let's build a bureau to do it for him.

Like the meadowlark, this substitute has its good points. It smells like success. It is satisfactory on poor land which bureaus can buy. The trouble is that it contains no device for preventing good private land from becoming poor public land. There is danger in the assuagement of honest frustration; it helps us forget we have not yet found a pheasant.

I'm afraid the meadowlark is not going to remind us. He is flattered by his sudden importance.

Why is it that conservation is so rarely practiced by those who must extract a living from the land? It is said to boil down, in the last analysis, to economic obstacles. Take forestry as an example: the lumberman says he will crop his timber when stumpage values rise high enough, and when wood substitutes quit underselling him. He said this decades ago. In the interim, stumpage values have gone down, not up; substitutes have increased, not decreased. Forest devastation goes on as before. I admit the reality of this predicament. I suspect that the forces inherent in unguided economic evolution are not all beneficent. Like the forces inside our own bodies, they may become malignant, pathogenic. I believe that many of the economic forces inside the modern body-politic are pathogenic in respect to harmony with land.

What to do? Right now there is a revival of the old idea of legislative compulsion. I fear it's another meadowlark. I think we should seek some organic remedy—something that works from the inside of the economic structure.

We have learned to use our votes and our dollars for conservation. Must we perhaps use our purchasing power also? If exploitation-lumber and forestry-lumber were each labeled as such, would we prefer to buy the conservation product? If the wheat threshed from burning strawstacks could be labeled as such, would we have the courage to ask for conservation-wheat, and pay for it? If pollution-paper could be distinguished from clean paper, would we pay the extra penny? Over-grazing beef vs. range-management beef? Corn from chernozem, not subsoil? Butter from pasture slopes under 20 per cent? Celery from ditchless marshes? Broiled whitefish from five-inch nets? Oranges from unpoisoned groves? A trip to Europe on liners that do not dump their bilgewater? Gasoline from capped wells?

The trouble is that we have developed, along with our skill in the exploitation of land, a prodigious skill in false advertising. I do not want to be told by advertisers what is a conservation product. The only alternative is a consumer-discrimination unthinkably perfect, or else a new batch of bureaus to certify 'this product is clean.' The one we can't hope for, the other we don't want. Thus does conservation in a democracy grow ever bigger, ever farther.

Not all the straws that denote the wind are cause for sadness. There are several that hearten me. In a single decade conservation has become a profession and a career for hundreds of young 'technicians.' Ill-trained, many of them; intellectually tethered by bureaucratic superiors, most of them; but in dead earnest, nearly all of them. I look at these youngsters and believe they are hungry to learn new cogs and wheels, eager to build a better taste in natural objects. They are the first generation of leaders in conservation who ever learned to say, 'I don't know.' After all, one can't be too discouraged about an idea which hundreds of young men believe in and live for.

Another hopeful sign: Conservation research, in a single decade, has blown its seeds across three continents. Nearly every university from Oxford to Oregon State has established new research or new teaching in some field of conservation. Barriers of language do not prevent the confluence of ideas.

Once poor as a church mouse, American conservation research now dispenses 'federal aid' of several kinds in many ciphers.

These new foci of cerebration are developing not only new facts, which I hope is important, but also a new land philosophy, which I know is important. Our first crop of conservation prophets followed the evangelical pattern; their teachings generated much heat but little light. An entirely new group of thinkers is now emerging. It consists of men who first made a reputation in science, and now seek to interpret the land mechanism in terms any scientist can approve and any layman understand, men like Robert Cushman Murphy, Charles Elton, Fraser Darling. Is it possible that science, once seeking only easier ways to live off the land, is now to seek better ways to live with it?

We shall never achieve harmony with land, any more than we shall achieve justice or liberty for people. In these higher aspirations the important thing is not to achieve, but to strive. It is only in mechanical enterprises that we can expect that early or complete fruition of effort which we call 'success.'

The problem, then, is how to bring about a striving for harmony with land among a people many of whom have forgotten there is any such thing as land, among whom education and culture have become almost synonymous with landlessness. This is the problem of 'conservation education.'

When we say 'striving,' we admit at the outset that the thing we need must grow from within. No striving for an idea was ever injected wholly from without.

When we say "striving,' I think we imply an effort of the mind as well as a disturbance of the emotions. It is inconceivable to me that we can adjust ourselves to the complexities of the land mechanism without an intense curiosity to understand its workings and an habitual personal study of those workings. The urge to comprehend must precede the urge to reform.

When we say 'striving,' we likewise disqualify at least in part the two vehicles which conservation propagandists have most often used: fear and indignation. He who by a lifetime of observation and reflection has learned much about our maladjustments with land is entitled to fear, and would be something less than honest if he were not indignant. But for teaching the fresh mind, these are outmoded tools. They belong to history.

My own gropings come to a dead end when I try to appraise the profit motive. For a full generation the American conservation movement has been substituting the profit motive for the feat motive, yet it has failed to motivate. We can all see profit in conservation practice, but the profit accrues to society rather than to the individual. This, of course, explains the trend, at this moment, to wish the whole job on the government.

When one considers the prodigious achievements of the profit motive in wrecking land, one hesitates to reject it as a vehicle for restoring land. I incline to believe we have overestimated the scope of the profit motive. Is it profitable for the individual to build a beautiful home? To give his children a higher education? No, it is seldom profitable, yet we do both. These are, in fact, ethical and aesthetic premises which underlie the economic system. Once accepted, economic forces tend to align the smaller details of social organization into harmony with them.

No such ethical and aesthetic premise yet exists for the condition of the land these children must live in. Our children are our signature to the roster of history; our land is merely the place our money was made. There is as yet no social stigma in the possession of a gullied farm, a wrecked forest, or a polluted stream, provided the dividends suffice to send the youngsters to college. Whatever ails the land, the government will fix it.

I think we have here the root of the problem. What conservation education must build is an ethical underpinning for land economics and a universal curiosity to understand the land mechanism. Conservation may then follow.

Courtesy of Outdoor Publications, Inc.

CONSERVATION ESTHETIC (1938)
Aldo Leopold

Barring love and war, few enterprises are undertaken with such abandon, or by such diverse individuals, or with so paradoxical a mixture of appetite and altruism, as that group of avocations known as outdoor recreation. It is, by common consent, a good thing for people to get back to nature. But wherein lies the goodness, and what can be done to encourage its pursuit? On these questions there is confusion of counsel, and only the most uncritical minds are free from doubt.

Recreation became a problem with a name in the days of the elder Roosevelt, when the railroads which had banished the country-side from the city began to carry the city-dweller, *en masse,* to the countryside. It began to be noticed that the greater the exodus, the smaller the per capita ration of peace, solitude, wildlife, and scenery, and the longer the migration to reach them.

The automobile has spread this once mild and local predicament to the outermost limits of good roads—it has made scarce in the hinterlands something once abundant in the back forty. But that something must nevertheless be found. Like ions shot from the sun the week-enders radiate from every town, generating heat and friction as they go. A tourist industry purveys bed and board to bait more ions faster, further. Advertisements on rock and rill confide to all and sundry the whereabouts of new retreats, landscapes, hunting-grounds, and fishing-lakes just beyond those recently overrun. Bureaus build roads into new hinterlands, then buy more hinterlands to absorb the exodus accelerated by the roads. A gadget industry pads the bumps against nature-in-the-raw; woodcraft becomes the art of using gadgets. And now, to cap the pyramid of banalities, the trailer. To him who seeks in the woods and mountains only those things obtainable from travel or golf, the present situation is tolerable. But to him who seeks something more, recreation has become a self-destructive process of seeking but never quite finding; a major frustration of mechanized society.

The retreat of the wilderness under the barrage of motorized tourists is no local thing; Hudson Bay, Alaska, Mexico, South Africa are giving way, South America and Siberia are next. Drums along the Mohawk are now honks along the rivers of the world. *Homo sapiens* putters no more under his own vine and fig tree; he has poured into his gas-tank the stored motivity of countless creatures aspiring through the ages to wiggle their way to pastures new. Ant-like he swarms the continents.

This is Outdoor Recreation, Model 1938.

Who now is the recreationist, and what does he seek? A few samples will remind us.

Take a look, first, at any duck marsh. A cordon of parked cars surrounds it. Crouched on each point of its reedy margin is some pillar of society, automatic ready, trigger finger itching to break, if need be, every law of commonwealth or commonweal to kill a duck. That he is already overfed in no way dampens his avidity for gathering his meat from God.

Reprinted from: Bird-Lore 40(2): 101-109.

Wandering in the near-by woods is another pillar, hunting rare ferns or new warblers. Because his kind of hunting seldom calls for theft or pillage, he disdains the killer. Yet, like as not, in his youth he was one.

At some near-by resort is still another nature-lover—the ,kind who writes bad verse on birchbark. Everywhere is the unspecialized motorist whose recreation is mileage, who has run the gamut of the National Parks in one summer, and now is headed for Mexico City and points south.

Lastly, there is the professional, striving through countless conservation organizations to give the nature-seeking public what it wants, or to make it want what he has to give.

Why, it may be asked, should such a diversity of folk be bracketed in a single category? Because each, in his own way, is a hunter. And why does each call himself a conservationist? Because the wild things he hunts for have eluded his grasp, and he hopes by some necromancy of laws, appropriations, regional plans, reorganization of departments, or other form of mass-wishing, to make them stay put.

Recreation is commonly spoken of as an economic resource. Senate committees tell us, in reverent ciphers, how many millions the public spends in its pursuit. It has indeed an economic aspect—a cottage on a fishing-lake, or even a duck-point on a marsh, may cost as much as the entire adjacent farm.

It has also an ethical aspect. In the scramble for unspoiled places, codes and decalogues evolve. We hear of 'outdoor manners.' We indoctrinate youth. We print definitions of 'What is a sportsman?' and hang a copy on the wall of whosoever will pay a dollar for the propagation of the faith.

It is clear, though, that these economic and ethical manifestations are results, not causes, of the motive force. We seek contacts with nature because we derive pleasure from them. As in opera, economic machinery is employed to create and maintain facilities. As in opera, professionals make a living out of creating and maintaining them, but it would be false to say of either that the basic motive, the *raison d'être,* is economic. The duck-hunter in his blind and the operatic singer on the stage, despite the disparity of their accoutrements, are doing the same thing. Each is reviving, in play, a drama formerly inherent in daily life. Both are, in the last analysis, esthetic exercises.

Public policies for outdoor recreation are controversial. Equally conscientious citizens hold opposite views on what it is, and what should be done to conserve its resource-base. Thus the Wilderness Society seeks to exclude roads from the hinterlands, and the chamber of commerce to extend them, both in the name of recreation. The gamefarmer kills hawks and the birdlover protects them, in the name of shotgun and field-glass hunting respectively. Such factions commonly label each other with short and ugly names, when, in fact, each is considering a different component of the recreational process. As I shall show shortly, these components *differ widely in their characteristics or properties.* A given policy may be true of one but false for another.

It seems timely, therefore, to segregate the components, and to examine the distinctive characteristics or properties of each.

We begin with the simplest and most obvious: the physical objects which the outdoorsman may seek, find, capture, and carry away. In this category are wild crops such as game and fish, and the symbols or tokens of achievement such as heads, hides, photographs, and specimens.

All these things rest upon the idea of *trophy*. The pleasure they give is, or should be, in the seeking as well as in the getting. The trophy whether it be a bird's egg, a mess of trout, a basket of mushrooms, the photograph of a bear, the pressed specimen of a wild flower, or a note tucked into the cairn on a mountain peak, is a *certificate*. It attests that its owner has been somewhere and done something—that he has exercised skill, persistence, or discrimination in the age-old feat of overcoming, outwitting, or reducing-to-possession. These connotations which attach to the trophy usually far exceed its physical value.

But trophies differ in their reactions to mass-pursuit. The yield of game and fish can, by means of propagation or management, be increased so as to give each hunter more, or to give more hunters the same amount. During the past decade a profession of wildlife management has sprung into existence. A dozen universities teach its techniques, conduct research for bigger and better wild animal crops. However, when carried too far, this stepping-up of yields is subject to a law of diminishing returns. Very intensive game- or fish-management lowers the unit value of the trophy by artificializing it.

Consider, for example, a trout, raised in a hatchery and newly liberated in an over-fished stream. The stream is no longer capable of natural trout production. Pollution has fouled its waters, or deforestation and trampling have warmed or silted them. No one would claim that this trout has the same value as a wholly wild one caught out of some unmanaged stream in the high Rockies. Its esthetic connotations are inferior, even though its capture may require skill. (Its liver, one authority says, is also so degenerated by hatchery feeding as to forebode an early death.) Yet several over-fished states now depend almost entirely on such man-made trout.

All intergrades of artificiality exist, but as mass-use increases it tends to push the whole gamut of conservation techniques toward the artificial end, and the whole scale of trophy-values downward.

To safeguard this expensive, artificial, and more or less helpless trout, the Conservation Commission feels impelled to kill all herons and terns visiting the hatchery where it was raised, and all mergansers and otters inhabiting the stream in which it is released. The fisherman perhaps feels no loss in this sacrifice of one kind of wildlife for another, but the ornithologist is ready to bite off ten-penny nails. Artificialized management has, in effect, bought fishing at the expense of another and perhaps higher recreation; it has paid dividends to one citizen out of capital stock belonging to all. The same kind of biological wildcatting prevails in game-management. In Europe, where wild-crop statistics are available for long periods, we even know the 'rate of exchange' of game for predators. Thus, in Saxony, one hawk is killed to each seven game-birds bagged, and one predator of some kind to each three head of small game.

Damage to plant-life usually follows artificialized management of animals—for example, damage to forests by deer. One may see this in north

Germany, in northeast Pennsylvania, in the Kaibab, and in dozens of other less publicized regions. In each case over-abundant deer, deprived of their natural enemies, have made it impossible for deer food-plants to survive or reproduce. Beech, maple, and yew in Europe; ground hemlock and white cedar in the eastern states; mountain mahogany and cliff-rose in the West are deer-foods threatened by artificialized deer. The composition of the flora from wild flowers to forest trees is gradually impoverished, and the deer in turn are dwarfed by malnutrition. There are no stags in the woods today like those on the walls of feudal castles.

On the English heaths reproduction of trees is inhibited by rabbits over-protected in the process of cropping partridges and pheasants. On scores of tropical islands both flora and fauna have been destroyed by goats introduced for meat and sport. It would be hard to calculate the mutual injuries by and between mammals deprived of their natural predators, and ranges stripped of their natural food-plants. Agricultural crops caught between these upper and nether millstones of ecological mismanagement are saved only at the cost of endless indemnities and barbed wire.

We generalize, then, by saying that mass-use tends to dilute the quality of organic crop trophies like game and fish, and to induce damage to other resources such as non-game animals, natural vegetation, and farm crops.

The same dilution and damage is not apparent in the yield of 'indirect' trophies, such as photographs. Broadly speaking, a piece of scenery snapped by a dozen tourist cameras daily is not physically impaired thereby, nor does any other resource suffer when the rate increases to a hundred. The camera industry is one of the few innocuous parasites on wild nature.

We have, then, a basic difference in reaction to mass-use as between two categories of physical objects pursued as trophies.

Let us now consider another component of recreation which is more subtle and complex: the feeling of isolation in nature. That this is acquiring a scarcity-value which is very high to some persons is attested by the wilderness controversy. The proponents of wilderness have achieved a compromise with the road-building bureaus which have the custody of our National Parks and Forests. They have agreed on the formal reservation of roadless areas. Out of every dozen wild areas opened up, one may be officially proclaimed 'wilderness,' and roads built only to its edge. It is then advertised as unique, as indeed it is. Before long its trails are congested, it is being dolled up to make work for CCC's, or an unexpected fire necessitates splitting it in two with a road to haul fire-fighters. Or the congestion induced by advertising may whip up the price of guides and packers, whereupon somebody discovers that the wilderness policy is undemocratic. Or the local chamber of commerce, at first quiescent at the novelty of a hinterland officially labeled as 'wild,' tastes its first blood of tourist-money. It then wants more, wilderness or no wilderness.

In short, the very scarcity of wild places, reacting with the *mores* of advertising and promotion, tends to defeat any deliberate effort to prevent their growing still more scarce.

It is clear without further discussion that mass-use involves a direct dilution of the opportunity for solitude; that when we speak of roads, camp-grounds, trails, and toilets as 'development' of recreational resources, we speak falsely in respect of this component. Such accommodations for the crowd are not developing (in the sense of adding or creating) anything. On the contrary, they are merely water poured into the already-thin soup.

We now contrast with the isolation-component that very distinct if simple one which we may label 'fresh-air and change-of-scene.' Mass-use neither destroys nor dilutes this value. The thousandth tourist who clicks the gate of the National Park breathes approximately the same air, and experiences the same contrast with Monday-at-the-office, as does the first. One might even believe that the gregarious assault on the outdoors en-hances the contrast. We may say, then, that the fresh-air and change-of-scene component is like the photographic trophy—it withstands mass-use without damage.

We come now to another component: the perception of the natural processes by which the land and the living things upon it have achieved their characteristic forms (evolution) and by which they maintain their existence (ecology). That thing called 'nature study,' despite the shiver it brings to the spines of the elect, constitutes the first embryonic groping of the mass-mind toward perception.

The outstanding characteristic of perception is that it entails no con-sumption and no dilution of any resource. The swoop of a hawk, for example, is perceived by one as the drama of evolution, by another as a threat to the full frying-pan. The drama may thrill a hundred successive witnesses; the threat only one—for he responds with a shot-gun.

To promote perception is the only truly creative part of recreational engineering.

This fact is important, and its potential power for bettering 'the good life' only dimly understood. When Daniel Boone first entered into the forests and prairies of "the dark and bloody ground," he reduced to his possession the pure essence of 'outdoor America.' He didn't call it that, but what he found is the thing we now seek, and we here deal with things, not names.

Recreation, however, is not the outdoors, but our reaction to it. Daniel Boone's reaction depended not only on the quality of what he saw, but on the quality of the mental eye with which he saw it. Ecological science has wrought a change in the mental eye. It has disclosed origins and functions for what to Boone were only facts. It has disclosed mech-anisms for what to Boone were only attributes. We have no yardstick to measure this change, but we may safely say that, as compared with the competent ecologist of the present day, Boone saw only the surface of things. The incredible intricacies of the plant and animal community—the intrinsic beauty of the organism called America, then in the full bloom of her maidenhood—were as invisible and incomprehensible to Daniel Boone as they are today to Mr. Babbitt. The only true development in American recreational resources is the development of the perceptive faculty in Americans. All of the other acts we grace by that name are, at best, attempts to retard or mask the process of dilution.

Let no man jump to the conclusion that Babbitt must take his Ph.D. in ecology before he can 'see' his country. On the contrary, the Ph.D. may become as callous as an undertaker to the mysteries at which he officiates. Like all real treasures of the mind, perception can be split into infinitely small fractions without losing its quality. The weeds in a city lot convey the same lesson as the redwoods; the farmer may see in his cow-pasture what may not be vouchsafed to the scientist adventuring in the South Seas. Perception, in short, cannot be purchased with either learned degrees or dollars; it grows at home as well as abroad, and he who has a little may use it to better advantage than he who has much. As a search for perception, the recreational stampede is footless and unnecessary.

There is, lastly, a fifth component: the sense of husbandry. It is unknown to the outdoorsman who works for conservation with his vote rather than with his hands. It is realized only when some art of management is applied to land by some person of perception. That is to say, its enjoyment is reserved for landholders too poor to buy their sport, and land administrators with a sharp eye and an ecological mind. The tourist who buys access to his scenery misses it altogether; so also the sportsman who hires the state, or some underling, to be his gamekeeper. The Government, which essays to substitute public for private operation of recreational lands, is unwittingly giving away to its field officers a large share of what it seeks to offer its citizens. We foresters and game managers might logically pay for, instead of being paid for, our job as husbandmen of wild crops.

That a sense of husbandry exercised in the production of crops may be quite as important as the crops themselves is realized to some extent in agriculture, but not in conservation. American sportsmen hold in small esteem the intensive game-cropping of the Scottish moors and the German forests, and in some respects rightly. But they overlook entirely the sense of husbandry developed by the European landholder in the process of cropping. We have no such thing as yet. It is important. When we conclude that we must bait the farmer with subsidies to induce him to raise a forest, or with gate receipts to induce him to raise game, we are merely admitting that the pleasures of husbandry-in-the-wild are as yet unknown both to the farmer and to ourselves.

Scientists have an epigram: ontogeny repeats phylogeny. What they mean is that the development of each individual repeats the evolutionary history of the race. This is true of mental as well as physical things. The trophy-hunter is the caveman reborn. Trophy-hunting is the prerogative of youth, racial or individual, and nothing to apologize for.

The disquieting thing in the modern picture is the trophy-hunter who never grows up, in whom the capacity for isolation, perception, and husbandry is undeveloped, or perhaps lost. He is the motorized ant who swarms the continents before learning to see his own back yard, who consumes but never creates outdoor satisfactions. For him the recreational engineer dilutes the wilderness and artificializes its trophies in the fond belief that he is rendering a public service.

The trophy-recreationist has peculiarities which contribute in subtle ways to his own undoing. To enjoy he must possess, invade, appropriate. Hence the wilderness which he cannot personally see has no value to him.

Hence the universal assumption that an unused hinterland is rendering no service to society. To those devoid of imagination, a blank place on the map is a useless waste; to others, the most valuable part. (Is my share in Alaska worthless to me because I shall never go there? Do I need a road to show me the arctic prairies, the goose pastures of the Yukon, the Kodiak bear, the sheep meadows behind McKinley?)

It would appear, in short, that the rudimentary grades of outdoor recreation consume their resource base; the higher grades, at least to a degree, create their own satisfactions with little or no attrition of land or life. It is the expansion of transport without a corresponding growth of perception which threatens us with qualitative bankruptcy of the recreational process. Recreational development is a job, not of building roads into lovely country, but of building receptivity into the still unlovely human mind.

Most students of wildlife ecology take hunting for granted. A growing group of dissenters sees no reason for man to continue this primitive and "barbaric" activity. This conflict will become increasingly significant. Both sides of the coin are examined—philosophically and practically—in the following five selections.

REVERENCE FOR LIFE
Albert Schweitzer

Reverence for Life

Slowly we crept upstream, [on one of the long African errands of mercy], laboriously feeling—it was the dry season—for the channels between the sandbanks. Lost in thought I sat on the deck of the barge, struggling to find the elementary and universal conception of the ethical which I had not discovered in any philosophy. Sheet after sheet I covered with disconnected sentences, merely to keep myself concentrated on the problem. Late on the third day, at the very moment when, at sunset, we were making our way through a herd of hippopotamuses, there flashed upon my mind, unforeseen and unsought, the phrase, "Reverence for Life." The iron door had yielded: the path in the thicket had become visible. Now I had found my way to the idea in which world- and life-affirmation and ethics are contained side by side! Now I knew that the world-view of ethical world- and life-affirmation, together with its ideals of civilization, is founded in thought.[1]

I Live for Other Life

Ethics is nothing else than reverence for life. Reverence for life affords me my fundamental principle of morality, namely, that good consists in maintaining, assisting and enhancing life, and that to destroy, to harm or to hinder life is evil. Affirmation of the world, that is to say, affirmation of the will-to-live which appears in phenomenal form all around me, is only possible for me in that I give myself out for other life. Without understanding the meaning of the world I act from an inner necessity of my being so as to create values and to live ethically, in the world and exerting influence on it. For in world- and life-affirmation and in ethics I fulfil the will of the universal will-to-live which reveals itself in me. I live my life in God, in the mysterious ethical divine personality which I cannot discover in the world, but only experience in myself as a mysterious impulse.[2]

The Highest Rationality

Today there is an absence of thinking which is characterized by a contempt for life. We waged war for questions which, through reason, might have been solved. No one won. The war killed millions of men, brought suffering to millions of men, and brought suffering and death to millions of innocent animals. Why? Because we did not possess the highest rationality of reverence for life. And because we do not yet possess this, every people is afraid of every other, and each causes fear to the others. We are mentally afflicted one for another because we are lacking in rationality.

There is no other remedy than reverence for life, and at that we must arrive.[3]

The Driving Force of the Ethical

Thought must strive to find a formula for the essential nature of the ethical. In so doing it is led to characterize ethics as self-devotion for the sake of life, motivated by reverence for life. Although the phrase "reverence for life" may perhaps sound a trifle unreal, yet that which it denotes is something which never lets go its hold of the man in whose thought it has once found a place. Sympathy, love, and, in general, all enthusiastic feeling of real value are summed up in it. It works with restless vitality on the mental nature in which it has found a footing and flings this into the restless activity of a responsibility which never ceases and stops nowhere. Reverence for life drives a man on as the whirling, thrashing screw forces a ship through the water.[2]

Life Has Value

It is in reverence for life that knowledge passes over into experience. . . . My life bears its meaning in itself. And this meaning is to be found in living out the highest and most worthy idea which my will-to-live can furnish . . . the idea of reverence for life. Henceforward I attribute real value to my own life and to all the will-to-live which surrounds me; I cling to an activist way of life and I create real values.[2]

Hindering or Helping

What shall be my attitude toward other life? It can only be of a piece with my attitude towards my own life. If I am a thinking being, I must regard other life than my own with equal reverence. For I shall know that it longs for fulness and development as deeply as I do myself. Therefore, I see that evil is what annihilates, hampers, or hinders life. And this holds good whether I regard it physically or spiritually. Goodness, by the same token, is the saving or helping of life, the enabling of whatever life I can influence to attain its highest development.[4]

The Principle Is Universal

Ordinary ethics seeks to find limits within the sphere of human life and relationships. But the absolute ethics of the will-to-live must reverence every form of life, seeking so far as possible to refrain from destroying any life, regardless of its particular type. It says of no instance of life, "This has no value." It cannot make any such exceptions, for it is built upon reverence for life as such. It knows that the mystery of life is always too profound for us, and that its value is beyond our capacity to estimate. We happen to believe that man's life is more important than any other form of which we know. But we cannot prove any such comparison of value from what we know of the world's development. True, in practice we are forced to choose. At times we have to decide arbitrarily which forms of life, and even which particular individuals, we shall save, and which we shall destroy. But the principle of reverence for life is none the less universal.[4]

Universal Ethics

The great fault of all ethics hitherto has been that they believed themselves to have to deal only with the relations of man to man. In reality, however, the question is what is his attitude to the world and all life that comes within his reach. A man is ethical only when life, as such, is sacred to him, that of plants and animals as that of his fellow men, and when he devotes himself helpfully to all life that is in need of help. Only the universal ethic of the feeling of responsibility in an ever-widening sphere for all that lives—only that ethic can be founded in thought. The ethic of the relation of man to man is not something apart by itself: it is only a particular relation which results from the universal one.

The ethic of reverence for life, therefore, comprehends within itself everything that can be described as love, devotion, and sympathy whether in suffering, joy, or effort.[1]

Respect for Life

There slowly grew up in me an unshakeable conviction that we have no right to inflict suffering and death on another living creature unless there is some unavoidable necessity for it, and that we ought all of us to feel what a horrible thing it is to cause suffering and death out of mere thoughtlessness. And this conviction has influenced me only more and more strongly with time. I have grown more and more certain that at the bottom of our heart we all think this, and that we fail to acknowledge it and to carry our belief into practice chiefly because we are afraid of being laughed at by other people as sentimentalists, though partly also because we allow our best feelings to get blunted. But I vowed that I would never let my feelings get blunted, and that I would never be afraid of the reproach of sentimentalism.

I never go to a menagerie because I cannot endure the sight of the misery of the captive animals. The exhibiting of trained animals I abhor. What an amount of suffering and cruel punishment the poor creatures have to endure in order to give a few moments' pleasure to men devoid of all thought and feeling for them![5]

THE PROBLEM OF ETHICS (1965)
Albert Schweitzer

An ethics that does not also consider our relation to the world of creatures is incomplete. The struggle against inhumanity must be waged wholly and continually. We must reach the stage at which killing for sport will be felt as a disgrace to our civilization.

In the course of the nineteenth and twentieth centuries, thinking men concerned solely with seeking truth were forced to admit that ethics has nothing to gain from a true understanding of the universe. The advancement of knowledge takes the form of an ever more precise understanding of the laws of phenomena. Science benefits us in that it enables us to put the energies available in the universe to use. But we are more and more led to abandon hope of being able to understand the meaning of phenomena.

Can altruism be justified within the terms of a world view? Ethical thinkers have constantly endeavored to do this. They have never succeeded. When they thought they had done so, they had in fact been constructing only the requisite naïvely optimistic world view that would accord with their ethical principles. However, a philosophy that proceeds from truth has to confess that no spirit of loving-kindness is at work in the phenomenal world. The universe provides us with the dreary spectacle of manifestations of the will to live continually opposed to each other. One life preserves itself by fighting and destroying other lives. The world is horror in splendor, meaninglessness in meaning, sorrow in joy.

Ethics is not in tune with this phenomenal world, but in rebellion against it. It is the manifestation of a spirit that desires to be different from the spirit that manifests itself in the universe.

If we attempt to comprehend the phenomenal world as it is and deduce principles of conduct from it, we are doomed to skepticism and pessimism. On the contrary, ethics is an act of spiritual independence on our part.

Early ethical thought had to create a world view in keeping with its values. It postulated a spirit that dominated the phenomenal world, and that, imperfect though it was, strove to achieve perfection. Our ethical strivings in the present world had meaning in view of that hoped-for goal.

But once ethical thought has come to see that concern for other wills to live is mandatory for us as human beings; that intellectually advanced men feel that concern and cannot escape it—once ethical thought reaches that insight, it has become completely autonomous. Henceforth, the fact that we possess only an imperfect and quite unsatisfactory understanding of the universe no longer seems so troubling. We possess understanding of the conduct our natures require. Faithful to that understanding, we proceed on our way.

The elemental fact, present in our consciousness every moment of our existences, is: I am life that wills to live, in the midst of life that wills to live. The mysterious fact of my will to live is that I feel a mandate to behave with sympathetic concern toward all the wills to live which exist side by side with my own. The essence of Goodness is: Preserve life,

Reprinted by permission from: Schweitzer, A. 1965. The teaching of reverence for life. Translated by Richard and Clara Winston. Copyright by Holt, Rinehart and Winston, Inc. N.Y.

74

promote life, help life to achieve its highest destiny. The essence of Evil is: Destroy life, harm life, hamper the development of life.

The fundamental principle of ethics, then, is reverence for life. All the goodness one displays toward a living organism is, at bottom, helping it to preserve and further its existence.

In the main, reverence for life dictates the same sort of behavior as the ethical principle of love. But reverence for life contains within itself the rationale of the commandment to love, and it calls for compassion for all creature life.

Only the ethics of reverence for life is complete. It is so in every respect. The ethics that deals only with the conduct of man toward his fellow men can be exceedingly profound and vital. But it remains incomplete. Thus it was inevitable that man's intellect should ultimately have reached the point of being offended by the heartless treatment of other living creatures, which had hitherto been considered acceptable, and should have demanded that ethics include them within its merciful purview. Ethical thought was slow and hesitant about taking this demand seriously. Only in recent times has visible progress been made along these lines, and only recently has the world begun to pay some regard to the undertaking.

But already the world is beginning to recognize that the ethics of reverence for life, which requires kindness toward all living organisms, accords with the natural feelings of thinking men.

By ethical conduct toward all creatures, we enter into a spiritual relationship with the universe.

In the universe, the will to live is in conflict with itself. In us, it seeks to be at peace with itself.

In the universe, the will to live is a fact; in us, it is a revelation.

The mind commands us to be different from the universe. By reverence for life we become, in profound, elemental and vital fashion, devout.

Courtesy of Outdoor Publications, Inc.

A DAMNABLE PLEASURE (1957)
Joseph Wood Krutch

It would not be quite true to say that "some of my best friends are hunters." Nevertheless, I do number among my respected acquaintances some who not only kill for the sake of killing but count it among their keenest pleasures.

To me it is inconceivable that anyone should think an animal more interesting dead than alive. I can also easily prove to my own satisfaction that killing "for sport" is the perfect type of that pure evil for which metaphysicians have sometimes sought.

Most wicked deeds are done because the doer proposes some good to himself. The liar lies to gain some end; the swindler and the thief want things which, if honestly got, might be good in themselves. Even the murderer may be removing an impediment to normal desires or gaining possession of something which his victim keeps from him. None of these usually does evil for evil's sake. They are selfish or unscrupulous, but their deeds are not gratuitously evil. The killer for sport has no such comprehensible motive. He prefers death to life, darkness to light. He gets nothing except the satisfaction of saying, "Something which wanted to live is dead. There is that much less vitality, consciousness, and, perhaps, joy in the universe. I am the Spirit that Denies." When a man wantonly destroys one of the works of man we call him Vandal. When he wantonly destroys one of the works of God we call him Sportsman.

Now, the typical Sportsman will not accept this parallel. He has his rules, his traditions, his protocols. Apparently he feels toward random slaughterers much as I feel towards even those who observe the rituals. The Sportsman is shocked by a man who will shoot a sitting bird. I am shocked by anyone who will, purely for "sport," shoot a bird at all. To no creature, man or beast, who is full of the desire to live is it any great comfort to know that killing him was done according to the rules. There is a rather well-known short-story (I have ungratefully forgotten the author) about a sportsman who came to the conclusion that man-hunting was the most challenging of all sports and used to give unsuspecting visitors to his island hideout a fair run for their money. Was this sport?

I am not a vegetarian and I am well aware that there are those to whom that makes me as shocking as the "true sportsman" is shocking to me and the mere slaughterer shocking to the Sportsman. I can only ask that we recognize not too scornfully the possibility of these differences of feeling. My position is a rather extreme one, though obviously not the most extreme possible, but I do not think it can fairly be called fanatical because, I freely admit, the Sportsman is not necessarily the monster my own logic seems to make him. Yet, though hunting for food and the destruction of certain animals is probably necessary to civilization, to me it still seems that any activity which includes killing as a pleasurable end in itself is damnable. Even the hunter-for-food may be as wicked and misguided as vegetarians say, but at least he does not kill for the sake of killing. To kill for killing's sake is a terrifying phenomenon—like doing evil not in the

Reprinted from: Saturday Review, August 17, 1957.

hope of gain but for evil's own sake—as strong a proof of that "reality of evil" with which present-day theologians are again concerned as we could have.

Examples of three different but typical ways of refusing to acknowledge that any defense of such killing is called for may be plucked out of recent popular periodicals.

In the spring of 1955 a magazine called *Sports Illustrated* distributed a questionnaire intended to determine the public attitude toward hunting. An answer received from a woman in Tampa, Florida, was as follows: "I am not the sloppy, sentimental type that thinks it's terrible to shoot birds or animals. What else are they good for?" And *The New Yorker,* which reprinted her reply, answered the question with an irony likely to be lost on the asker: "Bulls can be baited by fierce dogs, and horses sometimes pay money."

About a year before, *The New Yorker* had also, though without comment and merely in the course of report on the personality of the new British Permanent Delegate to the United Nations, quoted Sir Pierson Dixon as remarking genially, apropos of some articles on sport which he had written for English periodicals: "I like this shooting thing, stalking some relatively large animal or, even more enjoyable, shooting birds. It's like the pleasure of hitting a ball."

A little later *Time* magazine ran an article about how duck hunters near Utah's Bear River Migratory Bird Refuge (*sic*) "could hardly shoot fast enough" to bring down the ducks they found there and it adorned the article with a quotation from Ernest Hemingway's "Fathers and Sons": "When you have shot one bird flying you have shot all birds flying, they are all different and they fly different ways but the sensation is the same and the last one is as good as the first."

Of these three attitudes the first may seem the simplest and the most elementary, but perhaps it is not. The blank assumption that the universe has no conceivable use or meaning except in relation to man may be instinctive; nevertheless, the lady from Tampa is speaking not merely from naïveté. She is also speaking for all those minds still tinctured by the thought of the medieval philosophers who consciously undertook to explain in detail the *raison d'être* of the curious world of nature by asking for what human use God had created each species of plant or animal. If any given creature seems good for nothing except "sport" then it must be for sport that it was created.

Hemingway's utterance, on the other hand, is the most sophisticated of the three and the only one that seems to make the pure pleasure of killing a consciously recognized factor. The mental processes of the Permanent Delegate are neither so corrupt as those of Mr. Hemingway nor so intellectually complicated as those of the lady from Tampa. He is not, like the first, looking for madder music and stronger wine, nor, like the second attempting to answer the philosophical question of what animals and birds "are for." Because of the dreadful uncomprehending innocence sometimes said to be found most frequently in the English gentleman it has simply never occurred to him that the creatures whom he pursues are alive at all—as his phrase "like the pleasure of hitting a ball" clearly reveals.

Birds are simply livelier, less predictable clay pigeons. And it is in exactly the same light that those of his class have sometimes regarded the lesser breeds without the law, or even the nearly inanimate members of all the social classes below them.

For the attitude farthest removed from this Albert Schweitzer is the best-known contemporary spokesman. But one can hardly have "reverence for life" without some vivid sense that life exists even in "the lower animals" and it is this vivid sense that is lacking in the vast majority of sportsmen and equally in, say, the abandoners of pets and, not infrequently, one kind of biological scientist. Often not one of them is so much as tinged with the sadism which Hemingway's opinions and activities seem to suggest. It is not that they do not care what the abandoned pet or the experimental animal suffers but that they do not really believe he suffers to any considerable degree. In the case of the hunter it is often not so much that he wants to kill as that he has no vivid sense that he is killing. For him, as for Sir Pierson, it is more or less like "hitting a ball."

Hemingway would, of course, say that there was more to it than that. He feels more of a man out there with his gun, bringing down the birds. It's healthy out-of-doors, good for muscle tone, and there's the challenge of a contest, etc. These are exactly the common arguments which, until a few years ago, were advanced to defend war as a legitimate activity. None of the real goods is actually dependent upon the killing of another living creature. How anyone can profess to find animal life interesting and yet take delight in reducing the wonder of any animal to a bloody mass of fur or feathers is beyond my comprehension. You can go into the woods to share them with your fellow creatures just as well as to slaughter them. Photography is more difficult and challenging than gunnery. The air is sweeter without the odor of spilled blood. And in my opinion anyone who does not recognize this must fall into one of two classes, the one composed of the innocently and the other of the guiltily evil.

Thoreau once remarked that many a man went fishing all his life without realizing that it was not fish he was after. That is the type of the innocently evil who have simply never dissociated the pleasurable incidentals of hunting from the killing which comes at the end of it. But I rather suspect that these are a minority, and that the majority belong to the other class—the class of those to whom the final savagery is of essence. They are much like those drinkers who talk about either the fine bouquet of a wine or the conviviality of the cocktail but for whom the "kick" of alcohol is the real *sine qua non*. And I don't like blood lust even when tricked out in the philosophy of a Hemingway.

When Thoreau allowed himself to be persuaded to send a turtle as a specimen to the zoologists at Harvard he felt that he had "a murderer's experience in a degree" and that however his specimen might serve science he himself and his relation to nature would be the worse for what he had done. "I pray," he wrote, "that I may walk more innocently and serenely through nature. No reasoning whatever reconciles me to this act."

In general, however, professional students of living things are only somewhat more likely than the average man to feel strongly any "reverence for life." One of the most distinguished American students of birds told me that he saw no incompatibility whatever between his interest in birds and his love of "sport." Many, perhaps most professional students find no reason too trivial to "collect" a bird or animal, though their habitual use of this weasel word may suggest a defensive attitude. And I have often wondered that sportsmen who find themselves subject to many restrictions have not protested as unfair the "collector's license" rather freely granted and sometimes permitting the holder to shoot almost anything almost anywhere and at anytime.

Obviously the problem raised by all this is not solvable in any clearcut way. The degree of "reverence for life" which man or any other animal can exhibit is limited by the facts of a world he never made. When it was said that the lion and the lamb shall lie down together, the hope that they may someday do so carries with it the obvious implication that they cannot do so now. Even Albert Schweitzer's rule that no life shall be destroyed except in the service of some higher life will be differently interpreted almost from individual to individual.

Just how great must be the good that will accrue to the higher animal? Interpreted as strictly as possible, his law would permit killing only in the face of the most desperate and immediate necessity. Interpreted loosely enough, it might justify the slaughter of the 20,000 birds of paradise, the 40,000 humming-birds, and the 30,000 birds of other species said to have been killed to supply the London feather market alone in the single year 1914. After all, even fashionable ladies are presumably "higher" than birds and they presumably took keen delight in the adornments which the birds were sacrificed to provide.

Some pragmatic solution of the rights of man versus the rights of other living creatures does nevertheless have to be made. Undoubtedly it changes from time to time, and it is well that the existing solution should be re-examined periodically. Because the 1914 solution was re-examined, comparatively few birds are now killed for their feathers and it is not demonstrable that the female population is any the worst for the fact.

In India members of the Jain sect sometimes live on liquid food sipped through a veil in order to avoid the possibility that they might inadvertently swallow a gnat. There are always "anti-sentimentalists" who protest against any cultivation of scruples on the ground that they can logically lead only to some such preposterous scrupulosity. But there are extremes at both ends. Those who have scruples are no more likely to end as Jains than those who reject all scruples are likely to end as Adolf Hitlers. The only possible absolutes are reverence for all life and contempt for all life and of these the first is certainly no more to be feared than the second. If there is any such thing as a wise compromise it is not likely to be reached by the refusal to think.

In the old days, in this country, these lines were not infrequently drawn by those students who had interested themselves in old-fashioned natural history and were brought thereby into intimate association with animals and plants. Its aims and its methods demanded an awareness of the living thing as a living thing and, at least until the rise of behaviorism, the suffering and the joy of the lesser creatures was a part of the naturalist's subject matter. But the laboratory scientist of our modern supercharged day is not of necessity drawn into any emotional relationship with animals or plants, and the experiments which of necessity he must perform are more likely to make him more rather than less callous than the ordinary man.

At best, compassion, reverence for life, and a sense of the community of living things is not an essential part of his business as they are of the more vaguely defined discipline of the naturalist. And for that reason it is a great pity that the most humane and liberal of the natural sciences should play so small a role in the liberal arts curriculum. While still under the influence of an older tradition, field botany and field zoology were quite commonly taught in American colleges, even in the remoter parts of the United States. Today few liberal arts undergraduates know anything of such subjects and often would find no courses open to them if they did.

The most important things taught by these disciplines were not the shapes of leaves, or the calls of birds, but a philosophy, a certain attitude towards life. It is very hard to argue such a fundamental premise. The Sportsman, who kills living animals merely to re-create himself, obviously thinks that the right attitude is for man to use the life of the earth as he sees fit. This is not for me an acceptable premise. I do not believe that man has a divine right to the unlimited despotism of an oriental potentate; that he is justified when he says *"l'univers, c'est moi";* or that, like the Calvinist God, he may legitimately damn all inferior creatures merely for his own glory. I believe instead that all created things have their rights and that the right to live is one of theirs—unless there are compelling reasons why it should not be.

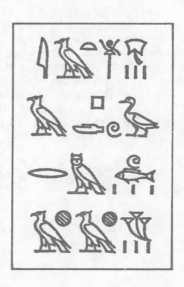

BUT IT'S INSTINCTIVE (1957)
Harold E. Anthony

I have been asked by the editors of *The Saturday Review* to comment on the views of Dr. Joseph Wood Krutch, which are typical of most anti-hunting criticism, on behalf of sportsmen and others who may taken exception to them. I may state at once that I have some fifty years of activity in two of the categories particularly specified by Dr. Krutch. During this half century I have hunted and fished on four continents and have also collected zoological material, principally mammals, for museum purposes. There is much of Krutch's thesis I can endorse and which I have been putting into practice. I have debated at length with myself as to whether I should come out in public with a foot in each camp. I do not believe in straddling, but the only way I can conscientiously react to the Krutch outburst is to go along with him until the parting of the ways is reached and then state the reasons for leaving his company.

Krutch maligns the sportsman as I understand the term. Wanton destruction is reprehensible to the principles of American sportsmanship both as I like to think they exist and as I interpret them when I call myself a sportsman. Certainly few of the large number of American hunters and fishermen included in the class of sportsmen would care to announce publicly that they fit the term as defined by Krutch. The term "sportsman," if used in its broadest sense, covers so many individuals that almost any allegation might be made and someone claiming to be a "sportsman" can be found to fit the crime. But the qualifications for a true sportsman, as I understand the term, require a respect for life that inhibits killing in excessive numbers, taking of life toward no useful end, and I would certainly deny that the act of killing per se should give the sportsman pleasure. I believe the great majority of persons who pride themselves on living up to fine sportsmanship make a conscious effort to conform to conventions in which killing itself is a subordinate part of the hunting pattern. Why does a true sportsman refuse to shoot a sitting bird or look over a number of possible shots before selecting the one to take, if the killing itself is the whole point of sport? But the feature which most disturbs Krutch is the fact that man can find "pleasure," "amusement," "fun" (dictionary synonyms for "sport") in taking life. This question cannot be solved as simply as it can be raised.

Many "sportsmen" simply give no thought to killing per se, but treat it as a routine action to reach the goal of capture or hitting the target. This is just as true as the fact that eating meat does not recall a slaughter-house nor putting on a pair of shoes a bloody hide. It is true, as a point in polemics, that once *killing* is introduced the reader has to face it and it has disturbing emotional consequences. But, in fact, there are quite a few of these tender and vulnerable spots in man's normal behavior pattern as it preys on organized life. I see nothing to be gained by denying that these emotional inconsistencies exist; I simply believe that, on balance, they do not have the significance that hunting's critics ascribe to them. As Krutch says: "Some pragmatic solution of the rights of man versus the rights of

Reprinted from: Saturday Review, August 17, 1957.

other living creatures does have to be made. Undoubtedly it changes from time to time, and it is well that the existing solution should be re-examined periodically."

I believe that most persons who have truly grown up will deplore the useless killing of a living creature. But man is a predator biologically and historically, and his mental processes are totally conditioned by this fact; everything about him is surveyed and appraised in terms of what the object or the circumstance can mean to man. The world today is as anthropocentric a universe as man can make it. With the discovery of atomic power we stand on the threshold of complete mastery of the physical environment and all living things in it.

I agree that it will be most deplorable if the criterion for preservation of any feature in the natural environment is to rest solely upon the answer to the question, "What good is it?"—meaning to man, of course. If man arrived at his decision as to "What good is it" after a calm analysis of all the factors involved my apprehension would not be justified. But all too often he destroys because it is instinctive to destroy anything he resents. But although the idea of an exclusively man-made environment is as distasteful to me as to anyone, I do not fancy the break with century-old inheritances. I believe that man is both biologically and mentally incapable of standing aside, as Krutch and the anti-sportsmen have done, to indulge in the introspection which calls forth the periodic blasts against hunting.

The average normal man (and I select the male sex as predominantly the hunter of the family) has passed through the boyhood stage which is heedless of animal life, thoughtless of what happens if a rock is thrown or a BB shot fired; he has reached a stage when regret follows a useless killing, and arrived at a period when he feels he has a justification if and when he kills a creature. Krutch does not criticize killing for food or some equally manifest necessity, for man long ago enslaved the rest of the animal kingdom and we might as well face it, but he bears down hard upon killing for "sport." This "reverence for life" finds expression in several religions and numerous cults and at times is associated with collateral effects that are inimical to man's interests and welfare as these aspects are considered on any logical and realistic basis. I have observed repulsive clouds of flies about the faces and on the eyes of Sudanese children because it was counter to the local mores to harm a fly. The resultant high incidence of infectious eye diseases was the price of reverence for the life of a fly.

I do not wish to decry a reverence for life for I have this myself, to the extent that I step aside to avoid stepping on any harmless insect. I think it would be a splendid thing if all men developed the respect for life which would make it second nature to shrink from a needless taking of life. But the very core of the point at issue rests upon the use of such adjectives as "harmless" and "needless." The application of these conditions is to man. Invariably man characterizes the life about him in terms that refer to his own personal likes and dislikes. One may believe that there is a greater concept and that man's interest should be considered as only a single link in a great chain, but a realistic approach forces one to the conclusion that human interest does and expects to exact tribute from all other organized life. Therefore, the wise sportsman does not defend himself by reminding us that certain animal populations, such as the deer in our West, must be periodically pruned, else the extermination of natural predators like cougars will bring an increase in deer population beyond the carrying capacity of the range. For otherwise unmanageable deer populations could be controlled by utilitarian state commissions: sportsmen shouldn't beg the issue by claiming that they are best serving the interests of deer by shooting them. Sportsmen shoot because they want to shoot, because they believe it is a good sport that enriches life—not for the deer, but for man.

The most disturbing charge is that killing for "sport" is degrading and unworthy of man. The disturbance arises only, however, if one enters upon the extreme soul-searching approach. I suspect most sportsmen just will not go along with this. They do not rationalize and try to answer to their own satisfaction the charges of anti-sportsmen. Why should they? That a basic inconsistency underlies the shooting of game is perfectly apparent: no one will deny that there is an inconsistency in cherishing a beautiful dog for many years, and going out every fall to shoot an equally beautiful deer. But, so far as we know, there is no escape from the tension of inconsistencies of which life consists. The most consistent of mortals, the medieval saints, allowed themselves to exist under layers of filth and neglect and emaciation, and to encourage infections and mutilations. These men were saints, but was this way of life "good," was it "healthy," is there a "lesson" in it for the rest of us?

The point here is that there is no black-and-white answer: what is meaningful to the saint is not necessarily meaningful to the great mass of mankind, which prefers to combine a moderate reverence for God with a moderate cleanliness. Probably the vast majority of men are fond of animals, and also are and have been for thousands of generations fond of a little hunting, which, when dressed up with rules and customs, they call sport; and the majority of men somehow reconcile the claims of these two affections in an amalgam which causes them no loss of sleep or agitation of conscience, but which strikes a Jain or Dr. Krutch as an intolerable offense against the intellect. If the "idealist" could so extirpate the contradictions from his own life his public effect would probably be greater; but, the most scrupulous of Jains kills bacteria in his nasal passages, and Dr. Krutch eats meat. There seems, in fact, no way to live a pure ideal.

When primitive man had only his own physical strength and crude weapons to overpower the life about him he was no great threat to the natural environment. He took what he wanted for the time being and mass slaughter was exceptional. When he learned to create all the material aids that modern technology has discovered he not only became capable of exterminating any life that stood in his way, but he deliberately did so. The millions of bison that roamed our Western plains a century ago were incompatible with man's occupation of that area: the bison were eliminated. Very recently active campaigns to reduce the big-game herds of Africa in an attempt to control the tse-tse fly have resulted in the killing of thousands upon thousands of splendid mammals. No sane person, if asked to weigh the life of a wild animal against the life of a man, has any doubt about the propriety of his decision, no matter how poignantly he regrets the end of an old order.

To sum up, man's attitude toward the organized life of the earth is to use it as he sees fit; he is completely dependent upon some of it for his physical existence.

Sportsman is not a synonym for hunter. A hunter has a strict practical purpose in mind; he kills for use or to protect something which might be damaged by the animal he hunts: the killing of the animal by the most direct means is the prime objective. No disparagement of the hunter is intended; his activities are analogous to those of the farmer who reaps his crops and pulls up the weeds. But there is vastly more to the activity of the sportsman than the killing of some living creature. The finest ideals of manhood, as they are currently accepted today, are based upon character- istics which are inseparably associated with the best expressions of sports- manship. Courage, hardihood, self-confidence, a sense of fair play are not only invaluable to a sportsman but if, as a beginner, he lacks these qualities the exposure of his mind and body as he pits himself against natural conditions will develop them. For his purposes the more primeval and less man-disturbed the environment the better. In this respect the good sportsman and Krutch see eye to eye.

The more man finds himself compressed into an urban existence the more he needs to break out of the pattern of modern high-pressured livelihood and move back into the ancestral inheritances which, it is true, make him a predator on his own account. In the city, whether he cares to acknowledge it or not, he is a predator by proxy. But when a man enters upon fair chase there can be, and under hoped-for conditions always is, a host of experiences, exposures to influences, and exalting contacts that often make the animal sought a very subordinate part of the operation. There can be a general sense of well-being that far transcends any "plea- sure" that a well-balanced sportsman feels in taking a life. As a matter of cold, hard fact, more and more sportsmen these days are giving up guns and hunting with cameras. I believe this comes about not so much because the camera hunter believes it would be "sinful" to kill his prey, but because in many instances a good photograph is a greater trophy than the dead animal, requires greater skill, and hence is more self-satisfying.

I agree that there is most definitely a need for an overall survey of man's relation to the organized life of the earth, both plant and animal. One of the most-to-be-desired expressions of man's advance in culture from his savage beginnings should be the breaking-away from the unjusti- fied exploitation of life which so often takes place. But there has to be a realistic balance between what we can postulate as an intellectual existence and what that same human mind will believe as it is housed in the body of a predatory animal—and in his profound essence man will forever be partly a predator. I believe the sportsmen will agree with Krutch in hoping for a more tolerant attitude between man and the animal life upon which he preys. At least I hope so, for I know I do.

IN DEFENSE OF THE SPORT HUNTER (1971)
Maynard M. Nelson

"Say Goodbye," the recent NBC television special about vanishing wildlife, capitalized on the new ecological conscience of our society. The ingredients were all there: beautiful close-ups of rare birds and animals, a popular theme, and a sad-voiced commentator.

Conservationists must endorse their distaste for the elimination of prairie dogs from vast regions by poisoned baits, the drastic decline of coastal pelicans by DDT, and the pressures brought to bear on numerous other species by ever increasing human populations.

But the producers of "Say Goodbye" failed to convey the differences between sport hunting and commercial harvesting of wild animals. It was the commercial hunter, not the sport hunter, who exploited the great blue whale, the sea otter, the egret and the passenger pigeon. Those who kill animals and destroy their habitat for quick profits are the ones who have endangered much of our wildlife.

The vast majority of rare and endangered wildlife species are not now, and never were, game animals.

As a sport hunter and career conservationist, I was saddened by the prejudice against sport hunting. True sportsmen do not slaughter female polar bears, leaving tiny cubs as orphans. But the producers of "Say Goodbye" apparently did this—and more. The hunter was one of their targets, and they used all the tricks of the camera to label the American sportsman as a part of the problem of vanishing wildlife.

Is such an indictment justice? Are sportsmen really this calloused, this intent on killing wild creatures?

Of course not. And the facts will bear this out.

Sport hunters were fighting for and paying for sound conservation programs long before the words "ecology" and "environment" came into everyday use. They have asked for and even insisted upon special charges, in addition to their license fees, to foster the well-being of the creatures they hunt. The duck stamp, the wetlands stamp, the 11 percent Pittman-Robertson tax on sporting arms and ammunition, and contributions to Ducks Unlimited are multimillion dollar examples.

Through their monies species such as the popular ring-necked pheasant have been successfully introduced. Thousands of acres of wildlife sanctuaries, breeding areas and recreational areas have been acquired and permanently set aside for all of our citizens. Games species and non-game species alike benefit from this habitat. Game laws are enforced to insure perpetuation of the species. Research has built a foundation of facts to bring game management from the trial and error methods of the past into the technical world of today.

Anti-hunting laws have more often been a curse than a blessing for wildlife. Our native prairie chicken has declined drastically even though the last Minnesota hunting season was over 29 years ago, the bobwhite quail is all but gone after 12 years of "protection," and further demands upon the land now threaten the exotic ring-necked pheasant with the same

Reprinted from: The Wildl. Soc. News No. 135.

fate. Sport hunting is too often blamed for scarcities caused by other forces in our technological society.

Where were those who cried for protection when the hunting seasons were closed and the flow of hunters' dollars stopped?

So what is the price extracted from the wildlife resource by the sport hunter? What does it take to satisfy his "primitive instincts"? Very little, believe it or not.

Years of surveys by biologists and game managers have consistently shown that pheasant and grouse hunters have done well to bag a single bird for a day afield. And the duck hunter's score is only slightly better. Or, consider the goose hunter who spends an average of four days afield to bag a single bird.

And how about the deer hunter? Even with the most modern high-powered rifle, he will probably hunt for four seasons before bringing home his venison—and if he chooses the bow and arrow it may take 25 years to connect. Hopeless odds? Not to 20,000 bow hunters!

Games species, like domestic animals or field crops for that matter, are a renewable resource. They produce an annual crop of young, some of which is surplus and some of which is needed for replacement of the parent stock. The surplus must perish, either by disease, starvation, predation, accidents, *or* by hunting. One way or another, death is assured. So which of the choices is the most practical and humane?

Hunting regulations typically are designed to take no more, and usually less, than the annual surplus. And when there is cause for doubt, the hunter is the first to protest. Witness the closed season on cock pheasants in 1969. The pheasant population fell to a historical low following severe losses from winter storms. Hens had been protected by law since 1943. Yet, the hunter insisted upon closure for both sexes in 1969. When he errs, the hunter errs in favor of conservation.

Not all men who carry guns are sportsmen. But neither are all motorists courteous, nor all athletes the epitome of fair play. The sport hunter is truly a conservationist. Virtually every environmental organization includes hunters among its leaders. To the sportsman, the killing of his quarry is almost anticlimactic. Hunting is a game of intense concentration, and a dedicated hunter is more carefully attuned to his environment—and holds far more esteem for nature—than do most other men.

AUTUMN THOUGHTS OF A HUNTER (1958)
C. H. D. Clarke

Hunting and fishing are sports that participants are inclined to take for granted. We are now beginning to realize that game and fish, and access to them, are not things that we can afford to leave to chance. How many have also stopped to think that hunting and fishing usually culminate in the death of some animal, that at the very least an attempt is made to molest or injure, and that there are many people who disapprove of all such things?

A recent survey in the United States (U.S. Fish and Wildlife Service, 1956) showed that in 1955 somebody in one of every three households hunted or fished. There were some twelve million hunters and twenty-one million fishermen. Included in both totals were eight million people who did both, for a grand total of twenty-five million people whose recreation was found in killing things. Most United States statistics apply to Canada, with due allowance for the fact that in the States there are ten times as many people. We are, therefore, on this continent, a large company, and we are not likely to be deprived of our sport in a hurry; but if one reasonable man speaks against us, we owe it to ourselves to seek the truth.

Down through the years the greatest writers of poetry and prose, the singers, dancers, painters, and sculptors, have found inspiration in field sports. The hunter, said the ancients, is not the one who will be found wanting in due reverence to the gods. The hours spent angling are not reckoned against a man's life span. "For," says Xenophon, "all men who have loved hunting have been good." The voices that have been raised against us have been charged with emotion, coming, not as they pretend, from philosophical heights, but from tight compartments, insulated from reality. For this reason, sportsmen have scorned them. On this continent there is no awakening of sympathetic responses from such dangerous passions as the class hatreds of Europe. From a distance it is easy to see the kinship of the perennial anti-blood sports bills in the British parliament to the Cromwellian ban on bear-baiting, which, as Macaulay said, the Puritans disliked not because it gave pain to the bear, but because it gave pleasure to the spectators. We do not provoke criticism on such grounds.

We are not, however, invulnerable, even to emotional propaganda. This was brought home to me as I watched a huddle of university professors on our Canadian television trying to argue propositions submitted to them by the viewing public. On this occasion the proposition was a statement by a former Toronto journalist, the late J. V. McAree, to the effect that anyone who could go out and kill innocent creatures for fun had something wrong with him, and in fact had not grown up. I was expecially interested because I had just finished reading an opposite view (*in* Voss, *et al.*, 1955), expressed in similar terms, by Gunther Schwab, poet and writer of the old festival city of Salzburg, who said that the chase should be only for the mature, others not being equipped to appreciate it. The professors all promptly agreed with McAree, and, in far less time than it takes to write it, they were quoting each other, until the whole thing was going round in

Reprinted from: J. Wildl. Mgmt. 22(4):420-427.

a nice tight little circle, like a stuck phonograph needle. It must be admitted that this happy state is by no means rare in such programs, and must be the bane of masters of ceremony, as it may simply signify that the debaters know little and care less about the subject debated. It is neither fair nor useful to expose their ignorance and then cry, in Izaak Walton's words, "I here disallow thee to be a competent judge." The interesting fact is that an emotional statement evoked agreement, to the point where nobody, in an obviously intelligent group, even for the sake of the program, was able to give the needle a push, much less turn the record over. To what degree do intelligent non-hunters accept the emotional arguments against hunting?

McAree's principal pronouncement on sport (McAree, 1951) may be cited to illustrate the quality of attacks on "blood sports." One could list many more like it. This one is printed in a secondary-school text, a fact that at one time caused me some apprehension. Now I am convinced that the interest in hunting is established before adolescence, and the young minds coming from at least one in three households would be resilient on this subject, however plastic in other respects. I am more concerned over the attitude of the textbook editors who chose this particular polemic from many. McAree justifies killing all predators, and all animals in any sense dangerous to man, but no others, and is sure that there are "proper ways" of regulating populations without hunting.

We have nothing to gain from controversy at the emotional level. In seeking truth in an emotionally charged atmosphere, one must be very careful of terms, and be as explicit as possible. In respect to the animals, we are dealing with two things, separable, although related. One is death. The other is pain. So far as man is concerned, we are dealing with the question of whether it is right or good for anyone to inflict either on a wild animal.

It might be contended that "right" and "good" are illusions, although whoever starts calling the things of the mind unreal may expect to end up in his own trap. If we abolished them, it would not matter what we did to animals, or what other people did to us. Society then would cease to exist, yet we know that it is older than our species. It must be confusing to try to reason from the premise of their nonexistence because the concept of a datum of excellence and justice, against which all conduct may be set, if part of the body and structure of the language in which our thoughts must be framed. It is equally difficult to abolish guilt, as some would do, in words that proclaim its existence. Without going into the arguments on this question, it is enough to say that I accept here the reality of the datum, and of the guilt implied in falling short of it. Lewis (1952) has argued it at some length in a discourse that I found stimulating. He sums it up by saying that humans "have this curious idea that they ought to behave in a certain way, and cannot really get rid of it," even though they "do not in fact behave in that way." Questions as to the nature, origin, variability, and absoluteness of this principle do not affect us here.

Thus, we may continue to speak of "right" and "good." As Lewis is a religious writer, I had hoped to get a religious slant on the question of animal treatment from him, especially as he deals with it in an earlier work (1940). It may be, he says, "that wild animals have no selves and no sufferings," in which case it would not matter what one does to them, but he leaves the question open. Domestic beasts, he says, are in a higher state, because they have achieved the true natural state of a beast, which is to be subordinate to man. This sort of rationalization carried to its logical conclusion is that of the proverbial Spanish peasant, who justifies his ill-treatment of beasts by saying, "¿Porqúe? !No es Cristiano!" My ethic forbids me such convenient justification. As a biologist, I think that a wild turkey has at least as much ego as a tame one. I would agree, however, that there is a stage in natural development beyond which there can hardly be much question of suffering. Anglers are not seriously accused of cruelty. At the same time, the perverse boy who pulls the wings off flies may have the intent to inflict suffering, and thereby come under our moral ban, even though flies do not suffer.

The intent is important, as we shall see later. Also, we must remember that, although both we and animals are alive and sentient, our living is only part of the life of an organic whole. In our other-worldliness we have lost the feeling of man's oneness with the earth, which modern faiths do not deny, but which early chthonic faiths saw most clearly, witness (Eliade, 1958) the original semantic unity of man (*homo*) and soil (*humus*), mother (*mater*), and matter (*materies*). Biologists, and most of all, wildlife biologists, know that any thought of man that he is apart from the rest of the living world is a perilous delusion. Here we face that part of our problem that concerns death. Death is a fundamental part of life.

The killing of an animal by another is harmful only if it is out of harmony with the functioning of the whole organic complex. Many other human activities are disruptive, and we can look at the face of earth and see that man has failed more often than not to achieve harmony with the land. This, surely, is the kind of savagery that we must outgrow, if we are to find any well-being. This figure of speech, incidentally, is from McAree *(op. cit.)*, and was applied to hunting.

A phrase that nowadays is tossed glibly at the hunter by his more sophisticated critics is the guiding principle of the gentle healer of Africa, Albert Schweitzer—*Ehrfurcht für dem Leben*. Untranslatable, as are all really profound expressions, it means both Honour and Awe for Life— much more than Reverence, as it is usually rendered. Schweitzer goes far beyond any question of pain: "A man is really ethical only when he obeys the constraint laid on him to help all life which he is able to succour, and when he goes out of his way to avoid injuring anything living. He does not ask how far this or that life deserves sympathy as valuable in itself, nor how far it is capable of feeling. To him life as such is sacred. He shatters no ice crystal that sparkles in the sun, tears no leaf from its tree, breaks off no flower, and is careful not to crush any insect as he walks. If he works by lamplight on a summer evening, he prefers to keep the window shut and to breathe stifling air, rather than to see insect after insect fall on his table with singed and sinking wings" (Schweitzer, 1923b:254 *et seq.*).

Schweitzer realizes the conflict of such a concept with the exigencies of human existence. He says, "The ethic of reverence for life recognizes no such thing as a relative ethic. . . . All destruction of and injury to life, from whatever circumstances they may result, are reckoned by it as evil. . . .

The absolute ethic of reverence for life makes its own agreements with the individual from moment to moment . . . [and] forces him to decide for himself in each case how far he can remain ethical and how far he must submit himself to the necessity of destroying and harming life and thus become guilty."

What his own decision would be in a rather critical case, he lets us know. He recognizes the similarity of his creed to the ahimsa of India, carried so far by the Jains, but says that it would be better to give cattle whose utility has ended a violent death than to let them starve (Schweitzer, 1936). At Lambarene he kept a gun, so he tells us, but used it only to shoot snakes and predatory birds (Schweitzer, 1922). The modern hunter's ethic would have justified him in destroying these creatures only as they were dangerous individually.

To me it is a relief to find the good doctor admitting the breech of his own law. The ice crystal, after all, is inanimate, and it would be better to stop working at night than to have the moth's "will to live" (and to reproduce) frustrated by an artificial light! We are brought to the old dilemma of the Pharisees, who, uncertain of what they might or might not do on the Sabbath, did nothing. In the one case there was a basic misconception of the Sabbath; and in the other, of life. Any concept of life that does not comprehend the whole organic cycle is inadequate. The reluctance to accept death, evidently a predominant Schweitzer characteristic (Russell, 1941), reveals an unseeing devotion to the vital spark. It is death that makes it glow, measure for measure.

At the risk of weighing this essay down with Schweitzer, I have quoted at length and must argue at length because he is one of the greatest thinkers of our time. His ideas cannot be ignored, especially as he has challenged (Schweitzer 1923b) his followers to action on the treatment of animals, and we are sure to hear from them as his shadow lengthens. *Ehrfurcht für dem Leben* is no Pharisaism. Schweitzer (1923a, 1923b) is right in affirming that the decay *(Verfall)* of civilization *(Kultur)* is caused by the lack of a proper relationship between man and other organic life, and its restoration *(Wiederaufbau)* can come only when such a relationship is established. I think that wildlife biologists would substitute "loss" for "lack," and "re-established" for "established." Man has lived, and in some places still lives, in harmony with nature, and the hunter and angler still cling to strong lines that connect us with the harmonious past. It is much more than not stepping on ants. One man, whether husbandman or forester, with a piece of land under his control, as mankind truly controls the whole earth, may go through life side-stepping ants and begging forgiveness of every blade of grass his mower touches; and in spite of his *Ehrfurcht,* because he has no feeling for the organic community, for the real life under his control, his land will have less and less life as the years pass, until, after generations of his kind, it may indeed die. Millenia of ahimsa have seen, and indeed contributed to, a man-made death for miles of land in India; and as the world of life shrinks in on the teeming mass of people, its individual elements cannot help growing more worthy of "reverence," until one day the remnant may be truly *furchtbar* (awe-inspiring). Another man, and he is very likely to be a hunter, will see to it that he leaves his land more truly alive and fruitful than he found it. Whose is the true reverence? Of course, one has no right to modify Schweitzer's concept in a direction so obviously rejected by him, but it seems to me that he was reaching out toward Leopold's "ecological conscience" (Leopold, 1947) and equally advanced conception of conservation ethics (Leopold, 1938), which are much closer to the heart of the problem of civilization.

As a biologist, then, I can accept *Ehrfurcht für dem Leben* only when life is interpreted as being the whole interwoven and interdependent association of plants, animals and soil, and the death that I inflict is right if harmony is maintained. The destruction of a whooping crane, for example, which would imperil the position of the species in the living community, or the violation of a game law, which, if nothing else, is a breech of trust with my fellow men, would be wrong.

With this clearly understood, I should be happy to see mankind guided by Schweitzer's maxim. Then the deliberate disintegrating of the beauty and productivity of our earth, so often hailed as "the conquest of Nature," will be abhorred. The true hunter, in the words of the old European hunter's pledge, "honours the Maker in His handiwork," but his honour, and awe, and reverence too, does not exclude delight, even in a doomed snowflake, a plucked daisy—or a wild goose headed for the platter.

In many areas of our own culture and in most primitive cultures, the chase is an integral part of a life where true harmony between man and nature exists. For example, the rural landscape of England, with its hedges and copses and beautifully managed fields, is, basically, a sporting landscape. Without fox hunting, the hedges would come down; without pheasant shooting, the copses would disappear. That is the civilized extreme. In the more primitive communities, where the power to destroy the landscape is less developed, the emotional, religious, and artistic life of the community is based to a remarkable degree on wildlife, and the chase is esteemed whether or not it is necessary for sustenance.

There is nothing remarkable about this. Man evolved as a hunter (Heberer, 1951). Forerunners of man are rather well known now. In South Africa, there were at one time two types of pre-men. One was a great shuffling hulk with a dentition that shows he was a vegetarian. The other was small and active, and fed on flesh as well as vegetable matter. This is the one that can be identified as having a place in the human pedigree. Vegetable gathering produced no tools, no forethought or planning, no tradition, no social organization. Pre-man the hunter, in developing and using all these for the chase, became man. He became cultured man, and culture grew as he ventured into cold regions, where animal fats and skins were a necessity. Finally, in the flood plains near the desert, he became a farmer. The relation of hunting to the development of cultural traits is expounded by Müller-Using (1951). You may wonder at my use of German references. I wondered myself at the amount of thought and space given to the ethics of hunting by German wildlife biologists and writers, until I remembered that their country still lies under the shadow of the leading antihunting fanatic of modern times, the late Reich Minister of the Interior, Heinrich Himmler. For him, all killing had to be purposeful and humane—gas chambers, not bullets.

There is still another point of view from which hunting and fishing have been pondered, namely, that of the Freudian psychiatrist. Thanks to Professor E. S. Carpenter, of Toronto, I have found one important work, by Menninger (1951), although there may well be more. Freud is another of the great thinkers of our time, and the validity of his early work on dreams and repressions is firmly established. He and his followers often wander beyond the discipline of science, and few concede the complete dominance of sex over the human mind, but because of the element of truth that it contains, the Freudian view must be considered seriously.

According to Menninger, a man who would have no deer killed, and I who kill them, may both be abnormal. The duck hunter who came to his clinic achieved, with the felling of each duck, the destruction of his own mother, for whom, in the slimy pit of his subconscious, and because of some outwardly forgotten chastisement, he had a consuming hatred. I wish that Menninger had gone into the subject of hunters who refuse to eat their game! His duck hunter may have been subject to just such a sub-conscious drive as he describes, but to imply that all hunters are so is to ignore the most powerful motivation of all. I am sure that hunting appeared to me in my childhood with all its prestige and magic intact, as it was in the beginning. In lands where it has been the prerogative of old families, to whom ancient communities have looked for leadership for centuries, and who can, even in poverty, retain a respect that money cannot buy, its prestige is enormous. I have seen one bedraggled mallard exalt a pros-perous immigrant as ranch-style house and Cadillac could never do.

In its broadest sense, we can best express the whole process in terms of play, which Huizinga (1949) shows to be deeply involved in the growth of culture in all its aspects. This all-embracing view of play is not original with him. It is inherent in the very word, which, in its imagery, is seen to include any meaningful activity that goes beyond simple physical need. It was in the play of words that abstractions developed, and many of these had their origin in the chase. Once man became an abstract thinker, the world of make-believe shielded, and assimilated, the serious business of life, which, in the most primitive economies, was largely the chase, so that the divine games of magic, ritual, religion, and law took their place on the stage of human life. Even when it was still necessary, hunting became a game to be played according to the rules, and man would sooner fail in his hunt than succeed by breaking the magic circle. In all this he never lost his place as a part of nature, and to maintain the old relationship is surely not a reversion.

I once called hunting an aesthetic pursuit, but I realize that if one restricts aesthetics to contemplation, as did Baumgarten (1735, 1739), the inventor of the term, then few even of the nonhunting naturalists can qualify as aesthetes. In the broader Socratic sense that assimilates the beautiful to the good and the useful, there could be such a thing as an aesthetic "pursuit," and the chase would certainly be an example. It may simply be enough to say that hunting is a form of play. It can, on occasion, be solemn, or serious, and it can be as exhausting and painful to the parti-cipant as the pancratium of the Greek games.

Müller-Using (*op. cit.*) points out that joy in hunting comes before hunting for joy. We find, though, that it is never a simple activity. The assimilation of play to real life is seen in the hunting play of carnivorous animals, but even the kittens on our hearth are ludicrously (the word comes from play) serious in their stalking and leaping, and may bite hard. We cannot, of course, impute cruelty to animals because we have not yet penetrated their minds to find out the quality of their intentions, and thus cannot apply the doctrine of *mens re* to their acts. However, the historian Froude's sometimes quoted "Wild animals never kill for sport: Man is the only one to whom the torture and death of his fellow creatures is amusing in itself," is matched in its unreality and apartness from nature only by Isaac Watts' (1777) "Birds in their little nests agree." Froude (1888) wrote much more eloquently in praise of hunting and fishing. The Russian word for hunt, *okhotit'sya,* which means something done willingly, goes to the root of the matter, and comes out right at the basic definition of play.

That hunting gives satisfaction is inherent in the play definition. The satisfaction is partly aesthetic but it goes much deeper, in that it is rooted in the maintenance by man of an old and harmonious relationship with nature, for wildlife is as truly his prey as it is that of any other predator. Furthermore, the role of the predator, including man, is still vital in the harmonious functioning of the natural community. Something has to happen to the fecund grasseating masses that Elton (1927) has called the key industries of nature's economy. The face of nature is so altered by man now that feral predators often find little room. The hunter becomes the alternate of disease and starvation.

So we have finished, I hope, with the question of death, and I can see no blame in the hunter, so long as his conscience, ruled by respect for nature, governs his actions. This respect is an emotion, and it must be admitted that the true climax of the hunt is, for most hunting, death. Personally I feel the same way about killing game as I do about felling a tree. The axe is still a symbol, with us; its skillful use carries prestige, and its ring on a trunk brings fulfillment both of a craft and a tradition. Were it used wantonly or wastefully, there would be guilt. The culmination is the cry of "Timber!" even though the pieces may contribute to art and industry in the four corners of the earth.

We still have to consider cruelty, as apart from death. Cruelty, or the willful infliction of pain, is no part of the purpose of hunting. As Lewis (1952) says, cruelty is either the act of a pathological pervert (whom one can pity, and wish cured), or, most reprehensibly, is done for some advantage. As no gain could possibly result from cruelty in hunting, cruel hunters must be perverts. The capacity for such perversion is innate in every human. I have often wondered if some antihunting fanatics, with an extreme preoccupation with the sufferings of animals, are not actually taking their cruelty vicariously. It is, of course, self-evident that there must be pervert hunters, and even fishermen, just as there are pervert clergymen, or boilermakers. No group is exempt, in spite of Xenophon, and we have to watch out for the pervert who deliberately takes up hunting. Primitive man knew and feared such persons, as likely to bring disaster on the tribe by offending the spirits of the animals hunted. When I was north, which is getting to be quite a while ago, there was still living an Eskimo who had been blinded deliberately by his people for just such a reason.

We come finally to the question of the incidental infliction of pain in hunting. In the chase, in the true sense of the word, with dogs, the natural predator is duplicated, and many observations indicate that Nature spares her children fear and pain under such circumstances. David Livingston (1858) remarked on this, after having been himself in the lion's jaws. A hunter who deliberately, ignorantly, thoughtlessly, or through lack of skill which an ethical sportsman would strive for, needlessly risks inflicting pain, is unethical and imperils his moral right to hunt. In shooting, the goal is a clean kill; if it is not achieved, there remains the knowledge that the death of the same animal in toothless old age would not be less painful. Man, who has the power to determine, in illness and injury, whether the death of his fellow-man is inevitable, refuses to sanction release. He bases his scruples on the very intelligence, which is the source of the fear and apprehension that make the process of death formidable. The starving cow, which even Doctor Schweitzer would permit us to kill, may fear man, whose blows she has felt, or the tiger, whose smell has terrified her kind for millenia, but not the abstract, death. It would be possible to list many things in addition to hunting that bring injury and death to animals, but it would be pointless, because we merely end with a knowledge of the inevitability and infinite variety of death itself, without which there is no life. Hunting remains, as it was in the beginning, completely assimilated to the basic processes of organic nature, in which death and life spring from each other.

It is because of this that hunting is still a life-giving, wholesome sport. Play, whether in ritual, law, religion, games, or any other of its manifestations can lose its roots and become degenerate. Hunting could lose its roots, too. Those who love it must clarify their own ideas as best they can, and become eternally vigilant, especially as the most artificial aspects of human culture spread like a cancer. Above all, we should esteem in ourselves and in our companions that maturity of spirit which alone places the right to hunt beyond question.

In the fantastic mass participation described at the beginning, we see some danger and some good. It is no good trying to make one of the basic activities of the human race on almost all land the exclusive property of a small cult. We have to let them hunt, even though we thereby include those who debase sport. They are the few. Of the rest, we must agree that few have the knowledge or perception to fit into nature as a hunter should. They are, however, willing and eager to learn, conscious of limitations to their own fulfillment imposed by their ignorance. By helping them we help ourselves, the game, and the whole world of nature.

Literature Cited

BAUMGARTEN, ALEXANDER GOTTLEIB. 1735. Meditationes philosophicae de nonnullis ad poema pertinentibus.
————. 1739. Aesthetica.

ELIADE, MIRCEA. 1958. Patterns in comparative religion. (Traité d'histoire des religions.) N.Y.: Sheed and Ward.

ELTON, CHARLES. 1927. Animal ecology. New York: The Macmillan Co.

FROUDE, J. A. 1888. On the uses of a landed gentry. *In* Short studies on great subjects. London: Longmans-Green.

HEBERER, GERHARD. 1951. Menschwerdung und Jagd. Schriftenreihe der Forstlichen Fakultät der Univ. Göttingen, Bd. 2; Vorträge der Hochschulwoche Hann. Münden, pp. 12-16.

HUIZINGA, JOHAN. 1949. Homo Ludens, a study of the play element in culture. London: Routledge and Kegan Paul.

LEOPOLD, ALDO. 1938. Conservation esthetic. Bird-Lore, 40(2): 101-109.
————. 1947. The ecological conscience. Bull. Garden Club of Amer., Sept. 1947, pp. 46-53.

LEWIS, C. S. 1940. The problem of pain. London: Bles.
————. 1952. Mere Christianity. London: Collins.

LIVINGSTON, DAVID. 1858. Missionary travels and researches in South Africa. New York: Harper.

MCAREE, J. V. 1951. They call it sport. *In* Prose for senior students, an anthology of short stories and essays; selected and edited by J. L. Gill and L. H. Newell, pp. 342-347. Toronto: D. Macmillan and Co. of Canada, Ltd.

MENNINGER, KARL A. 1951. Totemic aspects of contemporary attitudes toward animals. *In* Psychoanalysis and culture, essays in honor of Géza Roheim, pp. 42-72. New York: Int. Universities Press.

MÜLLER-USING, D. 1951. Kultur and Jagd. Schriftenreihe der Forstlichen Fakultät der Univ. Göttingen, Bd. 2; Vorträge der Hochschulwoche Hann. Münden, pp. 35-39.

RUSSELL, MRS. C. E. B. 1941. The path to reconstruction, a brief introduction to Albert Schweitzer's philosophy of civilization. London: Black.

SCHWEITZER, ALBERT. 1922. On the edge of the primeval forest. (Zwischen Wasser und Urwald.) London: Black.
————. 1923a. The decay and the restoration of civilization. (Verfall und Wiederaufbau der Kultur.) London: Black.
————. 1923b. Civilization and ethics. (Kultur und Ethik.) London: Black.
————. 1936. Indian thought and its development. (Die Weltanschauung der indischen Denken.) London: Hodder and Stoughton.

U.S. FISH AND WILDLIFE SERVICE. 1956. National survey of fishing and hunting, 1955. U.S. Fish and Wildlife Circular 44. 50 pp.

VOSS, R., ET AL. 1955. Wild und Weidwerk der Welt. Vienna: Marathon.

WATTS, I. 1777. Love between brothers and sisters. *In* Divine songs attempted in easy language for the use of children. London: Buckland.

ECONOMICS

Traditionally, wildlife biologists and "nature lovers" alike have assumed that everyone must or should share their emotional and "scientific" attitudes toward the whole outdoor complex—game, fish, plants, and scenery. To most, the placing of a price tag on a goose, a bass, or a river valley seemed impractical, if not impossible. And it was debasing at least.

Now that impact statements are required by law and counterstatements must be filed by competitive agencies and interests, we are all forced not only to find current price tags for everything, but also to project values into the future along with demographic considerations.

Some of the problems, needs, and computations required are expounded in the following papers.

WILDLIFE AND MAN (1966)
Ralph T. King

Like it or not, man is everywhere intertwined with wild animals—from the cockroach to the coydog.

Some of these relationships are biological because man is an animal, a biological organism, whatever else he may be. He, therefore, has physiological and psychological relations with other animals.

Man has an ecological relationship because he is but one kind of animal among more than a million other kinds sharing this earth, and, as a consequence, is interrelated with and dependent upon many of these other kinds. Also, to a very large degree, he is subject to the same forces and influenced by the same factors that rule them.

Another relationship is economic because man is to a woefully unrecognized degree affected by these other kinds of animals for good or ill. He is completely dependent upon them for certain essential services, benefiting from their innumerable values and suffering enormous losses in both health and wealth from their injurious activities.

Any discussion of wildlife and man must deal to some extent with all three of these relationships, but mostly with the latter two. In order to make clear at the beginning what is meant by economic relationships, it is necessary to define the term "total economic value" of wildlife, and then elaborate and illustrate the definition as we proceed. The total economic value of the wildlife resource is the sum of all its positive values plus the worth of the many services performed, minus the sum of all its negative values plus the cost of control and harvest.

Man has since his beginning been associated with wild animals, although more intimately in his early history than now, when he was dependent upon their flesh for food, their skins for clothing and shelter, their bones, teeth, antlers and sinews for tools, weapons and ornaments. In early civilization it was from this source that he derived his domestic animals; first the dog as an aid in hunting; later, goats, sheep, cattle, the ass, the camel, swine, the horse and poultry. Some of these provided materials for clothing and shelter, such as skins, hair and wool; of foods such as meat, milk, butter, cheese and eggs. Some served as beasts of burden, transport and war; and each of them provided additional materials utilized in the manufacturing of such essentials as waterbags, bowstrings, quivers, feathers for arrows, cordage and thread, tools, ornaments and even media of exchange.

In addition to the debt man owes wild animals for these very practical aids to his survival and development as a civilized creature, it is well for him to remember his ancestral relations in this connection and to keep in mind that wild animals constitute the very roots of his being, the source of his beginnings and as such are due some consideration, if not respect, as remote relations.

Today's Six Values

Man is still making much use of wholly wild animals and profiting to a very large extent from the services they perform, although most people

Reprinted from: N. Y. Conservationist 20(6):8-11, by permission from the New York State Department of Environmental Conservation.

are in large part, if not totally, unaware of these uses and services. All of these beneficial uses and services constitute the positive values possessed by wildlife and may be listed as six values: Commercial, recreational, biological, esthetic, scientific and social.

Commercial values include the income derived from the sale of wild animals or their products or from direct and controlled use of wild animals and their progeny. The best example of this type of value is provided by the commercial fisheries and all their products, such as food for human consumption, livestock foods, fertilizers, oils, pharmaceuticals, pearls and literally scores of by-products used in the manufacturing of paints, varnishes, glues, leather dressings, printing inks, soaps, explosives, fabrics and lubricants, as well as buttons, costume jewelry and numerous articles of wearing apparel and accessories.

Other examples are wild-caught furs and fur and game farming to the extent that these latter two are based on wildreared stock. The annual retail sales of products derived from these sources is well in excess of $2 billion and their harvesting, processing, wholesaling and retailing provide employment for thousands of people, to say nothing of the employment provided in supplying and subsidiary industries.

Recreational values are usually measured in terms of money expended in the pursuit of wildlife in connection with sports and hobbies such as hunting, fishing, hiking, touring, camping (to the extent that these last three are based on the attracting properties of wildlife), non-scientific and non-commercial collecting and wildlife photography. They, therefore, include sums spent for equipment, supplies, wearing apparel, license fees, transportation, provisions, board and lodging, hunting dogs, guide services and all other items required in connection with such sports and hobbies.

This is, however, actually only the measure of the worth of the wildlife resource as the economic basis for the industries and businesses catering to those who make purchases for the recreational use of wildlife. It is just another aspect of commercial values and is in nowise a measure of the true value of wildlife as a recreational asset providing as it does wholesome outdoor activities, absorbing interests, a sense of adventure, engrossing hobbies and renewed physical and mental health and vigor.

The fact is, these truly recreational values are intangibles and not amenable to measurement in terms of dollars. It is true, however, that sums so expended make up a considerable part of the income in some cases, and the entire income in many cases, of industries, businesses, communities and individuals, thus contributing significantly to the national income. On the basis of the most reliable figures, the addition to the national income annually from expenditures made by hunters and fishermen alone exceeds $1.75 billion.

It is quite probable that an equal amount is spent each year in connection with the recreational use of wildlife by those who neither hunt nor fish, although there are as yet no reliable figures available to substantiate such a claim. Another significant fact is that much of this income accrues to small businesses or is spent in small and poorer communities, thus making it even more important in the national economy.

102

Biological values include the worth of all the services rendered to man by wild animals. Unfortunately, they either are not obvious or so very obvious and taken so much for granted that they are not appreciated. It is impossible as yet to measure or express them in monetary terms, but they nevertheless are very real and very important—perhaps the most important of all wildlife values. Examples are pollination; reduction of losses from harmful insects, rodents and other injurious species; soil formation and enrichment; water conservation; sanitation; culling; suppression of diseases; recovery and conversion of materials not otherwise practically recoverable and utilizable. Pollination requires no explanation except to point out that it is not the exclusive prerogative of insects. Other kinds of animals serve in this capacity also, especially birds and some kinds of molluscs such as slugs and snails.

Insofar as harmful insects, rodents and other injurious species are concerned, it is true that their natural enemies do not exercise complete control. Because of their diversified feeding habits, predators never eliminate their prey. When one kind of prey has been reduced to the point where it is difficult to find, they transfer their feeding activities to a more numerous and easier to find species. Their predatory habits, however, do keep prey populations to much lower levels than would otherwise be the case. In the absence of the predators man would either suffer increased losses or be put to the additional expense of increasing artificial controls with all their attendant evils.

Anyone who has had the experience of growing domesticated plants, whether in connection with farming or gardening, knows that provisions must be made for maintaining a soil satisfactory in both physical and chemical make-up. The processes of cultivation and fertilization are necessary to counteract soil compaction and allow for the penetration of air and the percolation of water to the plant roots; to provide for the incorporation of humus; and to maintain a sufficient supply of plant nutrients. Without these provisions there would be little hope of growing much in the way of crops, and so man has devised many kinds of machines and devotes much labor to maintaining satisfactory soil tilth and fertility.

Wild plants such as forest trees, range forage and other natural growth are also dependent on the same soil conditions. But the way they grow and economic considerations make it impractical—in most cases actually impossible—to use the machines and the methods employed by the farmer and the gardener and the orchardist. How, then, are these essentials for plant growth provided in the case of wild plants? Through the agency of wild animals whose activities result in loosening, churning, and mixing the soil, bringing subsoil with its accumulated plant nutrients from the lower levels to the surface, and the incorporation of humus and the addition of fertilizing elements. Their combined activities accomplish exactly the same things in the way of cultivation and fertilization for wild plants that man's activities accomplish for domesticated plants.

It is commonly recognized that animals are dependent upon plants; it is not so commonly appreciated that plants are in their turn equally dependent upon animals. This is just one of the many examples of this interdependence.

To the extent that the processes mentioned above result in maintaining the porosity and penetrability of the soil and incorporation of humus, they enhance water conservation by retarding its runoff and providing for its retention in the upper layers of soil or its addition to the ground water supply. The activities of beavers in constructing dams and maintaining ponds also contribute in this respect.

The scavenging propensities of many species are important in maintaining sanitary conditions and esthetic appearances not only in isolated communities without benefit of public sanitation facilities, but also on our modern highspeed highways, along our recreationally important beaches and around our busy harbors and waterfronts. Here again, wild animals are performing a service without which man would suffer serious ill effects or be put to much additional expense in order to alleviate the condition.

The usually much-maligned predators serve to maintain the generally high genetic quality of wild populations through their culling effects, that is the early removal of the unfit and poorer quality individuals. Predators also aid in the suppression of diseases in wild populations. They hunt not as a matter of sport but because they are hungry and in need of something to eat. Usually their prey consists of those individuals easiest to catch, those whose reactions are just slightly less rapid than others of their kind. These are in many cases individuals whose responses are slowed by the effects of disease or parasitism and they are as a consequence removed from the population before their condition has run its course and resulted in the infection or infestation of numerous additional individuals.

Thus predators serve as the only natural agencies of isolation and quarantine functioning in wild populations. Admittedly, there are two sides to the predation picture; there must inevitably be some losses of healthy wildlife and domestic livestock. But except under quite unusual circumstances these are never large and much more than counterbalanced by the beneficial aspects. A predator that has been feeding on destructive rodents 99 per cent of its time may one day swoop down and take a barnyard fowl or a healthy pheasant, but it isn't customary in this country to shoot the hired man when he comes in to lunch.

Wild animals for the most part subsist on food materials—browse, forage, wild fruits, nuts, seeds, plankton—which, even though useful to man, are often so sparsely distributed or so inaccessible that harvesting is impractical or physically impossible. Oftentimes they cannot be profitably utilized by domestic livestock. In many cases these non-utilizable (from man's point of view) but otherwise useful materials are recovered and converted by wild animals into harvestable and useful products. Small and widely dispersed quantities of food, often produced on so-called wastelands, are converted into flesh by the small organisms which are in turn used as food by valuable fur and game species. It might not be wise policy to remind one's lady friends that their prized fox skins and mink stoles were originally mice and frogs, but this is literally the case.

Certainly the most important example of this recovery and conversion by wild animals of materials not otherwise practically recoverable or utilizable in their present state or location takes us back for a moment to consideration of the commercial fisheries. Ever since the beginning of geologic history the soils of the earth have been through the processes of erosion and leaching, losing chemical elements including those essential to plant and animal growth. These chemicals have for the most part accumulated in the oceans. Since the beginning of civilization, and more particularly since the beginning of industrialization, with their concommitants of sewage and waste disposal, these losses have been greatly augmented. Fortunately for the welfare of man this enormous quantity of rich "chemical soup" can, through the process of photosynthesis and the presence of plant and animal plankton, be drawn upon to replenish the nutrient materials lost from the land.

The plankton organisms convert the chemicals in the sea water into living substance; these small organisms are then eaten by somewhat larger organisms, and they in their turn by still larger ones, until finally they become food for the commercial fishes, which are returned to the land to supply these essential nutrients directly to man as food fishes, or indirectly as plant fertilizers to provide human food or food for livestock, to be used as human food.

In some instances the entire process is accomplished by wild animals, as in the case of the vast Chilean guano industry where enormous colonies of sea birds catch the fish and even perform a part of the conversion process. It is possible that man's ingenuity will enable him eventually to recover these chemicals from the ocean directly and economically, but for the present at least he is dependent upon fishes, a wholly wild resource, to perform this essential function.

Esthetic values are the values of objects and places possessing beauty, affording inspiration and opportunities for communion, contributing to the arts through music, poetry, literature, sculpture and painting and possessing historical and patriotic significance.

Regarding historical and patriotic significance, native species of wild animals in their natural surroundings are not different from sites or objects of physiographic, political, military and biographical interest. Some species of wild animals have played such an important role in our national development or entered to such an extent into our culture as a people that their consideration in this connection is amply justified. With no intention of being irreverent or unpatriotic isn't the same respect due the wild turkey that played such an important part in our Pilgrim Fathers' first Thanksgiving dinner as is due the rock upon which they supposedly landed?

Isn't the bald eagle, our national emblem, symbolizing as it does all our founders hoped for and all our country stands for, as deserving of preservation as are Mount Vernon and Monticello?

Isn't the beaver deserving of our everlasting gratitude and a permanent place in both our national memory and our country's fauna for the part it played in the early exploration, settlement and commerce of the continental United States? One American historian has gone so far as to say it "was the most important fact in American history."

There are few of us who do not retain childhood memories of native animals ranging from the heroes of Uncle Remus' tales to their prototypes in Thornton Burgess' bedtime stories, to be added to but not displaced in the current generation by Walt Disney's better efforts. These have entered into America's folklore, they are a part of America's history and heritage and as deserving of consideration, respect and preservation as its other national shrines, monuments and memorials.

Although esthetic values are intangible and purely personal, they are nevertheless of vital concern to everyone spending any time in the out of doors and in addition, are the values that induce a goodly number to become interested in the welfare of other natural resources and actively concerned in their conservation.

Scientific values are realized through the study of wild animals and associated widespread natural phenomena that may affect man's welfare either directly or indirectly. Examples are population behavior, diseases and their spread, varying virulence of pathogens, certain aspects of nutrition and reproduction, ecological relations, population dispersal, social organization, effects of stress induced by overcrowding, and so on. These values are of particular interest to the ecologist, ethnologist, pathologist, epidemiologist, demographer and sociologist and indirectly of value to all of us as we are benefitted by their investigations.

Social values can be disposed of briefly, not because they are unimportant but because they are not different from the values already discussed except in the one respect that the benefits in this case accrue to the community as a whole instead of to individuals, industries or businesses.

The difference between these values and those previously discussed will not be clear unless this distinction is kept in mind. The following examples will illustrate and perhaps clarify this point: Increased opportunity for wholesome and economical outdoor recreation, hobbies and adventure; utilization of leisure time; enhancement of interest in surroundings and required activities; increased real estate values; income from otherwise idle land; the offsetting of carrying charges incurred in other connections; creation of marketing possibilities for minor products; alleviation of monotony; improved physical and mental health.

Maintenance Costs

So far we have dealt with only positive values, but there is obviously an opposite side of the picture consisting of an equally imposing list of negative values. Due in part to space limitations and in part to that human perversity that so frequently makes us more familiar with the evil than the good, I am going to present a summary of negative values in the belief that it will suffice to both define and illustrate this category of values. It includes the value of property destroyed or damaged by wild animals and costs incurred in efforts to limit or reduce wild animal populations and prevent their access to or use of crops, stored products and structures. It includes losses to standing and stored crops on farms, forage and livestock on the range; standing, stored and manufactured timber and timber products; processed and stored foods, manufactured goods; damage to buildings, rights-of-way, dikes, levees, dams, irrigation and drainage ditches, terraces and other structures; losses from diseases harbored or transmitted by wild animals; costs of protecting, repelling, poisoning, trapping and other means of control; and harvesting costs.

106

In fairness, however, we must make some distinction between legitimate maintenance costs and negative values. In our daily living we do not ordinarily designate costs of operation, maintenance and repairs as negative values. We admit that these costs reduce profits, but we accept this fact, make allowances for it and consider ourselves fortunate to have those appliances and facilities that lighten our labors, provide us with the necessities for life and add to our comfort and pleasures. We do not discard our automobiles because their operation requires expenditures for gasoline, oil and repairs. We do not abandon our homes because we must pay for fuel, water, electricity, repairs and taxes. We realize that no good thing comes free of cost. When we apply these ideas of values to wildlife we must keep these distinctions in mind—the difference between normal allowable costs and losses incident to the use and enjoyment of the resource, and negative values—that is, excessive costs or losses due to abnormalities in or malfunctioning of the resource.

In concluding, I would like to paraphrase Professor Aldo Leopold: The objective of a wildlife conservation program is to retain for the average citizen the opportunity to see, hear, admire, enjoy and use and the challenge to understand the varied forms of wildlife living in his region. It implies not only that these forms be kept in existence, but that the greatest possible variety of them exist in each community. Wildlife management is, then, the art of making land produce sustained animal crops of wildlife in order that we (all the people) may realize the several values possessed by, and benefit from the many services performed by, this resource.

The admonition to "Be fruitful and multiply, and fill the earth and subdue it; and have dominion over the fish of the sea and over the birds of the air and over every living thing that moves upon the earth" (Gen. 1:28) implies not only use, enjoyment and control of the earth and its products, but understanding and appreciation and responsibility for these things as well.

BIONOMIC AND ETHICAL IMPLICATIONS OF COMMERCIAL GAME HARVEST PROGRAMS (1968)

James G. Teer and Nathan K. Forrest

In this paper we examine the impact of economic and social factors inherent in commercial hunting systems on the production, harvest, and management of game animals. The ethics of leasing programs now being used in Texas are evaluated. Our objectives are simply to demonstrate that leasing systems are widespread and important in Texas, and that these systems influence the ecology and management of several game species. Most of the data and discussion involve white-tailed deer (*Odocoileus virginianus*) and mule deer (*O. hemionus*): however, inferences and implications carry over to other species.

THE HUNTING LEASE SYSTEMS

Development and Increase of Hunting Lease Systems

Although no written records of the beginning of paying programs for harvesting game in Texas are known, many ranchers in central Texas and employees of conservation agencies state that commercial hunting began in the better white-tailed deer ranges in the Edwards Plateau and Central Mineral Region in the early 1920's. The 39th Texas Legislature

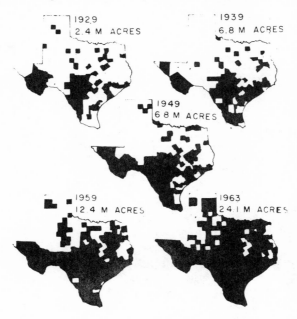

COUNTIES WHERE SHOOTING PRESERVE
LICENSES WERE SOLD

FIG. 15-1.—The spread of commercial hunting programs in Texas as indicated by the number of counties in which shooting preserve licenses were sold.

Reprinted from: Trans. N. Amer. Wildl. and Natural Resources Conf. 33:192-202.

in regular session passed the present "shooting preserve law" in 1925 (Texas Parks and Wildlife Department, 1963: p. 71). The law requires all landowners accommodating hunters on their lands for pay to buy a shooting preserve license and record the names, license numbers, addresses, and game killed by all paying hunters.

The first leasing arrangements were most likely made between a party of hunters and a rancher for hunting rights because the rancher desired to limit hunting and increase the number of deer on his rangelands. The hunters wanted to have exclusive access to the deer, and the price of the lease probably was a .30-caliber saddle gun or some such token of valuable consideration.

Whatever the circumstances and terms of agreement might have been, landowners discovered that wildlife, especially big-game animals, was a marketable commodity. Commercial systems of harvesting game have become the principal schemes of game cropping and hunter management in the State (Figs. 1 and 2).

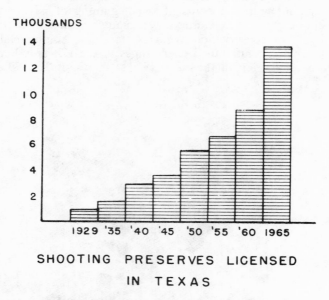

SHOOTING PRESERVES LICENSED

IN TEXAS

FIG. 15-2.—Number of licensed shooting preserves in Texas (after Lee, 1965).

The commercialization of hunting was made possible by the trespass statutes of the state, the American's traditional respect for private property, and perhaps most important, by the virtual lack of public lands on which the public had free access to hunt. Title to all public lands was retained by the State of Texas when she entered the Union in 1846, and less than 1,000 square miles of public lands now remain on which hunting is permitted. Thus a market for hunting rights on privately owned lands developed, and even though game is held in trust by the State for the people, access to game ranges is controlled by the landowners. Control of access has, for all practical purposes, transferred the custody of game animals from the State to the landowners.

From the small numbers of leases for taking white-tailed deer in central Texas in the early 1920's, commercial harvest programs have spread to other important game ranges. The number of game species involved has also increased. Today, leasing programs are involved in the harvest of practically all of the big game (white-tailed deer, mule deer, and pronghorn antelope) on ranges west of the 98th meridian. The harvest of deer was estimated at near 239,000 in 1967 in Texas (A. J. Springs, Texas Parks and Wildlife Department, personal communication), and of this number probably two-thirds were killed in that area. Those ranges comprise the great ranching area of Texas and such large land holdings lend themselves to leasing programs.

Leasing systems have spread to the Rio Grande Plains, the timberlands of the Post Oak and Pine Belts and Cross Timbers of east Texas, and to all other game ranges of the state that support huntable populations of deer and other game species. East Texas has been traditionally an open range for hunting. There, most private land holdings are small, but leases by groups of small operators as well as by large timber companies are increasing. Timber companies with large acreages are just now beginning to develop hunting programs through leasing for financial gain. In the past, most timber companies allowed free hunting primarily for public relations reasons. They now see opportunities for substantial income through sales of hunting rights.

Waterfowl hunting in the Texas coastal marshes, bays, and estuarine habitats and in the ricelands and prairies adjacent to the coast has also developed into highly commercialized hunting programs. Again, the primary reason for the development was the ability of landowners to limit hunter access to waterfowl habitats. Great concentrations of ducks and geese winter in these estuaries and bays and in the cultivated ricelands and grazing lands. The famous Lissie and Garwood Prairies, located within 50 miles of Houston, are closed to public hunting except through leasing privileges from landowners or "hunting outfitters."

Bobwhite quail (*Colinus virginianus*), scaled quail (*Callipepla squamata*), mourning doves *(Zenaidura macroura),* white-winged doves *(Zenaida asiatica),* tree squirrels *(Sciurus niger* and *S. carolinensis),* wild turkeys *(Meleagris gallopavo)* are beginning to figure more prominently in leasing arrangements in many game ranges in the state. Leases for hunting wild turkeys usually are made along with leases for deer because the two are ordinarily found on the same ranges. On the High Plains and Panhandle ranges, bobwhite quail is the most abundant game species. Many ranches are leased by quail hunters from as far away as Dallas, El Paso, and Houston.

Leases for hunting small game animals are also common in locations near large cities and population centers. Finding productive hunting areas near these population centers is becoming more difficult and competitive for city-dwellers. These urbanites wish to be in good hunting sites within a drive of an hour or two of their residences. Thus it is not surprising that farmers and ranchers in these favorable locations find a strong demand for hunting rights. These same locations, by the way, support the most successful put-and-take shooting resorts.

Types of Leasing Arrangements

Four general types of leasing programs, with several modifications for special situations, are used in commercialized harvest systems (Forrest, 1966). The first, and perhaps the most important, is a "season-lease" arrangement. Season leases usually provide that a hunter or group of hunters will have exclusive hunting privileges for specified game species for the season. Harvest quotas for the hunters are established by the landowner and are, of course, within the limits established by game regulations. The season-lease system has been and still is the most common hunting scheme used in big game harvest programs in the western half of the State, and many landowners provide hunting privileges for other species under similar arrangements.

Most landowners provide hunters with a camphouse or some type of living accommodations on the leased land. Some of these are little more than shacks, but others are fine lodges indeed, and it is not uncommon to find that many of them have been constructed by the hunters themselves. However, the stipulation is usually made that all permanent construction becomes the property of the landowner when the lease is terminated.

Some of the season leases go much beyond providing hunting recreation. Leases are becoming family-oriented weekend and holiday recreation centers. Landowners are beginning to attract more of the recreation market by improving facilities and offering additional activities for all members of the family. Fishing in streams and stockponds, horseback riding, hiking, camping, and photographing wildlife and nature are other facets of leasing programs that are becoming important.

The second, or day-hunting system, is becoming more popular with landowners in big game ranges and especially with landowners in wintering areas for waterfowl. This leasing system allows hunters access to game on a given area on a per-day basis. Hunters are usually not guided or provided with any particular equipment under day-lease arrangements for taking deer, but many landowners with waterfowl hunting may guide and provide decoys, boats and other equipment to the guests.

The hunting "broker" or hunting "outfitter" system is the third type of leasing system commonly used in the State. This system is being used predominantly in harvesting geese and ducks in the ricelands, marshes, and rangelands along the coast. Under such a program, a hunting outfitter will lease large blocks of favored wintering areas from the landowners. These blocks of wintering habitat will involve as many as 25 or more landowners' properties, and may be as large as 50,000 acres. All hunting rights are assigned to the outfitter, who operates the entire area under lease as a shooting preserve.

Outfitters offer waterfowl shooting on a day hunting basis. Ordinarily all equipment for hunting except guns, shells and dogs is provided; and often, food, lodging and other services are catered.

Outfitters manage their hunting programs to hold waterfowl throughout the season. Commonly, a mosaic of rice fields and irrigation reservoirs is flooded or filled to serve as sanctuaries and roosting sites for the waterfowl. Game laws allow morning and afternoon hunting, but most outfitters stop hunting at noon. The hunters are often distributed from day to day after the field-feeding patterns of waterfowl have been established by aerial or ground reconnaissance.

The fourth type of commercial hunting program is only now becoming important, and this is one in which the charge is made directly for the animal. These types of programs involve hunting introduced big-game animals. Such animals presently are not classed as game species under Texas statutes. Landowners or hunters can take them in any season using any means or methods desired. Such programs have a certain kinship to the traditional shooting resorts, but no regulations, such as are in effect for operating shooting resorts, are applied to hunting of exotic big game animals.

Axis deer (*Axis axis*), blackbuck or Indian antelope (*Antilope cervicapra*), aoudad or Barbary sheep (*Ammotragus lervia*), mouflon sheep (*Ovis musimon*), Sika or Japanese deer (*Cervus nippon*), and a few other antelope, cervids, and sheep are sold in these hunting programs. The quality of hunting in terms of natural conditions attendant to the hunt and the "wildness" of the game are sometimes below that of populations of native game animals. Yet the demand for such hunting is great and seems to be increasing.

Economic Returns for Hunting Leases to Landowners

Critical and exhaustive studies of the economics of game production and harvest programs in Texas have not been made. In this section we wish to report the trends of leasing prices under various leasing systems for particular game animals. Surveys of the economics of hunting and fishing have been made in Texas (Crossley S-D Surveys, Inc., 1956; and Bureau of the Census, 1961), but these studies did not consider income accruing to land operators for sales of hunting rights. An annual estimate of the number of hunting leases, acres in hunting leases, and income accruing to the landowners has been made since 1963 by County Agricultural Agents of the Texas Agricultural Extension Service, Texas A&M University. Klussmann (1966) reported that these estimates showed that 13,000 landowners leased 22,000,000 acres for hunting in 1965, and income to landowners for these leases amounted to $13,000,000. We feel that these are rough approximations, but these data do suggest that hunting income is substantial in the state.

Average income to landowners per acre for deer hunting in central Texas has increased steadily: $0.08 in 1938 (Tucker, 1939); $0.19 in 1948 (Hahn, 1951); $0.91 in 1959 (Teer *et al.*, 1965); and $1.07 in 1965 (Forrest, in litt.). These data represent gross receipts and do not include costs of hunter management or inputs of forage and other resources into the deer herd. Average prices of leases have increased over 1,000 percent in about 30 years, and the trend is still upward. On many ranches in the Edwards Plateau and Central Mineral Region net returns from the sale of hunting rights exceed the returns from the livestock enterprise on the same ranges.

Prices for deer leases range from a few cents per acre up to $3.00 per acre where excellent hunting and trophy animals are involved. For many years the average season lease for deer was made at the approximate rate of one man per 100 acres. Recent trends suggest that hunter densities are being increased with accompanying increases in price.

Some types of leasing arrangements are more profitable than others (Table 1). Forrest (*in litt.*) has shown that the day-lease system yields the highest return of all leasing programs. Combinations of season leases with day leases and of season leases with provisions for taking anterless deer are the next most profitable arrangements. The traditional season lease is usually the least profitable, but because of the limited inputs involved, it is still preferred by many landowners.

Day hunting for waterfowl along the Texas coast also is the most profitable leasing arrangement to landowners. However, leasing land to hunting outfitters or parties by the season may be equally as profitable to the landowner considering that he does not have the burden and expense of husbanding and providing gear for the hunters.

TABLE 1. Commercial Hunting Arrangements and Related Returns

Hunting Arrangement	Average Gross Return
	Dollars per acre
For white-tailed deer[1]	
Season	0.84
Day	1.51
Season with doe	1.07
Season and day	1.27
For ducks and geese[2]	
By landowners	
Season	0.62
Day	1.30
By outfitters	0.90

[1] Returns for white-tailed deer are for Llano County for the hunting season 1964.
[2] Returns for goose hunting are for Colorado, Wharton, Chambers, and Jefferson Counties for the hunting season 1966-67.

EFFECTS OF THE HUNTING LEASE SYSTEM
Economic Stimulus for Producing Game

The economic value of game to the landowner is unquestionably a great stimulus to the private sector of society to promote the growth, development, and welfare of game populations. Landowners enjoy having wildlife on their ranges for the same reasons that the average citizen enjoys wildlife on the parks, forests, and other public lands of the continent. But because these same animals also represent a substantial source of income, the stimulus for having high population densities of marketable game on private ranges is increased even more. In a sense, public enjoyment of the aesthetic values of game and wildlands is made possible on private property in Texas by the value of the leasing systems.

More deer are now found on Texas game ranges than were present when white men first came to Texas. Deer numbers dropped to an all-time low in the 1930's for many of the same reasons that they were reduced in numbers or extirpated from their ranges in other parts of North America —overshooting, encroachment of intensive agriculture, overuse and degradation of native vegetation, and perhaps predation and disease. Over 3,000,000 deer occur in Texas now (A. J. Springs, Texas Parks and Wildlife Department, personal communication), and while such great numbers cannot be attributed to the economic stimulus alone, hunting lease programs have certainly encouraged their numbers.

We have witnessed cases where economic considerations played a major part in restoration of deer numbers on areas as small as a section of a county or a single ranch. In choices of management programs for production of agricultural products and in the allocation of land resources, landowners are influenced by prices to produce the commodity having the strongest market potential. Such choices on a farm or ranch unit will often determine densities of game, and, in many situations, whether or not the species is present.

The economic stimulus to manage for production of small-game animals is limited at present but increasing yearly. Leases made for these animals are usually on lands that have not been manipulated for improvement of game numbers. However, as hunting areas become scarcer through encroachment of man's needs through intensive agricultural programs, urban sprawl, and hunter population increases, the impetus for intensive management to produce small game will surely increase.

Regulation of Hunter Conduct

Zealous husbandry primarily in the form of protection of game resources from poaching and overshooting are strong attributes of landowners having economically important hunting leases. Each landowner literally acts as his own conservation officer. Except for illegal entry, he usually knows who is in his pastures at all times. He is empowered by statute to file trespass cases. Considering the number of hunters and size of the deer range in the state, trespass cases are not especially common. Illegal kill has been reported to exceed the legal take on public lands in the Lake States and Northeast (Taylor, 1956; p. 178); illegal kill on leased lands simply never reaches such proportions.

Many parties of hunters have held season leases on single ranches for as long as 35 years in the deer ranges of central Texas. These lease holders develop proprietary interests and feelings about the wildlife and quality of hunting on their leases. Their conduct and ethics in sport hunting are made circumspect because they realize that they will be back next year. In such situations, there are no "landowner-sportsmen problems" that are becoming so prevalent in other systems of game cropping on private lands. Hunters that have an interest in the continued welfare of the game populations have often used their influence to cause the land operator to initiate or follow through on some desirable conservation and management program.

Safety of Hunters

Safety of hunters is another beneficial attribute of the hunting lease system. From 1954 through 1966, only two hunting fatalities occurred in Llano County, one of the heaviest hunted counties in Texas and a county in which virtually all hunting is done under leasing programs. In this same period over 128,000 white-tailed deer were harvested. Such an enviable record of low hunting fatalities surely was made possible by the leasing system. Hunting parties normally plan their hunts on leased lands so that each member will know where others are hunting. Moreover, parties of hunters that are acquainted with each other are probably more careful in the field and around camp than the average group of hunters on public lands.

On the Mark A. Moss Bar-O Ranch in southern Llano County 90 hunters per day were guided for many of the 46 days during deer season. The ranch contains 8,763 acres, and thus the density of hunters was almost one per 100 acres. They were positioned to take advantage of cover and terrain and were required to stay within a very small area while still-hunting for deer. There were no accidents, and the season's kill approached a deer per 10 acres. Guided hunts in day leasing programs can be safe hunts, as reflected by the above example.

Distribution of Hunting Pressure

The leasing system tends to distribute hunting pressure more evenly over large game ranges, and to a certain extent in relation to density of game. If unable to find a lease close to home, hunters are forced to hunt elsewhere, thus eliminating the problem of excessive numbers of hunters on any one area. On the better game ranges landowners tend to allow more hunters per given area of land. This is an important conservation measure in many situations. When game is in short supply and the animals cannot withstand large kills, hunting pressure can be controlled on individual ranches to prevent overshooting. Problems do occur on individual landholdings, however, in that not all landowners use game density as the criterion for determining the number of hunters to be accommodated.

Promotion of Conservatism in Kill Rates

An important detrimental effect of the economic value of game on certain game populations, particularly deer, has been the promotion of conservatism in kill rates. As game has become more valuable through leasing programs, the landowners have had a tendency to become more conservative. In the case of white-tailed deer and mule deer, this conservatism has created overpopulations and range abuse. Die-offs are frequent on many of the state's deer ranges.

Although does are harvested in leasing programs, they are often considered by landowners and hunters alike as the "producers" of the bucks which bring higher prices in leases. Obviously, not all of the cause and effect result can be laid to monetary value, but certainly the problem has been heightened. Literally no one wishes to kill the deer that is laying the golden egg.

Imbalances in sex ratios of deer have resulted from leasing arrangements where there was no price differential by sex. Under those arrangements hunters selected bucks. Does were harvested at much lower rates which resulted in sex ratios as divergent as one buck to eight or ten does (Hahn, 1945; Teer et al., 1965). However, with the advent of day hunting and the charge-per-animal type of leasing arrangements, ranchers have found that a price differential between the sexes is one means of solving the unbalanced ratios. By charging less for doe hunting, ranches provide

116

an incentive to hunters to harvest more does than would otherwise be the case.

ETHICAL CONSIDERATIONS OF LEASING PROGRAMS

At what point should society become concerned with the commercialization of hunting recreation? And when does the artificiality of game production and regimentation of hunting defeat the values derived from the sport?

The latter question can be answered only by the individual, who we are told, has less ability today in recognizing quality in hunting and purity in nature than our forebears did a generation or two ago. Nevertheless, who can say that the enjoyment of hunting by present-day hunters is not as great as that of their ancestors? Whatever the answer, leases for hunting recreation can prevent masses of hunters from overwhelming each other in concentrations that often develop on such hunting areas as public shooting grounds. Certainly, sport hunting is made safer through leasing programs. In this way too, some of the desirable qualities of hunting are retained.

We submit that landowners merit an economic return for animals in which costly inputs of resources are made. So far as land owners are concerned, forage consumed by big game animals might just as well be directed into production of domestic livestock. Changes in vegetative character to have game on livestock ranges can be made in most habitats, but who will stand the cost? Certainly, when encroachment on the livelihood of an individual results from game management, society will expect that the landowner be repaid for his losses when they occur in producing game for public benefit.

We consider unethical those commercial hunting programs in which management is only directed at attracting, holding, and concentrating game for harvest purposes. Society usually demands that rewards be given to only those who produce, and we feel that this axiom holds for commercial game harvest programs.

The special interests of hunting recreation will become more apparent to society as the demands for all kinds of outdoor recreation continue. Charging for hunting on private land is as ethically correct as charging for trailer space, campsites, canoe trips, or ski slopes when management is directed at production as well as harvest. For a society that is attempting to return to outdoor environments, if only on weekends, the economic stimulus to produce game can be a solution to overwhelming hunting pressures.

LITERATURE CITED

Bureau of Census
    1961. Second Texas survey of fishing and hunting. Prepared for Texas Game and Fish Commission. U.S. Dept. of Commerce, 35 pages.

Crossley, S-D Surveys, Inc.
    1956. Survey of hunters and fishermen. Prepared for Texas Game and Fish Commission, Austin, Texas, 31 pages plus appendices.

Forrest, N. K.
    1966. Some economic considerations of alternative deer lease arrangements. Pages 98-107 in Proceedings, The White-tailed Deer: Its Problems and Potentials. Texas A&M University, 110 pages.

Hahn, H. C., Jr.

    1951.   Economic value of game in the Edwards Plateau Region of Texas. FA Report Series—No. 8. Texas Game, Fish and Oyster Comm., 50 pages.

Klussmann, W. G.

    1966.   Deer and the commercialized hunting system in Texas. Pages 18-21 in Proceedings, The White-tailed Deer: Its Problems and Potentials. Texas A&M University, 110 pages.

Lee, Howard T.

    1965.   Preserved hunting. Texas Parks and Wildlife, 23 (12): 8-9.

Taylor, W. P.

    1956.   The deer of North America. The Stackpole Press, Harrisburg, Pa., and the Wildlife Management Institute, Washington, D. C., xvi + 668 pages.

Teer, J. G., J. W. Thomas, and E. A. Walker

    1965.   Ecology and management of white-tailed deer in the Llano Basin of Texas. Wildl. Mono., No. 15. 62 pages.

Texas Parks and Wildlife Department

    1963.   Full text of the game, fish and fur laws of Texas. Von Boeckmann-Jones Co., Austin. 538 pages.

Tucker, W. J.

    1939.   Game and fish research in Texas. Bull. No. 18. Texas Game, Fish and Oyster Commission, 12 pages.

CAN WE PUT AN ECONOMIC VALUE ON FISH AND WILDLIFE? (1965)

James Crutchfield

I would like to discuss three questions:

First, should we actually use economic evaluations as a sole or major basis for investment in outdoor recreation?

Second, can we derive meaningful economic values for fish and wildlife?

Third, if we do this, how do fish and wildlife come out in the competition with other renewable resources?

So far as the need for economic evaluation is concerned, I would like to put it as bluntly as I can, there is no alternative. Increasingly, fish and wildlife must compete with other users of water and land resources in particular. Fish, in particular, and wildlife in respect to land, use natural resources. They are rather special uses. And by doing so they impose costs in terms of other uses foregone. In a lot of cases groups have suggested, I think very popularly, that the costs foregone are so small that we may very logically and systematically fight for preservation of wilderness areas. In other cases, unfortunately, the cost can be very high.

Increasingly, water and land utilization are subject to more and more sophisticated techniques of evaluation and long-range planning. And as those plans, once under way, involve decisions with regard to fish and wildlife that for practical purposes are irreversible, then we must be in on the plans and we must be in on the plans using economic evaluation techniques that fall within the confines of the accepted practices of other water uses. If you do not use economic evaluations at all, your case is hopeless. If you use phony evaluations it is not much better. I think we do have to look at the problem in these lights.

To put it even more bluntly, I have never been able to understand why it should be that we allow people and encourage people to organize their business activities on the assumption that people are willing to spend, what they choose to buy, is one of the best estimates of what collectively we place in the way of values on particular goods and services. This is the very crux of a private enterprise economy and the kind of democratic government associated with it. Wildlife and fish involve services that are highly valuable to some of us and not to others. And the value that we place on them, simply puts them into their proper place in the only really widespread system of social choice that we have in our economy. The values that are placed on particular goods and services are the guide to our allocation and production.

I think we can still respect our Western attitude for the inherent right of every man and woman to fish or hunt or go camping or hiking free or virtually free, but this reflects the period when our resources available for these purposes were so abundant that there wasn't much conflict. Those days are gone and I think we are going to have to face the evaluation problem and do a better job than we have in the past if these values are to be preserved at all. Can it be done?

Reprinted from: Colorado Outdoors 14(2): 1-5.

I think that the only answer I can give you here is that it can be done but it has been made far more difficult by the insistence of many groups, including a good many very influential sportsmen's clubs, that hunting and fishing must be available free or nearly free. We do not have what would be by all odds the most useful source of information on how many people use these resources, where they use them, with what degree of intensity, how much they would be willing to give up rather than do without them. The sort of thing that I think we could develop quite easily and quite accurately if we were to move to a system of user fees, license fees if you like, that represent more accurately than our present licenses do the real value that people place on the right to fish, the right to hunt, the right to camp, the right to watch birds or anything else that you like in this area.

In effect, by insisting that it has to be free, we are undermining systematically the basis on which we can make our strongest appeal for an orderly place in land and water development for wildlife and the outdoor recreation field in general. We are denying ourselves access to the kind of long-term investment funds that we need.

We can substitute for that in part through what we call simulation studies—a number of people tell me that—Doug Gardner in Utah, a very excellent study in Oregon by Emery Castle and Joe Brown of Oregon State University, and several others as well. What these people have done is to try to use the cost of overcoming distance as a measure of what people would have been willing to pay for the use of a particular kind of recreation facility; the Oregon study, perhaps the most systematic and best, for the right to fish for salmon and steelhead. The difficulty with this type of operation, although it is conceptually perfectly correct, is that the studies are terribly expensive, they become out-of-date very rapidly and in many cases they involve technical difficulties that we haven't been able to overcome.

For example, when you use the willingness to travel as the measure of what people would have been willing to pay rather than do without, we are up against the fact that we can't separate mixed purposes. Frequently, when we get beyond the range where people can go to fish and hunt for the weekend we shift to an entirely different character of demand for outdoor recreation in our population. So that studies like Brown and Castle are making, although they are the best that we have, systematically understate the real economic contribution of fish, wildlife, and the activities associated with it. But, in fact, they are far better than the two most generally used and systematically phony techniques for valuing outdoor recreation.

One can use most expenses—the money spent on bait, tackle, beer and other necessities in a good orderly fishing and hunting trip. The assumption being, I presume, is that if people didn't buy these things they wouldn't spend their money at all. This is obviously not a fact and it is not accepted in legitimate techniques for evaluation of any sort of use.

The second is the technique of reaching deep into the hip pocket and pulling out a value. If somebody doesn't like it, you pull one out of another pocket, or something of the sort. You come out with a schedule of daily values for hunting, fishing, camping, hiking, rock collecting and so forth. This seems to rest on the assumption that where a number is needed a bad number is better than no number at all. Let me just point the nearest parallel that comes to mind. What do you suppose would happen if you asked a competent real estate appraiser for the real value of a square foot of earth and river? The answer, I think, would be that this is ridiculous. The value of a piece of real estate is determined by principles of evaluation that are unchanged but their application in any given area will bring you different answers as to how much they are worth. Steelhead in a river adjacent to Seattle or Portland or one of the large California metropolitan areas are worth vastly more than steelhead in a remote Alaskan stream—it is the same fish, they fight just as hard.

With the principle of evaluation, like the gross expenditure approach, we suggest that you follow it to its logical conclusion—that the farther away the fish are the harder and more expensive it is to get there, the more they are worth. This is as offensive to common sense as anything I know. It isn't going to get us far in competition with sound economic analysis which you will find in other water-using agents.

We can then use the simulations of what people are willing to pay. We can, and I think do, in some instances go to more realistic pressures for the use of resources for outdoor recreation purposes. The secretary of the Gill Netters Association of Puget Sound once made the remark to me that on the day the State of Washington goes to a $10 license fee for salt water salmon fishing the commercial fishery on the inner Puget Sound is dead. Until that time it is quite possible to obscure the issue sufficiently so that no one has any real idea how many salt water fishermen there are or how strongly they feel about carrying on their sport. We can then fix reasonably adequate values not on all but on many types of outdoor recreation including some of the most important, but we have made it much more difficult for ourselves than we might have.

I think it is vitally important for an economist working in this area to point out that dollar valuation in some instances may very well result in the complete and irreversible elimination of some kinds of outdoor recreation that are vitally important to small groups of people. In numbers they may not be very great but the intensity of their feeling and the fact that their feeling is part of a heritage in this country is something that we can afford to set aside on the basic principle of protection of minority rights. I see no particular conflict; in fact I have done work in the area in connection with the middle fork of the Salmon in Idaho. This pointed out that where commercial utilization is at best a marginal sort of proposition, that the cost of setting aside virtually untouched and completely nonreproducing segments of American fish and wildlife area is very small. So that an economic evaluation can play a consistent and logical part in this aspect of preservation of outdoor recreation.

There are a lot of cases where we need economic values in a more prosaic sense of the word. All of us are facing, although few of us face up to it, the necessity of making decisions about the relative value of sport vs. commercial fishing, primarily on our salmon species and, in one badly misguided thing, on our steelhead. The question of how we ought to use these is basically an economic question. These are natural resources used by, and essentially belonging to, the people of the state. And the question is which use or which combination of uses brings the greater benefits. I don't think you can do this without adequate evaluation techniques. And what we do is find it out with what we have in California, in Oregon, in Washington, in Alaska and in British Columbia—an emotional ground in which each tries to pull the plug in the other guy's tub no matter how many fishes go out with the dirty water. Oregon is facing precisely this kind of decision at the present time.

We also have equally serious conflict in game range use vs. some time very marginal grazing and agricultural operations. The magnificent game area in the Kootenay, for example, is crying out for some kind of moderate, conservative value to be placed on game in the Rocky Mountain trench area. The competition is marginal grazing of cattle, and Christmas tree production. It might be that the most elementary kind of guess as to the value of the game management possibilities in the area will indicate that it is a considerably better use. I do not know. I am just assuming this. I think it is very close. But we don't have even that kind of economic aspect and so nothing much is being done about it. The technique is to multiply and then pick one of them.

The area of water pollution and to some extent land pollution is one of serious concern to all of us. We have had some pretty bitter experience in Washington in connection with the pulp mills. To be blunt about it, we have been doing research for some 24 years in the area but as of the moment we cannot tell a court what damage to fish and wildlife is done by pulp mill waste material and what value is placed on that damage. Pollution, in brief, cannot be defined to the satisfaction of a court except in terms of economic damage to other uses of the water or land involved. Our inability to produce the kind of research that would make those estimates possible and defensible in court is handcuffing us in trying to deal with some of these urgent pollution problems that bear directly on fish and wildlife.

If, then, we do go to a more intensive use of economic analysis as a basis for an investment in fish and wildlife, how will we come out? I will argue, and again this follows the words of previous people, that where population and the mobility and incomes of our populations are rising, the demand for all types of outdoor recreation is going to continue to expand and the very nature of it is such that you cannot substitute for it as you can for almost all other types of industrial use of natural resources.

We are not short of agricultural land. We have too much of it under cultivation now and policies that seriously damage the nonsubstitutable recreational use with a rising future value are being compared quite illegitimately with land uses, the real economic need for which is in serious question unless you have a vested interest in piling up bigger surpluses.

I think, secondly, that where the alternatives to wilderness areas can be clearly spelled out in economic terms, where the alternatives would bring sport and commercial fishing to be clearly spelled out, the true conservationist has far more to gain and relatively little to lose from the application of expected professional treatise of economic evaluation. We'll lose some and we'll gain some but there is vastly more, I think, to be gained by concentrating our efforts on those cases where outdoor recreation needs are critical, where the competition is most intense and where our case can be spelled out strongly and convincingly as being the best, the most economical use of the land and water areas concerned. If we try to defend fish and wildlife everywhere under every circumstance, we lose not only the cases where we haven't really got a leg to stand on, but we lose the confidence of legislators and the general public in the integrity of the position we are trying to defend. I think we have been guilty of that in many areas.

Finally, I would like to make a point—we tend to be terribly defensive about the economic value of fish and wildlife. Why don't we put the shoe on the other foot and make the point that the economic evaluation of many of the competing uses of water and land is open to very serious question as to its validity, conceptually and in terms of the data employed. Before we start planning the level and intensity of further structural programs in water, the impact of which on fish and wildlife is usually negative, we ought to take a careful look at how much we can gain by using the water we have more sensibly.

Something in the neighborhood of 92 per cent of all water used in the Western States is for agricultural use, most of it for irrigation, a large part of it for irrigation and production of crops already in surplus supply. There are innumerable cases in my own state and others where water is being supplied at prices below the out-of-the-pocket cost to the user in a frantic, competitive race to get industries to settle in your particular area. The end result of this is a very much lower than logical level of water pricing in general.

The procedures used by the acting agencies in the water development fields for evaluation of multiple purpose projects are demonstratively and consistently overvaluing benefits and undervaluing costs. They are using an artificially low interest rate that systematically pushes in the direction of very large, very intensive water development programs even though others might be more efficient. Lest the representatives of the Corps of Engineers feel that I'm pointing the finger at them, I will hasten to add that the Bureau of Reclamation and the Soil Conservation Service are close touches.

Let's take a good careful look at the economic evaluation basis on which competing water uses and land uses rest. If we are in a position to say that our hands are clean in the sense that our own estimate of the value of our claims on this earth are conceptually legitimate and as good as the limited data available will permit, then we are in a position to get in and make sense.

So I don't think that the stand of the grim and irritating profession of the economist is in conflict with the theme of conservation as I would construe it. In the long run it may very well turn out that a hard-boiled kind of private enterprise look at the value of outdoor recreation may turn out to be the salvation of conservation.

METHODS FOR ESTIMATING THE VALUE OF WILDLIFE RESOURCES (1967)

John V. Krutilla

Wildlife is a valuable resource. This is implicit in the commitment of members of the wildlife management profession to their professional responsibilities. Yet, the profession has been staffed predominantly by biologists or ecologists whose competence as scientists has given them the ability, largely, to manipulate the environment to influence an "optimal" production of wildlife. The criteria for optimality in the management of wildlife resources have been obtained predominantly from biology and/or ecology and are of such character as "biological diversity," ecosystem "homeostasis," etc.

But the question which also often faces the wildlife managers is not, "does wildlife have a value"; but rather, in a specific case and for a specific configuration of wildlife resources in a specific area, "what *is* the value of the given wildlife resource?" In these circumstances the wildlife manager cannot discharge his responsibilities by a conviction that wildlife *has* a value. The problem of estimating *how much* value, however, does not fall within the normal competence of natural scientists. Moreover, an attempt by an ecologist to try his hand at valuing wildlife resources is likely to be as unsuccessful as a comparable attempt by an economist to measure the energy dissipated between trophic levels. His attempts to do so are bound to be amateurish and his attempts run the risk of being ridiculed by the "pro's." Nor is the statement "You can't put a value on a flowering Indian paintbrush" very persuasive for the behavioral scientist when, as he interprets the statement, it means only, "*I* can't put a value on a flower," and he would add, "Why should you be expected to?"

A more relevant dialogue between wildlife managers and social scientists might involve the question, "*Why place a value on wildlife resources?*" There are basically two reasons if the profession of wildlife management is to fill the void in professional attention to the *demand for* wildlife as it has in attention to the *production or supply of* wildlife.

Resources management in general involves two sometimes contradictory things: preservation of the works of nature and development of renewable resources. And often, as in the case of river basin work, the development of some resources comes at the expense of other natural resources. Thus, in order that we avoid the destruction of some resources having a greater value than the purpose for which an incompatible development is intended, the *comparative value of the two alternative purposes must be weighed.*

The second general case wherein the need for valuation of wildlife resources arises is not necessarily when a choice needs to be made between a wildlife resource and a mutually exclusive alternative, but rather when two or more wildlife resources compete. This may happen when a non-indigenous species like pheasants is introduced into quail habitat. Or, owing

Reprinted from a presentation to the Washington, D. C. Chapter, The Wildlife Society. John Krutilla, Resources for the Future, Inc., acknowledges Les Berner, Charles Dambach, Fred Dean, Ralph Hill, Larry Jahn and Jack Knetsch for helpful comments on an earlier draft of this paper.

to plant succession, at some seral stages elk and bighorn sheep may be found in competition. If wildlife managers need to make a choice between one or the other, or if not a choice *between* the two but only between a *little more of one* at a cost of *some of the other,* then a comparison of values is required. Now, if quantified values for competing resources are not available, the comparison is still made, but only implicitly and in ignorance of the value of what is being gained or given up.

Formally how does the process work? Let us consider as an example the prospect of a storage dam and reservoir which would inundate the prime wintering range for ungulates. The standard operating procedure (Eckstein 1958) requires that all of the benefits from a water resource project, commercial (like hydro power) and non-commercial (like flood control) alike be estimated, summed up, and compared with the costs. Costs, on the other hand, consist of things like planning and design expenditures, construction costs (namely, labor, supplies, and equipment), and the cost of land required for the reservoir. The latter is simply the value of the production foregone from diverting the use of the land from its present purpose alternatively to service as a reservoir. In the case of private farmland it is simply the market value of the land, which, in turn, is only the capitalized value of the annual net income stream.[2] If all of the benefits in total exceed the costs, the project is justified; if the costs exceed the benefits, the project fails to pass the evaluation test.

Now, if the land to be occupied prospectively by the reservoir does not happen to be privately owned farmland but, say, public domain, there is no explicit market value for the land. That does not imply that there is no cost associated with using such land just because the construction agency is not required to make a financial outlay for its use. The cost in this case is the value of the alternative uses foreclosed by construction of the storage project. If such land in its natural state gives rise to hunting, the free-flowing stream to fishing, and both to a variety of outdoor activities of value to recreationists, this value needs to be measured and entered as the "opportunity cost" *or the value of the recreation opportunities lost* before the full cost of converting the natural environment to some "developed" use can be assessed. This value must be measured if it is not to be lost by default. It is especially important to do so in cases where the preemption of wildlife habitat by a prospective mutually exclusive purpose results in the creation of another form of outdoor recreation. The reason for this is that under Senate Document 97[3] (Senate 1962), until a more adequate measure is developed, the same value is to be imputed to a "recreation day" irrespective of qualitatively different forms of recreation. Such a procedure will *always* favor the gregarious, mass recreation activities, such as picnicking along the reservoir shoreline, boating, swimming, etc., for which there are often numerous alternative opportunities, over such things as big game hunting, white water canoeing, fishing in free flowing streams, etc., unless a true economic value is substituted for the administratively imputed value.

---

[2] An example of capitalization, or computing the present value of an income stream, is provided later in the paper for illustrative purposes.

[3] Senate Document 97 is the official set of guidelines for the benefit-cost analysis associated with water resource and related land development for the Federal Agencies engaged in these activities.

In short, to the extent that outdoor recreation is composed of a variety of activities, some of which will command a greater willingness to pay on the part of their participants than others—and for which alternative sources are difficult to come by—to that extent it becomes important to measure the value of the specific kinds of recreation afforded by natural environments so that they do not get sentenced to extinction by a spurious "economic" evaluation.

Having made the case for the need to estimate the value of wildlife and related resources, I have doubtless left the impression that economists are the people who can show wildlife management how this can be done. Such an inference would place too great a burden on what has been said above. Economists should claim only that they are the ones who can make a strong case for the valuation of wildlife resources and that they, if anyone, should be able to develop a suitable method for doing so given sufficient perception and perseverance.

A very promising beginning has been made during the past relatively few years. It had its origin, however, twenty years ago when in 1947, A. E. Demaray, Associate Director of the National Park Service posed the following question to a cross-section of eminent economists: "What is the value of a National Park?" (Prewitt 1949). Of the many responses, one—Professor Harold Hotelling's—set off a line of work a decade later which has by now involved serious economists and which is adding an order of magnitude to our understanding of the economic significance of various aesthetic or recreational resources. Hotelling suggested that since there were generally no prices or markets associated with the use of national parks as recreation facilities, possibly an alternative means could be developed for imputing a price with an acceptable measure of accuracy. In this way the valuation could be made in the same dimension as the valuation of all other resources, and the measurement would be conducted in the same metric. He suggested in effect that note be taken of the distance from which people came to visit a park, and that this would yield a measure of the costs they were willing to incur. Now assuming the cost which the most distant traveler would incur to represent the upper bound, by appropriate treatment of the data a schedule of prices or a demand curve could be imputed. Hotelling did not spell out how this was to be done, but being a very eminent and imaginative econometrician no one doubts that had he set himself to undertake the task, his efforts would have been crowned with success.

As it turns out, the most significant thing associated with Hotelling's suggestion is that it stimulated Marion Clawson (1959) to think about the problem a decade later. Clawson eventually advanced the methodology of estimating demand for outdoor recreation a gigantic step by quite an improvement on Hotelling's suggestion. What did Clawson do?

The Clawson Approach

Clawson notes that the valuation of a resource derives fundamentally from the demand for use of the resource's services. That is, the value of the resource is the capitalized stream of annual revenues, the latter of which are the summation of individual valuations expressed by individuals' demands. In economics, a demand schedule is often drawn to show how the quantity of a good or service which is taken relates to (varies inversely as) the price that is charged. This demand relation represents the array of individual valuations in descending order of individuals' estimate of the value to them. This is shown diagrammatically in Figure 1.

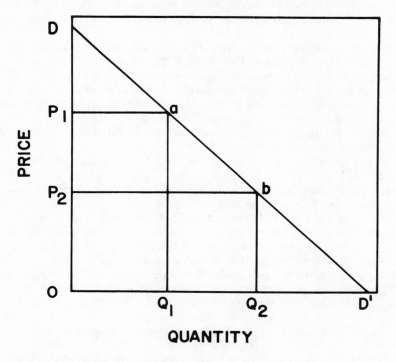

Fig. 17-1.—Illustrative demand schedule

The demand relation (DD') can be described as the relation between the quantity which would be purchased at each of the alternative prices. For example, at a price of P_1 we find point a on the demand schedule, and dropping a perpendicular to the horizontal, or quantity, axis we note OQ_1 as the quantity of the good in question which would be demanded at price P_1. Alternatively, were the price to be P_2 we move out to find b on the demand schedule, drop a perpendicular from that point to the quantity axis and obtain the indicated quantity (OQ_2) associated with a price of P_2. Similarly for all intermediate points between the price and quantity axes. Now, while the demand relation DD' can be described as the relation between the quantity which would be purchased at each of the alternative prices shown, it can also be described as a schedule which shows the maximum amount each consumer who has a demand for the good in question would be willing to pay rather than to go without. *Willingness to pay* is another expression for the individual's valuation. The sum of all individuals' willingness to pay (the integral under the demand schedule) gives the total value for the market clearing period, say, day, week, month, or year, whatever the relevant period.

The way Clawson came to estimate the demand schedule is as follows: let us consider a site which is visited for recreational purposes. Note the sources from which recreation seekers come (cities or towns). The latter can be segregated into mutually exclusive zones established by the equivalence of travel costs within zones, and non-equivalence among zones. Figure 2 illustrates this conceptualization with X representing the recreation site, the o's representing the towns, and the upper-case letters the zones into which the population centers are segregated.

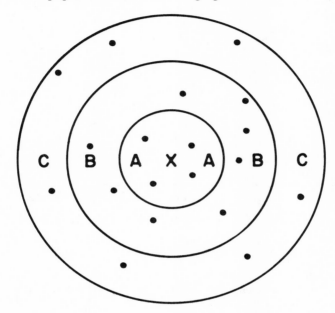

Fig. 17-2.—Illustrative distribution of recreation site (X) and sources of recreationists (●)

Now let us assume that the population by zone, cost per visit, number of visits, and number of visits per thousand population would appear as in Table 1.[4]

Table 1

Illustrative Data for Deriving a Demand Schedule
for Outdoor Recreation

Zone	Population	Cost/Visit	Number of Visits	Visits/1000 Population
(1)	(2)	(3)	(4)	(5)
A	2,000	$1	800	400
B	3,000	$2	900	300
C	5,000	$4	500	100

[4] The presentation below is adapted from Knetsch (1963) and represents a highly simplified relation for expositional purposes. One of Knetsch's (1964) actual equations is as follows: $\text{Log}(V + 0.80) = 3.82467 - 2.39287 \log C$, where V is visits/1000 in zone of origin and C is travel costs in dollars.

The numbers with which we illustrate the Clawson approach have been intentionally so chosen as to simplify the exposition. With the data given, it turns out that the visits per thousand population (V/1000) will plot out as a linear relationship given by the algebraic equation V/1000 = 500 – 100(c) (where c is cost in dollars) and illustrated graphically in Figure 3.

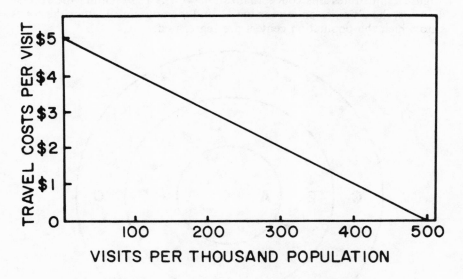

FIG. 17-3.—Relation between cost of visit and visits per thousand population

With such a relation between travel costs per visit and visits per thousand population, Clawson reasoned somewhat as follows: If one assumes that recreationists would regard added costs as equivalent whether they were incurred as travel expenditures on the one hand or as the price of admission on the other, the differences in visits per thousand population that appear as responses to the differences in travel costs could be used to estimate the change in the quantity of recreation services "purchased" as a result of the change in the "price" of the service. This, however, is precisely what the demand schedule represents. Hence, other things being equal, the differences in travel costs can be regarded as surrogates for prices, and a "demand relation" estimated. This estimation procedure would go as follows below.

Given the original data and the relation between travel costs and visits per thousand population, we can note that with no explicit entrance or admission fee there are 2,200 visits to the recreation site (Table 1, Column 4). On a typical demand diagram we would say that at zero price the quantity taken is 2,200 units, or visits in this case. We mark off 2,200 on the quantity axis (see Figure 4) and plot the point to correspond to zero price of admission. Assume now that a price of $1.00 is contemplated. We observe from Figure 3 that at $1.00 we have 400 visitors per thousand population, but at travel costs of $2.00 we have only 300. Now, if $1.00 in price were added to an experienced travel cost (Table 1, Column 3), the total cost for the three groups, by zones, would be $2:00, $3.00, and $5.00 respectively. From the first group (Zone A) we would expect visits at the rate of 300 per thousand, or a total of 600 visits; from the second group (Zone B) we would expect 200 visits per thousand for a total of 600 visits; from the third group (Zone C) we would expect no visitors, for at $5.00 per visit we see from Figure 3 that there would be no attendance. Thus, if we consider an admission price of $1.00 in addition to the costs incurred in traveling to the site, the total attendance would be 1,200. This is plotted as a second point in our schedule (Figure 4). We can go through the same procedure positing a $2.00 and a $3.00 admission price and would get respectively 700 and 200 visits to the site, as shown in Figure 4.[5]

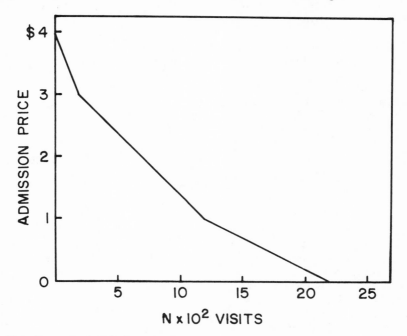

FIG. 17-4.—Demand schedule for recreation

[5] The specific points can be calculated directly from the expression $V/1000 = 500 - 100(c)$.

		V/1000 thousands
At zero price V/1000	= 500 – 100(1) or 400 x 2	= 800
	= 500 – 100(2) or 300 x 3	= 900
	= 500 – 100(4) or 100 x 5	= 500
	Total	2,200 visits
At $1.00 price	500 – 100(2) or 300 x 2	= 600
	500 – 100(3) or 200 x 3	= 600
	500 – 100(5) or 0 x 5	= 0
	Total	1,200 visits
At $2.00 price	500 – 100(3) or 200 x 2	= 400
	500 – 100(4) or 100 x 3	= 300
	Total	700 visits
At $3.00 price	500 – 100(4) or 100 x 2	= 200 visits

131

Figure 4 gives the demand schedule we seek in order to estimate the value of the recreation resource in question, to have an estimate which is comparable in concept and metric to the values obtained for the services of other uses of resources. How would we obtain the value of the resource now? Let us assume for convenience that the segments of the demand schedule between the dollar changes in prices are approximately linear as drawn. Then between a zero price and $1.00 we have 1,000 visits at an average value of $0.50 per visit or $500.00.[6] Between $1.00 and $2.00 there are 500 visits at an average imputed value of $1.50 for $750.00 in this bracket. Between $2.00 and $3.00 we have another 500 visits at $2.50/ visit or $1,250; and between $3.00 and $4.00, 200 visits at $3.50 for the block, or $700. If we could exact the maximum price each recreationist is prepared to pay which is the value of the visit to him and sum over all recreationists, then according to our imputation we would have a value under the demand schedule aggregating to $3,200. Now depending on whether the transaction period our data represent is a day, a season or what have you, the sum of the four segments under the demand schedule is multiplied by the appropriate factor to convert it to an annual value. This annual value is then converted to a capital sum by obtaining the present value of such an amount per annum for the appropriate time period, at an appropriate discount factor. If we are dealing with a non-depreciable resource, the period will be infinity.

As an example, let us calculate our capital value. Assume that the $3,200 represents the daily value and that we have a ninety-day recreational season. The annual benefit would be 90 x $3,200 or $288,000. To capitalize this stream of annual benefits, we make a present value computation and get $5,241,800 with an assumed discount rate of 5.5%.[7]

Well then, how does this method for valuing resources work out in practice? It has been used in a number of instances with good results. I shall not dwell on the studies where it has been applied successfully as the references to this paper cite the studies in question (e.g., Brown *et al.* 1964). What is equally important at this juncture is to indicate that it may not be applicable in every conceivable situation where an estimate of the value of a resource is desired. Recall that the Clawson technique was applied to a case where the resource in question was localized, so that travel cost from concentric zones could be calculated. In other circumstances, as for example the estimate of the value of the migratory waterfowl nesting habitat in the wetlands of the Central Mississippi flyway, conditions are not favorable toward its application. Here one would

---

[6] The use of "between price" intervals at the average of the two prices approximates integrating the area under the demand schedule when all interval values are summed.

[7] That is, the present value $P = \sum_{t=1}^{T} \dfrac{b_t}{(1 + r)^t}$, where b_t is the benefit in any year, r is the discount rate, and T is the period of time in years in which benefits are yielded. In the case of a flow resource or non-depreciating site, the period in years may be infinite, and the present value or capitalization can be taken out of any book of financial tables—in this case $288,000 x 18.18, the latter figure being the present value of 1 per annum at compound interest at 5.5% over an infinite time horizon.

expect to find numerous places (blinds) visited by numerous hunters all along the flyway, with different hunters taking routes to their blinds which represented cross travel from sources of hunters to destination blinds. Such cross travel makes the application of the method very difficult.

Fortunately there has been developed an alternative to the Clawson technique in connection with a study directed at valuation of the big game resources of the East Kootenay area of British Columbia (Pearse 1968). The method was developed in an effort to obtain comparable estimates, relying on fewer and less restrictive assumptions.

Pearse's method follows the Hotelling suggestion more closely than did Clawson and involves segregating hunters by income class. He assumes that within each hunter class grouped by income there would be a similar willingness to pay on the grounds that individuals with similar tastes (all big game hunters) had equal ability to pay. In each income class he identified the largest expenditure made by any individual in coming to hunt in the East Kootenay and attributed to that individual a marginal status. By marginal, of course, I mean that the individual in question was assumed to be on the margin of indifference between willingness to incur such high costs or avoiding them and foregoing the hunting. For such an individual there would be no willingness to pay an additional sum as a fee or price to hunt in the East Kootenay. The difference in expenditures between this individual and each of the other hunters with lower incurred expenditures was assumed to represent the amount which each would be willing to pay in addition to the cost incurred (his consumer's surplus) rather than to do without the hunting in the East Kootenay. The sum of all the differences in cost between the highest incurred and iteratively each of those with lesser expenditures, within each income class, produced an estimate of the aggregate willingness-to-pay for that class. The sum over all income classes will give the grand total as an annual value.

Having introduced the Pearse method, it may be of interest to give the main results of the East Kootenay study.

The East Kootenay area of British Columbia is a unique region insofar as wildlife is concerned. Not only does game abound, but the variety of species is reputed to exceed that for any other comparable area of British Columbia, and possibly anywhere else on the North American continent. Owing to the large number of big game species, the area is attractive to trophy hunters from distant parts of the North American continent as well as Europe. Pearse thus found that, in effect, he had three markets for big game hunting. First are local hunters in the East Kootenay. They are a group which typically hunt a day at a time on weekends, and the object of their hunting is meat as much as sport. The second group is the resident non-local hunters, which come from other areas of British Columbia, and finally there are the non-resident hunters, predominantly trophy hunters.

Taking the non-resident, trophy-hunter market first (593 in number), the results are as shown in Table 2.

The estimated annual value of the East Kootenay to non-resident hunters was put at $431,704, as shown.

Considering next the resident hunting population, the relevant figures are as shown in Table 3.

Table 2

Income group	Number in group	Highest fixed costs	Average willingness to pay
Less than $2,000	7	$ 263	$ 98
$2,000-$4,000	8	290	146
$4,000-$6,000	20	388	180
$6,000-$8,000	26	766	473
$8,000-$10,000	48	757	434
$10,000-$15,000	72	1,020	580
$15,000-$20,000	38	899	435
$20,000-$25,000	46	1,947	1,334
$25,000-$50,000	57	2,112	1,258
over $50,000	17	2,202	995

Total sample   339   Weighted average: $728

Total all non-residents; 593 x $728 = $431,704

(If the local demand were to be sought separately, Pearse found that approximately 5,500 local hunters participated and their estimated consumer surplus or annual value of the resource to them approximated $1,290,000.)

Now, while I did not go into all of the details, some quite elaborate, the model for estimating the value of the wildlife resources of the East Kootenay even so is a gross oversimplification. What are some of the weaknesses?

Perhaps the most serious weakness is the procedure used to estimate the willingness to pay. The total willingness to pay, or annual value which we convert to a capital sum by a discount factor depends very much on the choice of the size of the income classes. If, for example, we made so fine a classification as to leave only one member in each class, he would be both the marginal and average hunter and his willingness to pay something to hunt rather than do without would be nil. By this means we can be led to a result which shows no value for the wildlife resources.[8] On the other hand, if we do not stratify by income class but simply array all expenditures from highest to lowest—as was left implicit in Professor Hotelling's suggestion—the estimated annual willingness to pay would be much greater. *Accordingly, the estimate of the annual value of the wildlife resource for hunting depends on an arbitrary convention, i.e., upon the stratification procedure.* There is no denying that this is a serious criticism, and one which cannot be avoided when the conditions for application of the Clawson method do not exist.

Actually, there is yet another method developed by Robert K. Davis which does not suffer from the infirmities of either of the two indirect methods discussed above. This is the direct interview survey research approach successfully applied by Davis (1964) to the valuation of the several kinds of Maine Woods experiences. Although interviews are expensive, we may find ways of reducing the cost of the method by double sampling

---

[8] This does not apply to the Clawson approach.

134

Table 3

Income group	Number in group	Highest fixed costs	Average willingness to pay
Less than $2,000	25	$ 66	$ 47
$2,000-$4,000	67	186	149
$4,000-$6,000	219	287	224
$6,000-$8,000	109	320	221
$8,000-$10,000	32	267	152
over $10,000	33	355	196
Total sample	485	Weighted average: $197	

Total resident hunters: 14,346
Aggregate willingness to pay: 14,346 x $197 = $2,900,242

as Davis did or we find that the quality of the information developed by interviews justifies their costliness. Davis developed regression equations which not only demonstrate a structure and consistency in the interview responses, but can be used to estimate demand functions for the population using a recreation area. He concluded that recreation benefits, including hunting, comprise a substantial portion of the total value of the pulpwood forests of northern Maine.

In addition, the interviews were used to explore the quality dimensions of the recreation experience with the result that some useful insights were gained into the preferences of recreationists and the valuable characteristics of the areas. For example, he found that the opportunity to enjoy relative solitude and to escape from the usual clutter of tourist areas was an important aspect of the experience in using the Maine Woods.

Accordingly, we can say that very fruitful beginnings have been made but the different approaches applied to the same case will yield answers, all of which are plausible but all of which also differ to some degree from each other. The necessity of additional work in the field of wildlife-wildland resource valuation is inescapable. But let us not disparage the value of the work done to date merely because there are differences in the estimates depending on the technique used or approach adopted. These are only approximations; consider the usefulness of population censuses in wildlife management even though different techniques produce different results and all are subject to a wide range of error. The reassuring thing is that all techniques or methods fit results into the identical valuation framework and involve approximations measured in the same metric, as for example, benefits from resources employed in a mutually incompatible way.

This brings up the question raised at the outset, and it will help us gain some perspective. The results obtained are within the range of accuracy estimates obtained by engineers and earth scientists. Consider the hydrologist. With a thirty-year record of run-off he may do a fairly good job of estimating the average annual streamflow, but that is useful information for only a very limited range of problems. What the water resource managers need to know even more is how low is the low flow, how often will it occur, what is the maximum probable high flow, and what run of extreme events might one expect, etc. When hydrologists address the problem of estimating the tails of the frequency distribution, there is a wide margin of error involved depending on which of a number of different estimating techniques are involved. Here the natural scientist has reason to be every bit as humble as the social scientist regarding the accuracy of his estimates.

In summary, the methods which are being developed for putting a value in monetary terms on wildlife resources are crude. They have a great distance yet to go. Also additional work on them should be generously supported, the methods critically examined for purposes of exposing weaknesses and of identifying methodological issues requiring further development and additional refinement. But it is very necessary to keep in mind that they produce results probably well within the range of accuracy of the methods used for estimating the value of alternative uses for the resources and are thus useful for planning and management purposes.

REFERENCES

BROWN, W. G., AJMER SINGH, and EMERY N. CASTLE, *An Economic Evaluation of the Salmon Steelhead Sports Fishery*, Technical Bulletin 78, Agricultural Experiment Station, Oregon State University, September 1964.

CLAWSON, MARION, *Methods of Measuring the Demand for and Value of Outdoor Recreation*, Resources for the Future, Washington, D.C., 1959.

DAVIS, ROBERT K., "The Value of Big Game Hunting in a Private Forest," Transactions of the Twenty-Ninth North American Wildlife and Natural Resources Conference, March 9-11, 1964, Wildlife Management Institute, Washington, D.C.

————and JACK L. KNETSCH, "Comparison of Methods for Recreation Evaluation," *Water Research*, Allen V. Kneese and Stephen C. Smith, eds. (Baltimore; The Johns Hopkins Press for Resources for the Future, Inc., 1966).

ECKSTEIN, OTTO, Water Resources Development: The Economics of Project Evaluation (Cambridge, Mass.: Harvard University Press, 1958).

KNETSCH, JACK L., "Outdoor Recreation Demands and Benefits," *Land Economics*, Vol. XXXIX, No. 4 (November 1963).

————, "Economics of Including Recreation as a Purpose of Water Resources Projects," *Journal of Farm Economics* (December 1964).

PEARSE, PETER H., "A New Approach to the Evaluation of Non-Priced Recreation Resources," *Land Economics*, Vol. XLIV, No. 1 (February 1968).

PREWITT, ROY A., *The Economics of Public Recreation: An Economic Study of the Monetary Evaluation of Recreation in the National Parks*, U.S. Department of the Interior, National Park Service (Washington, D.C., 1949).

Senate Document No. 97, 87th Congress, 2nd Session, *Policies, Standards, and Procedures in the Formulation, Evaluation, and Review of Plans for Use and Development of Water and Related Land Resources* (Washington, D.C.: Government Printing Office, 1962).

COMMUNICATING COMPLETE WILDLIFE VALUES OF KENAI (1971)

Harold W. Steinhoff

The alliteration commenced in the caption can be continued by commenting that cogent communication must be both *comprehensible* and *comprehensive*. This paper will be a waste of your time and mine if I cannot tell you clearly about the wildlife values of Kenai. And you justifiably will feel cheated if I do not try to tell you all of the values.

Examples will come from a 1968 study of the wildlife values and related recreational values of the Kenai National Moose Range, Alaska. A 45 percent sample of recreational users of the Range, the managers of the area, local citizen leaders, and oil company representatives were questionnaired and interviewed. Data on expenditures, duration of visits to the Range, benefits, costs, and attitudes were gained from these groups. The results are used to illustrate the set of values described in this paper.

VALUES MUST BE COMPREHENSIBLE

Who must comprehend the values? Obviously the public, including congressmen and legislators, whose vote ultimately will determine broad resource use policies of any wildlife area. For communication we must have a mutually-understood vocabulary. I have tried in this paper to use terms understandable to a non-economist, because few of us truly understand economic terminology. For precise and efficient understanding in any specialized field, one needs the specialized vocabulary. But often these terms are so unfamiliar that a technically acceptable definition does not lead to true understanding. My aim is to use well-understood terms in a way which will be reasonably correct and efficient, if not completely so to an economist.

Definitions

Benefit—values received. In the case of wildlife the "purchaser," or user, buys an *experience,* measured crudely in visitor days. He buys a commodity which is not exchangeable for other commodities or money as if it were a diamond ring. No true market exists where he can pay one single price for the experience. No adjustment of price to value in a natural supply-and-demand system can exist. His experience is personal, so the value he receives is related to his knowledge and perception. The wildlife user is thus partly the producer as well as the consumer of the experience. The value he receives is non-negotiable, although some may share their experience via talks, but the user still retains the entire experience! The values received are mostly pleasurable feelings, including memories, but they may be partly tangible, in the form of venison or salmon steaks. Because they cannot be measured directly the benefits are assessed in special ways.

Cost—values yielded. The wildlife user incurs expenses for licenses and fees, equipment, travel, and subsistence required to consume

Reprinted from: Trans. N. Amer. Widl. and Natural Resources Conf. 36:428-438.

the experience. He also bears the loss of income he might otherwise have made, termed the "opportunity cost of time".

Profit—benefits minus cost. The cost of a wildlife experience can be measured rather logically and surely, but the benefits usually are without direct monetary measure because the user almost always gets more than he pays for. If a Kenai resident pays 100 dollars to hunt moose, and an identical non-resident pays 1000 dollars for the same experience, then the resident gets 900 dollars worth of value for which he didn't pay. This surplus is termed a *consumer's surplus* and may be considered equal to the profit. Methods of ascertaining the value of the consumer's surplus are based on a technique described by Clawson (1959).

Gross Income—the total benefit received.

Land Value—the worth of a defined unit of land. In the case of the Kenai National Moose Range, the land value for wildlife is the price for which the 1,730,000 acres would sell on the real estate market for the use of wildlife alone. The actual value is computed by determining the total profit, or consumer's surplus, from wildlife uses and capitalizing this at some logical rate, say 4 percent. This land value (or capitalized value, or real estate sale value) is the amount which a corporation would need to invest, at 4 percent interest, to gain the annual return equal to the total profit from wildlife use. This is also termed the "oportunity cost of money" invested in the Range.

An important view to keep in mind is that we must think of these as values *to someone.* One must have precisely in mind who the "someone" is before the value is correctly understood. In most cases we are expressing the values to the user of the wildlife experience. But these values accrue to society as well, so the sum of values to individuals is the value to society.

VALUES MUST BE COMPREHENSIVE

No "THE" value of wildlife exists. Many kinds of wildlife values are recognized. King (1947) has defined them in mutually exclusive categories as Recreational, Esthetic, Educational, Biological, Social, and Commercial. This is a comprehensive categorization, arranged according to the role played by wildlife in serving man's needs and wants. Another type of categorization relates wildlife values to comparable expressions of value of other commodities, such as oil or timber or football tickets. These categories may be described by the terms defined earlier. Obviously the choice of truly comparable values is important if one is to match the value of wildlife experiences on the Kenai to, say, oil.

The result can only be, that, when we try to express wildlife values, we must present a *catalog* of values, and indicate clearly the types of values of other commodities with which they can legitimately be compared.

Incommensurability

One further problem is incommensurability. Devine (1966) has distinguished between incommensurable, *i.e.* cannot be expressed in the common unit such as dollars, and intangible, *i.e.* incapable of quantitative measurement. Although some wildlife values may be truly intangible, most which cannot be expressed in money are incommensurable. When a non-consumptive user of wildlife says he would rather see the beauty of a moose feeding at the edge of Tustumena Lake than to see an oil derrick there, he is simply saying he is willing to forego the profit from oil, and thus is expressing the value of his moose viewing experience quite tangibly. Or when citizens through their Congress, vote to retain Echo Park undammed, they are valuing a natural Echo Park greater than the profit foregone from the dam.

Often the incommensurable values are most easily expressed as a vote, or the percentage of a group which expresses a certain view. For example, 90 percent of the owners of Tustumena Lake (*i.e.* the citizens of the United States) may say they prefer moose or salmon to oil production on the Lake, if there must be a choice. What, then, are the wildlife values and related recreational values, both economic and incommensurable, of the Kenai National Moose Range? Details of the method of deriving these values are found in Steinhoff (1969).

A CATALOG OF VALUES

Recreational Values

Profit—The total profit, or consumer's surplus, of recreational visitors to the Kenai National Moose Range in 1968 was $2,697,000. In effect this is value placed in the pocket of the recreationist as profit and is analogous to net income. A sole owner who charged the varying individual consumers' surpluses as entrance fees (a discriminating monopolist) could presumably recover this amount annually. The net annual income may be capitalized at 4 percent to $67,429,000 (or $39 per acre) as land value (or market value) of the Range for recreation.

A sole owner would more likely charge the same entrance fee to all recreationists and he would naturally seek the fee that would yield the maximum net return. The demand curve computed in Clawson's method permits computation of this value also. The optimum single fee would be $7 per recreation day, and recreationists would buy 131,737 days[1] at this rate, for an annual income of $922,000. The optimum annual fee per family unit would be $100. Some 2550 family units would purchase the use of the range at this figure and would spend 141,692 RD's there. The annual income would be $255,000.

Obviously few would pay the $100 fee if initiated next year, to say nothing of the public outcry at the idea. We assume that once the public became emotionally adjusted to paying for recreation they would be willing to pay this much. Obviously, though, the nation gains the greatest net return, ten times as much by letting each participant pocket his consumer's surplus for himself. Also, Seckler (1966) has made a strong case for considering the wildlife experience a welfare good, since the wildlife resource is owned by all. He advocated income-neutral rationing. A no-fee policy is the easiest way to do this. If we charge a fee, Seckler argues, we really should pay the low-income individual for the *loss* of harvest of the wildlife experience which he owns and can no longer afford.

Expenditures. Much condemned as the illegitimate child of the assessment family, critics call unfair the inclusion of food costs in recreational expenditures, because "one must eat anyway." A second complaint is that recreational expenditures do not add "new" money to the economy but

---

[1]A recreation day is a visit by one individual to a recreation area for recreation purposes during any reasonable portion or all of a 24-hour day.

simply reallocate what would otherwise be spent elsewhere. But other resources all charge the cost of food to the final product. The value of a log as it comes from the forest includes the cost of the logger's lunch, axe, and house trailer, just as the value of a recreational experience when it comes from the forest includes the cost of the moose hunter's lunch, rifle, and camper.

Several economists have pointed out that the second complaint is invalid because every expenditure, of any kind, for anything, is a "reallocation" from something else that might be purchased. So the expenditures method is a legitimate way to assess certain values of wildlife. Expenditures have been called "gross economic value" by some, but are more properly termed a "cost of production and harvest".

Recreational expenditures by visitors to the Kenai National Moose Range in 1968 totalled $7,543,000. They generated $5,656,000 in personal income, on which $1,131,000 were paid in Federal taxes. Contribution to the GNP is 1.2 times personal income, or $6,840,000. These figures are extrapolated from indices developed by Swanson (1969).

Gross Income (or Benefits). The recreationist is both producer and consumer of the recreational experience. His costs are his expenditures and the opportunity cost of time he invests. His profit is the consumer's surplus. The total is comparable to the sales price of other products. The recreational experience is analogous to the log, fresh salmon, barrel of crude oil, or sack of potatoes in the homesteader's truck.

$$\text{Expenses} + \text{Profit} = \text{Sales Price}$$
$$\text{(Recreational Expenditures} + \text{Opportunity Cost of Time)}$$
$$+ \text{Consumer's Surplus} = \text{RSP}$$

Sum of RSP's (Recreational Sales Price)
= Gross Income Volume or Gross Sales Volume

Expenditures	$ 7,543,000
Opportunity Cost	6,320,000
Consumer's Surplus	2,697,000

Gross Income Volume $16,560,000 (or Gross Sales Volume)

Opinions. Over 50 percent of a sample of 126 U.S. citizens, owners of the Range, who did not use the Range in 1968 said they would vote for a greater appropriation ($150,000 in 1968) for the Range, 40 percent indicated the same as current appropriations, and 7 percent said they would vote for less or none. These proportions were consistent among salary classes as shown by a non-significant chi-square. A vote by owners of a public resource is one important way to express value, and a vote involving appropriations is a very tangible evidence of it. This may be an example of "option demand"—willingness to pay for the option to use the resource later (Krutilla, 1967).

Fines. Though not intended by either donor or recipient as an economic expression, fines for violation of sport fishing or hunting regulations are a source of income to the state and express the cost of a "recreational" experience to the violator. In 1968, 53 convicted transgressors on the Moose Range paid $1475 in fines, an average of $28 each. The market

140

value of a recreation day is $46, so the miscreant made $18. A rational basis for setting fines might be at least the value of the stolen commodity, the recreational experience involved.

Incommensurable Values. Over 23,000 individuals, in 6090 families, used the Range for wildlife and related recreation in 1968. They spent 358,319 recreation days there. These figures alone represent a considerable, concrete expression of value. Most users rated "quality recreation" as the best use of the Range, "wildlife" as second, "general recreation" third, "other renewable resources" fourth, "non-renewable resources (oil and mining)" fifth, and "business and commercial" last.

Esthetic Values

Our materialistic society seems overwhelmingly to vote for esthetic values. Such values of wildlife are objects and associated environment possessing beauty, affording inspiration, and contributing to the arts (King, 1947). The average visitor scarcely distinguishes re-creation of mind, spirit, and body from the beauty of wildlife and environment which stimulates pleasure and satisfies artistic hunger. Visitors and managers of the area alike rated esthetic values of the Range as very high. Non-residents indicated esthetics as a major reason for their visit to the Range. A sizable portion of the $16 million dollar gross sales volume of recreation on the Range would be assignable to esthetic value, if I knew how to do it.

Diseconomies. Costs or losses to one resource because of another resource are known as "external diseconomies." The extra cost of oil exploration, development, and production on the Kenai National Moose Range in order to maintain esthetic values is an example. Extra costs accrue because of narrow seismic trails, lighter equipment, seismic operation only with snow cover and on frozen ground, careful containment and disposal of wastes during drilling, and restoration of areas by leveling, reseeding grass, and replanting trees after exploration, development, and pipeline construction. Although some of these measures are aimed at direct protection of wildlife (including commercial fisheries), most are aimed at preserving the esthetic beauty of the natural environment. The total extra cost for all oil operations on the Range in 1968 is estimated at $173,200. In earlier years the cost was greater because exploration and development activity was more intense, sometimes twice as great, or about $350,000.

Viewed nationally, this amount is profit which the public was willing to forego, and this is an expression of value of wildlife and related recreation on the Range. It should be added to the primary market value of wildlife, because it is a part of the expense of production of the wildlife experience.

The diseconomy oil imposes on wildlife and recreation includes loss of 20 square miles of habitat and recreational area due to oil roads pipelines, air strips, and oil well sites (Hakala,[1] personal communication). This totals 0.7% of the Range, a loss of $470,000 in land value, and an annual loss of $18,000 in profit from wildlife. This annual loss will continue as long as the land is occupied for oil production, whereas the diseconomy to oil will become minimal as soon as exploration and development cease.

---

[1] Refuge Manager, Kenai National Moose Range, 1969.

Educational Values

President Franklin D. Roosevelt declared in his Executive Order establishing the Range that "study in its natural environment of the practical management of a big game species that has considerable local economic value" was a major purpose of establishment of the Kenai National Moose Range. Thus the singular voice of the people spoke forcefully, from the first, of the educational value of the area. Educational values are those which add to man's knowledge, either collectively through research, or individually through personal learning.

Approximately $727,000 has been invested in 52 separate identified research projects on the Range. Moose were a primary interest in 28 studies, and 21 of these were concerned with moose range. Other research featured trumpeter swan, Dall sheep, goat, beaver, general and plant ecology, fisheries, fungi, spruce grouse, erosion control, ice fields, and lake morphometry.

Seventeen groups totalling 578 people visited the Range at least partly for educational reasons in 1968. Owners ranked education as the second greatest value of the Range, ahead of esthetic, social, and commercial values. Users, managers, and owners all rated education in the form of "wildlife observation" and "wildlife research" as a preferred use of the Range in relation to other resources.

Biological Values

King (1947) defined biological values as the worth of services rendered by wild animals. In the broad sense "wildlife" includes all wild animals,— beetles, nematodes, earthworms, and mosquitos, as well as moose, salmon, and ptarmigan. Each organism provides a service to the ecosystem, so each contributes to the value. All the ecology of a moose is integrated in one fact—the presence of the moose. Similarly the economics of the ecosystem of the Range is integrated in one value,—the value of the wildlife experience. The worth of a nematode which produces organic matter on which to grow moose food shows up in the expenditure of the moose hunter.

The ultimately expressed values in dollars in the pocket or gleams in the eye are affected just as much or more by changes in biological complexes as they are by immediate manipulation of moose herds and picnic tables. A change in biological values inherent in the moose-wolf relationship will change the wildlife value of the area subtly but profoundly. Thus any economic system devised, computerized, and dehumanized, must take into account the operative biologic systems. We must use bioeconomic systems.

Some biological values are negative ones (i.e. losses) to some groups. Moose-auto encounters and mosquito bites are examples. Officially recorded moose-auto accidents in 1968 totalled 42 and cost an estimated $42,000. Although these were losses to persons suffering the accident, they might be considered the amount society was willing to forego in order to have moose, thus a positive expression of wildlife value to society.

Social Values

Social values are those "accruing to the community as a result of the presence of wild animals" (King, 1947). These values are demonstrated by what people do, say, and commemorate. Buckley (1957) said that "well over half of the wage-earners in Alaska are dependent to a greater or lesser extent upon wildlife for their livelihood." Approximately one-third of the 1968 population living close to the Moose Range, or approximately 7500 people, are dependent directly on wildlife and related recreation. The dependencies come from commercial fishing, providing goods and services for recreationists, and from food provided by game meat. The entire flavor of the community is much affected by this dependence.

Fifty percent of nearby families use the Range for recreation. Family participation is shown by the average of 7 per party for swimming, 6 for picnicking, 5 for camping, 4 for fishing, 3 for general hunting (including moose), and 2 for sheep and goat hunting.

Wildlife and recreation rival the weather as a topic of social conversation on the Kenai Peninsula. Approximately 13 percent of the column inches of news in the *Cheechako News* (the principal newspaper near the Range) is conservation-related, and about 5 percent applies quite directly to the Kenai National Moose Range.

Names of local features such as lakes and streams indicate things held dear in the minds of namers. They continue to impart a character to the community throughout the following years. Wildlife place names occur at the rate of 3.4 per 100 square miles on the Moose Range, with each feature counted only once. These make up a very high proportion of place names of all kinds.

Socio-economic characteristics of users indicate segments of society which value the wildlife and recreation of the Range highly enough to use it, and those who receive the major benefit. Whether or not these are the kind of people we want to encourage and reward in our society is a matter of personal philosophy and value judgment. The greatest users of the Range, in proportion to their occurrence in the population as a whole, were skilled workmen, followed by professional, business (including sales and administrative), armed services, retired, and lastly other (including laborer, housewife, and student). Persons with over $10,000 annual income were proportionally more frequent visitors, as were those in the 26-55 age bracket for Alaskans, and the 46-65 age bracket for non-residents.

Commercial Values

Salmon produced on the Range contributed $1,122,000 or 25 percent of the commercial salmon income to the commercial fishermen of Cook Inlet in 1968, a "pink salmon year." The Range contributes 31 percent of the income, omitting pink salmon. Some years the proportion may be as high as 40 percent (Bureau of Sport Fisheries and Wildlife, 1963). Its retail value after processing at the cannery was $3 million. No indices exist to allocate the portion of this value actually produced on the Range. On livestock ranges of the western United States the value of a calf is 10 to 20 percent of the value of the marketed steer. If this analogy is valid, the value of the Gross National Product in 1968 of commercial salmon produced on the Kenai National Moose Range was $150,000.

Meat. An estimated 336,000 pounds of meat were harvested on the Range in 1968, about 75 percent moose (250,000 pounds) and most of the rest salmon at Russian River (76,000 pounds). At one dollar per pound, a conservative figure, the value in 1968 was $336,000. How is the value of game meat to be regarded in an economic analysis? Is it extra income to be added to the value of expenditures? Or an expected return on the recreational investment, to be deducted if one is computing the value of the recreational experience itself? To the extent that the meat was not a conscious goal of the recreational experience, it is a bonus, without cost. Thus its value is a commercial one, additional to the value of the recreational experience. If the meat was part of the purpose for the visit, its value should be deducted from the "recreational" category and tallied as a commercial value of wildlife.

Hides and Furs. Very few moose hides are salvaged or tanned, though some potential value exists in use of this resource. Fur trapping is primarily recreational, and its value has been included with recreational expenditures. Market value of furs harvested in 1968 totaled $4,014. The average annual income for 1963-67 was $4,669, at 1968 prices. Allocation of this value should follow principles discussed in the previous section, "Meat."

The Businessman. We deal with primary values to the nation at the point of consumption, in this analysis. Secondary benefits of those who sell wildlife goods and services—the multiplier effect—are not measured. However, the businessman's gain is roughly equal to the expenditures of $7.5 million annually. Of this, $2.4 million are current expenses which go largely to the local economy, $1.3 million are transportation expense in Alaska, $0.4 million is transportation elsewhere, $2 million for equipment in Alaska, and $1.4 million for equipment elsewhere. This totals $5.7 million spent in Alaska and $1.8 million spent elsewhere in 1968 by visitors to the Kenai National Moose Range and directly attributable to that experience.

ASSIGNMENT OF VALUES TO AREAS

Resource decisions of the future often will be made on smaller areas, rarely on the whole Range at once. If values are allocated to specified areas in proportion to recreation days generated, the Kenai-Russian River Campground, with less than 0.003 percent of the area generates 31 percent of the value. The Skilak Loop, a heavily used recreation area which has approximately 1 percent of the area generates 27 percent of the value. On the basis of recreation days of each activity, fishing accounts for 22 percent of the value, hunting 18 percent, camping and picnicking 15 percent, relaxation and driving 14 percent, wildlife observation and photography 12 percent, and all other recreational uses lesser amounts. This type of analysis may permit more rational selection of the best alternative use of specific areas where there is conflict, between oil and salmon, for example.

ESTIMATES OF FUTURE VALUES

I estimate that by 1980 the use of the Range will increase 184 percent over 1968, to 1,019,000 recreation days. Expenditures and consumer's surplus will increase 311 percent to $31 million and $11.6 million respectively. These figures are based on federal and state agency estimates of increases in population and tourist travel by 1980, and on expected construction of the Turnagain Arm Causeway. It also assumes continued development of recreational facilities at least at the present rate, and sufficient to meet the demand. They are believed conservative. The wildlife and related recreational resources of the Kenai National Moose Range are rare commodities. Many of them are unique. They are in short supply, and more cannot be produced at will on the assembly line. To paraphrase Cooley (1967), the acreage of the Moose Range in 1492 had almost no value to the white man because it was unknown and therefore unused and unvalued. Today the 1,730,000 acres have great value. In 1980 they will have proportionally much greater value because of 2.84 times the demand with the same number of acres.

LITERATURE CITED

BUCKLEY, JOHN L.
    1957.   Wildlife in the economy of Alaska. Biol. Pap. U. Alaska, No. 1, Revised. 33 pp.
Bureau of Sport Fisheries and Wildlife.
    (circa 1963).   Kenai National Moose Range. A plan for proposed management and development. BSFW, USDI, Wash., D.C. 54 pp.
CLAWSON, MARION.
    1959.   Methods of measuring the demand for and value of outdoor recreation. Reprint No. 10, RFF, Inc., Wash., D.C.
COOLEY, RICHARD A.
    1967.   Alaska, a challenge in conservation. U. of Wisc. Press, Madison.
HAKALA, JOHN.
    1969.   Personal communication. From Refuge Manager, Kenai National Moose Range.
KING, R. T.
    1947.   The future of wildlife in forest land use. Trans. N.A. Wildl. Conf. 12:454-467.
KRUTILLA, JOHN V.
    1967.   Conservation reconsidered. Reprint No. 67, RFF, Inc., Wash., D.C.
SECKLER, D. W.
    1966.   On the uses and abuses of economic science in evaluating public outdoor recreation. Land Economics 42(4): 485-494.
STEINHOFF, HAROLD W.
    1969.   Values of wildlife and related recreation on the Kenai National Moose Range. Mimeo rpt. to Div. Wildl. Res., BSFW, USDI, Wash., D.C.
SWANSON, ERNEST W.
    1969.   Travel and the national parks. U.S. Natl. Park Serv., Wash., D.C.

BIOLOGY AND POPULATIONS

Wise use of our wildlife resources requires knowledge of how animals and populations function—of how animals use their environment, interact with one another, reproduce and die. Each animal species is unique, having its own set of adaptations and functions in an ecosystem. Management of each species is therefore a unique problem requiring special knowledge.

The next paper emphasizes the concept of evolution and natural selection as a basis for studying wildlife biology. The remaining papers deal with many facets of the biology of species, emphasizing interrelationships, as among population density, behavior, disease, nutrition, reproduction and mortality.

ADAPTABILITY OF ANIMALS TO HABITAT CHANGE (1966)

A. Starker Leopold

The capacity of wildlife to adapt to changing environmental conditions varies among and within species. Leopold addresses the questions of what constitutes adaptability and what are the mechanisms by which animals adapt. Adaptive capabilities of each species determine responses of populations to management practices. Sophisticated manipulation of populations, either directly (controlled exploitation) or indirectly (habitat modification), requires an understanding of response of species to environmental change. Especially pertinent to wildlife biologists is the implication that rare and endangered species may be "nonadaptive", while more adaptive species provide for the bulk of recreation.

All organisms possess in some measure the ability to adapt or adjust to changing environmental conditions. But the degree to which different species are capable of adjusting varies enormously. This chapter concerns the nature and extent of adaptability and demonstrates the truism that in a world undergoing constant and massive modification by man, the animals with the highest capacity for adjustment are those that persist in abundance. Specialized animals with narrow limits of adjustment are those that have become scarce or in some instances extinct.

Relation of Ungulate Populations to Plant Successions

In any given ecosystem, there are animals that thrive best in the climax stages of plant succession and others that do better when the climax has been destroyed in some way and the vegetation is undergoing seral or subclimax stages of succession, working back toward restoration of the climax. This can be interpreted to mean that the climax animals are more specialized in their environmental needs, while the seral or successional species are more adaptable and able to take advantage of transitory and unstable situations. The principle can be well illustrated by considering the status of various native ungulates in North America.

The mass of data accumulated in studies of North American deer permits us to draw some general deductions about population dynamics in these animals, particularly in relation to food supplies. The following remarks apply equally to the white-tailed deer (*Odocoileus virginianus*) and the mule deer or blacktail (*O. hemionus*). The quality and quantity of forage available to a deer population during the most critical season of the year has proven repeatedly to be the basic regulator of population level. Usually this means winter forage, but not always. In desert areas or regions of Mediterranean climate, like coastal California, summer may be the critical season. In any event, the nutritive intake of the individual deer during the critical season determines both productivity of the herd (Cheatum and Severinghaus, 1950; Taber, 1953) and mortality in the herd,

Reprinted by permission from: Future Environments of North America, F. F. Darling and J. P. Milton, Eds. Copyright 1966 by The Conservation Foundation. Doubleday and Co., Inc., N. Y.

whether death be caused by starvation, disease, parasites, or even to some extent by predation or accidents (Longhurst et al., 1952, and others). Average population level is a dynamic function of these two opposing variables—rate of productivity and rate of mortality. Hunting is a source of mortality artificially interposed in the formula, and although it is inter-compensatory with other forms of loss (that is, hunting kill will reduce starvation losses, etc.) it is not regulated by nutrition, but by legislative fiat. However, since hunting is generally controlled in North America to remove no more than annual increment, and usually less, it cannot be construed as a primary determinant of population level in most areas. Putting all this in much simpler form, good forage ranges generally have many deer; poor ranges have few. All other influences are secondary.

Good deer ranges characteristically include stands of nutritious and palatable browse which as a rule are produced in secondary stages of plant succession (Leopold, 1950). Burned or cutover forest lands support most of the deer in the continent; some brush-invaded former grasslands are of local importance. In a few special cases, as for example that of the burro deer (*O. h. eremicus*) on the desert, sparse populations live in climax floras. But on the whole the association between deer and secondary brushlands (the connecting link being nutritional) is so general as to permit classification of deer as seral or successional species.

Assuming that range relationships are equally dominant in determining populations of other North American ungulates, and much evidence indicates that this is so, a general characterization can be made of each species, permitting classification along lines of range affinities, as had been done in Table 4-1.

This rather subjective classification requires some explanation.

Climax species

The northern caribou is a classic example of an animal that depends heavily in winter on undisturbed climax vegetation of the subarctic zone.

TABLE 4-1. General association of North American ungulates with climax or subclimax successional stages

	Biotic zone		
	Boreal	Temperate	Tropical
1. Associated primarily with climax forage types:			
Caribou *(Rangifer arcticus)*	x		
Bighorn *(Ovis canadensis* and allied species)	x		
Mountain goat *(Oreamnos americanus)*	x		
Musk ox *(Ovibos moschatus)*	x		
Bison *(Bison bison)*		x	
Collared peccary *(Pecari tajacu)*		x	x
White-lipped peccary *(Tayassu pecari)*			x
Tapir *(Tapirella bairdii)*			x
Brocket *(Mazama americana)*			x
2. Associated primarily with subclimax forage types:			
Moose *(Alces americana)*	x	x	
Elk *(Cervus canadensis)*		x	
White-tailed deer *(Odocoileus virginianus)*		x	
Mule deer *(Odocoileus hemionus)*		x	
Pronghorn antelope *(Antilocapra americana)*		x	

150

The lichens which supply much of the caribou's winter food grow either as an understory to the spruce forest or suspended from the spruce limbs. Any disturbance such as fire or grazing that depletes this particular vegetative complex lowers the carrying capacity for caribou.

Similarly bighorn sheep and mountain goats in their alpine retreats, bison on the great prairies, and musk ox on the arctic plains are adapted to feed on climax species of forbs, sedges, grasses, and a few shrubs.

In the southern reaches of the continent the two species of peccaries are generalized in their food habits, like other pigs, but the mast of oak and of many tropical fruit trees contributes heavily to their diet. Besides mast, the bulbous roots, palmettos, cacti, forbs, and grasses on which these pigs feed are on the whole characteristic of climax associations. The tapir and brocket are even more typical of climax rain forest (Leopold, 1959).

It is notable that of nine species of North American ungulates associated with climax vegetation, four are of boreal or arctic affinities, four are tropical, and only the bison and the collared peccary in part of its range occur in temperate latitudes.

Subclimax species

Nearly all of the ungulates that thrive best on kinds of weeds and brush that characterize disturbed vegetative situations are native in the temperate zone. This includes the two common deer, elk, and the moose, which extends northward through the boreal zones as well. The pronghorn antelope is predominantly a weedeater (Buechner, 1950), although it may consume much sage and other browse at times. On the Great Plains, the weeds and forbs that supported antelope originally may have resulted from local overgrazing by the native bison. On the deserts of Mexico, however, the antelope almost certainly depended on climax vegetation, but this is the fringe of its continental range.

Whereas most boreal and tropical ungulates have climax affinities, the temperate-zone species thrive largely on successional vegetation. In an evolutionary sense this would suggest that these adaptive species, all highly successful today, developed in an environment subject to frequent disturbance, presumably fire. Even the bison, here classed as a climax species, would fall in this category if one accepts the prairie as a subclimax, maintained by fire (Sauer, 1950).

Recognition of successional affinities of big-game species is basic to determination of sound management policy. The subclimax species (two deer, antelope, elk, moose) fit nicely into multiple-use land programs, including logging, grazing, and controlled burning. The climax species do not. Preservation of wilderness areas, without competing or disturbing uses, is particularly important in sustaining remnants of the climax forms designated in Table 4-1.

Plant Successions and other Wildlife

The principle illustrated above with ungulates applies generally to wild animals. In areas heavily modified by human action, the abundant species are those adapted to take advantage of disturbed ecologic situations. Over much of the United States, the upland game species that supply most of today's recreational hunting are the bobwhite quail, cottontail rabbit, ruffed grouse, mourning dove, and the introduced ringnecked pheasant—all typical subclimax or successional species.

Game species once abundant on the continent, but now localized and scarce because of shrinkage of particular climax vegetational types on which they depended, are the prairie chicken, sharp-tailed grouse, sage hen, upland plover, and wild turkey. Extinct are the heath hen and passenger pigeon.

The case of the passenger pigeon illustrates particularly well the dilemma facing an unadaptive species. The fabled legions that "darkened the sky" were supported in large part by mast crops produced in climax stands of mature timber, especially oak, beech, and chestnut. The flocks were highly mobile and searched the eastern half of the continent for favorable feeding grounds. When a good food supply was found, millions of birds would congregate to establish one of the massive colonial nestings so well documented by Schorger (1955). With the settlement of the country, two things happened concurrently that contributed to the swift collapse of the pigeon population: uncounted millions of the birds were slaughtered in the nesting areas, and the mature timber stands that produced the mast crops were felled to make way for farms. The demise of the pigeon is traditionally blamed on the market hunters; but had there been no hunting, it is doubtful that the pigeon would have survived the depletion of its food supply. So specialized was this bird that it seemingly had no capacity to adjust to the modest, scattered food source that certainly continued after the main hardwood forests were felled. When the big pigeon flocks were reduced, the survivors simply perished without a single pair exhibiting the ability to feed and reproduce under changed conditions. Its close relative, the mourning dove, on the other hand, adjusted very well indeed to the conversion from forest to farm, and today is undoubtedly much more numerous than in primitive times, despite heavy and persistent shooting.

The Nature of Adaptation

Precisely what is this character of "adaptability" that some animals have and others do not? What are the mechanisms by which animals adapt?

The paleontological record tells us that over the eons of time there have been enormous changes in climate and hence in habitat. With each major shift many animal species became extinct; these presumably were the unadaptable ones. Other animals persisted but evolved and were modified to meet the new conditions. One component of adaptability, therefore, is the capacity for genetic change.

At the same time, current experience offers many examples of individual animals learning new tricks of survival that contribute to longevity and hence to persistence of the population. A coyote can learn to be trapshy; a raccoon learns to search for eggs in wood-duck boxes; mallards learn the precise hour when legal shooting ceases, which signals the exodus from a refuge to go in search of food. Some species are quick to pick up new behaviorisms; others are not. Adaptability, therefore, may include the capacity to learn.

Genetic and learned adaptations will be discussed in that order.

Morphologic Adaptation

One manifestation of genetic adaptation to local environment is the demonstrable evidence of subspeciation in animals. Many widely distributed species are segmented into local populations that show marked and persistent differences in morphology. Some of the characters that vary and are easily observed and measured are body size, proportion of body parts, and color of plumage or pelage. The bobwhite quail (*Colinus virginianus*) is an example of a resident (nonmigratory) game bird that varies greatly from place to place. This bird occurs throughout the eastern half of North America, from New England and South Dakota south to Chiapas in southern Mexico. Within this range, twenty-one well-differentiated races or subspecies are recognized (Aldrich, 1955). In size, the bobwhite decreases from over 200 grams in the north to slightly over 100 grams in Chiapas. Likewise there is a general north-south gradient in plumage color, the palest birds occurring in the open or arid ranges, such as the Great Plains, the darkest forms being found in the wet tropics or subtropics of southern Florida, the coast of Veracruz, and the interior valleys of Chiapas. It is presumed that each population is particularly adapted to the local habitat in which it exists. The capacity to be molded genetically by local environment doubtless underlies the bobwhite's success in occupying such an extensive range in North America.

Commenting on this general question of genetic plasticity, Grant (1963, p. 434) states:

The great role of natural selection in the formation of races [subspecies] can be inferred from the observation that racial characteristics are often adaptive. The adaptiveness of the racial characters in many plants and animals is demonstrated by two sets of correlations. First, the different races of a species have morphological and physiological characters that are related to the distinctive features of the environment in their respective areas. Second, the same general patterns of racial variation frequently recur in a parallel form in separate species inhabiting the same range of environment.

He goes on to comment on some of the generally accepted "rules" of morphologic adaptation that have been summarized and analyzed by many other authors, including Mayr (1942, p. 90). These are,

1. *Bergmann's rule:* The smaller races of a species are found in the warmer parts of a species range, the larger races in cooler parts.
2. *Allen's rule:* Protruding body parts, such as ears, tails, bills, and other extremities, are relatively shorter in the cooler parts of the range of a species than in the warmer parts.
3. *Golger's rule:* Dark pigments (eumelanins) increase in the warm and humid parts of a range, paler phaeomelanins prevail in arid climates.

The bobwhite illustrates all of these rules of local adaptation. The same may be said of white-tailed and mule deer, the raccoon, the bobcat, hares of the genus *Lepus*, cottontails of the genus *Sylvilagus*, and many other widely distributed birds and mammals. In the case of the white-tailed deer, the size gradient is extreme: in Wisconsin an adult buck weighs well over 200 pounds, in parts of Mexico scarcely seventy pounds. The larger size and smaller ears of northern animals presumably give an advantageous ratio of body mass to exposed surface, for heat conservation. The opposite is true in warmer climates.

Physiologic Adaptation

More difficult to measure, but perhaps even more important in fitting local populations to their environments, are the physiologic adaptations. To be successful, a population must breed at the right time of year, produce only as many young as can be cared for, be able to digest and assimilate the foods locally available, and otherwise adjust its life processes to the local scene. Migratory birds lay on fat (fuel) for their travels and require elaborate navigational machinery. Research to date has scarcely scratched the surface of this enormously complicated area of animal adaptation.

A species that has been studied in some detail and that well illustrates several facets of physiologic adaptation is the common white-crowned sparrow of the Pacific coast (*Zonotrichia leucophrys*). There are two races of this bird, very similar in appearance, that winter together in central California; but in spring one race migrates to British Columbia to breed while the other breeds locally, on the winter range. Blanchard (1941) showed a number of differences in the life cycles of these two populations. Though living together all winter, the migrants laid on fat in spring and departed for the north; the residents did not accumulate fat but went leisurely about the business of nesting. The migrants, having less time on the breeding grounds, compressed the reproductive cycle into approximately two thirds of the time used by resident birds. Subsequent investigation by a number of workers has demonstrated that the mechanism triggering these events is changing length of day in spring, but the important differences in response reflect inherent, physiologic adaptations peculiar to the two populations.

Differences in timing of breeding are demonstrable in many other species. Black-tailed deer along the California coast fawn in May, mule deer in the Sierra Nevada in July, whitetails in northwestern Mexico in August. In each case fawning corresponds to the period of optimum plant growth—spring in California, summer rains in Mexico. Time of mating (seven months before fawning) is presumably timed by changing day length—in this case by shortening days, since the breeding occurs in fall or early winter. Ian McTaggart Cowan has kept a number of races of blacktailed deer in pens in Vancouver, and notes that the southern Alaskan and British Columbian stocks breed at almost the same time, whereas the Californian stocks have retained a response that induces antler growth, shedding of velvet, breeding, antler drop, and pelage molt a month or more in advance of the northern races kept in the same pens.

The number of young produced by a breeding population is regulated by physiologic controls. Lack (1954) presents examples of clutch size in birds varying apparently with food availability. He cites the work of Swanberg on the thick-billed nutcrackers, in which it was shown that in years when the autumn crop of nuts was below average, the birds laid only three eggs. In years of good or excellent nut crops, clutches of four eggs were normal. When the experimenter supplied nuts in winter for certain wild nutcrackers, those particular individuals had clutches of four eggs, even in years of poor mast crop. The change in number of eggs was therefore apparently a physiologic adjustment to the amount of food available. But in all cases the birds laid no fewer than three eggs, nor more than five, the limits presumably set by hereditary factors.

Clutch or litter size likewise may be a function of predator populations and the likelihood of losses of eggs or young due to predation. The mallard of continental North America lays eight to twelve eggs and predictable losses are high. The closely related Laysan duck, on isolated Laysan Island where there are no predators, lays only three to four eggs.

Certain deep-seated physiologic differences have been detected between wild and domestic turkeys which shed some light on how the wild birds are adapted to live successfully in the woods (Leopold, 1944). In the Missouri Ozarks the native turkey persists even under highly adverse circumstances and populations respond readily to protection and management. Domestic turkeys cannot exist away from farmyards. Hybrids between the two barely hold their own in refuges under intensive management. Differential reproductive success seemed to underlie the disparities in population behavior. Time of breeding is earlier in domestic and hybrid turkeys, leading to loss of eggs and chicks in late-spring storms. Behavioral differences between hens and chicks suggested other reasons why wild birds raised more young. These differential reactions were related to size of brain and relative development of some of the endocrine organs that control behavior, suggesting a few of the components that may be involved in "local adaptations."

Danger of Transplanting Local Races

If indeed some kinds of animals are delicately attuned to life in specific local environments, one may question the advisability of trapping and shifting these populations about in an effort to restock underpopulated ranges.

During the era 1920-40 there was a very large trade in Mexican bobwhites, imported into various midwestern states for release to augment local populations. Actual measurements of the results of this endeavor are lacking, but there seemed to be a consensus among observers that such releases never led to sustained increase in bobwhite numbers, and in fact some thought that in years following a liberation, local populations were depressed. This may well have been the case, since birds from the tropical coast of Tamaulipas (the main source of stock) and their progeny if crossed with northern birds, would not likely have been winter-hardy. In any event this program was abandoned, attesting to its failure.

Dahlbeck (1951) reported a similar failure when gray partridges from southern Europe were imported to Sweden and mixed with the hardy northern populations. A catastrophic drop in number followed. He also relates a case of shipping in Carpathian red deer stags to "improve" the stock on an island off the Scandinavian coast. The resulting hybrids apparently were unable to stand the rigors of the northern climate, and the population on the island fell to near extinction. Following these experiences Sweden adopted regulations to prohibit import of game birds and mammals from outside the country.

155

Individual Adaptability

Certain adaptive responses to a changing environment appear to be nongenetic. Some animals seem capable of internal physiological and behavioral adjustments and as a consequence can tolerate wide fluctuations in weather and other environmental factors. A classic example would be the mourning dove (*Zenaidura macroura*).

There is no more widely distributed or successful game bird in the North American continent than the dove. Its breeding range extends from the Atlantic to the Pacific and from the prairie provinces of southern Canada to Oaxaca in southern Mexico. Two weakly differentiated subspecies are recognized—an eastern and a western race. But each of these races successfully occupies a great variety of habitats. The western mourning dove, for example, breeds in the pine zone of the mountains, in the bleakest southwestern deserts, and along the tropical Mexican coast with equal success. If there are local physiologic adaptations, no one has detected them. In our present state of knowledge we must assume that the individual birds are capable of this range of adjustment.

The same can be said for some migratory birds like the mallard, which breeds from the arctic tundra to northern Baja California and from coast to coast. There are no detectable morphologic differences among North American mallards, nor is there any hint of local physiologic variation. Not only is the mallard adaptable in the sense of occupying a variety of breeding situations, but it has shown a remarkable capacity to adjust to the changes wrought in its wintering habitat. In primitive North America the mallard wintered in the natural marshes, sloughs, and backwaters and ate aquatic foods along with other ducks. Today most of these waterways are drained or otherwise made unattractive, and during the autumn much of the remaining habitat bristles with the guns of eager duck hunters. The mallard copes successfully with this situation by several adjustments in its habits. First, it feeds at night, spending the day in safety of a waterfowl refuge or on some open bay or sandbar. Secondly, it has learned to feed on the waste grain of stubble fields—wheat and corn in the midwest, rice and kafir in Texas and California. Each day with cessation of legal shooting the birds rise in great masses and fly to the stubbles for the evening repast. For a period in the 1940s shooting closed at 4 P.M. and the flight began at 4:15. When the law was changed to permit shooting till sunset, the birds adjusted their exodus to fifteen minutes after sunset, attesting to their capacity for quick reaction to circumstances. As a result, the mallard today is by far the most abundant duck in North America.

Some other species of waterfowl have learned the same tricks. The pintail and widgeon in the west, and various geese, feed on crop residues and avoid guns during the day by flocking in safe refuges. But many of the ducks have not adjusted and are steadily decreasing in number. The redhead, canvasback, wood duck, and shoveler continue to feed in the marshes and along shorelines where they are exposed to heavy shooting. These nonadaptive species require special protection and their situation will not likely improve in the future.

Another example of an adaptable species is the coyote. Originally it occurred in modest numbers through western North America, something of a hanger-on in the range of the wolf, scavenging scraps left by this lordly predator and catching such rodents as were available. In the remaining climax forests of the Mexican highlands, where wolves still occur, coyotes are scarce or absent (Leopold, 1959). But over most of the continent where the virgin flora and fauna (including wolves) have been eliminated, conditions for the coyote have been vastly improved. The scourge of rodents that came with agriculture and with over-grazing of the western ranges, plus the carcasses of domestic stock, offered a food supply much superior to that originally available. As a result, the coyote has thrived and extended its range far to the north and east. It invaded Alaska in the 1930s and currently has moved as far east as New York State. The coyote, in other words, is an example of a successional or subclimax predator that has profited from alteration in the climax biota, as much so as the deer. Because it occasionally preys on sheep and poultry, it has been the object of intensive control efforts, more so perhaps than any other carnivore in the world. Yet so adept is the coyote at learning the tricks of avoiding guns, traps, poisons, dogs, and even airplanes (from which it sometimes is shot) that it persists over nearly all of its original and adopted range, at least in modest numbers. The coyote will be among the surviving wild species long into the future.

Evolution of Behavior

When species like the mallard and the coyote show adaptive behavior, as described above, it is difficult to say what part of this adaptation may be genetic and what part is learned. Many mallards are shot and many coyotes are trapped or poisoned. Are these the slow-witted ones? Is man acting as a predator himself, applying a strong selective force to hunted species that may be bringing genetic changes in the survivors? If so, nothing is known of this force, but there is room for speculation.

Consider first the mallard. Much of a duck's behavior we know to be learned. The quick adjustment of the birds to a change in legal shooting hours could hardly be based on anything but experience. This quickly could become a tradition, transmitted from older experienced birds to young ones as some migratory habits are transmitted (Hochbaum, 1955). Yet over the years many individual mallards depart from this tradition and decoy into small ponds during shooting hours. They are among the missing when the breeders migrate northward in spring. Shooting, then, may be creating a new strain of mallard that tends to conform to mass behavior patterns and is less prone to make mistaken individual judgments.

In the southeastern United States, where the bobwhite has been heavily hunted for a century or more, it is generally reported that the birds have changed their habits. Old hunters claim to remember the day when a covey, flushed before a dog, would fly 100 to 200 yards and scatter in the broom-sedge or weed fields where they could be taken easily over points. Today covies tend to fly 300 to 400 yards and to seek shelter not in open fields but in dense oak thickets. Often such coveys put a "hook" on the end of their flight, turning to the right or left after entering the woods, thus being much harder to relocate. Is this change in behavior, if true, strictly learned and transmitted from adults to young? Or is there a genetic change involved as well, favoring the birds that fly far, seek woody cover, and change directions after entering the cover?

Much of the coyote's skill in avoiding peril is clearly learned. Individuals known to have escaped from a trap or to have survived a dose of strychnine become wary and are much more difficult to capture than young, inexperienced individuals. But the innate capacity for wariness may be strengthened and bolstered over the years by constant removal of the least wary individuals.

Thus, it may be that the hunted animals are evolving under a new selective force not affecting those animals that are permitted to live without persecution. In this sense, the adaptability which may be expressed as a genetic trait—or put in other words, as the ability to learn—is not a biological constant but a shifting attribute of a species.

Summary

There are notable differences in the response of wild animals to the sweeping changes in environment brought on by man. Some species are clearly associated with and dependent upon undisturbed climax situations, and these suffer the most from environmental change. They are here designated as nonadaptive species. The list includes all the rare or endangered species and some that have become extinct.

On the other hand, other animals adjust very well to changes in vegetation and in land use, and these on the whole persist or may even increase in abundance. Included in this group are many of the common game birds and mammals that supply the bulk of the recreational hunting in North America today. There appears to be a direct correlation between the affinity with seral or subclimax biotas and adaptability in the sense of the capacity to adjust to change.

The ability to adapt seems to involve two distinct components: (1) genetic plasticity, or the capacity for segments of a population to evolve rapidly to fit local conditions; and (2) the capacity for individuals to learn new habits of survival under altered circumstances. These cannot readily be separated, since the capacity to learn is itself a genetic trait.

BIBLIOGRAPHY

ALDRICH, J. W. 1955. Distribution of American Gallinaceous Game Birds. U.S. Fish and Wildl. Serv., Wash., D.C. Circ. 34.

BLANCHARD, B. D. 1941. The White-crowned Sparrows (*Zonotrichia leucophrys*) of the Pacific Seaboard: Environment and Annual Cycle. Univ. Calif. Pub. Zool. 46:1-178.

BUECHNER, H. K. 1950. Life History, Ecology, and Range Use of the Pronghorn Antelope in Trans-Pecos Texas. Amer. Midl. Nat. 43:257-354.

CHEATUM, E. L. and C. W. SEVERINGHAUS, 1950. Variations in Fertility of White-tailed Deer Related to Range Conditions. Trans. N. Amer. Wildl. Conf. 15:170-90.

DAHLBECK, N. 1951. [Commentary During U.N. Conf., Fish and Wild. Res.] Proc. U.N. Sci. Conf. on Conserv. and Utiliz. of Res. Lake Success, N.Y. Aug. 17-Sept. 6, 1949. 7:210.

GRANT, V. 1963. The Origin of Adaptations. Columbia Univ. Press, New York and London.

HOCHBAUM, H. A. 1955. Travels and Traditions of Waterfowl. Univ. Minn. Press. Minneapolis.

LACK, D. 1954. The Natural Regulation of Animal Numbers. Oxford Univ. Press.

LEOPOLD, A. S. 1944. The Nature of Heritable Wildness in Turkeys. Condor 46:133-97.

———. 1950. Deer in Relation to Plant Succession. Trans. N. Amer. Wildl. Conf. 15: 571-80.

———. 1959. Wildlife of Mexico: the Game Birds and Mammals. Univ. Calif. Press, Berkeley.

LONGHURST, W. M., A. S. LEOPOLD, and R. F. DASMANN. 1952. A Survey of California Deer Herds, Their Ranges and Management Problems. Calif. Fish and Game, Game Bul. 6.

MAYR, E. 1942. Systematics and the Origin of Species. Columbia Univ. Press, New York.

SAUER, C. O. 1950. Grassland Climax, Fire, and Man. J. Range Mgt. 3:16-21.

SCHORGER, A. W. 1955. The Passenger Pigeon: Its Natural History and Extinction. Univ. Wisc. Press, Madison.

TABER, R. D. 1953. Studies of Black-tailed Deer Reproduction on Three Chaparral Cover Types. Calif. Fish and Game Bul. 39(2):177-86.

Courtesy of Cornell Laboratory of Ornithology

A VIEWPOINT CONCERNING THE SIGNIFICANCE OF STUDIES OF GAME BIRD FOOD HABITS (1966)

Gordon W. Gullion

Identification of critical food resources requires study of food habits of all ages and sexes, throughout the year, and during years with diverse weather and different population levels. Gullion's paper illustrates that our knowledge of the biology of species will always be a dynamic mixture of accepted truths, opinions and hypotheses.

In the past six or seven decades there have been numerous studies concerning the food habits of North American game birds. However, in recent years food studies have become somewhat passé, partly as a result of the belief that little useful information is gathered that can be used in the development of wildlife management plans (Kalmbach, 1954). In place of understanding game bird food requirements, wildlife managers have turned to various forms of habitat manipulation to increase populations, and too often have found their efforts to be futile.

I can cite two examples from personal experience. First, an extensive water development ("gallinaceous guzzler") program in southern Nevada in the late 1940's failed to provide a hoped-for population expansion in Gambel's Quail (*Lophortyx gambelii*) because much of the area affected by development lacked an adequate food resource, and food is even more important than water to the desert quail. These quail can exist quite well in the proper environments without preformed drinking water but not without food (Gullion, 1960; Hungerford, 1962; Gullion and Gullion, 1964).

Second, we still apparently know too little about the food requirements of Ruffed Grouse (*Bonasa umbellus*), the voluminous studies of Bump *et al.* (1947) and others, notwithstanding, to understand fully the reasons for the periodic drastic fluctuations of population size, or to develop effective forest management plans that have resulted in significant, sustained, increases in Ruffed Grouse populations.

Three basic factors are believed to be responsible for this situation. First, most game bird food studies have been based on samples obtained in the fall from hunter-killed birds, and therefore represent items taken at the time of year when the greatest amount of food is normally available, both in quantity and variety. These fall-taken samples are often comparatively meaningless, even if carefully evaluated in terms of the variety and abundance of foods locally available to the birds (and this frequently is not done). Second, most studies are short-term, representing one or two years' thesis research, or a short-lived (2 or 3 years) intensive state game research project. Third, seldom are the food studies related to the status of the population of birds being sampled; that is, the investigators do not specify whether the population is static, rising, or falling; the density of the species (for comparison with other areas); and how the physical condition of the birds sampled compares with a normal or standard condition.

Reprinted from The Condor 68(4):372-376.

With these shortcomings it is hardly surprising that little has been learned that can be used significantly in developing long-range management programs for many native game birds. Indeed, there have been some published food studies of imported game birds that, in view of the species' failures to become established, can best be interpreted as reflecting diets that could not sustain the birds.

Food studies are needed that critically sample local game bird populations during times of stress as well as during periods of population upswing as was done by Lehmann (1953). Too often it has been assumed that a wide diversity of foods available, and taken, represents a desirable and adequate food situation, at least among the gallinaceous game birds. As Errington (1936:356) pointed out long ago, "The feeding tendencies of vertebrates generally may be rather indiscriminate . . . ." The presence of certain food items in the digestive system, even in abundance or with considerable frequency over a span of a year or two, is not prima facie evidence that the food items concerned were nutritious or even desirable. I have noted elsewhere (Gullion, 1964a:iv) that the thrift of a number of game animals depends largely upon the availability of a single species of plant, or at most a very few species. For these animals many other food items provide diversity, but lacking the critical plant species the game populations would be nonexistent, or in very low densities.

Among the North American grouse, for example, fall food intake of most species is similar, varying from area to area according to the species of plants locally available. Sage Grouse (*Centrocercus urophasianus*), Spruce Grouse (*Canachites canadensis*), Blue Grouse (*Dendragapus obscurus*), Sharp-tailed Grouse (*Pedioecetes phasianellus*), and Ruffed Grouse all feed in the fall on a large assortment of berries and succulent, green leaves. On the basis of fall food habits Sage Grouse should do as well in Spruce Grouse habitat as Spruce Grouse should do in Sharp-tailed or Ruffed Grouse habitat. It is not until the critical winter period that the availability of sagebrush leaves (*Artemisia* spp.) limits the distribution of Sage Grouse in the Great Basin; jack pine (*Pinus banksiana*) needles the distribution of Spruce Grouse in Ontario; limber pine (*Pinus flexilis*) needles the distribution of Blue Grouse in the Great Basin ranges of Nevada; and the availability of aspen (*Populus* spp.) catkins restricts the range of Ruffed Grouse in northern Minnesota.

Patterson (1952:201) lists 14 genera of plants utilized by Sage Grouse on a year-around basis, but in Great Basin areas where big sagebrush (*Artemisia tridentata*) or other closely related species of *Artemisia* are absent Sage Grouse are virtually nonexistent.

Alcorn and Richardson (1951), Christensen (1954), and Harper *et al.* (1958) list more that 100 plants utilized by Chukar Partridges (*Alectoris graeca*) in Nevada and eastern California; but the abundance and availability of cheatgrass (*Bromus tectorum*) on these cold desert ranges, more than any other single factor in their environment, determines the thrift of these partridge populations.

Koskimies (1955) notes that herbivorous species living in more extreme environments tend to specialize in the utilization of single species of plants. Recent studies of Capercaillie (*Tetrao urogallus*) and Black Grouse

(*Lyrurus tetrix*) in Finland (Seiskari, 1962) have shown a dependence by these species upon the needles of Scots pine (*Pinus sylvestris*) and the aments of silver and white birch (*Betula verrucosa* and *B. pubescens*), respectively, even though the total list of food items taken includes many other species of plants and animals. Jenkins *et al.* (1963:318) discuss in detail the dependence of Scotland's Red Grouse (*Lagopus lagopus*) upon heather (*Calluna vulgaris*). Crichton (1963) recently showed the importance of jack pine needles in the diet of Spruce Grouse in Ontario, as Hoffmann (1961) had done earlier for needles of white fir (*Abies concolor*) in the diet of Blue Grouse in California.

Recently (1964a) I have listed some 91 species of plants that are taken by Gambel's Quail on the desert ranges of southern Nevada. Yet of all these plants, the availability of only three small groups (*Lotus* spp., *Astragalus Nuttallianus* and closely related forms, and *Erodium cicutarium*) largely determines the abundance of quail on these desert ranges (Gullion, 1956:33).

I believe that much of our failure to understand many fluctuations of game bird populations has been the result of inadequate knowledge concerning food habits of the species involved during critical periods, and of improper interpretation of information that is available.

A study of Gambel's Quail in southern Nevada can be used to illustrate this point (Gullion, 1956). In 1950 and 1951, when quail populations were at a low level, the seeds taken as food represented a wide range of the species of plants growing on the desert. Particularly abundant among the items taken were crucifers, borages, and the Caprifoliaceae. Following a wet fall and winter in 1951-1952, the desert "bloomed," and a tremendous quantity of seeds were produced during March and April 1952. With a wide selection of seeds available the desert quail concentrated on those produced by the genera *Lotus* and *Astragalus* (and some *Lupinus*) and *Erodium cicutarium,* almost to the exclusion of all other plant genera. This selection of the seeds of a few species from among all those present continued through 1953. In 1954, when the stockpile of preferred seeds produced in the spring of 1952 began to diminish, a wide diversity of seeds again appeared in the crops of fall-taken quail. Seeds of red brome (*Bromus rubens*), although totally ignored by these quail in 1952, and used only sparingly in 1953, became a prominent item in these crops in 1954. Other seeds not previously utilized that began to appear in quantity included those of *Phacelia* and various crucifers. Also the consumption of dried catclaw (*Acacia Greggii*) leaves, pieces of dried grass leaves and stems, rodent feces, and other "stuffing" items became prevalent. By the spring of 1955, desert quail populations had dropped far below their 1954 levels.

Although there is a tremendous production of seeds on the southern Nevada desert when conditions are correct, the quail thrive only in those regions where the ephemeral legumes and filaree are abundant. The seeds of the many Compositae, Cruciferae, Onagraceae, Plantaginaceae, Cactaceae, and Gramineae the dominate the other desert areas will not sustain high-density populations of Gambel's Quail.

Current studies of the management of Ruffed Grouse in northern Minnesota indicate that the abundance and nutritional quality of the male aments of the aspens (*Populus tremuloides* and *P. grandidentata*) may be as important in determining the density of grouse populations as any other factor (Gullion, 1964b; Brander, 1965; Marshall, 1965). On the Cloquet Forest Research Center in northern Minnesota the Ruffed Grouse population has continued to decline during the past decade in spite of forest-cutting practices that conform with the widely prescribed recommendations for management (cf. Gullion *et al.*, 1962). Only one consistent change in the forest environment can be correlated with this decline in bird abundance, and that is the widespread elimination of mature aspen from the forest as the result of extensive selective cutting beginning in 1958–1959.

Moreover, there appears to be a definite pattern of *preferential feeding* by Ruffed Grouse wherein only certain male aspen trees or clones are repeatedly selected from among the many male trees available in a forest stand. In most instances the selected trees are the older, decadent, injured, or diseased trees that Grange (1949:220) recommended be cut in favor of younger, thriftier aspen. Nevertheless, we have been unable to document the use of young, thrifty aspen as food by grouse.

It appears likely that one reason game biologists have been unable to explain the basis of changes in Ruffed Grouse populations has been a result of the popular misconception that food is no problem for grouse in hardwood forests since grouse eat buds and twigs (Edminster, 1954:216). Failure to recognize a more restricted food requirement has led to dismissal of these population changes as "cyclic," implying an extraterrestrial influence, or some intrinsic factor (cf. Keith, 1963).

At least with respect to Ruffed Grouse, I feel that the belief that their winter diet is of low nutritional quality is probably incorrect. Although it is true that twigs and leaf buds are taken as food, it is also apparent that a major portion of the winter diet consists of male catkins of birch, alder (*Alnus* sp.), hazel (*Corylus cornuta*), and especially aspen. These catkins cannot be considered low-quality food items (Leopold, 1933:69), since they contain the organic and mineral nutrients necessary to produce flowers early the next spring. Probably the fact that Ruffed Grouse (and most other tetraonids, too, according to Kuzmina, 1961) do not put on a layer of fat in the fall reflects the richness of this winter diet. We suspect the grouse that cannot avail themselves of sufficient catkins and turn to leaf buds and twigs as stuffing represent a major portion of the 50 to 60 per cent of the population that has normally been lost during the winter.

Although we strongly believe that variation in the food supply is a major influence on Ruffed Grouse populations in northern Minnesota, we can not yet conclusively demonstrate this relationship. It will undoubtedly take many years of intensive study to demonstrate clear-cut relationships since various other factors tend to cloud the issue. There is possibly a periodic fluctuation in the nutrient content of the tree catkins (as postulated by Lauckhart, 1957), and there is possibly a periodicity in the quantity of catkins produced. However, records of the Lake States Forest Experiment Station, U.S. Forest Service, do not show a definite periodicity in this factor (Zazada, personal correspondence).

Also, the severity of winter weather may override favorable food conditions, or a period of cold, wet weather in June may cause heavy losses among newly hatched chicks, resulting in a population decline at a time when food conditions indicate the probability of an increase.

Wildlife managers have long regarded inadequate food as the most prevalent factor limiting the size of big game herds, and extensive management efforts have been directed toward the alleviation of this problem. But biologists dealing with the small game species seldom consider food resources as being limiting. Yet, intensive studies of several species in recent years (Patterson, 1952; Koskimies, 1955; Gullion, 1956; Seiskari, 1962; Jenkins et al., 1963) clearly indicate that lack of a single critical food resource is as important in limiting small game populations as it is in the big game species.

To understand these relationships and to be of significance in developing long-range management policy, studies of food habits must deal with the critical period of each year; they must compare the foods and feeding habits of birds living in populations showing increasing densities as well as stable and declining numbers; and they must deal with individuals known to be successful in surviving in their native habitats.

LITERATURE CITED

ALCORN, J. R., and F. RICHARDSON. 1951. The Chukar Partridge in Nevada. J. Wildl. Mgmt., 15:265-275.

BRANDER, R. B. 1965. Factors affecting dispersion of Ruffed Grouse during late winter and spring on the Cloquet Forest Research Center, Minnesota. Ph.D. thesis, Univ. Minn.

BUMP, G., R. W. DARROW, F. C. EDMINSTER, and W. F. CRISSEY. 1947. The Ruffed Grouse: life history, propagation, management. New York State Conserv. Dept., Albany.

CHRISTENSEN, G. C. 1954. The Chukar Partridge in Nevada. Nevada Fish and Game Comm., Biol. Bull., 1:1-77.

CRICHTON, V. 1963. Autumn and winter foods of the Spruce Grouse in central Ontario. J. Wildl. Mgmt., 27:597.

EDMINSTER, F. C. 1954. American game birds of field and forest—their habits, ecology and management. Charles Scribners, New York.

ERRINGTON, P. L. 1936. Differences in nutritive values of winter game foods. Proc. N. Amer. Wildl. Conf., p. 356-360.

GRANGE, W. B. 1949. The way to game abundance. Charles Scribners, New York.

GULLION, G. W. 1956. Let's go desert quail hunting. Nevada Fish and Game Comm., Biol. Bull. No. 2:1-76.

GULLION, G. W. 1960. The ecology of Gambel's Quail in Nevada and the arid southwest. Ecology, 41:518-536.

GULLION, G. W. 1964a. Wildlife uses of Nevada plants. U.S. Dept. Agr., Natl. Arboretum, Contributions toward a flora of Nevada No. 49.

GULLION, G. W. 1964b. Food and cover occurrence and availability as influenced by forest practices. Minn. Dept. Conserv., Div. Game and Fish, Quart. Prog. Report, 23:43-83.

GULLION, G. W., R. T. KING, and W. H. MARSHALL. 1962. Male Ruffed Grouse and thirty years of forest management of the Cloquet Forest Research Center, Minnesota. J. Forestry, 60: 617-622.

GULLION, G. W., and A. M. GULLION. 1964. Water economy of Gambel Quail. Condor, 66:32-40.

HARPER, H. T., B. H. HARRY, and W. D. BAILEY. 1958. The Chukar Partridge in California. Calif. Fish and Game, 44:5-50.

HOFFMANN, R. S. 1961. The quality of the winter food of Blue Grouse. J. Wildl. Mgmt., 25: 209-210.

HUNGERFORD, C. R. 1962. Adaptations shown in selection of food by Gambel Quail. Condor, 64:213-219.

JENKINS, D., A. WATSON, and G. R. MILLER. 1963. Population studies on Red Grouse, Lagopus lagopus scoticus (Lath.) in north-east Scotland. J. Anim. Ecol., 32:317-376.

KALMBACH, E. R. 1954. The continuing need for food habits research. Wilson Bull., 66: 276-278.

KEITH, L. B. 1963. Wildlife's ten-year cycle. University Wisconsin Press, Madison.

KOSKIMIES, J. 1955. Ultimate causes of cyclic fluctuations in numbers in animal populations. Finnish Game Found., Papers on Game Research, 15:1-29.

KUZMINA, M. A. 1961. [Adaptation of Tetraonidae and Phasianidae to climatic conditions.] Trans. Instit. Zool. Acad. Sci. of the Kazakh S.S.R., 15:104-114 (translation from the Russian).

LAUCKHART, J. B. 1957. Animal cycles and food. J. Wildl. Mgmt., 21:230-234.

LEHMANN, V. W. 1953. Bobwhite population fluctuations and vitamin A. Trans. N. Amer. Wildl. Conf., 18:199-246.

LEOPOLD, A. 1933. Game management. Charles Scribners, New York.

MARSHALL, W. H. 1965. Ruffed Grouse behavior. BioScience, 15:92-94.

PATTERSON, R. L. 1952. The Sage Grouse in Wyoming. Wyo. Game and Fish Comm. and Sage Books, Denver.

SEISKARI, P. 1962. On the winter ecology of the Capercaillie, *Tetrao urogallus,* and the Black Grouse, *Lyrurus tetrix,* in Finland. Finnish Game Found., Papers on Game Research, 22:1-119.

FACTORS LIMITING HIGHER VERTEBRATE POPULATIONS (1956)
Paul L. Errington

Effective conservation of wildlife necessitates understanding the factors which regulate growth and size of populations. Manipulation of populations is a primary function of wildlife management. In this article, Errington emphasizes compensatory interrelationships among factors contributing to mortality, natality and movements as they regulate population growth.

At times, in seeking to generalize, a student of animal populations may feel that almost anything can and does happen or that the one common propensity of animals is to live if they can and die if they must. Nevertheless, some patterns are coming to stand out in the population dynamics of many species of animals.

My own studies of such patterns have dealt with what are commonly thought of as limiting factors in mammal and bird populations, and, in this connection, I have observed that important aspects of competition and predation may be particularly misleading if certain natural relationships and adjustments are not adequately taken into consideration. The following discussions will therefore present some of my ideas of distinctions that are worth keeping in mind when one attempts to analyze effects of competition and predation on populations in at least mammals and birds.[1]

Competition and Habitat Selection

There may be circumstantial evidence seeming to link changes in distribution or abundance of animals with changed intensity of competition. Of two closely related or closely associated species, one gains as the other fades. But, is one species displacing the other or "competing it out", as through greater aggressiveness, or are both merely responding to such habitat changes as are favorable or unfavorable to one or the other?

We do know that ascendencies and declines of bobwhite quail and of certain species of grouse have accompanied different stages of human settlement in the north-central United States, and we know that, for the grouse—pinnated, sharp-tailed, ruffed, and spruce grouse—the habitats of one species grade off into habitats of the next species ecologically in line. Yet the segregation of these native gallinaceous birds into their own niches is not so complete that it rules out possibilities of tension zones where one species could well have a depressive influence on populations of another. In cases marked neither by overt antagonisms nor by destructive impacts of one species upon the other's food supply or general environment, evidences may be seen of differential mortality or of withdrawals of one species into poorer habitats. But, again, in so many cases of what *could* be significant interspecific competition, we must return to such questions as: How much may the observed phenomena be due to something else— for example, to responsiveness to habitat niches?

Reprinted from: Science 124(3216):304-307, by permission from the American Association for the Advancement of Science.

The distinguishing features of habitat niches for a species are often too elusive for human perception. The main criterion for judgment may be the behavior of the species, itself, considered over sufficiently long periods of time to be meaningful. Svärdson[2], writing of competition and habitat selection in Swedish birds, describes the establishment of wood-warbler breeding territories at the same places but by different individual male warblers each spring. Despite local differences in topography, vegetation, and light conditions, selection of the old territorial sites by newly arrived, strange birds proceeds according to pattern each year. After very intensive studies, McCabe and Blanchard[3] concluded that the three species of California deer mice with which they worked have an extreme sense of environmental specificity, which serves to keep members of each species segregated into niches.

It could be contended, I suppose, that it would be a peculiar animal that did not recognize its proper habitat when it found it, irrespective of the numerous examples that might be listed of animals pioneering into new habitats or otherwise trying to live somehow even when they find themselves outside of anything resembling a proper habitat. The gradations in suitability that habitat niches may show for their occupants may, however, lead one to ask just when enough is enough, when marginal habitability becomes submarginal or worse. Svärdson's studies of competition emphasize the tendency for strong *interspecific* competition or population pressure to cause a species to retreat to those habitats in which it is particularly adapted to maintain itself. Conversely, strong *intraspecific* pressure may force the species into a much greater variety of habitats, including those that may scarcely be defined as habitable for the species trying to live in them.

Of course, if we look for examples of animals either living in very restricted niches or showing spectacular mass increases of invasions or colonizations of new habitats, we can find them all the way down the phylogenetic scale from mammals and birds. We need only consult the vast entomological literature. Or, we can go down toward that nebulous line of demarcation between what is living and what is nonliving.

I have worked on the epizootiology of what can be an extremely contagious and deadly hemorrhagic disease of muskrats. The full etiology of this disease, in my opinion, remains undemonstrated; but, whether the available evidence suggests a viral or bacterial agency, or a combination of them, or something else, the manifestations of the disease in our Iowa study areas are all but restricted most of the time to certain special tracts of marsh or stream. In thinking over the long-term case histories of these foci of infection, I keep comparing them with our case histories of strategic habitats for the muskrats themselves, or with strategic habitats for bobwhites, pheasants, horned owls, minks, rabbits, foxes, and other higher vertebrates, or with those kinds of strategic habitats that Uvarov[4] and later authors call areas of permanent occupation for grasshoppers and locusts.

When we look for further parallels between population behavior of the muskrat disease, of the muskrats, of the bobwhites, the pheasants, the grasshoppers, we may often find them if we consider overflows from strategic habitats. The muskrat disease, if it spreads from a focus of infection into an adjacent part of a marsh having a dense contiguous population of the host animals, may virtually depopulate a large tract of its muskrats in a few weeks; but, when the dying subsides and the depopulated tract begins to draw in newcomers, about the only places where we may expect renewed flaring-up of the disease will usually be at or near the old foci of infection. At the risk of minor inaccuracies, we may say that the contagion seems to withdraw into its own areas of permanent occupation—at any rate, to these places that retain sufficient infectiousness over the years to be reservoirs.

When many animals overflow their strategic habitats, it may be only into places nearby or into places perhaps not differing greatly from the strategic habitats, or it may be into strange and inhospitable places. Muskrats of overpopulated desert marshes may engage in fatal movements into the surrounding desert in ways reminiscent of the famous migrations of Scandinavian lemmings into the sea. Overflows of muskrats often may be not very dissimilar to the overflowing of certain grasshoppers and locusts from their breeding grounds, the special aspects of the latter movements notwithstanding.[5] Pepper[6], in comparing thresholds of security and associated phenomena shown by our Iowa muskrats with what he had been seeing in Montana grasshoppers, brought out similarities that look very suggestive of common denominators in the population behavior of even such distantly related forms.

The main point that I would make here is that, whether a species is intrenched in the best of habitats or is trying to live where it really does not belong, whether it is highly versatile or has the most specialized of adaptations, the role of competition in its population dynamics may still be more difficult to appraise than may at first be apparent. To distinguish between cause-and-effect relationships and the merely incidental may require, for one thing, less emphasis upon what seems obvious and more emphasis upon trends indirectly suggested by long-term data.

Let us, for the time being, go on to other subject matter notable for the ease with which it may be misappraised.

Predation and Territoriality

Predation may have its superficial simplicities. It may look as simple as one animal killing and eating another animal. When the victim is dead, it is dead, and the species to which it belongs has one less living individual. From here, it is possible to make many speculations about the effects of predation on population, especially on the theme of how high the population levels of prey species would go were it not for predators preying upon them. It is frequently assumed that a predatory species exerts a limiting influence on a prey population about in proportion to the number of prey individuals it kills.

Predation, assuredly, can depress a prey population. Under special conditions, the impacts of a predator on its prey can be so severe that whole populations of a vulnerable prey species are wiped out. Predatory man has demonstrated this over and over again. On the other hand, the accrued evidence indicates that much predation may operate in an incidental fashion rather than as a true population depressant.[7] The distinction to be kept in mind is that predation centering on essentially doomed surpluses or wastage parts of prey populations is in a different category from predation that cuts right into a prey population and results in the prey's reaching or maintaining a significantly lower level than it would if it did not suffer such predation.

In analyses of the population dynamics of animals, we must not ignore the role of social intolerance as a limiting factor. Social intolerance may or may not be tied up with food supply or other of the more obvious needs of a population at a given time. The more dominant types of intolerance include those that we think of as territorial, even when habitat resources may appear to be only slightly utilized by the individuals claiming possession.

Territoriality is variously defined in the literature, but the definition of a territory as any defended area is one of the most acceptable.[8] In its manifestations, territoriality varies greatly with the species and the circumstances. It is not lacking among invertebrates and lower vertebrates, although, in those groups, its intensity may be weak, or we may have to strain a bit to apply the label of territoriality to certain intolerances. Nor are the more pronounced forms of territoriality to be perceived among all higher vertebrates. Still, the higher vertebrates include the most patently territorial groups of animals and those patently the most nearly self-limiting.

Self-limitation is about what strong territoriality adds up to in population dynamics. It allows *Lebensraum* for about so many animals of one or, sometimes, a combination of species at a given time and place. Compared with the basic role of territoriality in the population of many higher vertebrates, predation enters in as a secondary phenomenon and as one having, in more instances than are usually recognized, slight if any real depressive influence on prey populations—even when the predation may be severe in terms of numbers or proportions of the prey species killed by predators.

When a strongly territorial species fills up its habitat as much as the species will itself tolerate, and the surplus individuals cannot live anywhere else, the species may maintain its numbers with a high degree of independence of variations in kinds and numbers of predatory enemies. The muskrat in the north-central United States illustrates this sort of relationship and we may see, for this species, that a great deal of the frequently conspicuous and severe interspecific predation does not really count.[7]

If surplus individuals excluded from the better territorial sites can live in the less attractive places in the absence of but not in the presence of certain predatory enemies, the resulting predation may operate to some extent as a population depressant in the inferior habitats. This situation may be not uncommon when the prey species is one showing versatile behavior.

Some higher vertebrates may be sufficiently tolerant of crowding to increase up to the limits of their food supply in the absence of significant predation. North American deer are among the better known examples[9], but, on the basis of careful work on California deer herds[10], it would appear that the deer population is primarily determined by quality of habitat and that predators do little more than to remove the annual surplus. In many areas, striking increases in numbers of deer have been correlated with artificial reduction of the more efficient deer-killing predators. The deer populations have then built up to temporary levels above the carrying capacity of the land, with biological repercussions coming later, as from starvation or damage to the habitat. While territoriality exists for the deer and represents, for them, a self-limiting tendency, it does not limit enough to leave deer populations in quite the same category of independence from influence by predation that follows, for example, from the stronger self-limitation of the north-central muskrats.

It is quite to be expected that some animal species will show greater tendencies toward overpopulation, overuse of resources followed by population collapses, and, on occasion, by net depressions of population levels through predation, than do our more strictly self-limited species. The less that strong territoriality or other self-limitation enters population equations, the more something else must do the limiting.

Competition, Predation, Compensations, and Models

The quest for generalities in the population behavior of organisms has led to a substantial amount of laboratory experimentation.[11] Oversimplifications and artificialities need not detract very much from the interest and value of these experiments as long as the experimental results are not misapplied to relationships that are far more complex. In working with field problems, we may think of the better conceived laboratory experiments with populations as suggesting rules of order that we ought to know something about before we go on to consider the interplays, interruptions, deflections, and successions that characterize free-living populations.

Based either on experimentation or on purely theoretical grounds, many efforts have been made to express population relationships mathematically. I make no pretense of being able to examine the resulting mathematical treatments with any notable competence, but I have recognized that those of Nicholson[12] and Cole[13] seem to come the closest to depicting relationships that I, personally, have observed in nature—particularly the mathematical expressions of thresholds of security, overflows from favorable into unfavorable habitats, and compensatory trends.

Ideally, perhaps, everything that happens should be expressible mathematically, but, in the matter of population equations, I would say that the mathematicians have some distance to go. They have an imposing array of analytic pitfalls to avoid, and some of my mathematician friends confess that they do not see how anyone is ever going to put down on paper true-to-life mathematical expressions of the sorts of population relationships that are commonplace among higher vertebrates. But the potentialities of mathematics as an analytic tool in population studies should be far from exhausted at the present time. What I am stating here is not intended to discourage mathematicians from going ahead with any promising approaches that they might have. My purpose is only to emphasize that, to be true to life, the mathematical expression of a population equation must not assume constancies that are not constant or more randomness than exists, and that it must not fail to take into minimal account the capacities for adjustments that living species have acquired during the millions of years that they have lived their lives in their own ways.

Elton's[14] essay on animal community patterns emphasizes the grouping of populations around centers, in contrast to mathematical theories that treat populations as if they are randomly interspersed over major areas. Differences in soil types, warmth, moisture, plant successions, the location of a carcass or a rotten log, the segregation into habitat niches, and so forth, may leave scant uniformity in the natural distribution of a species and thus reduce the prospects for finding true-to-life formulas that apply to the more complex situations.

Let us consider the way in which the hemorrhagic disease may kill muskrats on a marsh when the muskrats are so few in number as to be barely present and when, according to some mathematical models, we should hardly expect continued dying. In nature, we can have the *entire* local population dying and newcomers dying about as fast as they come in. The reasons for these high mortality rates at times of very low overall population densities on the marsh are, in their gross aspects, quite plain—they chiefly reflect the fact that the deadlier foci of infection may also be among the more attractive places for muskrats on a marsh. The more that perfectly normal newcomers pick out and rehabilitate deadly burrow systems, the more die there, and the deadlier the burrow systems become over the years, until certain tracts of marsh may become all but uninhabitable for muskrats for years at a stretch. Under these circumstances, I cannot see that so very much of randomness is left in the population equations of either the hemorrhagic disease or its muskrat hosts.

Some remarkably definite patterns are shown by case histories of free-living wild populations, but it can be tricky to represent these in mathematical formulas. There can be much compensating in a population equation, or, in other words, automatic letting out and taking up of slack. Granted that many species can be sensitive to environmental changes of slight amplitude, we do have many populations maintained for long periods of time at notably uniform levels, more or less irrespective of a great many variations in breeding and mortality rates and in the weather, food supply, and other of what we consider ordinary environmental factors.[7,15]

The modern work with higher vertebrates perhaps illustrates as well as any how compensations operate, and, in order to remain within the philosophic bounds of personal familiarity, I shall draw my concluding examples from the results of our investigations of Iowa muskrats.[16] We find in our data on muskrats plenty of evidence of conformity to patterns that are definite enough to be expressible by segments of sigmoid curves[17], but which mean balancing and counterbalancing in population equations. The classical Darwinian view of the balance of nature is misleading with reference to population dynamics of the muskrat because it is so apt to put nature's resiliences and rigidities in the wrong places.

Instead of a population equation in which the end product varies directly and matter-of-factly and in an above-board manner according to variations in reproductive and mortality rates, we have end products that often look more or less predetermined. The latter may be a postbreeding population of around 400 muskrats on a 270-acre marsh, or 9000 muskrats on 1000 acres elsewhere, or some other comparatively definite number for another area. Or, when populations are well below saturation levels for an area, the annual rates of gain may conform to a sliding scale of values. When the end products of population equations show pronounced tendencies toward stability or conformation to patterns, the other parts of the equations are necessarily the parts in which adjustments occur whenever changes in reproductive or mortality rates would tend to disturb equilibria.

Although larger or smaller proportions of young muskrats may die from the attentions of predatory enemies or from weather vicissitudes or from attacks of other muskrats in one year than in another year, the population consequences of specific mortality factors seldom carry through long enough to affect appreciably the end products of our population equations. This, in particular, represents a departure from the Darwinian view. Instead of every agency of mortality each depressing the end product in proportion to the number of animals it kills, we have a lot of nullification of what we conventionally regard as limiting factors. Not only do we have natural substituting of one factor for another, but mortality may also precipitate natural population responses that tend to offset it.

Let us consider mink predation and the way it fits into our equations for muskrats insofar as this has been most intensively studied on a long-term basis.[18] Minks and muskrats may be closely associated in North American wetlands, and the minks are enterprising and able hunters that kill and eat muskrats about wherever they can. In some regions, they kill more muskrats than all other non-human predators combined. But, in analysis, mink predation on muskrats of the north-central United States turns out to be virtually centered on overproduced young muskrats, upon ailing and battered individuals of all ages, and upon those generally comprising the wastage animals of a population. The victims need not be manifestly unfit. Insecurity of position can impose as deadly a handicap on an animal in normal physical condition as can the sluggishness or weakness of an animal that is physically subnormal.

Particularly worth emphasizing in appraisals of net population effects of agencies of mortality is the evidence that the broad categories of muskrats most likely to be preyed upon by predatory vertebrates—excluding man—have poor life expectancies, anyway. They are the likeliest candidates for elimination through one agency or another, whether the minks are abundant, scarce, or absent, or whether the other common muskrat predators are abundant, scarce, or absent. In the frittering away of doomed surpluses, or of parts of populations doomed because of emergencies, it seems to make so little difference in the end what the specific agencies of mortality may be that I rarely feel sure of the logical propriety of ascribing true degressive influence to any one agency. Of what demonstrable population significance is any agency of mortality as long as much the same patterns in population trends continue to show up, seemingly irrespective of whether that agency operates or not?

If the effects of an agency are severe enough—if a deadly epizootic, a hurricane, or a drouth brings about a cataclysm for the muskrats over an immense area—the mortality can be sufficient to depress a population, but there still may be compensation. One of the commonest ways by which extraordinary losses are offset naturally is by accelerated reproduction.

The reproductive activities of our Iowa muskrats have an obviously close connection with psychological changes. Adult females giving birth to their usual maxima of four litters during a breeding season are typically animals living at low-to-moderate densities in a strong environment or those losing large proportions of their earlyborn young. On the other hand, those subject to the damping effects of crowding past their toleration limits just quit breeding early in the season after giving birth to a litter or two. As long as relief from the inhibiting effects of overcrowding remains such a stimulus to prolonged, late-season breeding—as long as heavy mortality among the early-born young, or special success of the early-born in keeping out of the way of intolerant elders, or the chance underpopulation of habitats may result in doubling the number born per adult female—the need for allowing for compensations in our pencil-and-paper figuring would not appear to be trifling. As long as the end product of a population equation remains unchanged, with reproductive and mortality rates serving as functions of each other in the ways indicated, more reproduction means more mortality, and vice versa.

In short, throughout any true-to-life equation representing population dynamics of the muskrat, there should be compensation after compensation, although it does not follow that all of the adjustments involved must be completely compensatory. Perhaps few of them are completely compensatory, but neither does it follow, if any one agency kills half of the muskrats during the breeding and rearing months, that relief from that agency will double the number of muskrats alive after the breeding and rearing months, nor does it follow that the appearance of a new and deadly agency that kills half of the muskrats must thereby reduce the end product of a population equation by half.

Solomon[15], in his review paper on natural control of animal populations, refers to the compensation principle as being of general applicability. This has not only been discussed in regard to vertebrate populations[7], but Nicholson and H. S. Smith, the entomologists, also have been expressing similar views for many years. In the literature on population, the idea of populations being to some extent self-controlled is therefore nothing wholly new. Still, the singular importance of considering automatic and compensatory adjustments in population dynamics is far too often neglected even in scholarly thinking, and a realistic approach in population studies calls for more attention to things that do not always work out with the inexorable precision that data tabulations might seem to imply.

REFERENCES and NOTES

1. This article is Journal Paper No. J-2854 of the Iowa Agricultural Experiment Station, project No. 1217, and it is also a contribution from the Iowa Cooperative Wildlife Research Unit, in which the U.S. Fish and Wildlife Service, Iowa State College, the Iowa State Conservation Commission, and the Wildlife Management Institute cooperate.
2. G. SVÄRDSON, *Oikos* 1, 157 (1949).
3. T. T. McCABE and B. D. BLANCHARD, *Three Species of Peromyscus* (Rood Associates, Santa Barbara, Calif., 1950).
4. B. P. UVAROV, *Locusts and Grasshoppers: a Handbook for their Study and Control* (Imperial Bureau of Entomology, London, 1928).

5. K. H. L. KEY, *Quart. Rev. Biol.* 25, 363 (1950).
6. J. H. PEPPER, *J. Econ. Entomol.* 48, 451 (1955).
7. P. L. ERRINGTON, *Quart. Rev. Biol.* 21, 144 (1946).
8. M. M. NICE, *Am. Midland Naturalist* 26, 441 (1941).
9. A. LEOPOLD, L. K. SOWLS, D. L. SPENCER, *J. Wildlife Management* 11, 162 (1947).
10. W. N. LONGHURST, A. S. LEOPOLD, R. F. DASMANN, "A Survey of California deer herds, their ranges and management problems" *Game Bull.* 6 (Calif. Dept. Fish and Game, San Francisco, 1952).
11. W. C. ALLEE *et al., Principles of Animal Ecology* (Saunders, Philadelphia, 1949): H. G. ANDREWARTHA and L. C. BIRCH, *The Distribution and Abundance of Animals* (Univ. of Chicago Press, Chicago, 1954).
12. A. J. NICHOLSON, *Australian J. Zool.* 2, 9 (1954).
13. L. C. COLE, *Quart. Rev. Biol.* 29, 102 (1954).
14. C. ELTON, *J. Ecol.* 37, 1 (1949).
15. N. E. SOLOMON, *J. Animal Ecol.* 18, 1 (1949).
16. P. L. ERRINGTON, *Am. Naturalist* 85, 273 (1951).
17. _____, *J. Wildlife Management* 18, 66 (1954).
18. _____, *Ecol. Monogr.* 24, 377 (1954).

EFFECTS OF WOLF PREDATION (1970)
L. David Mech

Predation long has held the interest of man; yet we understand little of the ecology of predation. Only during recent years has significant quantitative information been obtained concerning the role of predators in natural communities. L. D. Mech reviews current knowledge and hypotheses relevant to the ecological significance of wolf predation. Interaction between predator and prey is an important aspect of the population dynamics of both.

The interactions among members of the living community are so complex that a change at any point in the system can cause profound effects throughout the community. Obviously any animal that preys on others will bring about changes. Since the wolf is the dominant nonhuman predator on large animals in the Northern Hemisphere, it could be expected to exert especially strong influences. Some ideas about the nature of the wolf's effects can even be deduced.

Measuring the extent of the influences and proving that they were caused by the wolf is much more difficult. For example, one chain of events that might result from wolf predation on a moose follows: (1) where the moose falls, its blood, hair, bones, and stomach contents slowly disintegrate and add their minerals and humus to the soil, (2) as a result, the general area of the kill becomes more fertile and eventually supports a lush stand of small herbs and shrubs, (3) a litter of snowshoe hares pays frequent visits to the area to feed on the nutritious plants, (4) the presence of the hares draws foxes and other predators, and incidentally these remove many of the mice that live nearby, (5) a weasel that used to hunt these mice then shifts its activities to another area, and in doing so falls prey to an owl.

The above example could go on and on forever. The "chain" is endless and is interlinked with many others that have resulted from other effects of the same act of predation and from other unrelated events. Similar sequences of effects would result from the wolf's use of certain trails, its deposition of feces, and from various other activities. Although the study of the indirect effects of wolf predation would be fascinating, it is far too complex a subject to attempt to analyze in detail here.

At the present about all that can be discussed are certain occurrences, or changes in the living community, that are thought to be direct results of wolf predation. These effects fall into four groups: (1) the culling of inferior prey, (2) the control or partial control of prey populations, (3) the stimulation of productivity in herds of prey, and (4) the feeding of scavenging animals.

The "Sanitation Effect"

The culling of biologically inferior individuals from a population has been called the "sanitation effect" of predation. In Chapter VIII it was shown that wolf predation generally is selective, resulting in the removal of young, old, and otherwise inferior animals from prey populations.

The benefits that come from the culling out of certain segments of a herd are not well defined for the most part. The main exception to this generalization is in the case of diseased animals being removed from the herd. It is easy to see how the continued culling of individuals with contagious diseases could help prevent the diseases from spreading through the entire population.

A good example of this effect was provided by Fuller (1966:36) in his study of bison in Wood Buffalo National Park: "An adult male was autopsied on July 6, 1951. That animal had been seen alive the previous day when it appeared too weak to rise to its feet as a vehicle passed nearby. It had probably been dead less than 24 hours when examined, but most of the abdominal viscera had been removed by wolves. The autopsy showed retropharyngeal glands with tubercular lesions larger than oranges, lung lesions, and 'grapes' on the pleura, sufficient evidence on which to base a diagnosis of advanced generalized tuberculosis. That animal must have been a menace to any that came in contact with it. The wolves had actually performed a service in herd sanitation when they ended its career."

No doubt similar "services" are carried out every day throughout the wolf's range, for the diseases of hoofed animals are numerous. Internal and external parasites also plague the prey of the wolf, so in some cases wolf predation might help reduce their numbers by culling out the individuals carrying them. On the other hand, certain parasites such as the hydatid tapeworm discussed in the previous chapter are actually spread by the wolf when that animal eats prey infected with the larval stages. The larvae become adults in the wolf, and their eggs are expelled with the wolf's feces; when prey swallow vegetation or water contaminated with these eggs, the animals may contract the parasite and complete the cycle.

Other effects of differential predation on big game are less obvious. Wounded, injured, crippled, or old animals may be of little harm to the herd, so the only effect their removal might have is to relieve whatever misery they might experience.

If could be argued, however, that old, diseased, or injured animals are of little detriment to a herd as individuals but that as a group they form an inefficient part of the population. Perhaps such animals are less effective reproducers. Fuller found that only one-third of the aged bison in Wood Buffalo Park bred, compared to 100% of the younger adults. If this holds true for other species and for sick and injured animals, this class would be contributing little to the herd, yet would be using just as much, if not more, food, space, and cover as the effective reproducers. Their presence in the herd, therefore, might be of some disadvantage to the truly prime individuals, and their removal might have some long-range benefits.

The role of the wolf in the development and maintenance of various physical and behavioral traits in its prey species is also open to speculation. According to the principles of natural selection, species evolve as a result of environmental forces that tend to eliminate most quickly the individuals least adapted to living in a given environment. In the long run, this selective process allows the best adapted individuals to live longer and thus produce greater numbers of offspring with their more favorable traits.

Any environmental forces that affect the survival of a living thing would influence the development of the species to which it belongs. Because the wolf and its ancestors have long exerted such a direct effect on the survival of great numbers of prey, there can be no doubt that wolf predation has helped modify several prey species. Probably those traits most closely related to detection of danger, to defense, and to escape would be most affected.

It is obvious that if a genetic strain of caribou were to arise that has superior leg musculature, for instance, individuals with this trait would tend to survive longer and produce more offspring (assuming that such musculature had no disadvantages). No doubt the same is true for a strain that possesses superior senses. One would expect then that in most species of the wolf's prey increased alertness and running speed would be a direct result of millions of years of wolf predation. The defense formation of musk-oxen, the size and strength of bison and moose, the fleetness of deer, and the nimbleness and agility of mountain sheep probably developed in this way. In an informative discussion of the wolf's effect on the natural selection of Dall sheep, Murie (1944: 127) stated the additional possibility that "as an evolutionary force the wolf may function most effectively by causing the sheep to dwell in a rocky habitat."

An interesting contrast that might show the effects of the wolf on the defensive traits of its prey species is the comparison between the ease with which domestic animals are killed and the difficulty with which wild creatures are captured. It is reasonable to suggest that the difference results from the lack of continued predation pressure on domestic species, pressure that has ensured the persistence of traits such as alertness and fleetness in wild animals.

In addition to helping maintain the protective properties of the prey species, wolf predation probably would also help eliminate any tendencies toward congenital abnormalities or proneness to diseases and accidents. For example, any individual with shortened or missing limbs or incomplete heart valves would fall easy prey to a wolf pack. Any animal with low resistance to diseases or parasites, or any ill-co-ordinated creature would quickly be weeded out of the population.

Predation would exert its strongest selective effect in removing immature members of a herd. Any inferior animals killed before they breed would, of course, fail completely to pass their traits on to others. In this respect it is significant that such high percentages of prey killed by wolves are immature. Evidently a fairly thorough "screening" takes place during the prey animal's first year, because once an individual lives through that period its chances of dying from predation are very low until it grows old. Thus those prey that do survive their first year stand a much greater chance of passing their traits on to offspring and of furthering the process of the "survival of the fittest."

Control of Prey Populations

The field of interest known as "predator-prey relations" involves the study of the interactions between a great range of diverse predatory animals and their even more diverse prey. Some students of the subject believe that the principles that apply to the relations between one species of predator and its prey will apply to the relations between all species of

179

predators and their prey.

This view may hold true for some extremely general principles. However, the simple, unqualified question of whether or not predators control the numbers of their prey cannot, in my opinion, be covered by any broad generality. Rather, because of the extreme diversity of predators and prey, the question can only logically be asked of a given species of predator preying on a given species of prey under certain specified conditions.

Whether or not robins control earthworm populations has little relation to the question of whether or not wolves control deer numbers. (Indeed, whether or not wolves control deer numbers may have little relation to the question of the influence of wolves on caribou herds.) Because of this, I have made no attempt to discuss any other predator-prey relations than those involving the wolf.

The subject of population control itself is extremely complex and can only be treated superficially here, except as it applies to the wolf. The question of whether or not a specific mortality factor is controlling a population is especially confusing. At first glance it would seem that any factor causing death to even a single animal would be helping to control the population. However, when one finds that upon removing a known mortality factor no increase in population results, the plot thickens. Such a situation can arise because of the effects of a phenomenon known as "compensation" (Errington, 1946).

Compensation of mortality factors can be defined as the process in which one or more mortality factors increase in effect as the effect of another decreases. Complete compensation would take place when, for example, one of two mortality factors on a population was removed and the other then accounted for the same amount of mortality as both together did before. If the remaining factor accounted for more mortality than it did before the removal of the other, but less than the total of the two, this would be partial compensation.

In most, if not all, natural populations there are several mortality factors, and each usually is at least partly compensatory. For example, in a deer herd that has been greatly reduced by disease, few deer will die from other factors. But, if the disease is wiped out and the herd increases, more deer will be killed by such factors as hunting pressure and starvation. As Paul Errington (1967: 229) explained compensation, "The death of one individual may mean little more than improving the chances for living of another one."

A second element confusing the problem is the fact that some mortality factors are relatively light, such as accidents, whereas others are very important, such as hunting. A factor like disease may be of little consequence in a certain year or herd, yet in another herd or at some other time it may almost wipe out a population.

Still another problem that adds confusion is the fact that different mortality factors may become important at various population levels. For instance, starvation does not often kill many deer until the herd has built up to an unusually high level. This is frequently true with disease also.

In trying to discover how much effect any mortality factor has in controlling a population, one must consider all these problems. In addition, when trying to generalize about the role of wolf predation in population control, there are at least three other factors to be considered: (1) the extreme differences in individual and population characteristics of the various species of wolf prey, (2) the variation in prey-predator ratios with different prey species and with the same species in different areas, and (3) possible difference between the amount of food wolves must consume in order to survive and what they might consume if prey were more easily obtained.

Regarding the first factor, it is obvious that wolf predation might produce different effects on different populations that vary in such important aspects as density and reproductive potential. For example, to control a herd of deer, which may reach a density of thirty or more per square mile, many more animals would have to be killed than would be necessary to control a herd of moose, which may occur in a density of less than one moose per square mile. In addition, members of some species such as deer may bear young when only one year old and eventually may produce twins or triplets. A much higher mortality rate would be required to control such animals than to control bison, for instance, which may not breed until three or four years old and which then produce only one calf per year.

Another factor that would influence the degree of control among various species of the wolf's prey is size. This is because wolves would have to kill fewer large animals to obtain their food requirements than they would smaller ones. For example, on the average it would take four or five deer to supply as much food as one bison. This size factor, however, is at least partly compensated for by the fact that larger animals generally occur in lower densities.

The second major consideration that must be made in trying to generalize about the effects of wolf predation on population control is the relative prey-predator ratios in various populations. Reported prey-predator ratios have varied from roughly thirty moose per wolf on Isle Royale to three or four hundred head of big game (mule deer, elk, moose, caribou, mountain sheep, and mountain goats) per wolf in Jasper Park, Alberta. Further, the weight of the prey must also be considered. A ratio of thirty moose per wolf, for instance, may be similar in weight to a ratio of 150 deer per wolf.

The prey-predator ratio could even be important in influencing the effect of wolf predation on different populations of the same species of prey. Thus wolves might exert a much stronger control when their density is high and the prey density is low than in situations where the wolf density is low and the prey density is high.

The third factor to consider in examining the wolf's role in the control of any population is the possible latitude in the amount of food consumed by the wolf. As discussed in Chapter VI, the apparent food consumption rate for wolves in the wild may be more than twice the rate required for even very active wolves in captivity. It appears from this that wolves in the wild may eat more food than actually necessary when it is available; when prey is more difficult to obtain, they may be able to survive on much

181

less food than usual. This is just speculation, but the possibility must be considered.

All the above factors are discussed to show how difficult it is to tell whether or not wolves control their prey populations. Familiarity with these factors should also prevent the error of generalizing about this subject on the basis of information from a single population. In other words, if wolves were shown to be controlling caribou on a certain part of the tundra, this would not necessarily mean that they control the deer population in Michigan.

In philosophizing about the controlling effect of wolves on their prey, one is also faced with the fact that under primitive conditions there probably was no single factor that was consistently so important in big-game mortality as wolf predation was. Because of this, the wolf would be the prime suspect in a search for the controlling factor on big-game herds. However, several studies to be discussed below have indicated that wolf predation is not controlling all big-game herds. In fact, big game in numerous areas, with or without wolves, appear to be limited mainly by a lack of food at present.

For several biological reasons, starvation seems to be a very unnatural type of control on any population, and recently Pimlott has outlined a theory to explain the existing situation. In an article discussing the subject of wolf control on big-game herds, he wrote the following (Pimlott, 1967b: 275): "The question of whether or not wolves constitute an effective limiting factor on ungulates, and particularly on deer, moose, and caribou, is one that has only been partially answered. In considering the population dynamics of some big-game species, deer and moose in particular, the question arises, as to why intrinsic mechanisms of population control have not evolved to prevent them from increasing beyond the sustaining level of their food supply. It seems reasonable to postulate that it may be because they have had very efficient predators, and the forces of selection have kept them busy evolving ways and means not of limiting their own numbers but of keeping abreast of mortality factors.

"Contemporary biologists often have a distorted viewpoint about the interrelationships of ungulates and their predators. We live in an age when there is a great imbalance in the environments inhabited by many of the ungulates. In the case of deer and moose the environmental changes, or disturbances, have been favorable and populations are probably higher than they have ever been. Under such circumstances it is not much wonder that we have been inclined to argue that predators do not act as important limiting factors on deer and moose populations. I doubt, however, that it was a very common condition prior to intensive human impact on the environment. In other words, I consider that adaptations between many of the ungulates, particularly those of the forest, and their predators probably evolved in relatively stable environments that could not support prey populations of high density."

If Pimlott's theory is correct, as I believe it is, wolf predation could very well have been the main limiting factor on most, if not all, big game before man so greatly disturbed the habitat. Much of the information about big-game population control, then, might apply not to truly natural situations, but only to artificially high populations. This fact must be kept in mind in the following discussions.

Because of all the complications mentioned above, it is difficult to learn in any particular situation whether wolf predation is merely a contributing cause of mortality or whether it is the primary limiting factor. Two methods have been used by researchers for making this distinction. One is to compare a population being preyed upon by wolves to a similar one that is not. The other method is to compute the percentage of the herd killed by wolves per year and compare this figure with the annual reproduction of the herd. The latter method, unless used along with the first, does not consider the possibility that if wolf numbers were reduced other factors might compensate for predation and bring about the same number of deaths as formerly caused by wolves. Nevertheless, both methods furnish insight into the effect of wolf predation on prey populations.

Cases of control. Situations in which wolves are truly controlling a big-game herd can be defined as those in which removal of the wolves would result in a substantial population increase. In other words, they are cases in which other mortality factors cannot compensate fully for wolf predation.

This is thought to have been the situation in Mount McKinley Park, Alaska, when Murie conducted his study of wolf-Dall sheep relations from 1939 to 1941. During a period before this, there were few or no wolves in the area, and the sheep herd had increased to a point of overpopulation (about 1928). Widespread mortality then took place during the following winters. Eventually wolf numbers grew, however, and during Murie's study, the sheep population remained relatively stable.

In drawing his conclusion that the wolves were controlling the sheep herd, Murie (1944: 141) wrote the following: "The fact that sheep increased rapidly in the absence of wolves and have not increased during their presence strongly indicates that the wolves have been the factor preventing the sheep from increasing. I am fully aware how frequently 'obvious conclusions' are wrong, especially in prey-predator relationships. However, I found no other factor which seemed sufficiently operative to hold the sheep numbers in check. It seems, therefore, that the wolves are the controlling influence."

The prey-predator ratio in this situation was twenty-five to thirty-seven sheep (average weight about 200 pounds) per wolf, or 5000 to 7400 pounds of prey per wolf. A complicating factor is that these same wolves also preyed upon caribou. Nevertheless, the fact that the prey-predator ratio is so low compared to those from most other areas tends to make up for the fact that the wolves were also taking other kinds of prey.

The second area in which wolves were found to be controlling the numbers of their prey is Isle Royale National Park in Lake Superior (Mech, 1966a). There the prey-predator ratio is about thirty moose (averaging about 800 pounds each) per wolf, or approximately 24,000 pounds of moose per wolf. The 210-square-mile island supports at least 600 moose in late winter. The annual calf crop is calculated at approximately 225 animals, but only about eighty-five of these survive their first year and are added to the herd of adults. The wolf population, which has averaged about twenty-three animals each winter from 1959 through 1966, kills a calculated 140 calves and eighty-three adults per year. Comparison of these figures shows that the annual production of the moose herd and the annual kill by wolves are about the same and that therefore the wolves are taking enough moose to control the herd.

(Since publication of the above figures for the Isle Royale moose herd, Jordan *et al.,* in a 1967 article on the Isle Royale wolves mentioned incidentally that Jordan had estimated the moose population at 800 to 1000 animals. However, no documentation was given for these figures, nor was the type of sampling and censusing procedure described. Because of this and because moose censuses are usually thought to give gross estimates only, there is as yet little reason to believe that the size of the Isle Royale moose herd has changed between the times the two censuses were taken, 1960 and 1966.)

A stronger line of evidence that wolves are controlling the Isle Royale moose comes from the history of the herd. Moose have lived on the island for most of this century, but wolves did not arrive there until about 1949. Before that time, the moose herd increased to an estimated 1000 to 3000 animals in the early 1930s (Murie, 1934), decreased drastically through disease and starvation a few years later (Hickie, 1936), then built up and suffered starvation again in the late 1940s (Krefting, 1951). However, since the wolves arrived, moose numbers have been lower than they were previously, the herd has remained relatively stable, and the browse has begun to recover.

In Algonquin Provincial Park, Ontario, it also appears that wolves are controlling their prey population, in this case deer. Pimlott, using wolf food-consumption figures modified from the Isle Royale studies, calculated that it would require a deer density of about ten per square mile with an annual productivity of 37% to support a wolf population of one per ten square miles, which is the estimated wolf density in the park. If this is true, it also means that with these population densities wolves would be controlling the deer herd. According to Pimlott (1967b: 274), "The data on the deer population in Algonquin Park suggest a density of 10 to 15 per square mile, or a ratio of wolf to deer of between 1:100 and 1:150. The deer are primary prey of the wolves and predation may have been important in preventing major irruptions such as those that have occurred in many deer ranges where wolves are absent. . . ."

The prey-predator ratios mentioned by Pimlott would convert to about 15,000 to 22,500 pounds of deer per wolf, assuming average adult deer weights to be about 150 pounds.

In another wolf-deer study, it was concluded that the combination of wolf predation and human hunting was controlling the deer population in certain sections of Minnesota, with wolves accounting for about two-thirds of the control. The prey-predator ratio in this area was about 153 deer (approximately 23,000 pounds) per wolf, as calculated from figures by Stenlund (1955). It is interesting that this ratio is somewhat higher than that estimated by Pimlott to be the highest in which wolves alone could exert control.

Other areas in which wolves are thought to be limiting their prey are

184

certain of the islands in southeast Alaska. There the wolves' main prey is the black-tailed deer. Klein and Olson (1960), without giving documentation, stated that on wolf-free islands in that area overpopulation of deer was evident, whereas on wolf-inhabited islands winter mortality of deer was light and winter ranges were in better condition. In addition, when thirty-square-mile Coronation Island was stocked with four wolves, the deer population dropped over a period of four years (Merriam, 1964). Of course this latter situation was highly unnatural in that just the original stocking of wolves was at a higher density than has ever been reported for natural populations.

Wherever wolves are controlling the numbers of their prey, they do so primarily by removing the young from the herd. Murie considered that the loss of lamb and yearling sheep to wolves was the most important factor in the control of the Dall sheep population in Mount McKinley Park. On Isle Royale, an estimated 62% or more of the moose killed by wolves throughout the year were calves, and in Algonquin Park, Pimlott considered that fawns composed about 55% of the deer killed per year. It is only logical that mortality of young would have the most influence in population control by wolves because (1) this age class is almost always by far the largest in the population and thus could cause a great increase in any herd if not trimmed down, and (2) with young animals, many more individuals would have to be killed to fulfill the wolf's food requirements because of the great size difference between young and adults.

A second generalization that can be made from the above studies is that the highest prey-predator ratio in which control was thought to have occurred was the 24,000 pounds of living prey per wolf found on Isle Royale. Of course, if wolves were to eat only a small part of each prey animal and therefore were to kill many more individuals than they actually required, they could control populations with much larger prey-predator ratios. However, the very fact that wolves do not seem to limit populations with higher ratios, as discussed below, suggests that they probably do not often kill more than they eat.

Cases of noncontrol. In the Rocky Mountains of Canada, from 1943 to 1946, Jasper National Park supported a wolf population of about one wolf per ten square miles of winter range. Three other parks in the same general region contained almost no wolves. A study by Cowan (1947: 147) of big game in both areas revealed that "there is no discernible significant difference in the survival of young, or in the sex ratios within the two groups." Cowan concluded that wolves were not controlling the big-game herds. The prey-predator ratio in these parks was three to four hundred head of big game (bighorn sheep, elk, moose, deer, mountain goat, and caribou) per wolf. Assuming an average weight of all these species to be about three hundred pounds, the prey-predator ratio would be 90,000 to 120,000 pounds of prey per wolf.

During a study of deer populations in a wolf-inhabited area and a wolf-free area of Wisconsin, the same conclusion was reached. D. Q. Thompson (1952: 438) wrote the following: "The similarity in deer population behavior on the Oneida wolf range and the wolf-free range agrees with the inference drawn from range conditions within the wolf area; namely,

185

that the timber wolves at present densities did not prevent an overpopulation of deer from developing in the past two decades. Browse tallies and deer-yard inspections in the wolf range in Iron County reveal very similar conditions." The wolf density was about one animal per thirty-five square miles, and over a six-year period the density of deer increased from about ten to thirty per square mile on both wolf-inhabited and wolf-free areas. At just the lower deer density, the prey-predator ratio was about 350 deer (or 52,500 pounds) per wolf.

A third study from which the conclusion was drawn that wolves were not controlling the numbers of their prey was the caribou investigation in the Northwest Territories of Canada. Banfield (1954: 51) stated that in this region "the annual loss from wolf predation is probably not greater than 5 per cent of the total population, even during periods of wolf abundance." If this is true, wolves cannot be controlling the population because the annual reproduction of caribou is much greater than 5%. The wolf population in this area is estimated at about 8,000 animals (Kelsall, 1957), and the caribou herd at 670,000 (Banfield, 1954). This would be a prey-predator ratio of eighty-four caribou (or about 25,000 pounds) per wolf, by far the lowest ratio reported in a situation where wolves are *not* thought to be controlling their prey.

However, it is possible that the estimated number of wolves in this area is too high. Evidence that this might be the case comes from the wolf-control figures reported by Kelsall (1968). Control of the wolf population appeared to have been brought about after some 2000 wolves per year were taken. It was shown in Chapter II that over 50% of a winter population of wolves must be killed each year to effect control of the population. This would suggest that the number of wolves in the Northwest Territories when control was being applied was closer to 4000 than to 8000. If this is so, then the prey-predator ratio would be about 50,000 pounds of caribou per wolf.

Summarizing the results of the above studies, one finds that definite control by wolves is reported at prey-predator ratios of 7400 pounds; 15,000 to 22,500 pounds; and 24,000 pounds of prey per wolf; that about two-thirds control by wolves is reported at an estimated prey-predator ratio of approximately 23,000 pounds per wolf, and that little or no controlling influence is reported at ratios of 25,000 to 50,000; 52,500; and 90,000 to 120,000 pounds of prey per wolf.

Although most of these figures are rough, the tentative conclusion seems justified that wolf predation is the major controlling mortality factor where prey-predator ratios are 24,000 pounds of prey per wolf or less, but that at higher ratios wolf predation cannot keep up with annual reproduction; it then becomes only one of several other contributing mortality factors and cannot be considered a primary controlling influence.

Stimulation of Productivity in Prey

Big-game herds that have an adequate food supply and that include a minimum of old, sick, and debilitated individuals would be expected to reproduce the most vigorously. Unfortunately, few situations exist in which production figures for a big-game population that is heavily cropped by wolves can be compared with those from a similar population without wolf predation. The only place where such a comparison has been made so far is Isle Royale. Because the moose herd inhabited the island for decades before wolves became established, calf production before and after the advent of the wolf can be compared. The only figure for which enough data are available is the twinning rate, but this statistic is probably the most sensitive indicator of productivity in a moose herd. It is derived by taking the number of cows seen with twins as a percentage of the total number of cows seen with singles or twins.

Before wolves arrived on Isle Royale, about 1949, very few twin calves were observed. In 1929 and 1930, Murie (1934) saw only three cows with twins (6%) out of fifty-three cows that he observed with young. However, in 1959, after wolves had cropped the moose herd for ten years, I found a twinning rate of about 38%, and in 1960 approximately 15%. Shelton reported a twinning rate of 38% for the combined summers of 1961, 1962, and 1963 on that island. This rate is much higher than any of those recorded for other moose populations anywhere in North America (Pimlott, 1959).

Although there is no proof that the increased twinning rate of the Isle Royale moose herd is a direct result of wolf predation, no other possible cause has been found. The only known difference between the two eras in the history of the moose herd is wolf predation and the favorable changes it has brought to the herd. Thus it is logical to relate the wolf to the increase in the moose twinning rate.

Probably the high productivity of the Isle Royale moose herd is a direct result of the increased availability of food and/or space caused by the limiting influence of wolf predation. Level of nutrition is known to affect the ovulation rate in deer (Cheatum and Severinghaus, 1950), and it is also believed to influence the twinning rate in moose (Pimlott, 1959). Other authorities have shown that, within limits, the ovulation rate in animals of various other species also increases with the amount of space available to each individual.

Another pathway through which wolf predation might affect the productivity of a herd is by reducing the numbers of the less productive members of a population. In Wood Buffalo Park, Fuller showed that only one-third of the aged bison cows reproduced, whereas 100% of the younger adults bore young. If lowered productivity with old age holds true for other big game, then the wolf's removal of older animals would result in a more efficient production of young in these species also.

Supplying Food for Scavengers

A fourth direct effect of wolf predation is the providing of numerous scavengers with food. Whenever wolves leave a large carcass, either temporarily to go off and rest or permanently upon abandoning the kill, a wealth of food becomes available to smaller birds and mammals. Even a bone well chewed by a wolf can yield much nourishment for such an animal as a chickadee or a Canada jay.

Many scavengers depend a great deal on predators to provide their food, at least at certain times of the year. Some of these animals, such as crows, ravens, jays, and red squirrels, are poorly adapted for killing other animals themselves. Thus it becomes more efficient for them to spend most of their time gleaning bits and pieces of leftovers from the abandoned kills of predators. Other species, such as foxes, coyotes, bobcats, fishers, and eagles, are only part-time scavengers. Most of the time they prey on other animals themselves, but they do rely on scavenging to hold them over while their own prey is scarce or unavailable.

In many regions, including Isle Royale and Minnesota, it is common for ravens to follow wolf packs, wait for them to make a kill, and then feed on it as soon as the wolves leave. During winter a flock of ravens on Isle Royale seems completely dependent on wolves for their food. In Minnesota, most fresh kills are usually covered with two or three dozen ravens unless the wolves are still feeding, and often a bald eagle joins them. Once I saw several ravens, an eagle, and a wolf all sharing a freshly killed deer. Another time, on Isle Royale, I watched four foxes feeding together on the remains of a wolf-killed moose.

It is true that even where no wolves are present carcasses of big game would still be available to scavengers. However, without wolves the causes of mortality on big game are often catastrophic factors such as starvation or disease. These may provide vast amounts of food for scavengers during short periods. But for an area to support numbers of scavenging beasts there must be food available all year round, not just during a month or two of the year. Because wolf predation provides a relatively stable quantity of food throughout the year, it probably allows an area to support higher numbers of scavengers than other mortality factors would.

LITERATURE CITED

BANFIELD, A. W. F. 1954. Preliminary investigation of the barren ground caribou. Part II. Life history, ecology, and utilization. Can. Wildl. Serv., Wildl. Mgmt. Bull. Ser. 1, No. 10B. 112 pp.

CHEATUM, E. L., and C. W. SEVERINGHAUS. 1950. Variations in fertility of the white-tailed deer related to range conditions. Trans. N. Am. Wildl. Conf. 15: 170-89.

COWAN, I. M. 1947. The timber wolf in the Rocky Mountain national parks of Canada. Can. J. Res. 25: 139-74.

ERRINGTON, P. L. 1946. Predation and vertebrate populations. Quart. Rev. Biol. 21: 144-77, 221-45.

ERRINGTON, P. L. 1967. Of predation and life. Iowa State University Press, Ames. 277 pp.

FULLER, W. A. 1966. The biology and management of the bison of Wood Buffalo National Park. Can. Wildl. Serv., Wildl. Mgmt. Bull. Ser. 1, No. 16, 52 pp.

HICKIE, P. F. 1936. Isle Royale moose studies. Proc. N. Am. Wildl. Conf. 1: 396-98.

JORDAN, P. A., P. C. SHELTON, and D. L. ALLEN. 1967. Numbers, turnover, and social structure of the Isle Royale wolf populations. Amer. Zool. 7: 233-52.

KELSALL, J. P. 1957. Continued barren-ground caribou studies. Can. Wildl. Serv., Wildl. Bull. Ser. 1, No. 12, 148 pp.

KELSALL, J. P. 1968. The migratory barren ground caribou of Canada. Can. Wildl. Serv., Queen's Printer, Ottawa, 340 pp.

KLEIN, D. R., and S. T. OLSON. 1960. Natural mortality patterns of deer in southeast Alaska. J. Wildl. Mgmt. 24: 80-88.

KREFTING, L. W. 1951. What is the future of the Isle Royale moose herd? Trans. N. Am. Wildl. Conf. 16: 461-70.

MECH, L. D. 1966a. The wolves of Isle Royale. U.S. Nat. Park Serv. Fauna Ser. No. 7, 210 pp.

MERRIAM, H. R. 1964. The wolves of Coronation Island. Proc. Alaska Sci. Conf. 15: 27-32.

MURIE, A. 1934. The moose of Isle Royale. Univ. Mich. Mus. Zool. Misc. Publ. 25. 44 pp.

MURIE, A. 1944. The wolves of Mount McKinley. U.S. Nat. Park Serv. Fauna Ser. No. 5. 238 pp.

PIMLOTT, D. H. 1959. Reproduction and productivity of Newfoundland moose. J. Wildl. Mgmt. 23: 381-401.

PIMLOTT, D. H. 1967b. Wolf predation and ungulate populations. Amer. Zool. 7: 267-78.

STENLUND, M. H. 1955. A field study of the timber wolf (*Canis lupus*) on the Superior National Forest, Minnesota. Minn. Dept. Cons. Tech. Bull. 4. 55 pp.

THOMPSON, D. Q. 1952. Travel, range, and food habits of timber wolves in Wisconsin. J. Mammal. 33: 429-42.

THE SOCIAL ASPECTS OF POPULATION DYNAMICS (1952)

John B. Calhoun

Studies of animal behavior frequently are limited to elucidating behavioral mechanisms and their phylogeny. In this paper, however, Calhoun considers the application of behavioral studies to population phenomena. Social behavior is an important factor influencing mortality, natality and movement and some understanding of social behavior would enhance attempts to manage any species.

The subject of population dynamics is more commonly treated from the demographic point of view. This view stresses the fact that a population grows, remains stable, or declines, dependent upon the interrelationships of natality, mortality, and migration. Interactions of these phenomena determine density; that is, the number of organisms inhabiting a given space. Customarily, the results of such demographic studies are graphed as growth curves which pictorially show the change in density through time, or they are given as life tables from which such factors as life expectancy or age structure of the population may be derived.

In the analysis of those factors which alter the pattern of changes in density, consideration is normally given to the relative abundance of food or other prerequisites of life, to the incidence of disease and similar factors as they affect the general health of the population, and to the occurrence of favorable or unfavorable climatic conditions. Such factors are viewed as they depress or accelerate the growth and expansion of a population (Allee, *et al.,* 1949; Cole, 1948; Park, 1946). Scant attention is paid to the role of the individual or to the internal phenomena of those sub-groups of the population to which every individual of most species is normally a member, such as the family or other reproductive aggregates, feeding aggregations, harborage aggregations, and finally regional aggregations. This latter consists of individuals or groups which occasionally come in contact with each other without normally participating in the attaining of common goals. If social behavior really does alter the character of population dynamics, it is just such an understanding of the role of the individual and his group which we must seek. We might have rephrased our problem as "Does population dynamics alter the character of social behavior?" Both aspects will be examined here.

In the following discussion there is no attempt to review the literature. Rather, we shall hazard to discuss a wide variety of phenomena that are involved in a full appreciation of the interrelationship between sociality and population dynamics. Through such a "stock-taking" of relevant data from diverse fields of research, we shall endeavor to demonstrate the need for multi-discipline approaches to these complex problems. The writer, as an ecologist, no doubt expresses bias in his treatment of this discussion.

Reprinted from J. Mammal. 33(2):139-159.

We might first wonder if sociality really does have any influence at all on population dynamics. Perhaps it will be best for me to describe briefly a situation with which I have had intimate experience. This concerns the role of social behavior in limiting numbers among wild Norway rats. (This study of the Norway rat is still largely unpublished. It was a phase of the research program of the Rodent Ecology Project of the Johns Hopkins University School of Hygiene and Public Health, which was sponsored through a grant from the International Health Division of the Rockefeller Foundation.) (Calhoun, 1949a, 1949b.) For 28 months I observed a colony of rats (*Rattus norvegicus*) near Towson, Maryland, as it grew from a few individuals to the point of saturation in numbers. This colony was maintained in a 10,000-square-foot pen where there was a super-abundance of food at all times, and where harborage space was never completely utilized by the rats. At the time the colony was killed off there were considerably less than 200 adult rats, and all the evidence pointed to the fact that the adult population would never have exceeded 200 individuals. The number is particularly instructive when we compare it with the number of rats that might have been raised in the available space had each individual been isolated as a juvenile into two square feet of cage space, as is customarily done in the laboratory. Under such laboratory conditions 5,000 healthy rats might have been reared in 10,000 square feet of space instead of the 200 which utilized such space under free ranging conditions. This figure of 5,000 rats is actually a conservative one in regard to representing the biotic potential expected from this free-ranging colony. The studies of Emlen and Davis (1948) and Davis (1949) supplemented by my own observations indicate the following conditions for determining the potential reproduction were other limiting factors not in operation: (1) 8 per weaned litter with equal sex ratio; (2) first litter by 5 months of age; (3) one litter every two months; (4) no breeding during the four mid-winter months; (5) all rats born the first breeding season should be dead by the end of the third; (6) it is within the potential life span of a rat for all others to have been alive at the end of the experiment; (7) the study lasted from March 1947 to June 1949. With these conditions as a basis for judgment, 50,000 rats might have been alive in June 1949 as descendants from the original five females. Nevertheless, in the comparison above, it is believed that the figure 5,000 is a more realistic one in indicating the potential density of 10,000 square feet, although it is conceivable that 50,000 healthy rats could be maintained in a similar space by confining each to a cage somewhat less than eight inches on a side. What, then, was the cause of this 25-fold decrease in utilization of space under naturalistic conditions? The obvious explanation is that under free ranging conditions the rats expressed genetically determined and culturally modified behavioristic potentialities, which were impossible under caged conditions. This explanation has philosophically broad implications. Whenever the density of a population becomes increased beyond that level to which the heredity-to-environment relationship provides optimum adjustment, then the individual and the group must forfeit some of their potentials of behavior if all members are to maintain an adequate state of health.

There are three basic ways in which the social behavior of this colony of rats altered the population growth. They are as follows:

1. *Development of local groups which maintain their integrity restricts the utilization of space.*—Local colonies or aggregates were formed primarily on the basis of continued association in the locality of birth. There was sufficient conflict existing between these local colonies that there developed intermediate buffer zones in which burrows were never constructed and across which there was a reduced incidence of locomotion. The development of these social buffer zones seems essential to the maintenance of group integrity and it is a major factor in reducing the number of animals which utilize a given amount of space.

2. *Social stability favors successful reproduction.*—A stable group is one in which there is a well-developed dominance hierarchy, is one where there are well-established relationships between all the members of the group, and is one in which the individual members have experienced few behavioral disturbances and have exhibited favorable patterns of growth. Among such stable groups the frequency of conception is high, and most of the young born are successfully raised.

On the contrary, among socially unstable groups the frequency of conception is reduced and very few of the young born survive to weaning, and if they do the chances of their, in turn, leaving any progeny are very slim indeed. Socially unstable groups are those consisting of members who have had few associations in common, and/or who have experienced many behavioral disturbances and have exhibited retarded rates of growth. Such groups normally have an unstable or poorly defined hierarchial system.

3. *Social stability favors decreased mortality.*—Predation from flies was the chief direct cause of death. During the immediate post-weaning period, when the young rats are making their adjustments to colony life, flies frequently lay eggs in the fur of the young. The young most likely to succumb are those which have received excessive punitive action from their associates or who, for various reasons, have no permanent home. Flies also kill adults by laying eggs in open wounds, even fresh wounds. Rats low in the social order receive more wounds and are thus more subject to being consumed "alive" by maggots.

As the population increased in numbers there was an increase in the frequency, intensity, and complexity of behavioral adjustments necessitated among and between groups of rats. This forced more and more rats to be characterized by social instability with the accompanying result of lowering the biotic potential to the point where there was a balance between natality and mortality—all this in the continued presence of a superabundance of food and unused space available for harborage.

This influence of social behavior upon population growth in the Norway rat is exhibited in various degrees among other animals. However, in the time and space available here, no attempt will be made to present a critical review of the field. Rather, we shall examine the phenomena of social behavior and the condition of sociality as they relate to the broad

193

problem of growth exhibited both on the individual and on the population level. Through this discussion we shall place sociality in perspective to other biological phenomena and suggest avenues for further research.

Various concepts of levels or types of sociality exist. According to Allee (1940) these are: 1. "Sociality includes all integrations of two or more organisms into a supra-individualistic unity on which natural selection can act;" 2. Sociality is coextensive "with the existence of an innate pattern of a certain specialized appetite" whose satisfaction demands that animals live together and engage in common activities; 3. "True sociality occurs only in the presence of abstract values of which members of the group are more or less conscious." Thus, sociality ranges from unconscious automatic co-operation (Allee, 1945) to conscious co-operation in which the members react to socially conditioned symbols (Northrop, 1948). A bridging of this range of social characteristics is begun as soon as the association between a social behavior and its consequences is modified by the learning process. For example, when a mouse who has repeatedly lost in combat makes the adjustment of running away upon sight of his opponent, values are affecting social behavior. Approaching the opponent will result in pain, while avoidance prevents pain. Not only does such a behavior illustrate the realization of values, but also that such values may be generalized. A case (Allee, 1942) in point is that of an albino mouse, who submits to other albino mice on first encounter, after having previously been conditioned from repeated defeats by the more aggressive C57 black mice. To such a mouse any other mouse, and not just the one by which it had been beaten, serves as a symbol of the dire consequences which will result, if he fails to submit or run away. Such generalizations from prior experience form the major basis for the origin of abstract values.

For our consideration of the interrelationship of sociality to growth phenomena, the most important considerations cover those conditions permitting a population to develop and express those characteristics of sociality which are possible within the limitations imposed by the genetic potentialities of the species in question.

Wherever animals live they are constantly altering the environment about them. This occurs through such diverse phenomena as release of excreta, alteration of surrounding temperature and humidity, construction of trails and burrows, and the development of habits, all of which may alter the behavior of members of their own or later generations. These phenomena are spoken of as biological conditioning of the environment. Such activity has repeatedly been shown to alter the welfare of existing members of a population as well as the density exhibited by later generations (Allee, 1942, 1945; Allee, et al., 1949). Under essentially random dispersal of individuals through the environment, any effect of biological conditioning upon the welfare of the members of a population may be assumed to be dissociated from social phenomena. However, when such effects are associated with animals which live in aggregates (as opposed to different effects occurring when the same kind of animals live dispersed) we may, with assurance, infer that sociality is a factor in affecting the welfare of the group. There is a tendency among many animals toward group activity, the result of which ameliorates the environment so that their physiology is more efficient or that survival rate is increased. Such biologically conditioning phenomena are the result of co-operative activity. Beyond a certain point the same activity may become deleterious as the participating group increases in numbers, to the point that the formerly beneficial activity lowers survival rate or physiological efficiency. *The merits of any social behavior are thus relative to the condition and history of the group within which they occur.* For example, copulation among mammals is a desirable and necessary social behavior if the species is to survive. Yet, among certain socially disturbed groups of my Towson colony of rats, which lacked a well-integrated dominance-hierarchy, copulation rarely led to conception despite, or perhaps because of, its high frequency.

As soon as animals begin to condition their environment through the elaboration of relatively permanent artifacts such as trails, nests, burrows, and the like, biological conditioning assumes a more definite cultural aspect. To be sure, such artifacts satisfy primary organic requirements; dens are a place of retreat from enemies or inclement weather; nests are places where the young are safe; trails lead to food or harborage, and food caches serve to make food more accessible. However, beyond such primary functions, dens, nests, trails and the like further serve as a physical mold in which the social matrix takes its form.

It is with reference to the construction and utilization of these animal-made structures that many patterns of behavioral relationships become established. Where more than one animal uses one of these biological artifacts either conflict, tolerance, or the acceptance of rank-oriented priority develops (Collias, 1944). When two rats, who are familiar with each other, meet along a trail, each usually steps slightly aside and passage occurs with no sign of conflict, even where difference in rank occurs. Furthermore, young animals who develop within an artifact-conditioned environment find life much easier than did the original colonizers. They not only find previously established places of retreat and established pathways of movement between harborages, sources of food and the like, but they also encounter an artifact-oriented stabilized social structure within which their own integration during maturation is facilitated.

This alteration of the habits and social behavior of one generation by the activities of generations which precede it represents a cultural process, when culture is considered from a broad biological viewpoint. The term culture will here be used in this limited sense, without attempting to discuss the further elaborations which are expressed among human societies. If this restriction is placed upon the concept of culture, there exists the possibility of treating it comparatively in experiments with infra-human organisms. By so doing we may hope to arrive at generalizations which are useful on the human level. For such comparative purposes we can deal with effects and modifications produced by inherent behavior as well as those which are further structured through the process of learning.

There are striking similarities between the culture of man and that of some of the other vertebrates. Artifacts are constructed, learned patterns of social behavior are developed, and both are passed on to influence the life of later generations. Chance behavior or superstition may affect the pattern of learned social behavior (Skinner, 1948), and the character of vocalization may by handed down through cultural inheritance. Regarding the cultural modification of vocalization, Altmann (1950) has recently described an interesting situation among elk. In herds whose social structure has been upset by hunting, very little vocalization occurs. However, in a herd which lived far back in the Teton Mountains, where they had escaped being hunted, there was a continual calling back and forth between members of the herd.

Much in common exists between the patterns of culture among different species of vertebrates. Culture, particularly when continuity through many generations is insured, provides a stabilizing influence on the activities of the members of a population and permits them to make more effective use of their environment. Although there is as yet no experimental data to verify this postulate, it is quite likely that the genetic inheritance of many species is such that optimum adjustment by the individual or the group is made only under those conditions favoring the existence of a stabilized culture with its accompanying biologically produced artifacts. However, we must realize that cultural stability also restricts the potentialities of behavior, since other patterns of culture are automatically excluded.

It is through the alteration of the complexity and stability of culture that sociality exerts a controlling influence upon population dynamics. One of the inherent aspects of this concept concerns the relative continuity through space and time of both the population and the physical and social alterations which have been produced by the population. Discontinuities impose conditions of cultural instability as well as inhibit the maintenance of developing complexities of social organization. As mentioned previously, for the Norway rat such social control of population dynamics operates by influencing reproductive capacity, growth rate, mortality rate, incidence of disease, and behavioral adjustment. Our problem, then, resolves itself into a consideration of factors which may influence the complexity or stability of the culture of a population.

Analysis of operant factors must take into consideration the perception of the environment by the individual. The manner in which animals perceive their environment is socially important because it largely determines the rate and manner in which animals contact each other, and the manner in which they utilize the space about them. We often overlook the fact that the same physical environment, such as a mat of grass, may be differently perceived or is differently reacted to by different organisms (Schneirla 1949). Similarly, the same environment may have different meaning to two different individuals of the same species, due to differences in heredity or experience. In this discussion we shall treat the responses (or lack of responses) of animals as resulting from their perception of the environment. However, we must realize that the physiological state of the individual may alter the response regardless of how the environment is perceived (Fuller, 1950).

There are two phenomena relative to perception of the environment which must be kept in mind upon interpreting observations. First, an animal may react to an environmental situation as if it were complete, whereas portions of it are actually missing. Second, an animal may fail to perceive or react to portions of its environment which are actually present, and which it is capable of perceiving and reacting to. In either case, unfavorable usage of the environment, with resultant density effects, may occur.

The first phenomenon of reacting to an incomplete environmental situation is a derivative of the "releaser" concept developed by Lorenz and by Tinbergen (1948). A releaser is a structure of the environment or a behavior of one animal, which elicits a sequence of behavior by another animal. It is characteristic that the releaser is only a segment of the complete goal-object or goal-situation to which the reacting animal responds. Under usual conditions the behavior of the reacting animal proves satisfactory, since the complete goal-object or goal-situation is actually present. Tinbergen showed that the red belly of male stickleback fish during the breeding season served as a releaser, which elicited the female to follow the male to the spawning ground. Females will follow objects with ventral red areas which only remotely resemble fish in appearance. Under such conditions the behavior of the female can have no effective solution. Admittedly, much research needs to be done in the field of elicitation of behavior of social implication by releasers, but the releaser concept, nevertheless, provides a useful theoretical framework for orienting research.

Harris (1950) has made some interesting studies of spatial orientation in the deermouse, *Peromyscus,* which bears on the problem of the role of "releaser phenomena" on population dynamics. *Peromyscus maniculatus bairdi* inhabits grassland, whereas *Peromyscus maniculatus gracilis* inhabits woodlands. These two closely related subspecies may live in adjoining habitats and yet never interbreed, although they do so freely in the laboratory. Adjoining rooms with an inter-connecting passage were arranged to simulate the natural habitats. "Grassland" was made of bunches of thin strips of heavy paper, while "forests" were simply sections of small trees standing on end. When given a free choice of movement between these two rooms each of these subspecies of mice spent a significantly greater amount of time in the habitat simulating their natural one. Such orientation was just as efficient by mice born and raised in small laboratory cages as it was by mice trapped in the wild. It showed that these mice possess an innate capacity for tropistic behavior for which only a small segment of the environment is required as a *releaser.* This type of behavior is one of the keys as to why animals make differential usage of the available environment—space in particular being considered. Although extrapolating from experimental situations sometimes leads to false conclusions, one would strongly suspect that both the spacing and form of vegetation are important factors in both the occurrence of a deermouse in a habitat and the size of its home range, perhaps irrespective of the supply of food and harborage. Certainly, these ideas present a provocative subject for both observational and experimental studies. In fact, one is led to wonder how the behavior of animals is altered when they find themselves confined, as on islands, to habitats from which they cannot escape and to which their heredity does not permit their proper adjustment. Such an area of investigation might be designated as *"comparative esthetics."* Its ultimate analysis presumably would concern the manner in which the art forms of the material world about him affect man's behavior and peace of mind. Further theoretical aspects of releaser phenomena to social behavior have been pointed out by Ginsburg (1949). He says: "What interests me here is that a phylogeny of such releasers amounts to a phylogeny of symbolic behavior and indicates an innate capacity to derive meaning from abstract symbols. It is true that we do not know what this meaning is on an ideational level; nevertheless, it has its counterpart in human behavior if we accept the findings of orthodox Freudians."

The second phenomenon of failure to react to those existing portions of the environment, which potentially should contribute to the well-being of the organism, is one with reverberations in the dynamics of populations. The point involved here is that conditions arise which preclude the organism making the optimum use of available resources, whether they be physical, biological or social. In the field of psychology a large portion of the research in learning theory and abnormal behavior is actually involved with this problem. Likewise, it is the crux of the endeavors of psychoanalysis to reveal the origins of such situations. Field workers in ecology frequently observe animals whose reactions are out of harmony with their environment, and it is one of the aims of wildlife management to prevent their origin. In the experimental field we find such attempts to designate the problem, as in Tolman's (1949) concept of "perceptual blindness," or we find the conditions exemplified in such artificial situations as Liddell's (1942) work in producing "abnormal behavior" in his investigation of conditioned reflexes.

I would like to cite an observation of my own from my free-ranging colony of Norway rats. It exemplifies the complexities which may arise in an open society. Most rats, particularly those which have received mild degrees of punitive action from their associates, stored food in their burrows. The food might or might not be eaten immediately upon taking it to the burrow. Transportation of food in itself might satisfy a drive; however, it is to be noted that these rats deposited the transported food in locations where they themselves would have a good chance of securing it later. On the other hand, the storing behavior of rats who have experienced excessive punitive action from their associates is quite different. Repeated trips would be made from the food hopper depositing food at scattered points nearby, usually not more than 15 feet away, whereas the burrows were all further away. Once this food was left the rats which had done the transporting paid no further attention to it. Whatever the mechanism of development of this behavior may be, it is readily evident that the rats exhibiting it are no longer making a favorable use of this aspect of their environment.

An interesting aspect of this behavior, which is certainly abnormal from the individual's viewpoint, is beneficial with reference to the entire colony. (This type of behavior occurred in less than five percent of over 200 rats observed. Associated characteristics in such rats formed a syndrome which included (1) accentuated pre-weaning competition with older sibs, (2) inhibited growth during entire life span, (3) "freezing" when cornered in a trap or harborage, (4) lack of successful reproduction.) This scattering of the food made it more available and thus reduced competition at the main source of food. This observation raises the question, "how abnormal is abnormal behavior?" Though an individual rat may have its behavior so disturbed that its own effective reproduction is prevented and its own proper usage of food inhibited, it may, nevertheless, make a significant contribution to the welfare of its society through making the environment more favorable for its associates. For proper evaluation the range of variation in individual behavior needs to be viewed both as it affects the individual and the group.

Perception of spatial relationships and the manner in which animals utilize the space available to them have important social implications and exert a controlling influence on density. Territoriality, the active defense of a given tract, and home range, the occupancy of a preferred area, function as active or passive means of maintaining dispersion of individuals or groups (Allee, *et al.,* 1949, page 412; Burt, 1943; Nice, 1941). Although we lack sufficient knowledge to state exactly why an animal occupies a territory or home range of a given size, one rather general characteristic is that more food exists in the occupied area than is utilized.

This restriction of the privilege of occupying space irrespective of food imposes limitations to population growth not realized by the earlier students of this subject (Davis, 1950). Social hierarchies provide an elaboration to the complexity of territory or home range. The development of rank-order systems permits the organization of group integrity and stability which in turn leads to in-group and out-group status. Attraction between members of a group and antagonism between members of different groups produce local concentrations with intervening buffer zones which are little used by the members of adjacent groups (Keith, 1949; Scott, 1943; and author's observations on rats).

Perception of spatial relationships may have repercussions directly or indirectly on both social behavior and population dynamics, because patterns of locomotion through an environment alter the rate of contact between associates, as well as their orientation to the physical structures of the habitat.

At the Jackson Laboratory litters of dogs are raised in 20 x 70-foot pens. Snow trails reveal the manner in which the dogs utilize their confined area. Wirehaired Fox Terriers beat a single path about the periphery; Cocker Spaniels also beat a path about the periphery of the pen, but they also beat a few trails diagonally across the pen; Beagles and Basenjis form trails as do Cocker Spaniels, but in addition there are occasional to frequent wanderings away from the paths through the otherwise unbroken snow; and finally, the opposite extreme from the Wirehaired Fox Terriers is exhibited by Shetland Sheep Dogs—their tracks appear to be distributed completely at random over the pen with very little indication of a peripheral trail adjacent to the fence. Of course, we do not know what sort of natural population these breeds are capable of developing, but the snow-trail patterns exhibited indicate that these breeds would markedly differ in their utilization of their home range.

Another factor which has direct implications for population dynamics, particularly among social species, in that of *preadaptation* (Allee, *at al.*, 1949, page 642). Although natural selection may have been operating on a species with the result that this species exhibits the ability to make an optimum adjustment to some particular environment, the species may, nevertheless, make a very excellent adjustment to some new environment with which it has had no prior association. In fact, some animals prosper in the new situation, as indicated by expansion of the population into new areas or by increases in density. Such adaptation is particularly prominent among such birds as robins, chimney swifts, bluebirds, wrens, and kingbirds (Kennedy, 1915), which have utilized many man-made structures to increase their available nesting or feeding niches. This same utilization of environments, highly altered by man, is especially exhibited by such forms as the house mouse and the Norway rat. Preadaptation phenomena include the ability to engage in complex behaviors in entirely new situations. Under the artificial environment of the laboratory myriads of experiments with the derived strains of the Norway rat have amply demonstrated this ability. Under completely free-ranging conditions ground squirrels will engage and solve many intricate problems presented to them in their normal environment (Gordon, 1943).

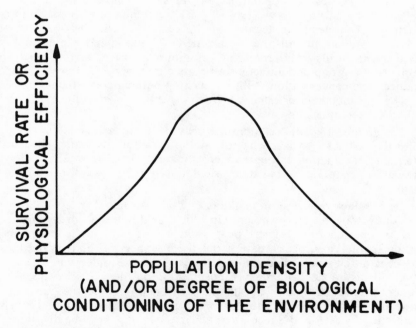

FIG. 23-1.—The relationship of population density to biological activity (after Allee). It is through the operation of this principle that sociality influences the rate of individual growth, biotic potential of population growth, and the permutations of behavior.

The phenomenon of preadaptation becomes of particular importance when the opportunity for it to be exhibited occurs in a population characterized by cultural continuity. Although the original manner of exploitation of a new environmental situation may be by chance, by learning, or by reasoning, its continued contribution to the welfare of the population is greatly enhanced by the new patterns of behavior being passed on to later generations through cultural processes. In time, the behavior may be further elaborated, so as to further the biological conditioning of the environment and also to modify the cultural pattern. In the long run, what preadapted and culturally modified behavior does is to permit the population to make more effective use of available energy. A striking example of this is reflected in the population growth (Fig. 2) of Germany (Dewey and Daikin, 1947). One cycle of growth during an agricultural economy had just about terminated at the beginning of the industrial revolution. At that time there arose a new growth curve which has only recently approached completion. Thus, the carrying capacity of an environment must also be considered from the ability and opportunity of its inhabitants to exploit the available energy. Each new type of exploitation gives rise to a heightened level of population density. (Many similar examples could be cited utilizing infrahuman animals. An outstanding one is that of the chimney-swift. Prior to the arrival of white man in North America it nested in hollow trees, and

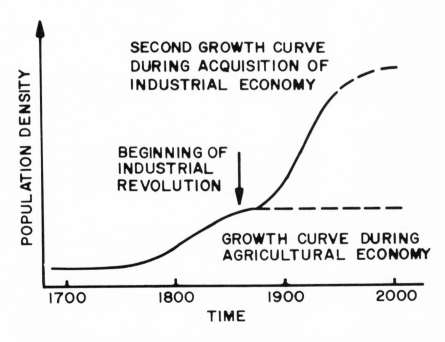

Fig. 23-2.—Population growth in Germany (after Dewey and Daikin). This figure typifies the influence upon the resultant population growth of the ability of an organism to utilize the available energy. Such changes in ability may arise through either genetic or cultural changes within the species.

during the migration seasons they aggregated in fairly large flocks which spent the night together. With the replacement of hollow trees by myriads of chimneys as a nesting niche, the abundance of this species has greatly increased. In addition to the increase in social contacts imposed by the proximity of chimneys, much larger aggregates—at times reaching many thousands—are formed in chimneys of large buildings during migration. Similar phenomena are characteristically observed in the changes of population densities during the succession of plant and animal communities (Allee, *et al.,* 1949). Animals or plants characteristic of a later stage of succession are commonly found as scarce invaders of an earlier stage. As the community structure changes and as conditions become more favorable for the invader its numbers increase. An important aspect of this situation is that the organism participates in the production of an environment more favorable to itself. From a research viewpoint the investigation of this phenomenon resolves itself into two aspects: (1) In what ways do organisms alter their environment to make them more favorable? (2) How can animals be induced to make more rapid and more efficient alterations and yet maintain their cultural stability?) The repetition of this process requires continued increase in complexity of the social organization. And as has been previously remarked, after a time there are continued restrictions to the development and expression of behavioral potentialities—a process, which we may anticipate, will terminate with the individual being only a hollow shell of his potential self. Opportunity for free expression of hereditary potentials of behavior and the drive toward increased utilization of available energy by the group are in part complimentary and in part conflicting tendencies.

Natural selection toward the survival of organizations of life which make more effective use of available energy is exhibited in the succession of plant and animal communities (Allee, *et al.,* 1949). The final stages are characterized by an increased rate of energy intake from the sun (by plants), by an increased rate of release of free energy (particularly by animals), by greater complexity of organization, and usually by a greater weight of living matter per area. In our search for guide posts for human civilization we would do well to examine more closely the dynamics of community succession whose terminal stage is self perpetuating as long as drastic changes in climate do not occur.

Nor can we consider the utilization of available energy without taking into account the growth of a population (that is, its density) with reference to the growth of the individual members of the population. Fishery research has shown that in a given body of water a relatively large number of stunted fish or a much fewer number of large fish may live. Density cannot be considered irrespective of the welfare of the individual. If the rat is at all typical, mammals behave much as do fish. In my Towson colony of Norway rats, as the population increased, more and more individuals were physically stunted despite having plenty of food available. Such stunted rats seemed healthy, as judged by the occurrence of fat—they simply failed to grow very large and attained their mature weight very slowly. These stunted rats were characterized by behavioral disturbances imposed by the increasing complexity of the social structure. Dwarfism or abnormal growth in man may also be associated with behavioral disturbances arising from unstable social environments (Binning, 1948; Fried and Mayer, 1948; Talbot, *et al.*, 1947).

Thus, we see that several growth processes are closely interrelated: (1) the rate of physical growth and skeletal maturation in the individual, (2) the level of mature growth of the individual, (3) the level of sexual and behavioral maturity in the individual, (4) the degree to which an individual or group is enabled to express genetic potentialities, (5) the growth rate of a population and its density at maturity, and (6) the social integration of a population—all these are inter-dependent variables whose expression is in turn influenced by the structure of the environment and the degree of cultural continuity possible.

The extent to which one of these growth phenomena may be enhanced through the partial suppression of the others raises the problem of value systems. Population density may be intensified at the expense of reduction in individual growth, and an increase in social tension. Maximum individual growth may be assured, through isolation with the resultant induced social sterility, irrespective of population density. A realization of the interdependence of these growth phenomena provides the viewpoint for the establishment of a truly comparative science of sociobiology.

As our human society becomes more highly technical, there arises the tendency to accentuate one of these growth phenomena without any consideration as to its effect on other aspects of life. This is particularly so as regards increasing population density, which in many quarters is accepted as a desirable objective. Bateson (1912) long ago realized the fallacy of this concept when he said: "It is not the *maximum* number but the *optimum* number, having regard to the means of distribution, that it should be the endeavor of social organization to secure. To spread a layer of human protoplasm of the greatest possible thickness over the earth—the implied ambition of many publicists—in the light of natural knowledge is seen to be reckless folly."

Yet such accentuation of a single aspect of the value systems relating to growth phenomena continues. E. G. Rochow (1949) predicts that it will be possible to feed a population of one billion persons (this is over five times the upper level indicated by the present trend) living within the boundaries of the United States. In a letter to me, Dr. Rochow made this further elaboration: "The chief difficulty arises, of course, in feeding so large a population, particularly if it is to spread over and inhabit a large part of the present farm lands. This is the part of the problem that becomes a challenge to chemists" and "I should also like to point out that the high population density in large cities is in part alleviated by purposeful isolation of many of the inhabitants." The choice before us is to develop a society whose numbers are limited, but whose members live a full life, or, as Rochow believes, to develop a society of maximum numbers whose members have had a restricted experience accompanied by an inhibition of many potentialities of expression. Maximum production of protoplasm is a valid concept and objective in the field of animal husbandry, but it is of doubtful value when applied to human society or even to game management. Current discussions of increasing agricultural production are also frequently so worded as to imply that what is possible is desirable— with little critical thought as to the consequences on the human population.

In this whole problem of the social aspects of population dynamics an important consideration is the individual's learning the nature of his physical and social environment. Although some behavior does not reach full development until an animal is quite mature, such as copulation and defense of territory, nevertheless, most contacts that an animal has with his environment begin very early in life. In fact, even where the complete behavior pattern or the full experience only occurs during adult life, the experiences of infancy and the juvenile period markedly alter later life (Hymovitch, 1949). The learning process among immature animals is qualitatively different; where the young are prevented from perceiving the environment, they, as adults, do not profit as well from similar experiences. Experiences during early life have a profound effect upon adult behavior and health. These conclusions apply to both physical and social aspects of the environment. Among dogs the latter part of the nursing period and the period just following weaning form a brief but critical one for the development of social adjustments (Scott and Marston, 1950). My own observations on wild rats were not such as to result in any clear-cut conclusions regarding the role of pre-weaning experience, but they amply demonstrated that the immediate post weaning and preadolescent periods were critical for future development. Among these rats social status, rate of growth, adult size, and stability of behavior were in large part determined during this juvenile period. In our observations of animals under natural conditions, in experimental studies of population ecology, and in laboratory studies of isolated animals or small groups, we need to give increasing attention to the manner in which the environment and experience of juvenile animals affect their behavior as adults.

In all species, regardless of their degree of sociality, natural selection operates on all levels of organic complexity from the individual to the population (Allee, 1945). *By a population we mean: any contiguously distributed grouping of a single species which is characterized by both genetic and cultural continuity through several generations.* Therefore, if we are to make real progress in understanding the interrelationships of sociality and population dynamics, our observations need to be focused upon the population as the major unit in which the lives of individuals find reality. Particular stress needs to be laid upon those factors which alter the maturation of the individual on the one hand, and, on the other, to the variations in the structure of the environment, which mold the fate of both individuals and populations. From an experimental standpoint this means that we must use populations as our experimental units; these to be followed from their inception with a few members to the maturity and possible senescence of the population, and to be studied in environments where many of the physical factors of the environment are controlled and organized into meaningful patterns. Fuller (1950), in his Situational Analysis, has provided a framework for the experimental manipulation of the field parameters of behavior (incentive, barriers, and complexity) into meaningful patterns. This framework coupled with Calhoun's (1950) approach to the experimental manipulation of population as the unit of investigation presents the necessary background for objective investigation of the social aspects of population dynamics. Many helpful suggestions for planning experimental studies of sociality are included in the "Minutes of the Conference on Genetics and Social Behavior" (Scott, 1946).

In the planning of such experiments we may rely on the great wealth of ecological field observations and the equally great wealth of laboratory studies of the psychology and physiology of individuals and small groups. At best, experimental studies into population dynamics, even with those vertebrates characterized by high reproductive potentials, take several years for completion. They require substantial sums of money and should be pursued simultaneously by investigators trained in several diverse disciplines. To be sure, this is a large order, but small in comparison to the likely contributions to the welfare of man and the world about him. Any interpretation of results pertaining to the interrelationship between sociality and population dynamics involves judgment values. This is as it should be. However, such judgment values can only gain reliability when viewed against a background of experimentation, which enables manipulation of the variables, as well as repetition of experiments with the view of determining the variability of the end results of social equilibrium, when the accompanying static aspects of the environment (and heredity) are maintained constant.

Initial studies under controlled conditions of the interrelationship between sociality and population dynamics are likely to be most fruitful if we utilize some of the common experimental mammals and their wild counterparts. Of these the most useful will be: (1) the mouse, *Mus musculus;* (2) the rat, *Rattus norvegicus;* (3) the rabbit, *Oryctolagus cuniculus,* (4) the dog-wolf complex, *Canis lupus;* and (5) the rhesus monkey, *Macaca mulatta.* This arises from the fact that there is a great backlog of biological information concerning them, and that scientists in several biological disciplines are accustomed to working with these forms. Four of these forms (mouse, rat, rabbit, and dog-wolf) are particularly suitable, since for them there is available a large number of highly inbred strains or genetically divergent breeds. This variability may be used to exploit the heredity parameter of the organism-environment complex. Scott (1949) has discussed in detail the value of inbred strains for experimental work relative to behavior, and Heston (1949) has similarly treated the usage of inbred strains in physiological studies. Inbred strains or breeds exhibit accentuation or inhibition of behavior characteristic of the wild form. It is this type of variability from the wild type which makes the use of such genetic derivatives useful. On the primate level we should have available breeds or inbred strains of a species suitable for use in the laboratory and in the field situation required by experimental population ecology. The rhesus monkey (Carpenter, 1942) is probably most suitable for such genetic work leading to further behavior studies. Although I have mainly stressed environmental influences in the present discussion, we must bear in mind that an analysis of the social aspects of population dynamics must be based upon a consideration of both heredity and environment. Sumner (1922) long ago ably pointed out that, insofar as the existence of life was concerned, neither heredity nor environment had reality in the absence of the other.

It so happens that all five of the species are characterized by rather complex social structure in comparison with many other representatives of their orders. To produce the fullest understanding of sociality and population dynamics some of those species with less complex social structure should also be thoroughly investigated.

Although present knowledge, derived from ecological studies of animals living in their native habitat, and from psychological studies of animals in the semi-isolated unsocial conditions of the laboratory, gives us a firm foothold for planning controlled studies of population ecology, much additional basic information is desirable. We particularly need many more detailed life-history studies of animals in their native habitats. These will be most effective when parallel life histories are made comparing related species known to differ in social structure. In practically all orders and many smaller taxonomic categories of mammals, there exists a wide range in the degree of sociality between different species. Table 1 presents examples of the wide range of sociality existing between related genera. In each instance the degree of sociality is judged on the basis of the size and permanence of groups, as well as the complexity of interrelationships between individuals and groups.

TABLE 1.—Comparative degrees of sociality between related genera[1]

COMMON NAME	ORDER	SLIGHTLY SOCIAL	MORE HIGHLY SOCIAL
Deer	Artiodactyla	Moose *(Alces)*	Elk *(Cervus)*
Rabbits	Lagomorpha	Cottontails *(Sylvilagus)*	European rabbit *(Oryctolagus)*
Rodents	Rodentia	Deermouse *(Peromyscus)*	Norway rat *(Rattus)*
Opossums	Marsupialia	American opossum *(Didelphis)*	Australian opossum *(Trichosurus)*

[1] Literature references: Moose (Denniston, 1949); elk (Altmann, 1950); cottontails (Trippensee, 1934); European rabbit (Southern, 1940, 1947); deermouse (Howard, 1949; Nicholson, 1941); Norway rat (Calhoun, 1949a, 1949b); American opossum (Lay, 1942); Australian opossum (Pracy and Kean, 1949).

The existence of wide ranges of sociality among many groups of mammals, even including the primitive marsupials, makes it highly likely that determination of social structure is in large part independent of the degree of evolution of the cerebrum.

Investigation of the following topics by those making life history studies will be most helpful in bringing about a better understanding of the relationship between sociality and population dynamics.

1. What are the goal-objects toward or between which animals orient?
2. How are these goal-objects distributed through space and time, particularly as they relate to the energy expenditure of the organism in re-encountering a goal-object?
3. What are the physical barriers of the environment and the complexity of their arrangement, which modify the likelihood of an animal perceiving or reaching a goal-object or of contacting other individuals?
4. What are the pain-producing barriers (both physical and social) which may occur between an animal and its goal-object?
5. How are the physical barriers or the pain-producing barriers distributed through space and time?
6. Describe each observed type of behavior in terms of:
   A. Composition of group involved (sex, age, relationship, etc.—see especially Carpenter, 1942).
   B. Type of behavior as regards its origin and function (see Scott, 1946, p. 23).
   C. Innate drives whose satisfaction depends upon the occurrence and distribution of goal-objects and barriers.
7. What are the conditions of juvenile life as related to:
   A. Relative maturity at birth.
   B. Length and pattern of dependency of young upon their mother or other associates, including frequency and kind of contact.
   C. Manner in which the young are integrated into the social structure.
   D. The maturation of each goal-object oriented behavior.
8. In what ways do the animals biologically condition their environment, and how does such conditioning influence the expression of either innate or learned behavior?
9. What is the social structure of groups in terms of rank-order relationships or other inter-individual adjustments?
10. What is the pattern of relationships between different groups?
11. How is the growth of the individual, its reproductive success, and likelihood of survival associated with the above types of data?

Whereas, other types (refer to the outlines appearing from time to time in Ecology, whose publication is sponsored through the Committee for Life History Studies) of observations are useful in preparing life history studies, the systematic accumulation of data of the above type will be of great usefulness in the next step of analysis—the planning and execution of controlled experimental studies into population ecology. Such data will facilitate a systematic arrangement of environmental components. In the native habitats of most animals goal-objects, barriers, and other physical structures are so irregularly arranged as to enable us to arrive at only vague approximations of their influence. From these life history-derived approximations we may logically plan the arrangement of goal-objects, barriers, and the like so that we may derive general principles as to their influence on population dynamics, social structures, and evolution of culture.

Concepts and techniques developed in the science of psychology will also be of great usefulness in planning and conducting experiments in population ecology. In its development, psychology has relied mainly on clinical studies of man and of experimental studies of various laboratory animals, the latter under essentially unsocial conditions. Both of these approaches are atomistic in the sense that they must perforce view the individual, whose past history and environment is little known, or which is living essentially out of context with its natural physical and social environment. Nevertheless, these two psychological approaches have given us great insight into the manner in which the individual perceives, learns, and adjusts, and to a more limited extent it has shown how individuals react to and with others of their kind in rather simple stereotyped environments. The time is now ripe to utilize this great host of information in planning experiments and analyzing results in which the unit of investigation is the population.

The potential contribution of psychology to the investigation of the behavioral aspects of population dynamics may not be realized by current trends in psychological research. Psychology has stressed the development of concepts at the expense of the descriptive aspects of behavior. Such comparative psychological endeavors can provide a cataloging of the range of behavior exhibited by a species and of the range of conditions which elicit such behaviors. Such data needs to be available both for the wild-type representative of each species and also for genetically similar isolated groups of the species, such as subspecies, inbred strains, or breeds. Such descriptive studies will form the building blocks of behavior with which we can proceed with greater assurance in planning experimental studies into group dynamics and population ecology.

With each new increase in complexity of life new properties arise, and the phenomena exhibited by the less complex forms of life take on new meaning. Thus, our knowledge of the behavior of individuals and small groups will assume richer connotations and reveal new concepts when applied to the social population level of organic organization. In turn, it is inevitable that investigation at this level of organization will produce new topics for investigation under strictly laboratory conditions.

Concepts of the social aspects of population dynamics are of potential value to three spheres of human activity. They contribute to man's management of himself through the development of a "preventive medicine" of mental hygiene, through its contribution to psychiatry by providing a better appreciation of the relationship of the total individual to his total environment (Cameron, 1948); through the provision of principles of community planning; and through the assessment of desirable population densities. They contribute, in the sphere of animal husbandry, to man's management of domestic animals, so that they will most economically provide him with sustenance. They contribute to the essential problem of man's management of the world about him in the broad fields of conservation and wildlife management; for man lives not alone, but in context with the "balance of nature," which he disrupts at his own peril. Admittedly, the concepts of the social aspect of population dynamics are as yet in an embryonic state. Their development to the point where we may safely and surely apply such knowledge presents a challenge to research. To meet this challenge we must plan long-term observational studies of the social ecology of man and other animals under their normal conditions of existence; we must plan long-term experimental studies of population ecology where conditions of the physical environment, which mold social structure, are systematically controlled, and where the history of the population is followed through the years from infancy to maturity; we must have the courage and foresight to depart from the laboratory in its customarily accepted sense, and take with us into the broader laboratory of field situations our extensive knowledge derived from analytical studies of the individual and small groups. Such procedures will lend greater insight into the dynamics of group behavior as well as provide new problems to carry back with us into the laboratory for other analytical treatment.

LITERATURE CITED

ALLEE, W. C. 1940. Concerning the origin of sociality in animals. Scientia, 154-160.

——— 1942. Social dominance and subordination among vertebrates. Biological Symposia, 8: 139-162.

——— 1945. Human conflict and cooperation: the biological background. Chapt. XX, pp. 321-367. In Approaches to National Unity, New York, Harper Bros.

ALLEE, W. C., A. E. EMERSON, O. PARK, T. PARK, and K. P. SCHMIDT. 1949. Principles of animal ecology. 837 pp. W. B. Saunders, Phila.

ALTMANN, MARGARET. 1950. Problems of social behavior in wapiti of Jackson Hole. Unpublished paper delivered at 1950 meeting of Amer. Soc. of Mammalogists.

BATESON, W. 1912. Biological fact and the structure of society. The Herbert Spencer Lecture. Delivered at the examinations Schools on Wednesday Feb. 28, 1912. 34 pp. Clarendon Press, Oxford.

BINNING, GRIFFITH. 1948. Peace be on thy house. The effects of emotional tensions on the development and growth of children, based on a study of 800 Saskatoon School children. 4 pp. reprinted from March-April issue of Health.

BURT, WM. H. 1943. Territoriality and home range concepts as applied to mammals. Jour. Mamm., 24: 346-352.

CALHOUN, JOHN B. 1949a. A method for self-control of population growth among mammals living in the wild. Science, 109: 333-335.

——— 1949b. Influence of space and time on the social behavior of the rat. (Abstract.) Anat. Record, 105: 28.

——— 1950. The study of wild animals under controlled conditions. Annals New York Academy Sci., 51: 1113-1122.

CAMERON, D. EWEN. 1948. The current transition in the concept of science. Science. 107: 553-558.

CARPENTER, C. R. 1942. Sexual behavior of free ranging rhesus monkeys (*Macaca mulatta*). Jour. Comp. Psychol., 33: 113-162.

COLE, LAMONT C. 1948. Population phenomena and common knowledge. Scientific Monthly, 67: 338-345.

COLLIAS, NICHOLAS E. 1944. Aggressive behavior among vertebrate animals. Physiological Zoology, 17: 83-123.

DAVIS, DAVID E. 1949. The weight of wild brown rats at sexual maturity. Jour. Mamm., 30: 125-130.

_____ 1950. Malthus—A review for game managers. Jour. Wildlife Mgt., 14: 180-183.

DENNISTON, R. H. 1949. Certain aspects of the development and behavior of the Wyoming moose—*Alces americana shirasi.* (Abstract.) Anatomical Record, 105: 25.

DEWEY, EDWARD R., and EDWIN F. DAIKIN. 1947. Cycles, the science of prediction. 255 pp., Henry Holt & Co., New York.

EMLEN, JOHN T., and DAVID E. DAVIS. 1948. Determination of reproductive rates in rat population by examination of carcasses. Physiological Zoology, 21: 59-65.

FRIED, RALPH, and M. F. MAYER. 1948. Socio-emotional factors accounting for growth failure in children living in an institution. Jour. Pediatrics, 33: 444-456.

FULLER, JOHN L. 1950. Situational Analysis: a classification of organism-field interactions. Psychological Review, 57: 3-18.

GINSBURG, BENSON E. 1949. Genetics and social behavior—a theoretical synthesis. pp. 101-124 in lectures on Genetics, Cancer, Growth and Social Behavior at the R. B. Jackson Memorial Laboratory Twentieth Commemoration. Bar Harbor Times.

GORDON, KENNETH. 1943. The natural history and behavior of the western chipmunk and the mantled ground squirrel. Oregon State Monographs, Studies in Zoology No. 5, 104 pp.

HARRIS, VAN T. 1950. An experimental study of habitat selection by the deermice, *Peromyscus maniculatus.* 157 pp. Ph.D. dissertation, Univ. of Michigan.

HESTON, W. E. 1949. Development of inbred strains of mice and their use in cancer research. pp. 9-31 in Lectures on Genetics, Cancer, Growth, and Social Behavior at the Roscoe B. Jackson Memorial Laboratory Twentieth Commemoration. Bar Harbor, Maine.

HOWARD, WALTER E. 1949. Dispersal, amount of inbreeding, and longevity in a local population of prairie deermice of the George Reserve, Southern Michigan. Contributions from the Laboratory of Vertebrate Biology, Univ. of Michigan. Ann Arbor, No. 43, 52 pp.

HYMOVITCH, B. 1949. The effects of experimental variations on problem solving in the rat (including an Appendix review of the effect of early experience upon later behavior). 71 pp. Ph.D. Thesis, McGill University.

KEITH, SIR ARTHUR. 1949. A new theory of human evolution. Philosophical Library, 451 pp., New York. Comments taken from a review by Dr. W. C. Allee: Concerning human evolution. Ecology, 31: 155-157.

KENNEDY, CLARENCE H. 1915. Adaptability in the choice of nesting sites of some widely spread birds. Condor, 17: 65-70.

LAY, D. W. 1942. Ecology of the opossum in eastern Texas. Jour. Mamm., 23: 147-159.

LIDDELL, H. S. 1942. The alteration of instinctual processes through the influence of conditioned reflexes. Psychosomatic Medicine, 4: 390-395.

MURIE, ADOLPH. 1944. The wolves of Mt. McKinley. Fauna of the National Parks of the United States. Fauna Series No. 5, 238 pp. U.S. Government Printing Office.

NICE, MARGARET M. 1941. The role of territory in bird life. Amer. Mid. Nat., 26: 441-487.

NICHOLSON, A. J. 1941. The homes and social habits of the wood-mouse (*Peromyscus leucopus noveboracensis*) in southern Michigan. Amer. Mid. Nat., 25: 196-223.

NORTHROP, F. S. C. 1948. The neurological and behavioristic psychological basis of the ordering of society by means of ideas. Science, 107: 411-417.

PARK, THOMAS. 1946. Some observations on the history and scope of population ecology. Ecological Monographs, 16: 313-320.

PRACY, L. T., and R. I. KEAN. 1949. The opossum (*Trichosurus vulpecula*) in New Zealand. N. Z. Dept. of Internal Affairs, Wildlife Branch Bulletin No. 1, 19 pp., Blundell Bros. Ltd., Wellington.

ROCHOW, EUGENE G. 1949. Chemistry tomorrow. Chemical and Engineering News, 27: 1510-1514.

SCHNEIRLA, T. C. 1949. Levels in the psychological capacities of animals. pp. 243-286, in Philosophy for the Future, edited by R. W. Sellars and V. J. McGill, the MacMillan Co.

210

SCOTT, J. P. (EDITOR). 1946. Minutes of the conference on genetics and social behavior. 35 pp. Published by the Roscoe B. Jackson Memorial Laboratory, Bar Harbor, Maine.

SCOTT, J. P. 1949. Genetics as a tool in experimental research. Amer. Psychologist, 4: 526-530.

_____ 1950a. The cause of fighting in mice and rats. Unpublished manuscript.

_____ 1950b. The social behavior of dogs and wolves; An illustration of sociobiological systematics. Annals New York Acad. Sci., 51: 1009-1021.

SCOTT, J. P., and MARY-'VESTA MARSTON. 1950. Critical periods affecting the development of normal and mal-adjustive social behavior of puppies. Jour. Genetic Psychol., 77: 25-60.

SCOTT, THOS. G. 1943. Some food coactions of the northern plains red fox. Ecological Monographs, 13: 427-479.

SKINNER, B. F. 1948. 'Superstition' in the pigeon. Jour. Exp. Psych., 38: 168-172.

SOUTHERN, H. N. 1940. The ecology and population dynamics of the wild rabbit (*Oryctolagus cuniculus*). Annals of Applied Biology, 27: 509-526.

_____ 1947. Sexual and aggressive behavior in the wild rabbit. Behaviour, 1: 173-194.

SUMNER, FRANCIS B. 1922. The organism and its environment. Scientific Monthly, 14: 223-233.

TALBOT, NATHAN B., E. H. SOBEL, B. S. BURKE, ERICH LINDEMANN, and S. B. KAUFMAN. 1947. Dwarfism in healthy children: Its possible relation to emotional disturbances. New England Medical Journal, 236: 783-793.

TINBERGEN, N. 1948. Social releasers and the experimental method required for their study. Wilson Bulletin, 60: 6-51.

TOLMAN, EDWARD C. 1949. The psychology of social learning. Jour. Social Issues, Vol. V, Supplement Series No. 3, 18 pp.

TRIPPENSEE, R. E. 1934. The biology and management of the cottontail rabbit. 217 pp., Ph.D. thesis. University of Michigan.

YOUNG, S. P., and E. A. GOLDMAN. 1944. The wolves of North America. Amer. Wildlife Institute, Washington, D. C. 636 pp.

211

PHYSIOLOGICAL AND PATHOLOGICAL CORRELATES OF POPULATION DENSITY (1964)

John J. Christian

Recent evidence indicates that physiological responses to change in population density and structure may play a role in regulating population growth. The review by J. J. Christian describes how physiological mechanisms which are sensitive to density-related aspects of social behavior may influence mortality and natality. Such physiological mechanisms are but one part of the complex array of phenomena which act in concert to limit the density and size of natural populations.

Pathopoietic Consequences of Increasing Population

A large body of evidence has accumulated over the past decade which supports the hypothesis that endocrine responses to increasing density, barring outside intervention, can regulate and limit population growth, largely by progressively decreasing natality and increasing mortality as population size increases (Christian 1950, 1961, 1963*a, c,* 1964*a*). It has also been established that these responses are engendered by social strife (Barnett *et al.* 1949, Davis 1953, Davis & Christian 1957, Christian 1956*a,* 1957, Mykytowycz 1960, 1961, Lockley 1961). Together social strife (or competition) and the endocrine responses to it constitute a regulatory feed-back system. Given a certain level of aggressiveness in the members of a population, social competition increases as a population increases. However, the amount of competition in a population of given size may vary widely, depending on the behavioural characteristics of the species, strain, or individuals. The physiological responses to increased numbers are often said to result from 'over-population' or 'crowding', but these undefinable terms are misleading, since some degree of response occurs at all levels of population and only becomes conspicuous at higher levels. We have used 'social pressure' to designate the total amount of social strife resulting from the combination of numbers and aggressiveness (Christian 1957). This phrase is conceptually useful, as it does away with the connotation of physical conflict, although it is unquantifiable at present. Thus, strictly speaking 'density' is incorrect. Perhaps 'social density' would be preferable. Presumably this feed-back system has evolved to prevent over-utilization of the environment and the threat of extinction it implies (Wynne-Edwards 1959, Christian 1961, Snyder 1961). However, a high price is exacted from an increasing proportion of the population for this regulation of population growth as population increases. It is this aspect of the problem that will be emphasized after first reviewing briefly the basic evidence.

Grouped male mice organize themselves into a social hierarchy often with, but sometimes without, fighting (Urich 1938, Christian 1959*b,* Davis & Christian 1957). The hierarchy is soon stabilized and fighting largely ceases (Christian 1956*a,* 1959*b*). Adrenocortical function is least in dominant and greatest in most subordinate mice, and increases more or less

Reprinted from Proceedings of the Royal Society for Medicine 57:169-174.

linearly with descending rank between these two extremes (Davis & Christian 1957, Vandenbergh 1960, Welch & Klopfer 1961, Bronson & Eleftheriou 1963, 1964). Somatic growth is inhibited in all but the dominant mice, increasingly with descending rank (Davis & Christian 1957, Christian 1961). It takes only two one-minute contacts per day with dominant mice to produce these effects (Bronson & Eleftheriou 1964). Reproductive function is depressed in all but the dominant mice (Christian 1961). Splenic weight, resulting from increased haemopoiesis, increases in subordinate mice (Rapp & Christian 1963). Injury from fighting cannot be ruled out as a factor in this effect, but it is unlikely to be an important one. Antibody production is partially inhibited in all but dominant mice (Vessey 1964). Dominant females do most of the successful breeding in a group (Retzlaff 1938). Some of these effects might have resulted from the dominant animal preventing others from acquiring sufficient food, but this possibility has been ruled out in several experiments (Davis & Christian 1957, Christian 1959a). However, decreased utilization of ingested food due to increased corticoid secretion cannot be ruled out. Inanition *per se* failed to increase adrenocortical activity in mice and a deficient or localized food supply had no effect on competition (Christian 1959a).

Similar results have been obtained with rats and rabbits (Calhoun 1950, Davis 1953, Barnett 1955, Myers & Poole 1959, 1961, Mykytowycz 1960, 1961, Lockley 1961), and dominant dogs secrete appreciably less hydrocortisone than subordinate dogs in a group (Eik-Nes 1959). Thus in several species, dominant animals show little or no endocrine response to grouping, whereas subordinate animals show increased adrenocortical function, decreased reproductive function and somatic growth, as well as secondary effects, in relation to their rank. All of these changes have been measured simultaneously only in mice. Reserpine in low doses suppresses the reactions to grouping, confirming the importance of aggressive behaviour in their genesis (Christian 1956a, 1963a).

With this background it is readily seen why increases in population are accompanied by increases in mean adrenocortical activity, decreases in reproductive function, &c., especially as population increases largely by the addition of subordinate animals. There is adrenal hyperplasia, decreased adrenal cholesterol and ascorbic acid, and increased corticoid secretion as numbers of mice per group increase (Christian 1955, 1963c, Welch & Klopfer 1961, Thiessen & Rodgers 1961, Bronson & Eleftheriou 1963, 1964). Increases in corticoid production were proportional to increases in adrenal weight (Bronson & Eleftheriou 1964), validating earlier conclusions on adrenocortical function in mice based on adrenal weight. Corticoid secretion of mature mice consists almost entirely of corticosterone (B), but an appreciable proportion of the corticoids of immature mice are 17-hydroxycorticoids with hydrocortisone (F) an important constituent (Varon, *et al.* 1963). Total corticoid secretion and the F/B ratio in immature male mice increase with grouping (Varon *et al.* 1964). Adrenal hyperplasia and thymic involution following grouping were greater in aggressive brown house mice than in more docile albino strains (Christian 1955). Thymic involution in brown mice was much greater than that produced by daily

214

injections of 400 μg of B. One unit of ACTH per day for ten days also produces greater involution in these mice than 400 μg of B (Christian 1963b, 1964b). These results suggest a more potent thymolytic adrenocortical steroid in the brown than in albino mice, although this must be established. However, it is clear that increased numbers of mice result in increased adrenocortical activity. The same is true for albino rats (Eechaute et al. 1962, Barrett & Stockham 1963) except that a fivefold to tenfold increase in corticoid secretion is unaccompanied by an increase in adrenal weight. This apparently is not true for *Peromyscus maniculatus bairdii,* a non-aggressive species (Bronson & Eleftheriou 1963). Likewise behaviourally 'compatible' *Peromyscus leucopus* show no increase in adrenal weight when placed together, whereas 'incompatible' ones show an increase (Southwick 1963). These results emphasize the importance of behaviour in eliciting endocrine responses to increased population size. Adrenal medullary hyperplasia occurs with increased density (Bullough 1952). Secretion of adrenaline and noradrenaline is greater at high densities and in subordinate animals. (Welch 1962a). Somatic growth is progressively inhibited with increasing numbers (Vetulani 1931, Christian 1955, 1961), as are sexual maturation as well as sexual function in mature mice (Christian 1956b, 1959c, 1961, 1964a). Size of the sex accessories and testes is decreased and spermatogenesis is partially inhibited and abnormal. In general, reproductive function appears to be more sensitive to changes in population than other endocrine function. Responses to injected gonadotrophins are altered by differences in density in rats (Chance 1956). Endocrine responses to increased numbers are not a function of density *per se* within broad spatial limits, as these responses to changes in numbers in a given strain of mouse are similar whether space per mouse is increased, decreased, or constant (Christian 1959c, Thiessen & Rodgers 1961.)

Similar changes occur on grouping females (Retzlaff 1938, Andervont 1944, Whitten 1959, Lamond 1959, Christian 1960). There is hyperplasia of the adrenal zonæ fasciculata-reticularis, accelerated involution of the X-zone (Jones 1957) (suggesting increased adrenal androgen secretion), anœstrus or delayed onset of œstrus, and inhibition of uterine development. Pseudopregnancy follows grouping in some strains of mice (Lee & Boot 1955, 1956).

In groups of mixed sex, the numbers of ovulations and implantations are decreased, intrauterine mortality is increased greatly, apparently occurring near mid-term, and lactation is diminished (Christian & LeMunyan 1958). Maternal behavioural changes also occur (Brown 1953, Lloyd et al. 1964), possibly as a result of altered endocrine function. Progeny of grouped females contract permanent behavioural defects *in utero* (Keeley 1962). Marked stunting of progeny, persisting into a second and possibly a third generation, results from inadequate lactation induced by grouping (Chitty 1955, Christian & LeMunyan 1958). The behavioural disorders originating *in utero* may reflect increased maternal secretion of corticosterone, as high physiological levels of it profoundly affect brain development in newborn mice (Howard 1963). Crowding can thus have prolonged and far-reaching effects which may take generations to dispel.

Complete inhibition of maturation is a striking result of greatly increased population size, whether in populations in the laboratory or in natural populations (Christian 1956b, 1961, 1963a, Crowcroft & Rowe 1957, Kalela 1957, Wijngaarden 1960). It seemed possible that increased secretion of adrenal androgens resulting from increased ACTH secretion might inhibit gonadotrophin secretion and explain the inhibition of maturation seen with increased densities. Grouping female mice produces evidence of increased adrenal androgen secretion other than accelerated involution of the adrenal X-zone, such as increased prevalence of an os clitoris and greatly increased preputial weight (Christian 1960, 1961). Another important point was that gonadotrophin secretion can be suppressed by much lower levels of steroids in immature than in mature rats (Byrnes & Meyer 1951, Ramirez & McCann 1963). Indeed, it proved possible to suppress pituitary gonadotrophin secretion and prevent normal maturation in female mice with low non-virilizing doses of adrenal androgens (Varon & Christian 1963, Duckett et al. 1963). However, ACTH also was found to inhibit normal ovarian development and thus maturation, in adrenalectomized and in intact mice (Christian 1963b). At least one other mechanism inhibiting reproduction, possibly purely nervous, is suggested by inhibition of reproduction with increased density in peromyscus without increased adrenocortical function (Terman 1963, Christian, unpublished).

The best example of the necessity for both numbers and behavioural aggressiveness to produce increases in adrenocortical activity was seen in a population of woodchucks (*Marmota monax*) (Christian 1962). During the breeding season the animals were aggressive and adrenal weight increased steadily as numbers in daily contact increased. Afterwards they became non-aggressive and tolerant of each other and adrenal weight declined sharply despite a continued increase in numbers. The increase in adrenal weight was not due to pregnancy, lactation, or other reproductive function *per se*. Furthermore adrenal weights were lowered by altering the age composition of the population and thereby reducing social strife and aggressiveness (Lloyd et al. 1964). Similarly decreased adrenal weight and increased reproduction of Norway rats and Sika Deer occurred after the population was reduced (Davis 1953, Christian & Davis 1955, Davis & Christian 1958, Christian et al. 1960).

The same physiological responses to increased numbers occur in freely-growing confined populations of house mice, voles and rabbits and in natural populations of voles, rabbits, deer and others (Clarke 1955, Christian 1956b, 1961, Louch 1956, 1958, Kalela 1957, Mykytowycz 1960, Wijngaarden 1960, Curr-Lindahl 1962, Patric 1962, Pearson et al. 1962, Welch 1962b). The responses of house mice were greater in these than in assembled populations of fixed size. Mean adrenal weight increased as much as 30-40% (Christian 1959c) in freely growing populations of mice or voles, and 45-60% in deer (Christian et al. 1960). Wild Norway rats of both sexes showed striking increases or decreases in adrenal weight with corresponding changes in population size (Christian 1959c).

In general birth rates are progressively lowered because of increased intrauterine mortality, decreased fertility and inhibited maturation as numbers increase in freely growing or natural populations; in addition there is usually a progressive increase in nursling mortality which may be attributed to intrauterine derangements, faulty lactation, maternal behaviour, or all of these from about the midpoint of the population growth (Clarke 1955, Crowcroft & Rowe 1957, Christian 1961, 1963a). Population growth may be limited mainly by declining birth rate, in which case the males are severely affected by increasing numbers, while females show little effect; or it may be limited mainly by nursling mortality, in which case the females are affected markedly (Christian 1963a). Thus, *in utero* losses and diminished fertility may be largely due to effects on males, but this is purely conjectural. Combinations of these factors are the rule in most populations and inhibition of maturation is always a factor.

With increased adrenocortical function accompanying increases in population one would predict decreased resistance to disease due to suppression of defence mechanisms by glucocorticoids. With increased density there is inhibition of inflammation, granulation (Christian & Williamson 1958), and antibody production (Davis & Prudovsky *in* Christian 1963a, Vessey 1964), decreased resistance to parasitism (Davis & Read 1958), increased susceptibility to infection (Retzlaff 1938, Mykytowycz 1961), and increased mortality following infection (Mykytowycz 1961), especially in subordinate animals. The appearance of spontaneous mammary carcinoma and onset of œstrus were delayed and mortality due to carcinoma decreased by grouping female C3H mice (Andervont 1944). Grouping also augments alloxan diabetes (Ader *et al.* 1963) and adrenal regeneration hypertension (Bernardis & Skelton 1963). It also enhances the action of amphetamine by increasing social stimulation of the animals (Chance 1946, 1947, Swinyard *et al.* 1961, Fink & Larson 1962). Grouping also affects the actions of other drugs and increases radiation mortality (Ader & Hahn 1963, Hahn & Howland 1963). Splenic erythropoiesis and the size of the intervertebral nucleus pulposus of voles were increased by social strife (Clarke 1953, Dawson 1956, Chitty *et al.* 1956). We have seen that increased population results in splenic hypertrophy and increased intrauterine and nursling mortality in mice.

Similar results were obtained from a study of a population of sika (*Cervus nippon*) that reached a density of one per acre and then experienced a die-off of two-thirds of the population (Christian *et al.* 1960). The deer were stunted without evidence of malnutrition. A proliferative, non-exudative glomerulonephritis first appeared in mild form three years before the die-off and reached maximum severity the year of the die-off. Viral hepatitis appeared the year of the die-off when one would expect decreased resistance. These diseases did not account for the observed mortality, but potassium deficiency from prolonged hypercorticalism may have been the major cause of death (Christian 1964c). Two years later normal growth was restored, adrenal weight decreased, renal disease ameliorated and hepatitis absent from deer born after the die-off. Glomerulonephritis was associated with high density, but otherwise its ætiology is unknown.

The above-mentioned woodchuck population had a high prevalence and incidence of proliferative, non-exudative intercapillary glomerulo-

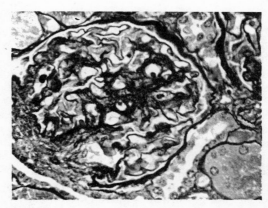

FIG. 24-1.—Woodchuck renal glomerulus with moderate intercapillary scarring, constriction of capillary channels and hyperplasia at base of the tuft. This degree of glomerular damage is less than average for the population. 3 μ thick, PAS-Allochrome stain. × 360

nephritis—often severe and in many animals with destruction to all glomeruli (Figs 1, 2) (Christian 1963a). Hypertension, ascites, hydrothorax, hydropericardium and diabetes were associated findings in varying frequency. Reducing social strife reduced the rate of development and mean severity of renal disease, and diabetes disappeared, despite immigration from surrounding dense populations which tended to obscure the changes (Christian 1963a and unpublished). Despite a number of studies, the ætiology of the glomerulonephritis remains unknown, although it was related to 'social pressure' and associated endocrine changes.

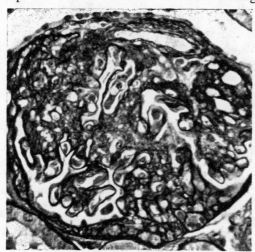

FIG. 24-2.—Chronic severe glomerulonephritis in a woodchuck. Note generalized adhesions of tuft to Bowman's capsule, severe scarring, occlusion of capillaries, and one instance (left) of organization with recanalization of vascular channel. All glomeruli in both kidneys were equally damaged. The epithelium covering the left surface belongs to an adjacent tubule. This animal was moribund and had gross cardiac enlargement, marked ascites, hydrothorax and hydropericardium. 3 μ thick, PAS-Allochrome stain. × 360

218

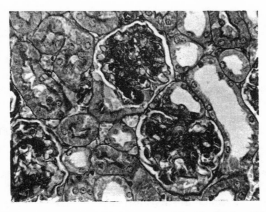

FIG. 24-3.—Section of renal cortex from a mouse treated with 4 units of ACTH daily for six weeks. Glomeruli are enlarged with severe PAS + fibrillar intercapillary scarring and moderate hyperplasia of mesangial cells, but without adhesions to Bowman's capsule. This scarring is similar in nature to that seen in woodchucks (Figs 24-1, 24-2). Distal tubules are dilated 4 μ thick, PAS-Allochrome stain. × 230.

The glomerulonephritis produced in mice by chronic treatment with ACTH gel may provide a clue to the pathogenesis of glomerulonephritis associated with high social pressure (Christian 1963*d*). Adrenals were necessary to produce this disease. The glomerular lesions (Fig. 3) resemble those seen in woodchucks (Figs 1, 2), but they were associated with necrosis of the papillary tips (Fig 4), which is unknown in woodchucks. (The renal papillary necrosis illustrated in Fig. 4 has not proven to be a regular feature of ACTH-induced nephritis: J. Christian, 1973.) The glomerular lesions are unlike those produced by deoxycorticosterone, growth hormone, or stress in sensitized rats. Some glomeruli, in addition to mesangial hyperplasia, intercapillary scarring, and capillary obliteration, had microaneurysmal dilatation of peripheral capillaries. Distal and collecting tubules were dilated (Fig. 3). Further details have not yet been studied.

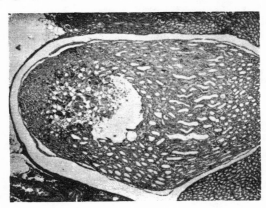

FIG. 24-4.—Renal papilla of same kidney as shown in Fig. 24-3. Note the large area of necrosis with little inflammatory reaction. 4 μ thick, PAS-Allochrome stain. × 23

Whatever the relationship between naturally occurring renal disease in woodchucks and various experimental nephropathies, there seems to be a relationship between social density and renal disease in woodchucks and probably sika. Increased 'social pressure' may be a factor in the genesis of some forms of glomerulonephritis and possibly of other diseases. The role of increased social density in reducing resistance to infectious disease and parasitism and therefore in increasing mortality is clear, and its role in increasing intrauterine and postnatal mortality has been discussed. It still is possible that crowding females during pregnancy and lactation may result in reduced viability of their young later on, as originally suggested by Chitty (1952).

In summary, populations of many mammals are evidently self-regulated and self-limited as a result of the operation of behavioural-endocrine feed-back mechanisms activated by changes in social density. These mechanisms regulate populations by altering mortality and/or natality. Social competition is an essential ingredient of such a system, although in some cases it may be too conventionalized or slight to be obvious. Movement, of course, also will result from competition. The pathopoietic consequences of increased social density are evident.

REFERENCES

ADER R & HAHN E W (1963) *Psychol. Rep.* 13, 211
ADER R, KREUTNER B A jr & JACOBS H L
(1963) *Psychosom. Med.* 25, 60
ANDERVONT H B (1944) *J. nat. Cancer Inst.* 4, 579
BARNETT S A (1955) *Nature, Lond.* 175, 126
BARNETT S A, BATHARD A H & SPENCER M M
(1949) *Ann. appl. Biol.* 38, 444
BARRETT A M & SOCKHAM M A (1963) *J. Endocrin.* 26, 97
BERNARDIS L L & SKELTON F R
(1963) *Proc. Soc. exp. Biol., N.Y.* 113, 952
BRONSON F H & ELEFTHERIOU B E
(1963) *Physiol. Zcöl.* 36, 161
(1964) *Gen. comp. Endocrin.* 3, 515
BROWN R Z (1953) *Ecol. Monogr.* 23, 217
BULLOUGH W S (1952) *J. Endocrin.* 8, 265
BYRNES W W & MEYER R K (1951) *Endocrinology* 48, 133
CALHOUN J B (1950) *Ann. N.Y. Acad. Sci.* 51, 1113
CHANCE M R A
(1946) *J. Pharmacol.* 87, 214
(1947) *J. Pharmacol.* 89, 289
(1956) *Nature, Lond.* 177, 228
CHITTY D
(1952) *Phil. Trans.* Ser. B. 236, 505
(1955) In: Numbers of Man and Animals. Ed. J B Cragg & N W Pririe, Edinburgh; p 57
CHITTY D, CHITTY H. & LESLIE P H (1956) *J. Path. Bact.* 72, 459
CHRISTIAN J J
(1950) *J. Mammal.* 31, 247
(1955) *Amer. J. Physiol.* 182, 292
(1956a) *Amer. J. Physiol.* 187, 353
(1956b) *Ecology* 37, 258
(1957) U.S. Naval Med. Res. Inst. Rep., Lecture & Rev. Series 57-2, 443
(1959a) *Endocrinology* 65, 189
(1959b) *Proc. Soc. exp. Biol., N.Y.* 101, 166
(1959c) In: Comparative Endocrinology Ed. A Gorbman. New York; p 71

(1960) *Proc. Soc. exp. Biol., N.Y.* 104, 330
(1961) *Proc. nat. Acad. Sci., Wash.* 47, 428
(1962) *Endocrinology* 71, 421
(1963a) *Milit. Med.* 128, 571
(1963b) *Fed. Proc.* 22, 507 (Abstract)
(1963c) *Proc. XVI Int. Congr. Zool.* 3, 8
(1963d) Proc. of Soc. for Endocrinol., Bristol, Nov. 15, 1963
(1964a) In: Physiological Mammalogy. Ed. W V Mayer & R G VanGelder. New York; 1, 189
(1964b) *Endocrinology.* (In press)
(1964c) *Wildl. Dis.* (In press)
CHRISTIAN J J & DAVIS D E
(1955) *Trans. N. Amer. Wildl. Conf.* 20, 177
CHRISTIAN J J, FLYGER V & DAVIS D E (1960) *Chesapeake Sci.* 1, 79
CHRISTIAN J J & LEMUNYAN C D (1958) *Endocrinology* 63, 517
CHRISTIAN J J & WILLIAMSON H O
(1958) *Proc. Soc. exp. Biol., N.Y.* 99, 385
CLARKE J R
(1953) *J. Endocrin.* 9, 114
(1955) *Proc. roy. Soc.* Ser. B. 144, 68
CROWCROFT P & ROWE F P (1957) *Proc. zool. Soc. Lond.* 129, 359
CURRY-LINDAHL K (1962) *J. Mammal.* 43, 171
DAVIS D E (1953) *Quart. Rev. Biol.* 28, 373
DAVIS D E & CHRISTIAN J J
(1957) *Proc. Soc. exp. Biol., N.Y.* 94, 728
(1958) *Ecology* 39, 218
DAVIS D E & READ C P (1958) *Proc. Soc. exp. Biol., N.Y.* 99, 269
DAWSON J (1956) *Nature, Lond.* 178, 1183
DUCKETT G, VARON H H & CHRISTIAN J J
(1963) *Endocrinology* 72, 403
Eechaute W, Demeester G, Lacroix E & Leusen I
(1962) *Arch. int. Pharmacodyn.* 136, 161
EIK-NES K
(1959) *Recent Progr. Hormone Res.* 15, 380
FINK G B & LARSON R E (1962) *J. Pharmacol.* 137, 361
HAHN E W & HOWLAND J W (1963) *Radiat. Res.* 19, 676
HOWARD E (1963) *Fed. Proc.* 22, 270 (Abstract)
JONES I C (1957) The Adrenal Cortex, Cambridge
KALELA O (1957) *Ann. Sci. Fennicæ,* Ser. A. IV. Biol. 34, 1
KEELEY K (1962) *Science* 135, 44
LAMOND D R (1959) *J. Endocrin.* 18, 343
LEE S VAN DER & BOOT L M
(1955) *Acta physiol. pharm. néerl.* 4, 442
(1956) *Acta physiol. pharm. néerl.* 5, 213
LLOYD J A, CHRISTIAN J J, DAVIS D E & BRONSON F H
(1964) *Gen. comp. Endocrin.* (In press)
LOCKLEY R M (1961) *J. Anim. Ecol.* 30, 385
LOUCH C D
(1956) *Ecology* 37, 701
(1958) *J. Mammal.* 39, 109
MYERS K & POOLE W E
(1959) *CSIRO Wildl. Res.* 4, 14
(1961) *CSIRO Wildl. Res.* 6, 1
(1962) *Aust. J. Zool.* 10, 225
MYKYTOWYCZ R.
(1960) *CSIRO Wildl. Res.* 5, 1
(1961) *CSIRO Wildl. Res.* 6, 142
PATRIC E F (1962) *J. Mammal.* 43, 200
PEARSON P. G, ANILANE J & GERLACH J
(1962) *Bull. ecol Soc. Anter.* 43, 134 (Abstract)
RAMIREZ D V & MCCANN S M (1963) *Endocrinology* 72, 452

RAPP J P & CHRISTIAN J J (1963) *Proc. Soc. exp. Biol, N.Y.* 114, 26
RETZLAFF E G (1938) *Biol. gen.* 14, 238
SNYDER R L (1961) *Proc. nat. Acad. Sci., Wash.* 47, 449
SOUTHWICK C H (1963) *Bull. ecol. Soc. Amer.* 44, 130 (Abstract)
SWINYARD E A, CLARK L O, MIYAHARA J T & WOLF H H
(1961) *J. Pharmacol.* 132, 97
TERMAN C R (1963) *Bull. ecol. Soc. Amer.* 44, 123
THIESSEN D D & RODGERS D A (1961) *Psychol. Bull.* 58, 441
URICH J (1938) *J. comp. Psychol.* 25, 373
VANDENBERGH J G (1960) *Anim. Behav.* 8, 13
VARON H H & CHRISTIAN J J (1963) *Endocrinology* 72, 210
VARON H H, TOUCHSTONE J C & CHRISTIAN J J
(1963) *Fed. Proc.* 22, 164 (Abstract)
(1964) *Endocrinology* (In press)
VESSEY S H (1964) *Proc. Soc. exp. Biol., N.Y.* 115, 252
VETULANI T (1931) *Biol. gen.* 7, 71
WELCH B L
(1962a) *Bull. ecol. Soc. Amer.* 43, 135 (Abstract)
(1962b) Proc. I Nat. Deer Dis. Symp., Athens, Ga.
Publ. Univ. of Georgia Ctr. Cont. Education
WELCH B L & KLOPFER P H (1961) *Amer. Nat.* 95, 256
WHITTEN W K (1959) *J. Endocrin.* 18, 102
WIJNGAARDEN A VAN
(1960) *Versl. Landbouwk. Onderz.* No. 66-22. Wageningen; p 1
WYNN-EDWARDS V C (1959) *Ibis* 101, 436

ECOLOGICAL SIGNIFICANCE OF TERRITORY IN THE AUSTRALIAN MAGPIE, *Gymnorhina tibicen* (1963)
Robert Carrick

The role of territorial behavior in many species is little understood. In this paper Carrick suggests that territoriality influences reproductive performance of both sexes and affects mortality, thereby contributing to stability in population size and density.

Much has been written on the possible significance of territorialism in birds and other animals; but, while some of the functions of territory appear self-evident enough, actual proof of their operation in nature has been difficult to obtain. In a comprehensive review of this subject, which cites the relevant literature to that time, Hinde (1956) was still able to write: "There is no direct evidence that territory limits the total breeding population in all habitats. . . . Territorial behaviour may reduce disease, but this is unlikely to be a significant consequence except in some colonial species. . . . The functions of territorial behaviour are extremely diverse, and the quality of the evidence available for assessing them is little different from that available to Howard." This last point is still substantially true, half a century after Howard. Wynne-Edwards (1962) has given a fully documented account of the territory habit, which he rightly interprets as no different in purpose from the other forms of social behavior that constitute the homeostatic machinery whereby populations of animals are widely dispersed and excessive increase of numbers, with consequent depletion of food and other resources, is prevented.

The two main questions arise from each side of the population equation, and each contains several others. *Firstly,* does territorialism reduce productivity (fecundity) significantly below the biotic potential of the species? To what extent does it do so, and how is the reduction achieved? Are adult females unable to breed through denial of suitable nest sites, mates, or food supply? Or is maturity prevented by lack of the necessary proximate stimuli, or even by inhibitory factors? *Secondly,* does territorialism buffer its adherents from important causes of mortality? Does it prevent or reduce the risk of starvation, i.e. what is the relation between territory and food supply? Does it confer safety from predators or protection from disease?

A main difficulty of research on this problem is that the effects of territorialism usually have to be inferred from the study of the territorial individuals alone; there is no nonterritorial element in the same species, or at least it is barely visible, to serve as a control and provide comparative data on natality and mortality under the two systems. This stems from the fact that those individuals that fail to attain territorial status are either excluded from the habitat that the species requires for food, shelter, and reproduction, and so they succumb, or else they live cryptically in and around the margins of the preferred habitat. In the case of the strongly

Reprinted from: Proc. Internat. Ornithol. Congr. 13: 740-753.

territorial Australian Magpie (*Gymnorhina tibicen*), however, there is a large and obvious overflow population outside the wooded breeding territories that is not territorial, at least in the same sense as the breeding birds, and that can maintain its numbers without recourse to migration. This stems mainly from the fact that this species is primarily an insectivorous ground-surface feeder, but is versatile enough to explore other food sources and even resorts to carrion and pasture foliage when necessary. The controlled experiment that we would like to set up in so many other species exists naturally.

Fig. 25-1.—Adult cock Australian Magpie *(Gymnorhina tibicen)* giving the aggressive carol at the boundary of its territory. Photo by E. Slater.

G. *tibicen* (Fig. 1) is a member of the Australo-Papuan family Cracticidae, allied to the Corvidae. It stands about 9 inches high; and its adult plumage pattern, with jet black underparts and white nape, rump, and wing-flash, advertises the fact that predation on it is unlikely to be important; so exposed habitats can be used. A reasonable solution to the problem of diurnal shelter from the elements, especially heat and wind, can usually be found even in open country, and these individuals resort to communal night roosts some distance from their feeding grounds. This magpie is a sedentary species, with conspicuous behavior; it is not shy and it is readily trapped. Its aggressive carol, energetic defense of the territorial boundary, and readiness to attack intruders, including ornithologists, further assist field study (Fig. 1). The immature first-year birds are distinguished by their grayish, not black, plumage, and the sexes by the grayish lower nape and rump and the shorter bill of the female. It nests typically in trees, but shows considerable adaptability.

Fig. 25-2.–The central part of the study area at Gungahlin, Canberra. Open savannah woodland (*Eucalyptus* spp., exotic conifers, and deciduous trees) and adjacent pasture are the habitat for permanent breeding territories. Photo by C. Totterdell.

The scene of the present study is 5 sq miles of open savannah, woodland, and pasture (Fig. 2 and 3) around Gungahlin, the headquarters of the Division of Wildlife Research, C.S.I.R.O., outside Canberra, Australia. The native gums, among which *Eucalyptus blakeleyi* predominates, form sparse cover with ground feeding places throughout and around them; exotic trees, including conifers and elms, are planted more compactly, and offer equally acceptable nest sites to the magpie. The study area was chosen to include samples of breeding habitat with intervening open ground. The basis of this study is individual color banding of territorial birds and group banding of others; over 650 of the former, and 2,500 of

FIG. 25-3.—A marginal part of the study area at Gungahlin, Canberra. The open pasture is populated by nonbreeding flock birds and groups in open territories; marginal territories form around isolated trees or brushes. Photo by C. Totterdell.

the latter, have been banded during 1955-62. Adults and young in territories on the study area have been banded annually, and in the four winters 1957, 1958, 1960, and 1961, about 80 percent of the nonterritorial birds living in the treeless pasture habitat have been banded. Since 1955, some 220 territorial groups have been studied. The area of woodland cover around Gungahlin (Fig. 2), which contains two-thirds of the territorial breeding groups in the study area, has been most intensively studied; every magpie there is color banded, i.e. about 150 birds in 40-45 territories. Over 1,000 specimens for dissection have been taken from comparable open and wooded terrain several miles from the study area, and experiments involving manipulation of internal or external environment have been made mainly outside the study area. Counts of the territorial birds in the area, with identification of color-banded individuals, are made every 3 months, and the free-flying juveniles still present in February receive their color combination then.

This is a preliminary account of the main findings that relate to the ecological significance of territorialism. These results are based on extensive data from birds of known identity and history, and a full account of this study will be published in a future issue of *C.S.I.R.O. Wildlife Research.*

Social Organization and use of Habitat

The Australian Magpie forms social territorial groups of 2-10 birds. Most territories fall within the 5- to 20-acre range, with an average of about 10 acres, but smaller areas are held where surrounding pressure is strong, and larger ones at the margins of the territorial area where there is no neighboring group. A group of two birds is always adult cock and hen; there may be six adults in a group, with any combination of sexes but a maximum of three breeding individuals of either sex in one group. The average number of adults per group is three, and males seldom outnumber females. Bigamy is common, and trigamy occurs. There is no relation between the size and quality of the territory and the number of birds that occupy it. At any time a large territory may have a small group, and vice versa; groups can fluctuate in time within the range of 2-10 birds without change of boundary.

The upper limit of territory size is, by observation, the largest area that the group can obtain and hold effectively; the better territories contain far more nest habitat and shelter than the group can use, and may well contain a food surplus also, although this requires to be tested by experimental alteration of food level. In a few instances the constant lateral pressure at territory boundaries enabled a group to increase its area when a neighboring group departed, but this gain was later surrendered, presumably through inability to defend the larger area. The lower limit of territory size is set by the amount of feeding pasture required to sustain the group, for a much smaller area than this can contain superabundant cover. Thus, territory size is largely determined by group size, although it is difficult to see what determines the level of the latter, which is similar throughout the range of the black-backed and white-backed forms of *G. tibicen* in eastern Australia. It is tempting to suggest that the group is limited by the number of birds that the dominant member can control, but the Western Australian Magpie (*G. dorsalis*) differs in having groups of up to 26 birds, with as many as six adult males in some groups, that occupy territories of 30-150 acres, and there are apparently no flocks (Robinson, 1956).

In many changes of territory ownership, no healthy reigning group has been dispossessed, regardless of the size of its territory or the relative strength of opponent groups. The members of defending and attacking groups fight as a team, with the advantage strongly in favor of the former.

It is convenient to recognize five social categories based on the quality of habitat occupied by each (Fig. 4 and 5), but these form a graded series and the system is anything but static, for birds and groups in the poorer environments are continually striving to improve their position in the habitat scale. Groups compete for tree cover with adjoining pasture feeding areas, which results in the open and marginal woodland, and also some open pasture, becoming subdivided into territories that are held for periods and defended with a tenacity proportionate to their quality as places to breed and feed.

1) *Permanent* groups hold territories that provide an adequate or surplus amount of all requirements all the year round. There are many more trees than the small number of birds requires for shelter, roosting, or nesting, and seasonal weights give no indication of food shortage at any time. Birds remain in these optimal territories all day and all year, and make no attempt to move. Virtually all successful breeding is done by these birds. A permanent group may contain birds of all ages.

2) *Marginal* groups occupy territories with an inadequate amount of either cover or feeding area. They form around one or two small trees or bushes (or even artificial nest sites such as telegraph poles or tall wireless masts) on the outskirts of better cover; also in open woodland poorly defended by the surrounding groups but with inadequate pasture for feeding at all seasons. Attempts to breed rarely succeed to the point of fledging. Marginal groups usually consist of adult birds only.

3) *Mobile* groups commute between a separate feeding area in the open and a nesting-roosting area among trees. The latter is held against the strong opposition of neighboring groups, and mobile groups exist mainly during the breeding season. Breeding always fails, usually at an early stage, and mobile groups do not contain first-year birds.

4) *Open* groups form in areas of treeless pasture that provide adequate feeding all year, except possibly during severe drought or hard frost. They roost in the denser woodland that is not otherwise used by this species; the daily flight is usually within a mile, and members of the same open group may go to different roosts. An open group can last several years, and some become mobile groups in spring. Open groups contain only adult birds, but they make no attempt to nest.

5) *Flock* birds are nonterritorial. They are birds of all ages and both sexes, and some may have bred as members of territorial groups now disbanded. They form loose flocks of a few up to several hundred individuals that feed in open pasture and roost in woods. More intensive study might well reveal that most flock adults are in fact in open groups with varying degrees of attachment to feeding area or constancy of membership, but more stable during the breeding season. The flocks show slight mobility throughout the year, and about half of the open terrain in the study area is occupied and the other half left untenanted by them at any one time. They do not attempt to nest.

Changes of Status

In this territorial system, there is considerable temporal and spatial stability of groups and individuals; in May 1962, 16 of the original 38 permanent groups present in 1955 still occupied the same territory, and 20 percent of males and 18 percent of females were in the territories where they were first banded as adults in 1955 or early 1956. These figures are rather low because they include losses from human activities that would not occur over most of the magpie's range. This stability is maintained by constant vigilance in a dynamic situation in which there is continual daily effort all the year round, with an upsurge of activity in July to October, i.e. before and during breeding, on the part of both groups and individuals to improve their social status.

Individual changes may result in increase, replacement, or decrease in the members of a group. Most birds leave their natal territory during their first year, some in the second, and a few in the third, but a small proportion continues to live and breed there. More females than males do this, and the oldest hen that has remained in the parental territory is now almost 7 years old, while the oldest cock is 3½ years old. It is exceptional for an adult to be added to an existing group, but this has occurred

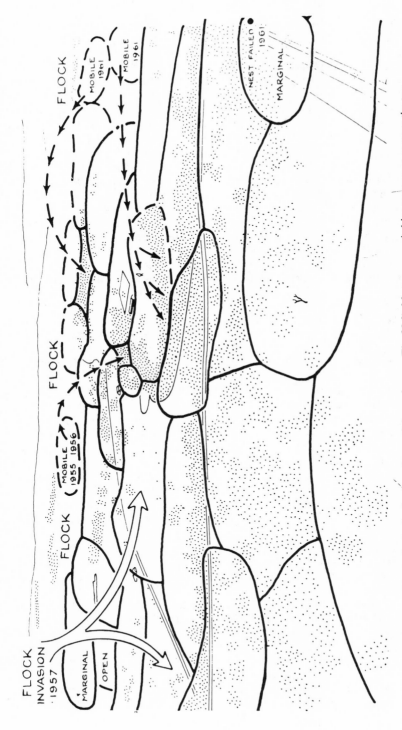

FIG. 25-4.—The territories in the central part of the study area (Fig. 25-2). Most are occupied by permanent groups; the two types of marginal territory are shown at top left (inadequate cover) and bottom right (inadequate pasture); small arrows show where mobile groups attempted to nest, and the large arrow shows where flock birds invaded breeding territories in the hard winter and spring of 1957.

229

when a sick hen was unable to repel a flock hen that became established in the group before the resident hen recovered. Members of a group repel their own sex, but each sex supports the other once a contest is under way. When a vacancy is created, as by mortality, for either sex, a replacement by one or more birds of the same sex may occur; this is more usual in the case of females than males, presumably because of the greater ability of the latter to hold on to their territory. Mortality causes decrease in a group, and either sex may emigrate from a group in an inadequate territory to one in a better territory where there is a sex vacancy for it.

A group preformed in the flock, or one in occupation of a poor habitat, may succeed in forcing its way into a better habitat, thus creating a new territory. Loss of the dominant adult, usually the male, often leads to break-up and displacement of a group by a new one. A group seldom becomes too large, but in one case a group of 3 males, 4 females, and 3 immatures became subdivided and the adult male and female, which separated from the others, continued to occupy part of the original territory. Expansion of territory with change in the composition of the group can occur when a neighboring group goes out and the territory is not immediately claimed by an incoming group; unless the first territory is small, the group is not usually able to defend the expanded area effectively and has to surrender all or part of it eventually.

The Gonad Cycle and Breeding

In the Canberra region, egg laying extends from August through October, and some seasons start earlier than others. This is preceded by increased epigamic activity of adult males from July onward, when many immatures are evicted from territorial groups and many open and marginal groups make determined attempts to secure adequate tree cover for nesting. The female alone selects the nest site and builds the nest; copulation occurs only at her invitation. The clutch contains 1-6, average 3, eggs, and some re-laying after failure occurs in earlier seasons, but little in a normal one. The cock does not brood, but may feed the hen on the nest and may play a variable part in feeding the young.

Males of all ages and all environments and social positions have motile sperm in the breeding season. Testes are largest in adult males in permanent territories, and much smaller in territory or flock 1-year-olds. Where nutrition is adequate, as it always seems to be, physical environmental stimuli alone appear capable of bringing the testis to maturity, after which age and social status in that order determine how far development will proceed. Testis size and sperm production do not appear to be affected by antagonistic relations between groups, or between a group and trespassing individuals, or within the group.

No 1-year-old female has been known to ovulate. Some 2-year-old hens breed, but even in permanent groups some females of this age or even older may not breed. In spring the ovary undergoes partial development in every case, and the final rapid increase in size of oocytes, with associated nest-building behavior, depends on the presence of certain critical stimuli as well as the absence of inhibiting factors. To attain ovulation, the hen must be a member of a social group in a territory that offers an acceptable nest site, but the threshold value of the latter in

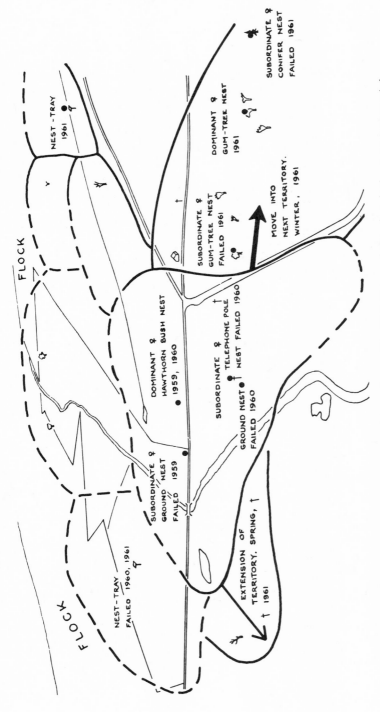

FIG. 25-5.—The territories in a marginal part of the study area (Fig. 25-3). The marginal territory in the center was occupied in 1959 and 1960 by a cock with two hens; the dominant hen nested in the single hawthorn bush and the subordinate one made abortive attempts elsewhere; in 1961, this group succeeded to the permanent territory on the right, but interference by the dominant hen still prevented the subordinate one from breeding successfully. A group of two cocks and three hens found the center territory inadequate for breeding in 1961, despite an extension to include a dead tree. A similar variability of response was shown by the open groups at top left and top right, and only the latter nested on the artificial tray provided.

Labels in figure:

NEST-TRAY 1961

FLOCK

SUBORDINATE ♀ CONIFER NEST FAILED 1961

DOMINANT ♀ GUM-TREE NEST 1961

SUBORDINATE ♀ GUM-TREE NEST FAILED 1961

MOVE INTO NEXT TERRITORY, WINTER, 1961

DOMINANT ♀ HAWTHORN BUSH NEST 1959, 1960

SUBORDINATE ♀ TELEPHONE POLE NEST FAILED 1960

SUBORDINATE ♀ GROUND NEST FAILED 1960

SUBORDINATE ♀ GROUND NEST FAILED 1959

FLOCK

NEST-TRAY 1960, 1961 FAILED

EXTENSION OF TERRITORY, SPRING, 1961

different individuals varies from a high tree to a low bush or post, and in one exceptional case the ground. Tradition is probably important, and preliminary experiments in open territories with artificial sites in the form of wooden trays on poles, bare or decorated with foliage, and with small trees, suggest that foliage as such sometimes has valency. Male stimulation of the female does not occur, for hens whose adult cocks were caponized with oestrogen implants and made effeminate to the point of building nests and soliciting, continued to build and lay (infertile eggs) normally on the same dates as control groups.

Even in the presence of adequate proximate stimuli, oocyte development and nest building can be inhibited by emotional factors, such as intrusion of a strange magpie of either sex into the territory, an undue amount of boundary fighting, or domination by another female of the same group. The psychosomatic effect of alien individuals, even on hens in first-grade permanent territories, has been observed as it occurred naturally in several situations, notably in 1957 when flock birds, which overran some territories (Fig. 4) during the frosty winter and were not evicted by spring, caused inhibition of nesting among the resident hens; this effect has been confirmed experimentally. The response of individual hens to similar stimulatory and inhibitory factors in the environment varies widely.

TABLE 1.—Numbers of *Gymnorhina tibicen* in the Gungahlin Study Area

Status . . . . When Censused	TERRITORY [a] AUG.-SEPT.		FLOCK [b] MAY-JULY		TOTAL IN POPULATION	
	No.	Percent	No.	Percent	No.	Percent
ADULT FEMALES						
1957 [c]	92	36	161	64	253	100
1958	103	35	189	65	292	100
1960	112	39	178	61	290	100
1961	111	40	168	60	279	100
AVERAGE DURING 1957-61						
Males	79	21	296	79	375	100
Females	107	38	174	62	281	100
Total adults	186	28	470	72	656	100
(Sex ratio males : females)	(43 : 57)		(63 : 37)		(57 : 43)	
1st-year birds [d]	ca. 15		ca. 70		ca. 85	
Total population	ca. 200		ca. 540		ca. 740	

[a] Territory birds include all hens that have an opportunity to breed, i.e. permanent, marginal, and mobile groups.

[b] Flock birds are nonterritorial individuals plus open groups.

[c] Owing to improved methods of observation and trapping in subsequent years, the numbers for 1957 may be rather low.

[d] Counts taken in midwinter.

No open group has reached the stage of nest building. The breeding performance of mobile groups varies from failure to commence building to an occasional successful hatching, but, because of predation while the adult is absent at the feeding ground, no hen in a mobile group has been able to fledge its young. Those mobile hens that become sufficiently established to build and lay often lose their eggs from the direct attack of neighboring magpies; or else the eggs become addled, or eggs or nestlings fall to predators when the hens are engaged in boundary fights or are absent in the feeding area. The most common predator of eggs and nestlings is the Australian Raven (*Corvus coronoides*). Marginal groups often fail to nest, but a small percentage rear young to the free-living stage. It is the permanent groups that produce the annual increment to the population, but even their breeding rate is reduced by aggression between groups and by sex dominance within groups, as well as by the usual factors not directly associated with social territorialism. The extent to which this system reduces breeding to one-quarter of the potential it would have in the absence of territorial capitalism of breeding sites and sociosexual aggression and dominance is shown in Tables 1 and 2.

Annual Productivity and Mortality

In a good breeding season about one juvenile magpie per adult territorial female reaches the free-flying stage in January, and the number is much lower in poor seasons. The high survival of adult birds during the course of this study indicates that a low annual death rate, especially in the permanent territorial groups, is adequate to cancel the normal increase from natality.

TABLE 2.—DEGREE OF BREEDING FAILURE CAUSED BY TERRITORIALISM

Year	1958		1960	
	No.	Percent	No.	Percent
Total number adult females in study area	292	100	290	100
Nonbreeding females in flocks	189	65	178	61
Failing females in territories, due to intergroup aggression	16	6	21	7
and intragroup dominance	13	5	14	5
Total reduction of nests	218	76	213	73

Starvation has not been evident in this study, although birds of all ages in the wide range of habitats, but each with good feeding pasture, have shown significant differences of body weight throughout the year. The same is true of stomach contents and fat reserves.

Predation by crows and hawks occurs up to the free-flying stage, and is more severe in poorer cover, but natural losses among older birds, even including those due to feral cats, are not considered serious. The Peregrine Falcon (*Falco peregrinus*) has occasionally hunted the area and taken adult flock birds in the open. Immature *Homo sapiens* of all ages take a steady but small toll of nestlings, which are popular if illegal pets, and of adults, which afford target practice in the absence of other game and, in the case of the cock during the breeding season, engender retaliation for their unprovoked attacks on people. Territories on main roads consistently lose their juveniles, and an occasional adult, in traffic accidents, and rabbit traps and other human agencies also account for a small number of birds, mainly in territories.

Diseases of many kinds have been identified during this study, some of them lethal, and at least one is considered to be an important primary cause of death. This is *Pasteurella pseudotuberculosis,* which killed large numbers of flock birds during the cold wet winter of 1956, but, being contact-spread, did not cause a single death among the territory individuals, all of which were banded, in woodland closely adjacent to open pasture where dead and dying birds could be picked up daily at the height of the epidemic. The flock birds exposed to this infection showed no sign of debility, as compared with territory birds, that might have predisposed them to mortality, and the conditions that favor the disease appear to occur too infrequently for development of resistance to it. During the harder winter of 1957, the food on the more exposed pastures became unavailable, and many flock birds concentrated on softer ground and haystacks, where they picked up the spores of the fungus *Aspergillus,* which became a secondary cause of death of some importance that year. Both of these diseases and several others take a constant low-level toll of magpies.

Conclusions

Territorialism and associated sociosexual interactions limit breeding to about one-quarter of the adult population of *G. tibicen.*

Territorialism buffers that element of the population against important mortality from disease, and probably also protects it from predation.

The completeness of the territorial habit in *G. tibicen,* in which the social group lives permanently within its territory, indicates that the food supply of this area is always adequate; nor is there evidence that flock birds come up against the food limit.

LITERATURE CITED

HINDE, R. A. 1956. The biological significance of the territories of birds. Ibis 98: 340-369.
ROBINSON, A. 1956. The annual reproductory cycle of the magpie, *Gymnorhina dorsalis* Campbell, in south-western Australia. Emu 56:233-336.
WYNNE-EDWARDS, V. C. 1962. Animal dispersion in relation to social behaviour. Oliver and Boyd, Edinburgh. 653 p.

EFFECT OF EXPLOITATION ON BIRTH, MORTALITY AND MOVEMENT RATES IN A WOODCHUCK POPULATION (1964)

David E. Davis, John J. Christian and Frank Bronson

Direct manipulation of populations through exploitation is a primary aspect of wildlife management. Exploitation may influence population density and structure. These population responses sometimes are counter to antici-pated results of management efforts. This paper illustrates the dynamic attributes of the response of a population to exploitation.

It is axiomatic that changes in the numbers of animals reflect changes in birth-rates, death rates, and movement rates that result in turn from changes in the environmental factors. A detailed examination of the changes in numbers and age composition of a population of woodchucks was an integral part of a continuing study of the role of social behavior in limiting population growth. Changes in age composition are recognized as an important manifestation of changes in the population itself. The experi-ment to be described was designed to determine the quantitative effects of removal of animals on population parameters. Therefore, changes in birth, mortality,.and movement rates in an area from which large numbers of woodchucks were regularly removed were compared with the same kinds of changes in a reference area from which few woodchucks were removed. High precision in estimating numbers has not been attained; hence the changes are indicated in magnitude and direction rather than in detailed counts.

The woodchucks were studied on the Letterkenny Army Ordnance Depot near Chambersburg, Pennsylvania, beginning in 1955. The research was conducted under grant H4836 from the U. S. Public Health Service. Certain early phases were supported by the Naval Medical Research Institute.

The annual cycle of woodchucks in this area consists of emergence from hibernation in February, breeding, parturition in early April, raising the young, and finally hibernation again in October (Snyder and Christian 1960).

Description of Area

The work was done on the ammunition storage section of Letterkenny Ordnance Depot. The storage section contains 10,000 acres subdivided into administrative areas. These areas, varying in size from 475 to 650 acres, contain ammunition storage bunkers in lines along a grid of hard-surfaced roads. The bunkers are of two types: (1) the open bunker, a U-shaped mound of earth, and (2) the closed bunker, a concrete shell covered by dirt. The usual distance between bunkers is 200 feet, and the lines of bunkers are generally about 1,000 feet apart. The terrain between areas, which is referred to as buffer strips, lacks bunkers and, usually, roads. The buffer strips vary in width from 1,500 to 2,500 feet. The areas compared

Reprinted from the J. of Wild. Mgmt. 28(1):1-9.

in this paper are Area C (605 acres) and Area D (537 acres). They are separated by a buffer strip about 900 feet wide at its narrowest point.

The woodchucks live on the bunkers and thrive on the lush vegetation. which consists chiefly of old-field associations interspersed with small woodlots, generally oak (*Quercus* spp.)—hickory (*Carya* spp.) associations. In order to determine whether the two areas were sufficiently homogeneous to permit comparisons, we analyzed 50 quadrats in each area for frequency of occurrence of plant species (Table 1). A chi-square test showed that the two areas did not differ substantially in this respect ($P < 0.05$). The quadrats, which were 9.5 x 21 feet each and were located on the flat tops of the closed bunkers, were also compared as to the mean number of species on each. The means and their 95-percent confidence limits for the two areas were as follows: Area D, 11.20 (10.92-11.48); Area C, 12.92 (12.50-13.34). In this respect, Area C differed significantly from Area D, probably because some of the closed bunkers were built at a later date than the others, and the newer ones usually had more plant species than the older ones. The most commonly appearing plants on the new bunkers were orchard grass (*Dactylis glomerata*) and alfalfa (*Medicago sativa*). In Area C, 18 percent of the bunkers were new, while in Area D there were no new bunkers, a fact which accounts for the differences in species composition. It was concluded, however, that the two areas were sufficiently similar for comparisons.

TABLE 1. Percentage of 50 quadrats in Areas C and D that contained each plant species.

Species	Area C (percent)	Area D (percent)	Species	Area C (percent)	Area D (percent)
Kentucky bluegrass, *Poa pratensis*	88	96	Creeping lady's sorrel, *Oxalis corniculata*	22	16
Wild onion, *Allium* sp.	76	82	Pennyroyal, *Hedeoma pulegioides*	22	8
Green foxtail, *Setaria viridis*	74	56	Buckhorn plantain, *Plantago lanceolata*	22	4
Foxtail, *Setaria glauca*	62	58	Wild strawberry, *Fragaria virginiana*	20	22
Canada thistle, *Cirsium arvense*	54	58	Poison ivy, *Rhus radicans*	18	6
Sheep sorrel, *Rumex acetosella*	54	38	Alfalfa, *Medicago sativa*	18	10
Bramble, *Rubus* sp.	50	40	Orchard grass, *Dactylis glomerata*	16	4
Cow cress, *Lepidium campestre*	38	30	Queen Anne's lace, *Daucus carota*	16	2
Climbing false buckwheat, *Polygonum scandens*	36	48	Indian hemp, *Apocynum* sp.	16	16
Poke, *Phytolacca americana*	36	22	Viper's bugloss, *Echium vulgare*	14	16
Goldenrods, *Solidago* spp.	36	10	Canada bluegrass, *Poa compressa*	14	2
Chinese mustard, *Brassica juncea*	36	22	Horse nettle, *Solanum carolinense*	12	20
Common ragweed, *Ambrosia artemisiifolia*	36	14	Upright cinquefoil, *Potentilla recta*	10	8
Blue waxweed, *Cuphea petiolata*	34	24	Quick grass, *Agropyron repeus*	8	44
Butter-and-eggs, *Linaria vulgaris*	28	36	Black nightshade, *Solanum nigrum*	8	20
Eyebane, *Euphorbia maculata*	26	66	Spanish needles, *Bidens bipinnata*	8	18
Brome grass, *Bromus racemosus*	24	8	Deptford pink, *Dianthus armeria*	6	0
Timothy, *Phleum pratense*	24	10	Flower-of-an-hour, *Hibiscus trionum*	0	4

Methods

The woodchucks were captured in treadle-type wooden box traps and were either killed for detailed examination or tagged in the ear with a numbered clip and released. In certain months, some were shot. Data on weight, age, sex, the various reproductive organs, and location were recorded in ledger books. Age (Davis 1964) was recorded in early spring as

236

yearling or *adult*; but after May 15, yearlings could no longer be distinguished with certainty from adults. Hence, after that date, individuals were recorded as adult and no age ratios were calculated. The young-of-the-year were easily distinguished in July, when they began to appear in traps. Since much of the analysis involves proportions of age groups, the method of calculating these proportions should be clearly understood. The fall (August or September) calculations of the percentage of young woodchucks in the population (Table 6) were made by multiplying the number of young-of-the-year by 100 and dividing by the total number of woodchucks, which included young yearling, and older animals. The spring (February-May) percentages of yearlings were calculated in the same way, that is, by multiplying the number of yearlings (surviving young of the previous year) by 100 and dividing by the total number of woodchucks.

TABLE 2. Mean interval in days between captures of the same animals during census periods (Areas C and D combined). No significant difference in susceptibility to capture was found to be due to sex.

SEASON	AGE	SEX	NUMBER CAPTURED	DAYS BETWEEN CAPTURES (MEAN)	SE
March-April, 1958	Yearlings	Male	6	4.2	2.27
		Female	4	16.2	4.37
	Adult	Male	23	11.2	1.56
		Female	23	9.6	1.52
May, 1958	Yearlings	Male	14	5.4	1.26
		Female	5	2.8	0.67
	Adult	Male	12	4.8	1.28
		Female	14	5.7	0.77
August-	Young	Male	22	7.8	1.14
September, 1958-59		Female	14	10.4	2.07
	Adult	Male	15	9.9	1.56
		Female	17	8.4	1.66

The possibility of bias in trapping was given careful consideration. First, the data on trapped woodchucks were analyzed with respect to sex and age ratios. To determine whether susceptibility to trapping is correlated with sex and age, the mean intervals between the first capture of an animal and subsequent recaptures were compared. (Equal trapping effort was expended in each area during the periods used for calculations.) This test of the data revealed no differences due to sex (Table 2) or age (Table 3). It did show that the woodchucks were more susceptible to capture in May than at other times of the year, but sex and age did not apparently contribute to this seasonal difference.

TABLE 3. Mean interval in days between captures of the same animals (areas and sexes combined). No significant difference in susceptibility to capture was found to be due to age.

SEASON	AGE	NUMBER CAPTURED	DAYS BETWEEN CAPTURES (MEAN)	SE
March-April, 1958	Yearlings	10	9.0	2.86
	Adult	46	10.4	1.09
May, 1958	Yearlings	19	4.7	0.82
	Adult	26	5.3	0.71
August-	Young	36	8.8	1.07
September, 1958-59	Adult	32	9.1	1.13

Further analysis (Table 4) compared weights of woodchucks trapped during selected periods in 1957 and 1958 with weights of woodchucks shot during the same periods. The percentage of animals under 6 pounds (a weight arbitrarily chosen to divide the young and yearlings from the adults) was significantly smaller in the animals shot than in those trapped. The problem then arose of deciding which data to use, those from trapped or from shot animals. Since woodchucks of all ages were equally susceptible to trapping (Tables 2 and 3), the data in Table 4 must mean that the number of young woodchucks shot was not in proportion to their numbers in the total population. Hence it was decided to use only data from trapped woodchucks in computing age ratios. It is not certain, of course, that trapping data accurately reflect the true age or sex composition of the total population. For example, although not many animals escaped from the traps, it is possible that large ones found it easier to escape than small ones did. It was assumed, however, that in the same months of different years, trapping produced the same proportions (whatever they might be) of the true age and sex composition, so that comparisons between years could be made.

TABLE 4. Relative percentages of small and large woodchucks trapped or shot at selected times in 1957 and 1958 (sexes combined). *Small* here means weighing less than 6 pounds.

	TOTAL NUMBER	SMALL (PERCENT)	P
1957			
Shot	101	19	0.001
Trapped	264	37	
1958			
Shot	87	14	0.001
Trapped	296	25	

Several methods were used and others considered to determine how many woodchucks were present. The recapture method was feasible since it was possible to tag and recapture woodchucks easily. As shown above, no bias was apparent in respect to age or sex in retrapping. However, soon after this study began, immigration attained a magnitude that violated the assumption of no differential movement of marked and unmarked animals and gave grossly inflated values. A deficiency of a recapture procedure is that assumptions, perhaps unwarranted, about immigration and births or emigration and deaths are necessary. These assumptions can be minimized quantitatively by the following procedure. First, woodchucks were trapped, tagged, and released for several weeks. Second, 50 traps were set for 30 days (census period). Third, woodchucks were trapped for several weeks after the census period. It was assumed that woodchucks captured before and after the census period were present during the census period. The efficiency of capture is the proportion trapped of those assumed to be present. The average catch per day (using 50 traps for 30 days) was divided by the efficiency to get the minimum number present. This method requires no assumptions about differential movement or mortality. The duration of trapping and the number of traps were constant. The estimates (plotted in Fig. 1) differ from the recapture estimates published in Snyder (1962:510) and are considered superior. Note that the plotted totals refer to only part (215 acres) of Area C and of Area D, not to the entire areas.

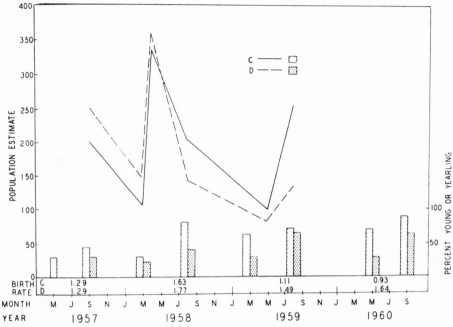

FIG. 26-1.—History of woodchuck populations from 1957-60, presenting the available estimates for part (215 acres) of the exploited Area C (solid line) and part (215 acres) of the reference Area D (broken line). The percentages of young or yearlings are shown by bars and the birthrates by numbers.

Sex ratios were calculated but no significant changes from 50 percent male occurred in these two areas (Snyder 1962:509).

Certain inferences can be made from recapture data and from calculations of age composition. A recaptured woodchuck has obviously lived long enough in the area to be retrapped. But if a woodchuck is not recaptured, it may have died, moved away, or avoided the traps. Thus, inferences based on woodchucks that "disappear" must be limited, particularly in analyzing age composition. An increase from one year to the next in the proportion of yearlings as compared with the proportion of young in the preceding fall may result from differential survival or from immigration or, more probably, from both. The numerical extent of survival or immigration is difficult to determine and will not be used in this paper.

Results

Fig. 1 shows no striking differences between the estimated population of Area C and that of Area D. Area C initially seemed to have fewer

	1957		1958		1959		1960	
	C	D	C	D	C	D	C	D
February	44	0	7	6	0	0	12	0
March	53	0	32	23	42	31	67	0
April	8	5	52	37	75	21	102	45
May	14	5	65	0	5	1	28	13
June	9	0	63	0	53	4	38	19
July	24	0	19	4	35	19	10	17
August	31	1	1	4	3	0	7	3
September	15	11	53	30	73	0	0	0
Total	198*	22	292*	104	286	76	264	97

* Totals differ slightly from those given by Snyder (1962) because he included poisoned animals.

woodchucks than Area D but later seemed to have more. Seasonal changes, however, are plainly shown in Fig. 1, especially the sharp increase each spring, caused by the birth of young.

Although 1,040 woodchucks were removed from Area C and only 299 from Area D (Table 5), the populations of the two areas remained numerically indistinguishable. The 1960 spring and fall population estimates are not shown on the graph because technical difficulties reduced their comparability, but the figures for the two areas were very close.

The percentages of young and of yearlings (Table 6, Fig. 1) increased greatly over the years. An unharvested population normally has about 30 percent yearlings in the spring. However, as animals were removed, the proportion of young and yearlings increased, until in Area C it reached 71 percent in the spring of 1960 and 90 percent in the fall, whereas in Area D, from which fewer animals were removed, the proportion remained near 30 percent in the spring and reached only 64 percent in the fall. It seems fairly certain that the removal of woodchucks tended to be compensated for by increased survival and decreased emigration of young.

TABLE 6. Percentages of yearlings in successive springs and of young in successive falls in Areas C and D (sample over 100 in all cases).

MONTH	AGE	AREA C	AREA D
May, 1957	Yearlings	30	—
September, 1957	Young	43	30
March, 1958	Yearlings	30	21
August, 1958	Young	80	40
Feb. 1-April 15, 1959	Yearlings	61	28
August, 1959	Young	74	65
May, 1960	Yearlings	71	29
August, 1960	Young	90	64

The survival rate may be roughly determined by comparing the numbers of tagged and released woodchucks recaptured in successive years. For example, in Area D in 1957, 41 young woodchucks and 84 adults were trapped, tagged, and released again. The next spring a fraction (0.24) of the young and a fraction (0.53) of the adults were recaptured. The ratio of recaptured young to recaptured adults was 0.24:0.53 or 0.45:1.00. Similar ratios were obtained for both areas in three successive years (Table 7).

About the same proportion of adults was recovered in Area D as in Area C, but Area C shows a consistently higher proportion of young recaptured,

TABLE 7. A measure of relative survival and residence of woodchucks in the two areas for different years. (See text for explanation.)

RELEASED IN	AND	RECAP- TURED IN	FRACTION OF YOUNG RECAPTURED FRACTION OF ADULTS RECAPTURED	
			AREA C	AREA D
1957		1958	1.28:1.00	0.45:1.00
1958		1959	0.89:1.00	0.73:1.00
1959		1960	1.08:1.00	0.81:1.00

although, to be sure, the proportion of young recaptured in Area D did show an increase in each of the three years. The higher recapture rate of young in Area C probably resulted from either greater survival or less emigration or both, suggesting that compensatory factors were at work to replace the woodchucks removed from that area.

The number of woodchucks emigrating from Area C to Area D can be compared with the number emigrating from D to C by determining how many of those marked in each area were recaptured in the other. Table 8 shows, for example, that of the many young males tagged in Area D in 1958, 18 were recaptured; 6 of these had emigrated to Area C and 12 had stayed in Area D. At the same time, all of the 36 recaptured young males that had been tagged in Area C were recaptured in the same area; not one was recaptured in Area D. The following conclusions may be drawn from the data in Table 8: (1) the majority of emigrants from both areas were young woodchucks, not adults; (2) the emigration from D to C was much greater than that from C to D, suggesting that immigration compensated at least in part for the removals from Area C; (3) emigration from Area D decreased in 1960, after the removal of more woodchucks from that area had begun to make the same kind of change in age ratio that had previously occurred in Area C.

It should be noted that Area D and Area C adjoin on only one side. The other three sides of each are bounded by other areas, which must have contributed their share of immigrants into both C and D.

TABLE 8. An indication of the extent of emigration from each area by age, sex, and year.

WOODCHUCKS MARKED IN AREA C								
YEAR . . .	1957		1958		1959		1960	
RECAPTURED IN AREA	D	C	D	C	D	C	D	C
Adult males	0	3	0	12	0	15	1	8
Adult females	0	8	1	12	0	5	0	0
Young males	0	8	0	36	0	21	0	9
Young females	0	17	1	31	2	44	1	25

WOODCHUCKS MARKED IN AREA D								
YEAR . . .	1957		1958		1959		1960	
RECAPTURED IN AREA	C	D	C	D	C	D	C	D
Adult males	1	15	0	23	1	18	0	0
Adult females	1	36	0	21	0	8	0	0
Young males	1	5	6	12	3	17	1	10
Young females	0	13	1	21	9	16	3	13

Comparisons can be made between the number of young removed, the expected number of young left, and the estimated number left for each year in each area. The approximations show large discrepancies in Area C and a gradual change in Area D. For example, in 1959, in Area C about 133 young were born and about 166 young were present in the fall, even though 124 had been removed during the summer. Obviously, immigration was great. Calculations of this type cannot be pursued in detail since two of the three numbers are estimates. However, it is clear that immigration was extensive and increased from 1957 to 1960 and seemed greater into Area C than into Area D. This difference, while not a precise figure, must be considered to show a greater extent of immigration into Area C than into Area D.

The fact that immigration played a large role in maintaining density in Area C becomes obvious when one realizes that the data (Table 8) show a net flow of animals moving into Area C. Woodchucks could and surely did move into Area C from Area D and the other three sides. Tables 7 and 8 suggest that (1) young animals made up the bulk of the immigrants into all areas; (2) young animals tended to stay in Area C instead of emigrating; and (3) young animals tended to emigrate at a higher rate from Area D than from Area C.

Birthrates for each area for each year were calculated from the mean number of embryos in a sample of females divided by a figure for the sum of males and females, which was obtained from the sex ratio. Birthrates clearly changed (Fig. 1). The rate increased at first in Area C and then declined. The decline was due to the removal of adult animals so that in later years the birthrate essentially represents the production by yearlings. Thus from Area C in 1959, 65 percent of 51 females captured were yearlings and, in 1960, 70 percent of 59 females were yearlings. Yearlings regularly produce fewer young than do adults (Snyder and Christian 1960: 655). For example, in Area C in 1960, 58 percent of all the females captured were pregnant while in Area D 84 percent were. The difference resulted from the difference in age composition (Table 6).

Discussion

The striking result is that the populations remained so similar in total number even though three times as many woodchucks were removed from C (1,040) as from D (299). Compensatory changes occurred in birthrate, mortality, and movements; especially in Area C.

The birthrate in Area C increased at first and then declined steadily, the decline being due to an increasing proportion of young animals, which have a low birthrate. Obviously, reproduction in Area C was too low to account for the maintenance of the population in the later years of the study. The problem then becomes one of determining the relative compensatory values of survival of young and of immigration. Since trapping was the main tool utilized for gathering data, survival and movement cannot be clearly separated. However, general trends can be indicated for movement and, by subtraction, to some degree for survival, since these two factors combine to produce the number of animals required. The increase in the percentage of young in Area C was presumably due at first to increased survival. The evidence shows that the percentage of young in an unmolested population of woodchucks is about 30; Area D had 30 percent in 1957, and in 1960 another un-exploited area (F) had 33 percent. The percentage in Area C increased to 43 even in the first year, while in Area D, where fewer woodchucks were removed, it took until August, 1958, for the percentage of young to rise to 40. The increase in the percentage of young results in part from an increase in survival and in part from immigration of young into the area. Increased survival is indicated (Table 7) by a difference in the percentage recovered. Unfortunately, in 1959 and in 1960, survival could not be separated from immigration, which had become very high.

These three forces—birthrate, survival of young, and immigration—compensated for the animals that were removed. The problem is to determine the extent of each. Unfortunately, for this purpose we would need the individual history of each woodchuck, which is not available. However, a comparison of the tabular data with Fig. 1 may show what happened in each area.

In 1958 in Area C, the population was kept stationary, in spite of removals, by an increase in birthrate (Fig. 1) and by some increase in survival (Table 6: compare 43 percent young in 1957 and 80 percent young in 1958). Some immigration into C occurred (Table 8). In 1958 in Area D, the birthrate also increased, but survival was low (40 percent young in the population). Emigration was high.

In 1959 in Area C, the birthrate dropped, but survival and residence of yearlings was high and survival of young until August was high. Also, immigration was high. In Area D, the birthrate dropped a little and survival of young increased. Emigration was high.

In 1960 in Area C, the birthrate dropped more and survival and immigration remained high. In Area D, the birthrate rose again and survival of young remained high, but survival from the preceding year was low. Emigration declined somewhat.

The history of these two populations shows that all three compensatory forces—natality, mortality, and movement—changed when woodchucks were removed. Removal of more woodchucks from Area C resulted in greater compensations. Large numbers of woodchucks may be removed repeatedly (Davis 1962), depending on the extent of compensation of these forces. Calculations show that under certain conditions as many as 78 woodchucks can be harvested annually from a population that numbers 100 at the start of breeding.

LITERATURE CITED

DAVIS, D. E. 1962. The potential harvest of woodchucks. J. Wildl. Mgmt. 26(2);144-149.
_____. 1964. Evaluation of characters for determining age of woodchucks. J. Wildl. Mgmt. 28(1):9-15.
SNYDER, R. L. 1962. Reproductive performance of a population of woodchucks after a change in sex ratio. Ecology 43(3):506-515.
_____, and J. J. CHRISTIAN. 1960. Reproductive cycle and litter size of the woodchuck. Ecology 41(4):647-656.

Courtesy of Ithaca Journal

VARIATIONS IN FERTILITY OF WHITE-TAILED DEER RELATED TO RANGE CONDITIONS (1950)

E. L. Cheatum and C. W. Severinghaus

This paper was one of the first to relate range quality to reproductive performance of big game. These authors recognized that fecundity may provide an index of population density with respect to adequacy of range. They provided a technique for periodically adjusting level of harvest to maintain "balance" between density of deer and available forage.

A considerable quantity of data has been gathered during the past decade on fertility of white-tailed deer in New York State. A significant variation in embryo counts has been described (Morton and Cheatum, 1946) between deer of the northern and southern parts of their New York range. Differences in the availability of essential nutrients were suggested as probably the most important factor causing this regional variation.

With the accumulation of more data, it is now possible to make fertility comparisons on the basis of a greater number of subdivisions of the deer range in the state. The topographic, climatic, forest and soil characteristics of the principal deer territory allow the distinguishing of at least five qualitatively different regions (Figure 1). In addition, winter range carrying capacities of these five regions differ, thus lending support to an hypothesis that these qualitative differences affect deer fertility. The present paper will deal with the degree to which fertility of deer may be correlated with the five qualitative variations recognized in New York deer range and with other related factors.

Since previous findings (op. cit.) had indicated significant effects of environmental conditions on deer fertility, it was assumed that growth also might be found to be affected to a measurable degree if comparisons were made of growth data from the additional qualitative subdivisions of deer range. A report pertaining to regional variations in deer antler growth will be presented elsewhere at this Conference (Severinghaus, Macguire, Cookingham and Tanck).

Materials and Procedures

Data regarding deer fertility were derived from a total of 911 does of which 608 were adult 1½ years old or older and 303 were fawns. These data were grouped according to five divisions of the state based on the general character of deer range prevailing in each. Information regarding range conditions was obtained from available literature and from the experience of department wildlife technicians.

Collection of specimens.—From 1939 through 1942, most of the reproductive tracts of doe deer were obtained from specimens sent to the Wildlife Research Laboratory at Delmar, New York, by state game protectors. The larger part of these were highway casualties and illegal kills during the hunting seasons. In addition, special collections were made

Reprinted from Trans. N. Amer. Wildl. Conf. 15:170-189.

from the Adirondack region by department personnel and some specimens were found dead from winter malnutrition.

During the antlerless deer seasons of 1943, deer checking stations were established on main highways in the Adirondacks and in certain counties of the western region of the state. These stations were manned by department personnel who intercepted hunters returning with deer. Since it is not compulsory in New York for hunters to stop with their deer at state checking stations, extensively advertised pre-season instructions were given for the hunters to leave the female reproductive systems intact when dressing out does and to stop at the checking stations with their specimens. A good collection of reproductive material was obtained in this manner.

In the winter of 1946-47 further collections were made in the central Adirondacks during winter mortality surveys. During the breeding seasons of 1947-48 and 1948-49 a sample of does was procured from the western and Catskill regions through the cooperation of game protectors as during the period of 1939-42. Also a fertility study of does from Allegany State Park in Cattaraugus County was made during the two antlerless deer seasons there in 1944 and 1948. This constituted a special study of deer reproduction in a locality which was being seriously overbrowsed.

The procedures used here for obtaining fertility data have been described in previous papers. Fertility of deer as indicated by average embryo counts was discussed by Cheatum and Morton (1942) and the technique of utilizing corpora lutea counts for determining ova production and breeding success was recently described by Cheatum (1949). The corpora lutea of the current breeding season and the corpora lutea scars of the preceding breeding season were determined from razor sections of each pair of ovaries after hardening in formalin preservative. Embryo counts were made only when macroscopic embryos were found. Adult does without evidence of embryos or current corpora lutea were counted as breeding failures when collected after January 1. Fawn does without evidence of breeding were counted failures after March 1. These dates were used since they represent the approximate termination of the mating season for the respective age classes (Cheatum and Morton, 1946).

Definition of range divisions recognized.—Fertility data have been analyzed on a regional and sectional basis. These regions and sections of regions in New York have been chosen and defined primarily according to the general character of the deer range prevailing in each. Four principal criteria have been used to define these sections, namely, topography, climate, forest characteristics and land use.

Topography is of importance not only in its shaping of drainage characteristics and influence on the stratification of vegetation types, but in its effects on deer movements and seasonal distribution.

Climate, especially winter weather, has been demonstrated to be a limiting factor to deer abundance in New York (Severinghaus, 1947). The length of the growing season roughly indicates the length of time succulent forage is available, and conversely the interval during which deer must depend on dormant vegetation for their food. The duration of

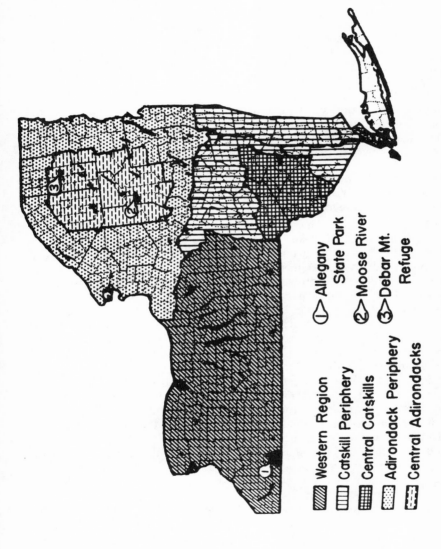

Fig. 27-1.—Distribution of five qualitatively different regions of deer range in New York State with locations of three special study areas.

Western Region

Catskill Periphery

Central Catskills

Adirondack Periphery

Central Adirondacks

① Allegany State Park

②> Moose River

③> Debar Mt. Refuge

real winter, snow depths and temperature conditions are the principal features to be considered.

The type of forest and the logging practices profoundly influence the quality of food and shelter characteristics of deer range. Regional differences in these features are considerable.

With respect to land use, deer apparently find their best environment in areas having a diversified pattern and good soil fertility. Land use is generally a good index to soil fertility over most of New York because the poorer soils either have never been used for agriculture or have been abandoned by farmers. Abandoned lands generally revert to brush, thence to forest cover. Land use is thus another index to range quality.

In addition, the status of the deer population in relation to range conditions, especially during the winter, is a measure of whether overpopulation exists or impends. Therefore, because too many deer can deplete their own food supply, this factor must be taken into account in defining the regions to be compared regarding the relation of nutrition to fertility.

On the basis of these criteria, five deer range divisions have been delimited in New York (Figure 1).[3] Following are descriptions of each according to the foregoing criteria.

Western Region.[4]—This region, lying west of and including Broome, Cayuga, Chenango, Madison and Onondaga Counties, is the best deer range in the state. Characterization of the southern section has been well presented by Gordon (1940), Cook and Hamilton (1942), and Darrow (1947-48). Excepting the Erie-Ontario Lake Plains this region is a rolling or hilly area with a moderate to mild winter climate. The growing season varies from 115 to 175 days, except for Allegany State Park and a narrow border around it which has a growing season of less than 115 days. Forested areas in the Southern Tier counties are interspersed with an almost equal amount of abandoned and farm land. The Lake Plains are relatively flat, contain some of the most fertile lands of the state, and are predominantly an agricultural area. Spot lumbering is generally practiced over most of the forested area, a practice which improves the environment for deer. Legal buck hunting, illegal killing and miscellaneous causes of death do not remove the annual increment of deer. As a consequence, periodic antlerless deer seasons are necessary to reduce agricultural damage as well as to keep the population within the long-term carrying capacity of the range. The quality of winter forage in relation to the deer population over most of the region has been adequate to excellent.

Catskill Region.—As a whole this region is delimited to accord roughly with the deer seasons of recent years but is altered somewhat along township boundaries to correspond with certain physiographic features. It embraces sufficient physiographic, ecologic and climatic differences to warrant dividing it into two sections. They are described separately as follows:

---

[3] Long Island has been omitted from this classification.

[4] This region comprises the area referred to in earlier publications as the Southern Tier and western counties of New York.

Catskill periphery.—This section of the Catskill region is a good deer environment and from the standpoint of range evaluation is akin to the Southern Tier section of the western region. The kinds and quantity of browse in both sections appear to be so similar that a difference in range quality is difficult to distinguish. This section extends from the foothills of the central Catskills to the Mohawk-Hudson Valley and also includes the area east of the Hudson River south of Washington County. The terrain is rolling, irregular and the elevation is low to moderate. The growing season varies from 115 to 190 days (although it exceeds 170 only in the lower Hudson Valley) and winter temperatures are mild to moderately cold. Low temperatures and deep snows are infrequent and of short duration. Possibly half of the area is farmland which varies from some of New York's best to some of its poorest. The other half is abandoned or forested land with soils of moderate to low fertility. West of the Hudson River and north of the central Catskill section wooded areas are generally spot lumbered. Deer can generally roam most of this range throughout the year but dogs cause heavy losses during some winters when the snow becomes unusually deep (Severinghaus, 1948). In the remainder of the area west of the Hudson River logging operations and clear cutting for acid wood distillation have created many areas of second growth even-aged hardwoods with a scattering of hemlock and other conifers. In addition illegal hunting, year around, keeps the sex ratio about equal in spite of the buck law, and the tendency to overpopulation is diminished.

Central Catskill.—This is the poorest deer range in southern New York. The section is roughly bounded by the Shawangunk Kill, the Delaware River and its West Branch, the southern margins of Schoharie and Albany Counties and the western border of the Hudson Valley some 10 to 15 miles from the river. This section has been described by Guyot (1880) and Bowman (1911). In the northeastern half there is a rugged, heavily forested, mountainous area supporting a predominantly hardwood cover. The southwestern half is rugged, less mountainous and is covered with a mixed stand of timber. The soils are acid and of low fertility. The growing season is 115 to 145 days long but winter temperatures are generally moderate and snow depths are seldom excessive. During some winters deer are restricted to their winter trials by snow which limits their movements on the steep slopes. Such occasional seasons sometimes cause winter losses from malnutrition. In general the wintering areas are small and scattered. The harvest of timber, impossible on state land representing about a quarter of the area and sometimes neglected on private lands because of personal indifference to practical forestry, is not continuous enough to make good deer environment. The deer population remains fairly static from one decade to the next in spite of the fact that only antlered deer are legal game in the fall.

Adirondack Region.—As in the Catskill region the Adirondack, or northern, region contains sufficient environmental differences to warrant its division into two sections. They are described as follows:

Adirondack periphery.—This section of the Adirondack region is poorer deer range than that of southern New York. It contains the outer flanks of the Adirondack Mountains, the Tug Hill Plateau, the valleys of the Black, St. Lawrence and upper Hudson Rivers, and the Lake Champlain Valley. The topography is rolling or hilly and in part mountainous. The growing season varies from 115 to 160 days and the winter season is moderately cold. Parts of the section are sometimes covered with snow of critical depths which remain for periods up to 4 to 8 weeks. There is a much greater diversification of timber types and land-use patterns in this section than is found in the central Adirondacks, next to be described. Excepting the Black River, St. Lawrence and lower Champlain Valleys where soils are of moderate to high fertility, the soils of the Adirondack periphery are generally acid and of low to moderate productiveness. A sizable proportion of the section is abandoned land or worked by subsistence farmers. However, the valley lands mentioned above support a good dairy industry. Much of the eastern edge of the section, and a narrow edge around the central Adirondack section on the west, falls within the Adirondack Forest Preserve. Logging of state-owned lands within the Preserve is prohibited. On the privately-owned lands lumbering is on a fairly sound rotational cutting cycle and quite often both hardwoods and softwoods are cut. There is little clear cutting. Deer wintering areas are mostly few in number, small and generally understocked so that little winter mortality has occurred, except in a few isolated winter areas, even during severe winters. The relatively high hunting pressure and the year around illegal killing keep the deer population in general within the carrying capacity of the winter range.

Central Adirondacks.—In general this is the poorest deer range in the State. It is of marginal quality and, prior to the elimination of wolves and panthers and the initiation of logging, contained very few deer. Most of the published information concerning the Adirondacks has involved this section. Merriam (1884) described central Adirondack conditions. Townsend and Smith (1933), Pearce (1937), Severinghaus (1947) and Darrow (1947-48) have also described conditions in various locations of the central section. It is a mountainous area characterized by acid soils of low fertility underlaid by granite. It has a rather short growing season of 80 to 130 days and a cold winter climate with deep snows. Most of the section is a dense northern forest, having a definite stratification of timber types. It includes most of the known wintering areas where malnutrition and winter losses have been chronic. Deer begin to congregate in valleys containing evergreen swamps or mixed stands as soon as snow becomes deep enough to make travel on the hardwood slopes difficult. Over-population of many wintering areas, in relation to the available winter browse supply results from a low hunting pressure in the fall and a virtual absence of illegal hunting. In other wintering areas reasonably close to roads and small settlements, the annual harvest of deer, legal and illegal, is heavy enough to prevent over-population in relation to available forage.

Local Study Areas.—In addition to data for the various range divisions as a whole, fertility records have been collected from three local study areas. These are the Allegany State Park in the Southern Tier county of Cattaraugus in the western region, DeBar Mountain Game Management Area in Franklin County, and the "Plains" on the South Branch of the Moose River in Hamilton County in the central Adirondacks (Figure 1).

Findings

Specimens from the five regions recognized were comparably distributed for both collection periods, and the age classes represented were also comparable. Data from these five regions and from the three special study areas are summarized in the following paragraphs.

TABLE 1. Comparative fertility of adult does from five regions of New York State, 1939-49[1]

	Embryo counts					Corpora lutea counts		
Region or section	Number does examined	Number pregnant	Per cent	Number embryos	Average per doe	Number pairs ovaries	Number corpora lutea	Average per doe
			1939-1943					
Western	88	81	92.0	141	1.60	71	136	1.92
Catskill Periphery	48	44	91.7	76	1.58	8	14	1.75
Central Catskill	20	19	95.0	33	1.65	16	30	1.88
Adirondack Periphery	14	12	85.7	18	1.29	14	24	1.71
Central Adirondacks	98	77	78.6	98	1.00	56	57	1.02
			1947-1949					
Western	52	51	98.1	99	1.90	52	106	2.04
Catskill Periphery	38	35	92.1	51	1.34	39	67	1.72
Central Catskill	18	14	77.8	19	1.06	16	25	1.56
Central Adirondacks	25	20	80.0	32	1.28	23	31	1.35
			Total					
Western	140	132	94.3	240	1.71	123	242	1.97
Catskill Periphery	86	79	91.9	127	1.48	49	81	1.72
Central Catskill	38	33	86.8	52	1.37	32	55	1.72
Adirondack Periphery	14	12	85.7	18	1.29	14	24	1.71
Central Adirondacks	123	97	78.9	130	1.06	79	88	1.11

[1] Average embryo counts are based on total number of does examined; average corpora lutea counts are based on the number of pairs of ovaries. Corpora lutea counts during 1939-1943 are only from does with corpora lutea and without visible embryos. Corpora lutea counts were made on all intact pairs of ovaries received during 1947-1949. No does were collected from Adirondack periphery during 1947-1949.

For adult does during the 1939-43 period (Table 1) the difference between the embryo counts for specimens from the western region and those from the central Adirondacks has a chi-square value of 6.03, a significant difference at approximately the 1 per cent level. An even greater difference between these two regions in the number of embryos

251

per doe fawn (Table 2) has a chi-square value of 21.66, which is highly significant at the 1 per cent level. In both cases the embryo production of deer sampled from the western region far exceeded that of those studied from the central Adirondacks during the same period. Ova production of adult does shows a similar difference.

TABLE 2. Comparative fertility of fawn does from five regions of New York State, 1939-49[1]

Region or section	Embryo counts					Corpora lutea counts		
	Number does examined	Number pregnant	Per cent	Number embryos	Average per doe	Number pairs ovaries	Number corpora lutea	Average per doe
			1939-1943					
Western Catskill	69	27	39.1	29	0.42	–	–	–
Periphery Central Catskill	30	8	26.7	8	0.27	–	–	–
Catskill Adirondack	20	4	20.0	6	0.30	–	–	–
Periphery Central Adirondacks	26	2	7.7	2	0.08	–	–	–
Central Adirondacks	89	3	3.4	3	0.03	–	–	–
			1947-1949					
Western Catskill	61	15	24.6	15[1]	0.25[1]	61	24	0.39
Periphery Central Catskill	35	11	31.4	11[1]	0.31[1]	35	13	0.37
Catskill	16	5	31.3	5[1]	0.31[1]	16	5	0.31
			Total					
Western Catskill	130	42	32.3	44[1]	0.34[1]	–	–	–
Periphery Central Catskill	65	19	29.2	19[1]	0.29[1]	–	–	–
Catskill Adirondack	36	9	25.0	11[1]	0.31[1]	–	–	–
Periphery Central Adirondacks	26	2	7.7	2	0.08	–	–	–
Central Adirondacks	89	3	3.4	3	0.03	–	–	–

[1] Includes yearlings containing old corpora lutea scars indicating their pregnancy as fawns. Embryo counts of these yearlings were recorded as a minimum of one for each specimen which showed pregnancy scars. The distribution among the three regions involved of the 41 such ovarian analyses of yearling deer was comparable to that of the fawn specimens examined.

The samples of adult deer obtained from the remaining three sections (Catskill periphery, central Catskill and Adirondack periphery) are not of sufficient size to show statistically significant differences. However, the 1939-1943 trend indicates deer from both Catskill sections as possessing fertility comparable with deer of the western region. The small sample of deer from the Adirondack periphery shows a higher average embryo count than that from the central Adirondacks and an ovulation incidence nearly comparable to that observed in the deer from the Catskill periphery.

The fertility data of 1939-1943 from fawns of the five range divisions (Table 2) roughly parallel the trend of the adult material.

The collections of does during the later period of 1947-1949 do not include representatives from the Adirondack periphery. However, adult does from the remaining four range divisions exhibit marked changes in fertility from that observed during the 1939-1943 interval (Table 1). The embryo and corpora lutea counts from the western sample show an increase in average-per-doe of 0.30 embryos and 0.12 ova. Does from the

Catskill periphery and central Catskills show a drop in fertility. The average number of embryos of Catskill periphery does dropped 0.24 while the drop in average ova production was only 0.03. The largest decline in fertility is to be noted in the does from the central Catskills where an embryo and corpora lutea average-per-doe of 1.65 and 1.88, respectively, for the 1939-1943 period dropped to 1.06 embryos and 1.56 ova for the 1947-1949 period. Does from the central Adirondacks showed an increase in average embryo and ova counts of 0.28 and 0.33, respectively.

The 1947-1949 collection of fawn breeding data shows a drop in the incidence of pregnancy among western fawns and a lower average embryo count. Both Catskill sections show a slight increase in the incidence of pregnancy and in average embryo counts, which is contrary to the declining trend observed in the adult does sampled from these two sections. No doe fawns were collected from either of the Adirondack sections during this later period.

Data from the central Adirondacks secured in 1947 came from two study areas in this region, the DeBar Mountain Game Management Area, and the "Plains" on the South Branch of the Moose River in Hamilton County (Figure 1). A comparison of data from these two areas during the two collection periods reveals a significant locality difference in 1947 fertility. Table 3 presents this analysis. During 1939-1943 the DeBar Mountain samples indicated a lower fertility than was found in the Moose River deer. In 1947 the DeBar Mountain deer exhibited a fertility over twice that reflected in the earlier samples while fertility of the Moose River deer remained relatively unchanged. The coincident history of deer populations in these study areas may explain this situation and will be presented in the discussion. It appears that the increased fertility in the central Adirondacks recorded for the 1947-1949 period (Table 1) resulted from inclusion of the DeBar Mountain deer whose fertility had more than doubled.

TABLE 3. Comparative fertility of adult does from Moose River and Debar Mountain areas, 1939-1949.

	Embryo counts					Corpora lutea counts		
Area	Number does examined	Number pregnant	Per cent	Number embryos	Average per doe	Number pairs ovaries	Number corpora lutea	Average per doe
			1939-1943					
DeBar Mountain	28	16	57.1	20	0.71	5	3	0.60
Moose River	43	39	90.7	43	1.00	45	44	0.98
			1947-1949					
DeBar Mountain	9	9	100.0	16	1.78	7	13	1.86
Moose River	16	11	68.8	16	1.00	16	18	1.13

All specimens from this period were obtained in 1947.

TABLE 4. Comparative fertility of adult does from Allegany State Park, 1944 and 1948.

Year	Number examined	Number corpora lutea	Average per doe
1944	22	30	1.36
1948	18	36	2.00

Reproductive data (Table 4) from deer in Allegany State Park, Cattaraugus County (Figure 1), were secured in 1944 during the first recent open season held in this park. Ovaries from 22 adult does were secured. Fertility data were derived from counting the corpora lutea of the current mating season. Since few embryos had grown to the point of visibility at this season (last 6 days of November) an embryo count was not included. All 22 does had ovulated and produced an average of 1.36 ova per doe. Since 1944 the same portion of the park with some additional area has been open annually to a short season on bucks. In 1948 when another antlerless deer season was declared, reproductive tracts were obtained from 18 adult does. Again only few embryos were visible and embryo counts could not be included in fertility data. All 18 does had ovulated, with an average of 2.00 ova per doe. This represented an average increase of 0.64 ova per doe over the 1944 findings.

A discussion of events and conditions which appear to have influenced the reproductive processes of deer in New York is now in order.

Discussion

The findings which have been presented show a considerable regional variability in the fertility of the deer examined which corresponds broadly with evaluations of range quality. From the high fertility of deer in the western region to the comparatively low fertility found in the central Adirondacks, there appear to be intermediate levels as exhibited by the does from the two Catskill sections and the Adirondack periphery.

It seems likely that the relative adequacy of the animals' nutrition, especially during the winter, may be a paramount factor governing such variations. There is a large body of literature which conclusively demonstrates the important influence of diet on the reproductive physiology of domestic and laboratory animals as well as of man. Much of this literature has been summarized in the excellent reference work edited by Allen, Danforth and Doisy (1939). The fertility of an animal appears dependent upon energy sources in excess of those required for its mere survival as an individual. Any curtailment of energy source, either in quality or quantity, below the requirement of the normal functioning of reproduction will be reflected in a lowered sexual vitality, abnormal sex function, or complete cessation of the sexual processes.

Moreover, insomuch as the reproductive physiology of animals is generally similar in its nutritional requirements, it is probable that their reproductive responses to changes in availability of nutrients are similar. The work of Davis (1949) and associates on population dynamics among wild rats shows a physiological response manifested by rate of growth and incidence of pregnancy which appears related to changes in population densities. In supersaturated rat populations, body growth was adversely affected and there was a reduction in incidence of pregnancy. It is possible that intensified intraspecific competition for food, among other factors, may have affected pregnancy rates.

In the case of the white-tailed deer, Gerstell (1938), Park and Day (1942), and Latham (1948) have reported on low productivity apparently associated with over-browsed sections of deer range in Pennsylvania.

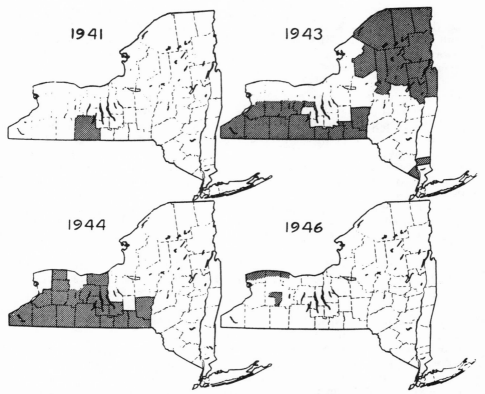

FIG. 27-2.—Distribution of antlerless deer seasons in New York (shaded areas), years 1941, 1943, 1944 and 1946.

O'Roke and Hamerstrom (1948) observed the behavior of deer populations on the George Reserve in Michigan and noted that the lowest fawn crops were produced during the period of the greatest concentration of deer and most extensive forage depletion. In the following discussion the fertility data presented here will be considered with respect to the hypothesis that the variations observed may be correlated with nutritional differences associated with the several range divisions involved and with the relative abundance of the deer occupying them.

It may be assumed that the more heavily a deer range is browsed the less the deer occupying it will be able to satisfy their nutritional requirements. Conversely, a reduction in deer population density should reduce competition for the available browse supply and improve the nutrition of the deer involved. The taking of antlerless deer in addition to antlered bucks usually results in such a reduction. Several seasons of this kind were held in New York during the years between the periods when fertility data were collected. Therefore, comparison of the data in relation to these and other events affecting population density affords a means of appraising the above hypothesis.

The distribution of recent antlerless deer seasons in New York during the years 1941-46 is shown in Figure 2. The reported legal kill of both antlered and antlerless deer during these years is given in the annual reports of the New York State Conservation Department to the Legislature (New York State, 1942-1947).

The southern and western portions of the western region were more intensively harvested than any other section of the state. Field observations left no doubt that these intensive harvests resulted in a reduction in the deer population. With the exception of the 1941 antlerless deer season in Steuben County they occurred after completion of the 1939-1943 samples, and could only affect the later 1947-1949 collection. As has been stated, fertility was higher among the adult does examined from this range during the second collection period than it was among those taken earlier. It is quite possible that the lower abundance of deer during the intervening years accompanied by lessened competition for the supply of choice foods, contributed directly as a cause to the increased fertility observed in the does collected from this region in 1947-1949.

The Catskill region, with the exception of two small counties (Figure 2), had no antlerless deer season. During the years between the two collection periods no substantial change in deer abundance took place. The data from the adult does examined show a decline in fertility between the first and second periods both for the peripheral and central sections of the region (Table 1). It is possible that this may be associated with a progressive deterioration in the relation between the supply of choice forage and deer density, especially in the central Catskills. It is known that in many localities good winter habitat is deficient. The number of deer in the samples, however, is too small for statistical support for such a relationship.

With respect to the Adirondack region, data for the two periods are available only for the central section where the records as a whole show a higher fertility for the adult does taken in 1947 than for those taken earlier. All the specimens examined during the second period, however, came from two localities and, as has been noted, the trend in fertility as indicated by the data resulted from the influence of one of these, the DeBar Mountain area. Other conditions were also radically different. Therefore, they will be discussed separately.

Although there was an antlerless deer season in 1943 which included the central Adirondacks, the "Plains" study area on the South Branch of the Moose River was relatively inaccessible to hunters and the harvest of antlerless deer in this area is known to have been light. Guides who operated big hunting camps in this area refused to lodge men who intended to shoot antlerless deer. Thus no appreciable reduction of the population was achieved and competition for browse was not lessened. Moreover, the data indicate no appreciable change in the degree of fertility for the deer in this locality.

The kill of deer in the vicinity of the DeBar Mountain area, on the other hand, was heavy during the antlerless season. In addition to this 1943 harvest, the nearly 8,000 acres of the DeBar Mountain Game

Management Area, normally kept as a refuge, were inadvertently opened to hunting for the first and only time during the buck season of 1945. On the management area alone about 250 deer were killed, of which nearly half were illegal (based on post-season counts of dead deer found and tallies of legal deer removed). This constituted a further reduction of considerable consequence to the deer population inhabiting the DeBar Mountain district. There can be little question that this resulted in an improved plane of nutrition among the deer that remained. It seems probable that the very significant increase in fertility which was recorded following these events reflected a greater availability of good forage as a result of the lowered deer pressure on it.

Another factor tending to improve the food supply in relation to numbers of deer was logging operations begun in the spring of 1946 on private lands in the immediate vicinity of the DeBar Mountain Game Management Area. This involved both softwood and hardwood cuttings. These cuttings have reduced the density of forest cover and increased the amount of food available for deer on about half of their wintering area by providing hardwood toppings and an increased sprout growth. As a consequence, winter mortality has been negligible during this latter period.

No observable change in the balance between deer population and winter forage in the Moose River area has occurred since the earlier (1939-1943) collections except during the two unusually mild winters of 1945-46 and 1946-47. During these years deer were not restricted to their usual wintering grounds and could roam throughout the hardwood areas for food. However, other factors being equal, these mild winters should have had approximately the same influence on deer of both areas. Yet negligible improvement in fertility was observed in the Moose River sample of 1947. Although the samples are small, it is estimated that they comprised at least 10 per cent of the total number of adult does occupying the immediate vicinities under study, and should, therefore, constitute an adequate representation of fertility.

The improved fertility of does sampled from Allegany State Park in 1948 is another example wherein alteration of deer densities in relation to available forage appears to find expression in altered rates of deer reproduction. The 1944 antlerless deer season in this park was held for the express purpose of reducing the excessive number of deer which had reached a level where over-browsing and severe winter losses were occurring (Shadle and Stulken, 1942; Severinghaus, 1945). Specimens collected in 1944 showed a low fertility. From 1944 through 1947, 270 legal deer were accounted for at the park checking station and 11 illegally killed during the open season were found. In addition to the harvests during the open season there is reason to believe that a considerable number of deer were illegally taken throughout the year. It is quite possible that the improved fertility noted in the 1948 sample of does from this park was a direct result of the deer harvests which must have had beneficial effects on the ratio of food to the number of deer competing for it.

With respect to the doe fawns examined, the trends in fertility shown by the data were contrary to those exhibited by the adult specimens for the western and Catskill regions. However, there is no reason to suspect that competition for adequate food during the summer and fall months was more severe in the western region than in the Catskills. Thus the early attainment of fertileness accompanied by ovulation, among fawn does, should show little difference between the Catskill and western regions assuming the summer and fall supply of forage remained adequate in both territories. The effects of competition for winter and spring forage might be reflected only in the fertility of deer which had had to subsist on it during that period and would, therefore, appear only in adult deer (1½ years and older). For this reason, neither the differences in embryo and ova counts between western and Catskill fawns nor the lack of agreement with trends in the fertility of adult deer are considered of great importance.

Records of fawn fertility for the Adirondack region were obtained only during the 1939-1943 period. They evidenced a very low fertility rate, especially in the central Adirondacks (Table 2). It is felt, however, that this condition has considerable significance with regard to the possibility of a positive correlation between fertility and nutrition among deer. Although fawns in this region are born at approximately the same time as are those in the south (Cheatum and Morton, 1946), they seldom ovulate in their first year in contrast to southern fawns. There is reason to believe that this may be due to poorer nutrition during their postnatal stage so that they are retarded in their over-all physical development at the time of the mating season. Weight measurements (Severinghaus, 1946) support this explanation. Fawns of both sexes from the Adirondack region showed significantly lighter weights than southern fawns at the time of the hunting season. Their skeletal dimensions were also somewhat smaller.

Although there is a shorter growing season in the Adirondack region which tends to limit the availability of succulent forage, there is another factor which may be more important as a cause of poor nutrition among fawns. This relates to the poor physical condition of many Adirondack does during the latter part of gestation. They frequently have passed a rigorous wintering period, especially in the central Adirondacks, and their poor state of nutrition may adversely affect not only the developing embryos, but also lactation (Maynard, 1937). An inadequate quantity and quality of milk would have a retarding effect upon the growth of their fawns. This may be an important factor in the slower physical development and delayed attainment of fertility observed in doe fawns of the central Adirondacks.

The low fertility of central Adirondack deer in general may bear a direct relation to the character of their winter nutrition. This section presents a serious problem in winter losses (Severinghaus, 1947). Deep accumulations of snow lead to yarding habits of deer which, in turn, lead to heavy over-browsing in many yarding areas. Death from winter malnutrition is extensive during severe winters. Figure 3 shows the distribution of known winter concentrations of deer and where mortality has been observed. The majority of areas showing mortality are grouped

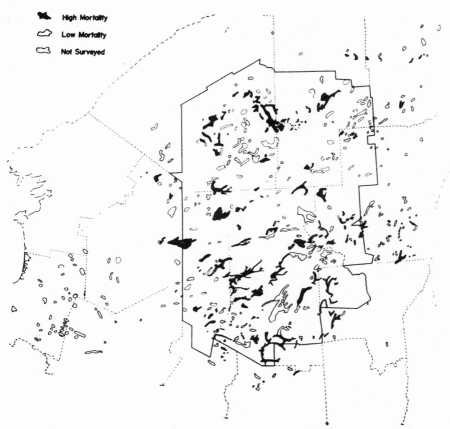

FIG. 27-3.—Distribution of known deer-wintering areas in the Adirondacks. Note frequency of mortality areas within the central Adirondack region (enclosed by heavy black line). Following average to severe winters, black areas yield 2 to 35 dead deer per square mile, areas enclosed by solid lines yield one or less per square mile, while areas indicated by dotted lines have not been surveyed for mortality. (Severinghaus et al, 1950, for further details).

in the central Adirondack section. It has been seen that deer from this section exhibit the lowest fertility. With the exception of the influence of the shorter growing season in this area, there is little field evidence that the Adirondacks is short in summer and fall deer foods. It seems probable, therefore, that the effects of winter malnutrition are carried over into the fall mating season and that the does, being burdened throughout the summer with suckling fawns, are not able to recuperate to their full reproductive capacity by the onset of the mating season.

From the foregoing discussion it seems evident that the data collected support the hypothesis that differences in forage conditions between the various divisions of deer range in the state, as well as changes which may take place in the quality and availability of the forage in the same section, are reflected in differences in the fertility of deer through their effect on the plane of nutrition of the animals.

The number of specimens from each region is admittedly small and scattered over wide areas. The error of applying results to a whole region, even though data are taken from what are considered typical localities, was demonstrated by the 1947 collections from the Moose River and DeBar Mountain areas in the central Adirondack section. Nevertheless, the facts represent strong evidence that the conclusion is valid.

Furthermore, it seems clear that excessive deer populations, through over-browsing, are often the chief cause of forage deficiencies. For example, the low fertility recorded for the specimens from Allegany State Park in 1944 demonstrates that this can happen in even the state's best deer range. Moreover, thinning of the excessive population there by controlled hunting led to a rise in fertility which closely approximated that which was found elsewhere in that range division. The reproductive response of this group of deer and of that in the DeBar Mountain area to changes in their nutritional environment strongly suggests that measures designed to reduce the deer population in such situations are to be recommended as good management.

Finally, the data suggest that measurements of deer fertility may afford a valuable index to trends in the status of populations in relation to the general adequacy of the range and that such measurements may be used as a tool in the management of this species. This includes the possibility of determining when and where deer harvests require adjustment to forage conditions on the range. It must be recognized, however, that further work will have to be done to determine the degree of lag to be expected between the actual occurrence of critical conditions on the range and the time they will be revealed in fertility data. It has been well established that there are important variations between regions in vital chemical constituents of soils and plants (Browne, 1938; McMurtrey and Robinson, 1938). It is highly desirable that chemical analyses of soils and forage plants be accomplished and correlated with variations in deer productivity, antler development and growth.

LITERATURE CITED

ALLEN, EDGAR, CHAS. H. DANFORTH and EDWARD A. DOISY
    1939. Sex and internal secretions. Second edition. Williams and Wilkins, Baltimore. pp. 1149-1196.
BROWNE, C. A.
    1938. Some relationships of soil to plant and animal nutrition—the major elements. Soils and Men. U.S. Dept. Agri. Yearbook. pp. 777-806.
BOWMAN, ISAIAH
    1911. Forest physiography. John Wiley and Sons, New York. pp. 691-694.
CHEATUM, E. L.
    1949. The use of corpora lutea for determining ovulation incidence and variations in fertility of white-tailed deer. Cornell Vet. 39(3):282-291.
CHEATUM, E. L., and GLENN H. MORTON
    1942. Techniques used in determining the period of the rut among white-tailed deer of New York State. Trans. Seventh N. Am. Wildlife Conf. pp. 334-342.

1946. Breeding season of white-tailed deer in New York. Jour. Wildlife Mgt. 10(3):249-263.

COOK, DAVID B., and W. J. HAMILTON, JR.
1942. Winter habits of white-tailed deer in central New York. Jour. Wildlife Mgt. 6(4):287-291.

DARROW, ROBERT W.
1947-48. The white-tail in New York (Part II). New York State Conservationist 2(3):10-13.

DAVIS, DAVID E.
1949. The role of intraspecific competition in game management. Trans. 14th N. Am. Wildlife Conf. pp. 225-239.

GERSTELL, RICHARD
1938. The Pennsylvania deer problem in 1938. Parts 1-3. Penna. Game News 9(5-7).

GORDON, ROBERT B.
1940. The primeval forest types of southwestern New York. N.Y.S. Mus. Bull. No. 321.

GUYOT, ARNOLD
1880. On the physical structure and hysometry of the Catskill mountain region. Am. Jour. Sci. Third Ser. 19:429-451.

LATHAM, ROGER M.
1948. Harvesting our deer crop. Penna Game News 19(2) :4-5, 17, 21.

MAYNARD, LEONARD A.
1937. Animal nutrition. McGraw-Hill, New York. pp. 395-447.

McMURTREY, J. E., JR., and W. O. ROBINSON
1938. Neglected soil constituents that affect plant and animal development. Soils and Men. U.S. Dept. Agri. Yearbook. pp. 807-829.

MERRIAM, C. HART
1884. The mammals of the Adirondack region. Holt, New York.

MORTON, GLENN H., and E. L. CHEATUM
1946. Regional differences in breeding potential of white-tailed deer in New York. Jour. Wildlife Mgt. 10(3):242-248.

New York State
1942-1947. Annual Reports, Conservation Dept. Division of Fish and Game Sections.

O'ROKE, E. C., and F. N. HAMERSTROM, JR.
1948. Productivity and yield of the George Reserve deer herd. Jour. Wildlife Mgt. 12(1):78-86.

PARK, BARRY C., and BESSE B. DAY
1942. A simplified method for determining the condition of white-tailed deer herds in relation to available forage. U.S. Dept. Agri. Bull. No. 840. pp. 1-60.

PEARCE, JOHN
1937. The effects of deer browsing on certain western Adirondack forest types. Roosevelt Wildlife Bull. 7(1):1-61.

SEVERINGHAUS, C. W.
1945. Report on deer of Allegany State Park. U.S. Dept. of Int., Pittman-Robertson Quart. 5(3):110-111.
1946. Comparison of the weight of Adirondack and Southern Tier deer. Pittman-Robertson Quarterly Report, New York Project 28-R, July 1 (attachment).
1947. Relationship of weather to winter mortality and population levels among deer in the Adirondack region of New York. Trans. 12th N. Am. Wildlife Conf. pp. 212-223.
1948. Winter deer mortality and this fall's hunting prospects. N.Y.S. Conservationist 3(1):29.

SEVERINGHAUS, C. W., H. F. MAGUIRE, R. A. COOKINGHAM, and J. E. TANCK
1950. Variations by age class in the antler beam diameters of white-tailed deer related to range conditions Trans. 15th N. Am. Wildlife Conf.

SHADLE, ALBERT R., and DONALD STULKEN
1942. The deer of Allegany State Park, New York. Jour. Wildlife Mgt. 6(1):27-30.

TOWNSEND, M. T., and M. W. SMITH
1933. The white-tailed deer of the Adirondacks. Roosevelt Wildlife Bull. 6(2):153-385.

FASTING METABOLISM OF
WHITE-TAILED DEER (1969)

Helenette Silver, N. F. Colovos, J. B. Holter and H. H. Hayes.

Wild animals are adapted behaviorally, morphologically, and physiologically to the unique ecological niches they occupy. Ecological studies have tended to be descriptive and have documented characteristics of habitat, behavior and morphology. Less attention has been afforded the equally important physiological adaptive mechanisms which integrate organism and environment. In the following paper, the authors provide fundamental information on energy metabolism in white-tailed deer and the adaptive significance of physiologic changes which accompany seasonal variations in the environment.

Detailed information on nutritional requirements under varying environmental conditions is requisite to intensive deer management. Feeding trials, and chemical composition analyses, and nutrition balances have contributed data on available nutrients and digestibility, and quantities of feed required by deer under specific conditions of the studies in which they were obtained (Maynard et al. 1935, Forbes et al. 1941, Davenport 1939, Bissell et al. 1955, Bissell and Weir 1957, Silver and Colovos 1957, Dietz et al. 1962).

There is, however, little basic knowledge of energy requirements of deer. Before the effect of factors that increase energy needs can be evaluated, it is necessary to know the amount of energy required for maintaining minimum vital activity. This minimum energy requirement, or basal metabolism, serves as a base from which to measure the increased energy demands imposed by activity and production, and is necessary for calculating energy exchange with the environment during adverse weather conditions (Moen 1968).

Basal metabolic rate (BMR) is the heat production of a resting animal in the post absorptive state in a thermoneutral environment. A respiratory quotient (RQ) of 0.7 (that of fat catabolism) and the absence of methane production are criteria of the post absorptive state. Temperatures near 20 C are within the zone of thermal neutrality for most species, and it is customary to measure BMR at approximately this temperature. Since complete repose can seldom be attained except with humans, animals are often measured over a period of some hours without regard to changes in position, or activity within the calorimeter. This measurement is called fasting metabolism (FMR), and is higher than BMR by the amount of energy expended in activity over the period of measurement.

Various correction factors have been used by nutritionists to adjust fasting metabolism to BMR (Ritzman and Benedict 1938:97-98). Blaxter (1962:80), writing of domestic animals, stated: "With ruminants, the difference between the two [BMR and FMR] is not, however, great, . . . provided the animal is not disturbed or frightened." He felt that the activity of animals kept in buildings was not much greater than when they were

Reprinted from the J. Wildl. Mgmt. 33(3):490-498.

263

in the calorimeter, and wrote that the normal outdoor activity of adult cattle and sheep was not great. The effect of activity on metabolism may last over a considerable period, and for this reason Kleiber (1961:175) preferred the use of FMR, in the belief that it represented reasonably well the heat production of animals under usual conditions. Whether this holds true for so nervous an animal as the deer, which by nature is much more active than domestic species, may be open to question. We might reasonably expect greater nervous tension and activity on the part of deer to be reflected in higher and more variable values than would be obtained on domestic animals under similar conditions.

Bissell et al. (1955:73), using the formula developed by Brody (1945), estimated BMR of a 100-lb deer to be 1,140 calories per day, or about 22 kcal/kg. BMR of two adult white-tailed deer reported by Silver et al. (1959:436) averaged 1,243 kcal/24 hrs, or 27.5 kcal/kg. Heat production of two adult deer measured in winter at ambient temperatures of −3.9 and 0.4 C, averaged 1,403 kcal/24 hrs, or 24.7 kcal/kg. Heat production per unit of weight was higher at the higher environmental temperatures. Measurements reported by Silver (1968:189) again showed BMR per unit of weight to be higher at higher environmental temperatures. She suggested (1959: 436-437) that (1) "critical temperature for fasting deer, in winter coat may be below 0 C.," or (2) BMR may be higher in spring than in winter. BMR was calculated by adjusting the measured FMR for activity in the chamber according to the formula used by Ritzman and Benedict (1938:101) for cattle.

This paper presents results of 20 recent measurements of heat production of white-tailed deer, and summarizes 32 total measurements made in the chamber described by Silver (1968) from 1961 through January, 1969. Values reported represent FMR, and are higher in some cases than results reported earlier for the same experiments when values were adjusted for activity and reported as BMR.

Special thanks are due A. N. Moen, Cornell University, and D. F. Behrend, Huntington Wildlife Forest Station, for helpful suggestions and criticism of the manuscript in its early stages.

Techniques

The experimental deer were hand reared from a few days of age, and trained to submit to handling and crating. They were penned out-of-doors, with open shelter available but seldom used. They were fed on an artificial ration of mixed small grains, and experienced winter weight losses typical of Northern deer. Unlimited feed was available at all times, but because of variation in feed intake accompanied by rapid weight changes they were seldom at the maintenance level of nutrition at which FMR of domestic species is ordinarily measured. Because of their voluntary regulation of feed consumption, it was not possible to maintain the deer on the customary standard intake for a period prior to measurement. Standardized maintenance is not a requisite for heat production measurements, but lack of standardization may produce variable results since metabolism is affected by level of nutrition.

Standard maintenance is, however, not a normal condition of life among wild deer. Maloiy (1968:5) notes that "the nutrition and behavior

264

of an animal under field conditions are influenced markedly by climate and other factors." Our interest was focused on energy requirements of deer living under natural conditions, and we attempted to produce deer as nearly like wild deer as possible under conditions of captivity, and consistent with ability to handle them during the experiments. We believe they were representative of their species, and of our native deer as judged by comparison with weights of deer taken in New Hampshire harvests, and accidental kills autopsied at other times of year.

Heat production was measured by indirect calorimetry. Experiments were conducted in all months of the year, but more frequently in winter season because of the emphasis on nutritional needs of deer at this season. Temperatures in the chamber ranged from 16.0 to 21.5 C. The animals were fasted in the chamber to permit adjustment to those temperatures. At the end of 48 hours, RQ's met the criteria described for post absorptive state. Fasts up to 60 hours did not result in lowered FMR. Length of the period of measurement varied from 4-10 hours. Changes in position and the proportion of time spent standing were recorded, but, for purposes of this report, no use has been made of these records to calculate the effect of activity in the chamber.

An attempt to determine the effect of coat on FMR was made in one instance. A 60-kg buck was measured in March in full winter coat. Following the experiment, he was put back on feed for a period of 7 days to recover from the effect of the fast. At the end of this time the buck was tranquilized, clipped as closely as possible with electric clippers, and placed in the chamber at an average environmental temperature of 20.9 C. Three days, during which feed and water were offered in unlimited amounts, were allowed for dissipation of the effect of the drug. The animal then was fasted for 48 hours, and heat production again measured.

Results

Average FMR of adult deer in summer coat from May through August (52.2 kcal/kg/24 hrs) was 1.5 times higher than that of adults in winter coat from September through April (33.8 kcal/kg/24 hrs) (Table 1, Fig. 1). Heat production of the clipped buck was nearly twice as high at an average ambient temperature of 20.9 C as it was in the previous test in full winter coat at an average temperature of 20.5 C (57.0 kcal/kg/24 hrs and 29.3 kcal/kg/24 hrs, respectively).

Species of larger size have a metabolic rate proportionally lower than small species. For this reason it is customary to express FMR in terms of heat production per unit of weight referred to some fractional power of the weight for comparison between species, and also for comparison between animals of different sizes within a species. Various powers of the weight have been suggested; $W^{0.75}$, proposed by Kleiber (1947:528), was adopted by the International Congress of Energy Metabolism in 1964.

A large difference in FMR of deer in summer and winter coats tends to override the difference attributable to size (Fig. 2). The data show only a slight tendency for higher heat production per unit of weight in deer of smaller size. All deer measured in winter coat, regardless of size, had a lower FMR than any deer measured in summer coat. Metabolic rate is, therefore, perhaps more realistically expressed as heat production per unit

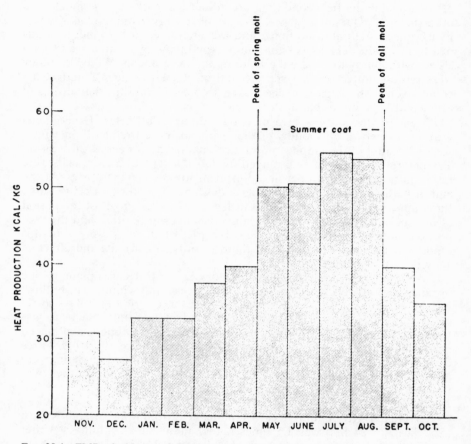

Fig. 28-1.—FMR of white-tailed deer by month of measurement.

of weight. Values obtained are shown in Table 1 both on the basis of kcal/ kg/24 hrs. and kcal/kg $W^{0.75}$/24 hrs.

Seasonal variability in FMR was not anticipated at the start of the project, so no records of dates of molt for either individuals or years were kept. Where the process is gradual, with length and density of coat varying over a considerable period, there can be of course, no precise cut-off date for change of coat.

Onset of the spring molt is variable, and its duration is always prolonged. Difference in condition is accepted as a prime factor in determining date of molt. Reference to journal entries and dated photographs as well as visual observations suggest that difference in condition of our deer between years was related to severity of the previous winter. Molt is generally well advanced in April, may start as early as the first of March, and in late-fawning does, occasionally is not completed before the end of June. Fall molt is more regular in appearance, and takes place over a shorter span of time. Major changes in coat are completed during the last week of August and the first week of September in adults. For purposes of data analysis, the end of April and the first of September were arbitrarily chosen to represent dates of coat change. Our records indicate that, in all years, all deer were in some state of molt on those dates, and for most years they represent the approximate peak of molt for the majority of the herd.

TABLE 1. FMR of white-tailed deer, 1961-1969.

				Heat Production/24 hrs.	
Weight (kg)	Sex	Month of Measure- ment	Total kcal	kcal/ kg	kcal /kg $W^{0.75}$
Adults, winter coat					
82.0	M	Dec.	2596	31.7	95.4
80.0	M	Apr.	3192	39.9	119.5
80.0	M	Jan.	2880	36.0	107.8
70.0	F	Dec.	1548	22.1	70.0
69.5	F	Sept.	3078	44.3	127.1
69.0	M	Jan.	2318	33.6	96.9
68.6	M	Oct.	2339	34.1	97.9
68.2	M	Oct.	2434	35.7	102.7
66.5	M	Nov.	2042	30.7	88.0
64.5	M	Jan.	1737	26.9	76.8
64.4	F	Sept.	2290	35.6	101.3
63.8	M	Jan.	2286	35.8	101.1
60.1	M	Mar.	1750	29.1	81.0
58.4	M	Feb.	1758	30.1	83.7
52.0	M	Jan.	1620	31.2	83.5
49.4	M	Feb.	1742	35.3	94.2
44.0	M	Mar.	1908	43.4	111.5
Avg.				33.8	97.1
Fawns, winter					
32.9	M	Feb.	1380	41.9	100.0
31.3	M	Feb.	1221	39.0	93.2
30.2	M	Feb.	1142	37.9	89.2
27.9	M	Feb.	958	34.3	78.5
Avg.				38.2	90.2
Adults, summer coat					
77.1	M	Aug.	4150	53.8	159.6
66.0	F	June	2945	44.6	126.9
60.6	F	Aug.	3268	53.9	149.9
58.8	F	July	3675	62.5	172.5
57.6	F	June	3134	54.4	150.6
54.6	F	June	2632	48.2	130.2
54.6	M	July	2543	46.6	125.8
50.1	M	June	2789	55.7	148.3
47.9	M	May	2393	50.0	131.4
Ave.				52.2	143.6
Fawns, summer					
36.5	M	June	2084	57.1	141.7
35.7	M	May	1764	49.4	120.0
Avg.				53.2	130.8

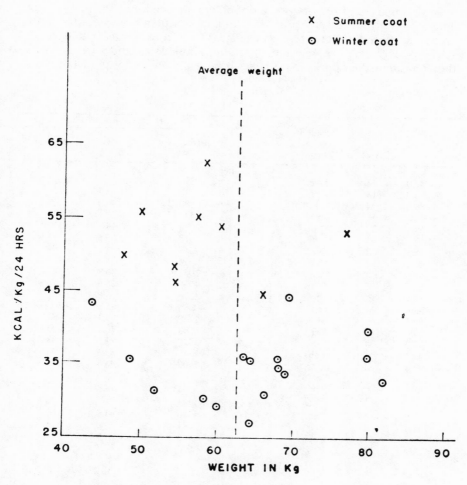

FIG. 28-2.—Effect of season on FMR of adult deer.

Graphed by month of measurement (Fig. 1), FMR increased from the first of March to reach a peak in July, followed by a sharp drop in September.

When the data are averaged by 2-month periods, they show a fairly smooth curve which reaches its lowest point during the coldest season of the year. Fig. 3 shows this curve compared to data on change in weights of thyroid glands of white-tailed deer presented by Hoffman and Robinson (1966: 271). Trends of the two sets of data correspond rather well except for the months of May and June, when thyroid weights dropped as FMR continued to rise.

Benedict (1938) noted that while differences in sex have usually been ignored in reporting metabolism measurements, with some animals, including ruminants, sex differences clearly have been shown. Game managers sometimes have speculated on possible differential nutritional needs of bucks and does in winter. Our data are inconclusive in this area. Only three of 17 winter measurements were made on does, one of which was pregnant. Where the additional influences of size and activity were necessarily present, although unmeasured, any attempt to show statistical difference between FMR of bucks and does in winter is unwarranted. There was no significant difference ($P > 0.05$) between mean FMR of does (52.7 kcal/kg/24 hrs) and bucks (51.5 kcal/kg/24 hrs) in summer coat.

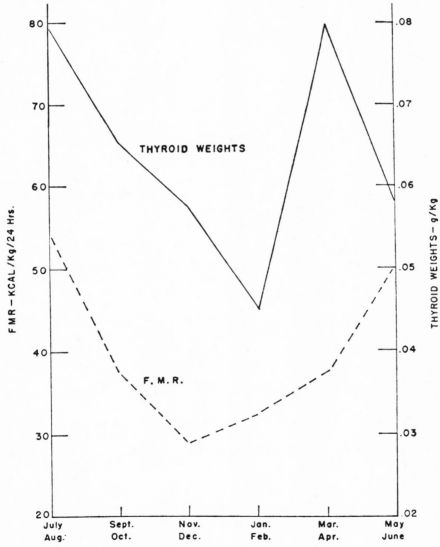

FIG. 28-3.—Seasonal changes in FMR and weights of thyroid glands in adult white-tailed deer. (Thyroid weights adapted from Hoffman and Robinson, 1966.)

Silver et al. (1959) questioned some results of their early experiments because of pregnancy of the does. Blaxter (1962) has since reported that, in sheep, metabolism of the fetus at term is approximately that of the adult ewe. Conversely, Hoffman and Robinson (1966:272), writing of white-tailed deer, reported that the "thyroid glands of animals *in utero* are more active than those of free-living animals measured during the same months and even more active than those of the pregnant females." Their fawn embryos were, however, collected during the last month *in utero*, and measurements of thyroid glands of fetuses were too few to show a consistent pattern. Even if thyroid activity were known to follow a consistent pattern, considering its small size, the embryo can not be expected to have much influence on total heat production of the doe during the first month of pregnancy.

The pregnant doe, measured in December, had the lowest FMR of any animal used in the experiments. This may be partially explainable by age (she was the oldest animal measured), and partially by date of measurement. Hoffman and Robinson (1966:272), "noted that during late pregnancy (April-May), and again during November-December, the thyroid glands of the females consistently exhibited a picture of extreme inactivity."

Young animals have a higher metabolic rate than adults. Results of six measurements of bucks under 1 year of age are shown separately in Table 1. Average FMR in February was 10 percent higher than for adults in winter coat, and 17 percent higher than for mature bucks in February. Average FMR, based on two measurements of the same animals the following May and June, was close to average value for adults in summer coat. The data are too few for drawing firm conclusions and the figures are presented only as a matter of interest. Higher relative energy requirements are a factor seldom considered in the high fawn mortality found in areas of winter feed scarcity.

Discussion

The cyclic variation in FMR found in our deer is not normal in domestic animals although instances have been reported. Benedict and Ritzman (1935:306) found variations of 10 to 90 percent in BMR of individual cows. The increase always occurred in cows measured during the pasture season. Hundreds of later experiments with cattle on standard maintenance programs have shown FMR of cattle to be remarkably constant (Colovos and Holter, in press).

Blaxter (1962:86) believed that the higher metabolic rate found in summer in cows by Benedict and Ritzman (1935), and in dogs by Lusk (in Blaxter 1962), resulted largely from differences in nutrition and freedom. Measurements of sheep gave higher values for BMR when they were fed at a high level prior to the preliminary fast.

Benedict (1938:26) states that "the animal must be in good nutritive condition at the time of measurement. If it is in a poor nutritive condition its metabolism will generally be depressed below the normal basal line, . . . undernutrition lowers the metabolism."

Although increased activity and a higher level of nutrition might account for the increased rate of metabolism in our deer during spring and summer, and the poor condition of Northern deer in late winter for the low values obtained at that time, such reasoning can not account for the abrupt drop of FMR in September, and a continuing low FMR during the fall period of high feed consumption and greatest activity.

Blaxter (1962:83) emphasizes the constancy of metabolic rate under standard conditions of feeding and management, a phenomenon strongly evident in the work of Colovos and Holter (in press) with cattle. Conditions for the deer were by no means standard between seasons because of voluntary limitation of intake and activity rather than restrictions imposed by our management program.

Our deer reduced both their feed intake and activity in winter, and experienced weight losses of 11-28 percent. They were, further, subject to natural fluctuations of weather not experienced to any similar degree by domestic animals.

Voluntary restrictions of feed consumption and/or activity have been reported for both penned and wild deer (Behrend 1966, Ozoga, unpublished data, Mattfeld, unpublished data). McEwen et al. (in Behrend 1966:146) suggested that " 'seasonal metabolic changes may have evolved as a means of adaptation to winter food scarcity.' "

Behrend (1966:146-147) believed "The strong correlation between deer activity and day length (or date) suggests a well-developed pattern with a firm physiological basis in which day length is the primary stimulus." He notes that "the pattern of the BMR in captive deer in New Hampshire is strikingly similar to the seasonal activity on the Huntington Forest, and the similar latitude of the study area ... would indicate a very similar regimen of daylight throughout the year."

Varying day length is the stimulus to molt, and is under endocrine control. Silver and Colovos (1957) observed that premature molt followed exposure of captive deer to artificial light. Further observations of excessive and premature hair loss were recorded (for deer not participating in the metabolism experiments) following a month of continuous sunshine; a doe maintained at the Dartmouth Medical School on a standard-length day, shed her coat in August, but remained almost hairless until lighting arrangements were changed to simulate natural day length (unpublished data, this study). French et al. (1960) concluded that reduced intake of captive white-tailed deer in winter was related to the shorter days of that season. BMR of three heifers exposed to artificial light was increased 23 percent compared to 0.6 percent decrease over the same period for controls (Ritzman and Colovos 1943:17).

The normality of the low metabolism found in winter is supported by Hoffman and Robinson (1966) who found that response, in deer, of the thyroid gland to cold is not comparable to that found in laboratory animals. Among several possible explanations for this Hoffman and Robinson (1966:278) suggest that: "the thyroid glands [may] undergo adaptive compensation, resulting in increased efficiency or elaboration of metabolic promotor substances as ambient temperatures decrease," or "the combination of cold and semi-starvation may lead to reduced signs and symptoms of thyroidal activity. . . ." Our finding of lower metabolism in winter refutes the possi-

271

bility of increased thyroid efficiency, but lends support to the latter possibility.

Seasonal variability of FMR may not be found in deer of other species, or in those maintained under conditions comparable to domestic stock. Eickhoff 1957 (in Hoffman and Robinson 1966:279) reported a picture of consistent thyroid inactivity in European red deer (*Cervus elaphus*). Brockway and Maloiy (1967) found no evidence of an annual rhythm of heat loss in a red deer measured every 2 months for 1 year. The red deer was housed indoors at a temperature of 18 C, and consumed a ration that either maintained weight or permitted a slight gain. It thus experienced neither the seasonal weather nor annual weight changes characteristic of white-tailed deer in northern forest habitats. Similar results were obtained on two other red deer (Maloiy 1968). Maloiy's data do not indicate what effect, if any, constant ambient temperature may have had on molt, or on the length and density of the hair covering.

Values of FMR obtained on our deer were variable, and high compared to the accepted interspecific mean. This is in conformance with findings of Brockway and Maloiy (1967:23), who note that variability and high values have been observed in the relatively few measurements of fasting metabolism of non-domesticated ruminants. According to Ritzman and Colovos (1943:9), "Marked differences in basal metabolism . . . denote either temperamental or functional differences, or both." That differences in temperament exist between such animals as deer and sheep or cattle is hardly open to question; individual differences in the deer are reflected in differences in activity in the chamber. In most cases, we used the same animals in winter and summer experiments, and in every case FMR measured in summer coat was higher than in winter coat. The influence of season appears to be greater than that of temperament as regards variability of FMR.

The influence of coat was demonstrated by the increased heat production of the clipped buck. The 5-day period between clipping and measurement must have been sufficient to allow the animal to reach thermal equilibrium with its environment, so that 20 C was below critical temperature in the near-absence of coat.

It seems reasonable to assume that seasonal changes in metabolism represent a physiological response to seasons and/or weather; and further to assume that the molt, the abrupt change in FMR, and changes in endocrine activity are in some way interacting. Together they probably represent part of a complex adaptation for survival of deer living near the northern extremity of their range, which may not be found in deer living in more southerly latitudes.

Additional studies of energy requirements of deer should undertake:

1. Determination of the limits of the zone of thermal neutrality for deer of varying size and condition, and at various times of year.

2. Measurement of heat production at effective temperatures below the critical temperature.

3. Measurement of the effect of level of intake, and feed temperature on heat production.

4. Investigation of the energy cost of activity and production.

5. Measurement of body temperatures at various seasons of the year, and under different conditions of activity.

LITERATURE CITED

BEHREND, D. F. 1966. Behavior of white-tailed deer in an Adirondack Forest. Ph.D. Thesis. Syracuse Univ. New York. Coll. Forestry, Syracuse, 206pp.

BENEDICT, F. G. 1938. Vital energetics. Carnegie Institution, Washington, D. C. 215pp.

_____, AND E. G. RITZMAN. 1935. Lability of the basal metabolism of the dairy cow. Proc. Natl. Acad. Sci. 21(6):304-308.

BISSELL, H. D., B. HARRIS, HELEN STRONG, AND F. JAMES. 1955. The digestibility of certain natural and artificial foods eaten by deer in California. California Fish and Game 41(1):57-78.

_____, AND W. C. WEIR. 1957. The Digestibilities of interior live oak and chamise by deer and sheep. J. Animal Sci. 16(2):476-480.

BLAXTER, K. L. 1962. The energy metabolism of ruminants. Charles C. Thomas, Springfield, Illinois. 329pp.

BROCKWAY, J. H., AND G. M. O. MALOIY. 1967. Energy metabolism of the red deer. J. Physiol. 194:22-24.

BRODY, S. 1945. Bioenergetics and growth. Rheinhold Publishing Corp., New York. 1,023 pp.

COLOVOS, N. F., AND J. B. HOLTER. 1969. Constancy of fasting (basal) heat production in ruminants. J. Dairy Sci. (In press.)

DAVENPORT, LaV. A. 1939. Results of deer feeding experiments at Cusino, Michigan. Trans. N. Am. Wildl. Conf. 4:268-274.

DIETZ, D. R., R. H. UDALL, AND L. E. YEAGER. 1962. Chemical composition and digestibility by mule deer of selected forage species. Colorado Game and Fish Comm. Tech. Publ. 14. 89pp.

FRENCH, C. E., L. C. McEWEN, N. D. MAGRUDER, T. RADER, T. A. LONG, AND R. W. SWIFT. 1960. Responses of white-tailed bucks to added artificial light. J. Mammal. 41(1):23-29.

FORBES, E. B., L. F. MARCY, A. L. VORIS, AND C. E. FRENCH. 1941. The digestive capacities of the white-tailed deer. J. Wildl. Mgmt. 5(1):108-114.

HOFFMAN, R. A., AND P. F. ROBINSON. 1966. Changes in some endocrine glands of white-tailed deer as affected by season, sex and age. J. Mammal. 47(2):266-280.

KLEIBER, M. 1947. Body size and metabolic rate. Physiol. Rev. 27(4):511-541.

_____. 1961. Fire of life: an introduction to animal energetics. John Wiley & Sons, New York. 454pp.

MALOIY, G. M. O. 1968. The physiology of digestion and metabolism in the red deer (Cervus elaphaus L.). Ph. D. Thesis, Rowett Research Inst., Aberdeen, Scotland. 192pp.

MATTFELD, O. O. 1967. Unpublished data. Archer and Anna Huntington Wildlife Forest Station, Newcomb, New York.

MAYNARD, L. A., G. BUMP, R. DARROW, AND J. C. WOODWARD. 1935. Food preferences and requirements of the white-tailed deer in New York State. New York State Conserv. Dept. and New York State Coll. Agr. Bull. 1. 35pp.

MOEN, A. N. 1968. Energy balance of white-tailed deer in the winter. Trans. N. Am. Wildl. and Nat. Resources Conf. 33:224-236.

OZOGA, J. J. (Nd) Unpublished data. Michigan Dept. Conserv., Cusino Wildl. Expt. Sta., Shingleton.

RITZMAN, E. G., AND F. G. BENEDICT. 1938. Nutritional physiology of the adult ruminant. Carnegie Institution, Washington, D. C. 200pp.

_____, AND N. F. COLOVOS. 1943. Physiological requirements and utilization of protein and energy by growing cattle. Univ. New Hampshire Expt. Sta. Bull. 80. 59pp.

SILVER, HELENETTE. 1968. Nutrition studies. Pp. 182-196. In Siegler, H. R. (Editor). The white-tailed deer in New Hampshire. New Hampshire Fish and Game Dept., Survey Rept. 10. 256pp.

_____, AND N. F. COLOVOS. 1957. Nutritive evaluation of some forage rations of deer. New Hampshire Fish and Game Dept. Tech. Circ. 15. 56pp.

_____, _____, AND H. H. HAYES. 1959. Basal metabolism of white-tailed deer—a pilot study. J. Wildl. Mgmt. 23(4):434-438.

THE DYNAMICS OF THREE NATURAL POPULATIONS OF THE DEER *ODOCOILEUS HEMIONUS COLUMBIANUS* (1957)

Richard D. Taber and Raymond F. Dasmann

Population analyses are used to discover characteristics of populations and to understand factors influencing those characteristics. Although this paper has been criticized (Caughley, G. 1966. Ecology 47(6):906-918), we include it here as an early example of the use of life tables to develop hypotheses pertinent to management. (See Eberhardt, L. 1969 in Wildlife Management Techniques, The Wildlife Society, for a recent discussion of methods of life table analysis).

In the course of an investigation of the ecology of the Columbian black-tailed deer [*Odocoileus hemionus columbianus* (Richardson)] in relation to chaparral management in Lake County, California, information on the dynamics of three natural populations has been obtained. These populations occupy different habitats. The original plant community and environment were common to all, but secondary modification has created three distinct range types.

The climax plant cover consists on south slopes of *chamise chaparral* and on the north slopes of *broad sclerophyll forest* as described by Cooper (1922). These associations are dominated by fire-tolerant shrubs which either sprout from the root-crown when burned or have seeds which germinate readily following heating.

On the southerly exposures the most abundant plant is chamise (*Adenostema fasciculatum*). Other species include yerba santa (*Eriodictyon californicum*), wedgeleaf ceanothus (*Ceanothus cuneatus*), and toyon (*Photinia arbutifolia*). Occasional burning apparently took place on these slopes during prehistoric times.

The northerly exposures were largely covered, before white settlement, with a broad-sclerophyll forest, in which the dominant trees were interior live-oak (*Quercus wislizenii*), canyon oak (*Q. chrysolepis*), California laurel (*Umbellularia californica*) and madrone (*Arbutus menziesii*). Since that time (1855-65) fires have become more frequent and at present much of the north-exposure vegetation must be called mixed or mesic chaparral, consisting of broad-sclerophyll species which have been reduced to shrub form by burning. The principal constituent of this association is interior live-oak *(Quercus wislizenii)*. A large assemblage of other woody plants including scrub oak *(Q. dumosa)*, Eastwood manzanita *(Arctostaphylos glandulosa)*, and deerbrush *(Ceanothus integerrimus)* is also found on north exposures.

At present the general cycle of events is that every five to twenty years or more a fire sweeps the region bare, except for isolated patches of brush and the bare, charred trunks of the burned shrubs. Within five to ten years the sprouts and seedlings have grown up to cover the ground with a dense thicket of shrubs. Two of the range-types that were compared in this study

Reprinted from Ecology 38(2):233-246, by permission of Duke University Press, Durham, N. Carolina.

are the two extremes of this burn-and-recover pattern: the newly burned area on which crown-sprouts and seedlings are abundant—here called the "wildfire burn"; and the area which has not been burned for at least 10 years—here called the "chaparral." The wildfire burn is admittedly a transient stage, but while it lasts it constitutes a special type of deer range, being rich in food and poor in cover.

Another modification of chaparral is possible. Certain portions may be burned deliberately in either the early spring or late summer, and the burned areas seeded to herbaceous species. After the rains, when the seedlings emerge, those of the herbaceous species compete successfully with those of the woody species. The brush-sprouts are kept hedged by deer use or reduced by re-burning. The net result is a scattering of shrubs with the intervening area occupied by herbaceous plants. When an area is managed in this way portions are left in heavy brush for cover. This range type is now called "shrubland."

The technique of managing chaparral to create shrubland is still in the experimental stage so the areas of shrubland are limited in extent. The area most intensively studied covered about 400 map acres (horizontal projection) and was followed from before burning, in 1949, until 1955. Areas which had been longer established were also studied.

Some discussion of the ecology of these chaparral cover types has been included in a previous publication (Biswell *et al.* 1952), and a fuller description of the plant cover, with special reference to use by deer, will form the body of a later report.

The three range-types under consideration may occur in close juxtaposition, and it was in such an area that the present studies were made. The area lies about five miles southwest of Lakeport, California, between the elevations of 1500 and 2500 feet. The substrate consists of Pliocene sandstones elevated in Pleistocene times (Manning and Ogle 1950). Erosion has been rapid and the soils are correspondingly thin. They are classified principally as *Maymen*, with lesser areas of *Los Gatos*. Small pockets of still other residual soils occur on the uplands, and alluvial soils are found in the stream-bottoms. The topography is moderately steep (average slope = 22 degrees), and consists of irregular drainages and ridges with rounded tops. Rainfall averages about 28 inches annually. Winter snows usually melt soon after they fall, especially on the warmer south exposures where the deer spend most of their time in winter.

The adjustment of the vegetation to the Mediterranean climate has a profound effect upon the food-regime of the deer. Most of the shrubs are evergreen, but do not grow in the winter, when it is moist enough but too cold, or in summer, when it is warm enough but too dry. Ordinarily there is some growth in crown-sprouts in late fall, but little or none in mature shrubs. The principal growth period, then, is spring. In April and May, the deer, feeding on the new shoots, gain weight rapidly. Most fawns are born in the second and third weeks of May. The last rains usually fall in May. Increasing drought dries the herbaceous plants and the shrubs become dormant in July. The moisture and crude protein levels in the browse fall steadily all summer, and the condition of the deer, especially lactating does, falls accordingly. Occasionally there is a heavy set of acorns and the deer begin to browse these directly from the low oaks in August and September, months when otherwise the forage is of low quality. In the fall come cool weather and the first rains. The timing of the first substantial rain is especially important in the shrubland, where large quantities of annual plants appear if about one inch of rain falls. Sufficient rain for germination usually falls in October, but occasionally the first heavy precipitation may be as early as August or as late as November.

The present study began in the fall of 1948 and continued through the fall of 1955. Many people aided the investigation: of the Field forces of the California Department of Fish and Game, Norman Alstot, Gordon Ashcraft, Bonar Blong, Herbert Hagen and Manley Inlay; of the State Fish and Game Laboratory, John Azevedo, Art Bischoff, Oscar Brunetti and Merton Rosen. Help in the field was also provided by Richard Genelly and Gerald Geraldson of the University of California. Aid, advice, and encouragement were constantly available from H. H. Biswell, Project Leader, A. M. Schultz, A. S. Leopold and W. M. Longhurst, of the University of California, and William Dasmann and Robert Lassen of the Department of Fish and Game. To these, and to Glen Keithley and Harold Manley on whose land much of the work was done, and to others too numerous to list, we are indebted for help.

In addition we wish to acknowledge the critical reading of the manuscript, with suggestions for improvement, by W. Leslie Robinette, J. J. Hickey, Robert F. Scott and staff members of the Museum of Vertebrate Zoology.

METHODS AND RESULTS

The basic data from which the life tables were derived consist of information on individual movement, population density, reproduction according to age-class, population structure, and mortality according to age and sex. These data were gathered seasonally for the three populations under study; notes on the methods involved are given below.

Movement

By studying the movements of marked deer daily, seasonally and annually, it has been found that the deer in the study region are nonmigratory and that most of them occupy home ranges with diameters of about one-half mile (does) to three-quarters of a mile (bucks). Populations occupying neighboring ranges may, therefore, be considered separately (Dasmann 1953).

Population density

Censuses were made at least twice a year, first by the pellet-group-count method and later by the sample-area-count method, both of which were found to be accurate when checked against populations of known density. These methods are described elsewhere (Dasmann and Taber 1955).

Table 5-1 shows population densities observed at various times on the three types of range under study. Counts in the chaparral give a summer density of about 30 per square mile. The wildfire burn, at the same season, showed 120 the first year after the fire. The summer density dropped to 106 the second year, 52 the third and 44 the fourth. The shrubland went from 98 the year following burning to 131 the second year and

TABLE 5-1. Deer density (individuals per map-square-mile) on three range types

A. Chaparral

	April-June	July-October	November-December
1949	28	..	30
1950	13	30	26
1951	..	..	30
Average	20	..	29

B. Wildfire burn

Growing season from time of burning	Early May	Mid-July	Early December
1	..	120	86
2	75	106	56
3	48	52	50
4	32	44	32

C. Shrubland

	Early May	Mid-July	Early December
1951	88	131	88
1952	69	112	99
1953	69	103	..
1954	53	85*	..
1955	55	82*	..

* mid-June

then down to about 84 the fifth and sixth years, at which level the population presumably stabilized.

Natality

Data on ovulation rates were obtained by collecting pregnant and post-partum does. Forty-eight does over 17 months of age were taken on the three range types. Younger does were also collected and were found not to breed under our conditions (Taber 1952).

The presence of *corpora lutea of pregnancy* is an indicator of the successful shedding, fertilization and implantation of ova, but not every *corpus luteum* represents a developing fetus. The ratio was found to be 94 fetuses per 100 corpora lutea, based on all pregnant does collected. No evidence of abortion or resorption was noted, so this six percent loss of ova must occur before fertilization or in very early pregnancy.

Does often breed first, in this region, at the age of 17 months, although on the poorest ranges some may not breed until the age of 29 or even 41 months. No yearling does (17-24 months) were collected in the poorest range type, the chaparral. Two from the shrubland had one fetus apiece and two out of three from the new wildfire burn had one fetus each. Two yearling does were taken from an older wildfire burn and neither was pregnant. These samples are so small that little confidence can be placed in them. However, some values for the contribution of yearling does to the annual fawn-increment must be assumed in the calculations which follow, so these figures for the shrubland and new wildfire burn will tentatively be accepted. In addition, since no data are available for reproduction in yearling does in the chaparral, it will be assumed that the rate of fawn production by them is 0.5 per doe.

Among adult does the samples are larger, ranging for the three range types from 10 to 16. Fawn production in the shrubland is significantly higher than that in the chaparral, the values being 1.65 and 0.77 fawns per doe respectively. The does on the new wildfire burn show an intermediate average of 1.32 fawns apiece. Fawn production is summarized in Table 5-2.

TABLE 5-2. Fawn production by yearling and adult does on three range types

Range Type	Yearling Does			Adult Does		Fawns produced per doe
	Number examined	Mean number of corpora lutea	Fawns produced per doe	Number examined	†Mean number of corpora lutea	
Chaparral	0	. . . .	*0.50	11	0.82 (0.42 - 1.22)	0.77
Wildfire burn after one growing season	3	0.66	0.62	10	1.40 (1.03 - 1.77)	1.32
Wildfire burn after three growing seasons	2	0.0	0.0	4	0.75 (0.00 - 1.54)	0.71
Shrubland	2	1.0	0.94	16	1.75 (1.51 - 1.99)	1.65

* Assumed (see text).
† Values in parentheses indicate the range with a confidence limit = 0.05.

Population structure

Population structure was determined by observing and classifying undisturbed deer at ranges consistent with accuracy, at times during which all age and sex classes were equally visible. The most favorable seasons were late July, when fawns were at heel and before hot weather caused the bucks to seek heavy cover, and early December, when the rut had subsided and the bucks had returned to their normal level of mobility but before the antlers were shed (Dasmann and Taber 1956). In shrubland, where a more intensive study was carried out, determinations were made throughout the year. The values in Table 5-3 are expressed in terms of ratios, where the number of adult does is always taken as 100.

The low density of deer and the high density of cover made herd composition counts difficult to obtain in the chaparral. Therefore use was made of the fact that when an area of chaparral is burned, and sprouts appear, as happened in 1949 and 1950, the deer whose home ranges impinge upon the burned area congregate on it to feed and are then (December) easily observed. This population may be taken to represent the population in the chaparral, so far as structure is concerned, if one correction is made. Since the home ranges of bucks are larger than those of does, a burned area attracts proportionally more bucks than does, if only those animals whose home ranges impinge upon the burned area come to it. The counts in Table 5-3(A) are corrected for this; i.e., adult buck counts were reduced one-third, because average buck home-range diameter is $\frac{3}{2}$ average doe home-range diameter.

TABLE 5-3. Population structure according to herd composition counts on three range types

A. Chaparral

Month	Number of deer classified	Adult males	Yearling males	Adult females	Yearling females	Fawns
Dec. 1949	124	72	23	100	38	85
Dec. 1950	47	20	5	100	25	60
Average	85	46	14	100	31	72

B. Wildfire burn (December counts)

During growing season 1 (1948 burn) counted in 1949	90	63	30	100	33	107
4 (1948 burn) counted in 1952	37	50	14	100	21	79
1 (1950 burn)	54	37	21	100	39	89
2 "	45	66	20	100	33	80
3 "	90	48	7	100	27	34

C. Shrubland

July, 1951	82	70	27	100	46	127
Dec., 1951	55	30	30	100	45	70
May, 1952	43	38	31	100	44	56
July, 1952	70	48	9	100	30	117
Dec., 1952	62	39	9	100	30	92
May, 1953	43	32	9	100	14	41
June, 1953	67	36	16	100	20	96
May, 1954	33	39	29	100	14	57
June, 1954	53	56	25	100	25	125
May, 1955	34	46	31	100	8	77
June, 1955	51	71	36	100	36	121

Mortality

Every carcass encountered was classified, if possible, according to age, sex, season of death, cause of death and range type. Occasionally special systematic searches were made for carcasses, especially along the beds of steep-walled canyons, where dead deer were most likely to accumulate. Altogether 222 carcasses were tallied; these are listed in Table 5-4. Aging was by tooth eruption and wear (Severinghaus 1949; Moreland 1952).

A carcass-count of this sort is not a true reflection of mortality in all classes; the very young deer are under-represented, because their fragile carcasses soon disintegrate. However, if this is taken into account, the carcass tally aids the study of mortality.

The principal cause of mortality was starvation, not caused by a quantitative lack of food, but rather by a seasonal drop in the quality of available forage (Taber 1956). The effects of starvation were often augmented by exposure to unfavorable weather and occasionally by disease or parasitism. Mortality from this cause was heaviest among fawns, but adults of both sexes were also affected. Principal starvation losses occurred in fall and winter. Next in importance as a mortality factor was hunting. Almost all adult buck mortality; except for old deer, was caused by bullet-wounds. A few deer of other classes were also affected. The loss of protected classes to hunting varies widely. It was found in the study region to be quite low. A few deer were killed in accidents or by predators, but these are relatively unimportant mortality factors.

TABLE 5-4. The classification of deer found dead on three range types

A. Chaparral

Sex	0-3 months	4-6 months	7-9 months	10-12 months	13-24 months	25-36 months	37 months and over	Total
males	0	7	6	0	8	3	9	33
females	1	6	4	0	1	1	23	36
?	16	0	0	0	0	0	0	16

Sub-total 85

B. Wildfire burn—one to four years after burning

males	7	1	2	0	1	6	12	29
females	1	4	1	0	1	1	11	19
?	16	0	0	0	0	0	0	16

Sub-total 64

C. Shrubland

males	3	7	1	2	5	4	4	26
females	1	5	0	0	0	4	18	28
?	19	0	0	0	0	0	0	19

Sub-total 73

Grand total 222

The hunting season extends from early August to mid-September and bucks usually become legal game during their third year and remain so for the rest of their lives. The kill at this time has a profound effect on the population structure. The ratios existing between two-year, three-year and older bucks in the kill, which are given in Table 5-5, are affected by three factors: the age distribution of bucks in the population; the relative vulnerability of the various age classes to hunting; and the deliberate selection of the larger (hence older) bucks by the hunter.

Where hunting pressure is only moderate and escape cover is adequate, bucks over four years old are much less vulnerable than two-year-olds, with three-year-olds being intermediate. For example, in an intensively studied area of shrubland the combined buck populations for the seasons of 1951 and 1952 were 14 two-year-olds, of which 10 were killed, and 13 older bucks, of which two were killed. This difference in vulnerability is probably above the average because little drive-hunting with dogs took place. This type of hunting results in a proportionally higher kill of old bucks.

Selective hunting, involving the deliberate attempt of the hunter to bag a trophy buck, is generally not practiced. Most hunters attempt to take the first legal target that they see. If the antlers are small and inconspicuous the hunter may not recognize the deer as legal game, or if two bucks appear together, the hunter will select the larger, but these factors do not appear to affect the kill appreciably. These remarks apply to hunters on public land, and private land with public access. All the areas studied except part of the shrubland could be so classed. However, there are certain lightly hunted areas of private land where there is a definite selection of larger (hence older) bucks by the hunter. Part of the shrubland of the present study was in this category, and for that reason the percent of old bucks in the kill (Table 5-5) is believed to be higher than would ordinarily be found.

TABLE 5-5. Distribution by age (in per cent) of bucks killed and taken home from three range types

Range type	Two years old	Three years old	Four years old and older	Number in sample
Chaparral	40	22	38	194
Wildfire burn after first growing season	36	22	*42	59
After second growing season	63	21	15	52
After third growing season	37	37	25	83
After fourth growing season	50	22	28	32
Shrubland	49	19	32	43

* Old bucks are unusually vulnerable during the first hunting season after a large wildfire has removed most of the escape cover.

In addition to the bucks which are killed and taken home by the hunters, there are those which are shot but not found. In the study region hunters often shoot across canyons at running deer at long range. This fact, and the heavy cover and the hard ground, which makes tracking difficult, lead to the loss of many wounded deer. Few of these recover. Intensive studies of small known populations have shown this loss to equal about 40 per cent, or slightly more, of the take-home kill.

RECONSTRUCTION OF POPULATION DYNAMICS

The information presented above has been used to deduce the detailed changes taking place within each population in the course of a year or, in the wildfire burn population, four years. In order that values per square mile may be readily derived, the tables of population dynamics given in this section are constructed to represent the deer population occupying 100 square miles of the range-type in question. In a later section, where life tables are presented, values in per cent may be more readily apprehended.

Annual population cycle: chaparral

From data presented above it may be seen that the deer population in the chaparral is one of low density, with low reproductive rate. Since the population is stable, this low reproductive rate is matched by a relatively low mortality. Does probably do not breed as early as they do on better ranges, and they certainly do not bear as many fawns in maturity. It is possible that some individuals breed only in alternate years. This partly relieves the population of the heaviest drain on adult vitality—gestation and especially lactation, where lactation takes place at a season of a falling nutritive plane. Mortality among fawns, though high, is not as high proportionately as it is on also fully stocked but better ranges, like shrubland. Presumably this is due in some measure to the fact that most fawns are born singly. Mortality among bucks during the hunting season is lighter than in more open range because the abundance of dense escape cover in the chaparral makes hunting difficult. The general pattern is of a population with a rather low rate of replacement and a correspondingly high life expectancy from adulthood. An annual cycle is shown in Table 5-6.

TABLE 5-6. The population dynamics, through one year, of a deer population inhabiting 100 square miles of chaparral

Season	4+ yr. Males	3 yr. Males	2 yr. Males	1 yr. Males	3+ yr. Females	2 yr. Females	1 yr. Females	Male Fawns	Female Fawns	Total
Late May (fawn-drop)	434	182	482	556	1935	706	858	2042	1810	9005
Early summer loss	...	...	...	...	29	...	...	350	224	603
July herd composition count	434	182	482	556	1906	706	858	1692	1586	8402
Hunting season bag	60	46	214	...	...	...	...	...	...	320
Crippling loss	24	19	86	...	...	...	...	...	...	129
Late summer and fall loss	...	...	...	20	115	37	20	856	547	1595
Dec. herd composition count	350	117	182	536	1791	669	838	836	1039	6358
Late winter loss	33	...	...	54	414	111	132	280	181	1205
Early May population	317	117	182	482	1377	558	706	556	858	5154
Late May (fawn-drop)	434	182	482	556	1935	706	858	2042	1810	9005

Annual population cycle: wildfire burn

The general trend of population density characteristic of wildfire burns is from a high point the spring following burning to lower and lower levels thereafter. Movement is the most important element in these population changes.

When the area burns the deer move ahead of the fire and are seldom directly injured. Lack of food, however, keeps them from re-occupying their home ranges, unless there happens to have been a heavy acorn crop. The brush on the warmer slopes sprouts from the root-crown about October or November, in areas burned in late summer. The wildfire burn thereupon becomes an attractive feeding area, and large numbers of deer appear on it. The deer densities observed on burned areas can be adequately explained by supposing that the deer feeding on the burned area are those whose home ranges included part of that area before it was burned. If this is true, deer are drawn to a burned area from a peripheral zone one-half mile wide for does and three-quarters of a mile wide for bucks; *i.e.*—the peripheral zone equals one home-range diameter in width. Thus if burns are small the deer density feeding upon them is high, whereas if burns are large the density is lower, because in the former case the peripheral zone is larger in proportion to the burned area and in the latter it is smaller.

Actual observations of increase in deer density following burning correspond, for the areas representative of wildfire burns, to that to be expected if a strip one-half mile in width were burned through the country. Therefore in the reconstruction of population dynamics (Table 5-7) it has been assumed that the burn consists of a strip one-half mile in width extending indefinitely across the country, and the population shown is that inhabiting 100 square miles of this burn.

In order to follow the dynamics of a deer population through four years, as has been attempted in Table 5-7, it is necessary to use some interpolated values for productivity. It has been seen (Table 5-2) that the average fawn production per doe in the new wildfire burn is about 0.62 for yearlings and 1.32 for adults. As the wildfire burn grows older the quality of the forage produced on it drops, and this is reflected in the reproductive rate. By the fourth year after burning reproduction appears, according to evidence from limited collecting and herd composition counts, to be about the same as that in the heavy brush, namely 0.5 fawns per yearling doe and 0.77 fawns per adult doe. It remains to interpolate intermediate values for productivity during the second and third years following burning. We will assume that yearling does each produce an average of 0.58 and 0.54 fawns and adult does 1.14 and 0.95 during the second and third years following burning, respectively.

Table 5-7 traces the dynamics of a deer population inhabiting a wildfire burn from the December following burning for four full years. The population, if there had been no fire, would have been about 29 per square mile. The influx of deer whose home ranges abutted on the burned area added another 53 per square mile. These deer, which bred in early November, showed a reproductive rate somewhat greater than that found in the chaparral. Presumably this was due either to a high-quality diet of new sprouts for a few weeks prior to breeding, or to the psychic stimulation of crowding in the periphery of the burn during the rut. The former seems more probable.

With the onset of cold weather there was apparently an exodus of a portion of the population from the burned area, where there was little heavy cover, to the periphery, and these did not return. There was apparently a similar movement the following winter. In both cases the population dropped but a lack of carcasses indicated that movement rather than mortality was the cause.

Mortality on new wildfire burns was found to be very low, as might be expected from the high quality of the feed there. However, as forage quality declined, mortality increased.

By the end of the fourth year the deer population in the wildfire burn had declined to about the levels in the chaparral both in density and reproduction.

Annual population cycle: shrubland

The management of chaparral to create shrubland resulted in the attraction of a heavy deer population, in much the same manner as has been described for the wildfire burn. There were, however, several important points of difference between the shrubland and the wildfire burn. In the shrubland there were areas of cover closely adjacent to feeding

TABLE 5-7. Dynamics of a deer population inhabiting 100 square miles of wildfire burn for the first four years following burning.

Season	4+ yr. Males	3 yr. Males	2 yr. Males	1 yr. Males	3+ yr. Females	2 yr. Females	1 yr. Females	Male Fawns	Female Fawns	Total
Original population (Dec.)	406	83	99	196	740	344	362	276	395	2901
Influx from periphery	406	83	225	444	1247	580	610	695	1003	5293
Early May population	812	−166	−324	−640	1987	924	972	971	1398	8194
Fawn-drop	978	324	640	971	2911	972	1398	2098	1856	12148
Early summer loss	...	...	...	...	...	...	...	92	56	148
July herd composition count	978	324	640	971	2911	972	1398	2006	1800	12000
Hunting bag	126	66	108	...	...	...	...	...	...	300
Crippling loss	50	26	43	...	...	...	...	...	...	119
Late summer and fall loss	...	...	...	...	...	...	...	100	61	161
Exodus	145	42	107	175	799	267	377	524	478	2914
Dec. herd composition count	657	190	382	796	2112	705	1021	1382	1261	8506
Exodus	46	11	29	48	117	39	57	77	70	494
Late winter loss	...	...	...	...	7	...	...	473	106	586
Early May population	611	−179	−353	−748	1988	666	964	832	1085	7426
Fawn-drop	790	353	748	832	2654	964	1085	2176	1925	11527
Early summer loss	...	...	...	...	...	...	...	589	437	1026
July herd composition count	790	353	748	832	2654	964	1085	1587	1488	10501
Hunting bag	66	92	277	...	...	...	...	...	...	435
Crippling loss	26	37	111	...	...	...	...	...	...	174
Late summer and fall loss	...	...	...	...	...	...	...	279	133	412
Exodus	259	69	55	386	1062	386	434	635	595	3881
Dec. herd composition count	439	155	305	446	1592	578	651	673	760	5599
Exodus	114	...	...	196	100	150	169	175	198	1402
Late winter loss	35	...	...	...	152	...	...	218	42	447
Early May population	290	−155	−305	−250	1040	428	482	280	520	3750
Fawn-drop	445	305	250	280	1468	482	520	1067	943	5760
Early summer loss	...	...	...	...	...	...	...	380	230	610
July herd composition count	445	305	250	280	1468	482	520	687	713	5150
Hunting bag	64	93	93	...	...	...	...	...	...	250
Crippling loss	26	37	37	...	...	...	...	...	...	100
Late summer and fall loss	...	...	...	...	18	...	...	165	101	284
Dec. herd composition count	355	175	120	280	1450	482	520	522	612	4516
Late winter loss	94	...	...	...	646	...	...	336	204	1280
Early May population	261	−175	−120	−280	804	482	520	186	408	3236
Fawn-drop	436	120	280	186	1286	520	408	822	727	4785
Early summer loss	...	...	...	...	...	...	...	261	174	435
July herd composition count	436	120	280	186	1286	520	408	561	553	4350
Hunting bag	44	34	104	...	...	...	...	...	...	182
Crippling loss	18	14	42	...	...	...	...	...	...	74
Late summer and fall loss	...	...	...	83	307	10	10	210	140	710
Dec. herd composition count	374	72	134	153	979	510	398	351	413	3384

grounds; the wildfire burn had little cover. In the shrubland there was an abundance of herbaceous forage, which the deer eat in quantity from December through March; in the wildfire burn there was little herbaceous forage. In the shrubland the browsing-pressure of the deer was sufficient to keep many shrubs hedged and within reach; the browsing pressure on the wildfire burn was not usually sufficient for this and shrubs tended to grow beyond reach. Because of these, and perhaps other factors, the shrubland continued to support a high deer density throughout the study. This density was very high during the first years due to influx and a high survival. By the fifth and sixth year following burning, however, it had stabilized at a lower, but still substantial density. It appears that this level, about 84 per square mile in July, can be maintained for some time, so it has been taken as the basis for the annual cycle of population dynamics reconstructed in Table 5-8.

The shrubland range is fully stocked and population gain is matched by loss. The reproductive rate is high. Most yearling does produce a fawn and adult does produce an average of 1.65 fawns apiece. The mortality in these fawns is high; during the first year of life 73 percent of the males and 53 percent of the females die. Among adult does mortality is also high—about 25 percent per year. Adult bucks, because of heavy hunting and the prevalence of open country, lost 62 percent of two-year-olds, 35 percent of three-year-olds and about 20 percent of older bucks to hunting, on the average.

Among yearling (12- to 24-month-old) deer not all the loss to the population was due to mortality. It is usual for a dispersal movement of yearlings to occur about fawning-time, when the adult doe become antagonistic toward their previous offspring. In a large, homogeneous area, of uniform deer density, this movement of yearlings from a local area would be balanced by others moving into it. A small area of dense population, however, would tend to lose more than it gained; this is the situation on the 400-acre shrubland study area. Here the average loss due to emigration during the four year period 1951-55 amounted to about 6 percent of the yearling class of bucks and 38 percent of the yearling class of does. It seems probable that this higher emigration rate in yearling females is connected with the tendency toward spacing and mutual antagonism among breeding does (Dasmann and Taber 1956).

Since this measurement of emigration was made on a small area of dense population, it is large. In Table 5-8, which is an attempt to describe shrubland population dynamics for a larger area, a yearling female emigration of 15 percent is assumed.

TABLE 5-8. Dynamics of a deer population inhabiting 100 square miles of shrubland

Season	4+ yr. Males	3 yr. Males	2 yr. Males	1 yr. Males	3+ yr. Females	2 yr. Females	1 yr. Females	Male Fawns	Female Fawns	Total
Late May (fawn drop)	343	121	190	239	1063	262	280	504	446	3448
Early summer loss	...	...	...	...	...	...	...	180	114	294
July herd composition count	343	121	190	239	1063	262	280	324	332	3154
Hunting season bag	39	27	49	...	...	...	...	...	...	115
Crippling loss	16	11	20	...	...	...	...	...	...	47
Late summer and fall loss	...	...	...	43	152	17	8	31	19	270
Dec. herd composition count	288	83	121	196	911	245	272	293	313	2722
Late winter loss	28	...	...	6	80	13	10	54	33	224
Early May population	260	83	121	190	831	232	262	239	280	2498
Late May (fawn drop)	343	121	190	239	1063	262	280	504	446	3448

Life tables for wild ungulates

It has been apparent, in preceding sections, that in any of the populations under study the dynamics of the male portion of the population differed from that of the female portion. This was due partly to a differential mortality in early life and partly to the fact that when adulthood was reached entirely different decimating factors were at work—physiological reproductive drain, coupled with reduced nutrient quality, for females, and predation (in the form of hunting) for males. In other populations it is probable that still other factors might be operative. As an analytical aid, then, it seems proper to consider the male and female components of each population separately.

The life table, as so ably described and used by Deevey (1947) and Hickey (1952), is a convenient vehicle for describing a population so that certain characteristics can be readily ascertained. The data, or values derived from them, are cast under the headings: x—the age-interval, in our case one year; l_x—the number alive at the beginning of each year; d_x—the number dying within the year; q_x—the rate of mortality during the year ($100 \, d_x/l_x$) and e_x—the mean length of life remaining to each individual alive at the beginning of the year—the life expectation.

Deevey *(op. cit.)* points out that sources of ecological data for the construction of life tables are of three kinds: (1) knowledge of age at death for a random and adequate sample of the population; (2) knowledge of the fate of individuals of a single cohort at frequent intervals; and (3) knowledge of the age-structure among the living. He goes on to remark that information of the first and third types can be used only if one is prepared to assume that the population is stable in time.

For the black-tailed deer we have accumulated data of all three sorts. The deer populations in the chaparral and shrubland we have considered, for the purposes of this analysis, as relatively stable. Those in the wild-fire burn are not stable. Life tables, then, may be constructed for the deer populations of the chaparral and the shrubland.

It is of interest to compare the elements of population dynamics displayed by these populations with those of other wild ungulates. Adequate information on which to base sex-separate life tables is available for relatively stable populations of the roe-deer *(Capreolus capreolus)* from Andersen (1953), the red-deer *(Cervus elaphus)* from Evans (1891), and the Dall sheep *(Ovis dalli)* from Murie (1944), providing that certain reasonable assumptions (stated in each case) are allowed.

TABLE 5-9. Life tables for the black-tailed deer of the chaparral

A. Males

x (years)	l_x	d_x	q_x	e_x
0 - 1	1000	526	526	2.3
1 - 2	474	97	204	3.3
2 - 3	377	137	363	3.0
3 - 4	240	75	313	3.4
4 - 5	165	20	121	3.7
5 - 6	145	14	97	3.2
6 - 7	131	14	107	2.5
7 - 8	117	30	256	1.7
8 - 9	87	35	402	1.1
9 - 10	52	52	1000	0.5

B. Females

x (years)	l_x	d_x	q_x	e_x
0 - 1	1000	372	372	4.2
1 - 2	628	41	65	5.3
2 - 3	587	66	112	4.6
3 - 4	521	68	131	4.2
4 - 5	453	67	148	3.7
5 - 6	386	54	140	3.1
6 - 7	332	54	163	2.6
7 - 8	278	54	194	2.0
8 - 9	224	33	147	1.4
9 - 10	191	191	1000	0.5

The black-tailed deer

In constructing life tables from the data previously presented, it has been necessary to extend Table 5-4 (the carcass-tally) so as to break down the 37 months-and-older category into annual age-groups from three to ten. The number of individuals in each age-group was small, but the general pattern seemed to be one of fairly constant mortality rates from three to nine years for does and four to eight years for bucks. This has been tentatively assumed. In extreme old age (arbitrarily considered by us to be about 9-10 years) there is an accelerated mortality, as the oldest deer all die. When techniques of aging become more accurate it may be found that senescence is reached at 12-15 years rather than 9-10, and that mortality is roughly constant all through adulthood. In other words, our assumption that no deer live beyond 10 years may create an artificially abrupt drop-off at the end of the survivorship curve.

TABLE 5-10. Life tables for the black-tailed deer of the shrubland

A. Males

x (years)	l_x	d_x	q_x	e_x
0 - 1	1000	728	728	1.3
1 - 2	272	36	132	2.5
2 - 3	236	147	623	1.8
3 - 4	89	31	348	2.9
4 - 5	58	12	207	3.2
5 - 6	46	9	196	2.9
6 - 7	37	7	189	2.5
7 - 8	30	6	200	1.9
8 - 9	24	6	250	1.3
9 - 10	18	18	1000	0.5

B. Females

x (years)	l_x	d_x	q_x	e_x
0 - 1	1000	526	526	2.4
1 - 2	474	83	175	3.6
2 - 3	391	82	210	3.2
3 - 4	309	77	249	3.0
4 - 5	232	58	250	2.8
5 - 6	174	44	253	2.5
6 - 7	130	32	246	2.2
7 - 8	98	25	255	1.8
8 - 9	73	18	247	1.3
9 - 10	55	55	1000	0.5

It may be seen (in Tables 5-9 and 5-10) that in both range types there is a higher proportional mortality in male fawns; this has been attributed to the higher metabolic rate and nutrient requirements among males (Taber and Dasmann 1954). There is a markedly unbalanced sex ratio by the time two years is reached. At this point the males become vulnerable to predation (hunting) and the females (individuals of which breed for the first time at either 17 or 29 months) to the strains of reproduction. The weight

288

of hunting falls most heavily on the two-year-old class of males, while the loss of females is roughly constant from two to nine years. Both sexes have a higher mortality in the shrubland than in the chaparral. In the adult males this is known to be due to the easier hunting conditions of the shrubland; the deer are easier to kill. In the adult females the higher mortality found in the shrubland is probably related to the higher reproductive rate there. The loss in yearlings from the shrubland range is due, in part, to emigration rather than mortality. This makes an interesting parallel to the situation in roe-deer, described below.

The roe-deer

In 1950 a relatively stable roe-deer population inhabiting some woods on the Danish Game Research Farm at Kalø was exterminated by shooting. Forty-six males, 76 females and 91 fawns were taken. Andersen (1953) has reported on the age-distribution and given data on the occurrence of corpora lutea of pregnancy in the females.

Assuming that the annual reproductive rate was relatively constant; that fawns born amounted to 90 percent of the corpora lutea of pregnancy and that the sex ratio at birth was 100 males: 100 females, we may construct life tables (Table 5-11) for the two sexes.

TABLE 5-11. Life tables for the roe-deer of Kalø (after Andersen)

A. Males

x (years)	l_x	d_x	q_x	e_x
0 - 1	1000	740	740	1.2
1 - 2	260	60	230	2.2
2 - 3	200	110	550	1.7
3 - 4	90	20	222	2.1
4 - 5	70	20	286	1.5
5 - 6	50	30	600	0.9
6 - 7	20	20	1000	0.5

B. Females

x (years)	l_x	d_x	q_x	e_x
0 - 1	1000	630	630	2.6
1 - 2	370	50	135	4.2
2 - 3	320	150	469	3.0
3 - 4	170	50	294	3.3
4 - 5	120	40	333	2.7
5 - 6	80	30	375	2.2
6 - 7	50	20	400	1.7
7 - 8	30	10	333	1.2
8 - 9	20	20	1000	0.5

It will be noted that there is a high loss not only in the first year of life, but also in the second and especially in the third, in both sexes. Andersen (1953 and personal communication) points out that the hunting kill at Kalø has averaged only 4 males, 4 females and 6 fawns per year, from 1943 to 1949. He accounts for the loss in young adults in terms of dispersal, citing as evidence the fact that each year roe-deer appear in small outlying woods which are normally uninhabited by roe-deer, and that as many as possible of these are killed. Thus the principal factor limiting this population is apparently not food, as it is in both examples of the black-tailed deer, but emigration. The woods of Kaløseem to have a saturation point for roe-deer, presumably based on intraspecific stress. Darling (1937) has commented on the intolerance of roe-deer for their young of previous years, which he attributes to the patriarchal nature of their social organization.

The red deer

From 1879 onward Henry Evans leased the red-deer shooting on the island of Jura, in Scotland. He conducted an annual census of males (in July) and antlerless deer (in February) and classified adult males, yearling (1-2 year) males and adult females and deer under one year of age.

TABLE 5-12. Life tables for the red deer of Jura (after Evans)

A. Males

x (years)	l_x	d_x	q_x	e_x
0 - 1	1000	610	610	2.9
1 - 2	390	. . .	. . .	5.6
2 - 3	390	5	128	4.6
3 - 4	385	26	675	3.6
4 - 5	359	65	181	2.9
5 - 6	294	86	293	2.4
6 - 7	208	61	293	2.2
7 - 8	147	60	408	1.7
8 - 9	87	35	402	1.8
9 - 10	52	22	423	1.7
10 - 11	30	13	433	1.5
11 - 12	17	8	471	1.3
12 - 13	9	5	556	0.9
13 - 14	4	4	1000	0.5

B. Females

x (years)	l_x	d_x	q_x	e_x
0 - 1	1000	485	485	3.1
1 - 2	515	60	117	4.5
2 - 3	455	. . .	. . .	4.0
3 - 4	455	126	277	3.0
4 - 5	329	91	276	3.0
5 - 6	238	65	273	3.0
6 - 7	173	48	278	2.9
7 - 8	125	35	280	2.8
8 - 9	90	25	278	2.7
9 - 10	65	18	277	2.6
10 - 11	47	13	277	2.4
11 - 12	34	10	294	2.1
12 - 13	24	7	293	1.7
13 - 14	17	5	294	1.2
14 - 15	12	12	1000	0.5

He kept a record of deer found dead and, having examined many pregnant females, estimated the production per female. During the first six years he did not burn the heather, and his deer population was roughly stable, the adult females increasing slightly. In the next five years, he was

active in heather-burning and his deer population had increased markedly and was still increasing at the time he drew up his report. For present purposes, the information from the first six years only has been used.
The basic data are (averages for 1879-1884 inclusive):

Stags (2 years and above)
    Alive in July—   460
    Shot—   60
    Dying from other causes—   31
Hinds (one year old and above)
    Alive in Feb.—   612
    Shot—   5
    Dying from other causes—   47

Hinds first breed at 2½ years, 100 hinds (one year old and above) bring 37
calves to February and 30 to one year of age. Of these 30, 13 are males—
these have little loss to 3 years, and 17 are females—these become 15 by
second birthday and are still 15 at third birthday. The sex ratio at birth
is 100 males: 100 females (Evans 1891).

A maximum life span is assumed as 15 years (by the present authors).
The life tables have been derived from these data (Table 5-12).

As in the black-tailed deer described above, these red deer died
principally of starvation and exposure, except for a light harvest of adult
stags. An effort was made by Evans to kill only mature stags, so there is
not the heavy mortality of young adult males noted for the black-tailed
deer.

The Dall sheep

From 1939 to 1941 Adolph Murie, working in Dall sheep habitat near
Mt. McKinley, where wolves were common, recorded the age, sex and
probable year of death of every sheep carcass he could find (Murie 1944).
Taking only those which died from 1937 to 1941, when the population was
relatively stable, it is possible to construct life tables (Table 5-13) for the
two sexes if the following surmises are accepted.

Ewes first breed at 2.5 years.
Average production per adult ewe is 1.0 lamb.
The sex ratio at birth is 100 males: 100 females.
The loss of yearlings is not more than 10 percent.

The sheep which could not be aged exactly because the horns were
missing, but which were known to be at least nine years old, had the same
age-distribution as the 9-year-plus-older sheep which could be aged from
the horns.

These data show for both sexes a low rate of loss between the first
and ninth year. The animals were not subjected to hunting, but they were
constantly under heavy pressure from wolves, which took mainly the
lambs and very old adults. This apparently left the prime animals, according to Murie's range observations, with ample food supplies and a
high life expectancy.

Table 5-13. Life tables for the Dall sheep of Mt. McKinley (after Murie)

A. Males

x (years)	l_x	d_x	q_x	e_x
0 - 1	1000	718	718	3.3
1 - 2	282	20	71	9.3
2 - 3	262	3	11	9.0
3 - 4	259	. . .	. . .	8.1
4 - 5	259	3	11	7.0
5 - 6	256	5	20	6.1
6 - 7	251	. . .	. . .	5.2
7 - 8	251	14	56	4.2
8 - 9	237	6	25	3.5
9 - 10	231	28	120	2.5
10 - 11	203	40	200	1.8
11 - 12	163	70	429	1.1
12 - 13	93	87	935	0.6
13 - 14	6	. . .	. . .	1.5
14 - 15	6	6	1000	0.5

B. Females

x (years)	l_x	d_x	q_x	e_x
0 - 1	1000	718	718	2.8
1 - 2	282	28	99	7.6
2 - 3	254	6	24	7.4
3 - 4	248	3	12	6.6
4 - 5	245	3	12	5.6
5 - 6	242	8	33	4.7
6 - 7	234	17	73	3.8
7 - 8	217	9	41	3.1
8 - 9	208	11	53	2.2
9 - 10	197	93	472	1.3
10 - 11	104	59	567	1.0
11 - 12	45	36	800	0.7
12 - 13	9	9	1000	0.5

Population characteristics

When survivorship curves, based on the l_x columns in the life tables, are plotted, as in Figures 1 and 2, various segments may be compared. Both sexes of all the species are alike in having a very steep initial slope, indicating a high mortality during the first year of life.

Among the males the loss during the second year of life is small in all species except the roe-deer, where there is emigration, and the black-tailed deer of the chaparral where some yearlings are lost, partly through being mistaken for older deer by hunters. During the third year of life there is a heavy loss among roe-deer and black-tailed deer from both range types. The roe-deer loss is due to emigration. That in the black-tailed deer is due to hunting. In the Dall sheep and the red deer there is little loss during the third year. From the fourth year onward to old age the hunted populations (roe-deer, black-tailed deer and red deer) show fairly steep losses. The rate of loss tends to become less in full adulthood in the black-tailed deer, because learning and behavior make these individuals less vulnerable to hunting. In the red deer the rate of loss becomes heavier in full adulthood because of the selection of prime stags by the hunter. The Dall sheep, which is not hunted, shows very little loss from adulthood to old age. If it were not for hunting, the other male populations would exhibit survivorship curves more nearly like that of the Dall sheep, but it is doubtful if they could ever attain as high a survivorship as long as their ranges were fully stocked and starvation was a common cause of death. The effects of competition are discussed below. The stress imposed by the annual growth and shedding of antlers, peculiar to the Cervidae, is another factor, of unknown magnitude.

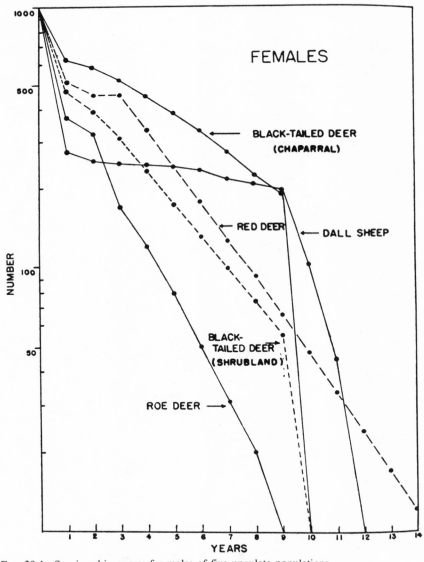

FIG. 29-1.—Survivorship curves for males of five ungulate populations.

In old age there tends to be a steepening of the survivorship curve—the accelerated loss due to senescence—especially in the Dall sheep. The red deer do not display this, because the high kill by hunting permits few individuals to grow old.

Among the females there is a small loss during the second year of life in all examples. In none of these populations do the females regularly bear young at one year of age. In the roe-deer and the black-tailed deer the usual time of first bearing is on the second birthday, although some

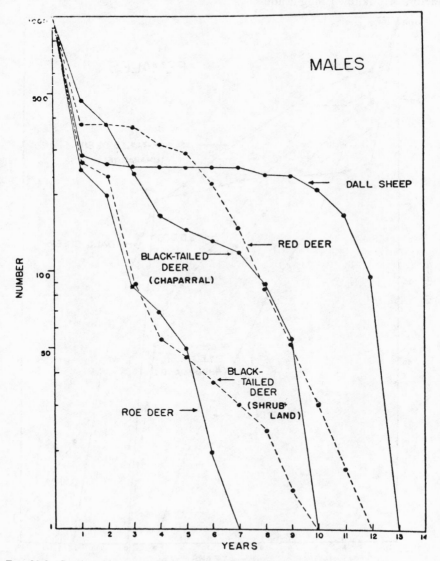

Fig. 29-2.—Survivorship curves for females of five ungulate populations.

294

black-tailed deer, especially from the chaparral, do not bear until three years old. The red deer and Dall sheep bear first at three years.

After the third year of life all examples have a rate of loss similar to that maintained until old age. In general, there is an inverse relationship between production of young and survival of breeding females. Presumably this is due to the fact that on any fully-stocked herbivore range there tends to be competition for forage, and the more successful is the reproduction, the keener is the competition. The survival of adult females may be lowered still further if they are hunted, as was true to a limited extent for the red deer of Jura. On the other hand, the survival of adult females may be raised if there is a removal of the competing members of the population. This was the situation for the Dall sheep of Mt. McKinley, where both the very young and very old were removed by wolves. The roe-deer population was also periodically lowered, reducing competition; the reduction there was caused by emigration. However, there was also a hunting loss among the adult females, and this tended to cancel the advantage conferred upon them by the emigration of the young.

The most clear-cut example among the present cases is the comparison of survival between the adult deer of the chaparral and those of shrubland. In December, when weaning is long past and the young of the year are in direct competition with the old for food, the chaparral population contains 0.53 fawn for every adult doe. The shrubland population contains 0.76 fawn for every adult doe (Tables 5-6 and 5-8). The values for life expectation of prime (3- to 6-year-old) does ranged in chaparral from 4.2 to 2.6 years and in shrubland from 3.0 to 2.2 years. Fawn production to December in chaparral is about 70 percent of that of shrubland; life expectation in shrubland is about 78 percent of that in chaparral. The comparison could be expanded to include the whole population of both sexes—taking the fawns plus yearlings on the one hand as the production, and all older deer together as the producers. The result would be much the same; the greater the proportional production, the shorter the life expectancy of the producers.

It seems that most of the differences between these various populations are not inherent in the species, but rather are imposed by environmental conditions. The limitation of the roe-deer population by emigration, for example, would be effective only if the population occupied an island of habitat, surrounded by uninhabited areas into which the emigrants could disappear and from which none would come to replace them. The situation in the shrubland is similar, but the island-like nature of the habitat is less marked, and an immigration from the surrounding low-density population may partially balance emigration. In the chaparral, which is merely an artificially designated area in a large region of similar habitat, emigration and immigration should balance.

If a roe-deer population is fenced, Andersen points out *(in litt.)* that winter mortality due to starvation is high. In such a case it would be expected that the population dynamics would be different from those found at Kalø, since the older deer would be competing with younger, physiologically more efficient animals.

Similarly, if a Dall sheep herd were not culled by predators, the population would presumably be limited by food supplies, and the mortality among prime adults would increase accordingly.

These considerations point up the danger of considering the population dynamics of a given animal under given circumstances as typical of that species in general.

SUMMARY

Population dynamics have been reconstructed for three natural populations of the Columbian black-tailed deer *(Odocoileus hemionus columbianus* (Richardson)) which differed from each other in habitat. The three habitats, chaparral, shrubland and wildfire burn, were all modifications by man of the chaparral association of the North Coast Range of California. Chaparral is a densely-growing association of shrubs; shrubland is a shrub-herb interspersion; wildfire burn is chaparral recently burned, where the shrubs are sprouting from the root-crown. These populations were compared for stability, density, structure, reproduction, mortality and movement. The principal causes of mortality were hunting (adult bucks) and starvation (other classes). The details of population gain and loss through one typical year (four years for wildfire burn) were reconstructed from these data. Some characteristics of the three populations are shown in Table 5-14.

TABLE 5-14.

	Chaparral	Shrubland	Wildfire burn (First year following burning)
Population density (Deer per square mile)			
July	33	84	112
December	27	64	86
Reproduction (fawns per 100 adult females)	0.77	1.65	1.32
Importance of movement in population gain or loss	none	little (yearling does)	great (all classes)

Populations in chaparral and shrubland were relatively stable, so life tables were prepared for them, the sexes being treated separately. The population on the wildfire burn was unstable, high at first due to influx and then dropping rapidly due to egress, increased mortality and decreased reproduction.

Sex-specific life tables for the deer of chaparral and shrubland were compared with those for: a hunted red-deer population on a fully-stocked island; a hunted roe-deer population from which there was heavy emigration; and an unhunted Dall sheep population under heavy predation by wolves.

Some characteristics of these populations are shown in Table 5-15.

On fully-stocked ranges there is an inverse relationship between production of young and survival of breeding adults, due presumably to

TABLE 5-15.

	Average annual population loss (per cent)		Loss during first year of life (per cent)		Life expectancy from birth (years)	
	males	females	males	females	males	females
Black-tailed deer						
Chaparral	36	22	53	37	2.3	4.2
Shrubland	55	34	73	53	1.3	2.4
Red deer	30	28	61	49	2.9	3.1
Roe deer	59	46	74	63	1.2	2.6
Dall sheep	42	30	72	72	3.3	2.8

competition for food between young and adults. When young (or senescent) are removed, by predation or emigration, the chances for survival of breeding adults appear to be improved.

The differences in dynamics between these various populations of different species, are apparently due more to environment than to heredity.

REFERENCES

ANDERSEN, J. 1953. Analysis of a Danish roe-deer population. Danish Rev. Game Biol., 2:127-155.

BISWELL, H. H., R. D. TAYLOR, D. W. HEDRICK, AND A. M. SCHULTZ. 1952. Management of chamise brushlands for game in the north coast region of California. Calif. Fish. and Game, 39:453-484.

COOPER, W. S. 1922. The broad-sclerophyll vegetation of California. Carnegie Inst. of Walsh., Pub. 319. 14 pp.

DARLING, F. F. 1937. A herd of red deer. London: Oxford Univ. Press, 210 pp.

DASMANN, R. F. 1953. Factors influencing movement of nonmigratory deer. Western Assn. State Game and Fish Comm., 33:112-116.

DASMANN, R. F., AND R. D. TABER. 1955. A comparison of four deer census methods. Calif. Fish. and Game, 41:225-228.

————. 1956. Determining structure in Columbian black-tailed deer populations. Jour. Wildl. Mangt., 20:78-83.

DEEVEY, E. S. 1947. Life tables for natural populations of animals. Quart. Rev. Biol., 22:283-314.

EVANS, H. 1891. Some account of Jura red deer. Privately printed by Francis Carter, of Derby, 38 pp.

HICKEY, J. J. 1952. Survival studies of banded birds. U.S. Fish & Wildl. Serv., Spec. Sci. Rept. (Wildlife) No. 15, Washington. [Processed.]

MANNING, G. A., AND B. A. OGLE. 1950. The geology of the Blue Lake quadrangle. Calif. Dept. Nat. Res., Div. Mines, Bull. 148.36 pp.

MORELAND, R. 1952. A technique for determining age in black-tailed deer. Western Assn. State Game and Fish. Comm., 32:214-219.

MURIE, A. 1940. The wolves of Mount McKinley. U.S. Dept. Interior, Nat. Park Serv., Fauna of Nat. Parks of the U.S., Series 5, 238 pp.

SEVERINGHAUS, C. W. 1949. Tooth development and wear as criteria of age in white-tailed deer. Jour. Wildl. Mangt., 13:195-216.

TABER, R. D. 1952. Studies of black-tailed deer reproduction on three chaparral cover types. Calif. Fish and Game, 39:177:186.

————. 1956. Deer nutrition and population dynamics in the North Coast Range of California. North Amer. Wildl. Conf., Trans., 21:159-172.

————, AND R. F. DASMANN. 1954. A sex difference in mortality in young Columbian black-tailed deer. Jour. Wildl. Mangt., 18:309-315.

HABITAT

Wild animals are adapted and limited to niches occurring only in suitable environments. Thus a suitable environment is the most fundamental need of every species and providing suitable environments for wildlife must be the primary concern of wildlife conservation. This requires understanding of structure, function and dynamics of ecosystems. The next four papers illustrate early and recent attempts to describe ecosystems. These papers range from descriptive and subjective, laced with philosophy, to quantitative and coldly objective. Both kinds are essential. We cannot afford an imprecise understanding of ecosystems when we manipulate them with the intensity and scope of today. Yet we must retain our willingness to look to ecosystems, not just for calories, proteins and materials, but also for beauty and for an understanding of nature and ourselves.

Usually a wildlife manager is primarily concerned with the food, cover, water and interspersion requirements of but a few species. For some species the literature on habitat requirements is scant, for others, enormous. The wildlife manager's job is to know and interpret this literature. The second four papers provide only a few ideas on the subject of habitat requirements of animals.

The next three papers emphasize the magnitude of change in wildlife habitat that is associated with fire, land use and successions.

Finally, Leopold's paper describes a conscience to guide our use of the land—a philosophy without which all our knowledge of wildlife habitats will be of no avail.

THE LAKE AS A MICROCOSM (1887)
Stephen A. Forbes

*Prior to 1940, only a few uncommon men, finding themselves in un-
common situations, were able to study and contemplate ecosystems with a
holistic viewpoint. These were naturalists—men with few tools, ever-ready
notebooks and tremendous insight. Their descriptions of ecosystems provided
necessary frameworks for quantitative studies that followed. Stephen A.
Forbes first read this paper in 1887 to the Peoria Scientific Association. It
illustrates early awareness of the complexities of ecosystems by describing
the roles of geology, natural selection, population dynamics, food chains
and pollution in ecosystems. Several pages have been omitted, the first and
last parts being sufficient to provide the reader with a classic example of
early descriptive ecology.*

A lake is to the naturalist a chapter out of the history of a primeval
time, for the conditions of life there are primitive, the forms of life are,
as a whole, relatively low and ancient, and the system of organic interactions by which they influence and control each other has remained substantially unchanged from a remote geological period.

The animals of such a body of water are, as a whole, remarkably
isolated—closely related among themselves in all their interests, but so
far independent of the land about them that if every terrestrial animal
were suddenly annihilated it would doubtless be long before the general
multitude of the inhabitants of the lake would feel the effects of this event
in any important way. It is an islet of older, lower life in the midst of the
higher, more recent life of the surrounding region. It forms a little world
within itself—a microcosm within which all the elemental forces are at
work and the play of life goes on in full, but on so small a scale as to bring
it easily within the mental grasp.

Nowhere can one see more clearly illustrated what may be called the
sensibility of such an organic complex, expressed by the fact that whatever affects any species belonging to it, must have its influence of some
sort upon the whole assemblage. He will thus be made to see the impossibility of studying completely any form out of relation to the other forms;
the necessity for taking a comprehensive survey of the whole as a condition to a satisfactory understanding of any part. If one wishes to become
acquainted with the black bass, for example, he will learn but little if he
limits himself to that species. He must evidently study also the species
upon which it depends for its existence, and the various conditions upon
which *these* depend. He must likewise study the species with which it
comes in competition, and the entire system of conditions affecting their
prosperity; and by the time he has studied all these sufficiently he will
find that he has run through the whole complicated mechanism of the
aquatic life of the locality, both animal and vegetable, of which his species
forms but a single element.

Reprinted from Illinois Natural History Survey Bull. 15:537-550.

It is under the influence of these general ideas that I propose to examine briefly the lacustrine life of Illinois, drawing my data from collections and observations made during recent years by myself and my assistants of the State Laboratory of Natural History.

The lakes of Illinois are of two kinds, fluviatile and water-shed. The fluviatile lakes, which are much the more numerous and important, are appendages of the river systems of the state, being situated in the river bottoms and connected with the adjacent streams by periodical overflows. Their fauna is therefore substantially that of the rivers themselves, and the two should, of course, be studied together.

They are probably in all cases either parts of former river channels, which have been cut off and abandoned by the current as the river changed its course, or else are tracts of the high-water beds of streams over which, for one reason or another, the periodical deposit of sediment has gone on less rapidly than over the surrounding area, and which have thus come to form depressions in the surface which retain the waters of overflow longer than the higher lands adjacent. Most of the numerous "horseshoe lakes" belong to the first of these varieties, and the "bluff-lakes," situated along the borders of the bottoms, are many of them examples of the second.

These fluviatile lakes are most important breeding grounds and reservoirs of life, especially as they are protected from the filth and poison of towns and manufactories by which the running waters of the state are yearly more deeply defiled.

The amount and variety of animal life contained in them as well as in the streams related to them is extremely variable, depending chiefly on the frequency, extent, and duration of the spring and summer overflows. This is, in fact, the characteristic and peculiar feature of life in these waters. There is perhaps no better illustration of the methods by which the flexible system of organic life adapts itself, without injury, to widely and rapidly fluctuating conditions. Whenever the waters of the river remain for a long time far beyond their banks, the breeding grounds of fishes and other animals are immensely extended, and their food supplies increased to a corresponding degree. The slow or stagnant backwaters of such an overflow afford the best situations possible for the development of myriads of Entomostraca, which furnish, in turn, abundant food for young fishes of all descriptions. There thus results an outpouring of life—an extraordinary multiplication of nearly every species, most prompt and rapid, generally speaking, in such as have the highest reproductive rate, that is to say, in those which produce the largest average number of eggs and young for each adult.

The first to feel this tremendous impulse are the protophytes and Protozoa, upon which most of the Entomostraca and certain minute insect larvae depend for food. This sudden development of their food resources causes, of course, a corresponding increase in the numbers of the latter classes, and, through them, of all sorts of fishes. The first fishes to feel the force of this tidal wave of life are the rapidly-breeding, non-predaceous kinds; and the last, the game fishes, which derive from the

302

others their principal food supplies. Evidently each of these classes must act as a check upon the one preceding it. The development of animalcules is arrested and soon sent back below its highest point by the consequent development of Entomostraca; the latter, again, are met, checked, and reduced in number by the innumerable shoals of fishes with which the water speedily swarms. In this way a general adjustment of numbers to the new conditions would finally be reached spontaneously; but long before any such settled balance can be established, often of course before the full effect of this upward influence has been exhibited, a new cause of disturbance intervenes in the *disappearance of the overflow*. As the waters retire, the lakes are again defined; the teeming life which they contain is restricted within daily narrower bounds, and a fearful slaughter follows; the lower and more defenceless animals are penned up more and more closely with their predaceous enemies, and these thrive for a time to an extraordinary degree. To trace the further consequences of this oscillation would take me too far. Enough has been said to illustrate the general idea that the life of waters subject to periodical expansions of considerable duration, is peculiarly unstable and fluctuating; that each species swings, pendulum-like but irregularly, between a highest and a lowest point, and that this fluctuation affects the different classes successively, in the order of their dependence upon each other for food.

Where a water-shed is a nearly level plateau with slight irregularities of the surface many of these will probably be imperfectly drained, and the accumulating waters will form either marshes or lakes according to the depth of the depressions. Highland marshes of this character are seen in Ford, Livingston, and adjacent counties (all now drained and brought under cultivation), between the headwaters of the Illinois and Wabash systems; and an area of water-shed lakes occurs in Lake and McHenry counties, in northern Illinois.

The latter region is everywhere broken by low, irregular ridges of glacial drift, with no rock but boulders anywhere in sight. The intervening hollows are of every variety, from mere sink-holes, either dry or occupied by ponds, to expanses of several square miles, forming marshes or lakes.

This is, in fact, the southern end of a broad lake belt which borders Lakes Michigan and Superior on the west and south, extending through eastern and northern Wisconsin and northwestern Minnesota, and occupying the plateau which separates the headwaters of the St. Lawrence from those of the Mississippi. These lakes are of glacial origin, some filling beds excavated in the solid rock, and others collecting the surface waters in hollows of the drift. The latter class, to which all the Illinois lakes belong, may lie either parallel to the line of glacial action, occupying valleys between adjacent lateral moraines, or transverse to that line and bounded by terminal moraines. Those of our own state all drain at present into the Illinois through the Des Plaines and Fox; but as the terraces around their borders indicate a former water-level considerably higher than the present one it is likely that some of them once emptied eastward into Lake Michigan. Several of these lakes are clear and beautiful sheets of water, with sandy or gravelly beaches, and shores bold and broken enough to relieve them from monotony. Sportsmen long ago discovered their advantages and club-houses and places of summer resort are numerous on the borders of the most attractive and easily accessible. They offer also an unusually rich field to the naturalist, and their zoology and botany should be better known.

The conditions of aquatic life are here in marked contrast to those afforded by the fluviatile lakes already mentioned. Connected with each other or with adjacent streams only by slender rivulets, varying but little in level with the change of the season and scarcely at all from year to year, they are characterized by an isolation, independence, and uniformity which can be found nowhere else within our limits.

.   .   .   .

It would be quite impossible, within reasonable limits, to go into details respecting the organic relations of the animals of these waters, and I will content myself with two or three illustrations. As one example of the varied and far-reaching relations into which the animals of a lake are brought in the general struggle for life, I take the common black bass. In the dietary of this fish I find, at different ages of the individual, fishes of great variety, representing all the important orders of that class; insects in considerable number, especially the various water-bugs and larvae of day-flies; fresh-water shrimps; and a great multitude of Entomostraca of many species and genera. The fish is therefore directly dependent upon all these classes for its existence. Next, looking to the food of the species which the bass has eaten, and upon which it is therefore indirectly dependent, I find that one kind of the fishes taken feeds upon mud, algae, and Entomostraca, and another upon nearly every animal substance in the water, including mollusks and decomposing organic matter. The insects taken by the bass, themselves take other insects and small Crustacea. The crawfishes are nearly omnivorous, and of the other crustaceans some eat Entomostraca and some algae and Protozoa. At only the second step, therefore, we find our bass brought into dependence upon nearly every class of animals in the water.

And now, if we search for its competitors we shall find these also extremely numerous. In the first place, I have found that all our young fishes except the Catostomidae feed at first almost wholly on Entomostraca, so that the little bass finds himself at the very beginning of his life engaged in a scramble for food with all the other little fishes in the lake. In fact, not only young fishes but a multitude of other animals as well, especially insects and the larger Crustacea, feed upon these Entomostraca, so that the competitors of the bass are not confined to members of its own class. Even mollusks, while they do not directly compete with it do so indirectly, for they appropriate myriads of the microscopic forms upon which the Entomostraca largely depend for food. But the enemies of the bass do not all attack it by appropriating its food supplies, for many devour the little fish itself. A great variety of predaceous fishes, turtles, water-snakes, wading and diving birds, and even bugs of gigantic dimensions destroy it on the slightest opportunity. It is in fact hardly too much to say that fishes which reach maturity are relatively as rare as centenarians among human kind.

As an illustration of the remote and unsuspected rivalries which reveal themselves on a careful study of such a situation, we may take the relations of fishes to the bladderwort—a flowering plant which fills many acres of the water in the shallow lakes of northern Illinois. Upon the leaves of this species are found little bladders—several hundred to each plant—which when closely examined are seen to be tiny traps for the capture of Entomostraca and other minute animals. The plant usually has no roots, but lives entirely upon the animal food obtained through these little bladders. Ten of these sacs which I took at random from a mature plant contained no less than ninety-three animals (more than nine to a bladder), belonging to twenty-eight different species. Seventy-six of these were Entomostraca, and eight others were minute insect larvae. When we estimate the myriads of small insects and Crustacea which these plants must appropriate during a year to their own support, and consider the fact that these are of the kinds most useful as food for young fishes of nearly all descriptions, we must conclude that the bladderworts compete with fishes for food, and tend to keep down their number by diminishing the food resources of the young. The plants even have a certain advantage in this competition, since they are not strictly dependent on Entomostraca, as the fishes are, but sometimes take root, developing then but very few leaves and bladders. This probably happens under conditions unfavorable to their support by the other method. These simple instances will suffice to illustrate the intimate way in which the living forms of a lake are united.

Perhaps no phenomenon of life in such a situation is more remarkable than the steady balance of organic nature, which holds each species within the limits of a uniform average number, year after year, although each one is always doing its best to break across boundaries on every side. The reproductive rate is usually enormous and the struggle for existence is correspondingly severe. Every animal within these bounds has its enemies, and Nature seems to have taxed her skill and ingenuity to the utmost to furnish these enemies with contrivances for the destruction of their prey in myriads. For every defensive device with which she has armed an animal, she has invented a still more effective apparatus of destruction and bestowed it upon some foe, thus striving with unending pertinacity to outwit herself; and yet life does not perish in the lake, nor even oscillate to any considerable degree, but on the contrary the little community secluded here is as prosperous as if its state were one of profound and perpetual peace. Although every species has to fight its way inch by inch from the egg to maturity, yet no species is exterminated, but each is maintained at a regular average number which we shall find good reason to believe is the greatest for which there is, year after year, a sufficient supply of food.

I will bring this paper to a close by endeavoring to show how this beneficent order is maintained in the midst of a conflict seemingly so lawless.

It is a self-evident proposition that a species can not maintain itself continuously, year after year, unless its birth-rate at least equals its death-rate. If it is preyed upon by another species, it must produce regularly an excess of individuals for destruction, or else it must certainly dwindle and disappear. On the other hand, the dependent species evidently must not appropriate, on an average, any more than the surplus and excess of individuals upon which it preys, for if it does so it will continuously diminish its own food supply, and thus indirectly but surely exterminate itself. The interests of both parties will therefore be best served by an adjustment of their respective rates of multiplication such that the species devoured shall furnish an excess of numbers to supply the wants of the devourer, and that the latter shall confine its appropriations to the excess thus furnished. We thus see that there is really a close *community of interest* between these two seemingly deadly foes.

And next we note that this common interest is promoted by the process of natural selection; for it is the great office of this process to eliminate the unfit. If two species standing to each other in the relation of hunter and prey are or become badly adjusted in respect to their rates of increase, so that the one preyed upon is kept very far below the normal number which might find food, even if they do not presently obliterate each other the pair are placed at a disadvantage in the battle for life, and must suffer accordingly. Just as certainly as the thrifty business man who lives within his income will finally dispossess his shiftless competitor who can never pay his debts, the well-adjusted aquatic animal will in time crowd out its poorly-adjusted competitors for food and for the various goods of life. Consequently we may believe that in the long run and as a general rule those species which have survived are those which have reached a fairly close adjustment in this particular.

Two ideas are thus seen to be sufficient to explain the order evolved from this seeming chaos; the first that of a general community of interests among all the classes of organic beings here assembled, and the second that of the beneficent power of natural selection which compels such adjustments of the rates of destruction and of multiplication of the various species as shall best promote this common interest.

A BIOTIC VIEW OF LAND (1939)
Aldo Leopold

A holistic view of ecosystem function is incompatible with an egocentric view. In the 1930's Aldo Leopold deplored studies of the environment motivated and restricted by desires for short-term economic gain. He warned that the knowledge and philosophy produced by economic biology would be inadequate to sustain a conservation movement and noted that the whole of an ecosystem is much more than the sum of its parts. This paper added breadth to the definition of wildlife environment. It also expanded our definition of wildlife, once restricted primarily to game, to include predators, songbirds and, in fact, all wild things.

In pioneering times wild plants and animals were tolerated, ignored, or fought, the attitude depending on the utility of the species.

Conservation introduced the idea that the more useful wild species could be managed as crops, but the less useful ones were ignored and the predaceous ones fought, just as in pioneering days. Conservation lowered the threshold of toleration for wildlife, but utility was still the criterion of policy, and utility attached to species rather than to any collective total of wild things. Species were known to compete with each other and to cooperate with each other, but the cooperations and competitions were regarded as separate and distinct; utility was susceptible of quantitative evaluation by research. For proof of this we need look no further than the bony framework of any campus or capitol: department of economic entomology, division of economic mammalogy, chief of food habits research, professor of economic ornithology. These agencies were set up to tell us whether the red-tailed hawk, the gray gopher, the lady beetle, and the meadowlark are useful, harmless, or injurious to man.

Ecology is a new fusion point for all the natural sciences. It has been built up partly by ecologists, but partly also by the collective efforts of the men charged with the economic evaluation of species. The emergence of ecology has placed the economic biologist in a peculiar dilemma: with one hand he points out the accumulated findings of his search for utility, or lack of utility, in this or that species; with the other he lifts the veil from a biota so complex, so conditioned by interwoven cooperations and competitions, that no man can say where utility begins or ends. No species can be "rated" without the tongue in the cheek; the old categories of "useful" and "harmful" have validity only as conditioned by time, place, and circumstance. The only sure conclusion is that the biota as a whole is useful, and biota includes not only plants and animals, but soils and waters as well.

In short, economic biology assumed that the biotic function and economic utility of a species was partly known and the rest could shortly be found out. That assumption no longer holds good; the process of finding out added new questions faster than new answers. The function of species is largely inscrutable, and may remain so.

Reprinted from J. Forestry 37(9):727-730 by permission from the Society of American Foresters.

When the human mind deals with any concept too large to be easily visualized, it substitutes some familiar object which seems to have similar properties. The "balance of nature" is a mental image for land and life which grew up before and during the transition to ecological thought. It is commonly employed in describing the biota to laymen, but ecologists among each other accept it only with reservations, and its acceptance by laymen seems to depend more on convenience than on conviction. Thus "nature lovers" accept it, but sportsmen and farmers are skeptical ("the balance was upset long ago; the only way to restore it is to give the country back to the Indians"). There is more than a suspicion that the dispute over predation determines these attitudes, rather than vice versa.

To the lay mind, balance of nature probably conveys an actual image of the familiar weighing scale. There may even be danger that the layman imputes to the biota properties which exist only on the grocer's counter.

To the ecological mind, balance of nature has merits and also defects. Its merits are that it conceives of a collective total, that it imputes some utility to all species, and that it implies oscillations when balance is disturbed. Its defects are that there is only one point at which balance occurs, and that balance is normally static.

If we must use a mental image for land instead of thinking about it directly, why not employ the image commonly used in ecology, namely the biotic pyramid? With certain additions hereinafter developed it presents a truer picture of the biota. With a truer picture of the biota, the scientist might take his tongue out of his cheek, the layman might be less insistent on utility as a prerequisite for conservation, more hospitable to the "useless" cohabitants of the earth, more tolerant of values over and above profit, food, sport, or tourist-bait. Moreover, we might get better advice from economists and philosophers if we gave them a truer picture of the biotic mechanism.

I will first sketch the pyramid as a symbol of land, and later develop some of its implications in terms of land use.

Plants absorb energy from the sun. This energy flows through a circuit called the biota. It may be represented by the layers of a pyramid (Fig. 1.). The bottom layer is the soil. A plant layer rests on the soil, an

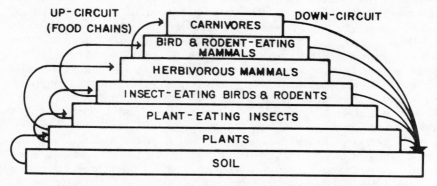

FIG. 31-1.—Biotic pyramid, showing plant and animal community as an energy circuit.

insect layer on the plants, and so on up through various groups of fish, reptiles, birds and mammals. At the top are predators.

The species of a layer are alike not in where they came from, nor in what they look like, but rather in what they eat. Each successive layer depends on those below for food and often for other services, and each in turn furnishes food and services to those above. Each successive layer decreases in abundance; for every predator there are hundreds of his prey, thousands of their prey, millions of insects, uncountable plants.

The lines of dependency for food and other services are called food chains. Each species, including ourselves, is a link in many food chains. Thus the bobwhite quail eats a thousand kinds of plants and animals, i.e., he is a link in a thousand chains. The pyramid is a tangle of chains so complex as to seem disorderly, but when carefully examined the tangle is seen to be a highly organized structure. Its functioning depends on the cooperation and competition of all its diverse links.

In the beginning, the pyramid of life was low and squat; the food chains short and simple. Evolution has added layer after layer, link after link. Man is one of thousands of accretions to the height and complexity of the pyramid. Science has given us many doubts, but it has given us at least one certainty; the trend of evolution is to elaborate the biota.

Land, then, is not merely soil; it is a fountain of energy flowing through a circuit of soils, plants, and animals. Food chains are the living channels which conduct energy upward; death and decay return it to the soil. The circuit is not closed; some energy is dissipated in decay, some is added by absorption, some is stored in soils, peats, and forests, but it is a sustained circuit, like a slowly augmented revolving fund of life.

The upward flow of energy depends on the complex structure of the plant and animal community, much as the upward flow of sap in a tree depends on its complex cellular organization. Without this complexity normal circulation would not occur. Structure means the characteristic numbers, as well as the characteristic kinds and functions of the species.

This interdependence between the complex structure of land and its smooth functioning as an energy circuit is one of its basic attributes.

When a change occurs in one part of the circuit, many other parts must adjust themselves to it. Change does not necessarily obstruct the flow of energy; evolution is a long series of self-induced changes, the net result of which has been probably to accelerate the flow; certainly to lengthen the circuit.

Evolutionary changes, however, are usually slow and local. Man's invention of tools has enabled him to make changes of unprecedented violence, rapidity, and scope.

One change is in the composition of floras and faunas. The larger predators are lopped off the cap of the pyramid; food chains, for the first time in history, are made shorter rather than longer. Domesticated species are substituted for wild ones, and wild ones moved to new habitats. In this world-wide pooling of faunas and floras, some species get out of bounds as pests and diseases, others are extinguished. Such effects are seldom intended or foreseen; they represent unpredicted and often un-traceable readjustments in the structure. Agricultural science is largely a race between the emergence of new pests and the emergence of new techniques for their control.

Another change affects the flow of energy through plants and animals, and its return to the soil. Fertility is the ability of soil to receive, store, and return energy. Agriculture, by overdrafts on the soil, or by too radical a substitution of domestic for native species in the superstructure, may clog the channels of flow or deplete storage. Soils depleted of their stores wash away faster than they form. This is erosion.

Waters, like soils, are part of the energy circuit. Industry, by polluting waters, excludes the plants and animals necessary to keep energy in circulation.

Transportation brings about another basic change: the plants or animals grown in one region are consumed and return to the soil in another. Thus the formerly localized and self-contained circuits are pooled on a world-wide scale.

The process of altering the pyramid for human occupation releases stored energy, and this often gives rise, during the pioneering period, to a deceptive exuberance of plant and animal life, both wild and tame. These releases of biotic capital tend to becloud or delay the penalties of violence.

This thumbnail sketch of land as an energy circuit conveys three ideas more or less lacking from the balance of nature concept:

(1)   That land is not merely soil.

(2)   That the native plants and animals kept the energy circuit open; others may or may not.

(3)   That man-made changes are of a different order than evolutionary changes, and have effects more comprehensive than is intended or foreseen.

These ideas, collectively, raise two basic issues: Can the land adjust itself to the new order? Can violence be reduced?

Biotas seem to differ in their capacity to sustain violence. Western Europe, for example, carries a far different pyramid than Caesar found there. Some large animals are lost; many new plants and animals are introduced, some of which escape as pests; the remaining natives are greatly changed in distribution and abundance. Yet the soil is still fertile, the waters flow normally, the new structure seems to function and to persist. There is no visible stoppage of the circuit.

Western Europe, then, has a resistant biota. Its processes are tough, elastic, resistant to strain. No matter how violent the alterations, the pyramid, so far, has developed some new *modus vivendi* which preserves its habitability for man and for most of the other natives.

The semiarid parts of both Asia and America display a different reaction. In many spots there is no longer any soil fit to support a complex pyramid, or to absorb the energy returning from such as remains. A cumulative process of wastage has set in. This wastage in the biotic organism is similar to disease in an animal, except that it does not culminate in absolute death. The organism recovers, but at a low level of complexity and human habitability. We attempt to offset the wastage by reclamation, but where the regimen of soils and waters is disturbed it is only too evident that the prospective longevity of reclamation projects is short.

The combined evidence of history and ecology seems to support one general deduction: the less violent the man-made changes, the greater the probability of successful readjustment in the pyramid. Violence, in turn, would seem to vary with human population density; a dense population requires a more violent conversion of land. In this respect, America has a better chance for nonviolent human dominance than Europe.

It is worth noting that this deduction runs counter to pioneering philosophy, which assumes that because a small increase in density enriched human life, that an indefinite increase will enrich it indefinitely. Ecology knows of no density relationship which holds within wide limits, and sociology seems to be finding evidence that this one is subject to a law of diminishing returns.

Whatever may be the equation for men and land, it is improbable that we as yet know all its terms. The recent discoveries in mineral and vitamin nutrition reveal unsuspected dependencies in the up-circuit; incredibly minute quantities of certain substances determine the value of soils to plants, of plants to animals. What of the down-circuit? What of the vanishing species, the preservation of which we now regard as an aesthetic luxury? They helped build the soil; in what unsuspected ways may they be essential to its maintenance? Professor Weaver proposes that we use prairie flowers to reflocculate the wasting soils of the dust bowl; who knows for what purpose cranes and condors, otters and grizzlies may some day be used?

Can the violence be reduced? I think that it can be, and that most of the present dissensions among conservationists may be regarded as the first gropings toward a nonviolent land use.

For example, the fight over predator control is no mere conflict of interest between field-glass hunters and gun-hunters. It is a fight between those who see utility and beauty in the biota as a whole, and those who see utility and beauty only in pheasants or trout. It grows clearer year by year that violent reductions in raptorial and carnivorous species as a means of raising game and fish are necessary only where highly artificial (i.e., violent) methods of management are used. Wild-raised game does not require hawkless coverts, and the biotically educated sportsman gets no pleasure from them.

Forestry is a turmoil of naturalistic movements.

Thus the Germans, who taught the world to plant trees like cabbages, have scrapped their own teachings and gone back to mixed woods of native species, selectively cut and naturally reproduced *(Dauerwald)*. The "cabbage brand" of silviculture, at first seemingly profitable, was found by experience to carry unforeseen biotic penalties: insect epidemics, soil sickness, declining yields, foodless deer, impoverished flora, distorted bird population. In their new Dauerwald the hard-headed Germans are now propagating owls, woodpeckers, titmice, goshawks, and other useless wildlife.

In America, the protests against radical "timber stand improvement" by the C.C.C. and against the purging of beech, white cedar, and tamarack from silvicultural plans are on all fours with Dauerwald as a return to nonviolent forestry. So is the growing skepticism about the ultimate utility of exotic plantations. So is the growing alarm about the epidemic of new Kaibabs, the growing realization that only wolves and lions can insure the forest against destruction by deer and insure the deer against self-destruction.

We have a whole group of discontents about the sacrifice of rare species: condors and grizzlies, prairie flora and bog flora. These, on their face, are protests against biotic violence. Some have gone beyond the protest stage: witness the Audubon researchers for methods of restoring the ivory-billed woodpecker and the desert bighorn; the researches at Vassar and Wisconsin for methods of managing wildflowers.

. . . .

Agriculture, the most important land use, shows the least evidence of discontent with pioneering concepts. Conservation, among agricultural thinkers, still means conservation of the soil, rather than of the biota including the soil. The farmer must by the nature of his operations modify the biota more radically than the forester or the wildlife manager; he must change the ratios in the pyramid and exclude the larger predators and herbivores. This much difference is unavoidable. Nevertheless it remains true that the exclusions are always more radical than necessary; that the substitution of tame for wild plants and the annual renewal of the plant succession creates a rich habitat for wildlife which has never been consciously utilized except for game management and forestry. Modern "clean farming," despite its name, sends a large portion of its energy into wild plants; a glance at the aftermath of any stubble will prove this. But the animal pyramid is so simplified that this energy is not carried upward; it either spills back directly into the soil, or at best passes through insects, rodents, and small birds. The recent evidence that rodents increase on abused soils (animal weed theory) shows, I think, a simple dearth of higher animal layers, an unnatural downward deflection of the energy circuit at the rodent layer. Biotic farming (if I may coin such a term) would consciously carry this energy to higher levels before returning it to the soil. To this end it would employ all native wild species not actually incompatible with tame ones. These species would include not merely game, but rather the largest possible diversity of flora and fauna.

Biotic farming, in short, would include wild plants and animals with tame ones as expressions of fertility. To accomplish such a revolution in the landscape, there must of course be a corresponding revolution in the landholder. The farmer who now seeks merely to preserve the soil must take account of the superstructure as well; a good farm must be one where the wild fauna and flora has lost acreage without losing its existence.

It is easy, of course, to wish for better kinds of conservation, but what good does it do when on private lands we have very little of any kind? This is the basic puzzle for which I have no solution.

It seems possible, though, that prevailing failure of economic self-interest as a motive for better private land use has some connection with

312

the failure of the social and natural sciences to agree with each other, and with the landholder, on a common concept of land. This may not be it, but ecology, as the fusion point of sciences and all the land uses, seems to me the place to look.

THE STRATEGY OF ECOSYSTEM DEVELOPMENT (1969)

Eugene P. Odum

Biotic succession is often the overriding force in wildlife environments. Undisturbed habitats, suitable for sharptailed grouse may become ruffed grouse coverts and eventually support only spruce grouse, a process described by Grange elsewhere in this section. Odum's paper reviews recent quantitative concepts of biotic succession. Wildlife biologists must master these concepts because manipulation of biotic succession is the most important method for producing or maintaining desired wildlife habitats. A portion of Odum's paper dealing with the relevance of successional theory to human ecology has been omitted here, but is recommended highly for further reading.

The principles of ecological succession bear importantly on the relationships between man and nature. The framework of successional theory needs to be examined as a basis for resolving man's present environmental crisis. Most ideas pertaining to the development of ecological systems are based on descriptive data obtained by observing changes in biotic communities over long periods, or on highly theoretical assumptions; very few of the generally accepted hypotheses have been tested experimentally. Some of the confusion, vagueness, and lack of experimental work in this area stems from the tendency of ecologists to regard "succession" as a single straightforward idea; in actual fact, it entails an interacting complex of processes, some of which counteract one another.

As viewed here, ecological succession involves the development of ecosystems; it has many parallels in the developmental biology of organisms, and also in the development of human society. The ecosystem, or ecological system, is considered to be a unit of biological organization made up of all of the organisms in a given area (that is, "community") interacting with the physical environment so that a flow of energy leads to characteristic trophic structure and material cycles within the system. It is the purpose of this article to summarize, in the form of a tabular model, components and stages of development at the ecosystem level as a means of emphasizing those aspects of ecological succession that can be accepted on the basis of present knowledge, those that require more study, and those that have special relevance to human ecology.

Definition of Succession

Ecological succession may be defined in terms of the following three parameters.[1] (i) It is an orderly process of community development that is reasonably directional and, therefore, predictable. (ii) It results from modification of the physical environment by the community; that is, succession is community-controlled even though the physical environment determines the pattern, the rate of change, and often sets limits as to how far development can go. (iii) It culminates in a stabilized ecosystem in which maximum biomass (or high information content) and symbiotic

Reprinted from: Science 164(3877):262-270, copyright 1969 by the American Association for the Advancement of Science.

function between organisms are maintained per unit of available energy flow. In a word, the "strategy" of succession as a short-term process is basically the same as the "strategy" of long-term evolutionary development of the biosphere—namely, increased control of, or homeostasis with, the physical environment in the sense of achieving maximum protection from its perturbations. As I illustrate below, the strategy of "maximum protection" (that is, trying to achieve maximum support of complex biomass structure) often conflicts with man's goal of "maximum production" (trying to obtain the highest possible yield). Recognition of the ecological basis for this conflict is, I believe, a first step in establishing rational land-use policies.

The earlier descriptive studies of succession on sand dunes, grasslands, forests, marine shores, or other sites, and more recent functional considerations, have led to the basic theory contained in the definition given above. H.T. Odum and Pinkerton,[2] building on Lotka's[3] "law of maximum energy in biological systems," were the first to point out that succession involves a fundamental shift in energy flows as increasing energy is relegated to maintenance. Margalef[4] has recently documented this bioenergetic basis for succession and has extended the concept.

Changes that occur in major structural and functional characteristics of a developing ecosystem are listed in Table 1. Twenty-four attributes of ecological systems are grouped, for convenience of discussion, under six headings. Trends are emphasized by contrasting the situation in early and late development. The degree of absolute change, the rate of change, and the time required to reach a steady state may vary not only with different climatic and physiographic situations but also with different ecosystem attributes in the same physical environment. Where good data are available, rate-of-change curves are usually convex with changes occurring most rapidly at the beginning, but bimodal or cyclic patterns may also occur.

Bioenergetics of Ecosystem Development

Attributes 1 through 5 in Table 1 represent the bioenergetics of the ecosystem. In the early stages of ecological succession, or in "young nature," so to speak, the rate of primary production or total (gross) photosynthesis *(P)* exceeds the rate of community respiration *(R)*, so that the P/R ratio is greater than 1. In the special case of organic pollution, the P/R ratio is typically less than 1. In both cases, however, the theory is that P/R approaches 1 as succession occurs. In other words, energy fixed tends to be balanced by the energy cost of maintenance (that is, total community respiration) in the mature or "climax" ecosystem. The P/R ratio, therefore, should be an excellent functional index of the relative maturity of the system.

So long as *P* exceeds *R*, organic matter and biomass *(B)* will accumulate in the system (Table 1, item 6), with the result that ratio P/B will tend to decrease or, conversely, the B/P, B/R, or B/E ratios (where $E = P + R$) will increase (Table 1, items 2 and 3). Theoretically, then, the amount of standing-crop biomass supported by the available energy flow *(E)* increases to a maximum in the mature or climax stages (Table 1, item 3). As a consequence, the net community production, or yield, in an annual cycle is large in young nature and small or zero in mature nature (Table 1, item 4).

Comparison of Succession in a Laboratory Microcosm and a Forest

One can readily observe bioenergetic changes by initiating succession in experimental laboratory microecosystems. Aquatic microecosystems, derived from various types of outdoor systems, such as ponds, have been cultured by Beyers,[5] and certain of these mixed cultures are easily replicated and maintain themselves in the climax state indefinitely on defined media in a flask with only light input.[6] If samples from the climax system are inoculated into fresh media, succession occurs, the mature system developing in less than 100 days. In Fig. 1 the general pattern of a 100-day autotrophic succession in a microcosm based on data of Cooke[7] is compared with a hypothetical model of a 100-year forest succession as presented by Kira and Shidei.[8]

During the first 40 to 60 days in a typical microcosm experiment, daytime net production *(P)* exceeds nighttime respiration *(R)*, so that biomass *(B)* accumulates in the system.[9] After an early "bloom" at about 30 days, both rates decline, and they become approximately equal at 60 to 80 days. The *B/P* ratio, in terms of grams of carbon supported per gram of daily carbon production, increases from less than 20 to more than 100 as the steady state is reached. Not only are autotrophic and heterotrophic metabolism balanced in the climax, but a large organic structure is supported by small daily production and respiratory rates.

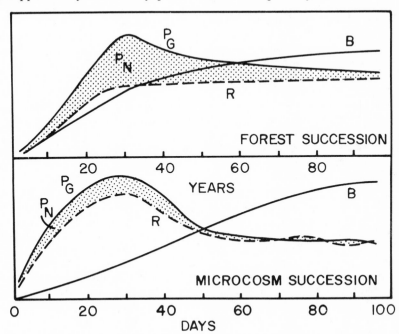

FIG. 32-1.—Comparison of the energetics of succession in a forest and a laboratory microcosm. *P*G, gross production; *P*N, net production; *R,* total community respiration; *B,* total biomass.

317

While direct projection from the small laboratory microecosystem to open nature may not be entirely valid, there is evidence that the same basic trends that are seen in the laboratory are characteristic of succession on land and in large bodies of water. Seasonal successions also often follow the same pattern, an early seasonal bloom characterized by rapid growth of a few dominant species being followed by the development later in the season of high B/P ratios, increased diversity, and a relatively steady, if temporary, state in terms of P and R.[4] Open systems may not experience a decline, at maturity, in total or gross productivity, as the space-limited microcosms do, but the general pattern of bioenergetic change in the latter seems to mimic nature quite well.

These trends are not, as might at first seem to be the case, contrary to the classical limnological teaching which describes lakes as progressing in time from the less productive (oligotrophic) to the more productive (eutrophic) state. Table 1, as already emphasized, refers to changes which are brought about by biological processes *within* the ecosystem in question. Eutrophication, whether natural or cultural, results when nutrients are imported into the lake from *outside* the lake—that is, from the watershed. This is equivalent to adding nutrients to the laboratory microecosystem or fertilizing a field; the system is pushed back, in successional terms, to a younger or "bloom" state. Recent studies on lake sediments,[10] as well as theoretical considerations,[11] have indicated that lakes can and do progress to a more oligotrophic condition when the nutrient input from the watershed slows or ceases. Thus, there is hope that the troublesome cultural eutrophication of our waters can be reversed if the inflow of nutrients from the watershed can be greatly reduced. Most of all, however, this situation emphasizes that it is the entire drainage or catchment basin, not just the lake or stream, that must be considered the ecosystem unit if we are to deal successfully with our water pollution problems. Ecosystematic study of entire landscape catchment units is a major goal of the American plan for the proposed International Biological Program. Despite the obvious logic of such a proposal, it is proving surprisingly difficult to get tradition-bound scientists and granting agencies to look beyond their specialties toward the support of functional studies of large units of the landscape.

Food Chains and Food Webs

As the ecosystem develops, subtle changes in the network pattern of food chains may be expected. The manner in which organisms are linked together through food tends to be relatively simple and linear in the very early stages of succession, as a consequence of low diversity. Furthermore, heterotrophic utilization of net production occurs predominantly by way of grazing food chains—that is, plant-herbivore-carnivore sequences. In contrast, food chains become complex webs in mature stages, with the bulk of biological energy flow following detritus pathways (Table 1, item 5). In a mature forest, for example, less than 10 percent of annual net production is consumed (that is, grazed) in the living state;[12] most is utilized as dead matter (detritus) through delayed and complex pathways involving as yet little understood animal-microorganism interactions. The time involved in an uninterrupted succession allows for increasingly intimate associations and reciprocal adaptations between plants and animals, which lead to the development of many mechanisms that reduce grazing—such as the development of indigestible supporting tissues (cellulose, lignin, and so on), feedback control between plants and herbivores,[13] and increasing predatory pressure on herbivores.[14] Such mechanisms enable the biological community to maintain the large and complex organic structure that mitigates perturbations of the physical environment. Severe stress or rapid changes brought about by outside forces can, of course, rob the system of these protective mechanisms and allow irruptive, cancerous growths of certain species to occur, as man too often finds to his sorrow. An example of a stress-induced pest irruption occurred at Brookhaven National Laboratory, where oaks became vulnerable to aphids when translocation of sugars and amino acids was impaired by continuing gamma irradiation.[15]

Radionuclide tracers are providing a means of charting food chains in the intact outdoor ecosystem to a degree that will permit analysis within the concepts of network or matrix algebra. For example, we have recently been able to map, by use of a radiophosphorus tracer, the open, relatively linear food linkage between plants and insects in an early old-field successional stage.[16]

Diversity and Succession

Perhaps the most controversial of the successional trends pertain to the complex and much discussed subject of diversity.[17] It is important to distinguish between different kinds of diversity indices, since they may not follow parallel trends in the same gradient or developmental series. Four components of diversity are listed in Table 1, items 8 through 11.

The variety of species, expressed as a species-number ratio or a species-area ratio, tends to increase during the early stages of community development. A second component of species diversity is what has been called equitability, or evenness,[18] in the apportionment of individuals among the species. For example, two systems each containing 10 species and 100 individuals have the same diversity in terms of species-number ratio but could have widely different equitabilities depending on the apportionment of the 100 individuals among the 10 species—for example, 91-1-1-1-1-1-1-1-1 at one extreme or 10 individuals per species at the other. The Shannon formula,

$$-\Sigma \; \frac{ni}{N} \log_2 \frac{ni}{N}$$

where ni is the number of individuals in each species and N is the total number of individuals, is widely used as a diversity index because it combines the variety and equitability components in one approximation. But, like all such lumping parameters, Shannon's formula may obscure the behavior of these two rather different aspects of diversity. For example, in our most recent field experiments, an acute stress from insecticide reduced the number of species of insects relative to the number of individuals but increased the evenness in the relative abundances of the surviving species.[19] Thus, in this case the "variety" and "evenness" components would tend to cancel each other in Shannon's formula.

While an increase in the variety of species together with reduced dominance by any one species or small group of species (that is, increased evenness) can be accepted as a general probability during succession,[20] there are other community changes that may work against these trends. An increase in the size of organisms, an increase in the length and complexity of life histories, and an increase in interspecific competition that may result in competitive exclusion of species (Table 1, items 12-14) are trends that may reduce the number of species that can live in a given area. In the bloom stage of succession organisms tend to be small and to have simple life histories and rapid rates of reproduction. Changes in size appear to be a consequence of, or an adaptation to, a shift in nutrients from inorganic to organic (Table 1, item 7). In a mineral nutrient-rich environment, small size is of selective advantage, especially to autotrophs, because of the greater surface-to-volume ratio. As the ecosystem develops, however, inorganic nutrients tend to become more and more tied up in the biomass (that is, to become intrabiotic), so that the selective advantage shifts to larger organisms (either larger individuals of the same species or larger species, or both) which have greater storage capacities and more complex life histories, thus are adapted to exploiting seasonal or periodic releases of nutrients or other resources. The question of whether the seemingly direct relationship between organism size and stability is the result of positive feedback or is merely fortuitous remains unanswered.[21]

Thus, whether or not species diversity continues to increase during succession will depend on whether the increase in potential niches resulting from increased biomass, stratification (Table 1, item 9), and other consequences of biological organization exceeds the countereffects of increasing size and competition. No one has yet been able to catalogue all the species in any sizable area, much less follow total species diversity in a successional series. Data are so far available only for segments of the community (trees, birds, and so on). Margalef[a] postulates that diversity will tend to peak during the early or middle stages of succession and then decline in the climax. In a study of bird populations along a successional gradient we found a bimodal pattern;[22] the number of species increased during the early stages of old-field succession, declined during the early forest stages, and then increased again in the mature forest.

Species variety, equitability, and stratification are only three aspects of diversity which change during succession. Perhaps an even more important trend is an increase in the diversity of organic compounds, not only of those within the biomass but also of those excreted and secreted into the media (air, soil, water) as by-products of the increasing community metabolism. An increase in such "biochemical diversity" (Table 1, item 10) is illustrated by the increase in the variety of plant pigments along a successional gradient in aquatic situations, as described by Margalef.[a, 23] Biochemical diversity within populations, or within systems as a whole, has not yet been systematically studied to the degree the subject of species diversity has been. Consequently, few generalizations can be made, except that it seems safe to say that, as succession progresses, organic extra-

TABLE 1. A tabular model of ecological succession: trends to be expected in the development of ecosystems.

Ecosystem attributes	Developmental stages	Mature stages
Community energetics		
1. Gross production/community respiration (P/R ratio)	Greater or less than 1	Approaches 1
2. Gross production/standing crop biomass (P/B ratio)	High	Low
3. Biomass supported/unit energy flow (B/E ratio)	Low	High
4. Net community production (yield)	High	Low
5. Food chains	Linear, predominantly grazing	Weblike, predominantly detritus
Community structure		
6. Total organic matter	Small	Large
7. Inorganic nutrients	Extrabiotic	Intrabiotic
8. Species diversity—variety component	Low	High
9. Species diversity—equitability component	Low	High
10. Biochemical diversity	Low	High
11. Stratification and spatial heterogeneity (pattern diversity)	Poorly organized	Well-organized
Life history		
12. Niche specialization	Broad	Narrow
13. Size of organism	Small	Large
14. Life cycles	Short, simple	Long, complex
Nutrient cycling		
15. Mineral cycles	Open	Closed
16. Nutrient exchange rate, between organisms and environment	Rapid	Slow
17. Role of detritus in nutrient regeneration	Unimportant	Important
Selection pressure		
18. Growth form	For rapid growth ("*r*-selection")	For feedback control ("*K*-selection")
19. Production	Quantity	Quality
Overall homeostasis		
20. Internal symbiosis	Undeveloped	Developed
21. Nutrient conservation	Poor	Good
22. Stability (resistance to external perturbations)	Poor	Good
23. Entropy	High	Low
24. Information	Low	High

metabolites probably serve increasingly important functions as regulators which stabilize the growth and composition of the ecosystem. Such metabolites may, in fact, be extremely important in preventing populations from overshooting the equilibrial density, thus in reducing oscillations as the system develops stability.

The cause-and-effect relationship between diversity and stability is not clear and needs to be investigated from many angles. If it can be shown that biotic diversity does indeed enhance physical stability in the ecosystem, or is the result of it, then we would have an important guide for conservation practice. Preservation of hedgerows, woodlots, non-economic species, noneutrophicated waters, and other biotic variety in man's landscape could then be justified on scientific as well as esthetic grounds, even though such preservation often must result in some reduction in the production of food or other immediate consumer needs. In other words, is variety only the spice of life, or is it a necessity for the long life of the total ecosystem comprising man and nature?

Nutrient Cycling

An important trend in successional development is the closing or "tightening" of the biogeochemical cycling of major nutrients, such as nitrogen, phosphorus, and calcium (Table 1, items 15-17). Mature systems, as compared to developing ones, have a greater capacity to entrap and hold nutrients for cycling within the system. For example, Bormann and Likens[24] have estimated that only 8 kilograms per hectare out of a total pool of exchangeable calcium of 365 kilograms per hectare is lost per year in stream outflow from a North Temperate watershed covered with a mature forest. Of this, about 3 kilograms per hectare is replaced by rainfall, leaving only 5 kilograms to be obtained from weathering of the underlying rocks in order for the system to maintain mineral balance. Reducing the volume of the vegetation, or otherwise setting the succession back to a younger state, results in increased water yield by way of stream outflow,[25] but this greater outflow is accompanied by greater losses of nutrients, which may also produce downstream eutrophication. Unless there is a compensating increase in the rate of weathering, the exchangeable pool of nutrients suffers gradual depletion (not to mention possible effects on soil structure resulting from erosion). High fertility in "young systems" which have open nutrient cycles cannot be maintained without compensating inputs of new nutrients; examples of such practice are the continuous-flow culture of algae, or intensive agriculture where large amounts of fertilizer are imported into the system each year.

Because rates of leaching increase in a latitudinal gradient from the poles to the equator, the role of the biotic community in nutrient retention is especially important in the high-rainfall areas of the subtropical and tropical latitudes, including not only land areas but also estuaries. Theoretically, as one goes equatorward, a larger percentage of the available nutrient pool is tied up in the biomass and a correspondingly lower percentage is in the soil or sediment. This theory, however, needs testing, since data to show such a geographical trend are incomplete. It is perhaps significant that conventional North Temperate row-type agriculture, which represents a very youthful type of ecosystem, is successful in the humid tropics only if carried out in a system of "shifting agriculture" in which the crops alternate with periods of natural vegetative redevelopment. Tree culture and the semiaquatic culture of rice provide much better nutrient retention and consequently have a longer life expectancy on a given site in these warmer latitudes.

Selection Pressure: Quantity versus Quality

MacArthur and Wilson[26] have reviewed stages of colonization of islands which provide direct parallels with stages in ecological succession on continents. Species with high rates of reproduction and growth, they find, are more likely to survive in the early uncrowded stages of island colonization. In contrast, selection pressure favors species with lower growth potential but better capabilities for competitive survival under the equilibrium density of late stages. Using the terminology of growth equations, where r is the intrinsic rate of increase and K is the upper asymptote or equilibrium population size, we may say that "r selection" predominates in early colonization, with "K selection" prevailing as more and more species and individuals attempt to colonize (Table 1, item 18). The same sort of thing is even seen within the species in certain "cyclic" northern insects in which "active" genetic strains found at low densities are replaced at high densities by "sluggish" strains that are adapted to crowding.[27]

Genetic changes involving the whole biota may be presumed to accompany the successional gradient, since, as described above, quantity production characterizes the young ecosystem while quality production and feedback control are the trademarks of the mature system (Table 1, item 19). Selection at the ecosystem level may be primarily interspecific, since species replacement is a characteristic of successional series or seres. However, in most well-studied seres there seem to be a few early successional species that are able to persist through to late stages. Whether genetic changes contribute to adaptation in such species has not been determined, so far as I know, but studies on population genetics of *Drosophila* suggest that changes in genetic composition could be important in population regulation.[28] Certainly, the human population, if it survives beyond its present rapid growth stage, is destined to be more and more affected by such selection pressures as adaptation to crowding becomes essential.

Overall Homeostasis

This brief review of ecosystem development emphasizes the complex nature of processes that interact. While one may well question whether all the trends described are characteristic of all types of ecosystems, there can be little doubt that the net result of community actions is symbiosis, nutrient conservation, stability, a decrease in entropy, and an increase in information (Table 1, items 20-24). The overall strategy is, as I stated at the beginning of this article, directed toward achieving as large and diverse an organic structure as is possible within the limits set by the available energy input and the prevailing physical conditions of existence (soil, water, climate, and so on). As studies of biotic communities become more functional and sophisticated, one is impressed with the importance of mutualism, parasitism, predation, commensalism, and other forms of symbiosis. Partnership between unrelated species is often noteworthy (for example, that between coral coelenterates and algae, or between mycorrhizae and trees). In many cases, at least, biotic control of grazing, population density, and nutrient cycling provide the chief positive-feedback mechanisms that contribute to stability in the mature system by preventing overshoots and destructive oscillations. The intriguing question is, Do mature ecosystems age, as organisms do? In other words, after a long period of relative stability or "adulthood," do ecosystems again develop unbalanced metabolism and become more vulnerable to diseases and other perturbations?

REFERENCES AND NOTES

1. E. P. ODUM, *Ecology* (Holt, Rinehart & Winston, New York, 1963), chap. 6.
2. H. T. ODUM and R. C. PINKERTON, *Amer. Scientist* 43, 331 (1955).
3. A. J. LOTKA, *Elements of Physical Biology* (Williams and Wilkins, Baltimore, 1925).
4. R. MARGALEF, *Advan. Frontiers Plant Sci.* 2, 137 (1963); *Amer. Naturalist* 97, 357 (1963).
5. R. J. BEYERS, *Ecol. Monographs* 33, 281 (1963).
6. The systems so far used to test ecological principles have been derived from sewage and farm ponds and are cultured in half-strength No. 35 Taub and Dollar medium [*Limnol. Oceanog.* 9, 61 (1964)]. They are closed to organic input or output but are open to the atmosphere through the cotton plug in the neck of the flask. Typically, liter-sized microecosystems contain two or three species of nonflagellated algae and one to three species each of flagellated protozoans, ciliated protozoans, rotifers, nematodes, and ostracods; a system derived from a sewage pond contained at least three species of fungi and 13 bacterial isolates [R. Gordon, thesis, University of Georgia (1967)]. These cultures are thus a kind of minimum ecosystem containing those small species originally found in the ancestral pond that are able to function together as a self-contained unit under the restricted conditions of the laboratory flask and the controlled environment of a growth chamber [temperature, 65° to 75°F (18° to 24°C); photoperiod, 12 hours; illumination, 100 to 1000 footcandles].
7. G. D. COOKE, *BioScience* 17, 717 (1967).
8. T. KIRA and T. SHIDEI, *Japan. J. Ecol.* 17, 70 (1967).
9. The metabolism of the microcosms was monitored by measuring diurnal pH changes, and the biomass (in terms of total organic matter and total carbon) was determined by periodic harvesting of replicate systems.
10. F. J. H. MACKERETH, *Proc. Roy. Soc. London Ser. B* 161, 295 (1965); U. M. COWGILL and G. E. HUTCHINSON, *Proc. Intern. Limnol. Ass.* 15, 644 (1964); A. D. HARRISON, *Trans. Roy. Soc. S. Africa* 36, 213 (1962).
11. R. MARGALEF, *Proc. Intern. Limnol. Ass.* 15, 169 (1964).
12. J. R. BRAY, *Oikos* 12, 70 (1961).
13. D. PIMENTEL, *Amer. Naturalist* 95, 65 (1961).
14. R. T. PAINE, *ibid.* 100, 65 (1966).
15. G. M. WOODWELL, *Brookhaven Nat. Lab. Pub. 924(T-381)* (1965). pp. 1-15.
16. R. G. WIEGERT, E. P. ODUM, J. H. SCHNELL, *Ecology* 48, 75 (1967).
17. For selected general studies of patterns of species diversity, see E. H. Simpson, *Nature* 163, 688 (1949); C. B. Williams, *J. Animal Ecol.* 22, 14 (1953); G. E. Hutchinson, *Amer. Naturalist* 93, 145 (1959); R. Margalef, *Gen. Systems* 3, 36 (1958); R. MacArthur and J. MacArthur, *Ecology* 42, 594 (1961); N. G. Hairston, *ibid.* 40, 404 (1959); B. C. Patten, *J. Marine Res. (Sears Found. Marine Res.)* 20, 57 (1960); E. G. Leigh, *Proc. Nat. Acad. Sci. U.S.* 55, 777 (1965); E. R. Pianka, *Amer. Naturalist* 100, 33 (1966); E. C. Pielou, *J. Theoret. Biol.* 10, 370 (1966).
18. M. LLOYD and R. J. GHELARDI, *J. Animal Ecol.* 33, 217 (1964); E. C. PIELOU, *J. Theoret. Biol.* 13, 131 (1966).
19. G. W. BARRETT, *Ecology* 49, 1019 (1969).
20. In our studies of natural succession following grain culture, both the species-to-numbers and the equitability indices increased for all trophic levels but especially for predators and parasites. Only 44 percent of the species in the natural ecosystem were phytophagous, as compared to 77 percent in the grain field.
21. J. T. BONNER, *Size and Cycle* (Princeton Univ. Press, Princeton, N.J., 1963); P. FRANK, *Ecology* 49, 355 (1968).
22. D. W. JOHNSTON and E. P. ODUM, *Ecology* 37, 50 (1956).
23. R. MARGALEF, *Oceanog. Marine Biol. Annu. Rev.* 5, 257 (1967).

24. F. H. BORMANN and G. E. LIKENS, *Science* 155, 424 (1967).
25. Increased water yield following reduction of vegetative cover has been frequently demonstrated in experimental watersheds throughout the world [see A. R. Hibbert, in *International Symposium on Forest Hydrology* (Pergamon Press, New York, 1967), pp. 527-543]. Data on the long-term hydrologic budget (rainfall input relative to stream outflow) are available at many of these sites, but mineral budgets have yet to be systematically studied. Again, this is a prime objective in the "ecosystem analysis" phase of the International Biological Program.
26. R. H. MACARTHUR and E. O. WILSON, *Theory of Island Biogeography* (Princeton Univ. Press, Princeton, N.J., 1967).
27. Examples are the tent caterpillar [see W. G. Wellington, *Can. J. Zool.* 35, 293 (1957)] and the larch budworm [see W. Baltensweiler, *Can Entomologist* 96, 792 (1964)].
28. F. J. AYALA, *Science* 162, 1453 (1968).

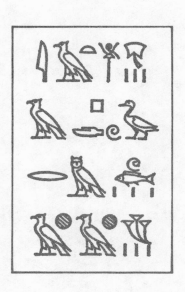

THE TUNDRA AS A HOMEOSTATIC SYSTEM (1969)

A. M. Schultz

In this paper, Schultz utilizes the holistic viewpoint (or "systems approach" in the new jargon) as did Forbes, Leopold and Odum. Schultz describes interactions between vertebrates and their environment concomitantly. Interestingly, Schultz' hypothesis of the role of phosphorus turnover in the lemming cycle was presaged by Leopold in A Biotic View of Land. Noting the importance of mineral nutrition in the biotic "up-circuit" (soil-plant-animal), Leopold asked, "What of the down-circuit?"

Cyclic Phenomena

Many of the activities of the tundra ecosystem under study are cyclic, with a periodicity of three or four years, but with varying amplitudes between cycles. We can think of a cycle as a series of transformations of state (Ashby, 1963). Thus, if a subsystem (compartment) has four clearly recognizable alternative states, a, b, c, and d, and the transformation always goes a → b → c → d → a → b, etc., then the sequence of states is a cycle. This can be shown kinematically:

or, when put on a time scale, as a sine wave:

and so on.

At Point Barrow we have good records of yearly lemming population densities, starting from 1946 (Fig. 1). Lemming peaks occurred in 1946, 1949, 1953, 1956, 1960, and 1965. Neither the amplitude nor the wavelength of these cycles is always the same. Yet there are some striking similarities. Using the systems language given above with a 1-year time interval, generally we can recognize four states: a, high density; b, very low density; c, low density; and d, medium density. The states can be named by reading the histogram, without any knowledge of lemming population dynamics or life histories. Sometimes c is missing and once c and d are transposed. Always the high year was immediately followed

---

Excerpted from: A study of an ecosystem: the arctic tundra *In* The Ecosystem Concept in Natural Resource Management (G. M. Van Dyne, Ed.). Copyright by Academic Press, Inc., N.Y. 383 pp.

by a very low year. But even during the low years, there were found local "pockets" supporting a denser population; for example, on the outskirts of the Eskimo village of Barrow, the fluctuations in lemming numbers have never been as pronounced as on the open tundra. Also of significance, some areas are out of phase with Point Barrow. At a point 100 miles east of Barrow, the population peaked in 1957, a year after the Point Barrow high. By 1960, it was in phase again.

What can be said about lemming population cycles? By Ashby's criterion, we have definitely observed cycles; but an engineer would say, if he saw the waves on an oscilloscope, that there was a lot of noise on the channel.

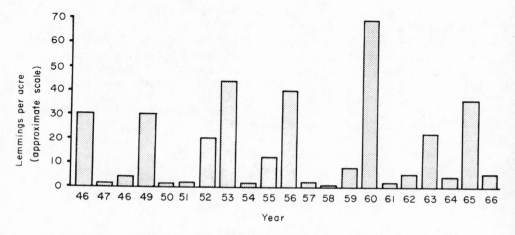

FIG. 33-1.—Lemming population cycles at Point Barrow, Alaska, from 1946 to 1966.

We have data on standing crop of plants (tops only), starting from 1958. Clippings were made in the vicinity of traplines used for the lemming census. Ninety percent of the dry matter was contributed by three species (*Dupontia fischeri, Eriophorum angustifolium,* and *Carex aquatilis*); these same species constitute the bulk of the lemming diet. When a graph is constructed for standing crop each year at phenologically equivalent dates, a cyclic pattern appears. Moreover, the pattern is in synchrony with that of the lemming population cycle, noise and all. A short lag develops between the two curves as the high point approaches. I do not want to explain the facts at this time, but I should say, in passing, that the high correlation between forage yield and lemming stocking rate would not come as a surprise to a range management audience.

Samples of the material clipped for production records were analyzed for total nitrogen, phosphorus, calcium, and several other elements. Concentrations of nutrients in the herbage, at any given phenological stage (i.e., date) increased through the year corresponding to the peak lemming year, then dropped to low values the year after, only to increase again.

Figure 6 shows the activity for phosphorus superimposed on the histogram of lemming population density. Within a season, nitrogen, phosphorus, and potassium decrease percentagewise as grasses mature, while calcium increases. The line in Fig. 2 should not be construed as a continuous increase in phosphorus level from 1957 through early 1960.

Calcium, potassium, and nitrogen show the same trends as phosphorus. Due to greater plot-to-plot variability, the nitrogen data are not as significant as are those of the other three elements, but the trend is nevertheless the same. Magnesium and sodium show no relationship to lemming numbers at all, nor were the data cyclic.

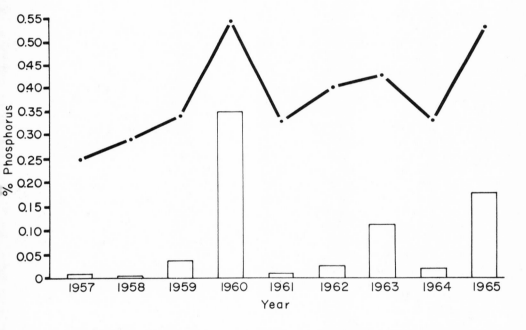

Fig. 33-2.—Phosphorus levels in forage at Point Barrow, Alaska. Bars represent relative lemming numbers.

Still another activity studied was decomposition of organic matter on the soil surface. This, too, turned out to be a cyclic phenomenon, and correlation with the activities already mentioned is high.

I have given a rough sketch of the behavior of the tundra, as discovered by survey techniques. The observations seem to fit closely a hypothesis of synchronous cycles. But at this stage, the results could be spurious. The close fit might result from artifacts of sampling. The transformation sequence a → b → c and/or d → a might occur frequently just by chance.

The next step is experimental: to introduce a disturbance at any one of the compartments and watch for reverberations throughout the system.

B. Experiments in Stressing the System

If the fluctuations in herbage production and nutrient level are related to immediate grazing history, then the cyclic aspect should disappear when grazing is eliminated. A simple exclosure, in effect, removes the herbivore from the system.

In 1950, a series of exclosed plots were established, alongside paired plots open to normal grazing (Thompson, 1955). Records kept for 13 years show cyclic variation on the outside paired plots, while the fenced plots show a constant decline. Since 1958, percentages of phosphorus, calcium, potassium, and nitrogen in the herbage from the grazed plots show the same marked cycles that occur elsewhere on the tundra (see Fig. 6). By comparison, year-to-year fluctuations inside the exclosures are slight and not cyclic.

With regard to decomposition of litter, the outside plots responded as did the tundra on the whole; inside the exclosures, decomposition rates were low and constantly decreasing.

An unexpected bonus came from the exclosure experiment. It gave an opportunity to assess the effect of lemming activity on the depth of thaw. By comparing, at the time of maximum thaw, soil depths inside and outside exclosures, I could separate the lemming-caused (within-system) effects from the summer temperature (environmental) effects. The results were most interesting. During a peak lemming year, the thickness of the active soil layer was maximum and it gradually diminished to the shallowest point the year before the next peak.

A second experiment was to stabilize artificially the fluctuating nutrient levels in the soil. This was done by fertilizing annually 6 acres of tundra with nitrogen, phosphorus, potassium, and calcium. Heavy applications were made to make sure that the variations in native soil nutrients were completely masked. What effect would this kind of disturbance have on primary and secondary production?

Net primary production, for the 4 years studied, was stabilized at a level 3–4 times that of the control plot. Annual variation was obliterated. Herbage quality was also stabilized. Protein levels, for example, were 4–5 times those of the vegetation of the control plot. Percent of calcium and phosphorus in the green tissue at equivalent dates remained high and constant in the four years.

The first fertilization was applied in 1961. No animals were seen either on fertilized or on control plots in 1961 or 1962. In 1963, animals were abundant all over the tundra (see Fig. 5 or 6), while in 1964, they were generally sparse. Immediately after the snowmelt in 1964, 30 winter nests per acre were counted on the fertilized area, none on the control plot, and less than 1 per 10 acres on the tundra in general. However, jaegers had found this 6-acre pantry and picked it clean. The few survivors observed at the time of the winter nest survey were large and fat. In 1965, a year of high lemming density all over the tundra, lemmings were abundant both on the fertilized and unfertilized control plot.

C. Hypotheses of Ecosystem Cycling

Only a fraction of the information collected so far can be presented in this paper. For the sake of brevity, I have shorn away all evidence of "noise" and shown, so to speak, only the slick regression lines. These represent the hypothetical behavior of the system compartments.

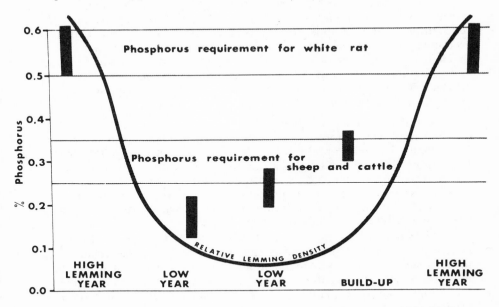

FIG. 33-3.—Hypothesis relating lemming populations and nutritional quality of forage. Lemming density curve is generalized, as are the black bars showing phosphorus in forage.

With the evidence at hand, let us develop a more general hypothesis to explain the synchronous cycles apparent in our ecosystem. Tentatively it might be called the nutritional threshold hypothesis (Fig. 3) but such a name places undue emphasis on just one part of the system.

Let us review a generalized 4-year cycle.

1. Early in summer of the high lemming year, the forage is calcium- and phosphorus-rich. Because of high production and consumption, much of the available calcium and phosphorus is tied up in organic matter. The soil has thawed down deep into the mineral layer because grazing, burrowing, and nest-building has altered the albedo and insulation of the surface.

2. The next year, not only is forage production low, but also the percent of calcium and phosphorus in the diet is below that which would be required for lactation by sheep or cattle. Nutrients in organic matter have not yet been released by way of decomposition.

3. The following year production is up, the plants are recovering from the severe grazing two years earlier, and dead grass from the previous year insulates the soil surface. At the same time, decomposition of that dead material is speeding up. Forage quality is still quite low. Whether there is enough calcium and phosphorus in the diet to support lemming reproduction and lactation depends on how closely the species resembles

331

domestic livestock, on the one hand, or the laboratory rat, on the other, in mineral requirements.

4. In the fourth year plants have fully recovered from grazing. Forage species accumulate minerals in their stem bases. Freezing action con-concentrates solutes in upper soil layers. Dead grass from several years has accumulated and plant cover is high; soil surface is well insulated and the thawed layer is very shallow. Decomposition rate is high. Calcium and phosphorus (and also potassium and nitrogen) content of forage is satisfactory for reproduction. There is enough food to support a large population of herbivores.

Next, the sequence is repeated.

Not until a nutritional threshold has been reached can a large lemming population build up. But the population does not keep getting bigger and bigger. This would be disastrous to the vegetation. So a deferred-rotation grazing scheme is built into the system. No grazing at all would also be disastrous to the vegetation and to the soil as well. Predators play a role at the time of herbivore decline. Indeed, all parts of the system play a role. It is a homeostatically controlled system.

This is only a hypothesis. It can be tested in the framework of the eco-system concept: First, by showing that all parts bear some relationship to all others; second, by experimentally stressing the system to see how it adapts to disturbance; third, by opening the black box and studying its physiology—that is, explanation of a phenomenon at a lower level of organization.

D. Contemporary Hypotheses on Cycling

Needless to say, the nutritional threshold hypothesis is at variance with several prominent hypotheses that have been advanced in recent years. The hypotheses of Christian and Chitty minimize the role played by energy and nutrition in controlling animal populations. The stress hypothesis of Christian (1950) associates population declines with shock disease and changes in adrenal-pituitary functions. The increase in adrenal activity at high population densities lowers reproduction and raises mortality. The hypothesis involving genetic behavior (Chitty, 1960) suggests that when animal numbers fluctuate, the populations change in quality. This is brought about through selection resulting from mutual antagonisms at high breeding densities.

All hypotheses concerning animal population cycles have in common the notion of feedback. There are two kinds of feedback, negative and positive. The kind generally involved in control mechanisms is negative or deviation-counteracting while the "vicious circle" kind is positive or deviation-amplifying (Maruyama, 1963). Most ecosystems have both kinds. We can think of loops running through a series of compartments so that the state of each compartment either counteracts (–) or amplifies (+) the change of state of the next (Fig. 4).

It is probable, in fact common, that any given element will be stationed on several loops. It may be checked via one loop and amplified via another. Consider the herbivore compartment of any ecosystem. Amount of forage, its quality, and availability of space are all positive; predators and pathogens are negatively related. In some cases, a density control

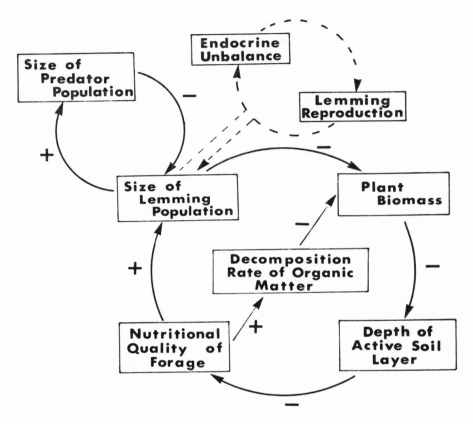

FIG. 33-4.—Feedback-loop model showing homeostatic controls in the arctic tundra ecosystem.

mechanism operates within the compartment itself—as described by the stress theory or the genetic selection theory. This is simply an additional loop in the system. There is no reason why a control system should have but one governor.

The idea of one cause–one effect is left over from the nineteenth century when physics dominated science. The whole notion of causality is under question in the ecosystem framework. Does it make sense to say that high primary production causes a rich organic soil and a rich organic soil causes high production? This kind of reasoning leads up a blind alley. We are dealing with the different dependent properties of the same system. Only things outside the system can cause something to happen inside. For the same reason, we cannot say that the lemmings are the driving force, any more than the vegetation, the soil, or the microflora, in making the ecosystem tick.

REFERENCES

ASHBY, W. R. 1963. "An Introduction to Cybernetics." Wiley, New York. 295 pp.

CHITTY, D. 1960. Population processes in the vole and their relevance to general theory. *Can. J. Zool.* 38, 99-113.

CHRISTIAN, J. J. 1950. The adreno-pituitary system and population cycles in mammals. *J. Mammal.* 31, 247-260.

MARUYAMA, M. 1963. The second cybernetics: Deviation-amplifying mutual causal processes. *Am. Scientist* 51, 164-179.

THOMPSON, D. Q. 1955. The role of food and cover in population fluctuations of the brown lemming at Point Barrow, Alaska. *Trans. 20th N. Am. Wildlife Conf.*, pp. 166-175.

THE ESSENTIALS OF A WILDLIFE RANGE (1938)
Ralph T. King

Here is an early attempt to describe the habitat requirements of wildlife. Although few game species had been studied King was able to synthesize this information into concepts still useful in the 1970's. His axiom that habitat must provide species' requirements for both sexes, all ages and all seasons —self evident though it may seem—is, unfortunately, still sometimes neglected.

Wildlife management consists almost entirely of environmental controls . . . Manipulations of the environment are usually referred to as "environmental controls" and they may be either wholly artificial or wholly natural or any combination of artificial and natural procedures. Generally speaking artificial controls are justified only as emergency measures and should not be used with a view to continuing them over any long period of time.

In the development of any wildlife management program the importance of environment must be kept constantly in mind. Much of the investigational work of the program must be directed toward environmental studies and practically all of the management practices must deal directly with the environment and thus only indirectly with the animal life.

. . . .

Every environment is made up of a multiplicity of factors. Fortunately the wildlife manager need not be concerned about many of them. Those that he is concerned with can be separated into two groups: first, the essentials, those things that must be present or provided on every range if it is to support any wildlife at all and second, the extraneities, those things that occur on practically every range and must perforce be recognized in the management program although they are not essential to the productivity of the range. These latter are often the most obvious of all the factors operating on the range and frequently the most important but they are never essential to the success of the range and are usually highly detrimental to its productivity; they are ordinarily decimating factors such as poaching, predation, disease and parasitism. The range essentials include such obviously necessary items as foods, coverts, and water. This distinction between the two groups of factors is made in order that no one can be accused of saying that only the essentials are important in a management program. That is not the case, the others are also important and must always be included in the program but it cannot be denied that their absence from the range would in no wise reduce its productivity.

The essentials of a wildlife range may then be listed as follows: foods, coverts, water resources, juxtaposition, and interspersion. The first three of these are materials, the last two are more in the nature of pattern. Every range must provide each of these materials in sufficient quantity and proper arrangement if it is to attain or even approach its highest state of productivity.

Excerpted from: J. Forestry 36(5):457-464, by permission from the Society of American Foresters.

It is thus seen that a wildlife range—insofar as non-migratory species are concerned—is a communal home, or rather, a communal home territory, the size of which is determined by the cruising radius of the species; and this home territory must contain all of the species' requirements—foods, coverts, and water, for both sexes and all age classes, for all seasons and for all the species' activities.

If one were to ask, "What constitutes a wild animal's home?" most persons, even those familiar with wildlife in the field, would reply, "A nest in the case of birds; a den or burrow in the case of most mammals." This answer, however, is far from being a true answer. These structures—nests, dens, and burrows—are usually only briefly existing parts of wild animals' homes. They are simply nurseries maintained and occupied for only a short period of the year while certain phases of reproduction are accomplished. Birds use their nests only while the eggs are being laid, incubated and hatched, and for a longer or shorter period after hatching until the young are able to follow the parent or parents; the length of this period depending upon the altricial or precocial properties of the species. In most cases there is no return to the nest once the young have left it; it has served its purpose as a nursery and is then no longer a part of the home. Dens and burrows are used by many mammals only during the period of parturition and for a short time thereafter until the young have gained sufficient strength to follow the mother. Usually there is no return to these dens or burrows once the young have begun hunting on their own, and in the case of some mammals there is nothing resembling either a den or burrow established.

These nurseries are of course an essential part of every wildlife environment, and any environment must provide satisfactory nursery sites if it is to remain productive, for regardless of how nearly optimum the conditions for individual existence, no environment will remain occupied for long unless there is proper provision for species continuance. The point is, however, that the nursery is only a part, a very important part it is true, but nevertheless a very transitory part of the wild animal home. Like the nursery in man's domicile, it is temporarily most important and apparently if not actually the center of all activity, but it does not constitute the entire home and would fail completely in its purpose if it were divorced from the other part of the home. The kitchen, the pantry, the livingroom, and the bedrooms are all necessary adjuncts and quite essential to a successfully productive home. These adjuncts are, in the case of wild animal homes, usually referred to as food and cover patches. The food patches constitute the kitchens, pantries, and dining rooms, while the cover patches function as living, recreational, and sleeping quarters, as nurseries and quite often also as transportation and communication routes.

But here again in connection with food and cover we have been too prone to remain satisfied with only a very superficial understanding. Every one is willing to grant the need for food and cover in wildlife economy but there has been little attempt to understand the physiological, sociological, and perhaps even psychological relations involved. It would perhaps be readily granted that the different species have different needs in these respects but isn't it probably equally true that the two sexes in any one species have different needs? It has been clearly shown in the case of some species that the cover requirements of the female during the reproductive period are vastly different from those of the male (whitetail deer for example); and it is equally well known that in some species the cover requirements of the male during the mating season are different from those of the female (for example, the drumming territory of the male ruffed grouse and the crowing ground of the cock pheasant). So also are the cover requirements different at different seasons. Winter cover is quite unlike summer cover; nesting cover may not be good feeding cover and very often is not satisfactory brooding cover; and mating cover in the case of some species is of no value at all for nesting, feeding or brooding. Cover requirements differ for the different age classes also; what suffices for adults may be and quite often is very unsatisfactory for the young.

The same marked species, seasonal, sexual, and age class differences are true in the case of foods. The differing food needs of different species are fairly well known although it is doubtful if we fully appreciate the true extent of these differences. It is also fairly well known that most wild animals eat different foods at different seasons and it has been assumed that this is due entirely to seasonal availability. It is doubtful if this is the complete explanation. It is, of course, true that they cannot obtain that which is unobtainable but it does not necessarily follow that they feed exclusively on those things that are easiest to get. In general wild animals make most use of those foods that occur in greatest quantity at a given time and place but there still remains, however, a fairly clear distinction between staple, preferred and emergency foods. It is not entirely unthinkable that certain foods are eaten at certain seasons because there is a particular need for them at that time and not simply because they occur at that time.

It is even more reasonable to suppose that there are different nutritional needs on the part of the different sexes. In the case of deer it is probably true that the buck utilizes as much energy in the production of a set of antlers as does the doe in developing a fawn but it is not likely that the same nutritional needs are experienced by both in process of accomplishing these two decidedly different ends. In the case of grouse it is possible that the males expend as much energy in the course of their mating antics as do the hens in the production of a clutch of eight to eighteen eggs, but it is doubtful if the same nutritive substances are required in both instances. Certainly it would not be surprising to find that there is some connection between the foods available to the female during the winter and early spring and the brood or litter produced later in the spring.

For example, it is known that the chick developing within the egg draws on the mineral content of the egg shell for the mineral salts necessary for its skeletal development. These salts must be provided from the tissues of the mother during the formation of the egg and her only source of supply is in the foods available to her. Certainly her requirements in this respect are much different than those of the male who is not called upon to meet this particular demand. The same general principle applies to nursing females in the case of mammals. Both gestation and lactation give rise to food needs peculiar to the sex.

As for the food needs of the different age classes they are almost too obvious to require discussion. In no species are the very young able to subsist on the same foods that suffice for the adults. Wild animals are no more able in this respect than are domestic species. Ruffed grouse, for example, are, as adults almost exclusively herbivores, but their young are just as exclusively carnivores, more particularly, insectivores, and unless softbodied insects are available to them during the first few days of their life they cannot hope to survive.

It is thus seen that food and cover are something different and more complex than they are ordinarily assumed to be. Each environment must contain all of the different types of cover and the various kinds of foods needed during the different seasons for the various activities of the several age classes of all the species it is intended that the environment should support. When all of these things needed by a single species are present in the environment they make of that environment a habitable range. If one of them is lacking it will seriously reduce if it does not totally destroy the productiveness of the range.

This, however, is only a part of the picture. A block of wildlife range may contain in its various parts all of the types of cover and all of the desirable foods necessary for a species and yet support that species in only limited numbers or not at all. This fact, that extensive environments apparently containing every food and cover requirement are frequently totally devoid of certain species or support only very limited populations of these species has occasioned much discussion and has seemed to make diagnosis an uncertain, if not an impossible, procedure. The difficulty, however, lies in our failure to understand the biological limitations of the species with which we are dealing. The explanation is to be found in species' properties, two of which we have just recently come to appreciate, namely, saturation points and cruising radii.

It is perhaps only natural for us to assume that wild animals, simply because they are wild and unfettered and possess the ability to fly or run great distances should utilize these abilities to cruise over wide areas in search of their daily and seasonal needs. We have unconsciously held to that belief for a long time but now we know we were in error. Work conducted during the past few years has proven conclusively the existence of very definite cruising radii as demonstrable properties of the various species. According to Leopold[4] Stoddard's work on bobwhite quail shows the average yearly radius to be not more than one-half mile for this species; Price with valley quail finds the average yearly radius to be one-fourth mile; Wight with ringneck pheasants finds one-half to one mile; Yeatter with Hungarian partridge believes three-fourths mile to be the yearly limit; Schmidt found one mile to be the limit in sharptail grouse, and my own work with ruffed grouse leads me to believe that the yearly average in this species will not exceed one-half mile.

It is thus seen that mobility varies greatly as between species but as Leopold[4] has said "it remains true that each species has a characteristic range of variation which differs from that of others, and which may accordingly be considered to be a property of that species." This new knowledge of cruising radii enables us to understand why certain wildlife ranges possessing all the necessary food and cover types may nevertheless support only sparse populations of wild animals.

Even though all of the required food and cover species are present in sufficient quantity they do not constitute a habitable range unless they are distributed in such a manner that every one of them occurs within the cruising radius of the animals requiring them, and unless they do so occur the range is valueless as far as those animals are concerned.

When all the food and cover requirements necessary for both sexes and all age classes of a species throughout the year are present on an area that does not exceed in size the cruising radius of the species then that area is a satisfactory communal home territory for that species. This distribution of all the species' requirements in relation to each other and in relation to the species' cruising radius is called juxtaposition. Proper juxtaposition simply means that all of the species' requirements are so distributed in space as to cause them all to occur on an area that does not exceed in size the area encompassed in the species' cruising radius.

Simple and obvious as this matter of juxtaposition may seem, it is nevertheless one of the five most important properties of wildlife environments. The various kinds of foods, the different kinds of cover, and water constitute three of these properties; juxtaposition is a fourth and equally important property.

The fifth property of a productive wildlife range is also one that has just recently been recognized. It has to do with maximum populations attainable on any block of range. Here again our failure to understand the true state of affairs was due to our lack of knowledge of species' properties. In the past we have assumed that the number of individuals produced or maintained on any area was wholly dependent on the amount of food and cover present on that area. Acting on this assumption we have frequently attempted to increase wild animal populations on given areas by increasing the amount of food and cover present on these areas. Usually this has resulted in some increase in the amount of wildlife; especially has this been true in those instances where consciously or unconsciously an improvement in juxtaposition was accomplished. Most environments have been so modified that they have suffered not only the effects of poor juxtaposition but also from an actual lack of food and cover; as a consequence the wildlife populations they supported were far below the potentialities of the environment. Any improvement of such environments was bound to result in some increase in the wildlife.

It was only natural to assume that if slight improvements in food and cover brought about an observable increase in the amount of wildlife then more extensive improvements should result in still larger increases. Our reasoning was something like this: Even though it takes 80 acres of poor pasture to support ten cows we can by providing sufficient food and proper shelter support that same number of cows on one acre. In other words, we were acting on the principle that it was wholly a matter of *carrying capacity*. Carrying capacity is exclusively a property of the environment and it is true that the populations of most domestic species and some wild species are determined by this property. If sufficient food and proper shelter are provided along with some provision for sanitation enormous populations can be produced and maintained on relatively small areas.

There is, however, in most wild species another property inherent in the species that supersedes carrying capacity and determines the level to which populations may rise on any or all areas. This property Leopold[4] has called *saturation point*. It cannot be better described at present than simply as something within the species that determines and regulates the number of individuals of that species that shall occur on any area at any one time.

Any figure expressing saturation point must of course be an expression of the population density at some particular time of year. In practice the overwintering population, which is also the breeding population in the case of most species, is accepted as the population density to which saturation point figures shall apply. According to Leopold[3] in bobwhite quail this maximum population appears to be one bird per acre over large blocks of range and no amount of improvement in the way of increased food, better cover and reduced predation or hunting will cause them to exceed this figure. A recent paper on ruffed grouse[1] states that optimum grouse environments in Minnesota do not support more than one grouse per four acres. It is obvious that it does not require one acre to produce the food and cover necessary for one quail and neither does it require four acres to produce the food and cover necessary for one ruffed grouse. These maximum populations of quail and grouse in optimum environments are not determined by carrying capacity, they are instead a measure of saturation point, a species property that regulates the height to which population levels may attain regardless of the excellence of the environment.

Knowing then that saturation point determines for many species the maximum populations possible on a wildlife range it is the business of good management to see that this maximum population level is attained or, at least, approached as closely as possible. He who attempts to surpass it is indeed foolish. Its attainment marks the successful rehabilitation of the range. All of the necessary food and cover species in proper juxtaposition will insure habitable and productive range, but one other requirement must be provided on every range if we are to build up and maintain maximum populations. This fifth range essential is practically perfect interspersion. Species' saturation points cannot be exceeded for the whole range, neither can they be exceeded for any part of the range except very temporarily. It is obvious, then, that each unit of the range as determined by the species' saturation point—one acre in the case of quail, four acres in the case of ruffed grouse—must produce its proportion of the total maximum population. There can be no permanent crowding of the animals into concentrations in excess of this saturation point; therefore, there can be no blanks in the sense of areas lacking in any single range essential if it is intended that the range shall maintain its maximum population.

This distribution of species' requirements in relation to saturation points is known as interspersion. Interspersion is the fifth of the five essentials of a wildlife range and may be defined as *the distribution over the entire range of all the food, water and cover requirements in a manner that renders it possible for each unit of the range, as determined by the species' saturation point, to produce its share of the total maximum population.*

The first four essentials mentioned—foods, coverts, water and juxtaposition—must be present on a range if it is to support wildlife in any quantity; the fifth interspersion, determines to a large extent the size of the populations present. Maximum productivity can be attained only when all of the essentials are at optimum.

By way of summary the five range essentials may be stated as follows: (1) foods, (2) coverts, (3) water, (4) juxtaposition to fit the cruising radii of all ages of all the species at all seasons, and (5) interspersion such as will enable each species to attain its saturation point. The first three essentials must meet the requirements for all the species concerned, for both sexes of all the species, for all age groups of all the species, for all seasons, and for all the species' activities.

LITERATURE CITED

1. KING, R.T. 1937. Ruffed grouse management. Jour. For. 35: 523-532.
2. LEOPOLD, A. 1931. Game range. Jour. For. 29: 932-938.
3. _____ 1931. Game survey of the North Central States. Madison.
4. _____ 1933. Game management. New York.

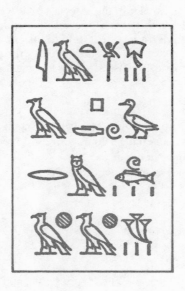

SNOW AS A FACTOR IN THE WINTER ECOLOGY OF THE BARREN-GROUND CARIBOU (1959)

William O. Pruitt, Jr.

Wildlife environments must supply food and cover. However, no widely accepted definition of cover is available and the use of and requirements for cover by wildlife have not been studied as adequately as have the food requirements of animals. Cover involves physical factors of the environment. Excerpts of Pruitt's paper on snow requirements of barren-ground caribou are included here to illustrate the importance of a physical factor to one species of wildlife.

Only a few northern biologists have fully understood the ecological importance of the arctic and subarctic snow cover. Possibly the first to bring this to the attention of biologists working only in the temperate zone were the naturalists Seton (1909) and Dugmore (1913). Others who have contributed substantially to our understanding of the ecological importance of snow have been Formozov (1946, 1948) and Nasimovich (1955) in the USSR, Vibe (1954, 1958) in Greenland, and Siivonen (1952, 1956) in Finland. A number of earlier Russian workers are cited by Formosov and Nasimovich. Murie (1935) noted the importance of snow in the migration and seasonal distribution of Alaska caribou, which are essentially mountain animals. Grinnell (1924) reproduced a letter dated November 17, 1846 from Thomas Lincoln of Dannysville, Maine to John James Audubon in which the nival environment of the woodland caribou *(Rangifer caribou)* was outlined in detail. Edwards and Ritcey (1956) discussed the effects of snow depth on the altitudinal migration of moose *(Alces alces)* in British Columbia and Edwards (1956) correlated snow depths and trends in ungulate populations.

· · · · · · · · · · · · · · · ·

From the foregoing exposition it is evident that the snow cover through which the caribou wade and from beneath which they gather most of their food exerts a profound influence on their behaviour, migration and species survival. Formozov (1946), in his classic work on the biological effects of snow, classified mammals as chionophobes (avoiding snow), chioneuphores (adapted to snow) and chionophiles (highly adapted to snow or even restricted to snow). Examples of chionophobes, according to Formozov, are the smaller cats and the steppe antelopes. Examples of chioneuphores are mice, wolverine, fox, voles, etc., whereas the varying or "hoofed" lemming and the snowshoe hare are examples of chionophiles. Formozov classified the Old World reindeer as a chioneuphore. Since the New World caribou because of its migrations, is subjected to snow factors for two-thirds of its annual cycle and because it exhibits behavioural and morphological adaptations to snow we are justified in classifying the Barren Ground caribou as

Excerpted from: Arctic 12(3):159-179.

a chionophile or an animal that is highly adapted to life on snow. Indeed, the name "snow caribou" would be more suitable for this species than is the term "Barren Ground caribou."

As my snow studies progressed it became evident that the wintering caribou in northern Saskatchewan were surrounded by a fence of snow having different characteristics from that in which they aggregated and that they were herded about over the countryside by this fence. To both the north and the south there was snow of greater depth than in the areas of concentration. To the south and southwest there was a sharp nival ecotone between soft, light taiga snow and hard, dense or iced snow almost temperate in its characteristics. The areas of caribou concentration had a snow cover that was softer, lighter, and thinner than that in the surrounding areas. Whereas the snow in the areas of occasional caribou was at times as soft and as light as that in the concentration areas it was at other times much harder and denser. The areas of no caribou had snow that consistently exhibited greater hardness, density or depth (occasionally all three qualities) than that of the areas of concentration. Variations in hardness appeared to influence caribou distribution more than variations in density. Obviously the presence of suitable food under the snow cover is also a factor of major importance as far as wintering localities are concerned. Under conditions of little modification of the winter range by man, probably the effect of nival factors was more prominent. Under such primeval conditions, before the extensive destruction of the winter range took place, nival factors probably were responsible for the location and density of wintering bands. Under present conditions the lack of food over extensive areas must be reckoned with.

Since snow conditions may prevent the wintering caribou from using extensive regions that are potential wintering grounds as far as food supply is concerned, it is obvious that winter range for any given number of animals must be substantially larger than the amount calculated from food intake per caribou per day and range recovery. In other words, a given amount of winter range can only support safely a much smaller number of caribou than that calculated on the basis of food intake and range recovery because snow conditions in different years may herd the caribou about so that they cannot use all the range that is vegetationally suitable. Calculations of the carrying capacity of caribou winter range must be related to the caribou's ability to dig feeding craters, the number of craters that can be dug per unit area in a given habitat type and the amount of food secured per crater.

Ideal snow conditions for caribou winter range appear to be (1) hardness not over 60 gm./sq.cm. for forest snow and not over 700 gm./sq.cm. for lake snow; (2) density not over 0.20 for forest snow and not over 0.32 for lake snow; (3) depth not over 50 or 60 cm.; (4) continuous low temperatures during the snow season (no invasions of moist tropical air masses) and low wind speeds during this period. Undoubtedly, if sufficient meteorological and climatological data were available, areas where such conditions are the rule could be mapped out. Of all the vegetationally suitable winter range those parts that are nivally suitable are the most valuable as far as species survival is concerned and should receive the maximum possible protection from artificial modification.

Nasimovich (1955) described similar reactions of Eurasian wild reindeer to nival conditions. The thresholds of sensitivity he recorded were in some instances significantly higher than those reported here. Thus it would appear that the behavioural responses of New World caribou to nival conditions are sufficiently different from those of Old World reindeer so that direct comparisons are not valid.

It is not by accident that all references to caribou in this paper are in terms of individuals or bands. Since the areas of wintering concentrations and the timing, direction and speed of migration are intimately related to the characteristics of the snow cover, I suspect that the actual geographic location of the migration routes themselves are governed by snow (and topography). Thus the "herds" of caribou (Banfield 1954) are actually the summation of individuals and bands aggregated because of the fencing or restricting action of snow. The discreteness of the several "herds" is but a biological reaction to areas or channels of softer, lighter, and thinner snow cover between and among areas of harder, denser, and thicker snow cover. If sufficient meteorological and climatological data were available this hypothesis undoubtedly could be tested.

Thus it appears that a profitable approach to the problem of caribou migration would be to develop further the idea of nivally suitable pathways and wintering areas or "deer passes." This approach has been singularly successful in dealing with the problems of migratory birds, resulting in the "flyway" concept.

REFERENCES

BANFIELD, A. W. F. 1954. Preliminary investigation of the Barren Ground caribou. Can. Wild. Serv. Wildl. Mgnt. Bull. 10A, 10B, mimeogr.

DUGMORE, A. R. 1913. The romance of the Newfoundland caribou. Philadelphia: J. B. Lippincott Co., 191 pp.

EDWARDS, R. Y. 1956. Snow depths and ungulate abundance in the mountains of western Canada. J. Wildl. Mgnt. 20: 159-68.

EDWARDS, R. Y. and R. W. RITCEY. 1956. The migrations of a moose herd. J. Mamm. 37:486-94.

FORMOZOV, A. N. 1946. The snow cover as an environment factor and its importance in the life of mammals and birds. Moskovskoe obshchestvo ispytatelei priroda. Materialy k poznaniyu fauny i flory SSSR. Otdel. zool. N. S. 5:141. (In Russian with French summary).

———— 1948. Small rodents and insectivores in Sharinski region of Kostroma Province during the period 1930-40. Moskovskoe obshchestvo ispytatelei priroda. Materialy k poznaniyu fauny i flory SSSR. Otdel. zool. N. S. 17:110 (In Russian).

GRINNELL, G. B. 1924. A letter to Audubon. J. Mamm. 5:223-30.

MURIE, O. J. 1935. Alaska-Yukon caribou. N. Am. Fauna 54, 93 pp.

NASIMOVICH, A. A. 1955. The role of the regime of snow cover in the life of ungulates in the USSR. Moskva, Akademiya Nauk SSSR. 403 pp. (In Russian).

SETON, E. T. 1909. Lives of northern animals. An account of the mammals of northern Manitoba. New York: Charles Scribner's Sons, 1267 pp.

SIIVONEN, Lauri. 1952. On the influence of climatic variations of recent decades on the game economy. Fennia (Fin. Geog. Soc.) 75:77-88.

———— 1956. The correlation between the fluctuations of partridge and European hare populations and the climatic conditions of winters in southwest Finland during the last thirty years. Pap. Game Res. 17:1-30.

VIBE, Ch. 1954. Problemerne omkring Grønlands moskusokser. Grønland, No. 11:401-14.

———— 1958. The musk ox in East Greenland. Mammalia 22:168-74.

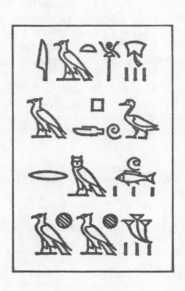

WILDLIFE RELATIONSHIPS TO SOIL TYPES (1944)
Aurthur H. Denney

*"Life is rooted in the soil"—an axiom too easily neglected. Denney
illustrates that soil fertility affects animal nutrition and, in turn, animal
quality. Animal quality influences rates of reproduction and mortality and
therefore the abundance of wildlife. Any land use depleting soil fertility also
reduces the soil's capacity to produce wildlife.*

*Soil fertility determines land use and thereby determines the quantity
and interspersion of foods and cover-types for wildlife. The very best soils
are most intensively used by man, resulting in poor habitat for many species
—on soil having the greatest potential for wildlife production! The best soils
are not for wildlife.*

We are told in our first course in biology that all animals are dependent upon plants for food, either directly or indirectly, and that plants in
turn obtain their food from the soil and process it in the presence of sunshine, air and water. This elementary law of nature is so simple and obvious
that its import to problems of wildlife conservation has been frequently
overlooked.

Environmental management—consisting of providing food, cover and
water, and protecting the breeding stock—is a well-established principle
of wildlife conservation. Recent studies in Missouri, however, indicate that
these practices are merely the superstructure of wildlife conservation, and
that wildlife populations are founded upon the soil and determined by a
sliding scale of declining soil fertility.

. . . .

Recently agronomists have observed that under identical climatic
conditions, the yield and quality of plants is directly related to the available fertility of the soil. Likewise the animal husbandrymen have noted
that the carrying capacity of pastures varies with the fertility of the soil
and it now appears that the soils through their influence on the quality
of vegetation, may have a pronounced effect on the reproduction and
growth of domestic animals.

Wildlife is a crop of the land and like domestic animals must depend
upon the quality and quantity of vegetation for its existence. However,
since wild animals must normally obtain their food entirely from the local
supply while livestock are frequently fed products of other regions, it is
only natural, therefore, to believe that wild animals will reflect even better
than domestic animals, the quality of the vegetation grown on different
soil types.

The Pittman-Robertson program in Missouri has approached wildlife management from the environmental aspect. After 3 years of careful
study, we reached the conclusion that the influence of climate, food, cover,
water and the protection of the breeding stock alone, would not explain

Excerpted from: Trans. N. Amer. Wildl. Conf. 9:316-322.

the irregular distribution of some species. Because these superficial environmental factors were inadequate to explain the status of some species, a new basis for game range classification was sought. It was found in soil types. . . . .

Soil types are an extremely durable physical classification of land areas, and yet every rain, snow, sleet and drought and every act of man has left tell-tale traces in the physical-chemical composition of the soil. The invasion of the seas and glaciers, the great dust storms and other earth and water movements have each contributed to the formation of the soil. Soils contain the remains of animal and plant bodies which in the process of evolution and development have gathered together the essential elements of life so that successively higher forms of life could survive.

Missouri is ideally suited to an examination of the relationship of soil to animal population, because of the great diversity of soil types within the state. This diversity of types was pointed out by Miller and Krusekopf (1929) when they said: "Missouri is the meeting ground of all of the important soil regions of the Mississippi Valley. Thus the extensive glacial and loessial soils of the northern part of the State are closely related to the glacial and loessial regions of the states to the north and east. The prairies of Southwest Missouri form the eastern edge of the Great Plains region extending to the Rocky Mountains. The limestone soils of the Ozark region are comparable to the soils of similar origin in Arkansas, Kentucky and Tennessee. The Southeast Lowlands represent the northern extension of that great belt of alluvial soils extending along the Mississippi River from Cape Girardeau to the Gulf of Mexico. The resultant of such varied soil conditions is a varied agriculture, of which it can be said that it is neither northern nor southern, eastern nor western. It possesses the characteristics of all of these regions."

Associated with these varied soils are regions of tall-grass prairie, pine, oak-hickory, and lowland hardwood forests. The average annual rainfall and temperature varies greatly within the state, and fluctuates violently from year to year.

With this variety of climatic, vegetative and soil conditions in Missouri, it has been only natural that we have observed variations in animal distribution and have been able to associate these variations with different soil types.

Our attention was first called to the relationship of animal distribution to soil types by the extremely low population of raccoon on a single soil type, and then later to a correspondingly low population of red fox on another soil type. In both cases the areas appeared to afford suitable habitat for the species.

Bennitt (1939) had previously traced the distribution of prairie chickens by soil types and noted that they were almost entirely confined to a few of the poorer prairie soils. In reporting certain studies of the wild turkey, Leopold and Dalke (1943) concluded: "It appears, therefore, that rough topography and associated extensive forests are not as closely correlated with turkey distribution as the type of soil (inherent fertility being perhaps the deciding factor) and the character of the vegetation itself." Rowe (1941) showed a marked variation in weight of cottontail rabbits collected from 14 widely scattered localities. Later analysis of these data showed that there was a greater correlation between rabbit weights and variations in soil type than with variation in climate and subspecies. Nagel (1943) showed that the average weight of raccoons increased with increasing soil fertility, but he found that the highest populations were associated with medium fertility soils. Honess (1941), working on the bighorn sheep in Wyoming, observed that, "It is obvious that the sheep are eating large quantities of soils from the various licks in an effort to correct the mineral deficiency."

Rucker (1942), after an exhaustive study of the Mobile Bay Delta in Alabama, stated that muskrats did not inhabit these marshes for reasons "which at this time are not known or understood." And he further remarked that "The only fact that seems certain is that the delta does not lie within the natural range of this species. Why, is not known at this time." This condition exists in spite of the fact that the natural range of muskrats comes within 25 miles of the area on the west, and that the muskrat is the number 1 fur bearer in the State of Louisiana. Could it be that the soil from northern farm lands deposited in Mississippi and Louisiana by the great Mississippi River has made conditions there suitable for muskrats, while the outwash from the Alabama and Tombigbee Rivers is deficient in some essential elements required for their support?

With all of the previously mentioned evidence as an indication of soil-wildlife relationships, we have undertaken in Missouri to measure the effect of variations in soil upon the abundance and quality of two species of wildlife—the cottontail rabbit and the raccoon. This investigation is still under way and will continue for several years, but sufficient progress has been made to present a diagram indicating the findings to date.

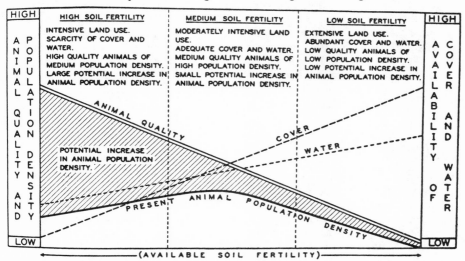

FIG. 36-1.—Diagramatic sketch of relationship of soil fertility, cover and water to animal quality and population density under present conditions of land use. If the intensity of land use is reduced and cover and water provided, the future animal population should increase in proportion to the shaded zone of potential productivity.

The base of this diagram represents available soil fertility which increases from right to left. The vertical axis of the diagram represents animal quality and population density, as well as the quantity of cover and water, and increases from the bottom to the top of the diagram. This generalized diagram shows that the quality of the animal as measured by size, increases directly with increasing soil fertility. The number of animals per unit area, however, increases up to a mid-point and then declines slightly. This decline is believed to be due to the more intensive use of the land and consequently less suitable habitat is available. It is also evident from this diagram that the amount of cover increases as the fertility of the soil decreases, and that this takes place in about the same proportion as the decline in quality of animals.

We have found in Missouri that water is relatively more abundant than cover in the high fertility areas, largely because of the many farm ponds constructed for livestock water supplies. Water is less abundant than cover in the low fertility areas, because these areas are not so well suited to farm pond construction and the livestock ranges over larger areas, depending for water mainly on spring seeps and permanent streams. We interpret the shaded portion of this diagram as reflecting the reduction in food, cover and water brought about by man's intensive use of the fertile soils for cultivation and we submit that it represents the potential of each soil type to support a larger population. No representation of the relative abundance of food is shown, but we believe that, under present land use, the greatest quantity of food is found in the area of medium fertility, but the highest quality food is associated with the highest soil fertility areas.

The data upon which this diagram is based consists of records from 175,864 live-trapped rabbits and from 66,636 raccoon. All of the rabbits and 15,806 of the raccoon were weighed. The variation in average weights of rabbits ranged from 2.1 pounds to 2.8 pounds, while the variation in average weight of raccoon ranged from 11.98 pounds to 18.54 pounds.

Not all of the relationships of soil to wildlife are of a chemical nature, but the importance of soil conservation practices as an aid to environmental management have long been recognized, and if I appear to pass swiftly over this phase of soil-wildlife relationships, it is only because I desire to touch upon some of the more basic relationships of soil to wildlife.

In Missouri we have used soil types as a basis of game range classification for all species, for the following reasons:

1. One of the greatest values of wildlife research and game management can accrue from the interchange of ideas between workers in the different states. This exchange of ideas is facilitated by the use of soil types as game range types. Each soil type has a fixed characteristic which will alter only slightly during the centuries, whereas man may quickly change the vegetative covering, or a cyclic fluctuation of the climate may cause wide variations within a short period of time.

2. Within each soil type there has been developed a relatively uniform land use pattern, and if this pattern should change in the future, it is reasonable to believe that the new pattern will also be uniform for each soil type.

350

3. Vegetative types show a close association with the soil types and individual species of plants have a distinct affinity for special soil and slope conditions.

4. The distribution of many animal species is almost synonymous with soil type boundaries. When the soil types upon which a species occurs are identified the range of the species may be traced on a soils map.

5. The quantity, quality and distribution of water takes on a characteristic pattern for each soil type, in Missouri.

6. The recommended wildlife management practices for any species will be limited by the primary land use on each soil type. Since most game management must be done upon private land, it is imperative that we devise our management techniques so that they will be compatible with and beneficial to the best use of the land for agriculture, grazing and forestry. Otherwise we can have little hope of seeing these practices adopted on a large scale by the individual landowner for the sole or primary benefit of wildlife.

7. The application of wildlife management practices is dependent upon recognition by agriculturists and foresters that these practices are compatible with their objectives. By basing recommendations for wildlife management on soil types we have demonstrated that wildlife really is a crop of the land and is subject to variations in yield and quality in the same manner that agricultural and forest crops are affected by the fertility of the soil. Thus by using terms familiar to landowners the principles of wildlife management can be more easily understood and more widely applied by landowners.

8. In most of the agricultural states detailed soil maps are available and represent an excellent base map for wildlife management. This use of soil type maps permits the classification of game range types quickly and at small cost.

The fundamental relationship of soil to animal life may be expressed in four statements:

1. The distribution of all species of wildlife is primarily determined by soil types and availability of the elements necessary for animal life; and only secondarily by cover and water, and climatic factors.

2. The abundance of any species of wildlife within an occupied range is basically determined by the fertility of the land, and secondarily by the type and intensity of land use, which we submit is also primarily determined by the fertility of the soil.

3. The quality and size of individuals of the species within the limits of its range are also fundamentally determined by the available fertility of the soil and are only slightly affected by the intensity of land use and the scarcity of suitable habitat.

4. Perhaps most important of all is the conclusion that wildlife production, like any other crop of the land, is in proportion to the available fertility of the soil and that land which is too infertile to produce satisfactory crops, grass or livestock is also marginal for wildlife.

In closing, I would like to offer the following suggestions to technicians in other states, in the hope that an aroused interest will result in the unfolding of many more secrets of animal life:

1. Review previous wildlife studies to determine whether or not beneath the cloak of variations in food, cover, water and climate, there is not a corresponding variation in soil types and conditions.

2. Investigate the relationship of high and low infestations of disease and parasites in animals in relation to soil types, and consider the possibility of controlling wild animal diseases and parasites by management of the soil or improving the resistance of the animal through improved diet.

3. Investigate the relationship of diet to color phases and the development of subspecies. If the New York Zoological Park (Bridges, 1943) can turn white flamingos pink, and if milady can brighten up her canary by a change in diet, what is the possibility that subspeciation is due to the response of animals to slight variations in the composition of their diet?

There may be many other relationships which may be traced to the soil, but if I have succeeded in arousing your curiosity and interest in these few points, I am sure that you will find for yourselves many ramifications and relationships hitherto ascribed to the more obvious environmental factors.

LITERATURE CITED

BENNITT, R. 1939. Some agricultural characteristics of the Missouri prairie chicken range. Trans. 4th N. Am. W. Conf., pp. 481-500.

BRIDGES, W. 1943. In the pink. Reader's Digest, July 1943, p. 38.

HONESS, R. F. 1941. The factors determining abundance of Rocky Mountain bighorn sheep in Northwest Wyoming. Pittman-Robertson Quar., Vol. 1, No. 1, January 1941, pp. 94-96.

LEOPOLD, A. S. and P. D. DALKE 1943. The 1942 status of wild turkeys in Missouri. Jour. For., Vol. 41, No. 6, June 1943, pp. 428-435.

MILLER, M. F. and H. H. KRUSHEKOPF 1929. The soils of Missouri. Univ. Mo. Coll. Agri. Exper. Sta. Bull. 264, 120 pp.

NAGEL, W. O. 1943. A study of the economic value, distribution, trends and soil relationships of Missouri fur bearers. (Unpub. report—Mo. Cons. Com., Pittman-Robertson Project.)

ROWE, K. C. 1941. Report of population study of the cottontail in Missouri and the effects of commercial shipments from Missouri in relation to need for control. (Mimeographed report, Mo. Cons. Com., 36 pp.)

RUCKER, H. C. 1942. Final reports of the muskrat investigation in Alabama. (Reviewed by W. J. Howard in Pittman-Robertson Quar., Vol. 2, No. 4, October 1942, p. 194.)

THE CONCEPT OF CARRYING CAPACITY (1955)

R. Y. Edwards and C. David Fowle

Every profession develops its own jargon. In wildlife management, perhaps no concept is more important than that of carrying capacity; yet perhaps no term has been more loosely used. This paper is, therefore, pertinent. The published discussion which followed the original paper is also recommended.

The term "carrying capacity" is well-established in the vocabulary of wildlife biologists as well as of many ecologists working in other fields. It is one of those terms often employed without strict consideration of exact meaning which is used to describe a general concept rather than to express an exact idea. As such it is useful, but as our knowledge of factors affecting the survival of animals grows it is wise to examine periodically the terms we use and to consider their adequacy.

In preparing this paper we set out to examine the term "carrying capacity" to determine its meaning and to assess its usefulness in wildlife management. If the term as currently used proved inadequate we hoped to redefine it to give it more useful precision. We have tried not to confine our thinking to herbivores, ungulates or to any particular group of animals, for it should be possible to develop a general concept which can be applied to a wide range of animals. If the term is to have value in wildlife management, it should recognize broad criteria within which must fit particular conditions pertaining to particular species.

Our conclusions can be briefly stated. We find that most definitions of carrying capacity are vague and that some are almost meaningless. There is a difference of opinion in that many have used, and are using, the term as if it applied to food alone, while others use it to denote more than limitation of food and include other factors. We find that carrying capacity is often considered a stable characteristic of environment despite the fact that nearly all limiting factors are known to vary constantly in their influence on populations.

Past and Present Use of the Term

In analyzing our thoughts as well as those of associates with whom we have discussed the matter, we have found that the most basic differences of opinion stem from whether carrying capacity has meaning only with reference to food supply or whether its meaning is broader. Most people have assumed the former meaning, especially those working with ungulates. A few have maintained that this is the only meaning possible and have cited Leopold (1933) as the basic reference on this point for wildlife management. His definition states (p. 450) that carrying capacity is:

"The maximum density of wild game which a particular range is capable of carrying."

Here food is not mentioned but elsewhere, in speaking of ungulates, he says (p. 54):

Reprinted from: Trans. N. Amer. Wildl. Conf. 20:589-602.

"... there is so far no visible evidence of any density limit except the carrying capacity of the food."

A somewhat different meaning is implied in another passage (p. 135) where he brings the importance of cover and "edge" into the definition. Although Leopold does not provide us with a specific definition it is apparent that he considered food as only one factor determining carrying capacity. This is illustrated by his use of the term "range" which, to him, included a variety of facilities in the environment, which are utilized by animals. He says (p. 135):

"A range is habitable for a given species when it furnishes places suitable for it to feed, hide, rest, sleep, play, and breed, all within the reach of its cruising radius. Deficiencies in such places are usually seasonal."

The last statement is significant because it shows that Leopold recognized the variability of environment in terms of variations in factors such as weather, season and plant succession, and that dynamic environment is reflected in fluctuations in populations of animals.

A number of authors have emphasized food in considering carrying capacity. Hadwen and Palmer (1922), speaking of reindeer *(Rangifer tarandus)* say that grazing or carrying capacity is (p. 29):

"... the number of stock which range will support for a definite period of grazing without injury to the range."

Here it is clear that food is the limiting factor under consideration. Trippensee (1948) also emphasizes the importance of food when referring to deer *(Odocoileus)*, saying (p. 196):

"The carrying capacity of a range, measured in terms of food availability, depends upon two factors; stand age and stand composition."

Elsewhere in his book he avoids the term. Alee *et al.* (1949:706) also stress food in discussing carrying capacity. Fowle (1950) in reviewing factors controlling deer populations says (p. 57):

"The environmental factor which has received the most attention in deer studies is food. Indeed, our concept of carrying capacity for deer centers around the adequacy of the food supply while our criteria of overuse have their basis in the rate of depletion of food supply."

Dasmann (1945:400) regards carrying capacity as:

"... the maximum number of grazing animals of a given class that can be maintained in good flesh year after year on a grazing unit without injury to the range forage growing stock or to the basic soil resource."

The same author modified this definition in a paper in 1948 (p. 189) by changing the words "grazing animals" to "foraging animals" and replacing "grazing unit" with "range unit." This definition, confined to foraging animals, represents the modern trend of confining the use of "carrying capacity" to ungulates and other herbivores.

Dasmann's definition adds two concepts to that of Leopold; first, the quality of the animals should be considered, and second, deterioration of range cannot be allowed. Because standards have been established, quality is relatively easy to deal with in domestic stock, but with wildlife species it is more difficult. Perhaps it has yet to receive the attention it deserves in wildlife studies. Fisheries biologists have employed the idea with some success in cases where an environment is found capable of producing a certain aggregate weight of fish (biomass) made up of either a few large fish or many small ones. Reference to the "maximum number" that the waters will hold is meaningless unless the quality (size) of fish required is stipulated. Similarly, a unit of environment may support a large number of deer living at a minimum subsistence level, or a lesser number of healthier animals.

If a population is sufficiently large to deplete the food supply faster than it is being produced, or injures the environment in some way, the size of future populations will be affected. This is an important concept in Dasmann's definition which is usually assumed in considering carrying capacity. In theory it is simple, recognizing that the animals should be in such numbers that they eat only the annual interest from food plants and none of the principal. Hence the environment should be stocked for perpetual maximum benefit rather than for a short period at its full capacity.

That Dasmann (1948) considers carrying capacity to be a dynamic concept is further illustrated when he says (p. 189):

"The number of animals that will take no more than the forage crop in all but poorest growth years is the maximum number a range unit will support on a sustained basis. Since range is dynamic, changing continually with fluctuations in precipitation, temperature, evaporation, and varying use-patterns, no rate of stocking can be considered final."

Leopold (1933:51) is careful to distinguish between "carrying capacity" and "saturation point." The former he regards as "a property of a unit of range" and the latter "a property of a species." However, Graham (1944) refers to both concepts as if they applied to range. He says (p. 60):

"Closely related to cruising radius is the idea of *carrying capacity* of the land, whether it relates to wild species or to domestic animals such as sheep and cattle. Many factors influence the number of animals an area can maintain. The ancients had this in mind when they remarked that 'one hill will not carry two tigers'. A knowledge of the number of animals a habitat can reasonably be expected to support —its *saturation point*—is useful to the land manager."

This statement and the discussion which follows show that Graham was considering all factors, including social intolerances, which can limit the number of animals in an area.

In this connection the definitions of Errington and Hamerstrom (1936: 308) are of interest. Speaking of bobwhite quail *(Colinus virginianus)* in winter they say:

"In its simplest form carrying capacity may be said to denote the upper limit of survival possible in a given covey territory as it exists under the most favorable conditions."

Later they state (309):

"The definition of carrying capacity may perhaps be restated as the level beyond which simple predation upon adult birds, their own territorial tolerances, and their tendencies to depart from coverts overcrowded with their own or some other species do not permit continued maintenance of population."

Reference to "upper limit of survival . . . under the most favorable conditions" suggests Leopold's phrase "maximum density." Inclusion of territorial tolerance and predation in the second definition gives it the wider meaning inferred in Graham's (1944) statement cited above.

The great importance of social interactions in limiting the number of animals within an area has been illustrated by work on rats *(Rattus norvegicus)* (Calhoun, 1949, 1950, 1952). Hodgdon and Hunt (1953) in defining carrying capacity for beaver also emphasize social tolerances when they say (p. 73):

"Carrying capacity, then, is a matter of available food, available water and degree of tolerance one beaver family has for another."

Allen (1954) gives no definition but uses the term frequently. He states (p. 44):

"Within limits a trained observer can make a fair-or-better estimate of what is likely to be a productive area for species he has worked with, but the final proof is *what it is actually supporting.* The biologist's term for this is 'carrying capacity'."

Again he states (p. 132):

". . . in the North the carrying capacity of a land unit usually declines during the cold season . . ."

Also (p. 259):

"In a given unit of range there probably will be an optimum density level where the population of prey animals will be reasonably safe from predation (i. e., the carrying capacity phenomenon). But variable factors, such as weather, may alter the condition of this range unit, for better or worse, in a given year."

On page 138 he states:

"Carrying capacity of deer country usually depends upon available food on the winter range."

It is clear that Allen's concept of carrying capacity is broad. He regards predation in relation to carrying capacity much as do Errington and Hamerstrom (1936). While food is acknowledged as the main limiting factor for deer, he recognizes that a number of factors may determine carrying capacity for other species. Of special interest perhaps is the statement from page 44 suggesting that the final proof of carrying capacity is what the area supports. He follows this statement by noting that an area with one quail per acre has a high carrying capacity for quail, but the same area may have a low carrying capacity for turkeys.

These examples will illustrate the general conception of carrying capacity as it has been developed in the literature. There is agreement that for various reasons it is impossible to crowd more than a finite number of animals into any unit of environment. This number will vary with the conditions for life existing in the unit concerned. It is not clear, however, whether all or only some of the many factors tending to limit animal populations should be included as factors determining carrying capacity. Some have stressed the importance of "quality" of the animals. It has been recognized that the ability of environment to support population varies from time to time, leading to fluctuations in population. The fluctuating nature of carrying capacity has not, however, been universally recognized, particularly by some earlier writers who inferred that it was a more or less stable attribute of environment.

What is Carrying Capacity?

Our review of the development of the concept of carrying capacity has shown that the original ideas were related to the role of such factors as climate and food-supply in controlling populations. Gradually, however, there has been a shifting of emphasis from a point of view holding that single factors, such as food, are the main controlling factors to a more comprehensive view in which it is recognized that: "The relationships of a population are with the whole ecosystem (which includes itself) rather than with the environment only." (Solomon, 1949:31; Tansley, 1935). The fact that populations do not grow beyond finite limits is the result of the limited capacity of the ecosystem to support organisms.

In view of the complexity of factors influencing populations it is impossible to make a generalization as to the factors which determine carrying capacity since these will vary with time, place and the species concerned. If, however, we include all the factors in the ecosystem which tend to limit populations as factors determining carrying capacity we are led to an apparent paradox; namely that the number of animals present at a certain time in a unit of environment within the main geographic range of the species concerned is in itself a measure of carrying capacity at that time or at a previous time. For example, the number of quail in an area in spring may be a measure of the carrying capacity of the area during the most critical period of the previous winter. Conditions in spring may be favorable to the maintenance of more quail than are present, but in the absence of reproduction or immigration the population remains below carrying capacity.

Hence carrying capacity may be expressed simply by the number of animals in a unit of environment, except when time has been insufficient to enable increase when it is possible and except where the distribution of the animals is such as to leave some parts of inhabitable environment vacant. The *desired* population may be smaller or larger, and it is the business of management to establish the desired levels through manipulation of the appropriate manageable factors in the ecosystem. Our approach leads us to conclude that management must deal with carrying capacities in order to control populations and not, as sometimes thought, with populations in relation to one carrying capacity.

For a given population in a unit of environment there are a number of factors and processes which are potentially capable of placing an upper limit on its size. Several of these may be acting simultaneously as, for example, in a population which is increasing. As the population density increases the food-supply may be gradually reduced, competition for space with associated intraspecific fighting will become keener, and there may be an increase in disease and predation. Some animals will be eliminated in fights, some may die as they are forced out into inhospitable habitat, some may starve, disease may kill some, and predators may take an increasing proportion beyond a certain threshold of density of prey. Severe weather may eliminate others. The net result will be to limit the population, but no one factor may be responsible.

On the other hand, the various factors may act separately in the sense that one may become critical in the manner described by Liebig's Law of the Minimum. Taylor (1934) suggested a somewhat similar idea when he restated the law to apply to environmental factors generally as follows (p. 378):

> "The growth and functioning of an organism is dependent upon the amount of the essential environmental factor presented to it in minimal quantity during the most critical season of the year, or during the most critical year or years of a climatic cycle."

The role of factors operating at a minimum are also considered by Hubbs and Eschmeyer (1938) who, in speaking of management procedures say (p. 21):

> "All the essentials of a large fish yield should be provided; none may be omitted because the lack of any one is sufficient to hold down production."

Later they say (p. 23):

> "When the least developed or most limiting factor has been built up and has increased the fish production, some other factor may then become under-developed in terms of the increased population."

Even here, however, it is virtually impossible to think of a factor acting independently of other factors or processes in the ecosystem. Indeed, as Rübel (1935) points out, factors operating at a minimum will have varying effects depending upon the other factors operating with them.

However, for purposes of management it is useful to approach the concept of carrying capacity from the point of view that populations are, in the last analysis, limited by some factor operating at a minimum. This approach focuses attention upon more or less measurable and manageable factors instead of complex environments regarded as entities. The latter can lead management into useless activity, improving environmental conditions which could be limiting, but which are not limiting in the situation at hand. For example, if 200 deer attempt to live in an area in a year when there is winter food for 100 and shelter at the height of winter for 300, and if we assume further that hunters will harvest 50, it is obvious that improving shelter or restricting hunting will neither maintain nor increase the herd. This can be done only be increasing the food. One detrimental factor alone can limit a population to a low level in what is otherwise superior habitat. Moreover, if the 200 animals are consuming their food supply faster than it is being produced, and the food supply cannot be increased, the aim of management should be to lower the level of critical operation of some other potentially limiting factor so that the herd is reduced to a number in balance with the food supply. Increase of the harvest to 100 would reduce the population to the desired level.

But what of a definition of carrying capacity? It is clear that populations are maintained by periodic recruitment of new organisms through reproduction or immigration. In the intervals between periods of recruitment there is a tendency for populations to decline because of many decimating factors which are operating against them at all times. These vary in the intensity of their effects with both time and density of population. For example, a population of ringnecked pheasants *(Phasianus colchicus)* may be reduced to half its size in winter because of shortage of food and shelter aggravated by severe weather. Again, a dense population of musk-rats *(Ondatra zibethica)* may develop in summer only to be reduced later by a reduction in water-level. Here water-level is the critical factor acting in accordance with Liebig's Law. These examples demonstrate that the most critical conditions for survival occur at intervals—in the cases cited, once a year. Thus, there may be definite periods of time in the life of a population in which the most critical controlling factors operate and it is in these critical periods that the population is reduced to minimum.

Hence, for practical purposes we may regard carrying capacity as represented by the minimum number of animals of given species and quality that can in a given ecosystem survive through the least favorable environmental conditions occurring within a stated time interval. For practical purposes this time interval is usually one year. This number of animals is an expression of the interaction of the properties of the species concerned and the total environment in which it lives. There is, of course, a maximum number of animals that can survive in the unit of environment under conditions existing at any given instant which might be called the current carrying capacity, but this does not seem to be as useful a concept as that for carrying capacity as we have defined it.

Perhaps a definition is not important in itself. The really important thing is to recognize that carrying capacity is not a stable property of a unit of environment but the expression of the interaction of the organisms concerned and their environment. Moreover, the carrying capacity of an ecosystem may fluctuate in response to the ebb and flow of interactions going on within it. The concept developed here requires management to determine, within the framework of local conditions, critical factors and periods in which they operate to limit populations, and to direct its energies into channels which will actually affect the operation of these critical factors.

LITERATURE CITED

ALLEE, W. C., A. E. EMERSON, O. PARK, T. PARK, AND K. P. SCHMIDT
    1949. Principles of animal ecology. W. B. Saunders. Philadelphia.
ALLEN, D.
    1954. Our wildlife legacy. Funk & Wagnalls. New York.
CALHOUN, J. B.
    1949. A method for self-control of population growth among animals living in the wild. Science. 190:333-335.
    1950. The study of wild animals under controlled conditions. Ann. N.Y. Acad. Sci., 51:1113-1122.
    1952. The social aspects of population dynamics. Jour. Mamm., 33:139-159.
DASMANN, W.
    1945. A method for estimating carrying capacity of range lands. Jour. For., 43:401-402.
    1948. A critical review of range survey methods and their application to deer range management. Calif. Fish & Game, 34:189-207.
ERRINGTON, P. L. & F. N. HAMERSTROM
    1936. The northern bob-whites' winter territory. Iowa State College Agric. & Mech. Arts, Res. Bull., 201.

FOWLE, C. D.
    1950.   The natural control of deer populations. Proc. 40 Annual Con. Int. Assoc. Game, Fish & Cons. Com. 56-63.

GRAHAM, S. H.
    1944.   The natural principles of land use. Oxford. New York.

HADWEN, S., and L. J. PALMER
    1922.   Reindeer in Alaska. U.S.D.A. Bull. 1089.

HODGDON, K. W. and J. N. HUNT
    1953.   Beaver management in Maine. Maine Dept. of Inland Fisheries & Game. Game Div. Bull. No. 3.

HUBBS, C. L. and R. W. ESCHMEYER
    1938.   The improvement of lakes for fishing. Univ. Mich. Inst. for Fish. Res. Bull. No. 2.

LEOPOLD, A.
    1933.   Game management. Chas. Scribner's Sons. New York.

RÜBEL, E.
    1935.   The replaceability of ecological factors and the law of the minimum. Ecology, 16:336-341.

SOLOMON, M. E.
    1949.   The natural control of animal populations. Jour. Animal Ecol., 18:1-35.

TANSLEY, A. G.
    1935.   The use and abuse of vegetational concepts and terms. Ecol., 16:284-307.

TAYLOR, W. P.
    1934.   Significance of extreme and intermittant conditions in distribution of species and management of natural resources, with a restatement of Liebig's Law of Minimum. Ecology, 15:374-379.

TRIPENNSEE, R. E.
    1948.   Wildlife management. McGraw-Hill. New York.

HABITAT CHRONOLOGY OF THE TOWN OF REMINGTON, WISCONSIN (1948)

Wallace B. Grange

A lifetime in one place is rarely long enough to appreciate the magnitude of land change caused by disturbance and biotic succession. A man's perception of environmental possibilities—of what the land once was, is becoming, or might become under a new land management is thereby limited. Grange beautifully described environmental changes covering 120 years and looked 50 years into the future. Economic and social changes of a growing Wisconsin and a growing nation had altered land use, creating vast changes in vegetation and obligating equally large changes in wildlife populations.

The main purpose which this chronology can serve is to bring home the fact that the fortunes of plants and animals are tossed about by the land uses and abuses of man. In exhibiting the panorama of change which has occurred, in attempting to point out the wildlife effects of these changes, we are close to the basic fundamentals of that game management understanding which such books as this strive to present. This chronology is many times more significant, in terms of management, than are a hundred tables of measurements or a hundred pages of life history studies on grouse. Measurements and life history studies, both of which were undertaken, are necessary. But the real problem which confronts us in game management (and never more formidably than in the management of prairie chickens and sharp-tailed grouse) is the question of land use, which is essentially the problem of controlling the plant covering of the land and thereby gaining control of the animals for which such vegetation is the habitat.

. . . .

The Wilderness Era

1827

At this time, Remington township was pure wilderness, inhabited by a few Indians in the vicinity of the Yellow river.

The peat areas were extensively covered with a fairly open stand of tamarack and some black spruce. The density of the stand varied greatly. Apparently there were numerous bog openings. The prevailing cover type was essentially bog, quite comparable to more northern muskeg, but with a smaller percentage of spruce. Sphagnum was almost universally distributed. Apparently, few tamaracks ever reached large size; most of them were stunted.

The sand islands and ridges were occupied by pineries of varying quality, some excellent, others inferior. The main species were white pine *(Pinus strobus)*, Norway pine *(Pinus resinosa)* and jack pine—the last named probably not abundant. There were also admixtures of soft maple *(Acer saccharinum)*, white birch, aspen, black ash *(Fraxinus nigra)* and a few

Reprinted from: Chapt. 18 *in* Wisconsin Grouse Problems, Pub. 328, Wisc. Dept. Cons., Madison. Literature citations have been omitted.

river birch *(Betula nigra)* near the river. At least one black ash swamp seems to have existed. On the best islands there were, also, both red and white oaks. How extensive it is impossible to say. In general, the small non-coniferous growth was limited to the juncture of bog and island. The prevailing condition of the uplands was pinery.

These conclusions as to original cover types are drawn from the field notes of government surveyors, who surveyed the township in 1857, and from stump evidence.

Standing water covered parts of the bog in spring but disappeared as the summer progressed.

Grouse: It is believed that ruffed grouse were present in small numbers; that spruce grouse were present and possibly fairly abundant. The latter conclusion is based upon habitat considerations; there is no record of the spruce grouse in the county. Prairie chickens definitely were not present. Sharp-tails may have been present. They probably were found at least within a few miles to the east, in openings created by the "annual Indian fires" mentioned by surveyors. It is believed that two species of grouse were present, possibly three.

Other Game: Deer, if present at all, must have been rare. There were bear *(Ursus americana),* lynx *(Lynx canadensis),* bobcat *(Lynx rufus),* porcupine *(Erithizon dorsatum)* and snowshoe rabbits, but no cottontails.

1852

First lands opened for settlement through land office at Mineral Point. Entry and settlement along the nearby Wisconsin river began almost at once.

1853

First land entry in present town of Remington east of the Yellow river by Daniel S. Ward in Section 27. Further entries in each subsequent year, a total of eight having been recorded through the year 1856. All of these were in Sections 22, 23 and 27, except for one in Section I.

1858

John W. King, in this year, took up portions of Sections 25 and 26 in what is now West Remington.

About this time H. W. Remington, then of Madison, is believed to have settled in Section 10, West Remington, along the west bank of the Yellow river. Local oldtimers believe that his was the first actual settlement west of the river, thus probably predating King, whose entry was in 1858.

Jones, McVean and others (1923) state that H. W. Remington experienced a perfect avalanche of misfortunes in 1857 and that shortly after his misfortunes Mr. Remington had moved into the cranberry marshes in the southwestern portion of Wood county, believing in their future value, and had made his home there, isolated from all appearance of civilization, but with the passing of the years a settlement grew up about him, and the surrounding township was named after him.

The site of his settlement is well known and the cranberry marshes lay to the west.

It is a moot question whether fire had occurred recently in this western marsh-bog country or whether the tamarack bog openings were caused solely by high water table. It is the author's guess that fire had already occurred. In any event, it appears that openings were common in the fifties. There is no reason to suppose that sharp-tails or ruffed grouse were not then present.

Some land clearing, cutting of timber for home consumption, splitting of shingles, harvest of cranberries and other activities were in progress by the close of the fifties

1864

Widespread fires were reported along the Black and Wisconsin rivers. Whether they entered the Remington country is unknown. If they did, they apparently did not burn the peat, merely removing some tamarack and spruce growth.

One land entry, by Louis S. Rustad, in Section 24.

1868

The town of Remington was organized on July 15, "at the store of McGlynn and Kruger near the residence of H. W. Remington" (Section 10). Since 1858 Remington had been a part of the town of Dexter.

According to Jones, McVean and others (1923), "at an early date, probably in the later sixties, a settlement called Remington was started on the west side of the Yellow river, opposite the present site of Babcock, and a little store was conducted there." This settlement was within Section 15, and hence within the present boundaries of the Wood County Public Hunting Grounds.

It can be assumed that this stage of settlement resulted in occasional fires from land clearing operations or carelessness, and that some land by now was under the plow.

1871

Land entries by George Hiles (Section 22) and by Eliphalet S. Miner (Sections 22-23).

The great passenger pigeon *(Ectopistes migratorius)* nesting of 1871 (Schorger 1937) had its northermost tip about a dozen miles to the east in present Wood county. At this time the Remington country commonly had many wild pigeons, at least as passing clouds, and very probably in all of the new clearings, as well as in the oaks (for acorns), the pines (for mast) and for all we know in the marshes for cranberries. It is an interesting speculation that the pigeons may have used the cranberry, a food eaten by virtually all game species.

The Settlement and Wiregrass Era

1872

Land entry by Henry Hamilton (Sections 26-28).

1873

The Chicago, Milwaukee and St. Paul Railroad ran its first trains through the settlement of Babcock which was by then relocated to the east of the Yellow river, the settlement of Remington thus dying. The railroad built a large hotel and a roundhouse and the settlement assumed considerable local importance, becoming division headquarters for the road, "and started trains from this place".

Jones, et al. (1923) likewise state that the heaviest settlement in east Remington (east of the river) occurred from 1870 to 1900.

1874-1880

This apparently was the period of first commercial development of wild cranberry marshes in the township by James Joy and William H. Bowden. One substantial dike with flood gates was constructed about this time. The main purpose was apparently to assure a supply of water as protection from frost. Numerous small planted marshes, using wild vines, were established before 1900, probably beginning in the seventies.

It is the author's judgment that the country was still solely a sharp-tail, ruffed grouse and spruce grouse range at this period.

1881-1885

Lumbering operations were in full swing on the higher land. Excellent pine spars were shipped from Meadow Valley (a few miles south of Remington township) and some may have been obtained from Remington. Records of the Jamieson Lumber Company, Poynette, Wisconsin provide this information.

At about this period prairie chickens are believed to have first invaded the area.

1893-1900

A disastrous fire swept much of the Remington country, destroying many of the cranberry marshes (most of which were never rebuilt) and eliminating most of the remaining tamarack and spruce in the bogs. There is some uncertainty as to whether a fire also occurred in 1892. The 1893 fire unquestionably burned into the peat, probably for the first time. If spruce grouse were previously present they apparently were extirpated by this fire.

Following the 1893 fire the country became predominantly open, with long vistas and with few woodlands except on the islands, which grew into pine and oak, both usually scattered. Blueberries were abundant on the islands. From this time on the two prairie grouse were abundant. According to local remembrance the proportions definitely favored chickens. As an aftermath of the fire, some settlers planted grains, clover and timothy *(Phleum pratense)* upon the peat ashes, producing rather spectacular crops. Success with farm crops gave first impetus to the later drainage programs.

A few cranberry beds were apparently re-established but seem to have failed.

The character of former sphagnum-tamarack bog country changed remarkably. Wiregrass *(Spartina pectinata)* developed extensive stands which were then cut for commercial manufacture of carpets. Much of this harvest was in late fall or winter. Until the ground became frozen it was necessary to "clog" the horses with large wooden or iron shoes. Scores of men were employed in this harvest.

This was a period of frequent and widespread fires. One wiregrass operator deliberately encouraged and set such fires. According to a local resident, this man traveled about in his horse and rig and "wherever you saw him go, a little later you would see the smoke roll up". Without much doubt, this was sound land management from the wiregrass production standpoint. It also had a direct and beneficial effect, in the long run, upon the prairie grouse populations.

364

1900

The first drainage boom was in the making. Promotion and organization proceeded.

1902

First drainage ditch dug in Remington. Before the boom ran its course some sixty or more miles of open ditch had been dug, profoundly and permanently altering the whole ecology of the territory. The ditches were dug with "floaters", which navigated the ditches, and with "walkers", which could travel laboriously overland.

Immediately on the heels of the dredges came the settlers.

1908

Deer were very scarce, but this was not a new condition. A party of nine hunted for two weeks from South Bluff to North Bluff and throughout the western territory but saw only one deer. (E. A. Van Wormer) This is in the same territory which, in the 1940's, has perhaps the greatest abundance of deer in Wisconsin.

1910

Drainage and settlement were in full sway. The country was being rapidly opened up. There were many new farms, roads, schools. The cropland expansion was great. Buckwheat, corn, hay, oats and rye were leading crops. Dairy cattle increased. Conditions for chickens and sharptails were nearly perfect. The ratio between species was "several chickens to every grouse" (sharp-tail). Ruffed grouse were not abundant, but occurred on the oak islands if undergrowth was sufficiently dense.

The fire of 1910 covered large acreages of wild land.

A rank growth of weeds was characteristic of most cultivated fields and of some fire-swept land. Among these, smartweed was noteworthy.

1912

By this year it was apparent that some of the drainage ditches were inadequate. Many farm fields were subject to flood. In numerous instances flooding prevented harvest of such crops as buckwheat, with the result that much wasted grain was left to the prairie chickens. The agricultural picture had by now developed some rough spots. The cure was thought to be deeper and better ditches, hence some re-dredging occurred which cut through the underlying rock cores of ridges in some cases. Drainage was thereby accelerated.

1919 or 1920

The drainage boom ran its course, the last ditches for agricultural purposes being dug in one of these years.

The tamarack and spruce, largely eliminated in 1893, were further subjected to drainage, fire and flood as the result of dredging. Wiregrass disappeared with the stagnated water which the ditches freed. It was replaced by farm weeds, goldenrod, bluejoint grass, wool grass, various sedges, willow and an increasing quantity of quaking aspen and white birch. Fires were frequent and often very patchy in this period. Considerable development of brush seems to have occurred on some islands, but for the most part fire kept the lower land and much higher ground from regenerating forest. Blackberries and blueberries were plentiful. At one time (exact dates unknown) many carloads of wild blueberries were shipped from nearby Mather and from Babcock.

This was a golden era for prairie chickens, which were still said to out-number sharp-tails.

The fire of 1920 covered a large part of western Remington and re-sulted in destruction of haystacks, buildings, etc.

In the year 1947 deer quickly jump out of sight in the protective shield of dense aspen woods (in which many trees now approach 35-45 foot heights); bitterns pump from the cattail-sedge marshes; teal and mallards nest along the ditch banks and in fall there are diving ducks on the open water flowages. It is difficult to look back and see accurately the enormous changes the years have wrought. To many persons the country has always existed as it is today. They have no conception of the transitions along the way. It is wild country, uninhabited, without farms except for a narrow belt along the Yellow river, for a rare straggler and for a few cranberry marshes. There are no cultivated fields. It is hard for many people to visu-alize the situation back in 1910, 1920 or even 1930.

In the heyday of agricultural development in this area some thousands of acres were planted to grains, hay and pasture crops. There were abun-dant weed supplies, clover for greens, grain gleanings at all seasons, well interspersed between wild hay meadows which the farmers assiduously cleared of tamarack stumps and mowed regularly. In addition, there were islands producing unbelievable yields of blueberries, plus small acreages in shrubbery and very young aspen, birch and oak, plus fire-swept open oak woods on the knolls and ridges with splendid crops of acorns, plus bluegrass and clover seeded pastures where open-loving birds prospered. There were grasshoppers aplenty and in winter adequate quantities of birch, aspen, cherry and hazelnut browse.

There was no lack of nesting cover in the stumpy fields in new pas-turelands and best of all along the newly made ditch spoils banks, forming untillable types of waste cover which came quickly in to grass, berries, sweet fern and other open-loving species of plants. In this golden prairie grouse era the country provided every element of bountiful food and limit-less cover which any covey could desire.

The woodlands were not then infested with foxes and coyotes or with numerous great horned owls, for the small amount of wooded cover was scattered. A few of these predators existed, but not in their present num-bers.

The general open condition, largely the result of widespread and fre-quent fire, passes present understanding or belief except to those few who saw and knew the Remington country in those days, or who are willing to piece together the story from the oldtimers. The writer has many times shown people an expanse of half killed, flooded aspen (a tract seemingly impenetrable because of the soft peaty bottom and the tangle of willows and sedges) saying, "there used to be a field of corn out there", only to note amazement and at first disbelief. The tile is still there in the muck, and long time residents are quick to tell of the corn, buckwheat and timothy they themselves saw grown on that very site. The author has been shown the old wiregrass marshes and knows where one of the ancient wiregrass mowers now stands half submerged in a recent flowage among water killed aspens. It is not easy to decipher all of the changes which have occurred, nor are the blocks of the picture puzzle easily assembled in retrospect.

The record, nevertheless, is as clear as the water of the streams which once rose back in the pineries to the northward, if one can read history, surveyors' notes, stumps, the tales told by long forgotten cement basements out in the brush and the stories of those persons still living who remember.

To read this record is to understand some of the reasons for the decline of prairie chickens in the area chosen for the grouse project's special studies. In this chronology, we pause back in the mid tens and early twenties of the century to look across the open vistas, hear the cries of sandhill cranes, experience the spring sound of thousands of cock chickens booming from all directions and watch school children on their way home along the narrow sand roads to do their chores. There is the tolling of school bells, the neighing of horses, the rare sputtering of a "Model T" and the barking of farm dogs. In winter there are sleighbells, while the farm teams jog along to town past fields of corn in the shock or alongside buckwheat which was nipped by the frost and abandoned. Wherever we pause in those days we are not far from the sight or sound of prairie chickens and of the rarer sharp-tailed grouse.

The Modern Era

1920

The fire of 1920 over-ran the Remington country, largely choosing its own course, unhindered except as farmers plowed around haystacks and buildings.

The agricultural depression of this and the next years spelled the doom of a country already beset by excessive taxes to pay for the drainage which often was over-drainage resulting in drought. Frost, flood, drought, fire, taxes and depression, in combination, forced abandonment of the farms, many of which were left forever to whatever fate might befall them. A peculiarity of the bonding system made each individual land parcel subject to the entire indebtedness of a whole drainage district so that no farmer, however diligent or successful, could escape from the perpetual drainage assessments.

The drainage tax rate was far beyond the productive capacity of the land. The sandy soils were subject to severe wind erosion and the peat to exhaustion of some chemicals essential to plant growth. With no adequate program of erosion control and fertilizing, any but the most skillful farmers were quickly put to rout. Those who learned the nature of the country and who depended upon livestock rather than upon grain survived for some time. Eventually, one by one, they too lost the struggle into which they had put life, funds and happiness. Many of them lost everything, and the bondholders or the drainage district officers in most instances did not benefit. It can be quite truly said that the only ones who made well financially in the whole agricultural venture were the dredge contractors who worked by the mile or the yard.

It is often said, unthinkingly in these days, that the agricultural venture in Remington (as in many other localities) was a promotional scheme through which any prudent citizen should have seen instantly. This is most unjust. Some seemingly comparable tracts were successfully settled and are today fine farms. Drainage projects were not universally failures as anyone can see in a drive through southern Wisconsin, Illinois, parts of Iowa, Ohio and elsewhere in the mid-west. The University of Wisconsin issued a bulletin *"Drainage District Farms in Central Wisconsin,"* (Jones and Packer, 1923), which was encouraging enough to prospective settlers. Most of the zealots who sought to make this a fine agricultural community were sincere, hard-headed and by no means fools. They failed, and by not too wide a margin, for under modern methods and without drainage taxes some of these lands could still be profitably operated.

1925

By this year abandonment was the rule, with only a few surviving farms left. Deserted buildings, where not burned up in the frequent fires, loomed up in the no man's land which none could claim, since the owners had abandoned the property and no new ownership was feasible due to the impossible accumulation of drainage and real estate taxes. An interval of years occurred here during which this was a deserted, ruined country, bankrupt beyond reclamation and visited mainly by those seeking salvage from the buildings, and by hunters.

The character of the country was again changing, especially in the rank growth of aspen, birch, cherry and oak on drier sites, and of wool grass, willow, hardhack and similar plants on the lowlands. Many of the wild hay meadows developed dense stands of bluejoint which went unmowed. The surviving farmers pastured large herds of cattle more or less generally over this unclaimed domain.

1929

The Jones-Van Wormer grouse food patches were instituted. Species ratios are unknown, but sharp-tailed grouse were now plentiful and may in some places have been first in rank.

1930

In September and October the most extensive fire occurred that central Wisconsin has ever known. The total acreage burned in this one fire was roughly 500 square miles, or in excess of 300,000 acres. The fire covered all parts of the West Remington territory as far as the Yellow river bottoms, except where it was locally put out in protection of property. During the days when it gained initial headway, the conservation department, although notified of the fire and requested to help, took no action. As the fire spread, some measures were taken to halt it. There was at that time no effective system of fire suppression in the area and no field organization to speak of.

This fire was unlike previous fires. It ate enormous holes in the peat, sometimes acres in extent and often 18 inches to 3 feet deep. Relatively few peat acres escaped heavy burning, although some, especially to the north, were but lightly touched. The sand islands were denuded of their humus and top soil in the majority of cases, although again some were spared this injury.

FIG. 38-1.—I. F. J. W. Schmidt, a former grouse investigator, looks over the 1930 burn in Wood county.

In company with Franklin Schmidt, the author saw much of this country at the time it was still smouldering, and in succeeding years. Thousands of acres of raw peat were exposed, black, bare and without living vegetation in the fall of 1930. The sand islands were generally devoid of good cover so that ruffed grouse were not numerous and were concentrated at remnant clumps of trees and groves. Many sharp-tails, some chickens and numerous deer were consumed by the flames of the fire, while other deer were shot by game wardens who found the suffering animals stump-legged after attempting to cross burning peat on their accustomed trails. Fish died in the ditches from the heat and possibly from the effect of the ashes. Many sizeable pickerel *(Esox lucius)* floated belly up, rotting.

FIG. 38-2.—II. The birth of an aspen forest on the 1930 burn.

FIG. 38-3.—III. Close-up of newly-seeded aspen, Wood county, 1931.

FIG. 38-4.—IV. "Closing in" of aspen on this tract occurred five years after fire. This is ruffed grouse habitat and an exclusion area for prairie chickens and sharp-tails.

FIG. 38-5.—V. The aspen forest has now thinned out. It is in good condition for ruffed grouse.

The fire of 1930 accomplished a more rapid transformation of the country than had any one previous factor. It succeeded in obliterating many of the traces of the recent agricultural settlement, burning houses, barns, silos, bridges, even roads and in some cases the peaty spoils banks themselves.

1931

During the first growing season following the fire some peat flats came directly to quaking aspen, noted in this year as seedlings, some of which reached a height of two or more feet within the season. Other peat areas remained bare.

Usually where farms had once existed there was immediate production of enormous quantities of weeds. Of these the smartweeds were most important, richly abundant and highly productive of seed. Ragweed, pigweed *(Chenopodium)* and all other common farm weeds also volunteered. Bluegrass and quack grass began to cover some of the ditch banks and were densely sodded in old pastures.

Meantime, in the previous year while the land was still smoking, there was held the first drainage sale, the Supreme Court having ruled that sale of the land for real estate taxes would forever wipe out the drainage taxes and other liens, thus opening the way for private ownership. Except for one case of purchase for game purposes, there was a poverty of interest in such ownership.

1932

The open grouse season produced one of the heaviest central Wisconsin kills on record (123,012 birds for the state). The Remington territory provided excellent hunting, for both chickens and sharp-tails made a very quick comeback after the fire. Much of the breeding stock was not wiped out by the fire. Sharp-tails were reported about as numerous as chickens. Revegetation of the burned lands was now visually rapid. The weed growths continued. Some peat acreage was still bare, some came slowly to a carpet of moss (not sphagnum) while the aspen grew very rapidly. The sand islands began to put on shrub growth. Many of the larger oak survivors of the fire produced acorns. Cottontail rabbits were extremely plentiful, almost unlimited in number, with few natural enemies and surrounded with a food supply of high quality. Snowshoe rabbits were a rarity.

The first flooding of the old marsh country was done in this year by E. A. Van Wormer and Franklin Schmidt, with funds raised by Haskell Noyes and associates of Milwaukee. This was an earth plug (a sand dam thrown across a drainage ditch) in Section 10, West Remington, in what is now the Wood County Public Hunting Grounds.

1933

The growth of young aspen by now was spectacular. At a distance, the aspen looked like vast cornfields.

The weed growth was diminishing. A greater percentage of grass now became evident.

Sharp-tails and chickens and ruffed grouse all remained numerous—the latter invading islands which held good shrub growth.

1934

The state food patch program ended, although Schmidt maintained a few stations. It is not known whether any remained in Remington.

The Civilian Works Administration undertook a program of firebreak, road and dike construction.

1935

The firebreaks and roads built in 1934 were thickly covered with solid masses of smartweeds and other farm weeds. Elsewhere, weed supplies were becoming deficient.

The U. S. Resettlement Administration undertook a central Wisconsin program of buyng out and eliminating farms. Much of their program affected Juneau, Jackson and Monroe counties, but three or more units were purchased in Wood county, of which two were in Remington. However, the farmers were permitted to stay on temporarily.

The state constructed a number of concrete dams across drainage ditches in Remington (and elsewhere), allegedly "in aid of agriculture", although everyone knew the work was for ducks. This work was financed largely through federal relief funds.

The Civilian Conservation Corps entered the Remington picture and began to build additional firebreaks, trails, roads and dikes.

A heavy kill of ducks was taken in the Remington territory. A combination of shallow water behind dams and dikes and the fire-made potholes together with enormous quantities of smartweed seed on the bottom was irresistible.

1936

On one of the CWA firebreaks the writer flushed 7 coveys of bobwhite in less than 2 miles; all feeding upon the plentiful smartweeds and other weeds. The numbers of sharp-tails and prairie chickens apparently declined but not below the plentiful level. Cottontails were on the downtrend.

The Civilian Conservation Corps established a few game food patches in the Remington area.

Deer became decidedly numerous with the increase of brush. Only a few deer, however, wintered in the area and in but one or two localities.

1937

The shift from chickens to sharp-tails had now taken place in at least part of the Remington area (based on kill recollections of hunters). Whether sharp-tails actually were more numerous is unknown; both were present and plentiful, but below their former high point. Ruffed grouse were increasingly common, despite the low of the cycle.

Sandhill Game Farm was established and fenced; a venture seeking to produce wild game on large natural acreage rather than in pens. It embraced about 7 square miles of the Remington country and some in adjoining townships.

The first controlled burning for game in Wisconsin was conducted on that area in April, 1937 by the author. This was for the control of excess vegetation in an area designated for grouse.

1938

The first extensive wintering of deer in Remington since the 1930 fire occurred in the winter of 1937-38, due to the profuse growth of brush.

Closing in of some aspen acreage occurred in 1937 or 1938.

Farm weeds had almost disappeared, except along roads.

The C. C. C. program of road, dike, dam and firebreak construction continued.

1939

A season on grouse was successful. The kill of sharp-tails and chickens was possibly one half that of 1932. Many ruffed grouse were taken, the species having literally mushroomed upwardly.

The waterfowl kill was likewise high.

The C. C. C. began a program of winter servicing of feeding stations for grouse, pheasants, quail and other upland birds.

Deer continued to increase.

The Wood County Public Hunting Grounds was established under joint county and state auspices.

Two remaining farms in the West Remington territory were liquidated, thus extinguishing almost all cultivation in the area except that by public agencies. Some food patches were put in by the C. C. C.

The loss of normal farm acreage is not easily offset by the provision of food patches, for each operating farm provides a year round program of some use to game. Pasturing, hauling of manure to the fields, cultivation at different seasons, mowing of wild meadows and other activities which affect from forty to one hundred acres annually is not compensated by planting buckwheat patches totalling a few acres. This year virtually marked the end of the settlement era in territory remote from the Yellow river, so far as ordinary agriculture is concerned.

1940

The open season on grouse produced a heavy kill of ruffed grouse and a much reduced kill of sharp-tails and chickens. The kill ratio was several sharp-tails per chicken. A large kill of deer was also taken. Hunting pressure had increased tremendously.

Much closing in of aspen growth occurred, resulting in some loss of range for sharp-tails. Extensive acres of aspen and of flowage were now unproductive for sharp-tails or chickens.

Project FA-5R Grouse was established. Work began in September.

1941

Another very heavy kill of ruffed grouse, but an unsatisfactory bag of sharp-tails and a very small bag of chickens was made.

The grouse project secured the use of part of the Wood County Public Hunting Grounds as an experimental area but with no regulation of hunting. Several miles of tractor-broken food strips were planted.

A considerable winter feeding program was conducted by the C. C. C., sportsmen's clubs, wardens and others.

The deer kill continued to rise annually. Deer were more and more plentiful.

The water areas created by dams and dikes played host to a white pelican *(Pelecanus erythrorhynchos)*, cormorants *(Phalacrocorax auritus)*, blue geese *(Chen caerulescens),* snow geese *(Chen hyperborea)* and Canada geese *(Branta canadensis),* egrets *(Casmerodius albus egretta)* and many ducks. A substantial muskrat harvest was taken.

1942

Forest reversion had now reached a stage where a very large exclusion area of aspen contained no sharp-tails or prairie chickens. The whole character of the country had become predominantly forest. Many aspen growths were closed at the top and were nearly barren of shrubbery below.

1943

In the winter of 1942-43 the first deer starvation occurred in the Remington country. An estimated 200 deer starved in the vicinity of South Bluff. The continued rapid increase in deer numbers combined with the rapidly shrinking acreage of good browse due to forest growth, resulted in insufficient food during the deep snow period of February-March, 1943.

The grouse trend was downward.

1946

Many booming-hooting grounds occupied in 1941 and 1942 were deserted. The population of sharp-tails and chickens was at the lowest ebb since settlement. Ruffed grouse, likewise, were extremely scarce.

The first controlled burning on the public hunting grounds was begun by Fred Benson, mainly on ditch banks and in marshes.

1947

A possible increase in prairie chickens occurred. Both species of prairie grouse remained at very low levels. Ruffed grouse showed a substantial pick-up from the previous year.

The deer herd appeared by spring to have multiplied beyond any previous record, despite the heavy illegal kill of does and fawns in 1946.

As of the summer of 1947, there are three cranberry marshes, one natural game farm and one ordinary farm in the West Remington area. Along the Yellow river are a number of other farms, but these lie largely outside the present ranges of either prairie grouse and are devoid of either sharp-tails or chickens so far as known. Most of the area is uninhabited by man, but is heavily used for hunting, trapping and to some extent for fishing.

Almost all sharp-tail and prairie chicken use is now limited to the vicinity of old farms, to the cranberry marshes, roadsides and to a few sterile uplands upon which vegetation growth has been unusually slow. Some of the sand islands exhibit a vegetative succession which may require from 20 to 40 years from denudation by fire to dense forest, and hence may potentially constitute suitable prairie grouse cover for another 3 to 23 years. In most cases such islands grow up to hazelnut, willow, cherry, birch and similar woody plants, often losing attractiveness to prairie grouse within a few years, depending upon density, even though not typically forested. Some old fields have been taken over by trees and shrubs but several are still in grass stage, partly due to various food patch planting programs.

Marshlands are now little used by either chickens or sharp-tails except where wild hay mowing has been practiced within the last years.

The area can no longer be considered favorable prairie chicken or sharp-tail habitat. It is now marginal, of steadily declining value and on the threshold of disappearance as prairie grouse range. On the other hand, it is excellent for ruffed grouse, which population should reach an unprecedented peak in the 1951-1953 period.

These changes have increased in rapidity since about 1937 and with greater acceleration since 1940.

In the absence of good grouse management, including the intelligent use of fire, the preservation of openings, the institution of some cultivation of crops and the probable necessity of evolving some method of preserving an adequate seed stock of birds under heavy mass hunting pressure, the future outlook for prairie chickens and sharp-tails in this studied area is extremely bleak.

The future course of events in the absence of management can be seen as follows:

The Future Era

1950-1953

Occurrence of the last real peak of chickens and sharp-tails in West Remington. The peak will be less than half that of the previous decade; possibly much smaller.

1956-1960

The low ebb of the cycle reduces both prairie grouse to the rare or uncommon bird level in this territory. From this low they never recover substantial numbers and are never again (at least justifiably) on the hunted open season list. The peak of the small game cycle in the sixties sees a decreased number of ruffed grouse, but this species is nevertheless abundant and remains so indefinitely, subject to the cyclic fluctuations. Deer are similarly decreased, but still abundant. People talk fondly of the "good old days" in the forties when deer were everywhere. The decline is generally attributed to the year or years when a one deer season was instituted.

1975

The prairie chicken, if found at all in the western part of the township is a rare bird. The sharp-tail still persists around cranberry marshes, but in numbers below the hunting level. Ruffed grouse are now the only common grouse.

Logging is again of real importance, the township gradually having assumed a typical forest region economy, aside from farms and increased recreational use. This latter may be due to effective control of the mosquito nuisance, the development of water areas for better fishing, and scenery.

The deer herd is by now under some semblance of management and may again show increase due to logging operations. Snowshoe rabbits are common, cottontails rare; lynx and wildcats are regular residents as are also black bear (all three species absent in 1947), while the porcupine is a numerous mammal after its long absence from about 1893 to about 1960.

It is possible that conditions may now justify the liberation of a few spruce grouse.

2000

Sometime between 1960 and 2000, prairie chickens and sharp-tails became extinct in the town of Remington. The prairie chicken may be an extinct species, remembered only by oldtimers and in the literature, at least so far as Wisconsin occurrence is concerned and quite possibly throughout its range.

Sharp-tails are not in danger of extinction. They are very abundant in some sections of Canada and Alaska which have recently been opened up by settlement, but in Wisconsin have reached the rare bird stage throughout all counties. Their occurrence is limited almost solely to sphagnum bogs not yet reforested with spruce. Few such openings remain.

FIRE AND THE DECLINE OF A MOUNTAIN CARIBOU HERD (1954)

R. Y. Edwards

While disturbance is necessary to maintain habitat needed by species adapted to developmental stages of vegetation, disturbance may destroy the habitat of species adapted to climax vegetation. Caribou are climax-adapted animals. Logging, fire and land-clearing have caused their extirpation from the northeastern and north-central United States and from much of southern Canada.

The mountain caribou *(Rangifer arcticus)* has decreased alarmingly throughout most of British Columbia. From the Kootenays in the southeast corner of the province to the Cassiar region in the north-west reports are much the same except that there is variation as to when the declines first occurred. Banfield (1949) has noted this condition in his treatment of the status of caribou in America.

Two features have characterized this decline. It has progressed from south to north, beginning in the south shortly after 1900 (Munro, 1947). In central British Columbia it began in the 1930's. The decline in the north appears to be quite recent but information from this wilderness is not detailed. Secondly, the decline has not wiped out most bands for which there is information. Apparently few caribou ranges have had their herds completely eliminated.

Many causes have been suggested for this decline, the most frequently heard being wolves, hunters including Indians, and moose which are said to be incompatible with caribou. None of these suggestions withstands careful scrutiny. Declines have occurred in wolf-free areas. The spectacular increase of moose throughout central British Columbia since 1920 has undoubtedly reduced hunting pressure upon caribou. Finally, every story of moose-caribou incompatibility, when examined, is based upon the caribou decline being concurrent with the moose increase, and not upon observation of the two species together in the field.

One of the decreased caribou herds inhabits Wells Gray Park (Lat. 52°N, Long. 120°W) in the Cariboo Mountains of British Columbia. For four years wildlife investigations in this park have gathered information on this herd, but it is difficult to study both from its wandering habits and the rough country that is its range. The data gathered are fragmentary but are sufficient to form a general history of the herd when combined with information obtained from homesteaders who have lived near the herd for many years.

Description of Area

The northern half of Wells Gray Park consists of rugged mountains up to 8000 feet high, with permanent snowfields and large glaciers covering extensive areas. Southward the country becomes less precipitous with more foothill topography and occasional isolated peaks. The whole area is

Reprinted from: J. Wildl. Mgmt. 18(4):521-526.

drained by the swift Clearwater River, flowing through a broad valley having sides oversteepened by glaciation. The headwaters of this drainage contain several large lakes which are opaque with glacial silt. These tend to be long, narrow and crowded by mountains.

The pattern of vegetation in the park is complex, due to variations in altitude, a longitudinal gradient in precipitation, and results of extensive fires. Before fires denuded many of the lowest elevations most of the valley floor and adjacent lower slopes were clothed in a mature coniferous forest of red cedar *(Thuja plicata)*, western hemlock *(Tsuga heterophylla)*, Engelmann spruce *(Picea engelmannii)*, and alpine fir *(Abies lasiocarpa)*. This is the Columbia Forest of Halliday (1937).

In dry areas with southern exposure in the southern part of the park, the humid forest was replaced by one of Douglas fir *(Pseudotsuga menziesii)* with grassy openings. This fir forest occurred mainly on exposed sites below 2500 feet.

At about 4000 feet, the Columbia Forest gave way to a sub-alpine forest of Engelmann spruce and alpine fir which became increasingly open and stunted with elevation. At about 7000 feet, openings enlarged to meadows. These tended to be of three kinds: thick mats of grasses and sedges, mats of heathers *(Cassiope* spp., *Phyllodoce* spp.), and lush growths of herbs such as false hellebore *(Veratrum viride)*, lupines *(Lupinus* spp.), anemone *(Anemone occidentalis)*, and Indian paintbrushes *(Castilleja* spp.). Rock lichens *(Cladonia* spp. and others) were not common above timberline although both the sub-alpine and Columbia forests at all elevations were hung abundantly with "tree moss" *(Alectoria sarmentosa* and perhaps other species) resembling *Usnea*.

Thus was the southern part of the park prior to 1926. Most of the lowland was in mature forest except where lightning fires of small size had created seral forests of various ages.

In 1926 a fire started in the dry Douglas fir forest to the south of the park, swept north up the Clearwater Valley with explosive intensity, and completely denuded some 200 square miles of forested land. It missed few lowland areas as it removed humus from the soil and even completely burned boles of mature trees over large areas. While it completely denuded most of the lowest elevations in the park, it did not make much headway in the sub-alpine forests on higher slopes. More recent smaller fires have enlarged the burnt area and reburned parts of the old burn.

Now, 27 years after the major fire, the lowlands are grown principally to open stands of willow, aspen, and birch in a poor, sandy soil generally with sparce herbaceous vegetation. Coniferous regeneration is evident mainly near the few unburnt coniferous stands, although isolated pioneers are scattered thinly throughout, mainly as young trees less than ten feet high.

In all, 60 per cent of the vegetation below 4000 feet has been reduced from climax forest to an early seral stage. Fire has drastically changed the vegetation of the valley. Catastrophic change in the ecology of the area is an inevitable result.

Fire and the Larger Mammals

Reliable local knowledge and study of present conditions provide a general history of the larger and better known mammals in and about the valley through the past thirty years. It is a history of change in mammalian populations concurrent with fire, and no less abrupt than the change of the land itself from dark forests deep in mosses and lichens to bare soils baking in the sun.

Mule deer and caribou were the main ungulates in the timbered valley. A small deer population wintered in warm canyons to the south among Douglas firs and dispersed in summer to open meadows above timberline or to small patches of young forest healing recent lowland burns. Deer avoided heavy forest except in travelling through it. A few goats occurred as outpost populations from larger herds in more rugged terrain to the north. Cougars and coyotes inhabited open areas used as winter range by deer, and coyotes, like deer, climbed to lush meadows in summer where mice were numerous and travelling was easy. Marten were common throughout the dense forests. Beaver and other fine fur species were well distributed. Wolverine ranged alpine meadows in summer and timbered lowlands in winter. Black bears were found sparingly throughout the lowlands, and grizzlies roamed in the high country, descending into the valley in spring. The whole scene was one that had been long established, with that evidence of permanence that has led to the concept of climax.

The fire that followed was catastrophic. In a few hours its destruction changed the scene in the valley from one of intricate complexity to one of relative simplicity. The changes that it wrought would fill volumes if all were known. Chemistry, structure, fauna and flora of the soil, vegetation with its dependent animal life, the very climate of the place were abruptly changed in a sudden fury of destruction. A tangled, wet forest penetrated only by miserable trails became a desert-like area where a horse could roam almost at will.

For a few years, the habitat was desolate, with some deer mice scurrying in the ashes and a few deer wandering among charred forest remains. Fireweed and willow began to heal the land in an environment suddenly suitable for them. Slowly the land that had been like a desert changed to one supporting an abundant growth of willow, birch and aspen. The new vegetation created a new world for mammals. The fire that had destroyed a rich vegetation with a varied mammalian community in which few species were abundant made new and extensive range for a number of species. The fire had totally removed the marten for decades, in destroying the dark forest. It had restricted the lowland wandering of wolverine and grizzly bear. At the same time it created new habitat for others. There was a spectacular increase in mule deer which almost swarmed in abundant browse. Dozens could be seen in a day where they were formerly infrequent wanderers in deep forest. Cougars became so common that one hunter took eighteen in one season where a few years previous it was unusual to see tracks. Coyotes suddenly flourished in this new, prairie-like valley where deer mice had increased and Columbia ground squirrels were abundant where previously unknown. Beaver found new food abundance and increased. Black bears found berries and other foods abundant as they never had been. Goats, among the few species whose ranges were mainly above the fires, were affected but little.

Moose were unknown in this valley before the fires. Wanderers colonized the valley in the early 1930's and increased until the winter of 1945, when homesteaders watched moose browsing close by and children on their way to school dodged them. Moose found extensive winter range in the hundreds of square miles of browse, and summered in the damp subalpine forests at and below timberline.

With the establishment and increase of moose, wolves increased markedly from a previously low population density. The new mammalian abundance probably figured strongly in this and other increases in mammalian predators of the valley.

Today the situation is only slightly changed. Shrubbery is older and higher, and the ground is not quite so bare. Young conifers are slowly repopulating the burn but are still absent from large areas. Deer are not so abundant, nor are cougars and coyotes, but moose in hundreds still wander down from the mountains to the lowland in autumn. Mice and ground squirrels are still abundant. The former are a major factor in arresting coniferous reinvasion, for they are efficient gatherers of tree seed.

The Caribou Decline

Through this time of change the caribou survived but their numbers were markedly reduced. In 1937, Game Department reports expressed concern over the future of the Clearwater caribou, and in 1940 hunting them became illegal.

The ranges inhabited by these caribou comprise the less precipitous foothill country bordering the mountains. The extensive meadows on the rounded foothill elevations seem better suited to this species than do precipitous slopes and permanent ice of the core of the Cariboo Mountains. The wide, heavily forested Clearwater Valley lay among and below these extensive alplands, and the caribou, following traditional trails through the forest, crossed regularly from one alpland to the other.

In summer and fall caribou were found in high meadows and in adjacent sub-alpine forests that were open and festooned with lichens. In winter and early spring they were usually encountered in valley bottoms in mature forests of cedar, spruce, hemlock and balsam. In these lowlands they seemed to favour the flat, poorly drained areas that were interspersed with open bogs, meadows and ponds, as well as those forests that were near the open ice of lakes. However, their altitudinal distribution was probably not quite as simple as this. At times during the winter they climbed to the high, wind-swept ridges of their summer haunts. This altitudinal movement, as in most such migrations of ungulates in mountainous terrain, was probably controlled by snow. According to several careful observers of this herd, the first deep snow of winter forces caribou down, just as it does elk, moose, deer, and in some areas mountain goats, throughout much of western America. If snows settle and harden the caribou travel the high country in mid-winter. Spring thaws which soften the snow drive them into poorly insolated lowland forests again, from which they move into snow-free alplands in May and June, there to spend much of the summer.

These caribou were forced to live in dense, lowland forests during part of each winter, 4000 feet below their summer range. It appears that just as deer, elk and moose in mountainous terrain must seek low elevations in winter, so must the mountain caribou, in some regions at least. Unlike more common and better-known ungulates this caribou descends to mature forest and not to young forest or to open grassy ranges. According to several observers their food in these forests is chiefly tree lichens. Browse is undoubtedly another food item.

The fires that created hundreds of square miles of new range for moose and deer reduced by 60 per cent the area of dense forests used by caribou in winter. It reduced forests with numerous boggy openings by 70 per cent. If these lowland forest ranges are as important to caribou as winter range is to most ungulates in Canada, the cause of the decline of the Clearwater caribou is no mystery. The same fire that allowed the increase of deer, and later of moose, burned from 60 to 70 per cent of the forest probably essential for caribou survival in winter.

Caribou did not become scarce immediately after the 1926 fire. The decline was first noted with alarm about 1935. It may actually have occurred earlier, for decreases are not easily detected in nomadic, gregarious animals inhabiting wilderness. It is probable, however, that the decline took place in the early 1930's, and it was perhaps accelerated by fires that followed that of 1926. Five fires burned an additional eighty square miles in the summers of 1930 and 1931, and another 100 square miles were burned before 1940. Now, except for three restricted lowland areas, mature Columbia Forest is gone from valleys bordering the caribou-inhabited highlands. The remaining forests are the only lowland areas where caribou are seen regularly in winter. Lowlands formerly frequented now contain only wanderers. They are rarely seen in burns where old antlers and local knowledge indicate winter abundance before the fires.

It appears that fire is the major cause of caribou decline in Wells Gray Park. The northward march of the decline through the province is suggestive of the same cause, since the trend of first human influence upon wilderness lands in British Columbia has progressed generally from south to north. In Alaska (Murie, 1951, p. 278), western Ontario (de Vos, 1948) and other areas where caribou declines or exterminations were followed by increases in deer or moose there is ample evidence to suspect fire.

Caribou Management

Before the fire of 1926, lowland Columbia Forest in the Clearwater drainage covered only 9 per cent of the country used by caribou, while the poorly drained areas which seemed to be preferred were only 3 per cent of the total. Fire has reduced these percentages to 3 and one respectively. These small areas appear to be the key to caribou survival.

When small areas of climax or near-climax vegetation are necessary to the survival of an animal species, any change in vegetation may doom the animal dependent upon it. In this case fire or clearcut logging completely eliminate caribou range, and the animals disappear as a result.

While caribou management in this area cannot tolerate fire or clearcut logging on winter range, it is possible that a form of selective logging would not endanger the herd. Much more study is necessary before this can be accepted as more than a possibility.

Whereas most game management yields quicker returns than does forestry, caribou management appears to require planning that is just as long-term as in forestry, or perhaps longer since the ideal caribou forest could be a senile forest well past ideal cutting age.

Our present incomplete knowledge suggests that three measures are necessary to manage caribou in Wells Gray Park. These are, in order of importance: (1) Protection of remaining mature forests from fire. (2) Protection of remaining animals, or cropping to remove annual increases should data be available to fix harvest levels with accuracy. (3) Vegetation management designed to increase the area of mature forest.

These measures are simply stated; but successfully implementing them in the field calls for research, planning and management, tempered by some of the convictions necessary for wilderness preservation.

LITERATURE CITED

BANFIELD, A. W. F. 1949. The present status of North American caribou. Trans. N. Amer. Wildl. Conf. 14:477-489.

DE VOS, A.   1948.   Status of the woodland caribou in Ontario. Sylva 4: 17-23.

HALLIDAY, W. E. D. 1937. A forest classification for Canada. Can. Dept. Mines and Resources, Dom. For. Ser. Bull. 89. pp. 1-50.

MUNRO, J. A. 1947. Observations of birds and mammals in central British Columbia. Occ. Papers B. C. Prov. Mus. No. 6. pp. 1-165.

MURIE, O. J. 1951. The elk of North America. Wildl. Mgt. Inst. Washington.

LEBANON: LAND-USE AND VEGETATION
HOW TO MAKE A DESERT (1960)

Lee M. Talbot

The productivity of wildlife, and indeed the fortunes of man, are in-extricably tied to the uses and abuses of land. This paper describes land abuses where agricultural man has resided for many centuries. It is a so-bering picture, but mankind has not yet fully learned its message.

In the historical past much of the Lebanon was forested. The higher parts, including most of the Lebanon and Anti-Lebanon ranges, were covered by pine, fir and juniper, with stands of the famous Cedars of Lebanon. The lower areas, the Bekaa Valley and the Coastal flats and foothills were of Mediterranean type oak-scrub grasslands.

Today, only four stands of the Cedars of Lebanon remain. They are fairly carefully protected but are too small to be significant in the forest economy. The other forests, except those in the Bekaa Valley are found in more or less inaccessible areas at from 6,000-10,000 feet in both the Lebanon and Anti-Lebanon ranges. The most extensive area is in the Kammouha region in the north of the Lebanon range. Here one can still see at work the unchanged processes which have denuded the forest cover of the rest of the country:

1. The more or less virgin timberlands are first invaded by wood cutters primarily interested in the hardwoods for making charcoal.

2. Where accessible, and removal to areas of demand is practical, the better conifers are cut. The most recent demand here was during the war for the Beirut-Tripoli railroad. The valley floors are cultivated, in-tensively and more or less destructively.

3. The population pressure becomes too great for the cultivated areas on the valley floor and they become so abused that their yield is lowered to the point where it fails to fulfil the needs of the population. Culti-vation then moves up the surrounding hillsides, removing all tree cover in the process.

4. The cultivation methods on these steep hillsides are extremely destructive—plowing straight up and down the hills, for instance. After about three years, the fields on the steepest sites are deserted, for their soil is so exhausted and their yield of grain so low that cultivation is no longer practicable.

5. In less steep areas and areas where terraces have been built, the cultivation may continue for many years.

6. Other areas, where cultivation is no longer or never was possible, are used for grazing. Goats are numerically and economically the most important animals. Then come sheep. A few cattle, horses and donkeys are also kept for transport.

Excerpted from: A Look at Threatened Species, A Report on Some Animals of the Middle East and Southern Asia Which are Threatened with Extermination. Published for the International Union for Conservation of Nature and Natural Resources in Oryx, J. of the Fauna Preservation Soc. 5(4): 275-278, 281.

The people in the highlands spend the summer months as nomads, as far up the mountains as food can be found for their flocks. They live in goat-hair tents and in shelters of fir branches. In winter, when weather makes this existence impractical, and grazing can no longer be found at the higher elevations, these people move down to their permanent stone villages.

Human and livestock concentrations are extremely high even on the summer ranges. In the grazing region above the Akkar villages, in an area of about 500 hectares, there are 5,000 people, who graze 12,000 goats, 4,000 sheep and the usual cattle, horses and donkeys.

All this results in the virtual destruction of the better grazing on the flats and the destruction of grasses and the more palatable forage on the hillsides. Both on the flats and slopes, sheep and goats browse off all the new bush shoots, leaving small frameworks of the heavier branches protecting the leaves in the center of the bush. Regrowth of tree or bush is impossible because all seedlings and shoots are immediately eaten.

7. To furnish food for the ravenous animals, especially towards the end of the season, the graziers climb the conifers, principally the firs and pull down the limbs for the goats and sheep to graze. This leaves straggly forests of scarred tree trunks each topped by one tassel of green branches. These trees are more susceptible to disease and unable fully to carry on their life processes in hard weather. Many soon die.

8. The final result is an extension of the deserts of the flatlands below —bare, treeless, windswept stretches of rocky land. The former rich profusion of useful grasses and herbs is completely destroyed, except where protected from grazing by rough terrain. Even the few bushes that remain are grazed into woody rounded balls, existing but not actively growing or reproducing. The soils, unprotected by vegetation and in many areas already diminished through previous agriculture, have eroded away, leaving rock and gravel.

Some authorities credit the loss of the extensive forest and vegetation of the Middle East to a gradual change in climate which has made such vegetal life impossible. This does not appear to me to be so for the following reasons:

1. Forest vegetation still exists in several parts of Lebanon.

2. In areas where the forests have long since been destroyed, a few small areas have been protected as holy places. These are either monastery enclosures or "sacred groves" where some holy man is buried. Here, where cutting of the trees is prohibited and goats excluded by fencing, there is lush growth of the remnants of the former forests, the oak in lower areas, or the conifers higher in the mountains.

3. The holy groves are usually on eminences or hill tops, in places where water would apparently be most difficult to obtain and where any extreme climatic change would first be felt and shown by loss of the vegetation.

4. Sir Julian Huxley, "From an Antique Land", 1955, has argued against the climate change theory by noting that one of the remaining groves of the Cedars of Lebanon exists in a walled-in monastry yard. Here, before the area was fenced, some cedars stood alone, their fellows cut and

all reproduction destroyed by goats. After fencing, these trees seeded successfully and produced a dense stand of some 400 vigorous young cedars.

5. At Terbol in the Bekaa Valley, in an area particularly devastated by agricultural and grazing misuse, a large enclosure has been made under the joint American-Lebanese "Point 4" (Technical aid to under developed countries) agricultural program. Here all grazing or agriculture was excluded, no water was provided or other modification made; the area was left alone to regenerate itself. At the time of my visit to Lebanon, after only two growing seasons, the results were spectacular. Even in such a short time the original vegetation had come up in great variety and density. The Point 4 report on the agricultural and forestry potential of the country says: "The ability of the land to respond to protection and lighter grazing use, as demonstrated in the Terbol Enclosure, is almost unbelievable".

Out of a total of 1,300,000 hectares (4,300 sq. miles) only 74,000 hectares (230 sq. miles) less than 6 per cent is now forest, made up as follows:—

Oak *(Quercus spp.)*	43,000 ha.
Nut pine *(Pinus pinea)*	12,000 ha.
Juniper *(Juniperus excelsa)*	11,000 ha.
Aleppo pine *(Pinus halepensis)*	5,000 ha.
Fir *(Abies spp.)* and cedar *(Cedrus libani)*	3,000 ha.

Forty-seven per cent of Lebanon's land area is unsuitable for cultivation. Another sixteen per cent is cultivated with great difficulty. Other areas are considered sub-marginal. Roughly, two thirds of the country is best suited to production of forests and pasture.

Considering the productive capacity of the land and its ability to respond to protection, it would seem that an effective program for management of the grazing and forest lands in Lebanon would show significant results in a very short period—possibly even in two seasons on parts of the pasture lands. From the economic standpoint, the need for such a program is obvious. The supply of timber from the Lebanese forests is estimated by their forest department to meet only 60 per cent of the country's needs. The program would also have great importance for Lebanese wildlife. If the half to two thirds of the country unsuited to agriculture were managed correctly and conservatively for grazing and forests, the presence there of wild animals, except for the larger predatory forms, would be quite compatible with good land use.

How to Make a Desert

In and near Lebanon's remote Kemmouha Forest, 6,000 feet high in the northern mountains, is evidence that man, and not changes of climate, is responsible for the growth of the desert—man and past practices of forestry and agriculture that forgot the long run, that probably seemed to be producing the greatest good for the greatest number at the time.

Short-term thinking about forests sent most of the Cedars of Lebanon out to the sea in ships, and overzealous search for food and fiber sent the soil out to sea after the ships. Adjacent to today's desert and in the same climatic zone is a handsome mixed forest which still exists because it was protected from exploitation by accident. It is a pitifully small island of an Eden, too small to ward off enduring poverty. All around there is the barren stone skeleton of the greater Eden, the Promised Land towards which Moses once led his people.

The Six Steps

The six steps of desert-making—about which no nation can be smug —are illustrated in Lebanon:

1. Resembling the forest of the Sierra Nevada, the uncut Kammouha forest still contains pine, juniper, and fir, with oaks on the lower flats.

2. Fields are cleared in the forest; cultivation remains on the deep fertile soil of the flats until population pressure or exhaustion of the soil forces use of the slopes. Here erosion is much more rapid; eventually cultivation is no longer profitable.

3. The abused flats are then grazed—and overgrazed—by sheep, cattle, and horses. Bedrock or hardpan appears.

4. Livestock, like cultivation, moves to the slopes when the formerly better flats are overgrazed. When the poorer feed here goes, branches are pulled down for forage. With seedlings eaten by ravenous livestock, forest regeneration ceases.

5. Goats finish off all traces of forest vegetation and nomads with their flocks constantly move about in search of the meagerest feed. Here in an area famed for its lumber in Roman times timber is now totally unavailable, even for the roofs of buildings, so "bee hive houses" are built of stones and mud heaped up in the fashion of an eskimo igloo.

6. And finally, abandoned terraces, irrigation systems, and cities blend with the sere landscape, to testify silently of the riches the land has lost.

THE ECOLOGICAL CONSCIENCE (1947)
Aldo Leopold

Leopold describes an ecological conscience, an extension of morality from governing only the man-to-man interaction to governing also those causes and effects which flow from man-to-land-to-man. Perhaps this is our only hope to preserve an environment where one may see, hear, enjoy and accept the challenge to understand this earth, its flora, its fauna, and man himself.

Everyone ought to be dissatisfied with the slow spread of conservation to the land. Our "progress" still consists largely of letterhead pieties and convention oratory. The only progress that counts is that on the actual landscape of the back forty, and here we are still slipping two steps backward for each forward stride.

The usual answer to this dilemma is "more conservation education." My answer is yes by all means, but are we sure that only the volume of educational effort needs stepping up? Is something lacking in its content as well? I think there is, and I here attempt to define it.

The basic defect is this: We have not asked the citizen to assume any real responsibility. We have told him that if he will vote right, obey the law, join some organizations, and practice what conservation is profitable on his own land, that everything will be lovely; the government will do the rest.

This formula is too easy to accomplish anything worthwhile. It calls for no effort or sacrifice; no change in our philosophy of values. It entails little that any decent and intelligent person would not have done, of his own accord, under the late but not lamented Babbitian code.

No important change in human conduct is ever accomplished without an internal change in our intellectual emphases, our loyalties, our affections, and our convictions. The proof that conservation has not yet touched these foundations of conduct lies in the fact that philosophy, ethics, and religion have not yet heard of it.

I need a short name for what is lacking; I call it the ecological conscience. Ecology is the science of communities, and the ecological conscience is therefore the ethics of community life. I will define it further in terms of four case histories, which I think show the futility of trying to improve the face of the land without improving ourselves. I select these cases from my own state, because I am there surer of my facts.

Soil Conservation Districts

About 1930 it became clear to all except the ecologically blind that Wisconsin's topsoil was slipping seaward. The farmers were told in 1933 that if they would adopt certain remedial practices for five years, the public would donate CCC labor to install them, plus the necessary machinery and materials. The offer was widely accepted, but the practices were widely forgotten when the five-year contract period was up. The farmers continued only those practices that yielded an immediate and

Reprinted from: Wis. Cons. Bull. 12(12):4-7.

visible economic gain for themselves.

This partial failure of land-use rules written by the government led to the idea that maybe farmers would learn more quickly if they themselves wrote the rules. Hence, in 1937, the Wisconsin Legislature passed the Soil Conservation District Law. This said to the farmers, in effect: "We, the public, will furnish you free technical service and loan you specialized machinery, if you will write your own rules for land-use. Each county may write its own rules, and these will have the force of law." Nearly all the counties promptly organized to accept the proferred help, but after a decade of operation, no county has yet written a single rule. There has been visible progress in such practices as strip-cropping, pasture renovation, and soil liming, but none in fencing woodlots or excluding plow and cow from steep slopes. The farmers, in short, selected out those remedial practices which were profitable anyhow, and ignored those which were profitable to the community, but not clearly profitable to themselves. The net result is that the natural acceleration in rate of soil-loss has been somewhat retarded, but we nevertheless have less soil than we had in 1937.

I hasten to add that no one has ever told farmers that in land-use the good of the community may entail obligations over and above those dictated by self-interest. The existence of such obligations is accepted in bettering rural roads, schools, churches, and baseball teams, but not in bettering the behavior of the water that falls on the land, nor in the preserving the beauty or diversity of the farm landscape. Land-use ethics are still governed wholly by economic self-interest, just as social ethics were a century ago.

To sum up: we have asked the farmer to do what he conveniently could to save his soil, and he has done just that, and only that. The exclusion of cows from woods and steep slopes is not convenient, and is not done. Moreover some things are being done that are at least dubious as conservation practices: for example marshy stream bottoms are being drained to relieve the pressure on worn-out uplands. The upshot is that woods, marshes, and natural streams, together with their respective faunas and floras, are headed toward ultimate elimination from southern Wisconsin.

All in all we have built a beautiful piece of social machinery—the Soil Conservation District—which is coughing along on two cylinders because we have been too timid, and too anxious for quick success, to tell the farmer the true magnitude of his obligations. Obligations have no meaning without conscience, and the problem we face is the extension of the social conscience from people to land.

Paul Bunyan's Deer

The Wisconsin Lumberjack came very near accomplishing, in reality, the prodigious feats of woods-destruction attributed to Paul Bunyan. Following Paul's departure for points west, there followed an event little heralded in song and story, but quite as dramatic as the original destruction of the pineries: there sprang up, almost over night, an empire of brushfields.

Paul Bunyan had tired easily of salt pork and corned beef, hence he had taken good care to see that the deer of the original pineries found their way regularly to the stewpot. Moreover there were wolves in Paul's day, and the wolves had performed any necessary pruning of the deer herd which Paul had overlooked. But by the time the brushfields sprang into being, the wolves had been wiped out and the state had passed a buck-law and established refuges. The stage was set for an irruption of deer.

The deer took to the brushfields like yeast tossed into the sourdough pot. By 1940 the woods were foaming with them, so to speak. We Conservation Commissioners took credit for this miracle of creation; actually we did little but officiate at the birth. Anyhow, it was a herd to make one's mouth water. A tourist from Chicago could drive out in the evening and see fifty deer, or even more.

This immense deer herd was eating brush, and eating well. What was this brush? It consisted of temporary short-lived sun-loving trees and bushes which act as a nurse crop for the future forest. The forest comes up under the brush, just as alfalfa or clover come up under oats or rye. In the normal succession, the brush is eventually overtopped by the forest tree seedlings, and we have the start of a new forest.

In anticipation of this well known process, the state, the counties, the U. S. Forest Service, the pulp mills, and even some lumber mills staked out "forests" consisting, for the moment, of brush. Large investments of time, thought, cash, CCC labor, WPA labor, and legislation were made in the expectation that Nature would repeat her normal cycle. The state embarked on a tax subsidy, called the Forest Crop Law, to encourage landowners to hang on to their brushfields until they were replaced by forest.

But we failed to reckon with the deer, and with deer hunters and resort owners. In 1942 we had a hard winter and many deer starved. It then became evident that the original "nurse-trees" had grown out of reach of deer, and that the herd was eating the oncoming forest. The remedy seemed to be to reduce the herd by legalizing killing of does. It was evident that if we didn't reduce the herd, starvation would, and we would eventually lose both the deer and the forest. But for five consecutive years the deer hunters and resort owners, plus the politicians interested in their votes, have defeated all attempts at herd-reduction.

I will not tire you with all the red herrings, subterfuges, evasions and expedients which these people have used to befog this simple issue. There is even a newspaper dedicated solely to defaming the proponents of herd-reduction. These people call themselves conservationists, and in one sense they are, for in the past we have pinned that label on anyone who loves wildlife, however blindly. These conservationists, for the sake of maintaining an abnormal and unnatural deer herd for a few more years, are willing to sacrifice the future forest, and also the ultimate welfare of the herd itself.

The motives behind this "conservation" are a wish to prolong easy deer hunting, and a wish to show numerous deer to tourists. These perfectly understandable wishes are rationalized by protestations of chivalry to does and fawns. As an unexpected aftermath of this situation, there has been a large increase of illegal killing, and of abandonment of illegal carcasses in the woods. Thus herd-control, of a sort, is taking place outside the law. But the food-producing capacity of the forest has been over-strained for a decade, and the next hard winter will bring catastrophic star-vation. After that we shall have very few deer, and these will be runty from malnutrition. Our forest will be a moth-eaten remnant consisting largely of inferior species of trees.

The basic fallacy in this kind of "conservation" is that it seeks to con-serve one resource by destroying another. These "conservationists" are unable to see the land as a whole. They are unable to think in terms of community rather than group welfare, and in terms of the long as well as the short view. They are conserving what is important to them in the immediate future, and they are angry when told that this conflicts with what is important to the state as a whole in the long run.

There is an important lesson here: the flat refusal of the average adult to learn anything new, i.e., to study. To understand the deer prob-lem requires some knowledge of what deer eat, of what they do not eat, and of how a forest grows. The average deer hunter is sadly lacking in such knowledge, and when anyone tries to explain the matter, he is branded forthwith as a long-haired theorist. This anger-reaction against new and unpleasant facts is of course a standard psychiatric indicator of the closed mind.

We speak glibly of conservation education, but what do we mean by it? If we mean indoctrination, then let us be reminded that it is just as easy to indoctrinate with fallacies as with facts. If we mean to teach the capacity for independent judgment, then I am appalled by the magni-tude of the task. The task is large mainly because of this refusal of adults to learn anything new.

The ecological conscience, then, is an affair of the mind as well as the heart. It implies a capacity to study and learn, as well as to emote about the problems of conservation.

Jefferson Davis's Pines

I have a farm in one of the sand-counties of central Wisconsin. I bought it because I wanted a place to plant pines. One reason for selecting my particular farm was that it adjoined the only remaining stand of ma-ture pines in the County.

This pine grove is an historical landmark. It is the spot (or very near the spot) where, in 1828, a young Lieutenant named Jefferson Davis cut the pine logs to build Fort Winnebago. He floated them down the Wis-consin River to the fort. In the ensuing century a thousand other rafts of pine logs floated past this grove, to build that empire of red barns now called the Middle West.

This grove is also an ecological landmark. It is the nearest spot where a city-worn refugee from the south can hear the wind sing in tall timber. It harbors one of the best remnants of deer, ruffed grouse, and pileated woodpeckers in southern Wisconsin.

My neighbor, who owns the grove, has treated it rather decently through the years. When his son got married, the grove furnished lumber for the new house, and it could spare such light cuttings. But when war prices of lumber soared skyward, the temptation to slash became too strong. Today the grove lies prostrate, and its long logs are feeding a hungry saw.

By all the accepted rules of forestry, my neighbor was justified in slashing the grove. The stand was even-aged; mature, and invaded by heart-rot. Yet any schoolboy would know, in his heart, that there is something wrong about erasing the last remnant of pine timber from a county. When a farmer owns a rarity he should feel some obligation as its custodian, and a community should feel some obligation to help him carry the economic cost of custodianship. Yet our present land-use conscience is silent on such questions.

The Flambeau Raid

The Flambeau was a river so lovely to look upon, and so richly endowed with forests and wildlife, that even the hard-bitten fur traders of the freebooting 1700's enthused about it as the choicest part of the great north woods.

The freebooting 1800's expressed the same admiration, but in somewhat different terms. By 1930 the Flambeau retained only one 50-mile stretch of river not yet harnessed for power, and only a few sections of original timber not yet cut for lumber or pulp.

During the 1930's the Wisconsin Conservation Department started to build a state forest on the Flambeau, using these remnants of wild woods and wild river as starting points. This was to be no ordinary state forest producing only logs and tourist camps; its primary object was to preserve and restore the remnant of canoe-water. Year by year the Commission bought land, removed cottages, fended off unnecessary roads, and in general started the long slow job of recreating a stretch of wild river for the use and enjoyment of young Wisconsin.

The good soil which enabled the Flambeau to grow the best cork pine for Paul Bunyan likewise enabled Rusk County, during recent decades, to sprout a dairy industry. These dairy farmers wanted cheaper electric power than that offered by local power companies. Hence they organized a cooperative REA and applied for a power dam which, when built, will clip off the lower reaches of canoe-water which the Conservation Commission wanted to keep for recreational use.

There was a bitter political fight, in the course of which the Commission not only withdrew its opposition to the REA dam, but the legislature, by statute, repealed the authority of the Public Service Commission and made County Commissioners the ultimate arbiters of conflict between power values and recreational values. I think I need not dwell on the irony of this statute. It seals the fate of all wild rivers remaining in the state, including the Flambeau. It says, in effect, that in deciding the use of rivers, the local economic interest shall have blanket priority over statewide recreational interests, with County Commissioners as the umpire.

The Flambeau case illustrates the dangers that lurk in the semihonest doctrine that conservation is only good economics. The defenders of the Flambeau tried to prove that the river in its wild state would produce more fish and tourists than the impounded river would produce butterfat, but this is not true. We should have claimed that a little gain in butterfat is less important to the state than a large loss in opportunity for a distinctive form of outdoor recreation.

We lost the Flambeau as a logical consequence of the fallacy that conservation can be achieved easily. It cannot. Parts of every well-rounded conservation program entail sacrifice, usually local, but none-the-less real. The farmers' raid on our last wild river is just like any other raid on any other public wealth; the only defense is a widespread public awareness of the values at stake. There was none.

The Upshot

I have described here a fraction of that huge aggregate of problems and opportunities which we call conservation. This aggregate of case-histories show one common need: an ecological conscience.

The practice of conservation must spring from a conviction of what is ethically and esthetically right, as well as what is economically expedient. A thing is right only when it tends to preserve the integrity, stability, and beauty of the community, and the community includes the soil, waters, fauna, and flora, as well as people.

It cannot be right, in the ecological sense, for a farmer to drain the last marsh, graze the last woods, or slash the last grove in his community, because in doing so he evicts a fauna, a flora, and a landscape whose membership in the community is older than his own, and is equally entitled to respect.

It cannot be right, in the ecological sense, for a farmer to channelize his creek or pasture his steep slopes, because in doing so he passes flood trouble to his neighbors below, just as his neighbors above have passed it to him. In cities we do not get rid of nuisances by throwing them across the fence onto the neighbor's lawn, but in water-management we still do just that.

It cannot be right, in the ecological sense, for the deer hunter to maintain his sport by browsing out the forest, or for the bird hunter to maintain his by decimating the hawks and owls, or for the fisherman to maintain his by decimating the herons, kingfishers, terns, and otters. Such tactics seek to achieve one kind of conservation by destroying another, and thus they subvert the integrity and stability of the community.

If we grant the premise that an ecological conscience is possible and needed, then its first tenet must be this: economic provocation is no longer a satisfactory excuse for unsocial land-use, (or, to use somewhat stronger words, for ecological atrocities). This, however, is a negative statement. I would rather assert positively that decent land-use should be accorded social rewards proportionate to its social importance.

I have no illusions about the speed or accuracy with which an ecological conscience can become functional. It has required 19 centuries to define decent man-to-man conduct and the process is only half done; it may take as long to evolve a code of decency for man-to-land conduct. In such matters we should not worry too much about anything except the direction in which we travel. The direction is clear, and the first step is to throw your weight around on matters of right and wrong in land-use. Cease being intimidated by the argument that a right action is impossible because it does not yield maximum profits, or that a wrong action is to be condoned because it pays. That philosophy is dead in human relations, and its funeral in land-relations is overdue.

RESEARCH

There are many definitions of research and some exceedingly diverse opinions about just what constitutes wildlife research. However, there is general agreement that research is valuable if not hallowed or even sacrosanct. Therefore its conception, direction and application are of concern to all. Yet few have hesitated in their headlong rush for results long enough to contemplate the direction of research and fewer have put their ideas into print, especially in the discipline of wildlife ecology. We have selected one paper on a philosophy of research and two on research methods.

THE OBLIGATIONS OF THE BIOLOGIST (1961)

Harold E. Alexander

In discussing this subject before this select group, it might be more appropriate to refer specifically to the wildlife biologist or resource manager, since most of us like to think of our job status in such terms. My reference to the larger designation, the biologist, is deliberate. Because, in this world of science and scientific marvels, which have vastly increased the scope and quality of our existence, and have, likewise, brought us to the edge of "Doomsday", there is no longer a point at which any segment of biology, or, for that matter, any aspect of science may be separated from any other science, or from the social or ethical codes or systems by which we live. Only a few years ago, the lives of people (and of biologists) were relatively insulated from what went on outside the immediate scope of their endeavor. Today, in this age of jetplanes, antibiotics, synthetics, high speed presses, pesticides, and the megaton bomb, nobody, and least of all the scientist who has been largely responsible for the creation of such a world, is any longer separated from what goes on outside the realm of his particular speciality. But as we acknowledge the mighty force of science, and take pride in the advances it has brought about in human welfare, we are, likewise, aware of the limitations of science. The physical scientist has made us particularly aware of this; for with the development of the atom bomb, he created a force which threatens man's extinction, and which does not acknowledge or enlarge on the limitations of his moral and ethical responsibility. Neither the biologist, or any other scientist, can longer lead the "ivory tower" existence, with which they have been credited in the past, but most acknowledge their obligations not only to their professional codes, but also to their situations in the social and moral world of other men. They must assume a personal responsibility for the end results of what they do. They can no longer escape responsibility through the divisions of labor they have set aside for themselves.

We would note, too, that science, which is concerned with the discovery of truth, can be perverted. Its findings have often been exploited, not necessarily for the betterment of mankind, but for military, industrial and political purposes, and to exalt the prestige of nations (AAAS Comm. 1960). It has been used by promotors and charletans to attain their nefarious objectives. In view of this, the scientist cannot fail to be concerned about the uses to which his knowledge is put.

The scientist must be concerned with the "interaction of science and society" (Stewart, 1961). Even in the field of wildlife management we have maintained a separation between what was found out, and what was done. In the light of our experience, such a separation is no longer possible. The researcher has a moral obligation to promote the application of his knowledge to the best interest of society.

The biologist today is, I believe, in a unique position. Although we have been concerned primarily with technological advancements, we are discovering that technology is not enough. We are discovering that we, like other forms of life, have "biological" limitations; that we have en-

Reprinted from: Proc. Ann. Conf. S. E. Assoc. Game and Fish Comm. 15:173-178.

vironmental and esthetic needs which are necessary, to our physical and emotional welfare; and that ethical considerations, goodness and truth, and beauty, are essential to the fulfillment of our destiny and even to the survival of man. For the wildlife biologist I believe there is a particular place in the future of science and society, for by training he is concerned with the interrelationships of living things, and people are among those things.

The biologist, through his understanding of resource limitations, must be a conservationist. In the future he must be more and more concerned not only with resource management, but with what one writer has called "social conservation". Today, the subject of conservation is people (Romney, 1960).

In the future the biologist must be more than a technician. He must function as an educated man who is able to apply his special knowledge to the betterment of society and the advancement of welfare. As a bio-ecologist, whose business is the study of environment, he is well adapted to a role in the investigation and preservation of a balanced world in which men may live a satisfying beneficient life. In introducing the subject we have touched on the obligations of the biologist to his profession and to society. It shall be our purpose to elaborate further on these principles.

The Ethic

The biologist, first of all, is, as a member of the science profession, concerned with the discovery of truth. Further than that, he is obligated to the expression of the truth. He cannot, as a scientist or as a citizen, ignore that obligation. He must, also, be willing to assume risk to arrive at the truth. He must be willing to encounter adversity. He must acknowledge error, and be willing to accept criticism and ridicule. He must attempt to envision the end results of the application of his findings, be able to evaluate those results in terms of other scientific systems of analysis and other actions; and he must understand the social problems which stand as obstacles to the application of his knowledge to social betterment.

The scientist has been criticized by other men, and with reason. He has been accused of social neutrality, moral incompetence, and ridicule of areas of knowledge "not subject to precise measurement" (Quimby, 1954). Science has been feared because it represented change and "destructive force". He has been criticized for being "particularized", to the extent that his vision was myopic, and he could not see beyond the criteria which surrounded his specialty. He can no longer let specialization warp his vision. He must, in this time, become a socially integrated person concerned with the ramifications of his knowledge as it is related to other knowledge, and the end results of the application of all knowledge. He is not only a scientist, he is a man with moral responsibilities.

In this complicated world the biologist must extend his knowledge to include the vast realms of scientific possibilities. He must recognize, too, that his specialty is only a segment of the whole. To quote Poincare, "We cannot understand an elephant by restricting ourselves to thin slices of him seen under a microscope."

Further, the biologist must understand that there are realms of knowledge to which the techniques of science cannot be applied. Somebody said "that you cannot extract the square root of a sonnet" (Dryden, 1954). In the application of our specialties to courses of action, we need to keep this concept in mind. In this connection, I believe the wildlife worker is prone to concern himself too much with numbers and bag limits. He needs to recognize that sport and recreation are primarily esthetic in nature. If this is not true, then all the efforts we give to perfecting fine tackle for fishing, skill in wing shooting, and our efforts to hunt in wilderness and seek out beauty in nature are wasted. We had best fish with seines and poisons, and kill our game by the most effective and lethal means. With this consideration in view, we need to give more attention to "quality" in sport as well as within other phases of our life.

I believe we have given too much precedence to what science can and has produced. Romney (1960) commented on "the dilemma of man enmeshed in the asphyxiating environment of his own creation (as presenting) the greatest challenge conservation has ever known. . ." As has been suggested, scientific findings and their results are only tools which may be used for human betterment or degradation. Their first use should be in the preservation of a wholesome environment for man. Sometimes the preservation of such an environment is best accomplished not by altering things, but by leaving things as they are.

Possibilities of perverting the uses of science knowledge were thoroughly demonstrated by the Nazi ideology, which used anthropology to prove Arian superiority, biology to carry out ghastly experiments on suffering humanity, and scientific techniques to destroy millions of helpless people. Studies in biology have led not only to the control of disease, but also to the development of biological warfare. Reverence for technological achievement has a hollow sound, without the application of ethical and moral principles, to which the criteria of truth, goodness and beauty are basic. Of these, truth is fundamental to scientific endeavor. To quote (Piel, 1954), "We can know with assurance only to the extent that we are informed on all the known alternative views." It is in the presentation of alternative views that the biologist must call upon another quality essential to his profession, and to his obligations. That quality is courage.

It has been said that a "serious man ought not to waste time stating a majority of opinion" (Weaver, 1961), which has already been stated many times over. The important thing is to examine the alternatives to established or proposed systems of action. In this connection, it can be observed that industry has used the benefits science has produced for profit, and this has been its main purpose. The military have used that knowledge to develop larger and better means for destruction, (and we acknowledge the necessities of the moment), and governments have used scientific developments for political purposes without concern for ethical motivations. Many times, as in the case of pesticides or atomic developments, the commercial interests or developers have insufficient knowledge of the effects of the use of these agents, or were unconcerned about such effects, subordinating them for profit motives. I believe both insufficient knowledge of their effects and indifference on the part of the producer and sellers have led to a dangerous application of pesticide poisons to crop and forest lands.

397

Even though he will be criticized for retarding "progress", I believe it is the obligation of the biologist to evaluate the effects of these pesticides, of nuclear products on life and on social welfare.

We have other problems resulting from the "progress" of technology, such as pollution and water developments for limited purposes with unknown and often detrimental and long term results, which need careful study; and such studies are the business of the natural scientist (biologist). But those who dissent, who present a point of view at variance with established or material objectives are sure to be criticized, ostracized or driven from their positions. Nevertheless, it is their moral obligation to state what they know, to present their findings so that we can know all the alternative views, and men can make intelligent choices from among the possibilities. The biologist has the obligation to give society the benefits of his position and that takes courage, without which the scientist is only a follower.

It has been observed that "conformity can be a cloak for the timid" (Weaver, 1961). The true scientist cannot retreat behind that "cloak of conformity". Courage is basic to the application of principle and to the very purpose of his existence. The only alternative is retreat from society and from his obligations.

Purpose And Knowledge

The first criteria for judging the worth of any action is purpose. Science and culture cannot be separated. "Science is but one section of our culture." (AAAS Rept. 1957). Biologists and other scientists often seem to be more concerned with "method" and the "mechanizations of science" than with its relation to the cultural whole. The separation of knowledge and culture has been brought sharply to our attention through that development of the physical sciences, the atom bomb. Today the atomic scientist is fully aware that what he does cannot be separated from other affairs of men.

Thus, the philosophy and purposes of science have forced themselves on this group of scientists as a major consideration. But, the preoccupation with method and technique is still too apparent in the science journals. In seeking references for this paper, only three references pertaining to the purposes and philosophy of science were reported in a major abstracting journal covering a three year period. In that same period, approximately 25 such references were listed in "Reader's Guide". These, almost invariably, were written by physicists concerned with the relation of nuclear research to human survival.

Although the primary effects of radiation are biological, the biologist is only just beginning to concern himself with the relation of the social and physical sciences to his field of endeavor. This lack of concern with social obligations is as apparent among wildlife biologists as among workers in other science fields. Preoccupation with techniques and methods of census, for example, is of little use to the wildlifer unless he can solve the social dilemma of the "buck law", and population counts of ducks or fish are unimportant unless the larger social factors, which result in vast drainage programs and in water pollution, can be solved. The problem of pesticide use and its effects on living things is unsolved, but it is a problem concerned with the application of biological data to social ethics. The fact that

6,000 commercial brands of pesticides are sold suggests that the commercial worth of these chemicals is the major consideration in their use. The primary purpose is profit; human welfare is considered secondarily.

The preoccupation with research for "practical" purposes is of concern to the scientist. It has been estimated that 10 billion dollars per year (Holton, 1960) are spent on research, of which only 7% is spent on basic research, defined as the "roots of the tree". Industry allocates large sums to practical research, only 3% of which is spent on basic studies. For them, research must pay off in quick returns. In applied research, there is little consideration of the fact that all we know stands on a broad base of knowledge obtained through man's primary interest in the discovery of truth. Our knowledge of atoms or cells is basic to nuclear development and to advances in the science of medicine. Without these basic data, a progression to applied science is impossible. Of Federal appropriations, only 11% goes to biological and 2% to social studies. Yet the preservation of biological balances and social order are essential to preservation of those resources essential to man and to his survival.

Regardless of its necessity, it should be of concern to us that 84% of our research was motivated by military considerations in 1957 (AAAS Prelim. Rept., 1957). This, in part, accounts for our preoccupation with physical research, and neglect of biological and social studies. Such motivation warps the scope of our knowledge, and imposes restrictions on our intellectual, social and personal freedom, which are fundamental to scientific achievement.

Of concern to many scientists and to us all is the problem of communications. For the scientists, there are 50,000 scientific and technical journals published annually. (Holton, 1960). They are poorly abstracted, and their results are available only to the select group interested in that phase of scientific subject matter reviewed. There is little or no effort to correlate the findings into any common fount of knowledge. It has been suggested that one of the great needs is a meeting of representatives of the various sciences to "bridge the barriers of specialization". Further hampering the dispensation of knowledge are restrictions on free communication, industrial, military; and due to the lack of any common "language" of communication, which can be understood by all scientists regardless of their specialty.

But of even greater concern is failure to communicate scientific information to the social groups which shape the uses to which knowledge is put. It has been pointed out that newspapers give only 5% of space to factual data, and T.V. programs allocate only 0.3% of their time to presenting scientific information (Holton, 1960). Scientists, themselves, fail to convert what they know into common knowledge, forgetting that men like Newton took pains to communicate their findings in popular form so that they became commonly understood. Since the scientist has a moral responsibility to other men, he must not forget that what is done with his knowledge is conditioned by political, economic considerations, and the character and motives of the users. He cannot escape responsibility for the application of his knowledge to purposes which may be good or evil.

In discussing this problem of communications, we finally get back to that basic ethical consideration, that the scientist is, first of all, a member of the human community, with moral and social and professional responsibilities, which are not divisible. As a solution to the problem of communications, several actions are suggested. These include the establishment and observance of a general code of ethics for all scientists, similar to the oath of Hippocrates, which provided standards and principles for the practice of medicine; the organization of general science societies which could integrate and relate the various fields of science to each other, and to the mental, spiritual, and physical needs of men; and more concern with the means and methods of communicating scientific knowledge so that all scientists and all men can profit from such knowledge. The world of science needs an active conscience that does not stand aloof from human needs, and self criticism to make that conscience an ethical force.

REFERENCES

1. COMFORT, ALEX, "Morality, Science and Art", Commonweal LV (15): 367-369, Jan. 18, 1952
2. DECKER, FRED W., "Scientific Communications Should Be Improved", Science 125 (3238) : 101-105, Jan. 18, 1957
3. DRYDEN, HUGH L., "The Scientist in Contemporary Life", Science 120 (3105) : 1052-1055, Jul. 2, 1954
4. HOLTON, GERALD, "Modern Science and the Intellectual Tradition", Science 131 (3408) : 1187-1193, April 1960
5. HILL, A. V., "The Ethical Dilemma of Science." Vital Speeches 19: 110-114, Dec. 1, 1952
6. IHDE, AARON J., "Responsibility of the Scientist to Society.", Scien. Monthly 77:244-249, Nov. 1953
7. MEIER, RICHARD L., "Toward Social Responsibility." Sat. Review 41:41-45, Nov. 1958
8. PIEL, GERARD, "The Scientists in American Society.", Symposium, Scientific Monthly 78:129-133 Mar., 1954
9. QUIMBY, FREEMAN, "Unpopular Science.", Science 119:162-163, Jan. 29, 1954
10. ROMNEY, HENRY, "A New and Human Science." Sports Ill. 12:72-82, Mar. 1960
11. ROWLAND, JOHN, Mysteries of Science. A study of the limitations of the scientific method. 214 pp. Philosophical Library, Inc. New York 16. 1957.
12. SEARS, PAUL B., (Review) Human Nature and the Human Condition. by Joseph Wood Krutch, Random House, Nation Jan. 3, 1960, pp., 81-82
13. SKUTCH, ALEXANDER F., "The True Conservationist." Nature 46(3): 258-261, May 1953
14. STEWART, BRUCE, "Science and Social Change." Bull. of the Atomic Scientists xvii (7): 267-270, Sept. 1961
15. WAGER, J.V.K., "Quality Standards for Forest Recreation and Wildlife Production and Harvest." Proceedings, Soc. of Amer. For. Meeting, 1954
16. WEAVER, WARREN, "The Moral Un-neutrality of Science." Science 133 (3448) :255-262, 1961
17. News & Notes "Communication of Research Results", Science 120 (3105) :1055, July 2, 1954
18. Preliminary Report of A.A.A.S. Interim Committee, "Social Aspects of Science", Science 125 (3239) :143-147, Jan. 25, 1957
19. Report of A.A.A.S. Committee on Science, "Science and Human Welfare", Science 132 (3418) :69-73, July 1960.

A PATTERN OF SCIENTIFIC INQUIRY
FOR APPLIED RESEARCH (1952)
H.G. Wilm

Ever since people started thinking they have expended effort on the solution of problems encountered in life; and almost as much effort on figuring out more effective ways to gain these solutions. This has led to the development of scientific inquiry: a complex system of thought and action that is employed by trained people as they attempt to solve their problems.

For a long time—perhaps up to John Stuart Mill—work on the methods of scientific inquiry was dominated by philosophers, who paid most of their attention to the metaphysical aspects of the subject. These methods became more and more formalized, until by Mill's time they were shaped into a well-organized pattern. Since then other philosophers and logicians have reformed and polished this pattern, so that it has assumed relatively perfect form in the writings of John Dewey and his contemporaries.

One feature of this kind of scientific method is striking to workers in applied research: The collection and analysis of factual data are quite subordinated to the philosophical processes. From a logician's viewpoint, most of the job of solving human problems lies in the mind of a trained person. Accordingly, his scientific method features the use of pure reason to evolve principles and to examine relationships among factors in the problem at hand; and it treats the collection and analysis of experimental evidence only as an incidental part of the scientific method.

This kind of approach opens rewarding avenues to knowledge; but it is not likely to supply a complete solution to practical problems. When he studies the conventional patterns of inquiry, the worker in applied research finds himself lost in a maze of unfamiliar language. The older literature on logic devotes attention to the intricate details of categorical argument, the character of induction, and the weakness of Mill's experimental methods; and recent writers seem to take delight in weaving a new and strange vocabulary, replacing the arguments of the classicists with the abstruse reasoning of a philosophical Gertrude Stein. And both earlier and current logicians enter only slightly into the earthy realm of empirical evidence, which a practical researcher requires to satisfy his customers in the farming or manufacturing world.

To meet this real need, investigators in the fields of applied research have turned away from the endeavors of pure logic. Instead they devote a major part of their attention to quantitative work, depending more on experimental data than on rational processes for the solution of problems. Perhaps they have gone too far in this direction. At least they have taken on a large additional burden, for the skilled use of the mind is a more streamlined way to attack problems than is the laborious collection and analysis of data.

Even so, the structure of quantitative scientific methods was not excessively complicated in fields like physics and chemistry, where the prob-

Reprinted from: Journal of Forestry 50(2): 120-125, by permission from the Society of American Foresters.

lems of natural variation are not ordinarily serious. But with the development of biological research, it became more necessary to sort out the effects of the variables being tested from all the sources of variation which could not be subjected to experimental control. Over the last half-century this has led to the growth of an intricate pattern of quantitative study, with its accent on skillfully designed experimentation. By now these techniques, employing mathematical statistics as their tools, have been developed to a high degree of perfection. As an inevitable result, present-day research workers are inclined to devote an excessive amount of attention to correlation analyses, designed experiments, and related procedures, and not nearly enough to the philosophical aspects of a complete scientific method.

In applied research there seems to be a need for these two schools of thought to be brought together into a single generalized pattern for scientific inquiry, combining the rapid techniques of logic with the solid facts of experimental evidence. While such an amalgamation does not contain original contributions to knowledge, perhaps it will supply the worker in applied research with more powerful weapons in his search for solutions to practical problems.

A suggested pattern for a scientific method of this kind is sketched below, under each of a series of topic headings. It will be evident that the successive headings represent formal steps in a research procedure. In solving any problem, however, not all of the steps may be necessary; some of the intermediate ones may be omitted. Where the problem is not very important or the solution is clearly provided by the experience of other workers, the steps of controlled experience and experiment may not be necessary: it may be possible to move directly from exploration to the solution of the problem and thence to the pilot project. But where human life, large expenditures of money, or a major change in natural-resource management depends on the correctness of the solution, the research worker may go through all these steps and even repeat some of them before he is willing to make a final recommendation. In any investigation the appropriate combination of research steps depends on the importance of decisions which rest on the solution of the problem, and on the degree of certainty which can be reached by any of the steps.

Setting Up the Problem

As a research worker approaches a problem to be solved, he has to define it in clear-cut terms. This is true whether he is starting from an indeterminate situation in a completely new field, or planning to sharpen up his knowledge on one aspect of a problem about which much is already known. In either case he has to specify the problem which he is to study, so that he can organize his thinking and action in the most efficient manner. Suppose a range-management researcher is concerned about improving the condition of deteriorated grassland in ponderosa pine forests of the western United States. Right there is stated a general research problem, but it is so broad in scope that it would be difficult for any research worker to get hold of it. The ponderosa pine zone extends from Mexico to Canada and from South Dakota to the Pacific Coast; and it is grazed by cattle, sheep, and big game in every season of the year. So the problem has first to be brought down to manageable size, by defining some aspect of it which can be attacked in a single piece of research. In this case, for example, the worker might state his specific problem to be the improvement of natural range vegetation in the ponderosa pine forests of the Blue Mountains in Oregon, through better grazing management.

When he has defined his special problem to any degree such as this, the research worker examines it to see whether a reasonable solution can be worked out with the resources of personnel, money, and land at his disposal. If not, he may have to circumscribe the problem even further; but otherwise he is ready to go ahead and develop an hypothesis to be tested. So he puts his feet on the desk and speculates on the variables which may have a bearing on the problem. In doing so, he reviews his experience with related problems on similar range lands, or even in other areas and climates; and he asks other workers in his own field of research what their experience has been. This includes a careful review of the results of previous research and observation.

Some of the classical tools of inquiry may be of value at this and other stages in the research technique. An adaptation of Mill's "method of agreement and difference" may, for example, help extend experience gained in other areas and climates to the range country of eastern Oregon. Suppose previous experiments have been conducted on ponderosa pine range land in the Rocky Mountains, with conclusive findings as to desirable methods of land management. Our research worker looks for similarities in the two areas: the composition of their range vegetation, and the character of the pine overstory; similarities in ordinary management and past history, in soil and topography and climate. Then, before he draws inferences as to his Blue Mountain problem, he makes equally detailed comparisons of differences between the two areas. The fact that the growing season of range vegetation in the central Rockies is characterized by frequent rains, whereas the Blue Mountains are much drier during this season, may have a profound influence on decisions as to good land management.

A variation of this technique is the method of analogy, which has gained increasing popularity in engineering research. The behavior of bodies moving in water or other fluids is found, for example, to be very much like their behavior in air—with easily recognized restrictions and adjustments associated with the differing effects of temperature, pressure, and viscosity. This similarity facilitates qualitative and even quantitative inferences on airfoil behavior, developed from observations in the denser fluids.

After he has gone through analyses like these our range worker may reason as follows: "The ponderosa pine range in the Blue Mountains of eastern Oregon is badly deteriorated, due to past and present overgrazing. Therefore reductions in grazing intensity should encourage recovery." This oversimplified statement of the relation may or may not be right. As an ecologist realizes, its correctness will depend on the degree to which the climax forage species have been eliminated by past overgrazing. If, as he may know from study of the areas involved, the remaining forage on large tracts of land consists only of annual weeds and other plants representing an early successional stage, reductions in grazing intensity could not accomplish recovery in any reasonable period of time. Then the research man abandons his idea of building up this kind of range land through management of natural vegetation. Instead he begins to delve into the possibilities of artificial revegetation through the seeding of desirable plant species. If, on the other hand, climax plants are still present in numbers sufficient to make recovery possible, he inquires whether it is simply overgrazing that has caused the trouble, or whether the seasonal timing of grazing use has had an important effect.

And so the worker goes on, using his mental capacities and experience to consider a number of variables associated with his problem. He picks up and rejects some and retains others, until finally he has organized the remaining variables into a small group whose manipulation promises a relatively high degree of success in attaining the solution of the problem. Then he is ready to formalize his thinking by stating a concrete hypothesis, definitely circumscribing the "population" to be used in testing it; and specifying how the results of his test may be used in the practical management of range land. The hypothesis might be expressed in terms like this: "Successful long-term management of pine range land, under conditions corresponding to those in the Blue Mountains of eastern Oregon, can be accomplished by reducing the use of forage by cattle to a point at which the climax species can build up in number and vigor until they dominate the general aspect of the range. This adjustment in use can best be accomplished by two means: cutting down the number of livestock, and avoiding any use during the spring months when the forage and soil are not ready to sustain the impact of livestock. Because the studies of timing and intensity of use will be relatively limited in area, the results will not be used directly to aid land managers. Instead, they will assist in the planning of pilot projects elsewhere in the ponderosa pine zone, which will serve as more quantitative guides to land managers."

In a more elaborate form, this process of elucidating a problem may be built up into project or problem analyses, some of which may outline a whole series of related problems needing research in any given region and field of knowledge.

As you review these patterns of reasoning you will notice their use of the principle of the "calculated risk," commonly employed by military men and by civilians in ordinary life as well as by scientists. As the range investigator reviews possible leads and examines variables associated with his general problem, he consciously eliminates those which, in his judgment are less likely to yield fruitful results. By this process he may close the door to avenues leading toward the best answer to his problem. But if he makes good use of judgment and experience, the odds against such an outcome are relatively large; and he insures, on the average, more certain returns from his investment in time and money devoted to research.

Testing the Hypothesis by Exploration

When the investigator has organized his thinking by analyzing the variables involved in his problem, setting up a formal hypothesis, and describing the limitations of its solution, he is ready to start solving the problem. One way to approach this job is by a process of exploration, part of which is like the mental processes used in defining the problem. Again, the research worker examines his own and other peoples' knowledge, making an exhaustive review of past work and publications. While doing so he is likely to find that a surprising amount is already known on problems like his. Occasionally the need for new research may even be eliminated: a sufficiently good solution can be worked out from available knowledge. If not, at least the information that has already been gained will assist the worker in further circumscribing the work which needs to be done in his own investigations.

During this preliminary exploration the investigator probably finds gaps in knowledge which can be filled without the need for formalized experimentation. In order to close these gaps he schedules trips to areas in which his particular problem exists, or in other ways searches for useful new information. Our range investigator goes into the ponderosa pine forests of the Blue Mountains, organizing his travel so that he can study range deterioration under a variety of conditions. He visits areas with different soils, elevations, and exposures, and he keeps track of variations from normal conditions, noting how they may have affected range succession and retrogression. As a result of this work, the researcher is able to build up a set of strong impressions as to desirable range management techniques.

It should be emphasized that observations by trained people form one of the most valuable tools of applied research. Compared to better controlled techniques, observation is relatively subjective. But it is a rapid and inexpensive way to acquire knowledge, and it offers maximum opportunity for the use of intelligence and judgment in attacking problems. Therefore this technique is useful not only in the preliminary stages of research, but as a valuable accessory to the most controlled kinds of experimentation.

In exploration, as in other phases of the scientific method, the ideas that are developed may call for adjusting or even completely revamping an hypothesis and its attendant reasoning processes. Variables originally considered important may not be worth retaining, or expected solutions may be found impractical. Hence the investigator needs to preserve flexibility in his attitudes, and to be ready to adjust his thinking whenever necessary.

These exploratory steps in research—perhaps even including the analysis of literature—might be called uncontrolled experience, in the sense that the information gained is not subjected to control by careful experimental planning. Experience of this kind formed the stock in trade of many earlier investigations, and it is still one of the most valuable assets of men doing applied research. As it is accumulated over the years, it generates a feel for what is right, and for the most profitable attack on any problem. Much knowledge has been gained through the use of uncontrolled experience without experiments; but it has sometimes led to the development of unsound beliefs, which have carried administrators and research workers into unproductive and often damaging by-lanes.

Guiding the way into these unfruitful paths are two weaknesses of experience. First, it is hard for even the most careful thinker to separate true experience from unconscious prejudice. Second, it may be equally hard to divorce the subject of investigation from the effects of all the variables that surround it. As the range investigator looks at the ponderosa pine zone, areas that he finds in good condition may easily have been the best land originally, where the most progressive and intelligent pioneers obtained ownership long ago. There the effects of good management may be confounded with the inherent potentialities of site and soil. Because of difficulties like these—perhaps more obscure but equally dangerous—the investigator knows that experience alone cannot be depended upon to tell the whole story; that he needs an unbiased test which will transform his hypothesis into relatively certain knowledge. This thought leads to the more quantitative steps in the scientific method.

It is at this stage, incidentally, that the worker in applied research ordinarily prepares a working plan for his further investigations. In doing so, he reviews all the impressions that have been acquired by reasoning, observation, and uncontrolled experience, and then lays out a detailed plan for new work in either of two directions. Of these, the first can be called controlled experience; the second is the use of "designed" experiments.

Testing the Hypothesis by Controlled Experience

In this research technique, as in the observational part of exploratory studies, the investigator works with variables as they occur in nature. In our range management problem, for example, he goes into the ponderosa pine forests and studies the effects of past and present land use. But he subjects his observations to a higher degree of control—and makes his studies more expensive—through quantitative measurements of the variables involved in the problem. And he puts these measurements under further control by either or both of two general techniques: classification or correlation.

When the classification method is used, the investigator examines the population of variables which he wants to study, and sorts it into a number of discontinuous classes, each of which is relatively homogeneous with respect to the main variables to be examined. In testing a range-management hypothesis, the worker may find it profitable to select a varied sample of grazed areas in the ponderosa pine zone, and to classify them according to soil types, elevation, apparent productivity, and present condition. Then he will analyze the intensity of past and present grazing use on each of these strata, comparing these figures with data on the relative abundance and vigor of the desirable climax forage plants. Measurements of vegetation are necessarily taken on relatively small sample plots, distributed by some scheme of randomization and stratification. The purpose is to supply unbiased and representative sample averages for each of the important plant species on each of the land strata. From the results, comparisons among the strata may lead to inferences on the relation of livestock use to the development and survival of vegetation.

The correlation technique is obviously related to classification, in that quantitative measurements are taken in a number of places and under differing conditions, so as to supply a well-organized array of empirical evidence. Then the data on measured variables are subjected to simple or multiple correlation analyses, from which the necessary conclusions can be drawn.

In many cases the classification and correlation techniques can be combined for maximum efficiency. The population to be studied is first subdivided into discrete classes with respect to those variables that are

406

not characterized by continuous variation. Differences in exposure or soil type, for example, fall naturally into clear-cut strata. At the same time measurements may be taken of other factors such as soil depth, forage volume production, intensity of use, and precipitation. These can be included in correlation analyses within the areal strata, and thus a large amount of information can be obtained from the study.

Still these investigations are subject to some of the same criticisms that were made of exploration techniques, however well organized and executed they may be. Personal biases can be largely removed by careful planning; but no matter how many subclasses a population is divided into, or how many variables are used in a multiple correlation analysis, the investigator is working with phenomena as they occur in nature. Thus he is still risking the possibility of both natural bias and the confounding of variables. As a result, even the most exhaustive investigations conducted by the methods of controlled experience require discretion and judgment by the investigator, as he weighs the chances of confounding and bias and interprets the results of his studies. in terms of practical land management. These remaining risks obviously lead to the need for controlled experiments, in which bias and uncontrolled confounding of variables are removed as completely as possible through experimental design.

Testing the Hypothesis by Controlled Experiments

Developed partly as an outgrowth of correlation-analysis techniques, the procedures of controlled experimentation form the most unbiased and reliable, as well as the most expensive kind of quantitative research. Because of their relatively high cost, ordinarily controlled experiments should be resorted to only where simpler procedures have failed to provide satisfactory solutions, and where the expected results are sufficiently valuable to warrant the cost. From this viewpoint any investigator can think of numerous cases in which controlled experimentation has been overdone or unnecessarily applied. As a rule, in approaching any problem the research worker should first try to see how far he can get with simpler and cheaper techniques.

The principles of controlled experimentation are widely known and need not be discussed in detail here. But it may be commented that this research method has several objectives: to give each variable that is to be tested an equal chance to exert its effects, if any; to minimize extraneous variations which might obscure these effects, by the use of efficient experimental designs; and to provide unbiased estimates of both the effects being tested and the remaining uncontrolled variations, or experimental error.

In modern research techniques the first and third of these objectives are met through various processes of randomization and replication, accompanied by quantitative measurement of the variables involved. The second is attained by provision for both experimental and statistical control of variables that are not associated with the effects to be tested. By experimental control is meant the organization of experimental units, such as plots on range land, in such a way as to minimize extraneous variations. A simple example is the familiar randomized-block design which is used in field and laboratory research. A number of relatively homogeneous "blocks"—tracts of land, or batches of experimental material—are chosen for experimental treatment within the general population to be studied. Each of these blocks is subdivided into smaller units—as plots—equal in number to the treatments that are to be investigated. Within each block the various treatments are assigned at random to these smaller units. Because all the treatments appear relatively close together within each block, extraneous variations like those due to differences in soil or exposure are reduced; and by randomization each treatment is given the same chance to exert its effects. Then the total variation in the experiment can be partitioned into that attributable to effects of the treatments; to variations among the blocks; and to the failure of the different treatments to behave alike in the different blocks.

Frequently the remaining uncontrolled variation in an experiment of this kind can be still further reduced by statistical control: the measurement and analysis of some of the variables that make up the experimental error. When this technique can be applied, it leads to the maximum amount of information which can be obtained from a designed experiment. A good example is the use of "past performance" as a concomitant variable in the analysis of experimental results. In a harvest-cutting study in a forest stand, for instance, the average growth rate of trees on each experimental plot for several years before treatment can be used to integrate all the complex of site factors that are associated with tree growth, except for the timbercutting treatment itself. When pre-treatment growth is used to supply statistical control in a covariance analysis, it is commonly found that the remaining experimental error is considerably reduced. Other variables may also be chosen for this purpose; it is only important to make sure that they have no relation to the treatment itself.

This leads to one more interesting thought—the possibility of using variables that do have a relation to the treatments; not to reduce the uncontrolled experimental error, but to help explain the effects of the treatments. As an example, a study may be conducted to ascertain the effects of timber cutting or of heavy grazing on the infiltration capacities of the soil on watershed land. We may assume that such a study has been completed, and that statistically significant treatment effects were found. The precision of the experiment has already been built up to a satisfactory degree by experimental and statistical control. In addition, however, it is desired to estimate the effects, if any, of several factors which may have been associated with the effect of vegetation removal on infiltration of water into the soil. In order to find out, when the experiment was conducted measurements were made of these variables, including the volume of plant litter and humus on the surface of the mineral soil. Through a covariance analysis of experimental results, this particular factor was found to be significantly related to the variations in infiltration induced by the experimental treatments.

The scrutiny and interpretation of explanatory data play an extremely important role in applied biological research, as they do in other aspects of science. Often, as a worker seeks for explanations of natural phenomena or of experimental effects, his search will lead him deep into the realm of "fundamental" research. This is entirely appropriate, as long as his inquiry or his more abstract research bears a direct relation to the testing of his original hypothesis. Although administrators frown at him, there is even a place in applied research for the sound scientist who spends all of his time delving into the uncharted courses of true fundamental research. But such freedom should not be misused. In general, a safe guiding rule for the worker in applied research is to start with a clear-cut hypothesis which points toward the solution of a practical problem; to keep his inquiries directed toward that solution; but not to hesitate to explore any branching paths of fundamental research which, by the calculated-risk principle, offer a fair chance of helping him to arrive at a usable answer.

The Experimental Solution

When the research worker has completed his investigation, whether by observation, experience, or experiment, he has either verified his hypothesis or failed to do so. If he failed, there may have been one or more of several reasons. Perhaps he had not acquired the background necessary to pick the most promising treatments; or perhaps there simply were not any treatments that would yield usable results. Techniques employed or concomitant variables selected may have been inadequate to express the real effects of treatment or relationships among variables. Chemical soil analyses, for instance, may by no means express the real relation of mineral nutrients to plant growth; or data on total storm precipitation may be poorly related to flash-flood discharges. Or it may easily be that the experiment was not efficient enough to make the treatment effects stand out above the experimental error. These troubles are all common enough so that they deserve careful attention; one of the secrets of successful research lies in the design and execution of suitably efficient experiments.

Even if the hypothesis was verified, it was only in relative terms. As in ordinary life, the results of the investigation have simply led the worker to a conclusion or decision, which may be either right or wrong. In order to assist him in judging its correctness, he sets up various probability levels which serve to suggest the chance that the solution may be wrong. If the results of the investigation are not very vital, the investigator may choose to work against relatively low odds. But if the penalties of a bad decision are likely to be severe, he will ordinarily require a higher level of probability against such an eventuality. Then he will set up a more precisely controlled set of tests or a larger number of them, or he will demand a larger measured effect of treatments before it is judged significant. With such a background of skillful planning, the investigator has real cause for satisfaction when experimental results stand out clearly above experimental errors.

In any case, when an experiment has been concluded it will generally have exposed new problems or interesting variables, some of which may be considered more important than the subject of the original tests. This may call for more experiments, or it may mean resuming the faster paths of logic, exploration, and experience. Using these tools as far as possible the investigator goes on, adding more new impressions to the facts gained from his experiment, until he needs to resort to quantitative tests again.

Extension of the Solution

In applied biological research especially, the investigator has to work with an extremely varied population under changing climatic and economic conditions. On his route toward an experimental solution he tries to encompass this variation as thoroughly as possible by the combination of exploration, experience, and experiment in an efficient pattern of inquiry.

Even so, he cannot often cover a substantial part of the population, and some of his experiments must necessarily be artificial or small in scale. Consequently, experimental findings can seldom be recommended for practical application before they are tested by means of pilot projects, to see how usable they are and how widely they can be applied.

Ordinarily pilot projects should be carried out first under conditions similar to those of the experimental solution, but on a more practical scale. The study units in a pilot project may have to be large in size, and it is desirable to have administrative people or land managers as well as research workers take part in laying them out and conducting the investigations. In forest areas, for example, such a project may include one or more logging units in a timber sale; on range land the units are large enough so that livestock can be handled in a natural manner. Then, if no hitches in procedure develop from this larger-scale application, similar projects may be set up on sites or materials differing from the original experiments. Timber-cutting pilot projects may be replicated on widely different areas in the same general forest type, so as to show how recommended treatments may vary in their effects under different environmental conditions.

The results of such pilot projects do not change the validity of an experimental solution, within the limits prescribed by the original hypothesis and experimental procedures. But they may demonstrate that the solution is not practical when tried out on a larger scale or under different conditions. Then further investigations must be directed toward reorientation of the solution or reformulation of the hypothesis, with any necessary movement back through a part or all of the steps of scientific inquiry.

Like other parts of the general pattern, the pilot-project step may sometimes be omitted; or it may be reached directly from logical analyses or exploratory work, without recourse to the more detailed and expensive processes of controlled experience and experiment.

The Pattern in Review

In the preceding discussions we have gone through a complex pattern of inquiry which is particularly intended for use in applied research. None of the steps are new in themselves; if there is anything intriguing in this presentation, it is the interweaving of these techniques into a single, organized scientific method, with logic, exploration, experience, and experiment assuming their proper places. This, it would seem, is an efficient way to do research. The steps may be contracted or expanded, but the pattern remains the same. Like a mountaineer, the research worker looks over his task and plans a practical route. Secured by the protecting rope of training, he moves rapidly up over the rocky obstacles until he feels unduly exposed—especially if the footholds of his observations seem a little shaky. Then he stops and drives a spike, fastening himself to the cliff with the firm anchor of a quantitative experiment. And so he proceeds upward, keeping just the right balance between climbing and anchoring. If he anchors too often, all his time is consumed in driving spikes—or making statistical analyses—and he may never reach the summit. But if he climbs too fast and far between anchor points, sooner or later he will fall. For the mountain climber or the research worker, the first course means lack of progress; the second may be fatal.

BIOLOGICAL EXPERIMENTS AND STATISTICS (1964)
Edward Batschelet

The importance of statistical methods in biological research is probably as often overestimated as underestimated. Opinions vary widely so that biologists and statisticians do not always work effectively together. This article is intended to contribute to a better mutual understanding.

Statistical considerations enter into almost any kind of scientific research, even field observations which are naturally made under special circumstances, in a restricted area, and at a particular time. In the following, however, we shall confine ourselves to biological experiments in which, in general, some effects are studied as dependent on one or more factors.

Planning of experiments is a controversial topic. Statisticians often complain that data they are asked to analyze are outcomes of a poorly planned experiment. They feel that they could have contributed essentially if the experimenter had consulted with them in advance. On the other hand, the biologist's view might be quite different. In searching for new results, he may face various difficulties of a financial, technical, or even psychological nature. In addition, many features of the planned experiment may be vague in the beginning. A clarification is possible only by trial and error, that is, by an initial series of experiments which we call *pilot experiments*. They are frequently indispensable and the experimenter is well advised if he proceeds stepwise, each time carefully checking the new situation and providing a flexible arrangement. There are decisions like the following to be made: improve the precision of measurement, adjust the sample size, study the influence of a previously neglected factor, etc. Intuition is here a basic tool since there exists no general method to plan pilot experiments. Can we honestly blame a biologist in this phase of his work if he forgets the statistician and if he wants to go his own way?

Although pilot experiments may violate the rules of modern design of experiments, the data should be statistically analyzed. Graphical approaches as well as the computation of means, variances, covariances, and other quantities will help the experimenter to get some information. The appearance of a significant difference gives him some hope that a certain effect is real and not due only to chance fluctuations.

We have just used the word "hope" to indicate that a test of significance applied to data from pilot experiments does not lead to a definite conclusion but merely to a tentative statement or to a working hypothesis. As a rule, nothing can be proved from it. The reason for this strange fact is not quite obvious. If a test of significance should be more than a guiding tool, if actually the level of significance should have the true meaning of a probability, we have to know the hypothesis to be tested in advance, that is, before we make the experiment. Very often this condition is not satisfied. *It is a common abuse of statistics to "prove" a hypothesis from data that have just been exploited to create this hypothesis.* Therefore, a pilot experiment can hardly lead to a well established scientific result and it is wise to admit this in a publication. A similar idea has been expressed by L. C. Cole (1957, p. 875): "Biologists commonly award that certificate of

Reprinted from: Bioscience 14(10): 30-31.

accuracy known as 'statistical significance' to any experimental result that has odds of 19 to 1 against its occurrence as a result of chance alone. Consequently, it appears that anyone who has experimental data and sufficient patience to compute different indices and to match these with several independent environmental fluctuations should have a reasonable expectation, in 20 or so trials, of obtaining at least one 'statistically significant' result."

Pilot experiments are of a heuristic nature. They are most frequently indispensable in discovering new ground. They are inspiring and guiding and many lead to an interesting hypothesis. However, they should be clearly distinquished from those experiments that finally furnish well established results. We call them *principal experiments*. If preliminary experimental or theoretical investigation has produced a certain hypothesis, it is the purpose of a principal experiment to prove or to disprove it. The experiment has also to answer the question under what conditions the result can be reproduced over and over again. In fact, a principal experiment has to satisfy a respectable amount of requirements. Let us study some of them in detail.

First of all, the experimenter should be concerned with those factors that essentially influence the outcome of his experiments. Neglect of a factor may produce such a large systematic error that the result is of no scientific value even if the statistical analysis was correctly performed. We call such factors *major factors*. In searching for them the experimenter has to free himself from any kind of prejudice. He has to consider even his own person as a possible source of major influence on the experiment. His staff, his laboratory, his equipment, everything has to be declared suspect. Planning of a principal experiment may force the experimenter to make some other pilot experiments. Serious troubles may arise, especially if two major factors are confounded, that is, if a change of the level of a known factor causes a simultaneous change of an unknown factor that might be more important than the first one. Not until all the major factors have been brought under control can the principal experiment be started. Then there is a guarantee that an effect is reproducible within the limits of random fluctuations.

In the actual performance of a principal experiment, some major factors will be kept at a known level. Their influence may not be of main concern. At least one factor will be varied in its level to produce a desired effect. If two or more factors are varied, observations for several combinations of levels are required in order to study possible interactions.

In addition to the major factors there always exists a great number of *minor factors* that will influence the outcome of an experiment to a low degree. It is practically impossible to bring more than a few minor factors under control. They will produce small systematic errors as well as random deviations. They are inevitable even in the most precise physical or chemical experiments. Sometimes a minor factor may be of great theoretical interest. If a principal experiment is planned to study the influence of a minor factor, still more precautions are required. Control of factors and elimination of confounding are most essential. In addition, the sample size has to be increased to such an extent that the effect of a variation of the minor factor can be proved to be significant.

412

The amount of work required to perform a principal experiment looks prohibitive. Biologists may feel that the time and expense involved are exorbitant. In fact, we have here an economic problem par excellence. It can certainly not be solved by a simple neglect of the major requirements. In the past, too many resources have been wasted on so-called results that could never be reproduced by other experiments. We should clearly face the dilemma of finding and insuring new results, even though the effort required looks tremendous. It is at this point that modern methods of experimental design enter the picture. Today there exist a great many designs which are tailored to a variety of situations. Their main purpose is economic efficiency. Reliable information should be obtained with the least possible amount of work and within the shortest possible time. Although these methods are relatively young and need still more development, they are today very useful tools. They also provide a clear logical structure as well as an effective statistical analysis.

Few biologists are well acquainted with the theory of experimental design. As this area is growing rapidly, even fewer biologists will be able to keep abreast of it in the future. A well-trained expert in experimental design should be consulted whenever a principal experiment is planned. He will use preliminary experience from pilot experiments to propose a proper linear or nonlinear model, to determine the number of parameters, to decide on things like the degree of homogeneity and the sample size. The entire procedure of a principal experiment together with the methods of statistical analysis should be well determined before the experiment starts. Any change that might be unavoidable while the experiment is proceeding will jeopardize the reliability of the result.

The biologist and the statistician have to share in the careful and effective planning of a principal experiment. While the biologist is competent in mastering the experimental technique and in knowing the approximate influence of major and minor factors, the statistician is responsible for the logical and statistical aspects. They will both profit by the joint effort. Only free exchange of ideas between life scientists and statisticians has created the powerful methods which are available today.

The following diagram may summarize schematically this article:

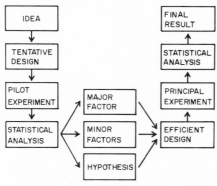

REFERENCE:
L.C. COLE (1957). Biological Clock in the Unicorn, Science 125:874-876.

413

EDUCATION

Although these papers are over three decades old, their information is pertinent today and may help the undergraduate in wildlife conservation to put his coursework and personal goals in perspective.

WHAT CONSTITUTES TRAINING IN WILDLIFE MANAGEMENT (1938)

Ralph T. King

This paper is concerned only with college or university training in the art of wildlife management. It does not include any consideration of training obtainable from other sources or in other manners. This restriction is due entirely to the limitations of time and the author's limited knowledge, not because it is held that such other training is either impossible or undesirable. Furthermore, the paper is confined to a discussion of training in the art or *practice* of wildlife management. It does not deal with the so-called vocational aspects of the subject and neither is it concerned with the training of research men as such. Errington[3] has already ably presented the case for this last mentioned group.

Leopold[5] has called attention to the three kinds of training desirable in wildlife education and pointed out how we may profit by the experience of forestry. He says: "Game education can avoid one of the mistakes made in forestry. It should foresee the desirability of an early choice between the various possible degrees of education. Training for game research, game administration and game keeping are three very different things, not necessarily combined to advantage in a single institution." May I add— impossible to combine in a single curriculum.

To completely divorce these three fields during the student's academic career is neither possible nor desirable; but it is equally impossible and undesirable to fully combine them effectively and economically. One or the other of these three fields must be given primary consideration in the case of each individual and when the choice has been made only such training as is complementary and accessory to this major interest should be included from the two remaining fields.

Because we are here dealing with a consideration of training in the application of the art of wildlife management it will be well to consider for a moment the nature of this art. Art is the application of knowledge, and knowledge is an accumulation of facts. Every art must be based upon a science if it is to have a firm foundation. Science is systematized knowledge. The science upon which the art of wildlife management must be built is wildlife research. This systematized accumulation of facts in regard to the life histories, ecology, growth, habits and needs of wild animals is the science of wildlife research on which an exact art of wildlife management can and must be based.

Welch[9] in his discussion of the essential nature of limnology has furnished us with an explanation that applies equally well to wildlife research and management. Paraphrasing his remarks the case is stated as follows: To qualify as a science, wildlife research must possess some central, unifying feature which ties the whole subject into a coherent, orderly, organized field. Lacking this requirement, wildlife research will be merely an accumulated mass of data. It is held that the central unifying influence of wildlife research is the *problem of biological productivity*. Wildlife research

Reprinted from: Trans. N. Amer. Wildl. Conf. 3:548-557.

417

may therefore be defined as that *branch of science which deals with biological productivity of natural environments and with all of the causal influences which determine it.* Wildlife research is essentially a synthetic science composed of elements some of which extend well beyond the limits of biology as ordinarily conceived. It depends upon the proper application and integration of certain facts, principles, and methods of geology, meteorology, zoology, botany, forestry, agriculture and others to the solution of problems which are, in the end, biological in nature. It is, of course, primarily ecological in its bearing.

This synthetic nature of the science upon which the art is based must carry over into training for the art. Time spent in debating the question of whether a wildlife manager is a zoologist, botanist, forester or member of some other previously formally recognized profession or art is time wasted. He is none of these things if he is a good wildlife manager, and yet he is at the same time to some extent or degree all of these things and more. Training in wildlife management must include something from each of these fields but it must also include something not contained or available in any of these fields. Wildlife management is not a new deck of cards but it is a reshuffling and recombination of the cards in the old deck and results in a hand not previously held by any group playing the scientific game.

The statement made by Harris[4] in a slightly different connection perfectly states the case. He says: "In grappling with these problems more than science as we conceive it today is required. These are not problems of biology alone—they are problems of the application of the results of biological research under difficult economic and political conditions. It is here that some new type of man must establish his interests on the frontiers of biology and economics."

Referring again to the definition of wildlife research as that branch of science which deals with biological productivity of natural environments and with all of the causal influences which determine it, we may accept as the central thesis of wildlife management this matter of *productivity*. Leopold[6] has defined productivity as "the rate at which mature breeding stock produces other mature stock, or mature removable crop." Training in wildlife management must, therefore, be primarily concerned with these causal influences determining productivity and methods of controlling them.

The general subject of the conservation of organic resources is commonly divided (although this is not necessarily the most natural division) on the basis of the several resources it includes. These are soils, waters, forests, grazing, wildlife and mankind. The primary concern of wildlife management is wildlife and its conservation. This, however, cannot be its only concern. Wildlife is so intimately related to other organic and inorganic resources, and so utterly dependent upon them that any consideration of its welfare must perforce include some consideration of the welfare of these other resources. It should be obvious that every wildlife conservation effort is predetermined by the nature, the needs and the activities of the animals we are attempting to conserve. Unless these conservation efforts are based on a knowledge of wild animal biology there can be little hope of success.

In addition it must be realized that all wildlife conservation is wholly dependent upon the provision of satisfactory environments, for all wild animals are totally dependent upon the environment in which they live. Every need of the individual and the species must be supplied by the environment; if the environment provides poorly wildlife will be scarce, and if it provides not at all, even in the case of a single need, wildlife will not exist there. And finally, the demands made upon both the environments and the wildlife, the innumerable influences brought to bear upon them, and the various uses to which they are subjected conditions every effort we make at conservation and every response we obtain. These last mentioned conditioning factors and influences are all included under the term land uses.

The essential nature of wildlife conservation or management as just outlined is illustrated in some degree by the accompanying diagram (Fig. 1). The three arms of the triangle representing *animal biology, environments* and *land uses* are of equal length, thus signifying that these three sets of factors are of equal importance in any wildlife management program. The arm chosen to serve as the base will vary according to the training and interests of the one doing the choosing. The zoologist would choose animal biology; the botanist and perhaps some foresters would choose environments; while other foresters, agriculturists and economists would no doubt choose land uses. The important thing in our management thinking is not which of the three serves as the base but rather are all three given sufficient consideration and are their intimate relations recognized and fully appreciated? The triangle will rest solidly on any one of them if neither of the remaining two is either shortened or lengthened.

Any sound training in wildlife management must include knowledge from all three of these general fields; and any balanced program of wildlife management must derive that balance from equal attention to these three fields.

Each of these fields includes a large body of knowledge which is now subdivided and treated in our various curricula as numerous highly specialized courses. No attempt has been made to list all of these courses or to arrange those listed in the order of their importance; and no attempt will be made to discuss these many courses or subjects. The object is to make as clear as possible the complexities involved in wildlife biology and the important interrelations existing between wildlife and its environments and the other uses to which these environments are subject. Certainly this is the minimum amount of knowledge permissible in any wildlife manager.

To what extent should the wildlife manager know animal biology and what phases of the subject should he be especially proficient in? Briefly he should know species' requirements, life histories, behavior patterns, and species' and population properties. He must have engrained within him the following biological conceptions: First, that each environment must contain that great variety of foods, coverts, water and special factors needed during the different seasons for the various activities of both sexes and all age groups of all the species it is intended that the environment shall support. This applies not only to the materials necessary for the animal's physical well being but also to the pattern or arrangement of these materials in a

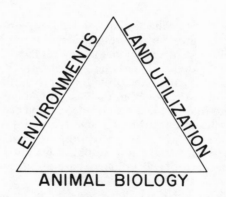

ENVIRONMENTS	ANIMAL BIOLOGY	LAND UTILIZATION
Botany	Zoology	Economics
Morphology	Vertebrate	Sociology
Taxonomy	Invertebrate	History
Ecology	Morphology	Geography
Field Botany	Taxonomy	Forestry
Limnology	Physiology	Policy and Admin.
Geology	Embryology	Forest Man.
Soils	Genetics	Grazing
Forestry	Ecology	Silviculture
Silvics	Zoogeography	Agriculture
Dendrology	Mammalogy	Agronomy
Chemistry	Ornithology	Grazing
Organic	Ichthyology	Soils
Physiological	Entomology	Recreation Eng.
Biochemistry	Field Zoology	Wildlife Man.
Meteorology	Pathology	
Biometry		

FIGURE 1

manner suited to the animal's physical abilities. Second, that adaptations are just as truly limitations, and that these restrictions on behavior give rise in animals to definite sets of habits; these habits constitute the animal's behavior pattern—or expression of the animal's abilities—and ordinarily it can be modified only slightly for it is in reality the sum of the responses the animal is compelled to make to its environment. To know the limitations imposed by the various morphological, physiological and behavioristic adaptations, and to know in addition the limitations resulting in and from the several phases of the more or less complicated life histories of animals requires a considerable knowledge of animal biology and a detailed knowledge of the various species one is attempting to manage. Third, as expressed by Leopold[6] that "many characteristics of wild species are so manifestly a fixed attribute that they may, without unduly stretching the term, be called 'properties' in the same sense that the specific gravity, or the coefficient of expansion, is a property of various chemical substances, or of industrial materials." It is understood that he must know these properties and take account of them in his management practices.

What must the wildlife manager know of ecology and in what phases of the subject must he be especially well-versed? He must appreciate fully that environments have both their physical and biological phases and he must understand quite well both of these phases as they relate to the species with which he is concerned. Perhaps the ecological concept of most impor-

420

tance to the wildlife manager is that of succession. The wildlife manager must look upon both animals and environments not as things static and having only linear dimensions, but as things happening in nature and in a state of constant change. Adams[1] has expressed this point-of-view as follows: "The environment is not to be considered as static, not as an unchanging medium; it has both a past and a future, not merely horizontal extension. The problem as to its *dynamic status*—whether in a condition of stress, in the process of adjustment, or in relative equilibrium must be faced." It is frequently necessary in management to hasten or reverse succession, and once a desired stage has been attained it is necessary to retard succession on the area in question or have other areas approaching the same stage. For these and other reasons a clear conception of succession and the dynamics of environments is essential to every wildlife manager. To understand the simple fact that animals are dependent upon their environment is important but far from sufficient; to make this knowledge the basis of a sound management program requires an understanding of the innumerable relationships involved and the constantly changing pattern of these relationships.

To what extent must the wildlife manager be familiar with land uses? Certainly to the extent that he appreciates the following named governing principles: First, that wildlife is an organic product and that it is just as much a product of the land on which it lives as are forest trees, range grasses or farm crops. Second, that wildlife management practices are conditioned by the other uses to which the land is subject and also by economic and sociological considerations. Third, that wildlife has numerous values all of which must be taken into consideration.

Perhaps every one associated in any way with wildlife recognizes most of the values of wild animals and has a deep appreciation of some of them. It is doubtful, however, if anyone without special training in economic zoology recognizes and appreciates all of the values possessed by wildlife. This degree of training is not essential for one's personal enjoyment of wildlife, but it is necessary if one is to prepare management programs that will bring the greatest possible returns from management and provide the best assurance of multiple land use and sustained yield. The several values of wildlife may, for the sake of brevity be listed under six general headings, these are: Commercial, Recreational, Biological, Social, Esthetic and Scientific. Unfortunately most individuals, including too many wildlife managers, recognize only one, or at most two or three of these values, and insist that those they do recognize be given primary if not exclusive consideration. This has led to the present situation wherein various organized groups all intensely interested in wildlife conservation advocate and demand conservation programs that are antagonistic to each other, incomplete in their provisions, and very apt to do more harm than good should they be enacted. There can be no improvement in the public's attitude and no provisions for the proper management of this resource unless and until those responsible for its management are informed as to the various values possessed by wild animals, the various services performed by them, and unless they are aware also of the values of this resource to at present inarticulate and apparently uninterested groups. Those are my reasons for insisting that such knowledge be considered an essential part of the wild-life manager's training.

These several considerations arising from the major concept of multiple land use may be expressed as the seven premises on which wildlife management must be based, these are:

1. Wildlife values include all the rights and interests that the various groups of our population have in this resource. Whether or not these groups are organized is a question of no fundamental importance.

2. Wildlife is an organic resource and can be managed on a sustained yield basis.

3. Wildlife is a product of the land, therefore, management practices are conditioned by the other uses to which the land is subject.

4. Wildlife is a commodity and as such is answerable to the ordinary rules of investment.

5. Wildlife cannot be considered separate and apart from its environment, as a consequence its management must make provisions for satisfactory environments.

6. Wildlife environments in most instances have values in themselves in addition to their value to wildlife.

7. Income from wildlife may in some instances be sufficient to offset carrying charges accruing on wildlife environments that are being managed for purposes in addition to wildlife production.

What, then, are the subject matter courses that should be included in the wildlife manager's curriculum? We may for convenience consider them in three groups—basic courses, applied courses and complementary courses.

The basic courses are those included under zoology, botany, geology, economics, history, etc., that provide a knowledge of the fundamentals of biology, ecology, values and human relations as they apply to lands; they need not be enumerated for they are listed in connection with figure 1.

The applied courses are those furnishing training in technics and they should be kept at a minimum. Although formal training in wildlife management has existed as such for less than a decade we are already overcrowding our curricula with "shop courses" at the expense of training in basic sciences. We can profitably apply in our teaching of wildlife management the principles laid down by Dr. Karl T. Compton[2] in a recent paper wherein he discusses the development of engineering education. He says: "In the early days the professional (engineering) curriculum consisted of pure science, the applied science of the day and the techniques of practical work in shops or in the field. As great industries developed, based on technological advances, the curriculum took on more of systematic training in the processes and techniques of these industries, became more crowded with newer and newer specialties, with some tendency to crowd out the basic sciences and much pressure to stuff the student with all the factual knowledge and techniques which he might later be called upon to use. This trend finally broke for two reasons: it became impossible, unwieldy and it became out of tune with industrial demands. . . . Now the larger industries can, and prefer, to do much of the training of their new employees in the particular techniques and operations which they use. Their great demand is for young engineers who are so well grounded in the sciences and in the fundamental theories of engineering as to be capable of grappling effectively with the new problems and ever-advancing arts that are associated with technological progress. So the recent tendency of the engineering schools has been to reduce emphasis on shop practices . . . also to postpone the more specialized training into postgraduate years; and to concentrate chiefly on basic science and fundamental engineering, together with more attention to the economics and social science which are becoming more and more the concern of the engineer. In this program, such specialization as remains in the undergraduate curriculum is more for the purpose of training the student how to specialize than for producing a specialist."

If teachers of wildlife managers are as wise as they should be they will profit by this experience of engineering schools, and if employers of wildlife managers are as wise as they should be they will realize that a knowledge of shop practices and techniques will have to be largely acquired "on the job" if their young men are to come to them properly trained in the fundamentals of the science which it is their business to apply.

Taylor[7] has summed up the situation in his statement that "our present practice, of turning out technical assistants who are ultra-specialists, is unfair both to the young graduates, to the community, and to the natural resources for which they may be responsible."

Complementary courses include those in which the student obtains training in speaking, writing, preparation of specimens, and introductory courses in certain highly specialized fields with which he should have some familiarity. Public relations work makes some training in public speaking highly desirable. The preparation of reports will be facilitated by proper training in writing. A knowledge of how specimens should be prepared and what data should be submitted with them will prove valuable to most field men. Although the wildlife manager is not supposed to be a pathologist he should have a sufficient knowledge of both parasitology and bacteriology to know when the services of specialists in these fields are necessary and how best to cooperate with them.

As pointed out in connection with the diagram each of the three general fields mentioned includes a large body of knowledge, some quite general and some highly specialized, but far more in each case than any one individual can hope to master in detail. It isn't necessary that every item of knowledge in each subdivision of each field be mastered and retained. A body of workable knowledge is never thus obtained. Acquiring knowledge is an essential step in education and acquiring an education is in some respects analogous to the construction of a building. Certain materials are essential to the completion of the building and when it is finished they are an integral part of it. There are, however, other materials just as essential to the completion of the building during the process of construction but once their function is performed they are discarded and forgotten and form no part of the completed structure. These last are usually in the nature of scaffolding; they are very necessary in the process of building but would be a serious liability if retained in connection with the completed structure. The larger and more pretentious the building the more of this scaffolding required.

Likewise, in any curriculum there are certain courses known as pre-requisites; these are essential to sound training and the attainment of the student's objective, but it is neither necessary nor desirable to retain forever all the information acquired in these courses. It is usually these courses that the student has in mind when he complains that he was compelled to take work that is of no value to him after graduation. He has forgotten, if he was ever aware of, the value of this work to him in completing his educational structure.

In conclusion I would like to quote once more, this time from Van Hise[8]. This matter of training as applied to the work of a geologist, but applying with equal force to the wildlife manager, has been concisely expressed by him as follows: "I have heard a man say: 'I observe the facts as I find them, unprejudiced by any theory.' I regard this statement as not only condemning the work of the man, but the position is an impossible one. No man has ever stated more than a small part of the facts with reference to any area. The geologist must select the facts which he regards of sufficient note to record and describe. But such selection implies theories of their importance and significance. In a given case the problem is therefore reduced to selecting the facts for record, with a broad and deep comprehension of the principles involved, a definite understanding of the rules of the game, an appreciation of what is probable and what is not probable; or else making mere random observations. All agree that the latter alternative is worse than useless, and therefore, the only training which can make a geologist safe, even in his observations, is to equip him with such a knowledge of the principles concerned as will make his observations of value."

There will be differences in the titles of the courses taught in the name of wildlife management, and differences in the semester and quarter hours of credit allotted them. There must, however, be agreement on fundamentals or wildlife managers will never get along with themselves, and they will most assuredly never get along with the public. These fundamentals are submitted as one man's point-of-view. Honest differences of opinion are invited in the belief that only in this way can our teaching be improved, our practices be made more effective, and our profession advanced.

REFERENCES

1. ADAMS, CHARLES C. 1913. Guide to the Study of Animal Ecology, N.Y.
2. COMPTON, KARL T. 1937. Engineering in an American Program for Social Progress. Science, 85, pp. 275-280.
3. ERRINGTON, PAUL L. 1934. Wildlife Research as a Profession. Scientific Monthly, 38, pp. 554-560.
4. HARRIS, J. ARTHUR. 1930. Frontiers. Scientific Monthly, 30, pp. 19-32.
5. LEOPOLD, ALDO. 1931. The Role of Universities in Game Conservation. DuPont Magazine, June.
6. LEOPOLD, ALDO. 1933. Game Management, N.Y.
7. TAYLOR, WALTER P. 1936. What is Ecology and What Good is It? Ecology, 17, pp. 333-346.
8. VANHISE, C. R. 1904. The Problems of Geology. Journal of Geology, 12, pp. 589-616.
9. WELCH, PAUL S. 1935. Limnology, N.Y.

THE STATE OF THE PROFESSION (1940)
Aldo Leopold

One of the ironies frequent in history is a group of men attempting one thing and accomplishing another. We are attempting to manage wildlife, but it is by no means certain that we shall succeed, or that this will be our most important contribution to the design for living.

For example, we may, without knowing it, be helping to write a new definition of what science is for.

We are not scientists. We disqualify ourselves at the outset by professing loyalty to and affection for a thing: wildlife. A scientist in the old sense may have no loyalties except to abstractions, no affections except for his own kind.

Moreover, some of us entertain heresies and doubts. We doubt whether science can claim the credit for bigger and better tools, comforts, and securities without also claiming the credit for bigger and better erosions, denudations, and pollutions. We doubt whether the good life flows automatically from the good invention.

The definitions of science written by, let us say, the National Academy, deal almost exclusively with the creation and exercise of power. But what about the creation and exercise of wonder, of respect for workmanship in nature? I see hints of such dissent, even in the writings of the scientifically elect—Fraser Darling, for example. Of course, we have always had such writers (David, Isaiah, John Muir) but they were not scientifically elect; they were only poets. Is Fraser Darling only a poet?

The peculiar pertinence of this to our profession is that we deal with science, but we have no prospect of inventing new tools or powers. Our job is to harmonize the increasing kit of scientific tools and the increasing recklessness in using them with the shrinking biotas to which they are applied. In the nature of things we are mediators and moderators, and unless we can help rewrite the objectives of science our job is predestined to failure.

I daresay few wildlife managers have any intent or desire to contribute to art and literature, yet the ecological dramas which we must discover if we are to manage wildlife are inferior only to the human drama as subject matter for the fine arts. Is it not a little pathetic that poets and musicians must paw over shopworn mythologies and folklores as media for art, and ignore the dramas of ecology and evolution?

There are straws which indicate that this senseless barrier between science and art may one day blow away, and that wildlife ecology, if not wildlife management, may help do the blowing. We have, at long last, an ecological novel—Peattie's "Prairie Grove." Darling is not the only ecologist whose scientific writings have literary quality. In our profession, and on its fringes, are a growing number of painters and photographers who are also researchers. These intergrades in human taxonomy are perhaps more important than those which so perplex the mammalogists and ornithologists. Their skulls are not yet available to the museums, but even a layman can see that their brains are distinctive.

Reprinted from: J. Wildl. Mgmt. 4(3):343-346.

In its external trappings of printed knowledge, our profession has attained in four years a maturity which might well have taken a decade. I refer, of course, to THE JOURNAL OF WILDLIFE MANAGEMENT and the *Wildlife Review*. Some journal papers are still a bit thin, but the average is high and getting higher. No other conservation profession has the equal of the *Wildlife Review*.

One of the weak points in our profession is the low proportion of private employment. Even among the publicly employed the proportion dealing directly with practice on private lands is small.

I think there are more opportunities in private practice than we foresee.

A few industries are already set to go ahead. The guano industry of Peru has employed an American ornithologist to manage its birds, and thus to put guano on "sustained yield." The number of guano birds on these very small Peruvian islands is nearly as great as the number of ducks in North America. This comparison may help convey the heroic proportions of this venture, and incidentally, the low estate of our ducks.

The Hudson's Bay Company is, I think, about set for fur management in the Canadian Arctic. They must be, for the wild fur is gone. Canadians, I think, will do well to encourage the venture, else they will have more acres on relief than we have. Incidentally, a boom in beavers will do much for the ducks.

Why do large private holdings retain wildlife managers in the Southeast, but not elsewhere? If our profession can give valuable service on strings of quail preserves, why not to other game species in other regions where large holdings exist? At least one reason harks back, I think, to a lack of respect for private property. In most regions the public puts all land-owners, large and small, under moral suasion not to post. The public does not realize that this is moral suasion not to manage.

Some day the hunter will learn that hunting and fishing are not the only wildlife sports; that the new sports of ecological study and observation are as free to all now as hunting was to Daniel Boone. These new sports depend on the retention of a rich flora and fauna. Management of private holdings to rebuild the fauna and flora is one of the opportunities offered our profession today. There is a growing number of private sanctuaries, private arboreta, and private research stations, all of which are gropings toward non-lethal forms of outdoor recreation. But few such gropings are skillful. Wildlife managers, acting in a consulting capacity, could help owners find what they are looking for.

Some fear that we are getting too much research and not enough management into our journals and (by implication) into our programs. I do not share in this view; in fact, I think the shoe is on the other foot. We know how to manage only a few easy species like deer and pheasants. In other species we know a few fragmentary treatments which are *probably* beneficial, but this is not enough. Until we know more it is proper that a high proportion of our professional effort should go into research.

Too much research, however, is superficial and aimed at quick returns. The high proportion of sporting funds in both the ten unit system and the new Pittman-Robertson structure tends to perpetuate this distortion. So does the low proportion of research groups which have as yet demonstrated capacity to execute more fundamental investigations. So does the series of inter-bureau treaties which confine federal research to a single bureau. Is it not just as illogical to confine wildlife research to a single bureau as it is to confine conservation to a single department?

If anyone doubts that we are trying to eat our research dessert before starting the soup-kettle, let him appraise the national situation in terms of the following questions: In how many species do we know the sex and age composition of a population, and its rate of turnover? In how many species do we have criteria of age? In how many species have we followed the behavior of a sample population for ten years?

The research program is out of balance in other respects. One is the paucity of research of an ecological nature in such groups as rodents where the problem is to manage downward rather than upward. Stockmen and farmers quite naturally want direct action in the form of control, while absentee conservationists protest at any action at all. It is probable that both are wrong, and that the eventual answer in rodents, as in game, lies in indirect environmental manipulation. But where is the research aimed to develop and implement this concept? Concepts do not help to manage land.

The research program is out of balance in that certain kinds of wildlife are omitted altogether; for example, wildflowers and other non-economic vegetation. It would be interesting to see one of the Ten Units get into a huddle with the botany department and propose to the Director of Conservation that something be found out about the management of lady-slippers in farm woodlots. Would the checkbook snap open or shut?

It is encouraging to note that one erstwhile orphan, innocent of economic utility, is no longer high-hatted by his useful conservation cousins. I refer to rare species.

Lastly, the research program pays too little attention to the history of wildlife, and our system of publications makes no provision for historical monographs. We do not yet appreciate how much historical evidence can be dug up, or how important it can be in the appraisal of contemporary ecology. I have in mind such historical work as that of A. W. Schorger in Wisconsin, most of which is not yet in print. I would like to see the Society set up a basket to receive funds for the publication of historical wildlife monographs. I believe that both the monographs and the funds would eventually be forthcoming.

One problem which now faces the profession is how to organize extension. I use that word in its agricultural sense, *i.e.,* sending out trained men to help landowners to help themselves.

Most extension efforts in wildlife have been aimed at helping sportsmen to help themselves. It represents real progress to see states like Texas and Missouri sending out young technicians to deal directly with landowners. The coordination of this new enterprise with the parallel enterprises in agriculture and forestry remains to be worked out.

The problem of teaching conservation to laymen is distinguishable from extension only in name. State after state is legislating conservation courses into the curricula of public schools. But where are the local teaching materials, and who is to teach the teachers how to use them?

In those states which have wildlife research units the production of teaching materials is presumably under way, but what of the teaching of teachers? Why do so many universities spend most of their wildlife funds and use their ablest men in training professional managers when the greater need is for wildlife courses for the general student body and for prospective teachers?

These are problems of educational policy far wider than our own profession, but the speed and skill with which they are solved will depend in large degree on the statesmanship of wildlife managers.

In this little list of unanswered problems and dilemmas there lies concealed, but I hope not undiscovered, a story of almost romantic expansion in professional responsibilities.

Our profession began with the job of producing something to shoot. However important this may seem to us, it is not very important to the emancipated moderns who no longer feel soil between their toes.

We find that we cannot produce much to shoot until the landowner changes his ways of using land, and he in turn cannot change his ways until his teachers, bankers, customers, editors, governors, and trespassers change their ideas about what land is for. To change ideas about what land is for is to change ideas about what anything is for.

Thus we started to move a straw, and end up with the job of moving a mountain.

PUBLIC RELATIONS AND EXTENSION

For many years biologists have appreciated the importance of "people problems" in conservation. Yet, sophisticated efforts to create a more favorable climate of human interests and attitudes in which to practice wildlife management have been slow to emerge. The following selections reflect historical trends and philosophies in extension and public relations aspects of wildlife conservation. The findings of Smith and Berryman reflect attitudes of professional biologists toward extension work. Papers by Calkins and by Schoenfeld outline fundamental approaches and ideas in attempting to sway public opinion. Woolf's case history illustrates the potential role of public relations in decision-making by management agencies. Finally, a challenge of the present and future is available in the work of Rettie.

WILDLIFE EXTENSION—PAST, PRESENT, AND FUTURE (1962)

E. H. Smith and J. H. Berryman

It is the purpose of this paper to critically examine the past performance and present status of wildlife extension programs in the United States and, on the basis of this examination, to suggest its most productive future role. Obviously we are "sold" on wildlife extension and it is our hope that through a critical examination and a reorientation, more states can be encouraged to adopt wildlife extension as an educational and management tool.

First, we should briefly explain the Cooperative Extension Service. It is primarily an educational service, organized with offices and professional staff members on a federal, state and county partnership basis. It was created by the Smith-Lever Act of Congress in 1914 and originally aimed primarily at the rural populations. Extension now aims to serve all of the people and it has been broadened to engage in program planning on a broad, long-term basis.

Extension is the off-campus arm of Land Grant Universities. All Extension Services have a staff of specialists in a wide variety of fields—agronomy, agricultural economics, radio and television, veterinary science, sociology, farm planning, recreation, and so on. The services of this staff are made available to the public through the County Agents. County Agents in turn are generally among the most influential and respected men in their communities.

Obviously, this is an extensive organization with its nerve center on a university campus, grass root ties in local communities and channels extending to the nation's capital. Here is an organization that is in touch with every agricultural activity, and with its expanding program it will soon touch on every phase of community life.

The Past

Wildlife Extension is one of the newer subject matter fields covered by the Extension Services. It was only natural that as wildlife was included within the extension program, it would fall into the traditional extension approach. Originally, and over much of the nation at the present time, this approach was one of in-service training and providing direct assistance to either individuals or small organized groups. Originally the wildlife extension worker, following the pattern of the agricultural extensionist, made new findings available through pamphlets and by bringing information on wildlife to a small segment of the public through public appearances and the traditional farm visit.

Faced with changing times, changing patterns of land-use, a shifting economy and a rapidly expanding population, extension is taking a fresh look at itself. It is now in a period of evolution. Extension has learned that the traditional approach is inadequate. Wildlife extension, caught up in the same impetus, is going through a similar process.

Wildlife extension faces an even newer set of problems peculiar to

Reprinted from: Trans. N. Amer. Wildl. and Natural Resources Conf. 27:450-459.

the resource. Wildlife management was once concerned with protective legislation and law enforcement, control of predators, and the stocking of fish and fowl. These were operations over which game departments had direct control and were able to handle. These functions also took place at a period in our history when there was more open land and fewer people. Game departments now, however, are faced with problems and situations over which they have no control. The use of pesticides, drainage, highway planning, pollution, and a score of other accelerated activities directly affect wildlife. Game departments and other wildlife management agencies have little or no control over such activities. We have arrived at the time when these management agencies cannot solve wildlife problems alone. Wildlife resource needs must be considered in a broader sphere by industry, education and agriculture.

The Present

With newer and broader problems the sphere of activities, responsibilities, and techniques required of wildlife specialists has been enlarged. If we believe otherwise, if we believe we can restrict ourselves to the old traditional extension approaches alone, we are fooling no one but ourselves.

Believing that although we may not think *alike,* we should at least think *together,* questionnaires were recently sent to Extension Wildlife Specialists and to Fish and Game Departments in states having a wildlife extension program. The replies were illuminating, constructive, and largely encouraging. Questionnaires were also sent to Federal Bureau chiefs of related agencies.

Replies were received from fifteen extensionists in fourteen states. Seventeen states are known to have individuals employed in this type of work. Specialists are financed in a variety of ways. Six are paid entirely from fish and game department funds. Two are financed by extension funds alone. Four are financed jointly, although not necessarily in equal amounts, by Extension Service and fish and game department funds. Two are financed jointly by fish and game department and university funds. One is jointly financed by Extension Service and Agricultural Experiment Station funds.

Twelve specialists stated adult education was their primary responsibility. Obviously, adult education has many facets. Classification of the various attitudes, philosophies, and procedures entailed in this phase will be discussed later.

Two specialists considered youth education their primary responsibility. One specialist named animal damage control as his major area of operation. Other major activities named included farm pond management, coordination and liaison, and in-service training. Obviously, the majority of the specialists operate in the area of adult education.

What are they attempting to do in this area? Their objectives are summarized as follows:

1. *Present* people with factual information about the interrelationship between wildlife management, soil, water, plants and people.

2. *Develop* appreciation of the recreational, esthetic, and economic values of wildlife.

3. *Stimulate* ecological approaches to land management activities and problems.

4. *Create* appreciation, understanding, and willingness to properly utilize the wildlife resource and support sound management principles.

5. *Influence* the adoption of land and water use practices that provide consideration for, and are beneficial to wildlife.

6. *Discuss*, with agencies, organizations, and individuals, the public issues affecting resource use, thus broadening the understanding and cooperation on these issues.

Apparently the approaches of wildlife specialists are to present, develop, stimulate, create, influence, and discuss wildlife resource problems. Selecting key phrases from the broad objectives previously summarized, these techniques will be applied in the areas of (1) factual information, (2) recreational, esthetic and economic values, (3) ecological approaches, (4) utilization, (5) land and water use practices, and (6) involvement in public issues.

We believe that these objectives are valid and progressive. However, objectives mean little unless they are attained. How to attain them? Replies from the various wildlife specialists were varied, but the main ideas can be summarized as follows:

1. Place greater stress on mass media methods of communication.

2. Do not scattergun information—concentrate on training county extension agents.

3. Involve local people in local problems, in developing goals, and initiating action programs for settling their own problems.

4. Require better program direction and coordination of specialists between states by direction from wildlife specialists at federal level.

5. Require that specialists be better trained in the areas of adult education and public relations.

6. Specialists must take the bull by the horns—one way, instigating and promoting research in areas where factual information is lacking or questionable.

7. Specialists must have better comprehension of the extension role, structure, function, and proprieties. Extension has a long history of not attempting to "sell" any specific program. Stay detached from agency policies, procedures, and programs; sell resource management, not someone's program unless they coincide.

8. Do not subjugate the development of projects and programs to informational type activities.

9. Develop active, cooperative programs with other personnel in and out of Extension. Encourage appointment to committees, boards, commissions, etc.

10. Avoid duplications of activities of wildlife techniques—broaden scope of activities to include more esthetic and non-harvest aspects.

11. Call a spade a spade; do not compromise principles.

12. Keep abreast of developments in own field; interpret and adapt them to needs of clientele.

13. Extension wildlife specialists should be administered by educational institutions, not resource agencies.

14. Get dynamic people for a dynamic program; people with better than adequate training and experience. Work on big issues, do not fritter away time, energy, and money on rat-hole projects of a trifling nature.

15. Specialists must use all legitimate means at their disposal to influence agencies and policies, including the traditional educational approach, but with more emphasis on influence and pressure. Obviously this must be carefully done. In attempting to influence agencies and policies the specialists must maintain their respect by holding firm to an objective, unbiased position.

16. Develop aggressive administrative support on a par with commodity groups—including support at Federal Extension Service level.

17. Develop specific educational programs which face the *issues* in wildlife resource development.

The foregoing suggestions are wide ranging and varied; from training, through technique, to philosophy.

Obviously no single idea represents a complete program that will fit all occasions, and they were not intended to. The majority are complementary, some are contradictory. We skate on thin ice for a moment in an attempt to apply these ideas to the construction of a wildlife extension specialist and a wildlife extension program from the component parts submitted.

The specialist will have more than adequate professional experience and technical training with equivalent skills in communication and educational techniques. He will be a dynamic individual with the courage to stick to principles in spite of personal and political pressure. He will be an astute diplomat with the ability to remain objective and unbiased. He will be able to evaluate research findings and promote and instigate research where required to further his educational program.

The wildlife extension program will be based on sound objectives and established priorities as determined by proven needs and developments. The program will include the traditional educational approach, but also recognize the advantages of applying legitimate influence and pressure through the medium of committee, commission, advisory board, and personal contacts, both inside and outside the extension service. His program will be based upon sound principles of wildlife and related resource management, which may or may not coincide with current policies of resource management agencies or users of natural resources. His program will attempt to resolve such differences when they occur. His program will recognize the competitive demands upon soil, water, plants and space, and intimately relate the wildlife resource to total resource development. His program will be based upon the conviction that the wildlife resource is a recreational, esthetic and economic asset to our nation and is worth fighting for.

It is axiomatic that the educational responsibilities of the wildlife specialist cross the lines of management responsibility legally assigned to a variety of public agencies. Among these agencies, state fish and game departments are most directly involved.

If we are to follow our own recommendations regarding bias and objectivity, the state fish and game departments should be heard from.

Consequently, questionnaires were sent to fish and game administrators in those states known to be employing extension wildlife specialists. Replies were received from thirteen states.

One of the questions asked state wildlife administrators was "What do you believe the current and future role of wildlife extension programs should be?"

All replies followed one main theme. Wildlife extension programs should utilize other extension specialists and county extension agents to the maximum degree. This would not only take advantage of an already existing, widespread organization, but would encourage the dissemination of sound land use and wildlife management to a portion of the public directly concerned with natural resources, but often not reached through regular wildlife department channels.

Several administrators either stated or inferred that wildlife specialists should assume the responsibility for providing adequate inservice training to extension personnel, thus to provide coordination and prevent chaos.

We are frankly surprised that only two fish and game administrators discussed the potentialities and values for coordination and liaison inherent in the wildlife extension program outside the extension organization itself. In the words of one, "I feel wildlife extension should continue along the present levels of educating the county agents and the farmers to encourage them in good wildlife practices. However, I think there is a real challenge for the extensionist to work with certain influential groups, such as the editors of newspapers, policy making people of different departments and bureaus, etc. They can certainly aid the wildlife management program by helping these people to understand wildlife problems and establish their programs so they are compatible to wildlife."

Insofar as only two of thirteen fish and game department administrators discussed either the efforts put forth or the potential involved in liaison and coordination activities of wildlife specialists in their states, we believe a question is appropriate. Why does this discrepancy exist between the emphasis placed by specialists on this type of activity and the apparent recognition of its value and desirability by fish and game administrators? One answer may be that specialists are giving lip service, but little action to this type of activity. An additional deduction is that fish and game administrators feel this type of activity is of so little importance that it does not merit comment, or on the other hand, they believe this activity is an inherent part of the extension process, and no discussion is required or expected. Last, cooperation and coordination between fish and game administrators and wildlife specialists may be so poor that each does not know what the other is accomplishing.

Some objective self scrutiny by administrators and wildlife specialists in the various states may be appropriate on this question. On the basis of the questionnaire, replies from both state administrators and specialists, there is evidence that there is considerable room for improvement in the area of formal coordination and cooperation between the state fish and game administrators and the specialist. This may provide a partial answer to the question.

To summarize the questionnaire replies from both sources regarding cooperation and coordination a bit further, the majority indicated the level was good to excellent, but usually with reservations regarding certain areas. The remainder suggested there was considerable room for improvement, with no reservations. We gained the distinct impression that cooperation and coordination was most active at field levels and tapered off, rapidly in some instances, as administrative levels were approached.

In spite of the obvious deficiencies in this area, eleven of the thirteen administrators answering the question, "Is wildlife extension aiding you in accomplishing your management goals?", answered in the affirmative. One state indicated aid was limited and one declined to answer.

In reply to the question, "Is wildlife extension an effective educational tool in your state?", nine administrators answered in the affirmative, two felt it was not what it could be, two declined to answer the question.

Several of the miscellaneous ideas forwarded by administrators relating to the last two questions may be of interest. Some indicated lack of coordination required rationalizing a positive affirmative answer. Others felt affirmative answers were appropriate only if applied to certain specialist areas of operation. Two suggested that the extension programs would be more effective, management-wise, if the specialists restricted themselves more to adults and specific problems.

Obviously, the area of coordination requires more attention, insofar as deficiencies in this area are being reflected in evaluation of program effectiveness. However, as one state administrator pointed out, "It is realized that there can be no compromise in teaching a good wildlife management practice. However, in actual practice, the department cannot always place into effect the practice that the best management would dictate because of lack of public understanding."

The fact that a state fish and game department is basically a political organization must be recognized by the wildlife specialist. Snap judgments are inappropriate coming from either the administrator or educator. The objectives of both can only be served by mutual understanding and consistent and aggressive efforts leading toward a mutual objective.

The Future

Our survey reveals that wildlife extension is not well understood and does not enjoy the cooperation of the extension services or the game departments in some states. Furthermore, Wildlife Extension has made no obvious impact on the leaders of responsible Federal resource agencies. Under such circumstances it cannot be expected to perform effectively. It is incumbent upon the university, the extension service and the game department to join a cooperative effort. Developing such cooperation is largely a responsibility of the specialist, but there must be a favorable climate among the cooperators. This is not always the case.

Several extension programs are focused on a small facet of wildlife resource management. They fail to "probe the heart of basic problems."

Obviously, wildlife extension has a most important future role to play. Also, this will be an expanded role as time goes by and complexities increase. It is equally obvious extension is not meeting present needs in some areas and is not geared for its future challenge in others.

Cooperative extension, including wildlife extension, cannot adequately meet today's or tomorrow's needs using the old, conventional and traditional tools in extension any more than in outer space investigations. There is urgent need for a reorientation of objectives, priorities and approach.

In terms of objectives, extension must attempt to reach areas not covered by the responsible management agencies. Here it must define its specific problems and shape its working program to accomplish these objectives.

Priorities must be carefully examined and selected in any program whether it be wildlife extension or wildlife management. There are far more needs than can be satisfied, far more activities than can be successfully pursued. It is only through careful selection of a limited number of high priority needs that careful aim can be taken and a fruitless waste of time and energies be prevented.

Now, what are the legitimate areas of concern to wildlife extension? Land use planning is a high priority with involvement in public issues such as pollution control, the proper use of pesticides, the impact of highway planning, and urban and rural development deserving of equal attention. Here there is need for creating an aware public and for influencing policy determinations. Here the Extension Wildlife Specialist can bring the talents of the Extension Services and the university as a whole to bear on problems beyond the normal scope of the management agencies.

The tremendous boom in outdoor recreation, including fishing and hunting, provides an opportunity, in fact demands attention from the Wildlife Specialist in fully developing the economic potential of our wildlife resources. Fishing and hunting are now important to rural and urban communities. They can become more so. This is a challenge in land use and outdoor economics that will require a joint effort with the specialist assuming responsibility for consideration of the wildlife resource.

The new rural area development program provides a special opportunity. Fishing and hunting are built-in attractions that can mean more in rural area development and in community development programs. This too is a field that should receive the time and attention of the specialist.

Obviously, and to repeat, the traditional extension approach is inadequate for an effective contribution in these areas. It is physically and practically impossible to effectively reach an adequate number of people. More reliance must be placed on the use of mass media in creating an informed public.

Extension must turn more to influencing opinion leaders. This might be termed the legitimate use of influence and pressure. The extensionist must maintain the necessary contacts to secure committee assignments, maintain good working relationships with key community and organization leaders, and, the more difficult qualification, that he remain respected and influential without antagonizing these various groups.

The involvement in land use and other issues is a legitimate function and one where a concrete contribution can be made through the definition of objective policy and through influencing policy makers and the public at large.

Extension has a role in reaching publics not normally reached by the management agencies and for attacking problems not normally within the scope of these agencies. This will require a fresh approach, a reorientation, and a continuing evaluation. Once this evaluation is accomplished with the full cooperation of the universities, the fish and game departments, and other responsible agencies, extension can begin to perform its proper role in the management of our wildlife resources. This responsibility must rest equally upon the cooperators, but responsibility for initiation remains with the existing wildlife extension program.

PUBLIC RELATIONS AND EDUCATION IN THE WILDLIFE MANAGEMENT FIELD (1960)

R. D. Calkins

The pressures and competition of civilization during the past few generations have brought into being two new arts.

One is that of wildlife management. The other is that of public relations.

They came into being for different reasons. But today wildlife management is looking to public relations for help in getting its job done better and faster.

Those who ply these two arts—wildlife managers and public relations men—have one thing in common. They both have been educated in the sciences and from them seek answers.

Sciences Provide Foundation

Wildlife managers rely on such sciences as botany, zoology, pathology and ichthyology while public relations men turn to psychology, sociology, economics and semantics.

Almost every sportsman and conservationist thinks of himself as an expert in the wildlife management field. Similarly most human beings believe in their hearts that they are expert public relations practitioners.

The fact remains, however, that education in the sciences and practice in the application of the laws and principles places the wildlife manager and public relations men in a category outside that of the self-anointed experts in both these fields.

Within the wildlife management field itself, full acceptance of this fact has yet to be accomplished.

At this point we must look to the educator who is the key, not only to providing better qualified people to serve wildlife management, but also to providing the foundation upon which full public understanding and acceptance of the philosophies and principles of wildlife management must be built.

Basic Concepts Needed

In the long run, citizens who have been educated in the basic concepts and needs of sound resource use and conservation are more amenable to supporting wildlife management than are those in ignorance.

Long range education programs which build solid foundations for understanding of resource use problems are essential to the future of the wildlife managers' programs. If today everyone had a solid conservation education background, chances are the problems of wildlife managers would be fewer than they are and their public relations better.

While we may dream about such a time in the future, we must work aggressively to create a nation filled with people who understand and insist on conservation philosophies being carried out for the public benefit.

Realities Must Be Faced

The realities of today too often evaporate this dream of the future.

An old cliché in the business is that the wildlife manager could get

Reprinted from: Trans. N. Amer. Wildl. and Natural Resources Conf., 25:481-487.

his job done without too much trouble if there were no human animals in the natural habitat.

To better cope with humans, who are here to stay, the wildlife manager is turning more and more to people trained in dealing with human relations, public opinion and communication of information. These are the people who work at the art of public relations. Products of industrial competition, the wares of these people are being readily adapted to fill the needs of the wildlife administrator and manager in solving many problems.

The employment of public relations techniques and tools to expedite wildlife management is a relatively new field.

The essentials which make them work for industry also are effective in this area of wildlife management.

Public Confidence—The Key

Public confidence in an organization, program, policy or project is essential to good public relations. To create this confidence, industry usually aims its public relations efforts toward reflecting to the public an accurate, attractive picture of company policies, personnel management practices or of a product for sale. From the outset a planned course is set with public acceptance the goal. By repeating the image, keeping it accurate and up-to-date, identifying it with other things and ideas already having public acceptance, and by sticking to a straight course, public confidence is built, and good public relations are realized and the idea or product is sold.

The same principles work for wildlife management. Our policies are those of our agency, our products are management programs and projects.

Sound Policies Needed

Good public relations can be built only on basically sound, forward looking programs, projects and policies. Public relations is not a "silver wand" which can be waved to convert poor programs and policies into good ones. Public relations people aren't magicians who can make a silk purse out of a sow's ear, although I'm sorry to say some have tried unsuccessfully.

Pitfalls on this path to good public relations which wildlife managers so often encounter, however, include unsound programs and policies set for expediency, or to evade a crisis.

Another malady is the palpitating program or policy, the image of which most often looks to the public like the circus fat lady reflected in The Hall of Distortion Mirrors.

Still another is lack of policy which leaves the wildlife manager operating in a vacuum.

One of the most important things public relations people often can do effectively is to dig out and demonstrate for the wildlife administrator that his programs or policies do not appear to be sound and the kind upon which public confidence can be built.

Honesty Is Essential

Complete frankness and honesty is essential in efforts to reflect the items in which an agency would build public confidence. Bad news, such as errors in judgment or operations, frankly discussed with the public, often can strengthen an organization's public relations. Hiding and trying to cover up, sooner or later leads to disaster both to the public relations on the outside as well as to the internal well-being of an organization.

To build public confidence in his work and his agency, the wildlife manager could well seek to develop a confident attitude in presenting not only the successful but also the unsuccessful aspects of his efforts. It is human nature to avoid unpleasant news, particularly if one is a part of that news. But introversion on the part of wildlife managers must be replaced with aggressive presentation of all the facts, good and bad, if the public is to understand, accept and support the goals of wildlife management.

Proven Principles

There are other proven principles which lead to good public relations and successful programs adaptable to the needs of the wildlife management field. Among these are action by top management to construct policies and programs in terms understandable to the general public. People won't accept things they don't understand. This does not mean, however, that only those policies and programs which are immediately understandable and acceptable should be adopted. Policies, programs or projects which might be unpopular and give rise to charges of "poor public relations" can be developed into acceptable ideas and "good public relations" if they are sound and given proper, planned public relations treatment.

Work According to Plan

Essential to such treatment is a comprehensive information program conducted according to plan to solve specific problems of understanding among various groups or publics. This program should give attention not only to specific individuals or groups primarily concerned and vociferous on the subject at hand, but also to less interested groups which make up the public at large. Too often wildlife managers concern themselves only with the understanding of, say, sportsmen, while other publics and the people at large who actually own the resource involved are ignored. Good, lasting public relations depends on public understanding—not only understanding and acceptance by a tiny percentage of the public.

Methods, timing and media must be judiciously selected to fit the problem at hand to accomplish a given goal of public relations or education. Arbitrarily to set down a formula as to how to go about getting good public relations and educated understanding of wildlife management and to follow that formula under every circumstance is a common fault. Few of us in the business like to admit that this happens, but it does. Too often we race around going through identical motions trying to put out public friction fires. Instead we should be working to prevent the fires from starting by planned use of the informational and educational tools available.

Tools Being Improved

The form and techniques of using these tools which influence the thoughts, opinions and actions of people are constantly being improved and are increasing in number. There is an effective use for every media of communication in the wildlife management public relations and education business. At this stage of the work, however, adolescence rather than maturity is often reflected in the tools we choose and how we employ them to do specific jobs.

The illustrated written word, made available to the public in newspapers, pamphlets, bulletins, magazines and books, remains the proven backbone upon which lasting public understanding of wildlife management must be built. Speeches, television, radio, moving pictures, visual displays and various attention-getting gimmicks all are useful for special purposes. These latter media, however, should not be accepted as informational or educational panaceas, nor should their use result in the sapping of effort, time and money directed toward the printed word.

Talent Is Available

Wildlife managers and administrators today have within their own organizations unused or misused talent to employ these tools to assist materially in improving public relations problems. This talent needs to be given the time and opportunity to perform. To be effective this talent must be made an integral part of the head man's team, in a place where advice can be given and heard on what, when and how the signals should be called.

Similarly, the education specialist in wildlife management could be much more effective if he could work as a team with the public relations specialist on the first team in wildlife management. Too often in wildlife conservation organizations we find these talents buried so deep on organization charts they're hard to find. And in such cases, chances are the public doesn't have much confidence in the organization.

Wildlife management, education and public relations people are teaming up to get a better job of wildlife management done in North America. They are demonstrating every day that this combination works. Given greater opportunity tomorrow, they'll do even better.

PUBLIC RELATIONS ASPECTS OF WILDLIFE MANAGEMENT (1957)
C. A. Schoenfeld

Quite as much as the management of game itself, wildlife management involves human factors. This complication has always been with us, but its deeper ramifications have only begun to be appreciated.

P.S. Lovejoy was a pioneer in understanding the public relations aspects of wildlife management. Gordon (1944:7) has noted this "human element—the public relations problem" in conservation. Leopold (1946:4) wrote near the close of his career that "a conservation commission can operate up to the level of public opinion, but finds a drag when it attempts to proceed beyond that point." King (1948:10) is one of a number of modern biologists who see that "the real core of the (wildlife management) problem seems to be that the public does not understand our program and so is not ready to adopt it."

A generation ago, we were confident that once we had collected a body of scientific knowledge about wildlife crops and cropping, all would be well. Today we realize that wildlife management cannot function in America without public support, or at least without public sufferance, and that the development of a favorable climate of public opinion must accompany or even precede the management of game.

Why and how the change in attitude?

We began this century with convictions about the usefulness of bounties, refuges, and restrictions on the take. Our wealthy people copied the British techniques of artificial propagation and release. Then, as we picked up the idea that wildlife is a crop that is grown on the land, we came to realize the important role of the land owner. Today, with our increasingly heavy hunting and fishing pressure, and a clearer knowledge of the carrying capacity of our game range, we are embarked on involved schemes of controlled hunting. At the same time we have had to drop such widely accepted ideas as the inviolability of refuges, the threat of overfishing on lakes, and the efficiency of bounty systems.

In the face of all these developments we are being asked to manage game in a scene of intricate economic phenomena involving subsidized drainage, the popularity of gigantic engineering schemes, and the efforts of both engineers and agriculturists to put more and more wild land under the plow. Conservation in 1907 was predicated on a few simple biological facts; in 1957 it is involved in a vast socio-economic complex in which the taxpayer is a key factor.

This evolution has complicated immensely the task of the wildlife manager. As Gabrielson (1941:110) saw, "The most uncertain factor (in wildlife management) is not management (of game) itself but public support for a suitable and effective program." Henderson (1954) reports that "seldom in the history of human events have so many known so little about so much as the public knows about official conservation operations." MacQuarrie (1948) said "trained men are doing things they do not want to do but are forced to do" by ill-advised sportsmen.

Reprinted from: J. Wildl. Mgmt. 21(1):70-74.

The management of rabbits in Pennsylvania, of trout in Maryland, of deer in Wisconsin, of panfish in Kentucky, of ducks in the Dakotas, of antelope in Wyoming—these are not exclusively or even primarily problems in biology today; they are problems in public relations. They are problems because the development of public opinion has not been kept in pace with the development of scientific knowledge. Outdoor America is full of conservation programs that are sputtering along, not because they are based on inaccurate or insufficient research but because they lack sufficient public understanding and support.

To apply to public relations an ecological term, public opinion has come to constitute a *threshold* which effectively controls the application of game-management techniques to public conservation problems. The resulting bottleneck in American wildlife management is less an inadequate research base for operations than an adequate public support of sound management practices. When the practice of wildlife management learns to invest as much time and talent in the study and application of public relations as in the study and application of ecology, we can expect some progress on Leopold's "back forty."

As he moves out to study public relations, the wildlife manager will find that public relations and wildlife management have much in common. Public relations is defined by public-relations men as those functions and policies designed to bring about the communication and interpretation of ideas and information to all the various publics of an enterprise; and the communication and interpretation of information and ideas from those publics to the enterprise, in an effort to bring the two into harmonious and fruitful adjustment (Schoenfeld 1954:26). In principle this is not unlike the task of so adjusting species and environment that you wind up with a shootable crop. The public-relations process involves fact-finding, planning, and communicating (Cutlip and Center, 1952:126). This is not unlike the research-development-engineering sequence inherent in wildlife management.

As a discipline, public relations, like wildlife management, is a creature of the 20th century. Like wildlife management, public relations is rooted in fundamental research, yet in itself is as much an art as a science. Both professions are as yet unstabilized; both are cursed with fanatics and quacks; and both number among their practitioners some of the most able and devoted public servants in the country.

The "laws" of public relations are as untested and as transient as the "laws" of wildlife management, yet some of the basic "PR" principles which can be postulated can be stated in terms abundantly familiar to every wildlife manager.

Deep Digging. The basic public-relations principle is this: effective public relations is primarily a matter of policy and only secondarily a matter of publicity. What you are will always speak louder than what you say. This is exactly the same principle under which Leopold (1948) called for "deep-digging" research programs in wildlife management. "It is futile," he said, "to attempt the practical in advance of the fundamental." This is as true in public relations as it is in conservation. Publicity cannot attract public support for wildlife management unless the basic policies and practices of the enterprise are such that public support can be built upon them.

Multiple Factors. In the management of game the wildlife scientist has learned long ago there is no royal road to abundance. The pheasant crop, for example, is conditioned by the interaction of many forces, and the wildlife manager who fails to reckon with the complexity of his task is in for disappointment.

In the influencing of public opinion the public-relations man has learned there is likewise no magic key to success. The factors conditioning public opinion are even more numerous and complex than those obtaining in wildlife management. Gaus (1947:42) has pinpointed these key "ecological" factors, affecting the ebb and flow of the relations between an enterprise and its constituents, as "people, place, physical technology, social technology, wishes and ideas, catastrophe, and personality."

To try to oversimplify these public-relations forces is to court disaster. Every conservation department, for example, has a dozen windows open to the world, and every department policy has a dozen points of view—some positively contradictory, some quasiconflicting, others mutually supporting, all of them important to somebody, each of them meriting decent attention if not full allegiance.

Biologists may be coming more and more to suspect that it is the wholly fortuitous piling up of favorable factors or the chance pyramiding of unfavorable forces which produce many record peaks and valleys in game populations. Public-relations men see no reason to believe that chance does not play a role in public relations also. Neither the public-relations man nor the wildlife manager, however, can afford strictly to gamble. Theirs is the common task of considering, balancing, and adjusting many perspectives.

Key Factors. Although both wildlife management and public relations involve multiple factors, there are in both pursuits certain key factors which are more basic than others. Graham (1947:69) says it is a *home* which wildlife needs above all else. The public-relations man has a related principle: "Public relations begins at home" (Reck, 1946:7). Ripples of discontent and irritation radiating from biologists, wardens, technicians, and secretaries will ultimately be seen or heard by the public at large, to the detriment of a conservation department. Wherever old-time wardens still look askance at scientific procedures, wildlife management remains emasculated, no matter how popular it may be in other circles. Until its relations with its internal publics are sound, wildlife management cannot hope to achieve complete rapport with its external publics.

Indigenousness. Most biologists take a dim view of exotics. So do more public-relations men. To be effective, a public-relations program should be "native, inherent, natural"—at home in the environment of the enterprise for which it is planned. Occasionally an alien public-relations program will, like the ringneck pheasant, succeed tolerably; more likely, it will do as much damage to native flora and fauna as the carp. A public-relations program for Michigan conservation, in other words, must be indigenous; it cannot borrow at will from Texas.

Population Mechanics. Ever since Errington described the phenomenon of inversity, wildlife managers have known that so-called "internal" factors play a major role in establishing wildlife population levels, despite "the human tendencies to over-estimate the population effects of conspicuous or demonstrably heavy predation" (Errington, 1946:236). The related public-relations phenomenon may be stated in this way: public relations is not the job of a single individual; it is a way of life for an entire enterprise (Reck, 1946). Every contact between an enterprise and its constituency is an episode in the complex flow of public relationships. Despite the splash which a single performer may make, wildlife management's voice in the final analysis is a composite of many individual acts. The public relations of wildlife management is an "all hands" job. A conservation department's public-relations program can no more be delegated to a chief of information than its total research program can be effected solely by a chief of research.

Air Pressure. In public relations, as in the physical universe, nature abhors a vacuum. When the reticence of wildlife scientists creates a news vacuum, the vacuum never stays empty. "Science fiction" rushes in. An American enterprise simply cannot live in a world apart. If it does not seek to fill news columns with constructive releases, the law of air pressure will fill those columns with less desirable material. There is no vacuum in public relations. You may have good public relations or poor public relations, but you will always have public relations. Until wildlife managers supply the public prints with continuous, clear, and candid summaries of their activities, they can expect to be harassed by hairbrained stories.

Missing almost entirely from the periodical literature of wildlife management is the synoptic article summarizing in relatively intelligible language, either on a species, a topical, or a regional basis, the progress in research and development. Russell Lord has said that biologists write in "a rather spurious or pretended jargon of objectivity which they impose upon themselves as a mark of scientific respectability" (Shaw, 1946). Yet "quite as necessary as research (in conservation) is (public) education" (Vogt, 1948:152).

Equal Stresses. A related public-relations law is the law of equal stresses. Like a gun that compensates by recoil for the forward velocity of its projectile, the public accommodates the publicity efforts of an enterprise by focusing on it an inordinate interest. When a publicity seeker plunks a news release on the city desk, he is saying to the editor, in effect, "My enterprise is news!" He must not be surprised when that editor proposes to make news out of an institutional foible that the enterprise would prefer to keep buried. There is as yet no recoilless rifle in public relations. All the public-relations man can do is keep his powder dry.

Carrying Capacity. The ecological law of carrying capacity operates in public relations. Flood a newspaper with too many releases, and the editor loses his receptivity. Paint too strong a picture of an enterprise and the public loses its capacity to cherish that undertaking. The overzealous wildlife manager who promises the moon on the basis of one research finding is doing as much damage public-relationswise as is the warden wildlife-managementwise who feeds deer in an already depleted winter yard.

Carrying capacity has a specific application in the public relations of wildlife-management training. The carrying capacity of a university campus effectively limits the kind of instruction that campus will support. By enrolling more wildlife students you can raise the quantity of students but not their total quality. Crowded conditions on a campus will produce the same complaints from disappointed parents and employers that a crowded pond will elicit from disappointed anglers.

Momentum. What Walter Lippman (1922) called the pictures in people's heads are among the most fixed states of matter. Once an enterprise gains a favorable reputation, the momentum of its bandwagon is tremendous. Counterwise, the toughest public-relations job is the job of erasing a widespread misconception. So effectively did the conservationists of yesteryear sell the efficacy of the buck law that modern wildlife managers have had to start from below scratch in selling the idea of the any-deer season.

Gravity. As in nature, the public-relations law of momentum is opposed by the law of gravity. What goes up can come down. Initial momentum is not enough to keep a favorable picture fixed in the public mind indefinitely. There must be constantly renewed those accelerating policies and functions which built effective public relations in the first place. Neglect them and the balloon falls. The conservation department which built a reputation on stocking pheasants 30 years ago cannot expect to ride along forever on the strength of this popularity. There will be new projects to tackle and new publics to cultivate.

The "law" of gravity operates also in public relations to prevent public sentiment from rising higher than the source of its inspiration. Confine your public addresses to the minutia of statistics, and you fail to stimulate that broad interest which wildlife management needs. Emphasize stocking projects in your news releases at the expense of developments in research, and you appeal to meat hunters but not to discriminating sportsmen. Build a program exclusively for the benefit of trout fishermen, and beaver trappers ignore your pleas for support. Try to muddle through without vigorous leadership, "with letterhead pieties and convention oratory," and you take two steps backward for every step forward. The quality of its men makes the quality of wildlife management and its public-relations program. You may have your offices and laboratories, you may create committees, and you may find and spend money; yet you will add nothing substantial to America's outdoor resources unless you are equipped with at least a few professors, administrators, and public-relations men who are leaders. When leaders come together in conservation today, the whole country feels the higher pressure which they generate.

Nitrogen Cycle. In the public relations of wildlife management there is a nitrogen cycle that requires the same kind of attention as the nitrogen cycle in agriculture. Research is the leguminous plant, and scientists are the root-nodule bacteria which draw conceptual schemes and "fix" new facts. Practical conservation thrives on this new knowledge. Without it, conservation becomes necrotic and withers. The conservation department which tries to operate without constant refertilization by basic research is like the farmer who never rotates his crops. There can be, however, such a thing as too much nitrogen. In concentrated form it "burns" plants. And there is such a thing as a consuming emphasis on research which draws too much time and talent away from the practical application of wildlife knowledge and from the communication of wildlife facts to the public. The public-relations law here is the law of balance—achieving reciprocal action in fact-finding, planning, and communicating.

Ecology. An enterprise is always a reflection of the food and cover of its environment. To say that a state has a better—or a worse—conservation department than it deserves is to defy both a law of ecology and a law of public relations. On the other hand, to say that a conservation department cannot improve on its "natural habitat" is untrue. Just as a wildlife manager can manipulate flora and fauna by altering land-use practices in order to produce bigger and better game crops, so can a conservation department, over the years, alter its environment through effective public relations in order to develop surroundings more hospitable to wildlife-management progress. Like the wildlife manager, however, a public-relations man can go only so far so fast, lest drastic changes of the landscape result in unforeseen flash floods and vegetative excesses which place the public-relations biota virtually beyond control.

Heliotropism. A plant's leaves reach toward the light. So with a university wildlife-management department. If the "sun" of the department is a record enrollment, the department will be twisted and stunted in a hunt for students and a scramble to keep them eligible. If the "sun" is research money, undergraduate teaching and adult education may grow yellow and frail in the shadows. If the "sun" is a passion to please every hunter or fisherman who comes along demanding something absurd, then the department wilts under the heat of artificial public relations. But if the "sun" of the department is that balance between responsibility for great academic traditions and responsiveness to public needs, then the department's public relations are on sound footing.

Overturn. The limnological phenomenon of seasonal overturn has its public-relations applications. The outdoor public exhibits "mixing" characteristics similar to those of an inland lake. In the fall, stimulated by the hunting season, sportsmen's activities produce turmoil and public-relations headaches. As winter sets in, public relations becomes marked by a lack of turbulence; but the fishing season brings springtime "mixing." The public relations of wildlife management will always reflect this semiannual swing from stratification to instability.

Cycles. If the Wisconsin situation is diagnostic, the public relations of wildlife management also exhibits cyclical tendencies, with irruptions occurring in each decade. In the '20s, the '30s, the '40s, and the '50s the state of Wisconsin has changed conservation directors. (In Wisconsin, the state conservation director is exceeded only by the university football coach as the hero—and whipping boy—of the public.)

Symbiosis. A final public-relations law to be considered here is the law of symbiosis. Just as in nature certain species live intimately associated lives because such a relationship is necessary or advantageous to both, so a commonwealth and its wildlife-management enterprises constitute a natural partnership. Public problems and public funds have built wildlife management. In turn, wildlife management has enriched the public's recreational resources. It is the continuing objective of public relations for wildlife management to cement this mutually advantageous partnership.

Public support for wildlife management can be brought about by a combination of bringing the ideas and aspirations of the wildlife manager down to the level of the public's grasp, and bringing the sentiments of the public up to the plane of wildlife management's possibilities. This meeting of minds will come about when the wildlife manager adds public relations to his management techniques. It is only a question of time before a course in public administration becomes quite as much a part of the required regimen for the wildlife student as Zoology 1a. That the wildlife manager with a public-relations flair is within the realm of possibility there is present evidence. In the profession of wildlife management, and on its fringes, are a growing number of scientists and administrators with a bent toward communicating with their constituents.

"These intergrades in human taxonomy," wrote Leopold (1940:346), "are perhaps more important than those which so perplex the mammalogists and ornithologists. Their skulls are not yet available to the museums, but even a layman can see that their brains are distinctive."

LITERATURE CITED

CUTLIP, S., AND A. CENTER. 1952. Effective public relations. Prentice Hall, New York. 502pp.
ERRINGTON, P. 1946. Predation and vertebrate populations. Quart. Rev. Biol., 21(2):144-177; (3):221-245.
GABRIELSON, I. N. 1941. Wildlife conservation. Macmillan, New York. 250pp.
GAUS, J. 1947. Reflections on public administration. University of Alabama Press, University, Alabama. 217pp.
GORDON, S. 1944. Pennsylvania bags 700,000 deer in ten years. Our deer—past, present, and future. Pa. Game Comm. Bull. 42pp.
GRAHAM, E. 1947. The land and wildlife. Oxford University Press, New York. 232pp.
HENDERSON, D. 1954. Conservation news reaches but few. (Madison, Wis.) Capital Times, Nov. 26.p.10.
KING, F. 1948. The management of man. Wis. Conserv. Bull., 13(9):9-11.
LEOPOLD, A. 1940. The state of the profession. J. Wildl. Mgmt., 4(3):343-346.
————. 1946. The deer dilemma. Wis. Conserv. Bull., 11(8-9):3-5.
————. 1948. Why and how research? Trans. N. Amer. Wildl. Conf., 13:44-48.
LIPPMAN, W. 1922. Public opinion. Wiley, New York. 151pp.
MACQUARRIE, G. 1948. Right off the reel. Milwaukee (Wis.) Journal, Jan. 6. p.16.
RECK, E. 1946. Public relations for colleges and universities. Harpers, New York. 286pp.
SCHOENFELD, C. 1954. The University and its publics. Harpers, New York. 284pp.
SHAW, R. 1946. Technical journalists wanted. The Quill, 23(7):15-16.
VOGT, W. 1948. Road to survival. Sloan, New York. 335pp.

THE YELLOWSTONE ELK CONTROVERSY (1971)
Alan Woolf

OBJECTIVES

This case study will include the history of the Yellowstone elk controversy, and an attempt will be made to focus attention on the events and opinions leading to the decision by the National Park Service to terminate the direct-reduction program during the winter of 1967.

CASE SITUATION

Policies

The policies involved will be presented in two parts: first, the policies of the National Park Service; and second, the policies of the other natural resource agencies involved in the management of the Northern Yellowstone elk herd. The policies adopted by the Park Service are the heart of the controversy. These policies have not been fully presented and explained to the many publics that are involved and concerned with the management practices of the Park Service. Following are some of the more important aspects of National Park Service policy pertinent to the Yellowstone elk controversy, and the sources of these policies:

Act of August 25, 1916 establishing the Park Service:

"The service thus established shall promote and regulate the use of the Federal areas . . . by such means and measures as conform to the fundamental purpose of the said parks, ..., which purpose is to conserve the scenery and the natural and historic objects and the wild life therein and to provide for the enjoyment of the same in such manner and by such means as will leave them unimpaired for the enjoyment of future generations."

"That the Secretary of the Interior . . . . may also, upon terms and conditions to be fixed by him, sell or dispose of timber in those cases where in his judgement the cutting of such timber is required in order to control the attacks of insects or diseases or otherwise conserve the scenery or the natural or historic objects in any such park, monument, or reservation. He may also provide in his discretion for the destruction of such animals and of such plant life as may be detrimental to the use of any of said parks, monuments, or reservations."

Advisory Board on Wildlife Management appointed by Secretary of the Interior Udall (The Leopold Report) March 4, 1963:

"In recent years the National Park Service has broadened its concept of wildlife conservation to provide for purposeful management of plant and animal communities as an essential step in preserving wildlife resources . . . . unimpaired for the enjoyment of future generations."

"As a primary goal, we would recommend that the biotic associations within each park be maintained, or where necessary recreated, as nearly as possible in the condition that prevailed when the area was first visited by the white man, a National Park should represent a vignette of primitive America."

". . . observable artificiality in any form must be minimized and obscured in every way possible . . . . In the same category is artificial

Reprinted from: Natural Resources and Public Relations, D. L. Gilbert. The Wildlife Soc. Washington, D.C. 320 pp. References have been omitted.

feeding of wildlife . . . . Fed elk deplete natural ranges. Forage relationships in wild animals should be natural."

". . . every phase of management itself be under the full jurisdiction of biologically trained personnel of the Park Service . . . Reducing the numbers of elk in Yellowstone . . . is part of an overall scheme to preserve or restore a natural biotic scene. The purpose is single-minded. We cannot endorse the view that responsibility for removing excess game animals be shared with state fish and game departments whose primary interest would be to capitalize on the recreational value of the public hunting that thus could be supplied. Such a proposal imputes a multiple use concept of park management which was never intended, which is not legally permitted, nor for which can we find any impelling justification today."

"Direct removal by killing is the most economical and effective way of regulating ungulates within a park. Game removal by shooting should be conducted under the complete jurisdiction of qualified park personnel and solely for the purpose of reducing animals to preserve park values. Recreational hunting is an inappropriate and non-conforming use of the national parks and monuments."

The contents of the Leopold Report are extremely important because it has been accepted by the Park Service as a guideline for park policies and objectives.

A Cooperative Management Plan for the Northern Yellowstone Elk Herd and its Habitat—December 1963:

"The animals indigenous to the parks shall be protected, restored, if practicable and their welfare in a natural wild state perpetuated. Their management shall consist only of measures conforming with the basic laws and which are essential to the maintenance of populations and their natural environments in a healthy condition."

This cooperative management plan is signed by the National Park Service, Montana Fish and Game Commission, Wyoming Game and Fish Commission, and the U.S. Forest Service.

Long-Range Wildlife and Habitat Management Plan for Yellowstone National Park—September 1964:

"Objective: To attain a balanced relationship between plants and animals and between different species of animals, thus providing an optimum opportunity for the park visitor to observe and enjoy wildlife and plant resources of Yellowstone National Park under conditions which will reflect healthy animals in an appealing, natural environment."

The specific programs for the Northern Yellowstone elk herd can also be considered Park Service policy. The policies of the other natural resource agencies concerned with the management of the Northern Yellowstone elk herd are stated in the cooperative management plan that was formulated and signed in 1963. The policy statements of the agencies co-signing with the Park Service are:

Montana Fish and Game Commission: "To produce and maintain a maximum breeding stock of big game on all suitable lands of Montana, public and private, in harmony with all other uses of such lands, and consistent with the available forage supply, and to utilize, through public

452

hunting, the available crop of big game produced annually by this breeding stock."

Wyoming Game and Fish Commission: Their policy statement conforms closely with the statement of the Montana Fish and Game Commission.

U.S. Forest Service: "The Forest Service recognizes that responsibility for elk stocking rests with the states. In order to insure coordination of uses, the Forest Service will determine the appropriateness of individual projects . . ."

"Breeding stock now exists on most National Forest areas where elk production and management is desirable. It rarely will be necessary to build up additional supplies of elk by artificially stocking. Of more importance is the determination and correction of environmental or other factors that limit the natural increase. . . . The agreement will also provide for herd controls to keep populations in balance with the habitat."

"This policy does not provide for widespread stocking without individual study agreements. Future stockings will depend on individual study findings."

The important statements regarding this controversy are contained in several documents, none of which have been given a great deal of publicity. They are the "Leopold Report," a cooperative management plan for the Northern Yellowstone elk herd (Leopold, 1963), and the long-range wildlife and habitat management plan for Yellowstone National Park. Another important document containing figures on the current elk status and the reasons behind the reduction program is the 1966-67 wildlife management plan for Yellowstone National Park.

Budgets

Until 1964, no specific provision was included in the Park Service budget for wildlife management, and all expenses for management came from contingency funds within individual parks. Wildlife management measures received money from the Park Service budget only if they were related to other park activities.

The costs of live-trapping elk are shared by the Park Service and the agencies receiving the elk. The receiving agencies pay helicopter and shipping costs, with no charge being made for the animals. Helicopter charges have varied from two to ten dollars per animal trapped. The Park Service pays all other costs related to the elk reduction program. This includes salaries, trap construction (estimates for new traps, specifically designed for trapping elk with helicopters, are approximately $15,000 each) and related expenses. Additionally, approximately $100 per hour rental for helicopters used for driving elk to hunters beyond the park boundary and elk censuses are paid for by the Park Service.

Leopold (1963), in the advisory board report to the Secretary of the Interior said that trapping and handling of a big game animal usually costs from $50 to $150 and in some cases, much more. Even with receiving agencies paying a small portion of the cost, this amounts to a large sum of money spent by the Park Service to trap elk. In addition to the financial burden on the Park Service, Jack Richard, author of an article in February 21, 1965 Sunday Empire, the magazine of the Denver Post, also pointed out the economic problems of Montana and Wyoming. Richard wondered how long these two states could afford to accept live-trapped elk costing from $12 to $20 per head and still charge their resident hunters $5 for a license. Of course every elk hunter is not successful. Much additional money is spent by hunters for food, lodging and other items.

Basis for Opposing Arguments

The arguments revolve around several basic problems and approaches to these problems. One view is that elk reductions in the park are not necessary. One aspect of this view is that there may be an over-population, but since it is a National Park, the herd should be left alone for nature to take its course.

The Park Service in turn can point to research, including range exclosures, that indicates the harmful effects the elk herd has had on Northern Yellowstone winter ranges. Very little controversy exists over whether or not a reduction is necessary. As for letting nature take its course, it has been pointed out by the Leopold Report that management is necessary in National Parks if park objectives are to be met; namely, to preserve the flora, fauna and scenic features of the area.

Another argument against letting the animals starve was well put by Pengelly (1963). He pointed out the inevitable cycle of overpopulation, overgrazing, moisture retention, soil deterioration and the replacement of desirable plant species by less nutritional species. This cycle would further damage the range and reduce the carrying capacity for all ungulate species. While elk normally can reproduce their number in five years, it takes up to 50 years or more for vegetation to re-establish itself, and from 100 to 500 or more years for soil building and replenishment on eroded ranges.

Most arguments revolve around how the reduction should be carried out by the Park Service. Basically, there are five possible methods of herd reduction: 1. public hunting north of the park boundary; 2. live-trapping and transplanting; 3. "direct-reduction" by park personnel; 4. public hunting in the park which is not within the existing legal framework; and 5. introduction of large predators.

The first method of control, public hunting outside the park, presently is used and has been for many years. However, it is not an effective control measure because the success of the hunt depends on weather, date of the hunt and the extent of elk movements. The widely varying kills shown in Table 9 indicate the lack of dependable herd reduction by this method. However, this method may be preferred by the Park Service as a method of herd control. The hunt is important to the economy of Gardiner, Montana, a small town just north of Yellowstone Park headquarters at Mammoth. The Park Service and the Montana Fish and Game Commission have cooperated for many years to achieve a maximum harvest from this hunt consistent with weather conditions and the live-trapping program in the park. The Gardiner-Jardine "Firing Line" has achieved nationwide fame and is talked about nearly as much as the direct-reduction in the park itself.

The local residents of Gardiner have mixed feelings about the elk situation in the park and the "Firing Line." Most residents recognize that the overpopulation exists but question if large reductions in the park are necessary. They would prefer to have the elk driven out for hunters. Although they do not think much of the "hunt" and the "sportsmen" involved, the Gardiner residents can not afford to have the hunt ignored as the main reduction method. Christopherson, writing for the Saturday Evening Post, (1952) gave a description of the Gardiner-Jardine Firing Line. He called it "one of the sorriest spectacles known to hunting."

Live-trapping and transplanting is the method of reduction strongly advocated by state conservation agency personnel of Montana and Wyoming. Again, the Park Service prefers this method to direct-reduction, but the success is limited by weather conditions. Beginning in 1963, helicopters were used to herd the elk into traps. This technique has greatly improved the success of live-trapping (Table 9). However, live-trapping and transplanting of surplus elk, in number large enough to have a great deal of effect is, at the present time—with present methods, impractical and uneconomical. Most of the nation's tenable elk range is already occupied and has all the elk it needs and can support (Madson, 1966).

The Leopold Report also considered the solution of live-trapping. The report stated: ". . . Trapping and transplanting has not proved to be a practical method of control, though it is an appropriate source of breeding stock as needed elsewhere." The discussion of budgets, earlier in this case study, pointed out some of the costs of the live-trapping operation, both to the Park Service and the agencies receiving elk.

Direct-reduction by Park Personnel is the center of the Yellowstone elk controversy. This method was first used by the Park Service in 1934. Direct-reduction is used only when hunter harvest outside the park and live-trapping fail to reduce the herd to the desired level. Most of the opposition to direct-reduction comes from those who believe that live-trapping can accomplish the necessary reduction without resorting to direct-reduction and those who believe that the Park Service is usurping a recreational resource that should belong to sportsmen.

Public hunting in the park is not permitted under existing laws. Most Park Service personnel generally believe that the law should not be changed to permit hunting because it would endanger other park values. The Park Service policy follows the policy statement in the Leopold Report: ". . . Such a proposal imputes a multiple use concept of park management which was never intended, which is not legally permitted, nor for which can we find any impelling justification today."

Sportsmen argue that the precedent for public hunting in National Parks has already been set in Grand Teton Park. However, the Park Service also points out that public hunting would not accomplish the necessary reduction. In addition, other park values are endangered. During the 1961 Teton hunt, 23 illegally killed elk, 11 moose, 2 bears, and several coyotes were found by park rangers. As for hunting success, only half of the permits authorized from 1951 to 1962 ever were used with a hunter's success of 27 per cent (Trueblood, 1963). To accomplish the 5,000 herd reduction of 1962, nearly 20,000 hunters would have been needed. This figure is only a rough estimate because the Grand Teton winter range is much smaller and more accessible than the Northern Yellowstone winter range.

TABLE 9. National Park Service Elk Reductions, Northern Yellowstone Elk Herd, Yellowstone National Park.

Period	Hunter kill	Direct Field Reduction	Live trapping	Winter kill	Total Reduction	Actual spring count
1934-35	2,598	223	444		3,265	10,647
1935-36	2,287	6*	551	89	2,933	10,112
1936-37	257	394	180	15	846	10,281
1937-38	3,587	11*	225	89	3,912	8,794
1938-39	2,971	—	307	533	3,811	10,976
1939-40	122	—	16	68	206	
1940-41	275	—	12	10	297	
1941-42	2,071	—	145	108	2,324	
1942-43	6,539	691	—	872	8,102	
1943-44	125	—	10	100	235	8,235
1944-45	403	—	—	300	703	
1945-46	2,094	—	73	250	2,417	
1946-47	3,069	—	76	475	3,620	8,513
1947-48	970		39	375	1,384	
1948-49	2,837	—	49	300	3,186	7,815
1949-50	40	518	316	184	1,058	
1950-51	1,265	500	312	217	2,294	
1951-52	3,198	52*	563	500	4,313	
1952-53	110	7*	165	50	332	
1953-54	422	171	216	241	1,050	
1954-55	763	13*	593	289	1,658	
1955-56	3,900	1,974	645	—	6,519	6,963 (helicopter)
1956-57	345	717	227	—	1,289	
1957-58	50	536	—	—	586	
1958-59	372	1,051	319	—	1,742	4,848 (fixed-wing)
1959-60	50	674	135	—	859	
1960-61	25	1,287	147	—	1,459	8,150 (helicopter)
1961-62	125	4,309	301[1]	476	5,220	5,725 (helicopter)
1962-63	530	619[2]	671	negligible	1,820	
1963-64	30	215[5]	906[3]	11	1,151	
1964-65	1,012	205[5]	687[4]	11	1,904	4,865 (helicopter)
1965-66	30	181[5]	1,059[6]	11	1,270	
TOTALS	42,472	14,354	9,398	5,541	71,765	

* Taken for museum specimens or biological studies.
[1] Includes 13 trap loss.
[2] Includes 215 for biological studies.
[3] Includes trap loss of 40.
[4] Includes trap loss of 22.
[5] Biological studies only.
[6] Includes trap loss of 35.

Artificial feeding has been suggested as an emergency measure, but this would be in complete opposition to Park Service objectives. The artificiality and additional problems in range management it would cause make this alternative undesirable.

Introduction of large predators, wolves and cougars, has been advocated by some. This method appears to have several serious drawbacks. Predators would be hard to obtain in the numbers necessary. They probably would kill other animals in addition to, and perhaps instead of, the elk. There is no reason why they should stay within the Park confines. Stockmen in the vicinity probably would lose animals and the National Park Service would have additional problems.

Present Park Service policy is to carry out the necessary herd control using public hunting outside of the park as the primary method. This is supplemented by live-trapping. Direct-reduction by rangers is used only when the other two methods fail to achieve the desired and needed reduction. This is the same policy first established and used in 1934. Table 9 shows the official Yellowstone Park elk reduction figures from all herd control methods from 1934 to 1966.

Politics

Politics enter the Yellowstone elk controversy from two aspects. As with all public agencies, the National Park Service is responsible to the people. This responsibility is manifested in the form of Federal legislators who exert financial control over the Park Service operations and political pressure at the higher administrative levels. Legislators are an important internal public of the Park Service. They can do much to help management practices or bring them to a quick halt. The influence of Senator McGee (D-Wyo.) in the 1967 controversy is an example of how a Senator can influence park management policies.

Another effect of politicians came from the elected officials of Montana and Wyoming. The Governors of these states were leading the opposition to the direct-reduction program. The Governor of Wyoming made the first public out-cry against the policy and his condemnation of the Park Service quickly gathered support for his contentions and charges.

HISTORY

Background

The Northern Yellowstone winter range that supports the controversial elk herd includes a maximum area of nearly 120,000 acres in the northern half of Yellowstone National Park east of the Gallatin Mountain range. This area is reduced to less than 90,000 acres of winter range during severe winters (U.S. National Park Service, 1964). The Northern Yellowstone elk herd shares this limited winter range with mule deer, bighorn sheep, antelope, bison and moose. White-tailed deer also were once present on this range and their extinction is blamed on competition with elk.

The present winter ranges of elk in the Lamar and upper Yellowstone River drainages were not traditional wintering grounds in 1872 when Yellowstone National Park was created (Pengelly, 1963). By 1881, park records show that 400 elk wintered in the Lamar Valley. The winter herd increased rapidly and by 1892, the elk herd on the northern winter range was estimated to number 25,000. Heavy winter losses of approximately 5,000 elk were reported in 1892 and 1899, but the herd quickly recovered (Pengelly, 1963). The herd reached its peak in 1914, numbering an estimated 35,200 head. During the severe winter of 1919-20, two thirds of the elk herd died. Since then, the herd size has fluctuated between approximately 15,000 and 6,000 animals (Table 10).

The following estimates of the number of elk in the Northern Yellowstone elk herd for the years shown are the most accurate available. It must be understood that these are estimates, and that over such a long period, correspondence, news releases, etc., may have included figures that are somewhat varied.

TABLE 10. National Park Service Estimates of the Size of the Northern Yellowstone Elk Herd, 1892-1965.

Year	Estimated number	Year	Estimated number
1892	25,000	1941	12,500
1893	25,000	1942	11,700
1897	15,000	1943*	9,100
1907	25,000	1944	10,500
1908	25,000	1945	11,500
1909	30,000	1946*	10,700
1910	30,000	1947	9,600
1912	30,100	1948	12,400
1913	32,200	1949	11,000
1914	35,300	1950	12,000
1916*	29,500	1951	12,000
1923*	14,500	1952	9,200
1926	14,000	1953	10,600
1927*	13,000	1954	11,500
1928*	14,200	1955	11,800
1929	13,300	1956*	8,300
1930	10,600	1957	8,200
1931	10,600	1958	9,000
1932	10,600	1959*	7,200
1933	12,500	1960	7,600
1934*	13,000	1961*	10,000 (helicopter)
1935*	11,000	1962*	6,800 (helicopter)
1936*	11,000	1963	6,100
1937*	9,700	1964	6,700
1938*	11,000	1965*	6,900 (helicopter)
1939	10,800	1966	7,000
1940	12,000	1967	7,200

* Years in which actual count was made; figure printed is estimate based on count.

Park Service officials recorded their first observations of range damage due to elk abundance in 1911 (Pengelly, 1963). Important range investigations first were carried out in 1917 (Graves and Nelson, 1919), and again in 1930 (Rush, 1932). Although the problem was recognized, little was done to improve the situation. Authorization for the removal of elk by killing first was received in 1934 and 223 elk were removed by direct-reduction. Since that time, direct-reduction has been used as needed to reduce the herd when other methods have not produced the necessary success. However, it was not until 1949 that the first soundly thought out management program for the Northern Yellowstone elk herd was approved (Yellowstone National Park, 1964). The goal of this plan was to reduce the herd to 5,000 elk and maintain it at that level. Relatively large direct-reduction programs were undertaken in 1955-56 (1,974 elk); 1958-59 (1,051 elk); and 1960-61 (1,287 elk). These programs were met with some adverse reaction by some publics, but generally the press emphasized the Park Service's views and assessments of the situation and little opposition came to the surface. Most of the opposition came from sportsmen's groups who desired public hunting in the park.

The approximate goal of 5,000 elk on the northern winter range was not reached until the winter of 1961-62, when a total reduction of 5,220 was attained with 4,309 taken by direct-reduction. This reduction was much publicized and touched off an emotional explosion. The opposition consisted of two groups. They either had vested interests in the Yellowstone elk, or they were well meaning but poorly informed. Trueblood (1963) stated that "public understanding of the need of management is the most difficult problem of all. A vast number of people still grow misty-eyed because of the Bambi myth." Protests were made against the extermination of the elk. "Organizations were formed, and one of them—the Gallatin Elk Protective Association—sent out a bulletin: 'Dear Sportsman: Hang up your rifle forever . . . Even as you read this letter the most magnificent of American big-game animals, the elk, is rapidly on its way toward complete extinction" (Trueblood, 1963). This reaction was typical of the emotions generated by the 1961-62 reduction.

The Montana Fish and Game Department fearing adverse publicity, refused to cooperate with an extended season for hunters outside the park and the rangers carried out the reduction themselves. The opposition to the reduction relied primarily on emotions to halt the Park Service, but even legal action was attempted. An injunction to halt and prohibit further shooting was brought against Yellowstone National Park Superintendent L. A. Garrison by three Cody, Wyoming guides and outfitters represented by former Wyoming Governor, Milward Simpson. The injunction was dismissed in court, but U.S. Congressional pressure was threatened by Senator Joe Hickey (D-Wyo.) when the court action failed. This Congressional pressure also failed to stop the direct-reduction.

Although the controversy and its resulting publicity subsided, the situation was not resolved. The reduction ended for the year, but the elk problem remained. However, some efforts were made to solve the problem. An advisory board (Stanley A. Cain; Clarence M. Cottam; Ira N. Gabrielson; Thomas L. Kimball; and Chairman, A. Starker Leopold) was appointed to study the problem of wildlife management in National Parks. This board made its report (Leopold Report) to the Secretary of the Interior on March 4, 1963. The findings of the board formed the basis of present

Park Service policy regarding wildlife management and park objectives and values.

To solve the elk problem further, a cooperative management plan for the Northern Yellowstone elk herd and its habitat was initiated. This cooperative plan was endorsed and signed by personnel of the U.S. National Park Service, Montana Fish and Game Commission, Wyoming Game and Fish Commission, and the U.S. Forest Service. In 1964, two additional steps were taken by the Park Service to improve the situation. First, money was allocated for wildlife management for the first time in the Park Service budget. With funds now included in the budget, Yellowstone Park initiated a long-range wildlife and habitat management plan. This plan set goals and removed management from a year to year basis.

The last direct-reduction until 1967 was carried out in 1962-63. Only one year after the major controversy, little opposition was voiced, and 619 elk were shot by park rangers.

Reasons for the 1967 Controversy

The 1967 controversy was merely a continuation of the attitudes, opinions, and beliefs that remained unchanged since the beginning of the Yellowstone Park direct-reduction program. The controversy reached its peak during the 1961-62 reduction, and emotions completely dominated any attempts to rationally evaluate the possible alternatives. The elk problem remained but the issues were permitted to become dormant. When the 1967 reduction was announced, political leaders in Wyoming and Montana (particularly Wyoming) claimed a lack of communication and cooperation on the part of the Park Service and quickly rallied support to halt the 1967 direct-reduction program short of its goals.

PUBLICS INVOLVED AND THEIR TENDENCIES

Proponents

Internal publics: National Park Service (includes numerous subpublics such as administrators, rangers and naturalists, office staff, maintenance personnel, etc.). With the exception of one important internal public that will be discussed under opponents, the Park Service is united behind the concept of direct-reduction as a management tool. Most personnel do not like the job and regret the need to do it; however, they recognize the necessity.

External publics: Professional managers (this public also includes many sub-publics, some of which are opponents of the direct-reduction program). For the most part, professionally trained wildlife investigators recognize the practicality and economic advantages of the program and support the Park Service management plan for elk.

Park and Recreation "Conservation" groups: Although numerous and having diverse interests, most of these groups support the Park Service policy. They are strongly against public hunting in the park. However, many would favor live-trapping to reduce the herd.

Opponents

Internal publics: Some federal legislators are included because they approve budgets and policies. This important internal public of the Park Service generally is strongly against the direct-reduction program in Yellowstone. Almost all the pressure is from the legislators from the surrounding states of Montana and Wyoming, especially Wyoming. The legislators have advocated the live-trapping program and have not been trying to gain public hunting privileges in Yellowstone.

External publics:

State of Montana —Elected Officials
        —Fish and Game Department
         —Commission
         —Administrators
         —Biologists, wardens, and others

State of Wyoming —Elected Officials
        —Game and Fish Department
         —Commission
         —Administrators
         —Biologists, wardens, and others

Both of these states went on record as being opposed to the direct-reduction program. They prefer a live-trapping and transplanting program to control the herd. Wyoming even suggested artificial feeding as an emergency measure rather than direct-reduction.

Rocky Mountain States Game and Fish Departments: The personnel of these departments favor trapping and transplanting. Many administrators also advocate more state control of game management in National Parks. Some employees do recognize the need for direct-reduction and support the Park Service as individuals.

Local residents of Gardiner, Montana: This public includes many sub-publics such as guides, businessmen, motel operators and others. For economic reasons, they want the Park Service to devise means to provide more hunting opportunity, either outside the park, or inside the park. Most of these people do recognize the need to control the northern elk herd, either by hunting or other means if needed.

Montana and Wyoming guides, outfitters and other businessmen: These sub-publics favor public hunting in the park for economic reasons. Some will support live-trapping but more are strongly opposed to direct-reduction.

Sportsmen's groups (Montana, Wyoming, and other groups throughout the country): These groups for the most part, advocate public hunting in the park.

Media personnel: They recognize the need for some type of herd control but generally favor live-trapping or public hunting. A few persons completely support the present program, and some oppose any sort of reduction.

"The Great American Public:" This ill-defined and ambiguous public, consisting of numerous and unidentifiable sub-publics is against direct-reduction with only a few exceptions. The reasons are mostly emotional and because of publicity put out by opponents of direct-reduction. However, their support could be won by a

461

well-planned public relations effort to foster a greater understanding of the reasons, issues and alternatives.

CAMPAIGNS AND COMMUNICATIONS

Media Used

Newspapers were the major medium used by both the National Park Service and the various opponents to the 1967 direct-reduction program. The Park Service relied heavily on news releases, while the opponents used statements and interviews very effectively. Because of nationwide interest in Yellowstone National Park, the issue was given extensive coverage from coast-to-coast. News media personnel also were quick to editorialize the issue since it generated much interest and was very controversial. Television also was used to disseminate information about the issue. However, the coverage given on TV was not sought by either side, information merely was used because of public interest.

The elk controversy has been given coverage in national magazines, Sunday supplements to newspapers and semi-technical publications for many years. Most of the reports stressed the need for reduction, but few gave support to the program of direct-reduction. Many technical publications and papers have been written about the issue stressing the various aspects of the controversy. They are perhaps the most objective reports; however, they have a limited readership.

Other Techniques

Personal contact, meetings, field-trips and other methods to explain their problem on a face-to-face basis have been used by the Park Service. Tours or interviews also were used. In most of the cases that were investigated, the media personnel frequently requested the interview or tour.

The only regularly scheduled meetings concerning the northern elk herd are those scheduled each Spring under the terms of the 1963 cooperative management plan. According to a Park Service press release dated December 6, 1966, consultations were made with cosigners of the agreement before firming up management plans for the Northern Yellowstone elk herd.

A public meeting on the controversy was held in Casper, Wyoming on March 11, 1967. This was a hearing requested by Senator McGee (D-Wyo.), a member of the Senate appropriations subcommitee. When this hearing opened, Senator McGee announced the end of the direct-reduction program for 1967.

Propaganda was used very effectively by those opposed to the direct-reduction program. In all of the newspaper articles that were reviewed, the only statements that could be considered propaganda by the Park Service were two that mentioned "saving the herd," and it "is the humane thing to do." Both of these statements may have been attempts to arouse the sympathy of the public. One other propaganda attempt by the Park Service was to use the testimonial technique. The original date to begin reduction was delayed so the Park Service advisory board (the Leopold Board) could investigate and report on the situation. This effort completely backfired when the press reported that the members of the board never even entered the park. This discredited the report of the board that endorsed a continuation of direct-reduction.

462

The opposition used a well-planned propaganda effort to halt the direct-reduction. They used "name-calling" effectively to appeal to the "common man" and termed the board an "aesthetic, intellectual group." They made many efforts to discredit the Park Service. Repetition was used often, and charges of "lack of cooperation with state officials;" "laxity in the trapping program;" and "lack of an adequate, responsible, and effective management technique" were leveled against the Park Service. Particular emphasis was placed on the "admitted goof" by the Park Service Director when he failed to pursue the live-trapping program further before initiating direct-reduction. Also, Wyoming was pictured as "experts" in the field of elk management, and inferences were made that they could have solved the problem had the Park Service sought advice.

The "testimonial" and "band-wagon" techniques were both used with effectiveness. Constant references were made to the "public" and the "people of Wyoming" by well-known state and federal officials of Wyoming. According to these officials, everyone but the Park Service was opposed to the direct-reduction. Loaded words were also used by the opposition, and the media personnel writing articles. Terms such as "butcher," "slaughter" and "wanton killing" were used in nearly every statement and printed article. Appeals to public emotions were also made by describing "frightened animals being herded and shot" from helicopters and snowmobiles. Verbal appeals to the public's emotions were supplemented by well-chosen pictures.

Economics or the "money angle" also were brought into the battle. Many references were made to the economic advantages public hunting possessed in contrast to the "costs" of direct-reduction.

"Card stacking" and the "red-herring" technique were used in statements by the opposition. Only part of the story was told and the complexities and consequences of the various alternatives never were mentioned.

The issue is complex and not all newspaper articles opposed the direct-reduction. Some articles recognized the complex problems involved and tried to give the public some knowledge of the situation. Generally, however, the press reported the Park Service management program in a negative light. Although recognizing the need to reduce the herd, either public hunting or increased live-trapping was preferred. Since the opposition made a determined effort to be heard, they monopolized the news reports and the Park Service was usually presented as: "but the Park Service said. . . ." Some articles that were opposed to the direct-reduction were either written by well-meaning, but ill-informed people or by those capitalizing on the sensationalism of the issue.

RESULTS

Analysis of Techniques and Their Effectiveness

The opposition forced a halt to the 1967 direct-reduction program with an effective public relations effort that employed propaganda to make strong emotional appeals to the public. The Park Service was portrayed as "having an autocratic and untenable attitude" in carrying out the slaughter program in spite of overwhelming public protests.

The Park Service did not make a sufficiently planned and organized attempt to sell their elk management program to the publics involved.

Their efforts mainly were to answer charges made by the opposition. The defensive posture taken by the Park Service did little to win public support. The opposition won by capitalizing on the lack of public knowledge and understanding, and was able to present their views in a favorable light.

Sequence of Events

December 6, 1966— Press release by the National Park Service announcing 1966-67 elk management plans.

February 13, 1967— The orginal announced date to begin the direct-reduction program. This date was postponed on February 11, 1967 so the advisory board could investigate the situation and report to the Secretary of the Interior.

February 27, 1967— Second date scheduled to begin direct-reduction. Reduction started.

March 11, 1967 — Public hearing in Casper, Wyoming. Senator Gale McGee (D-Wyo.), a member of the Senate appropriations sub-committee, acted as chairman. The halt of the 1967 direct-reduction program was announced at this hearing.

Basis for Success or Failure

Under the heading, Analysis of Techniques and Their Effectiveness, reasons were given for the failure of the direct-reduction program. However, the failure also was caused by other reasons. One major problem seemed to be a lack of successful communications with the state agencies concerned with the issue. The either real, or apparent indignation displayed by the state officials of Wyoming suggests that additional conferences and coordination with these officials could do much to reduce active opposition. Although a cooperative management plan has been in existence since 1963, either the provisions for cooperation are not being followed, or the Park Service is failing to publicize meetings and management decisions.

Perhaps the best reason for the failure was well stated by Trueblood (1963). "Probably nowhere in all the fields of human activity does the shadow of the past lie more heavily upon the present than in game management. Tradition's chilling taboos force administrators to do short-sighted things, blind the public to the true status of our game populations, and furnish politicians with emotion-charged issues."

Summary, Alternate Solutions and Future Possibilities

The basis for arguments, both pro and con were discussed early in this case study. The possibilities open to the Park Service basically constitute the same program that has been used since 1934. The need for direct-reduction remains dependent on the success of hunting outside the park and the live-trapping program in the park. Continued pressure undoubtedly will be put on the Park Service to permit public hunting in Yellowstone Park. This will not solve the elk problem, and it may endanger park values and goals if permitted. The economic disadvantages of large scale live-trapping, as well as the inherent short-comings of the technique, may limit this method as an effective herd control measure.

The only solution to the problem is a dedicated effort to inform the public of the complexities of the situation and win their support to develop and carry out an effective herd control program on the Northern Yellowstone winter range. This program should be coordinated and in cooperation with the states of Montana and Wyoming. However, the Park Service should bear the responsibility for the program and should direct it. Above all, the management program, changes and the status of the elk herd should be well publicized.

Two quotes from Pengelly (1963) are the best summary of the situation, and hope for the future:

"Whether the agencies involved and the general public understand the biological, social, and legal aspects of this special case will largely determine its future handling. Public reaction will depend in part on the efforts of responsible and courageous conservationists who must conduct more basic research and explain the entire history and course of events—choices, costs, and consequences—in such a way that the public (hunters and non-hunters) will want to support proper management. There are some issues that cannot be resolved by popular vote, and this appears to be one of them."

"Management can only proceed as fast, and as far as the public will support it, and with complex issues such as these it will take time, skill, and courage to achieve such support. The initiative, however, rests with the agency entrusted with management responsibility."

Where do we go from here? The elk program has been around for a long time. Until public support is won, it will continue to be a problem plaguing the National Park Service and their attempts to manage the elk herd on the Northern Yellowstone winter range.

465

LET'S URBANIZE CONSERVATION EDUCATION (1968)
D. F. Rettie

Most major meetings on important conservation topics begin with:
"Ladies and Gentlemen, today we are fighting to save the last remaining stand of virgin redwoods . . ." or

"Ladies and Gentlemen, we have now a last chance to save the bald eagle . . ." or

"Ladies and Gentlemen, when is America going to clean up the mess it has made of its rivers? . . ."

The purpose of these inflammatory beginnings is to get people excited about major conservation issues and mobilize public opinion for effective conservation action. The most noble goal of conservation education is to prepare the citizenry at large with a background of knowledge and a basic system of values capable of understanding and forming intelligent opinions on conservation issues when they are raised.

Today I want to raise another kind of conservation issue that I think we as conservation educators have too long ignored.

I think conservation education is, on the whole, out of touch with about seven out of every ten Americans.

The seven people I have in mind live in cities. They are the vast bulk of our population whose interests lie in the urban community and whose livelihood, whose homes, and whose major recreation goes on in our major metropolitan regions.

Our metropolitan areas account for less than one percent of the land area of the United States, and they account for almost no percent of the focus of conservation education efforts. The exceptions are important but on a scale so small as to be pathetic.

Conservation education in the United States has been traditionally concerned with the issues and values that have speared the Movement since the days of Theodore Roosevelt and Gifford Pinchot.

We have worried about sustained-yield forest management, and we have spent decades developing technologies and educating farmers in practices that save soil and preserve water supplies. We have made tremendous progress in reducing man-caused forest fires. We have developed a genuine concern of national proportions for the preservation of wilderness values and areas as samples of our natural environment. We have made very large public investments to preserve wildlife species, to study their habitats and their diseases, and to manage their populations. We have developed in this nation a conservation land ethic which today is surprisingly non-controversial. Who today would argue that indiscriminate agricultural settlement on arid lands is a good thing?

And let me say that I feel much a part of this Movement; I claim it as my own and have spent most of my professional life in it.

Perhaps a couple of numbers can put my views in perspective.

In 1965 there were 125 million people in the United States age 18 and over. In that same year some 14 million hunting licenses were sold in the 50 states. The waterfowl hunting population totalled some 1.6 million

Reprinted from: Trans. N. Amer. Wildl. and Natural Resources Conf. 33:465-470.

hunters. There were some 20 million fishing licenses sold that year. It is likely these figures include a lot of double counting.

I cite these figures, not because I want to downgrade the importance of these groups, or downgrade the importance of the conservation issues which they represent. I mention them because I think it important to keep the issues in perspective, especially as we carry out decisions in conservation education which will form the foundation of understanding which will influence the decisions of others in the future.

Conservation education, like the majority of the interpretive programs of the great conservation agencies at all levels of government, is geared in large part to the identification and articulation of rural outdoor values. Most of our outdoor activities have some connection with our earlier rural and farm life. Camping. Fishing. Hunting. Picnicking. Hiking and horseback riding.

Government programs and conservation education efforts at all levels have traditionally placed public investments in support of these activities and these values. We must, of course, continue and expand these programs. But I think we need to expand our view of the world of conservation issues, to include the crises that are today so critical in our cities and in their surrounding suburbs. We need to broaden our view of conservation to include the land environment under our feet as well as that at the horizon of our view.

First, I think it is necessary to understand that most of the people who live in cities do not do so against their will. Most of them want to live there because life in the city has for them a job, a home, a sense of neighborhood, and a way of life they choose. If there are some of us who see monotony in the average suburb, who see waste in lengthy commutes to and from work, who complain about the lack of cultural life in the endless sprawl of new subdivisions, and who yearn for architectural boldness we are all dissatisfied urbanites who would improve the city, not people who have given up and want to abandon it.

Most of what we have so far done to translate conservation values and attitudes into the experience of city people has focused on the idea of instilling awareness of our dependence on natural resources for the good life and things we need and use. We have emphasized resource use and the interdependencies of life systems. We have tried to help a city resident know and understand that the trees in a far away forest provide the material for his house or his newspaper or his furniture. We have worked to provide for people far removed from our Nation's prime wilderness areas a sense of identity with them—linking people's loyalties to the natural resource assets in which they have citizens' ownership and interest.

These are good, but they are remote. They will ring responsive bells with the highly mobile suburbanite, but will have only a distant vagueness to those whose experience does not include them.

The foundation for such a new thrust in conservation must be a new urban conservation ethic, comparable in scope, in purpose, and in vitality to the set of conservation values we have so successfully applied to our rural and farm landscape.

It is not well understood that while contour furrows and cropping are an established theorem of modern farming, there is no comparable principle or practice to stop massive soil erosion in new city subdivisions. Farmers would not think of leaving hundreds of acres bare to the ravages of wind and rain for one, two or more years. Most developers do. Not because they are deliberately malicious, but because the issues have been only barely defined, and there is no broad public understanding of the consequences of such thoughtless action. No public understanding exists which would recognize the added costs of providing temporary cover, catch basins, and other protective measures. Virtually no local governments have ordinances which would equalize such actions—if one developer did it, because he felt a sense of public duty, he would have no reason to believe his competitors would follow suit.

If conservation education has ever had a challenge greater, I cannot name it. To bring to the American people a new sense of urban land values, a new urban conservation ethic for our cities and their people. Not instead of the traditional set of conservation goals and values but as an extension of them. Not a new kind of value, but a new dimension to a set of values whose truth and utility no longer need proof.

What are its horizons? Let me briefly list the issues in their urban context. I have already mentioned soil erosion. That's big and it's important, because improper land use in urbanizing areas can make our rivers unswimmable and clog reservoirs with needless silt. The loss of top soil in the new suburbs will in the long run substantially increase the costs to the public of cleaning up the water courses, dredging the silt, hauling in new top soil for lawns and gardens. In addition, upstream siltation from urban developments may substantially increase municipal water supply costs for downstream communities, ruin recreation and scenic values, destroy fish resources.

Closely related to the issue of soil erosion are issues of urban land use and geology. Today an uncounted number of new urban developments, sometimes whole communities, are being built on lands geologically unfit for development. Lands subject to rock and mud slides. Lands on or near major earthquake zones and fault lines. Flood plains. And irreplaceable swamps and marshes. The long-term private and social costs of many of these unthinking land use decisions will be large. How large we do not know. But they are avoidable. We need to build expertise in urban geology, in urban hydrology, and in the dynamics of earthquake prediction. We need better zoning or other measures to protect areas from development that should be left undeveloped. The best of present flood plain regulations are a starter.

In other urban land-use decisions, we need to strengthen the values assigned to open spaces, both public and private, in the urban environment. So-called planned unit developments, or cluster zoning, are one type of partial answer for preserving part of the urban landscape in its natural state. With this development technique it is possible to do very dramatic things with trees and undeveloped buffers.

We need better planning for public open spaces in urban areas—not only in the new communities we are building, but also in the older parts of our cities and suburbs where yesterday's planning errors are coming home to roost.

We need to heighten the sense of awareness and willingness to preserve major natural resource assets in our urbanizing areas—the swamp and salt marsh, the old remnant forest, sand dunes, streams and swales.

The air in many of our great cities is virtually unfit to breathe. On bad days it kills people. The rest of the time it just keeps adding to the costs of things and making life miserable for people.

I can probably add little to your understanding of the dimensions of the problems of water pollution and water quality. Not only does the health and vigor of our population depend on it, our whole society from top to bottom requires that we clean up our rivers and waters. We are started, but there is a long road ahead.

How many times has the conservationist listing the resources of nature included on that list one of nature's almost vanished elements—silence? Consider the extinction of silence. It is endangered now. By the din of city life and the whine of jet aircraft silence is almost now extinct.

One of those smoldering crises of urban conservation is sending up its warning signals even now as we prepare for quantum expansions in air travel and the introduction into commercial service of the Boeing 747, the SST Concorde, and the Boeing 2707. Where will we put our needed jetports? And what of the development we will permit around them?

Let me add another of what seems to me to be one of the most important new frontiers in urban conservation—the location and design of our urban freeway system. Just now the great interstate highway network is crossing the urban threshold. Where will these highways be located? To what physical and design standards will they be constructed? How wide will they be? How will they avoid those parts of the city we seek to preserve? And what costs are we willing to pay to preserve (say) a historic building or neighborhood? And what of those irreplaceable historic assets that must stand in the way of the new freeways, or in areas of blight and decay designated for renewal?

Is the world of conservation in tune with these issues or our cities? The new President's Council on Historic Preservation, established under terms of the Historic Preservation Act of 1966, sees these issues as items of major significance. Do our programs in conservation education treat historic preservation as a full partner in the conservation ethic?

I can do no more than briefly list some of the other issues:

—what will be done to rebuild our urban waterfronts, perhaps one of the most mis-used assets of many of our major cities?

—how can we reverse the process by which we have in the past taken up all the high quality land for development, then, when we ran out of things to use it for, painted the remaining dregs green and called it open space? In many cases there was none left to paint green at all. In others, the land remaining had neither form nor relationship to people and their lives.

—how can we preserve a viable segment of agricultural land use at the periphery of our cities, or mingled in with other forms of urban development—not as a museum, but as a permanent part of our landscape?

—how can we harness the Nation's dedication to the values of natural beauty as manifest in the countless beautification efforts going on around

470

the country? We must nowhere be satisfied to settle for planting trees and flowers as our national expression of concern for the total quality of our environment.

—how can we conserve those great cultural and humane values of our central cities that have over the centuries given our cities such life and creative vitality? Are our central cities doomed to decay and death?

—in addition to undergrounding electric utilities, why not extend the principle to refuse collection, mail distribution, and other services?

The issues of conservation in the cities can be lengthened far more. These are, it seems to me, the new frontiers for the national conservation movement, of which this Conference holds a position of vigorous leadership. They are your issues, no less abstract than the drive to save the redwoods or the ivory-billed woodpecker.

Conservation education has the challenge. It has the opportunity. And I think the idea is nearing the time it can no longer be put off.

POLICY

Policies concern goals. There must be a policy before there can be a management program to achieve any goal. While some aspects of policy are well-rooted in our culture, policies are still subject to question, review and change. In North America, wildlife policy is essentially a public definition of goals through the usually slow-moving democratic process. Changes in policy require a clarification and orderly presentation of the issues involved so that people may judge the decisions.

The first paper in this section describes broad wildlife policies of the United States. Four subsequent papers have clarified the consequences of wildlife policies and have led to formulation of new policies.

Biologists in the field are often most aware of the wildlife resource and its values. Often, they must inform the public of the consequences of decisions, so that policies are not created—or neglected—through ignorance or apathy. The sixth paper of this section describes activities of a state agency influencing wildlife policy.

The section concludes with policy statements of The Wildlife Society on environmental issues.

THE CONSERVATION OF FISH AND WILDLIFE (1970)
Richard D. Taber, Richard H. Cooley and William F. Royce

This review of federal and state wildlife policies describes their historical roots, notes some inadequacies, and suggests some policy changes to accommodate new needs and new public attitudes toward wildlife.

This brief survey deals with wild populations of animals—fish and wildlife—as a natural resource used by citizens of the United States, and the mechanisms through which this resource is administered and perpetuated.

The status of fish and wildlife as a natural resource is equivocal, since some species are abundant and important, some are abundant but unimportant, and others are so rare as to be almost extinct, with every shade of variation between these extremes. But since events may make the common rare, and the rare more abundant, we will take all fish and wildlife species together as a natural resource of at least potential significance.

We believe that there are four interrelated problems in the use of fish and wildlife as natural resources in the United States: ownership, habitat, cropping, and husbandry.

Ownership

Our present pattern of fish and wildlife ownership has its roots in the distant past, in the preliterate state of human culture when men were organized in bands and fish and wildlife constituted primary and essential resources. Generally, under such conditions, the band hunted or fished over a rather definite territory. This territory and the fish and wildlife to be found on it were considered to belong equally to the members of the band. This concept, that the resource was in common ownership, remained entrenched in human cultures in northern Europe even after the rise of agriculture. As rulers grew stronger, they claimed ownership of *ferae naturae,* and enforced this claim forcibly against the common man's tendency to act as though fish and wildlife were still a common resource.

As human populations increased, with attendant pressures on wildlife habitat, there was also a gradual development of the concept that those who owned land were rightfully the owners of the fish and wildlife that sheltered upon it. In England, for example, the lawyers would argue thus:

. . . a wild animal is practically the property of no one, though theoretically it may be deemed that of the crown; but when any individual exercises the right of ownership over it by curtailing its natural freedom, supplementing its food supply, or protecting it from the ravages of its natural foes, he establishes a title to it which converts it into more or less of a domestic creature.

These sentiments found no great sympathy among the common folk, who kept right on taking fish and wildlife when they could get away with

Reprinted from: No Deposit—No Return; Man and his environment: A View Towards Survival. Edited by Huey D. Johnson. Addison-Wesley Publ. Co. Reading, Mass. (Anthology of papers presented at 13th National Conf. of U.S. National Commission for UNESCO, Nov. 1969, San Francisco.)

it, in spite of penalties designed to chill their blood. This difference of opinion between the privileged and the common classes naturally became a political issue. When Wat Tyler led a rebellion of English peasants in 1381, for example, he

> . . . insisted on the total repeal of the forest and game laws. All warrens, woods, waters, and parks were to be common, and the poor as well as the rich were to have rights of venison, vert, piscary, and hawking. (Russel M. Garnier, *Annals of British Peasantry.* Swan Sonnenschein & Co., London, 1895.)

They hung him, of course, but these demands reflect the conviction that fish and wildlife are, or should be, common property.

When King George reigned over the original thirteen colonies, he claimed a sovereign right over the fish and wildlife in his domain, and in some of the southern colonies there were real efforts to tie the right to use these resources to land ownership. But when these same colonies had successfully broken away from British dominion, each colony took unto its citizens the former sovereign rights of the King, and fish and wildlife came to be owned in common, once again, by the citizens of the state where they were found.

As each new state was added to the United States, this same legal provision was repeated, and so it stands today—the citizens of each state own in common all fish and wildlife residing in that state.

This public ownership of the fish and wildlife resources becomes private ownership when some private person gains possession of the animals. With a virgin continent before him, the American went with a characteristic zest into the business of turning this public property to his private account. As settlers increased, as railway lines were pushed across the country, as firearms became more efficient, and as markets grew in the industrial cities, the exploitation of fish and wildlife for commercial profit intensified. The decades following the Civil War saw a rapidly mounting pressure on these resources, both by the widespread population existing on subsistence agriculture and by commercial hunters. The tremendous fish and wildlife wealth of the new continent could not stand this strain, and most of the exploited species went into a sharp decline. Law upon law was passed to provide protection, but since these were not enforced, the pressure on the resource grew.

By the 1880's the buffalo were almost gone, by the 90's the passenger pigeon was virtually extinct, and many other exploited animals were in similar straits.

Shortly after the turn of the century a wave of reaction from uncontrolled exploitation permitted the establishment of an effective system of administration for fish and wildlife resources.

On the level of state government, the sportsmen were for the first time charged a fee for the hunting or fishing license. This provided a source of earmarked revenue for the state departments of fish and game. One consequence was that funds were now available to hire full-time officers to enforce protective regulations. These regulations had two main aims— to prevent over-harvesting, and to equalize opportunity among the harvesters. Another consequence was that the sportsmen came to act as stockholders in a corporation. Since the sportsman paid the cost, fish and wild-life resources should be managed for his benefit. And since state departments of fish and game were dependent for income on license sales, they were quite responsive to the sportsmen, devoting their attention primarily to those species of interest to sportsmen, and to the preservation and increase of the sportsmen themselves. Meanwhile, the citizens of each state, legal owners of all the free living fish and wildlife in the state, support this resource with virtually nothing from the general funds.

As part of the protection provided for the sportsmen, most species of game fish and wildlife were removed entirely from commercial markets.

Commercial fishing was regulated separately. But even here the thrust of the regulations was the same—to prevent overharvesting and to equalize opportunity among the harvesters.

The administration by state departments of fish and game, described above, is only partially effective as a means of administering fish and wildlife resources. There is little interest in the multitude of species which are not important for game or commerce. There is little interest in the control of pest situations involving fish and wildlife. There is no effective means for dealing with populations which pass in migration from state to state, or nation to nation, or which are found in international waters. All of these aspects of administration of the fish and wildlife resource, which were largely excluded from the conservation activities of the states, were gradually taken over by the federal government.

These federal activities have been supported partly from the sports-men—through taxes on sporting equipment, through the "duck stamp," and partly through general appropriations. The federal fish and wildlife conservation structure, then, is not tied quite so tightly to the sportsman's interest as is the state.

Habitat

Fish and wildlife populations, when reduced, will rapidly increase again to fill their habitat. But habitats can change and become less suitable for animal species, which thereupon decline.

There has been an ever-increasing spectrum and intensity of uses by man of the lands and waters of the North American continent. These uses have changed fish and wildlife habitat, often for the worse.

On any particular piece of the landscape, there will be some use which will yield a tangible and immediate reward to a definite group of human beings. At the same time, its value as fish or wildlife habitat is spread over an indefinite period of time during which it will yield fish and wildlife benefits of unknown magnitude to the citizens as a whole, present and future.

Privately owned land is private property. Wildlife living on that land, in the United States, is public property. Access to this public property—that is, to the wild animals—might be considered a common right of ownership—that is, of citizenship.

The land owner, though theoretically protected by trespass laws, is in reality faced with an army of sportsmen and a state agency devoted to the welfare of these sportsmen. The effects are several. The landowner is inhibited by his own cultural attitudes from charging fees for use of his lands by sportsmen; and state government has long reinforced this cultural inhibition by promoting free use.

The results are clear: the land owner makes his land management decisions with little regard for fish and wildlife. Since these do not provide him with any income, they are not part of his profit-making decisions. Considerations far removed from the perpetuation of the fish and wildlife resource are fed into his calculations. His fields become larger as more powerful farm implements become available to him; irregularities and obstructions are eliminated from his fields; he no longer needs a woodlot for fuel and posts; weeding and insect control through pesticides are suited to his increasingly mechanical system of husbandry. As a result of these improvements in the efficiency of agriculture the quality of wildlife habitat, and consequently population of wildlife, declines.

To date all the efforts made in the United States to overcome the consequences of this system—mainly through the purchase and management of wildlife lands and the improvement of wildlife habitat on private lands with state funds—have failed to counterbalance the steady deterioration of wildlife habitat on private lands. Consequently the states, in licensing hunters, are selling them the right to pursue an ever-dwindling resource. Hunters resist governmental efforts to charge more for this scarce resource, and eventually some of them give up these sports altogether. The result is that the state has, at best, a static income from sportsmen, with no prospects for this income to increase. If this trend continues, the services offered by the state can only decline.

There is one exception to this general pattern which provides some food for thought. The State of Texas has exceptionally rigorous trespass laws, and little public land. This has permitted the land owner to charge fees for entry to hunt. The wildlife resource upon his land has thus become a source of revenue for him. The consequence is that many Texas landowners protect and improve wildlife habitat as part of their overall business-management plan. The actual changes in land-management practices which would enhance rather than destroy wildlife habitat are often not difficult or expensive to achieve, so the landowner has the potential to realize a rather good return upon his managerial investment in the wildlife resource.

The lesson is clear. If the wildlife resource means income to the landowner, he will consider it along with his other sources of income. And although the sportsman is reluctant to pay the state substantial fees, he will, if necessary, pay the landowner.

A different pattern has emerged for most of the fish habitat. A major part of the sport fishery has always been pursued in the public waters of the sea, the estuaries, the large rivers, and the lakes. Recently a large expansion of the public fish habitat has occurred in the multipurpose reservoirs that are being built in all sections of the country. But even though habitat and fish are both clearly under public control, other uses of the water create problems.

Of increasing importance is the problem of pollution. Pollution has many forms, among which we instantly think of waste materials dumped into waters, pesticides widely spread through all our ecosystems, and the

478

results of such industrial accidents as oil or chemical spills. These are private acts diminishing public values. If there were clear evidence of the responsibility for these acts and their detailed effects upon fish and wildlife biology, and if we knew the resultant losses in public property, the effective remedies, and their costs—if we had knowledge of all of these things the problem would be largely solved, because the polluters could be held financially responsible for their acts. But the polluters and their pollutants are many, the effects of pollution are often subtle and only partially understood, and remedies, if such exist, are not yet found.

Finally, fish and wildlife habitats are suffering from the massive ecological changes connected with our expanding population with its even more rapidly expanding demands for space and power. Everywhere we turn, marshes are being filled, streams are being straightened, estuaries are being dredged, strip-mines are operating, suburbia is spreading into the forest, and new highways, new dams, and new subdivisions are on the drawing board. Losses of wild animals are sometimes spectacular, as in the case of the migratory fish of the Columbia or the resident wildlife of the Everglades. Even more important, on a continental scale one can see the summation of the many small changes continually going forward—particularly changes in streams, which are becoming increasingly channelized, with a greater high-low water differential, and small ponds and marshes which are continually being filled to provide a base for construction. These losses are greater than the gains, and we have a problem. Solution lies in a realistic evaluation of both the gains and the losses. Our ability to evaluate fish and wildlife resources, particularly in any terms other than pounds of meat or quantity of furs, is still rudimentary.

Cropping

There are values in fish and wildlife resources alive and free, and there are values in harvesting an annual crop. The magnitude of this crop must obviously be controlled if excessive exploitation is to be avoided. Controlling the magnitude of the crop is one major objective in administration of fish and wildlife resources. At the same time, it will be recalled, we here in the United States strive for maximum participation in the cropping process, and equality of opportunity among the participants. Both state and federal administrators, then, are forced to control cropping by indirect means, through regulation of seasons and equipment. The present wide participation in fish and wildlife cropping, described above, does not lend itself well to attaining a close control over cropping magnitude.

It would not be far from the truth to say that a goodly share of the time of fish and wildlife conservation agencies is devoted to determining what the annual crop should be, and tinkering around with the regulations to achieve a harvest which approximates, but does not exceed, this allowable crop. The tendency, since control is uncertain, is to err on the conservative side, and under-crop. This is often of little practical consequence, but under certain circumstances it leads to trouble. Principal among these is the case in which there is some population of fish or wildlife which is involved in a pest situation. The population, often, should be reduced. However, the species involved is usually dear to the heart of some group of consumers. One familiar example is the great increase in populations of white-tailed deer over the past half-century, the damage often done by excessively heavy populations to forest and farm crops, and the public resistance to effective measures for deer population control. There has been similar opposition to needed control of many other populations of native animals.

This focus on harvesting an annual crop by the regulatory agencies, and saving the lives of individual animals by the sympathetic public, tends to distract attention from the need for fish and wildlife husbandry: the protection, maintenance, and enhancement of this renewable resource.

Husbandry

Fish and wildlife resources can be husbanded most successfully if the habitat is controlled.

There are two sorts of lands or waters on which fish and wildlife husbandry is seriously attempted. One consists of publicly owned landscape units such as major waters and national forest and range lands. The other consists of those relatively small units of private land on which fish and wildlife are intensively managed for private benefit. Over most of our private lands and waters, which cover the most productive regions of the United States, husbandry of fish and wildlife resources is minimal, to say the least.

In the case of the many species of fish and wildlife which are adapted to life on publicly owned lands (usually forest, range and recreational lands) minor adjustments in management can perpetuate at least fair habitat. Then there are the species of fish and wildlife which have habitat requirements which are not met in this way; the numerous species of water-birds provide a good example. For these there must be special habitat preserved, or else created and maintained. Since our system has discouraged us from attempting to preserve habitat on private lands, we have left ourselves with only one alternative: buy up the needed lands with public money and manage them to provide habitat for those species which would otherwise have none.

One result of this policy is our national system of waterfowl refuges. Another is our system of sanctuaries for species threatened with extinction.

But the national system of waterfowl refuges is only half established because of a shortage of funds, and as more and more species become threatened with extinction, can we expect to obtain larger and larger sums of money to establish sanctuaries for them?

The prospects of accommodating all the fish resources we would like to have in the United States in public waters seem reasonably good. The prospects of accommodating all the wildlife resources we would like to have in the United States on public lands seem poor indeed.

Recommendations

From this review of the administration of fish and wildlife resources in the United States, we can draw the following conclusions:

1. The state departments of fish and game need a broader base of responsibility and the appropriate public funding to free them from their present dependence on the sportsmen.
2. Both state and federal fish and wildlife resource agencies need a substantial increase in research support and improved means of feeding research findings into husbandry.

3. Means should be devised to reverse the deterioration of wildlife habitat on private lands, probably through income from the sportsman to the landowner for this service.
4. Pollution of fish and wildlife habitats should be fought at both state and federal levels with increased research funding and more effective regulation.
5. Although this brief review has been intentionally limited to the United States, it must be recognized that the problems of ownership, habitat, cropping, and husbandry present serious international complications. These can be expected to greatly intensify in the years ahead, and their equitable resolution will require much more effective international cooperation and control than presently exists.
6. Finally, and most important, none of these recommendations will be practical if we continue to pack more and more of mankind and his works into the landscape of North America. The control of human populations is the first necessity if the multitude of populations of other forms of life is to survive.

EXOTIC BIG GAME ON PUBLIC LANDS (1966)

Frank C. Craighead, Jr., and Raymond F. Dasmann

Transplantation of native game and introductions of exotic game have been the hoped-for panacea, the solution for declining stocks of native game on dwindling habitat. This paper, dealing solely with introductions of big game, describes what is at stake when exotics are introduced. The paper contains the following foreword:

"Dr. Craighead and Dr. Dasmann were retained as consultants by the Bureau of Land Management to investigate the advisability of the introduction of exotic big game species on public lands; and to recommend guidelines to be followed in considering proposed releases. The report was submitted to an Advisory Committee appointed by Secretary of the Interior, Stewart L. Udall. The Committee was composed of representatives from State and Federal agencies, private conservation organizations, and the National Advisory Board Council of the Bureau of Land Management. The Committee, after a review, recommended that the report be adopted; former Bureau of Land Management Director, Charles H. Stoddard concurred in this recommendation. In August 1966, the guidelines and recommendations contained herein . . . were approved by Secretary Udall as public land policy".

The purpose of this report is to provide information for determining if, where, and under what conditions, exotic mammals, particularly big game species, might be released on federal lands and to suggest guidelines for consideration in specific release proposals. The approach has been to analyze the effects and results of past introductions, to study and assess field conditions and to evaluate these on a basis of ecological knowledge and principles. The authors wish to acknowledge the contribution of numerous scientists and writers most of whom cannot be individually credited in a report of this kind.

A rapid survey of the literature on introductions, reveals certain generalities concerning the release or transplantation of exotic animals. A better understanding of the subject of exotic mammal introductions can be achieved within the context of this broader view.

1. There is a worldwide trend toward dissemination and establishment of exotic plant and animal species. This is progressing through both planned introductions, accidental escapes and natural spread. Though it can be accelerated or retarded, the facts of the case and the forces at work indicate that the trend will continue indefinitely into the future.

2. There are still "wild" areas of the world where the endemic fauna and flora are relatively unmodified by recent introductions of exotics. For a variety of reasons it seems desirable to maintain such areas in their virgin condition.

3. The history of animal introductions reveals dismal failures and disastrous and disruptive consequences; as well as both successful introductions and those that quite definitely can be considered beneficial. A well-defined but flexible policy appears needed.

Reprinted from: a report submitted to the U. S. Bureau of Land Management.

4. Most introductions have not been made in the public interest. They have been haphazard affairs, not scientifically planned or executed. The history of exotic releases vividly points up the need for a systematic approach to the subject.

5. It is evident that we have not had in the past and still do not have sufficient information and knowledge to introduce exotic species with any assurance that they will be successes or failures, prove detrimental or beneficial. We cannot as yet predict consequences, especially long-range side effects.

6. The principal dangers resulting from the successful introduction of an exotic species are the establishment of nuisance and pest species, the establishment and spread of diseases, the initiation of forces bringing about disruptive ecological changes, added competition with native forms, and hybridization resulting in inferior species or the elimination of species.

7. There is evidence that vacant ecological niches exist, some created through natural processes and others brought into existence by the activities of man. There is a growing demand to fill these with game species. Almost nothing is known about the existence, nature and extent of vacant ecological niches.

8. Most of the introduced species that are now abundant were not established as a result of the first introduction.

9. Participation in outdoor recreation activities, including big game hunting, will grow. Accompanying stepped-up demand by sportsmen for increased game supplies is to be expected. The introduction of exotics is one possible approach toward satisfying the demand.

10. The main causes of failure of past introductions were failure to consider the characteristics of the species to be introduced, failure to determine in advance climatic and habitat requirements and failure to liberate a sufficient number of healthy individuals under conditions comparable to the original environment.

Opinions on Exotics

Exotic ungulates in America have a history dating back to the first explorations and settlements in the New World. Soon after the Americas were colonized, the horse and hog became established as feral animals and were to be followed in some areas by representatives of many other domestic groups. The introduction of wild game came later, but dates back at least to the 18th century. It is too late, therefore, to decide whether exotic ungulates should or should not be introduced. They are already here. We can only determine the extent to which further introductions might be beneficial or desirable.

A dearth of fact provides a wide field for the expression of emotional opinion on the subject of exotics. There are excellent reasons why the introduction of exotics should be considered seriously for certain lands, and equally good reasons why such introductions should be unfavorably considered in other areas or under other circumstances.

Those who oppose introductions of exotics often base their opposition on one or more of the following grounds: (a) Exotic species can create further land use conflicts in areas already fully stocked by domestic ungulates and native wild game. (b) Exotic big game may displace native species from habitats where these natives still exist. (c) Exotic species can disrupt the balance existing within natural communities, and thus destroy those areas that we hope to maintain in a primitive or representative natural state. (d) We should concentrate on preserving an American biota in America, an African biota in Africa, an Asian in Asia, and not accelerate an already world-wide trend toward biotic uniformity. (e) The money spent for exotic introductions would go much further if used in improving habitat conditions and preserving environment for native species. (f) Exotic ungulates can be difficult or impossible to control where circumstances favor their rapid spread and increase.

Those who favor the introduction of exotics base their arguments on the premise that North America has many vacant ecologic niches, not occupied or only partially filled by native species. Exotic animals could fill these niches and thus promote faunal diversity in this continent. This would be of value for: (a) Making available to the sportsmen a greater abundance and variety of shootable game. (b) Increasing yields of meat and other economically useful products from wild lands. (c) Providing an opportunity to preserve in America species that are in danger of extinction in their native lands.

Conflicting opinions on the desirability of exotic introductions have led game departments of some States to come out in firm opposition to exotic ungulates, and have led other States to start a vigorous program aimed at widespread introductions of exotics. Those who strongly oppose exotic ungulates often offer enthusiastic approval of exotic game birds. Decisions should be based logically upon knowledge of the effects of earlier introductions on the land and its native biota, and on detailed studies of the ecology of the species proposed for introduction. But such knowledge and studies are limited and at present, there is inadequate information to support any firm conclusions. In the absence of such knowledge, and to protect the public interest on federal lands, it is important for the agencies concerned with the conservation of these lands to develop an interim policy governing the introduction of exotic ungulates on lands under their administration. It is also desirable that they support the studies needed to acquire the necessary information.

Regulation and Control of Exotic Big Game

Federal regulations prevent the direct introduction and release in the United States of big game animals from foreign countries. Such animals can be imported by zoological gardens, or similar institutions, but may not be released from these places. The offspring of these zoo animals can be sold to private game farms or used to stock private or public land, subject to State regulation and agreement of private land owners or public land administrators. State regulations governing the movement and release of exotics vary greatly. In Texas, private land owners can purchase, transport, and release exotic big game. In California, since 1963, the importation, transportation, or release of such animals by private individuals is prohibited. California, therefore, has tight control over exotic big game releases; Texas has virtually no control. Both States have well-established populations of exotics over which no effective control has been exercised.

New Mexico and Nevada propose releases of exotic big game on public lands. Arizona and California propose to restrict or prevent such releases.

States that favor the release of exotic big game believe that they can control the numbers and distribution of these animals through hunting. However, few States have actually demonstrated the ability to consistently control the numbers of any species of big game, native or exotic, that makes effective use of cover, is abundant, and widely distributed. Such species as the horse, zebra, or perhaps oryx, that occupy an open habitat, perhaps can be easily controlled. Species such as the kudu, various deer, and small antelope that prefer dense, brushy cover, can be difficult to control under most conditions. Departments of Game that are willing and able to attempt control over the numbers of exotics, can be readily prevented from doing so by the action of Fish and Game Commissions or State legislatures just as some State departments have been prevented from efforts to control the numbers of native deer. The lack of uniformity of State regulations and the probability of exotic release and spread on federal lands creates a problem for Federal land management agencies.

Evidence from Recent Exotic Introductions

The Texas Situation: More species of exotic ungulates have been introduced into the State of Texas than into any other comparable area of North America with which these writers are familiar. Exotic big game animals are now established in 48 of the 254 counties in the State, from the arid west to the humid east. Jackson (1964) has listed the following species of exotics found in Texas with the approximate numbers of each:

Axis deer (*Cervus axis*)	2,196
Sika deer (*Cervus nippon*)	634
Fallow deer (*Cervus dama*)	220
Sambar deer (*Cervus rusa*)	38
Barasingha deer (*C. duvauceli*)	32
Red deer (*Cervus elaphus*)	21
Barbary sheep (*Ammotragus lervia*)	1,588
Mouflon sheep (*Ovis musimon*)	1,846
Blackbuck (*Antilope cervicapra*)	3,693
Nilgai (*Boselaphus tragocamelus*)	3,334
Eland (*Taurotragus oryx*)	5
Oryx (*Oryx gazella*)	3
Wild boar (*Sus scrofa*)	Over 575

Except for the smaller numbers, all of the above figures are estimates and probably conservative. The rate of introduction, spread and increase of exotics has been accelerating. Although most species are on private ranches under fence, some are now well established and increasing in the wild. The axis deer, fallow deer, red deer, Barbary sheep, mouflon, blackbuck, nilgai, and wild boar all have unfenced populations. With the exception of the red deer, which is doubtful as yet, all of these must be considered successful introductions into unfenced land. Species that have shown little increase or have remained static in numbers are the sambar, barasingha, red deer. The eland and oryx, recently introduced, have thus far failed to reproduce.

There is little information available on competition between native and exotic ungulates. A paper by Sanders (1963), based on a study near Laredo, reports that the blackbuck, sika deer, mouflon, axis deer and native white-tailed deer tend to seek out different, non-conflicting habitats. In this area, however, the exotics were barely maintaining their numbers, and not increasing. White-tailed deer were abundant and thriving. "Deplorable range conditions due to chronic overgrazing by cattle" were said to exist on the ranch used as a study area.

An example of the rate of increase and spread of an exotic ungulate is provided by the nilgai. This species was introduced in 1930 to a ranch on the lower south Texas coast. The original broodstock was thought to be twelve. The species now occupies 1,425,000 acres on six adjoining ranches and numbers 3,334.

The California Situation: The vegetation of California has been drastically modified through overgrazing, mostly attributed to domestic livestock, but added to by feral ungulates. Most of the grasslands are now dominated by exotic annual grasses and forbs brought in, mostly, along with domestic animals. Soon after Spanish settlement, feral horses and cattle spread over the grasslands of California. Early explorers from the American States found herds of wild horses and cattle existing along with abundant populations of native elk, deer, and antelope. Most of the damage to the rangelands must be blamed on the combination of drought and unchecked increase in domestic livestock.

Since its early history, many species of wild exotic big game have been introduced into California. A survey by the California Department of Fish and Game shows that twelve species of exotic wild ungulates have been established in the State. These include:

Fallow deer *(Cervus dama)*	500 plus
Spotted deer *(Cervus alfredi?)*	60
Black deer (?)	20
Sambar deer *(Cervus unicolor)*	10
Axis deer *(Cervus axis)*	?
Sika deer *(Cervus nippon)*	?
Barbary sheep *(Ammotragus lervia)*	300
Tahr *(Hemitragus jemlahicus)*	60
Burchell Zebra *(Equus burchellii)*	15
Wildebeest *(Connochaetes taurinus)*	?
Mouflon *(Ovis musimon)*	15
Wild boar *(Sus scrofa)*	3,000 plus

Of these species only the wild boar can be considered as widely and successfully established in the wild. It has maintained itself, increased and spread from the original introduction site since it was first brought into the State in the 1920's. It now ranges from the Carmel Valley south through the Santa Lucia Mountains as far as Nacimiento Lake, a distance of at least 70 miles from the original site. Throughout the area occupied by the wild boar, the native black-tailed deer remains abundant.

For nearly twenty years, white fallow deer have been present on the Ridgewood Ranch near Ukiah. Fifty animals were introduced, and an estimated 250 to 300 are now present. The species has not spread widely. The black-tailed deer remains very abundant in the same area.

Near Drake's Bay, the Ottinger Ranch supports three kinds of deer said to be fallow, spotted and black deer. These were introduced around 1940 and have increased from 65 to an estimated 220. They have not dispersed widely. The native black-tailed deer remains abundant in the same area.

The greatest variety of exotic big game exists on or has escaped from the Hearst Ranch near San Simeon. Here the fallow deer, sambar, axis deer, Barbary sheep, tahr, zebra, wildebeest and perhaps other species are to be found. The Barbary sheep and tahr are said to have spread into the Santa Lucia mountains. Both numbers and distribution are only a guess.

New Mexico: Much publicity has been given to proposals for the introduction of exotic big game into New Mexico. One species, the Barbary sheep, has been successfully introduced, and the introduction of others is planned. It has been claimed that New Mexico could provide a haven for species threatened with extinction in Africa. Kudu, gemsbuck and ibex have been brought from Africa to the Albuquerque zoo. When sufficient offspring have been produced, it is planned to release these three species into wild areas.

The Barbary sheep was deliberately released in the Canadian River canyon of northeastern New Mexico in 1950. Since then, there have been two releases of Barbary sheep in western and southern New Mexico. The Canadian River introduction has been studied. Little is known of the status of sheep in the two other areas. In the Canadian River canyon, the Barbary sheep population increased from 52 to more than a thousand between 1950 and 1961. From the original release site, near Roy, they have spread northward as far as Colorado, a distance of 80 miles, and southward beyond the Conchas Reservoir, a distance of at least 50 miles. The spread has mostly been confined to the habitat provided by the brush-covered, rocky rims of the canyon. East and west of the canyon, rolling grassy plains occur and these have not been occupied by sheep. The habitat characteristic of the Canadian rims, however, continues on mesa slopes over a large area of New Mexico. There is no real barrier to the continued spread of the sheep.

In 1962 it was thought that the Barbary sheep had decreased since hunters failed to find sheep in places where they had been located in earlier years. In 1963 and 1964 hunting was discontinued. In the absence of hunting, it has been virtually impossible to keep up with the numbers or distribution of the sheep. Some believe that the sheep have not decreased, but have dispersed more widely. Only further study will reveal the truth. The kind of habitat occupied is rough and hard to traverse, making it difficult to control the Barbary sheep if they once become both widely dispersed and numerous. In the absence of hunting, the use of radio-tagged sheep might provide the needed information on dispersal and population ecology.

Nevada: Nevada has no reported populations of exotic big game, although feral horses and burros are widely distributed. The Fish and Game Commission, however, has proposed the introduction of the Barbary sheep into the State. Since it was planned to release these animals on federal lands, it was thought advisable by the Bureau of

Land Management, the agency in charge of the administration of this land, to have an impartial committee review the situation and the possible problems involved. The introduction of Barbary sheep has, therefore, been postponed until such time as a policy governing future introductions of exotic big game can be decided upon for lands under BLM administration.

The proposed release site for Barbary sheep lies in the Seven Troughs Range northwest of Lovelock. The area was chosen because it seemed to present a minimum chance for conflict between Barbary sheep and native big game. It is bounded by deserts, saltbush flats, alkali lakes and other habitat thought poorly suited to the sheep and likely to serve as a barrier to their spread. Big game animals are scarce in the area. A few mule deer occur in mountains near the western boundary; a small band of antelope has been reported near the eastern boundary; small bands of mustangs and wild burros range over the area. The State, itself, has scattered populations of the desert bighorn sheep *(Ovis canadensis nelsoni)* as well as the largest remaining concentrations of this animal.

The proposed release area is poor habitat for native big game since the mountains do not rise high enough to support the better browse-plant communities. The entire region is dry, overgrazed, and probably overstocked with domestic livestock. It forms a summer range for cattle and a winter range for sheep. Grass cover is dominated by exotic annuals, such as cheat grass, and red brome. The exotic chukar partridge is well established and numerous. There is little question, therefore, of interference with an undisturbed native biota. The nearest native bighorn sheep occur 125 air miles away in the country west of Walker Lake. With the introduction of bighorn to the Sheldon Refuge, native sheep will be located within 100 miles of the release site.

If Barbary sheep are to be introduced into Nevada, the Seven Troughs Range provides a site least likely to provide conflict with other more important land uses. There is no way, however, for predicting whether the sheep will survive in, or remain in, the area in which they are to be released. If they should become established, their impact on the range is not likely to improve conditions.

The greatest danger from such an introduction lies in the possibility of spread to existing desert bighorn ranges. If this occurred, it could be a very real threat to the survival of the native species.

Niches and Competition

Some problems involved with exotic big game are best viewed in the light of happenings over the past 8,000 to 9,000 years. The ungulate populations of North America were vastly different 9,000 years ago from what they were when the Europeans first arrived in America. The variety and abundance of American ungulates at the end of the last glacial age equalled that to be found in the savannas of Africa today. For reasons not fully understood, most of these animals became extinct. Some believe that primitive man was a factor in causing these extinctions. The botanical evidence suggests that the plant communities that supported the post-Pleistocene abundance and variety of big game were not different from those that exist today. From these and other data, it can be postulated that the extinctions of native ungulates left ecologic niches that have not yet been filled by those species that survived in America.

The introduction of exotic species to America differs only in degree from the normal changes that have taken place in modern man's absence. The moose, caribou, mountain sheep, elk and bison, for examples are exotics in the sense that they are relatively recent immigrants from Eurasia. They have moved into a continent previously occupied by such long-established residents as the mule deer, pronghorn and white-tailed deer. Presumably, they have survived here only because they were more adaptable, better competitors or found vacant niches that could be occupied.

The success of various feral ungulates might be considered further evidence for vacant niches. The speed with which the horse increased in numbers and spread over the Americas suggests that it found a niche not occupied by any competing species. There is no evidence that it has anywhere displaced native ungulates. Feral hogs and feral burros have also adapted to North America with apparent ease and have occupied extensive areas. The evidence for competition with or displacement of native ungulates is inconclusive. By contrast, except for islands, the feral goat and feral sheep have not done well in the Americas, although small populations hold out in some places.

In addition to feral ungulates, there have been many introductions of wild exotic ungulates into North America. These introductions have met with varying degrees of success. There is as yet little evidence of serious conflict between native big game and the exotic wild species. However, the situations involved have not yet been adequately studied.

In considering the arguments for the introduction of exotics, the basic premise, that vacant niches do exist, seems to be supported by the available evidence. The assumption, however, that suitable species can be found to fill these niches finds less support. Most exotic big game introductions have been only partial successes, and many have failed. Costs are relatively high. It is virtually impossible to predict whether a species will adapt to an American environment in advance of its actual introduction. Even when a species has been introduced, it may take many years, or decades, before we can know whether or not it will ultimately survive, increase and spread, or alternatively, fail.

Maintaining the Primitive Scene and Native Biota

An opposition to the introduction of exotics based on a desire to maintain, or restore, the primitive scene in America, as it was before civilized man began to modify it, is certainly legitimate. It should be realized, however, that it is a desire to maintain the pre-Columbian, or pre-settlement scene, with the natural communities that existed at that time. Further back in time other natural communities did exist. There can be an equally legitimate desire to attempt to restore a much earlier American biota through introduction of the near relatives of now extinct American forms. The scientific value of such an attempt is as obvious as the value of preserving or restoring the Pre-Columbian biota.

Disruptive Effects of Exotics and Land-Use Conflicts

Thinking on the subject of exotic big game is colored by the unfortunate consequences of exotic introductions on islands. The examples of Hawaii and New Zealand, where severe disruption of the native biota took place when exotic ungulates were introduced, are well known. Australia, island-like in its isolation from other continents, provides similar illustrations. In Europe, hybridization has caused the extermination or near loss of native ungulate races and species. Evidence of disruptive effects from the larger continents similar to that from islands is not available. Nevertheless, since this threat is always present, the burden of proof must rest on those who would introduce new species. Before an exotic is turned loose, it should be demonstrated that it will not cause disruption or displacement in the native biota or serious conflict with other, more valuable forms of land use. This does not rule out the introductions of exotics in areas that do not have primary value for preservation of native biota, or high economic value for other conflicting land uses. Introductions into such areas should be preceded by evidence that the new species can be confined to these areas.

Guidelines for the Introduction of Exotic Big Game Animals

When an animal species is introduced into any environment, it has both the potential to produce disruptive, often uncontrollable forces as well as to fill a vacant niche and fit into an existing ecological pattern with beneficial rather than deleterious effects. Big game releases, therefore, should be preceded by scientific study with the findings carefully evaluated and the release systematically planned. It should be determined that the introduction will fulfill a desirable objective, and that maximum safeguards have been taken to protect native biota. Provision should be made for follow-up in the form of scientific investigations on the status of the released animal.

Some factors and conditions that should be considered as a guide to introductions are:

1. It should be objectively determined that there is a real need for a proposed introduction, and it should appear likely that the introduction will have desirable ecological, recreational and economic impacts.

2. The introduction should fill a definite vacant ecologic niche, one not filled or suitable for a native species. The probable existence of such a niche should be reasonably well documented.

3. An introduction should not be considered if there is any danger, even apprehension, over the action leading to drastic reduction or regional displacement of indigenous populations. Pending future study, the introduction of exotic big game species on federal lands should be governed by the necessity for protecting the native biota and for preventing conflict with other existing or proposed land uses.

4. Studies of the ecology of the animal considered for release should precede and guide introductions. Studies should, likewise, be made to determine the suitability of the proposed release area.

5. Every effort should be made to study disease interrelationships and to take steps for assuring effective quarantine resulting in disease-free game.
6. Precautions against hybridization should be taken by selecting animals that do not have close relatives in this country and rejecting those that do.
7. Small trial introductions in suitable areas using adequate numbers of stock should first be conducted on an experimental basis under controlled conditions such as in a fenced area. The results should be carefully studied using the latest and best research methods. An evaluation of this introduction should serve as a basis for further action.
8. Before an exotic is introduced, positive assurance should be obtained that adequate control methods can be instigated to prevent overpopulation or spreading.

Recommendations

In view of the foregoing discussion and considerations, the following recommendations are made:

1. The introduction of an exotic species should be considered as a crucial decision taken only after thorough research and competent and unbiased evaluations. To insure this, the federal government should institute studies or encourage cooperative studies with the States as soon as feasible, to gather data on the ecology of big game animals proposed for, or potentially suitable for, introduction into the United States. Studies should be instituted as soon as possible in areas where exotic big game are already established in the United States with a view toward determining their impact on the native biota and the characteristics of their population ecology, including rates of increase and distances of movement and dispersal, predation effect, disease status, degree of control and change in habits.
2. No exotic big game animals should be permitted in national parks, wilderness or primitive areas, wildlife refuges, native game ranges or other areas designated for the preservation of native flora and fauna in an undisturbed, or relatively undisturbed condition. To protect the above areas, exotic big game animals should be excluded from a buffer area surrounding each of these areas. The width of the buffer strip should be determined by the mobility of the exotic big game animals concerned, type of terrain and the ease with which it can be controlled.
3. Exotic big game animals should be excluded from the vicinity of any area in which rare or uncommon native big game species occur until such time as it can be conclusively demonstrated that no conflict will occur between the native and the exotic species.
4. Exotic big game animals should be excluded from any area of federal land that is of primary value as livestock range and is already fully stocked with domestic livestock. Exceptions to this should be made only when it has been shown conclusively that

the exotic animal will not compete significantly with domestic species.

5. To prevent conflict with other uses of the land such as timber production, farming, urban development, or intensively used recreation sites, exotic big game animals should be excluded from the vicinity of areas of primary value for these other purposes, except where it can be demonstrated that uses can be fully coordinated.

6. On other federal lands, exotic big game may be introduced under permit from the federal land management agency. The terms of such an agreement must include a commitment by the state agency concerned to maintain numbers of exotics at levels determined by the federal agency to be within the safe carrying capacity of the habitat, and to use every means for preventing the spread of such exotics into any of the areas from which they are excluded for the reasons listed above.

7. Individuals or organizations that introduce exotic big game animals that spread from state, from other public, or private lands into federal lands, without permit or prior agreement, should be held liable for any damages that result from the spread of these exotics, and responsible for any expenses incurred in their control.

8. Policy in regard to the introduction of exotic mammals on public lands should be flexible, that is, periodically reviewed and if necessary, revised in light of new knowledge, new technology and the numerous and tremendous changes that are rapidly, and in some cases, permanently altering our environment. It should also reflect that the introduction of exotics is itself a force capable of causing drastic changes in environment; that considered in its totality, we are a part of this environment as well as being dependent upon its proper functioning for our existence.

SELECTED BIBLIOGRAPHY

(These are but a few of the papers in the original, extensive bibliography)

ANDERSON, R.M. 1933. Effect of the introduction of exotic animal forms. *Proc. 5th Pac. Sci. Cong.* 1:769-778.

BALDWIN, P.H., C.W. SCHWARTZ, and E.R. SCHWARTZ. 1952. Life history and economic status of the mongoose in Hawaii. *Jour. Mammal.* 33(3): 335-356.

BRYAN, E.H. 1947. The introduction of birds into Hawaii. *Hawaii Ent. Soc. Proc.* 2(4): 169-175.

BUMP, G. 1951. Game introductions—when, where and how. *Trans. 16th N.A. Wildlife Conf.* pp. 316-325.

CAHALANE, V.H. 1949. Some effects of exotics on nature. *U.S.D.I. Nat. Park Ser.* pp. 1-14 (mimeographed).

COTTAM, C. 1949. The effects of uncontrolled introductions of plants and animals. *Proc. Inter. Tech. Conf. Protec. Nature.* U.N.E.S.C.O. Paris, France. pp. 408-413.

DE VOS A., R.H. MANVILLE, and R.G. VAN GELDER. 1956. Introduced mammals and their influence on native biota. *Zoologica* 41(4): 163-194.

ELTON, CHARLES. 1959. The ecology of invasions by animals and plants. John Wiley, New York. 191 pp.

HALL, E.R. 1963. Introduction of exotic species of mammals. *Trans. Kans. Acad. of Science,* 66: 516-518.

JACKSON, A. 1964. Texotics. *Texas Game & Fish.* April. pp. 7-11.

KING, R.T. 1940. Is it a wise policy to introduce exotic game birds? *Audubon Mag.* 44: 136-145, 230-236, 306-310.

LINDEMANN, W. 1956. Transplantation of game in Europe and Asia. *Jour. Wildl. Mgt.* 20(1): 68-70.

SANDERS, C.L., JR. 1963. Habitat preferences of the white-tailed deer and several exotic ungulates in South Texas. *Ecology* 44: 803-805.

STORER, T.I. 1934. Economic effects of introducing alien animals into California. *Proc. 5th Pac. Sci. Cong.* (1933) 1:779-784.

TURCEK, F.J. 1951. Effect of introductions on two game populations in Czechoslovakia. *Journ. Wildlife Mgt.* 15(1): 113-114.

WILDLIFE MANAGEMENT IN THE NATIONAL PARKS (1963)

A. Starker Leopold, Stanley A. Cain, Clarence M. Cottam, Ira N. Gabrielson and Thomas L. Kimball

In 1962, Secretary of the Interior Stewart Udall requested advice on management of wildlife in National Parks. The subject was receiving lively discussion at the time as opposing views on managing Yellowstone elk were published and broadcast across the nation. Udall's advisory board recommended goals and policy for wildlife management in National Parks. This policy was accepted and now influences management of all resources within Parks. It is a policy of protection and maintenance without harvest.

In the Congressional Act of 1916 which created the National Park Service, preservation of native animal life was clearly specified as one of the purposes of the parks. A frequently quoted passage of the Act states ". . . which purpose is to conserve the scenery and the natural historic objects and the wild life therein and to provide for the enjoyment of the same in such manner and by such means as will leave them unimpaired for the enjoyment of future generations."

In implementing this Act, the newly formed Park Service developed a philosophy of wildlife *protection,* which in that era was indeed the most obvious and immediate need in wildlife conservation. Thus the parks were established as refuges, the animal populations were protected from hunting and their habitats were protected from wildfire. For a time predators were controlled to protect the "good" animals from the "bad" ones, but this endeavor mercifully ceased in the 1930's. On the whole, there was little major change in the Park Service practice of wildlife management during the first 40 years of its existence.

During the same era, the concept of wildlife management evolved rapidly among other agencies and groups concerned with the production of wildlife for recreational hunting. It is now an accepted truism that maintenance of suitable habitat is the key to sustaining animal populations, and that protection, though it is important, is not of itself a substitute for habitat. Moreover, habitat is not a fixed or stable entity that can be set aside and preserved behind a fence, like a cliff dwelling or a petrified tree. Biotic communities change through natural stages of succession. They can be changed deliberately through manipulation of plant and animal populations. In recent years the National Park Service has broadened its concept of wildlife conservation to provide for purposeful management of plant and animal communities as an essential step in preserving wildlife resources ". . . unimpaired for the enjoyment of future generations." In a fewparksactivemanipulationofhabitatisbeingtested,asforexamplein the Everglades where controlled burning is now used experimentally to maintain the open glades and piney woods with their interesting animal and plant life. Excess populations of grazing ungulates are being controlled

Reprinted from: Trans. N. Amer. Wildl. and Natural Resources Conf. 28:29-42.

in a number of parks to preserve the forage plants on which the animals depend. The question already has been posed—how far should the National Park Service go in utilizing the tools of management to maintain wildlife populations?

The Concept of Park Management

The present report proposes to discuss wildlife management in the national parks in terms of three questions which shift emphasis progressively from the general to the specific:

1) What should be the *goals* of wildlife management in the national parks?

2) What general *policies* of management are best adapted to achieve the pre-determined goals?

3) What are some of the *methods* suitable for on-the-ground implementation of policies?

It is acknowledged that this Advisory Board was requested by the Secretary of the Interior to consider particularly one of the methods of management, namely, the procedure of removing excess ungulates from some of the parks. We feel that this specific question can only be viewed objectively in the light of goals and operational policies, and our report is framed accordingly. In speaking of national parks we refer to the whole system of parks and monuments; national recreation areas are discussed briefly near the end of the report.

As a prelude to presenting our thoughts on the goals, policies, and methods of managing wildlife in the parks of the United States we wish to quote in full a brief report on "Management of National Parks and Equivalent Areas" which was formulated by a committee of the First World Conference on National Parks that convened in Seattle in July, 1962. The committee consisted of 15 members of the Conference, representing eight nations; the chairman was Francois Bourliere of France. In our judgment this report suggests a firm basis for park management. The statement of the committee follows:

"1. Management is defined as any activity directed toward achieving or maintaining a given condition in plant and/or animal populations and/or habitats in accordance with the conservation plan for the area. A prior definition of the purposes and objectives of each park is assumed.

"Management may involve active manipulation of the plant and animal communities, or protection from modification or external influences.

"2. Few of the world's parks are large enough to be in fact self-regulatory ecological units; rather, most are ecological islands subject to direct modification by activities and conditions in the surrounding areas. These influences may involve such factors as immigration and/or emigration of animal and plant life, changes in the fire regime, and alterations in the surface or subsurface water.

"3. There is no need for active modification to maintain large examples of the relatively stable "climax" communities which under protection perpetuate themselves indefinitely. Examples of such communities include large tracts of undisturbed rain-forest, tropical mountain paramos, and arctic tundra.

"4. However, most biotic communities are in a constant state of change due to natural or man-caused processes of ecological succession. In these "successional" communities it is necessary to manage the habitat to achieve or stabilize it at a desired stage. For example, fire is an essential management tool to maintain East African open savanna or American prairie.

"5. Where animal populations get out of balance with their habitat and threaten the continued existence of a desired environment, population control becomes essential. This principle applies, for example, in situations where ungulate populations have exceeded the carrying capacity of their habitat through loss of predators, immigration from surrounding areas, or compression of normal migratory patterns. Specific examples include excess populations of elephants in some African parks and of ungulates in some mountain parks.

"6. The need for management, the feasibility of management methods, and evaluation of results must be based upon current and continuing scientific research. Both the research and management itself should be undertaken only by qualified personnel. Research, management planning, and execution must take into account, and if necessary regulate, the human uses for which the park is intended.

"7. Management based on scientific research is, therefore, not only desirable but often essential to maintain some biotic communities in accordance with the conservation plan of a national park or equivalent area."

The Goal of Park Management in the United States

Item 1 in the report just quoted specifies that "a prior definition of the purposes and objectives of each park is assumed." In other words, the goal must first be defined.

As a primary goal, we would recommend that the biotic associations within each park be maintained, or where necessary recreated, as nearly as possible in the condition that prevailed when the area was first visited by the white man. A national park should represent a vignette of primitive America.

The implications of this seemingly simple aspiration are stupendous. Many of our national parks—in fact most of them—went through periods of indiscriminate logging, burning, livestock grazing, hunting and predator control. Then they entered the park system and shifted abruptly to a regime of equally unnatural protection from lightning fires, from insect outbreaks, absence of natural controls of ungulates, and in some areas elimination of normal fluctuations in water levels. Exotic vertebrates, insects, plants, and plant diseases have inadvertently been introduced. And of course lastly there is the factor of human use—of roads and trampling and camp grounds and pack stock. The resultant biotic associations in many of our parks are artifacts, pure and simple. They represent a complex ecologic history but they do not necessarily represent primitive America.

Restoring the primitive scene is not done easily nor can it be done completely. Some species are extinct. Given time, an eastern hardwood forest can be regrown to maturity but the chestnut will be missing and so will the roar of pigeon wings. The colorful drapanid finches are not to be heard again in the lowland forests of Hawaii, nor will the jack-hammer of the ivory-bill ring in southern swamps. The wolf and grizzly bear cannot readily be reintroduced into ranching communities, and the factor of human use of the parks is subject only to regulation, not elimination. Exotic plants, animals, and diseases are here to stay. All these limitations we fully realize. Yet if the goal cannot be fully achieved it can be approached. A reasonable illusion of primitive America could be recreated, using the utmost in skill, judgment and ecological sensitivity. This in our opinion should be the objective of every national park and monument.

To illustrate the goal more specifically, let us cite some cases. A visitor entering Grand Teton National Park from the south drives across Antelope Flats. But there are no antelope. No one seems to be asking the question— why aren't there? If the mountain men who gathered here in rendezvous fed their squaws on antelope, a 20th century tourist at least should be able to see a band of these animals. Finding our what aspect of the range needs rectifying, and doing so, would appear to be a primary function of park management.

When the forty-niners poured over the Sierra Nevada into California, those that kept diaries spoke almost to a man of the wide-spaced columns of mature trees that grew on the lower western slope in gigantic magnificence. The ground was a grass parkland, in springtime carpeted with wildflowers. Deer and bears were abundant. Today much of the west slope is a dog-hair thicket of young pines, white fir, incense cedar, and mature brush—a direct function of overprotection from natural ground fires. Within the four national parks—Lassen, Yosemite, Sequoia, and Kings Canyon—the thickets are even more impenetrable than elsewhere. Not only is this accumulation of fuel dangerous to the giant sequoias and other mature trees but the animal life is meager, wildflowers are sparse, and to some at least the vegetative tangle is depressing, not uplifting. Is it possible that the primitive open forest could be restored, at least on a local scale? And if so, how? We cannot offer an answer. But we are posing a question to which there should be an answer of immense concern to the National Park Service.

The scarcity of bighorn sheep in the Sierra Nevada represents another type of management problem. Though they have been effectively protected for nearly half a century, there are fewer than 400 bighorns in the Sierra. Two-thirds of them are found in summer along the crest which lies within the eastern border of Sequoia and Kings Canyon National Parks. Obviously, there is some shortcoming of habitat that precludes further increase in the population. The high country is still recovering slowly from the devastation of early domestic sheep grazing so graphically described by John Muir. But the present limitation may not be in the high summer range at all but rather along the eastern slope of the Sierra where the bighorns winter on lands in the jurisdiction of the Forest Service. These areas are grazed in summer by domestic livestock and large numbers of mule deer, and it is possible that such competitive use is adversely affecting the bighorns. It would seem to us that the National Park Service might well take the lead in studying this problem and in formulating cooperative management plans with other agencies even though the management problem lies outside the park boundary. The goal, after all, is to restore the Sierra bighorn. If restoration is achieved in the Sequoia-Kings Canyon region, there might follow a program of re-introduction and restoration of bighorns in Yosemite and Lassen National Parks, and Lava Beds National Monument, within which areas this magnificent native animal is presently extinct.

We hope that these examples clarify what we mean by the goal of park management.

Policies of Park Management

The major policy change which we would recommend to the National Park Service is that it recognize the enormous complexity of ecological communities and the diversity of management procedures required to preserve them. The traditional, simple formula of protection may be exactly what is needed to maintain such climax associations as arctic-alpine heath, the rain forests of Olympic peninsula, or the Joshua trees and saguaros of southwestern deserts. On the other hand, grasslands, savannas, aspen, and other successional shrub and tree associations may call for very different treatment. Reluctance to undertake biotic management can never lead to a realistic presentation of primitive America, much of which supported successional communities that were maintained by fires, floods, hurricanes, and other natural forces.

A second statement of policy that we would reiterate—and this one conforms with present Park Service standards—is that management be limited to native plants and animals. Exotics have intruded into nearly all of the parks but they need not be encouraged, even those that have interest or ecologic values of their own. Restoration of antelope in Jackson Hole, for example, should be done by managing native forage plants, not by planting crested wheat grass or plots of irrigated alfalfa. Gambel quail in a desert wash should be observed in the shade of a mesquite, not a tamarisk. A visitor who climbs a volcano in Hawaii ought to see mamane trees and silver-swords, not goats.

Carrying this point further, observable artificiality in any form must be minimized and obscured in every possible way. Wildlife should not be displayed in fenced enclosures; this is the function of a zoo, not a national park. In the same category is artificial feeding of wildlife. Fed bears become bums, and dangerous. Fed elk deplete natural ranges. Forage relationships in wild animals should be natural. Management may at times call for the use of the tractor, chain-saw, rifle, or flame-thrower but the signs and sounds of such activity should be hidden from visitors insofar as possible. In this regard, perhaps the most dangerous tool of all is the roadgrader. Although the American public demands automotive access to the parks, road systems must be rigidly prescribed as to extent and design. Roadless wilderness areas should be permanently zoned. The goal, we repeat, is to maintain or create the mood of wild America. We are speaking here of restoring wildlife to enhance this mood, but the whole effect can be lost if the parks are overdeveloped for motorized travel. If too many tourists crowd the roadways, then we should ration the tourists rather than expand the roadways.

Additionally in this connection, it seems incongruous that there should exist in the national parks mass recreation facilities such as golf courses, ski lifts, motorboat marinas, and other extraneous developments which completely contradict the management goal. We urge the National Park Service to reverse its policy of permitting these nonconforming uses, and to liquidate them as expeditiously as possible (painful as this will be to concessionaires). Above all other policies, the maintenance of naturalness should prevail.

Another major policy matter concerns the research which must form the basis for all management programs. The agency best fitted to study park management problems is the National Park Service itself. Much help and guidance can be obtained from ecologic research conducted by other agencies, but the objectives of park management are so different from those of state fish and game departments, the Forest Service, etc., as to demand highly skilled studies of a very specialized nature. Management without knowledge would be a dangerous policy indeed. Most of the research now conducted by the National Park Service is oriented largely to interpretive functions rather than to management. We urge the expansion of the research activity in the Service to prepare for future management and restoration programs. As models of the type of investigation that should be greatly accelerated we cite some of the recent studies of elk in Yellowstone and of bighorn sheep in Death Valley. Additionally, however, there are needed equally critical appraisals of ecologic relationships in various plant associations and of many lesser organisms such as azaleas, lupines, chipmunks, towhees, and other non-economic species.

In consonance with the above policy statements, it follows logically that every phase of management itself be under the full jurisdiction of biologically trained personnel of the Park Service. This applies not only to habitat manipulation but to all facets of regulating animal populations. Reducing the numbers of elk in Yellowstone or of goats on Haleakala Crater is part of an overall scheme to preserve or restore a natural biotic scene. The purpose is single-minded. We cannot endorse the view that responsibility for removing excess game animals be shared with state fish and game departments whose primary interest would be to capitalize on the recreational value of the public hunting that could thus be supplied. Such a proposal imputes a multiple use concept of park management which was never intended, which is not legally permitted, nor for which we can find any impelling justification today.

Purely from the standpoint of how best to achieve the goal of park management, as here defined, unilateral administration directed to a single objective is obviously superior to divided responsibility in which secondary goals, such as recreational hunting, are introduced. Additionally, uncontrolled public hunting might well operate in opposition to the goal, by removing roadside animals and frightening the survivors, to the end that public viewing of wildlife would be materially impaired. In one national park, namely Grand Teton, public hunting was specified by Congress as the method to be used in controlling elk. Extended trial suggests this to be an awkward administrative tool at best.

Since this whole matter is of particular current interest it will be elaborated in a subsequent section on methods.

Methods of Habitat Management

It is obviously impossible to mention in this brief report all the possible techniques that might be used by the National Park Service in manipulating plant and animal populations. We can, however, single out a few examples. In so doing, it should be kept in mind that the total area of any one park, or of the parks collectively, that may be managed intensively is a very modest part indeed. This is so for two reasons. First, critical areas which may determine animal abundance are often a small fraction of total range. One deer study on the west slope of the Sierra Nevada, for example, showed that important winter range, which could be manipulated to support the deer, constituted less than two per cent of the year-long herd range. Roadside areas that might be managed to display a more varied and natural flora and fauna can be rather narrow strips. Intensive management, in short, need not be extensive to be effective. Secondly, manipulation of vegetation is often exorbitantly expensive. Especially will this be true when the objective is to manage "invisibly"—that is, to conceal the signs of management. Controlled burning is the only method that may have extensive application.

The first step in park management is historical research, to ascertain as accurately as possible what plants and animals and biotic associations existed originally in each locality. Much of this has been done already.

A second step should be ecologic research on plant-animal relationships leading to formulation of a management hypothesis.

Next should come small scale experimentation to test the hypothesis in practice. Experimental plots can be situated out of sight of roads and visitor centers.

Lastly, application of tested management methods can be undertaken on critical areas.

By this process of study and pre-testing, mistakes can be minimized. Likewise, public groups vitally interested in park management can be shown the results of research and testing before general application, thereby eliminating possible misunderstanding and friction.

Some management methods now in use by the National Park Service seem to us potentially dangerous. For example, we wish to raise a serious question about the mass application of insecticides in the control of forest insects. Such application may (or may not) be justified in commercial timber stands, but in a national park the ecologic impact can have unanticipated effects on the biotic community that might defeat the overall management objective. It would seem wise to curtail this activity, at least until research and small-scale testing have been conducted.

Of the various methods of manipulating vegetation, the controlled use of fire is the most "natural" and much the cheapest and easiest to apply. Unfortunately, however, forest and chaparral areas that have been completely protected from fire for long periods may require careful advance treatment before even the first experimental blaze is set. Trees and mature brush may have to be cut, piled, and burned before a creeping ground fire can be risked. Once fuel is reduced, periodic burning can be conducted safely and at low expense. On the other hand, some situations may call for a hot burn. On Isle Royale, moose range is created by periodic holocausts that open the forest canopy. Maintenance of the moose population is surely one goal of management on Isle Royale.

Other situations may call for the use of the bulldozer, the disc harrow, or the spring-tooth harrow to initiate desirable changes in plant succession. Buffalo wallows on the American prairie were the propagation sites of a host of native flowers and forbs that fed the antelope and the prairie chicken. In the absence of the great herds, wallows can be simulated.

Artificial reintroduction of rare native plants is often feasible. Overgrazing in years past led to local extermination of many delicate perennials such as some of the orchids. Where these are not reappearing naturally they can be transplanted or cultured in a nursery. A native plant, however small and inconspicuous, is as much a part of the biota as a redwood tree or a forage species for elk.

In essence, we are calling for a set of ecologic skills unknown in this country today. Americans have shown a great capacity for degrading and fragmenting native biotas. So far we have not exercised much imagination or ingenuity in rebuilding damaged biotas. It will not be done by passive protection alone.

Control of Animal Populations

Good park management requires that ungulate populations be reduced to the level that the range will carry in good health and without impairment to the soil, the vegetation, or to habitats of other animals. This problem is world-wide in scope, and includes non-park as well as park lands. Balance may be achieved in several ways.

(a) *Natural predation.*—Insofar as possible, control through natural predation should be encouraged. Predators are now protected in the parks of the United States, although unfortunately they were not in the early years and the wolf, grizzly bear, and mountain lion became extinct in many of the national parks. Even today populations of large predators, where they still occur in the parks, are kept below optimal level by programs of predator control applied outside the park boundaries. Although the National Park Service has attempted to negotiate with control agencies of federal and local governments for the maintenance of buffer zones around the parks where predators are not subject to systematic control, these negotiations have been only partially successful. The effort to protect large predators in and around the parks should be greatly intensified. At the same time, it must be recognized that predation alone can seldom be relied upon to control ungulate numbers, particularly the larger species such as bison, moose, elk, and deer; additional artificial controls frequently are called for.

(b) *Trapping and transplanting.*—Traditionally in the past the National Park Service has attempted to dispose of excess ungulates by trapping and transplanting. Since 1892, for example, Yellowstone National Park alone has supplied 10,478 elk for restocking purposes. Many of the elk ranges in the western United States have been restocked from this source. Thousands of deer and lesser numbers of antelope, bighorns, mountain goats, and bison also have been moved from the parks. This program is fully justified so long as breeding stocks are needed. However, most big game ranges of the United States are essentially filled to carrying capacity, and the cost of a continuing program of trapping and transplanting cannot be sustained solely on the basis of controlling populations within the parks. Trapping and handling of a big game animal usually costs $50 to $150 and in some situations much more. Since annual surpluses will be produced indefinitely into the future, it is patently impossible to look upon trapping as a practical plan of disposal.

(c) *Shooting excess animals that migrate outside the parks.*—Many park herds are migratory and can be controlled by public hunting outside the park boundaries. Especially is this true in mountain parks which usually consist largely of summer game range with relatively little winter range. Effective application of this form of control frequently calls for special regulations, since migration usually occurs after normal hunting dates. Most of the western states have cooperated with the National Park Service in scheduling late hunts for the specific purpose of reducing park game herds, and in fact most excess game produced in the parks is so utilized. This is by far the best and the most widely applied method of controlling park populations of ungulates. The only danger is that migratory habits may be eliminated from a herd by differential removal, which would favor survival of non-migratory individuals. With care to preserve, not eliminate, migratory traditions, this plan of control will continue to be the major form of herd regulation in national parks.

(d) *Control by shooting within the parks.*—Where other methods of control are inapplicable or impractical, excess park ungulates must be removed by killing. As stated above in the discussion of park policy, it is the unanimous recommendation of this Board that such shooting be conducted by competent personnel, under the sole jurisdiction of the National Park Service, and for the sole purpose of animal removal, not recreational hunting. If the magnitude of a given removal program requires the services of additional shooters beyond regular Park Service personnel, the selection, employment, training, deputization, and supervision of such additional personnel should be entirely the responsibility of the National Park Service. Only in this manner can the primary goal in wildlife management in the parks be realized. A limited number of expert riflemen, properly equipped and working under centralized direction, can selectively cull a herd with a minimum of disturbance to the surviving animals or to the environment. General public hunting by comparison is often non-selective and grossly disturbing.

Moreover, the numbers of game animals that must be removed annually from the parks by shooting is so small in relation to normally hunted populations outside the parks as to constitute a minor contribution to the public bag, even if it were so utilized. All of these points can be illustrated in the example of the north Yellowstone elk population which has been a focal point of argument about possible public hunting in national parks.

(e) *The case of Yellowstone.*—Elk summer in all parts of Yellowstone Park and migrate out in nearly all directions, where they are subject to hunting on adjoining public and private lands. One herd, the so-called Northern Elk Herd, moves only to the vicinity of the park border where it may winter largely inside or outside the park, depending on the severity of the winter. This herd was estimated to number 35,000 animals in 1914 which was far in excess of the carrying capacity of the range. Following a massive die-off in 1919-20 the herd has steadily decreased. Over a period of 27 years, the National Park Service removed 8,825 animals by shooting and 5,765 by live-trapping; concurrently, hunters took 40,745 elk from this herd outside the park. Yet the range continued to deteriorate. In the winter of 1961-62 there were approximately 10,000 elk in the herd and carrying capacity of the winter range was estimated at 5,000. So the National Park Service at last undertook a definitive reduction program, killing 4,283 elk by shooting, which along with 850 animals removed in other ways (hunting outside the park, trapping, winter kill) brought the herd down to 5,725 as censused from helicopter. The carcasses of the elk were carefully processed and distributed to Indian communities throughout Montana and Wyoming; so they were well used. The point at issue is whether this same reduction could or should have been accomplished by public hunting.

In autumn during normal hunting season the elk are widely scattered through rough inaccessible mountains in the park. Comparable areas, well stocked with elk, are heavily hunted in adjoining national forests. Applying the kill statistics from the forests to the park, a kill of 200-400 elk might be achieved if most of the available pack stock in the area were used to transport hunters within the park. Autumn hunting could not have accomplished the necessary reduction.

In mid-winter when deep snow and bitter cold forced the elk into lower country along the north border of the park, the National Park Service undertook its reduction program. With snow vehicles, trucks, and helicopters they accomplished the unpleasant job in temperatures that went as low as $-40°$ F. Public hunting was out of the question. Thus, in the case most bitterly argued in the press and in legislative halls, reduction of the herd by recreational hunting would have been a practical impossibility, even if it had been in full conformance with park management objectives.

From now on, the annual removal from this herd may be in the neighborhood of 1,000 to 1,800 head. By January 31, 1963, removals had totalled 1,300 (300 shot outside the park by hunters, 600 trapped and shipped, and 406 killed by park rangers). Continued special hunts in Montana and other forms of removal will yield the desired reduction by spring. The required yearly maintenance kill is not a large operation when one considers that approximately 100,000 head of big game are taken annually by hunters in Wyoming and Montana.

(f) *Game control in other parks.*—In 1961-62, excluding Yellowstone elk, there were approximately 870 native animals transplanted and 827 killed on 18 national parks and monuments. Additionally, about 2,500 feral goats, pigs and burros were removed from three areas. Animal control in the park system as a whole is still a small operation. It should be emphasized, however, that removal programs have not in the past been adequate to control ungulates in many of the parks. Future removals will have to be larger and in many cases repeated annually. Better management of wildlife habitat will naturally produce larger annual surpluses. But the scope of this phase of park operation will never be such as to constitute a large facet of management. On the whole, reductions will be small in relation to game harvests outside the parks. For example, from 50 to 200 deer a year are removed from a problem area in Sequoia National Park; the deer kill in California is 75,000 and should be much larger. In Rocky Mountain National Park 59 elk were removed in 1961-62 and the trim should perhaps be 100 per year in the future; Colorado kills over 10,000 elk per year in open hunting ranges. In part, this relates to the small area of the national park system, which constitutes only 3.9 per cent of the public domain; hunting ranges under the jurisdiction of the Forest Service and Bureau of Land Management make up approximately 70 per cent.

In summary, control of animal populations in the national parks would appear to us to be an integral part of park management, best handled by the National Park Service itself. In this manner excess ungulates have been controlled in the national parks of Canada since 1943, and the same principle is being applied in the parks of many African countries. Selection of personnel to do the shooting likewise is a function of the Park Service. In most small operations this would logically mean skilled rangers. In larger removal programs, there might be included additional personnel, selected from the general public, hired and deputized by the Service or otherwise engaged, but with a view to accomplishing a task, under strict supervision and solely for the protection of park values. Examples of some potentially large removal programs where expanded crews may be needed are mule deer populations on plateaus fringing Dinosaur National Monument and Zion National Park (west side), and white-tailed deer in Acadia National Park.

Wildlife Management on National Recreation Areas

By precedent and logic, the management of wildlife resources on the national recreation areas can be viewed in a very different light than in the park system proper. National recreation areas are by definition multiple use in character as regards allowable types of recreation. Wildlife management can be incorporated into the operational plans of these areas with public hunting as one objective. Obviously, hunting must be regulated in time and place to minimize conflict with other uses, but it would be a mistake for the National Park Service to be unduly restrictive of legitimate hunting in these areas. Most of the existing national recreation areas are federal holdings surrounding large water impounds; there is little potentiality for hunting. Three national seashore recreational areas on the East Coast (Hatteras, Cape Cod, and Padre Island) offer limited waterfowl shooting. But some of the new areas being acquired or proposed for acquisition will offer substantial hunting opportunity for a variety of game species. This opportunity should be developed with skill, imagination, and (we would hopefully suggest) with enthusiasm.

On these areas as elsewhere, the key to wildlife abundance is a favorable habitat. The skills and techniques of habitat manipulation applicable to parks are equally applicable on the recreation areas. The regulation of hunting, on such areas as are deemed appropriate to open for such use, should be in accord with prevailing state regulations.

New National Parks

A number of new national parks are under consideration. One of the critical issues in the establishment of new parks will be the manner in which the wildlife resources are to be handled. It is our recommendation that the basic objectives and operating procedures of new parks be identical with those of established parks. It would seem awkward indeed to operate a national park system under two sets of ground rules. On the other hand, portions of several proposed parks are so firmly established as traditional hunting grounds that impending closure of hunting may preclude public acceptance of park status. In such cases it may be necessary to designate core areas as national parks in every sense of the word, establishing protective buffer zones in the form of national recreation areas where hunting is permitted. Perhaps only through compromises of this sort will the park system be rounded out.

THE NATIONAL WILDLIFE REFUGE SYSTEM (1968)

A. Starker Leopold, Clarence Cottam, Ian McT. Cowan,
Ira N. Gabrielson and Thomas L. Kimball

*This is another effort of Secretary of Interior Udall's advisory board.
It is a policy proposed for management of a refuge system in North America.*

In 1903 President Theodore Roosevelt designated Pelican Island in
Florida as a federal refuge to protect the nesting pelicans, herons and
egrets from molestation by plume hunters and fishermen. From that
humble beginning there developed in the ensuing 65 years a National
Wildlife Refuge System comprising 317 major units and additional small
acreages with a combined area of nearly 29 million acres. The system is
administered by the Bureau of Sport Fisheries and Wildlife, under the
Secretary of Interior.

Growth over this period has been opportunistic. From time to time the
objectives of the system have changed. The most important continuing
objective has been the protection and husbandry of the continental migratory waterfowl population, for which the Federal Government assumed
primary responsibility in the Migratory Bird Treaty Act of 1918. During
the period of the New Deal, a number of game ranges were added to the
system representing samples of landscape not otherwise protected at that
time (desert, grassland, Alaskan conifer forest, and mountains). Likewise
blocks of submarginal land, retired from agriculture by Resettlement
Administration, were turned over to the refuge system. Offshore islands or
whole chains of oceanic islands have been incorporated into the refuge
system, largely to protect the habitat of colonial sea birds or mammals.
Some refuges serve also to protect rare or endangered species, such as
whooping cranes, Key deer, and subspecies of clapper rail and seaside
sparrow.

There is no ambiguity regarding the desire or intent of Congress to
perpetuate the National Wildlife Refuge System. The Inter-American
Treaty of 1942 committed the United States to a continuing program of
wildlife protection and husbandry, and refuges were specified as one of
the protective devices. The Endangered Species Preservation Act of 1966
provides for a program of conservation, protection, restoration, and propagation of endangered species, including refuge units to protect vanishing
vertebrates. It goes on to redefine the National Wildlife Refuge System
as including all lands administered by the Secretary of Interior that are now
designated as wildlife refuges, protection units for endangered species,
wildlife ranges, game ranges, wildlife management areas, and waterfowl
production areas.

What is still lacking, however, is a clear statement of policy or philosophy as to what the National Wildlife Refuge System should be and what
are the logical tenets of its future development. This report suggests a viewpoint to guide refuge administration and management.

Reprinted from: Trans. N. Amer. Wildl. and Natural Resources Conf. 33:30-53.

As of July 1, 1967, the refuge system comprised the following units:

	Number	Approximate Acreage
Migratory Bird Refuges (waterfowl) established primarily for wild ducks and geese	250	3,783,000
Migratory Bird Refuges (General) for migratory birds other than waterfowl, including colonial nesting species and some endangered species...........................	45	3,717,000
Big Game Refuges, primarily for big game species, established by acts of Congress or purchased...........................	14	5,191,000
Game Ranges, primarily for big game species withdrawn from the public domain	5	4,005,000
Alaska Wildlife Ranges set aside to conserve a variety of wildlife	3	11,185,000
Additional Waterfowl Production Areas (N. and S. Dakota, Minn., Neb.)	—	677,000
	317	28,558,000

A Philosophy for the Refuge System

Nearly everyone has a slightly different view of what the refuge system is, or should be. Most duck hunters view the refuges as an essential cog in perpetuation of their sport. Some see the associated public shooting grounds as the actual site of their sport. A few resent the concentration of birds in the refuges and propose general hunting to drive the birds out. Bird watchers and protectionists look upon the refuges as places to enjoy the spectacle of masses of water birds, without disturbance by hunters or by private landowners; they resent any hunting at all. State fish and game departments are pleased to have the federal budget support wildlife areas in their states but want maximum public hunting and fishing on these areas. The General Accounting Office in Washington seems to view the refuges as units of a duck factory that should produce a fixed quota of ducks per acre or of bird days per duck stamp dollar. The Bureau of Outdoor Recreation sees the refuge system as 29 million acres of public playgrounds. All of these views are valid, to a point. Yet the National Wildlife Refuge System cannot be all things to all people. In America of the future, what are likely to be the highest social values that the refuges can serve?

This Board recognizes the primary importance of protecting and perpetuating migratory waterfowl, as subjects of hunting and as objects of great public interest. Public shooting on parts of the refuges is another important function. Likewise we acknowledge the significance of refuges in serving the needs of rare or endangered species. But beyond that we view each National Wildlife Refuge in the old-fashioned sense of a bit of natural landscape where the full spectrum of native wildlife may find food, shelter, protection and a home. It should be a place where the outdoor public can come to see wild birds and mammals in variety and abundance compatible with the refuge environment. It should be a "wildlife display" in the most comprehensive sense.

For each refuge there will always be some primary or transcending function that receives and deserves major attention. The duck breeding refuges, like the Upper and Lower Souris are managed mainly as production areas. Wintering refuges like the Sacramento or Bosque del Apache are developed to shelter and feed wintering waterfowl. The Kofa Game Range is operated to favor perpetuation of the desert bighorn. And so on. But additionally, without impairing primary functions, virtually all refuge areas can be so managed as to produce a wealth of secondary wildlife values. A mudflat maintained for shorebirds, a woodlot supporting a heron colony, a tule border left for yellow-headed blackbirds or a thicket for transient warblers represents a value over and beyond the cloud of ducks and geese that occupy the central ponds. The number of Americans concerned with viewing or photographing wildlife is increasing at least exponentially with population. Their interests should be served by the refuges, along with the interests of the hunting public.

In essence, we are proposing to add a "natural ecosystem" component to the program of refuge management. Wherever a fragment of some native biota remains on a refuge it should be retained or expanded and restored insofar as this is practicable and in conformance with the primary function of the refuge. Native plants would be as much a part of this concept as native animals, and should where possible be used in landscaping and in development of wildlife coverts.

With this broad view of refuge function in mind, we urge the Bureau of Sport Fisheries and Wildlife to reappraise the goals of the National Wildlife Refuge System and to provide for maximum value of the system to the broadest possible spectrum of interests. Director Gottschalk recently made this excellent statement of the objectives of the Bureau in managing migratory birds:

The Bureau's general policy is to assure the management and perpetuation of the migratory bird resource for the benefit and enjoyment of all the people and as an important component of a healthy environment. Such management will provide, when possible, optimum hunting recreation of some species in adequate supply. . . . The Bureau will continue to work to safeguard the ecological, recreational, cultural, scientific and economic values of game and non-game migratory birds and their habitats, including raptorial species. The Bureau will seek to preserve endangered birds so that no species or subspecies will knowingly be allowed to become extinct through man's actions.

If this enlightened point of view characterized the management of all the national refuges there would be no problem. But such is not the case, as will be shown presently. A redefinition of refuge goals and objectives is very much needed.

Developing and Financing the Refuge System

The nature of a refuge system is quite naturally influenced by the manner of its origin and of its financing.

Most of the original units in the National Wildlife Refuge System were islands designated as sanctuaries for colonial nesting birds, or game ranges intended to prevent extermination of native big game mammals. Thus on Jan. 24, 1905 Congress authorized the President to set aside a portion of the Wichita National Forest for the protection of game animals and birds. No funding was authorized in the Act, and the area was managed by the Forest Service until 1935, when it was transferred to the Bureau of Biological Survey.

The first refuge to be specifically authorized by Congress was the National Bison Range by the Act of May 23, 1908. Again no funding was authorized, but provision was made for compensating the confederated tribes of the Flathead, Kootenai, and Upper Pend d'Oreille for the appraised value of the lands. The act provided for fence and shed construction and buildings for the proper care and maintenance of bison.

The Act of March 4, 1913, authorized the establishment of the National Elk Refuge, including the purchase of lands and improvements, the erection of necessary buildings and enclosures, and the right to incur other expenses necessary for the maintenance of the reserve.

The first waterfowl unit of the system to be authorized and funded by Congress was the Upper Mississippi River Wild Life and Fish Refuge. In 1924 Congress appropriated 1.5 million dollars for purchase of bottomlands along the Mississippi River between Wabasha, Minnesota, and Rock Island, Illinois, primarily to preserve waterfowl habitat. In the next decade several more refuges were created by Congress, and in the period of the New Deal a great expansion of the refuge system occurred, supported by direct appropriations and by emergency relief funds.

In 1934 the Migratory Bird Hunting Stamp Act was passed, imposing a tax of $1.00 on waterfowl hunters, the income of which was earmarked for marshland purchase, development and administration. At this point in history waterfowl management became a dominant objective of the National Wildlife Refuge System. Concurrently, Congress shifted the burden of financing the refuges from general tax revenues to the tax on waterfowl hunters. In the ensuing three decades the cost of the duck stamp was raised to $2.00 and then to $3.00; the current annual income of about 5 million dollars is still marked for acquiring waterfowl habitat.

But it seems that marshland drainage still proceeds faster than marshland restoration, so in 1961 Congress authorized a seven-year accelerated program of purchasing duck marshes with the understanding that funds advanced for this purpose would ultimately be repaid from future duck stamp sales. The seven-year accelerated program was designed to add 2.5 million acres of waterfowl habitat to the refuge system at an estimated cost of 105 million dollars additional to current duck stamp revenues. Only 46 million dollars have been appropriated, however, and 1.1 million acres purchased—far below target. In 1967 Congress extended the funding authorization another eight years, so that repayment is scheduled to begin in 1977.

Since the pattern of financing growth of the refuge system is harnessed closely to the hunting tax paid by waterfowl hunters, it follows that all lands purchased with these funds are expected to be of maximum value to waterfowl. Other interests and values are entirely secondary. Duck stamp funds are insufficient to acquire needed marshlands—especially production areas—with current escalation of land prices. Aside from limited funds to acquire habitat for rare and endangered species, there is no support nor clear authority for the Bureau of Sport Fisheries and Wildlife to extend the refuge system in relation to wildlife needs other than for migratory birds.

In viewing the refuge system as a network of wildlife habitats, each serving many public interests, we are suggesting that more support from general funds is called for. Duck stamp money should indeed continue to be used for purchasing waterfowl management areas, but that allotment of itself supplies only part of the total refuge need.

Meeting Waterfowl Habitat Needs

Some difficult questions, raised by Congress and by the General Accounting Office, are: When will the federal refuge system be complete? What portion of the continental waterfowl population should it support? How much more land is needed? How much more money will it cost?

As regards migratory waterfowl numbers, the Bureau of Sport Fisheries and Wildlife has chosen as a management target the continental population in the period 1956 (high) and 1962 (low), with an average fall population of about 150,000,000 ducks. To provide permanently for such a population will require preservation of considerable habitat now in private ownership and subject to drainage. Especially is this true of breeding habitat in the north-central prairie states and the adjoining prairie provinces of Canada. Allocation of funds in the accelerated wetland habitat preservation program has placed great emphasis on breeding ground preservation (80 percent of acreage in the prairie states). The program has two aspects. The larger and more permanent potholes and lakes are purchased outright. Smaller, temporary wetlands are left in private ownership but are protected as duck breeding habitats by perpetual easement under which the owner agrees, for a single payment, not to drain, burn, fill or level his wetlands. Under this program a substantial number of breeding marshes have been protected. In autumn they serve additionally as hunting grounds. In Canada there are parallel though less extensive programs to preserve breeding marshes, conducted by the Canadian and provincial governments and by Ducks Unlimited. But it is by no means assured as yet that the total endeavor in both countries is adequate to maintain an average fall population of 150 million ducks. For the moment therefore the reply concerning breeding grounds preservation and restoration is that the end is not in sight. Considerable help could be rendered by land and water use agencies whose agricultural programs affect the future status of prairie marshlands.

The problem of supplying refuge habitat along flyways and on the wintering grounds is not so acute, but may be critical for some subpopulations, especially of geese. Waterfowl that are highly territorial and widely spread out during nesting, become gregarious in fall and winter, concentrating on smaller areas. Existing federal, state and private refuges supply most of the resting areas now needed by migrating and wintering birds. The accelerated purchase program allocates about 7 percent of the acquisition acreage to additional stop-over points and 13 percent to more wintering grounds. Brackish bays and estuaries for diving ducks are still poorly represented in the National Wildlife Refuge System; new units might be added as wintering areas.

Even though the ultimate dimensions of the federal system of waterfowl areas are still obscure, it would seem timely for the Bureau to make further rigorous analyses of land needs as a guide to long-range planning. Habitat shrinkage is still proceeding faster than habitat restoration. Further expansion of federal holdings, especially of breeding grounds, will clearly be needed. But the process of refuge expansion should be subject to orderly planning, leading ultimately to a more or less stabilized network of management units, serving the full spectrum of waterfowl needs.

Managing Waterfowl Refuges

When a refuge property is acquired it rarely is in a stage of optimum development to serve as waterfowl habitat. Levees and water control structures are usually needed, roads must be built to facilitate patrol and other aspects of management, and agricultural crops may be grown to provide food for the migrant birds. An active and ambitious staff of engineers and managers attend to these aspects of development.

But because some engineering and agricultural development is good, it does not necessarily follow that more is better. On many refuges the Board noted a tendency to equate any *development* with *improvement*. Some refuge plans were stronger in principles of agricultural engineering than of wildlife ecology. The refuges are intended to serve certain biological and social objectives, and their development should be guided primarily by the professional managers who are to make them function. Ecological engineering is needed, rather than strictly agricultural engineering. Frequently the same techniques are involved, but the ecological framework maintains and blends natural relationships with man-designed improvements.

In the light of our plea for naturalism in refuge management, we suggest thoughtful moderation in physical development of terrain. A refuge property can be overdeveloped. For example, it is not necessarily the best practice to impound every possible acre foot of water to serve the needs of waterfowl. Some meadows and swales may better be left in puddles rather than be escalated into lakes.

Ducks and geese are attracted to grain, but a waterfowl feeding regime based solely on grain culture may have serious drawbacks. Some of the most difficult management problems with Canada geese have arisen when concentrations gathered on refuges where generous quantities of corn were grown to attract the birds. This happened first on Horseshoe Lake Refuge in Illinois in the early 1940's and was repeated in much the same form on Horicon Refuge in Wisconsin in the mid-1960's. Despite these lessons, many other midwestern goose refuges are competing in the corn-feeding derby. Some, like Squaw Creek Refuge in Missouri, have cleared additional woodlands to increase the acreage of corn and other grains.

One of the effects of refuges is to dictate the distribution of waterfowl. This is accomplished in part by protection from disturbance, but likewise by the food regime on the refuge. A well managed network of refuges should serve to achieve a general spread or distribution of waterfowl over wide regions. As presently operated, refuges seem to be competing with one another to concentrate waterfowl. Undue concentration of birds may lead to crop depredations, excessive hunter kill, or spread of disease. Recent experiences at the Horicon Refuge demonstrate the adverse effects on agriculture and on the goose population, of attracting too many Canada geese to one place. We strongly recommend that excessive concentrations of waterfowl, such as the Horicon goose flock, be purposefully scattered to encourage earlier migration and wider distribution of the population. Reducing the intensity of the feeding program would seem to be an initial step in this process, along with regulated hunting on the refuge itself and possibly drawdown of water levels. The tag system now in force at Horicon can be used to regulate total kill until the tradition of concentration is broken.

In the long run, a more varied and low-key feeding program may be in the best interests of waterfowl. A number of agricultural crops are attractive and nutritious for waterfowl, and in appropriate marshlands, natural foods can often be grown with forage yields approaching those of the agricultural crops. A good stand of smartweed (*Polygonum*) or of pond weed (*Potamogeton*) may yield a surprisingly high poundage of seed per acre. Alkali bullrush *(Scirpus paludosus)* is one of the most productive of all waterfowl foods where it occurs on western marshes. Variety in foods will meet the nutritional needs of many species. It is impossible to write a generalized formula for food management on waterfowl refuges. But on any area, a varied offering would seem to have advantages over a one-crop diet, however palatable the single crop might be.

On breeding refuges, the management of nesting cover is of prime importance. Manipulation may be achieved by patterns of mowing, of livestock grazing, of burning, of manipulating water levels, or by topographic manipulation such as building islands in ponds. On Malheur Refuge a skillful pattern of mowing followed by grazing has created superior nest grounds for ducks while at the same time yielding an income to the government and to the neighborhood. By and large, manipulated areas kept in early successional stages seem to be more productive of nesting waterfowl than are climax marshes. Continuing manipulation therefore is a concomitant of managing most duck nesting areas.

In the refuge system are many superb examples of good habitat management for waterfowl. Our brief commentary on this facet of refuge administration is intended merely to question excessive artificialization where it occurs.

Managing Refuges for Wildlife Other than Waterfowl

Each refuge, though part of a network, should be viewed as an independent microcosm with many biological features and values of its own, all of which should be appreciated and if possible sustained in some harmonious combination. This overview of the refuge as an oasis for wildlife in general has not been especially evident in the management of the National Wildlife Refuges to date.

Management of the rough upland portions of waterfowl refuges (non-marsh, non-agricultural) is sometimes sadly neglected. Native wildlife that could be supported on these upland areas is often scarce or absent. To cite two examples: (1) Malheur Refuge in Oregon has been mentioned as a case of excellent management of waterfowl nesting habitat; yet the upland sagebrush areas constituting a substantial portion of the 181,000-acre area are largely sterile of wildlife. Antelope and sagehens occur on the adjoining ranches but rarely are seen on the refuge. This curious situation may relate to the intensive grazing program. Whatever the cause, it is probably subject to correction. (2) When the Necedah Refuge in Wisconsin was taken over from Resettlement Administration it was excellent range for prairie chicken and sharp-tailed grouse. Until very recently little effort was made to maintain the openings. As a result of rigid fire exclusion the area is now a thicket of little value to prairie grouse. A general policy urging and supporting management of the total wildlife resource on all refuges would lead to identification and solution of many problems such as these.

The national refuges should stand as monuments to the science and practice of wildlife management. To do so they should display wildlife in its greatest diversity, as well as in reasonable abundance.

Managing Game Ranges and Other Types of Refuges

By comparison with the waterfowl refuges, the intensity of management on game ranges, island refuges, and preserves for rare species is very low indeed—perhaps too low in some situations. For these areas collectively, present management consists largely of protection from undue disturbance or change.

In the case of the bird islands, protection or isolation is indeed the crux of management. This is true also of islands harboring oceanic mammals and sea turtles.

On mainland game ranges, where ungulate populations are concerned, there is often required some control of numbers. Bison, moose, elk and deer are all likely to exceed the capacity of their ranges, especially on refuge areas. Nothing can be more deleterious to the habitat and to the animals themselves than carrying too many on the range. Reduction normally is accomplished most effectively through public hunting, although removal of small numbers may be more easily done by refuge personnel. In wilderness-type areas still supporting a reasonable quota of predators one may hope for homeostasis in the predator/prey interaction, but it rarely lives up to expectations because predators are seldom prey-specific. The gun is usually needed in management sooner or later.

Intrusion of exotic ungulates may constitute a major management problem on some ranges and refuge areas. Trespass cattle, burros, goats and pigs often need control or preferably elimination.

Whereas there is general recognition of the need to protect big game ranges from overgrazing, there is much less attention paid to the possibility of raising range capacities for wildlife through plant manipulation or water development. We are aware of some experimental burning on the Kenai Moose Range in Alaska and the National Bison Range in Montana. Some modest reseeding trials have been attempted on several other game ranges. But the point of view toward management has been predominantly one of protection rather than manipulation. For example, on the Desert National Wildlife Range in Nevada, carrying capacity for bighorn sheep could be greatly increased with development of some well-situated water holes, but little effort has been made to assist the sheep in this manner.

Presumably the game ranges could receive, at least locally, more intensive habitat management than in the past.

Development of food resources on wildlife refuges is a logical way to attract and support wildlife. But there is a fine line between supporting wild animals and prostituting them. One example of the latter will suffice here.

The National Elk Refuge was created in Jackson Hole in 1913 to perpetuate an elk herd whose winter range was largely expropriated for cattle ranching. To hold elk on the refuge, a program of hay feeding was begun which has become a fixed ritual. The elk stream down from South Yellowstone and the Tetons, to gather on the feeding grounds where they spend all winter without making any effort to find natural forage. The daily arrival of the hay sled signals the only activity, namely, a jostling among the animals to be first in line as the bales are dropped. Tourists ride among them on sleighs. These elk have lost their independence. Like the Canada geese at Horseshoe Lake, and more recently at Horicon, they have developed a tradition of dependency. Fear of man is lost. Wilderness is forfeited.

A cooperative program is underway between the Bureau of Sport Fisheries and Wildlife, the Park Service, the Forest Service and the State of Wyoming to rehabilitate this herd by breaking the hay habit. Limited hunting on the refuge is eliminating the earliest arrivals and pushing the main herd back into the hills where good winter forage is available. Hopefully the herd can be weaned to natural foods, precluding the need for the feeding program.

Again, the lesson to be derived seems to be, avoid excessive artificiality in refuge management.

Administration and Planning

When the refuge system was smaller, it was operated successfully from a strong, central administrative office in Washington. This form of management gave way in recent years to an almost completely decentralized system in which the operational policies and goals of the refuges were delegated largely to the regional offices and in some cases were assigned in turn to individual refuge managers. The refuge system has lost much of its cohesiveness, in fact it can scarcely be designated functionally as a system. The morale of the personnel has decreased accordingly.

It is the strong recommendation of this Board that the Division of Wildlife Refuges be given far more centralized authority in setting policies and objectives of the refuge system and in seeing that individual refuges are managed in compliance with the updated goals of the Bureau. The size and complexity of the system dictate that normal administrative channels be followed, utilizing the machinery of the regional offices. But the reconstruction of an integrated, vitalized refuge system can only be done from a central office with considerable authority and responsibility.

Broad views are required to plan and align management efforts on the network of refuges to meet ecological and distributional patterning needs of migratory birds ranging throughout North America. Greater planning effort must be focused on satisfying ecological requirements of subpopulations and specific flocks. This task logically falls to the Washington office, where regional and local views can be aligned to an overall continental perspective. In our opinion this accelerated, coordinated planning would (1) facilitate full analysis and use of existing management facts, (2) help pinpoint specific voids in knowledge, (3) provide a broad framework within which individual management efforts can be fitted, (4) identify strategic locations where additional refuges are needed, (5) help refuges function as a coordinated system for some migratory birds, as well as individual cases for a wide variety of wildlife, and (6) permit reduction of the large regional staffs of refuge administrators and add manpower on the refuges where the work must be done. Information from well coordinated efforts should shed more light on the basic questions on refuges asked by the Congress and the General Accounting Office.

Planning of the national system in any given locality obviously takes cognizance of the number, distribution, and carrying capacity of refuge units operated by other organizations.

One weakness characteristic of some individual refuges is lack of full jurisdiction on the part of the Bureau of Sport Fisheries and Wildlife. Split administrative authority with other federal agencies is an unsatisfactory arrangement. Thus for example, Gray's Lake Refuge in Idaho is jointly administered with the Bureau of Indian Affairs, Chas. M. Russell Refuge in Montana is jointly administered with the Bureau of Land Management, and so on. No refuge in split jurisdiction encountered by this Board was really properly managed. Every unit of the National Wildlife Refuge System should if possible be incorporated fully into jurisdiction of the Bureau. Moreover, in one way or another each refuge should acquire the water rights needed to manipulate water levels required for wildlife purposes. A refuge with inadequate water rights, like the Stillwater in Nevada, is scarcely better than no refuge at all.

We further recommend that the in-service training program, begun in 1965, be extended and intensified to bring an improved sense of order and unity into the Division of Wildlife Refuges. Whatever concepts and policies are adopted in Washington should be brought quickly and forcefully to the attention of the regional offices and the field force. Within the past year the Division has begun to assume more directional force in formulating the refuge program, but this has not fully percolated down to the field level.

Public Recreational Use

The demand for pleasuring grounds in America is going up even faster than the population because of extended leisure time, higher income, and improved transportation. The National Wildlife Refuges are attracting their share of attention by the recreating American public. Nearly 14 million visitors came to the refuges in 1966 for purposes of outdoor enjoyment. The classification of visitors was as follows:

Purpose	Visits	Per cent of visits
Hunting	541,210	4
Fishing	3,777,051	27
General recreation	9,485,040	69
	13,803,301	100

In 1967 the total visits had increased to 15.6 million according to incomplete reports now available.

Questions facing refuge administrators are: How far to go in attempting to help meet this popular demand for public playgrounds; secondly, what kind of recreation should be offered on the refuge areas; and thirdly, who is going to pay the bill for the greatly increased cost of administration, service, and development?

In 1962, Congress expressed its intent that the National Wildlife Refuges be used for outdoor recreation (Public Law 87-714), provided that the primary purpose of the refuges was not compromised and that the cost of the recreational program was funded. Subsequently in 1964, the Fish and Wildlife Service issued a printed leaflet entitled "Recreational Policy on National Wildlife Refuges" which interprets and delineates the Congressional mandate. The 1964 policy is well stated and closely conforms to the concepts of recreational policy held by this Advisory Board. The problem remains however, of interpreting the written policy into operational procedure on a given refuge.

It seemed to this Board that there is a great deal of variation throughout the refuges of the country in the manner and extent to which recreation is being developed and incorporated into operational plans. On the one hand, there are refuges maintained largely in closed status with little or no attention paid to recreational demand; the public is not encouraged to enjoy these wildlife areas, or is permitted to do so only under highly restrictive conditions. Several national refuges in the Sacramento Valley of California record only a few hundred visits by general recreationists whereas nearby state refuges attract tens of thousands who come to see the waterfowl. On the other extreme, some refuges, particularly those situated in highly populated areas of the East and Midwest, have become so oriented to mass recreation that there is a question whether these areas are serving their original function as wildlife reserves. Crab Orchard Refuge in Illinois is an example, with nearly 1.5 million visits recorded in 1966. The problem facing the administrator of a refuge is one of finding a reasonable compromise between isolationism and over-use.

We concur with the policy statement of the Fish and Wildlife Service that recreation on the refuges should in all cases be secondary to the primary purpose of management for wildlife enhancement, and under no circumstances should general recreation be permitted to interfere with this primary dedication. Moreover, the sorts of recreation appropriate on a National Wildlife Refuge should be oriented toward the appreciation, enjoyment, and in certain cases the harvesting, of wildlife and fish. Hunting and fishing will be discussed subsequently. Wildlife viewing, hiking, sightseeing, nature observation, study, and photography can be enhanced by well-labeled self-guided tours, wildlife trails, observation points or towers, and by construction of interpretive centers and natural history exhibits. It is these types of recreation and associated ecologic teaching that should be emphasized on the refuge areas.

Members of the Board visited Brigantine Refuge in New Jersey and consider the facilities there an appropriate example for refuge development. A one-way loop road on a levee permits visitors to observe waterfowl and wading birds without interfering with the birds or with each other. Simple, inexpensive picnic facilities serve the 78,000 visitors that come to enjoy the natural scene.

Some of the larger game ranges and other refuges are being examined under the terms of the Wilderness Act for possible dedication to wilderness status. On the Kenai Moose Range in Alaska wilderness designation was made informally some time ago, and canoe trails have been developed to encourage primitive forms of travel. It seems appropriate that portions of the larger refuge areas meeting the criteria for wilderness be added to the National Wilderness System so long as the refuge function is not thereby inhibited.

Unfortunately, the proximity of urban masses leads inevitably to pressure for larger picnic grounds, camping facilities, improved swimming beaches, motorboat marinas, water skiing, baseball fields, bridle paths, target ranges, and other assorted forms of play which are only obliquely related to refuge purposes. Once any of these forms of public use becomes established, it is difficult to terminate. Therefore the master plan for each refuge should have a firm and definite program of development for recreational programs and facilities favoring those activities appropriate to the refuge area and excluding or firmly limiting those that are inappropriate. Also included in the master plan should be a clear statement of budgetary needs to develop recreational facilities and to administer the program. Recreation cannot be allowed to draw excessively from funds intended for general refuge purposes.

The central theme of this report emphasizes the great recreational, educational, and inspirational value of the refuge system to Americans who find an interest in wildlife and natural history. But the recreation of which we speak must retain a qualitative element of naturalism. The value is gone if the refuges are permitted to become mass playgrounds.

Hunting and Fishing

As originally conceived, the national wildlife refuges were sanctuaries where all sport hunting was prohibited. The first departure from this policy occurred in 1924 when the Upper Mississippi River Wild Life and Fish Refuge was created, with provision for hunting and fishing. Subsequently in 1948 Congress passed the Lea Act providing for the purchase of crop lands in California to grow duck food with the idea of keeping the birds away from commercial crops. This Act also authorized public waterfowl hunting on lands so purchased. The following year Congress revised the Duck Stamp Act and provided for public waterfowl hunting on 25 percent of any refuge in the system, if authorized by the Secretary. With the further revision of duck stamp legislation in 1958, hunting was authorized on 40 percent of any refuge. In short, the waterfowl refuges have for a long period served a function as public shooting grounds. In an era when less and less marshland is open to public hunting, the availability of shooting privileges on portions of the larger refuges is a boon to the unattached waterfowler. In 1966 the refuge system supplied 541,000 hunting visits, an important recreational contribution.

In situations where demand for waterfowl hunting is high and daily quotas of hunters must be regulated, the function of administering public hunting, enforcing the local hunting rules, and checking hunters in and out is sometimes assumed by the state game department, as for example in California. The ultimate decision of where waterfowl hunting is to be permitted and how it should be regulated on the National Wildlife Refuges remains with the Secretary of Interior, but cooperative administration with state officials is mutually advantageous where operational details can be worked out.

A more complex problem is the allowance of public hunting of non-migratory game species living on refuge areas. A legal question has arisen as to the proprietary interest and regulatory responsibility of federal vs. state government in these situations. Whichever way this legal technicality is resolved, we would hope and expect that public hunting on the federal refuges will be cooperatively operated by the state and federal wildlife agencies. Legal ownership need not preclude cooperative management.

Controlled deer hunts are commonly used to regulate deer numbers. Bow and arrow deer hunters are allowed on Malheur, Aransas, and many other refuges, more with the idea of supplying some recreation than reducing deer populations. Moose, elk, caribou, mountain goats, various kinds of mountain sheep, and bears are hunted on different refuge units and game ranges. This leads logically to proposals to extend the concept of harvest to lesser species such as pheasant, quail, sage grouse, prairie chicken, sharptails, doves, rabbits, raccoons, opossums, coyotes, bobcats and any other species whose pursuit may furnish sport. Whereas there is no doubt of the ability of these diverse populations to absorb a regulated kill, there arises the question of whether a so-called refuge is indeed a sanctuary where the non-hunter can go to observe undisturbed wildlife. If all possible surplus populations are hunted, the refuge becomes little different from the rest of the countryside.

We take the view that the National Wildlife Refuges should be conciously developed as show places for all kinds of wildlife. All forms of disturbance, including hunting, should be so regulated in areas of visitor concentration as to favor an optimal display of wild birds and mammals, gentle enough to be easily seen by the visiting public.

The bodies of water encompassed in the national refuge system offer some fine fishing. In 1966, 3¾ million refuge visitors came to partake of this sport. On most refuges, fishing is restricted during the seasons of waterfowl use to minimize interference with nesting or wintering populations of ducks, geese, or other wildlife. By and large, fishermen respect these limitations, and within prescribed limits, fishing is a conforming use. There may be local interference between fishing and bird watching. At times special regulations are needed to separate these functions. On a levee on Bear River Refuge is a sign saying "Fishing beyond this point reserved for the birds." The levee serves as part of a tour route for bird watchers. On more northerly refuges, ice fishing is a sport generally compatible with the waterfowl function since it takes place when the birds are absent. As in the case of managing hunting of non-migratory game, we recommend that fishing programs on the national refuges be cooperatively regulated with state authorities.

By and large, hunting and fishing are highly significant forms of public use on the National Wildlife Refuges, to be encouraged and permitted insofar as they do not interfere with primary refuge functions. The larger the refuge, the more liberal can be the regulations for hunting and fishing without likelihood of impinging on primary functions.

Protecting Refuges from Invasion

However carefully refuge sites may be selected, the lands are forever subject to invasion by government agencies with higher rights of eminent domain, such as military services, Atomic Energy Commission, Corps of Engineers, Bureau of Reclamation, and the Bureau of Public Roads. After a refuge is acquired and developed, it often has to be defended.

A few examples will suffice to illustrate the problem. In 1955 the Army proposed to extend its artillery range at Fort Sill, Oklahoma, by taking over part of the Wichita Mountains Wildlife Refuge. In 1951 irrigation interests set about to drain part of Tule Lake National Wildlife Refuge in northern California to extend grain and potato agriculture in that basin. These two proposals were stopped by massive action on the part of conservation organizations. In 1960 the Alabama Highway Department, supported by the Bureau of Public Roads, designed a highway that bisected the Wheeler National Wildlife Refuge in Alabama. The road was built nearly to the refuge boundary before negotiations to transect the refuge were initiated; the crossing could have been prevented by earlier consultation with the Bureau of Sport Fisheries and Wildlife.

In 1964 the Department of Defense and the Atomic Energy Commission arranged to fire an underground atomic shot on Amchitka Island, one of the central islands in the Aleutian Islands National Wildlife Refuge and the stronghold of the northern sea otter herd. "Project Longshot" led to detonation in 1965, but instead of terminating the project the agencies followed with plans for five more atomic blasts, some possibly powerful enough to blow the side out of the island and endanger life in the adjoining seas. Amchitka has been converted from a wildlife refuge to an atomic testing ground without benefit of democratic process and over the objections of Governor Hickel of Alaska, filed in September of 1967.

There is no way in which the sanctity of refuge lands can be guaranteed other than by continuing public interest and by spirited public defense as required. Sometimes these do not suffice.

Research on Refuges

If, as here proposed, the national refuges become centers of management of the full spectrum of native wildlife, they logically should serve also as centers of investigation. There is advantage in continuity and long-term study on areas permanently sustained as wildlife habitat.

Just as in the case of the national parks, the refuges should be made available for legitimate field study by any qualified scientist, whatever his affiliation. University groups as well as government scientists can contribute to knowledge of a refuge and thus indirectly to better management. Some talented laymen without official trappings may help as well. Refuge administrators should do everything possible to assist and facilitate such field investigations, so long as they do not interfere with the primary refuge functions nor endanger the existence of any native species. Scientific collecting of plant and animal specimens, under proper authorization and control, should be recognized as a legitimate and important research procedure.

There has been considerable variation among refuges in the extent to which management personnel are permitted to participate in research. On some refuges all research initiative is discouraged as detracting from the management function. On others research is encouraged, which is the view that we urge be uniformly adopted. Clearly the day-to-day operations must go on, but limited time made available for serious and relevant research can yield significant information and moreover may keep many biologists content in management jobs. It may indeed sharpen their interest and increase their competence in the management job. As an outstanding example of wildlife research conducted by refuge personnel we mention the work being done on the breeding and migration of Alaskan black brant by personnel of the Clarence Rhode and Izembek refuges.

Role of State and Private Refuges

In emphasizing the function of the federal refuges, particularly as regards migratory waterfowl conservation, we do not overlook the great importance of refuge units established and operated by other agencies, largely state game departments. In a number of states, the federal and state refuge units together form a cohesive and effective refuge network. California is a case in point, with migratory waterfowl being served by 15 national and 7 state refuges. Additional municipal and private refuges offer sanctuary for waterfowl, as for example in the San Francisco Bay area, Lake Merritt operated by the city of Oakland and Richardson's Bay Refuge operated by the National Audubon Society. The aggregate pattern of rest areas is thus amplified considerably beyond the National Wildlife Refuges. For refuges to act as an effective network, however, it is imperative that the respective administrators cooperate in defining collective goals and striving to achieve them. We encountered too many examples where cooperation was not in evidence.

Recognition should be accorded to the extensive areas of waterfowl habitat privately maintained and managed by hunting clubs. The three and one-third million acres of marshlands which they manage contribute substantially to the maintenance of the continental populations of ducks, geese, and other marsh birds.

Canadian and Mexican Refuges

Recognition of the joint interest of Canada, the United States and Mexico in the welfare of migratory birds is expressed in international treaties ratified between Canada and the U. S. in 1916 and the U. S. and Mexico in 1936. To what extent does the refuge system extend north and south of the United States border?

The Canadian Government has designated 15 "migratory bird sanctuaries" in Northwest Territories. These sanctuaries, with an aggregate area of about 27 million acres, serve primarily to protect nesting populations of geese from hunting on the breeding grounds. A few ducks and some colonial birds are protected as well.

In the tier of provinces extending across southern Canada, establishment of wildlife refuges is a provincial rather than a federal prerogative. A number of provincial sanctuaries serve to protect waterfowl during the hunting season, but in general these areas are not managed nor administered on a year-round basis comparable to the federal or state refuge systems in the United States. The purpose is simply protection of migratory waterfowl from excessive shooting. There is relatively little habitat improvement undertaken.

Details of the number and distribution of provincial refuges were not available to us. However, in spite of the vast area of Canada, the relatively low human population and low gun pressure, the naturally extensive marshlands, the system of legal restrictions and of provincial and federal sanctuaries is probably inadequate at present to protect waterfowl from overshooting. Considerable evidence points to serious overshooting of mallards in Manitoba, for example. Special restrictions were added in 1967 to reduce the kill. Habitat preservation, largely for duck nesting, is a much more serious matter still not resolved.

Mexico has just started a program of bird protection through refuges, with establishment of a sanctuary on Raza Island in the Gulf of California. The island is a major nesting ground for terns and gulls, and until given protection was regularly raided by commercial egg gatherers. The Mexican Government was assisted in this undertaking by the National Audubon Society.

In terms of migratory waterfowl, there is serious need in Mexico for a system of wintering refuges comparable to those in the southern United States. The interior marshlands originally scattered over the uplands from Chihuahua and Tamaulipas down to the Valley of Mexico have largely been dried up and converted to agriculture. Refuge areas might be used to restore local marshes, which, with protection from hunting, could be safe and attractive concentration points for migrating birds. Along the tropical coast there is adequate marshland habitat remaining, but hunting pressure is spreading. At least some spots should be reserved for the undisturbed use of waterfowl. Scammon Lagoon in Baja California, now the gathering point for most of the Pacific black brant of the continent, would be a logical beginning point for a refuge system. There are a number of other potential sites, equally attractive. The continental program of waterfowl protection cannot be fully effective until Mexico provides protection and assured habitat for the winter visitants.

Some Questions About the Refuge System

Refuges for migratory waterfowl certainly attract and hold the birds and protect them from excessive harassment during the hunting period. In some areas they keep hungry migrants out of commercial crops. It is easy to assume, therefore, that the impact of refuges on ducks and geese is all good. But there remain some troublesome and puzzling questions about this impact, some of which follow:

To what extent does the present pattern of refuges alter the species mix by favoring some species over others? It seems that the stubble feeding birds profit most, by using the refuges for sanctuary and seeking feed on dry stubbles for a radius of many miles. This may explain the dominance in the continental population of mallards, pintails, and various geese, despite the fact that these are the species most sought by hunters. The traditional or compulsory marsh feeders like redhead, shoveler, wood duck, etc. do not use the refuges so effectively and probably will decrease in the long run. Aside from differential hunting regulation, is there any way to manage the little ducks more effectively?

Refuges concentrate populations of ducks and geese and change their food habits for a long, and perhaps critical period, prior to migration and reproduction. We know next to nothing about the nutritional needs of these birds, particularly the role of winter nutrition on subsequent reproduction and juvenile survival. We know too little about the possible dangers of communicable disease, such as fowl cholera, in winter populations that are clustered on refuges.

If there were no refuges where would the birds be? Would they find other protective devices as have European waterfowl that seek tidal flats to escape hunting? Would they migrate farther, or earlier? The pattern of movement certainly would be different. The refuge network in the upper Mississippi Valley has shortstopped the movement of Canada geese and created a dangerous problem of hunting regulation. This subspecies no longer visits its former wintering grounds south of Illinois in large numbers. Is the balance positive, negative, or only different?

Can the refuge system be designed more effectively to protect locally decimated populations, such as, for instance the breeding mallard population of the upper Mississippi drainage or the honker and redhead populations along the eastern base of the Sierra Nevada? Is the land acquisition program thoughtfully geared to meet these local, specific protection problems? Can these problems be solved just by hunting regulation?

Unanswered questions of this sort point to the need for a continuing program of study and reappraisal of the actual functioning of the refuge system.

WILDLIFE DAMAGE AND CONTROL (1970)

National Academy of Sciences Committee on Agricultural Land Use and
Wildlife Resources

*Attitudes toward wildlife and wildlife values continuously change. New
methods for pest control evolve. Intensification of land use creates wildlife
problems where none previously existed. In reviewing the problem of wildlife
damage and control from an historical viewpoint, this paper provides an example of the dynamics of wildlife conservation policy.*

Just as agriculture and land use have changed tremendously in the
United States during the past 100 years, so have attitudes toward wildlife. This has been as true of the scientist as of the general public and the
agriculturist. The early premise was simple, i.e., animals were either harmful or beneficial, in varying degrees. The government program, begun in
the 1880's by the Division of Economic Ornithology and Mammalogy to
determine which birds and mammals were harmful and which were beneficial, concentrated for years upon the food habits of birds and mammals
in order to establish their economic relationship to man.

These attitudes naturally were reflected in the legislation of that day.
State bird protection laws left unprotected or even provided bounty pay-
ments for destroying birds considered harmful, such as the hawks and owls
that were known to feed upon smaller birds.

Many factors have contributed to the changing attitude toward wildlife, so that no longer can a species be designated simply as friend or foe.
Increasing emphasis on ecology and recognition of many of its principles
by the public as well as at the congressional level have been important.
At the same time there has been an increasingly widespread interest in
conservation and a recognition of the value of preserving our natural environment. The Wilderness Act and the Rare and Endangered Species Act
reflect the concern of Congress, and President Nixon has established an
official council of environmental advisors to the Executive Office.

As public and official attitudes have changed, the pressures upon resources have increased and become more complex. These factors combine
and result in a number of situations where wildlife and agriculture are in
some degree of conflict.

Predation and the Livestock Industry

Predation upon livestock by large carnivores is one of the earliest,
most sustained, and most widely recognized types of wildlife damage. As
early as the 1600's colonists shot, trapped, and offered bounties for the
destruction of wolves and cougar to protect their livestock, so these large
predators were eliminated rather early over most of the East. Even in the
western states the timber wolf has been exterminated, and the red wolf of
the South is considered an endangered species. In several states the cougar
and the black bear have now come to be recognized as valued game species,
rather than pests. The coyote is the species against which most predator

Reprinted from: Chapter 7 in Land Use and Wildlife Resources, Publ. ISBN 309-01857-9,
Committee on Agricultural Land Use and Wildlife Resources, National Academy of Sciences—
National Research Council, Washington, D.C. 1970.

control is now directed. In some situations its depredations upon sheep are unquestioned, but unbiased assessments of the extent of damage are difficult to obtain because many sheepmen tend to attribute most or all of their losses to coyotes. Accurate evaluation of coyote damage is complicated by the animal's carrion-eating habits. It is often difficult to determine whether a fed-upon lamb was dead or moribund from some other causes when the coyote found it. The magnitude of the coyote control program is indicated in the Leopold report (1964), which shows that in the federal and cooperative predator control program nearly 90,000 coyotes were taken in one recent year, out of a total of 190,763 predators of all kinds.

Another species widely accused of predation upon lambs is the golden eagle, especially in Texas and New Mexico. After World War II literally thousands of these raptors were killed, largely by private gunners in aircraft. Federal protection was accorded the golden eagle in 1962, but the law provides that governors of states where ranchers could show evidence of eagle predation upon livestock, primarily young sheep and goats, can obtain permission from the Secretary of the Interior for the ranchers to shoot and trap the birds (but not to hunt them from airplanes or to employ poisons).

The economic effects of golden eagles are being studied by biologists from several agencies. Most recently the National Audubon Society, the National Wool Growers Association, and the Department of the Interior have sponsored a study by Texas Technological College, on the basis of which the subject of golden eagle regulation is being evaluated by the Department. However, more information is still needed on the economics of the golden eagle, and studies should continue.

Wildlife Conflicts with Crops

Birds may often cause severe damage to fruit or agricultural crops, and for several reasons the incidence of damage seems to be increasing. The nature of modern agriculture, with its emphasis upon monoculture and highly specialized crops, and the high cost of bringing the crop to the harvesting stage, when bird damage usually occurs, are among the factors involved.

Accurate estimates of the value of fruit or grain destroyed by birds are extremely difficult to obtain. Numerous field surveys have been made; among the most convincing are those involving ducks and small grain in the Canadian Prairie Provinces and California, blackbirds and rice in Arkansas, and blackbirds and corn in Ohio and several other states.

Losses of grain in Canada have become so serious that major efforts have been made to alleviate them. Devices of various kinds to frighten the birds, and spreading grain near the marshes to lure the birds from the unharvested grainfields, are two methods that have been used. Both are cumbersome and expensive, and they are not always effective.

Another program, inspired by the success of crop insurance against losses from hailstorms and similar "acts of God," was initiated by Saskatchewan in 1953 and by Alberta in 1961. Paynter (1966) summarized the experience of the first 13 years of the Crop Depredations Insurance program in Saskatchewan, showing that 4,395 farmers had been insured for

526

liabilities totaling $9,557,828. They paid insurance premiums of 2 percent (over $180,000), and claims that totaled more than $745,000 were paid. Claim payments beyond those covered by the 2-percent premiums are covered by a $1 surcharge on each hunting license sold in the province.

The insurance plan alone, however, cannot be considered completely successful in Canada. Many farmers feel they should not be required to pay any premium to defend their interests against legally protected birds, and such a high proportion of those insured are being paid claims for damage that the fund appears likely to be inadequate.

Although waterfowl depredations upon grain in the Dakotas, Minnesota, and Nebraska have been estimated at hundreds of thousands of dollars in some years, the Canadian insurance plan, though considered, has not actually been tried in the United States.

Jahn (1969), in an excellent review of crop depredations by migratory birds, has pointed out that in some counties of the United States the all-risk crop insurance available through the Federal Crop Insurance Corporation of the U.S. Department of Agriculture includes losses to bird depredations among the items eligible for payment. The arrangement is different from that in Canada, since the policy guarantees a specified number of bushels per acre and quality of crop harvested. The number of farmers taking out the all-risk crop insurance has increased since 1937, when it was first made available, so that in 1968 nearly a third of a million farmers insured almost 20 million acres of crops. However, the losses due to wildlife depredations are so minor compared to those from drought, excessive rainfall, hail, insects, and similar causes, that they are included only among the "other causes" that comprise 5 percent of the total.

Farmes (1969) reports that an interagency team, after evaluating waterfowl crop depredations in Minnesota, concluded that with appropriate changes the federal crop insurance program might be more effective in handling losses caused by waterfowl, and that the Federal Crop Insurance Corporation has the staff and experience to deal with a wildlife insurance program.

In California, damage to rice and other small grains by waterfowl has been reduced through a combination of several management procedures. Plantings of waterfowl foods on areas purchased especially for this purpose attract ducks from nearby commercial crops. Improvements in rice-farming practices have also been aided by creating more continuous stands and reducing openings, which are especially attractive to ducks. Finally, state and federal officials have developed with farmers a "self-help" crop protection program that includes bird harassment and the use of fright devices.

Depredations by several kinds of blackbirds upon rice, especially in Arkansas (Neff and Meanley, 1957), and upon corn in several states in the eastern half of the country are still exceedingly serious and, despite a long-term research program, the problems remain unsolved. Only a few examples of the many other situations in which birds or mammals cause damage to fruit or agricultural crops can be included here.

Lesser sandhill cranes, strictly protected since the Migratory Bird Treaty Act of 1918, have been reported in several western states to cause damage to sorghum, alfalfa, winter wheat, and peanuts. Experimental hunting seasons, in strictly limited areas in New Mexico and Texas, were initiated in 1961, and complaints of damage have decreased. This suggests that the institution of hunting seasons has provided successful control.

In Maine, blueberries are a multimillion-dollar crop on 80,000 acres, and depredations on the ripening fruit by gulls are estimated by specialists at the University of Maine at 2 percent of the crop annually. The total damage appears small, but individual growers may lose the greater part of their crop in a single day.

In California several specialized crops are damaged by legally protected birds of many kinds. Horned larks destroy lettuce; linnets (local name in California for house finch) eat the buds of apricot and almond trees; band-tailed pigeons damage several orchard and truck crops; and coots feed upon hay and truck garden produce.

The problems of bird conflicts with crops are so numerous, complex, and varied that no one solution can be expected. Some effective control measures have been developed, but many more are needed, adaptable to the peculiarities of the problem faced. Nonlethal methods are particularly appropriate, for many of the birds that cause trouble in one situation are valued in others. Where lethal methods are deemed necessary, it is important that they be specific, or selective, so that they will not needlessly destroy nontarget species or have a long-lasting effect upon the environment as do so many of the pesticides now commonly employed.

Wildlife Problems Involving the Forest and Range

Damage to the forest by wildlife is widely scattered and usually attracts little attention. Perhaps the commonest effect is upon tree reproduction, because a large number of birds and mammals feed upon tree seeds (Smith and Aldous, 1947). Both artificially seeded and natural forest reproduction have been severely damaged by a variety of small mammals, particularly mice, chipmunks, and squirrels. Areas cleared through logging or fire are particularly vulnerable to wildlife damage during the stage of reseeding and growth of seedlings and saplings, because many species of wildlife are attracted into the openings (Kverno, 1964).

Two other types of damage widespread in the forest are clipping and browsing of timber species by big game, rabbits and hares, and others; and the bark and root damage caused by rodents, such as pocket gophers, mice, and porcupines.

Deer, elk, and other ungulates have frequently become so numerous that their feeding has caused severe damage to forests, especially to seedlings and saplings. In most areas, however, population control is now being achieved through regulated hunting and this type of damage is far less widespread than in the past.

Studies of the effect of rabbit and rodent activity on range forage have shown that rabbits eat mostly leaf and stem material as do meadow voles *(Microtus)*, pocket gophers *(Thomomys, Geomys)*, and some species of ground squirrels *(Citellus)*; most other rodents eat such foods as seeds and insects and may have a beneficial effect on rangelands.

In north-central Colorado studies have shown that the plant genera *Vicia, Lathyrus,* and *Agoseris* are important foods for meadow voles; these plants also are consumed by cattle. Pocket gophers eat some of the same plants as do cattle, and show a high preference for certain grasses (e.g., *Stipa comata*) at the very season when cattle show similar preference. In a variety of areas pocket gophers, ground squirrels, and jack rabbits all compete to some degree with cattle for food.

It is clear that small mammals consume range forage plants, but to what extent? In some annual grassland areas in the Central Valley of California, jack rabbits commonly reach a population level of one rabbit for every two acres. At this level rabbits would eat approximately 115 pounds of air-dry herbage per acre per year. In the same areas pocket gophers occur regularly at population densities of approximately 10 per acre; at this level they would eat about 220 pounds of air-dry herbage per acre per year. The aggregate consumption of these small mammals—about 330 pounds per acre per year—is about a third of the total allowable annual forage utilization.

In the subalpine parklands of the Rocky Mountains the two small mammals of greatest importance as consumers of vegetation are the northern pocket gopher *(Thomomys talpoides)* and the montane vole *(Microtus montanus)*. In studies made in the summer of 1965 in Colorado, these rodents occurred at population levels of about 20 and 8 animals per acre, respectively. In such numbers, they would consume about 460 pounds of air-dry herbage per acre per year, or approximately one quarter of the yearly herbage production.

Not all of the vegetation eaten by these rodents is suitable for livestock forage and it is likely that their most important effect is not from consumption of herbage, but from their burrowing, mound building, and food storage activities. Jameson (1958) has estimated that the California vole destroys as much vegetation through these activities as in its food consumption. Fitch and Bentley (1949), in their work on the rodents of a California annual grassland, showed that they ate but 10 percent of the vegetation they destroyed. In a 1966 study of subalpine rangeland in north-central Colorado, about 22 percent of the ground was found to be covered with soil brought to the surface during winter or spring by pocket gophers, and only a few plants were able to establish themselves on the fresh workings.

The total ecological impact of rodents on rangelands is clearly the result of a variety of factors. Both native and domestic animals affect vegetation; it is of primary importance to determine precisely what these effects are and how they are brought about. A final and more difficult step is to develop management practices that maintain a vegetational complex such that there will be minimum rodent and rabbit damage and maximum forage for livestock and game animals.

Nonagricultural Wildlife Problems

Wild birds and mammals act as carriers or reservoirs for certain diseases of man and domestic animals. A few of these, such as rabies, are of great economic importance, but the majority are local or temporary and do not usually result in control demands of any magnitude.

In certain urban and industrial situations, however, birds have become serious pests and have created unusually difficult control problems. Best known are starling and pigeon roosts on buildings or the roosting in city shade trees of tremendous aggregations of starlings and other birds. A variety of control methods are partially successful, but most are awkward, expensive, and ineffective.

Perhaps the most spectacular conflict between birds and man involves the bird-airplane problem, which was brought dramatically to public attention in 1960 when a jet plane crashed at Logan International Airport, Boston, killing a number of persons. In this instance a flock of starlings was sucked into the jet engines.

In Canada one commercial airline (Air Canada) has maintained records of strikes with birds and costs of repairing the damage. Strike rates are highest during the spring and fall bird migrations, and the greatest annual damage was $350,000, sustained in 1961. Since then the damage and costs have declined as a result of habitat modification and other measures to disperse birds from the vicinity of the airports.

In The United States, records appear to be less accurate, but at 28 of the nation's busiest commercial airports from 1962 through 1966, approximately 1,000 bird strikes were recorded. In 1965 the U.S. Air Force recorded 839 strikes, necessitating 75 engine replacements at a cost of four to five million dollars (Seubert and Solman, 1968; U.S. Air Force, 1966).

More accurate data must be obtained as a basis for remedial action, but the one simple fact that has come through most clearly is that habitat conditions particularly attractive to birds cannot be tolerated in the immediate vicinity of jet airports.

Positive Values of Predators and Rodents

Predators and rodents have positive values as well as the negative ones discussed above. This, in fact, was the first tenet of the Leopold report (discussed later in this chapter) and it underscores the expressed policy of the Department of the Interior that control measures when instituted must be specific and selective and must avoid destroying the innocent individuals with the guilty.

The American public, as it has become more affluent with more leisure time for recreation, has developed a stronger and more sophisticated interest in nature and the out-of-doors. This interest is expressed in many ways. While the number of hunters and fishermen continues to grow, the number of people interested in the "nonconsumptive" uses of wildlife has shown a far greater increase. National parks and other nature reserves are used far more than ever; and books, binoculars, and cameras sell as never before to the growing number of bird-watchers and other amateur naturalists.

Not many decades ago, few would have challenged the statement that "the only good coyote is a dead coyote," but today many thrill to hear or see a coyote. It is a common sight in some of the national parks to see traffic jams where motorists have stopped to enjoy the sight of a coyote hunting. The timber wolf population in Algonquin Provincial Park, only 200 miles from Canada's largest city, is regarded by many as the park's proudest possession, and hundreds have gathered in an evening along the road through the park to hear the wolves respond to recorded howling.

While the value is sometimes intangible and difficult to translate into monetary terms, it is clear that the American public has come to place a high premium on wildlife in general, and particularly upon predatory species that only recently were almost universally condemned as pests and that, in certain situations, must still be controlled to prevent damage. In this context the growing interest in the predators for sport has special significance, especially if their use in sport can aid in necessary control.

Potential of Large Predators for Sport Hunting

The value of large predators for sport has received little attention in the United States, though the contrary is true in northern Europe. Where the Europeans hunted such carnivores for sport, the American tradition was to trap, poison, and bounty them. This attitude was understandable on the frontier, where wildlife was more important for food than for recreation; therefore, deer, turkey, or ducks were far more welcome quarry than a fox. Neither economic nor social conditions in the United States favored a leisure class that could afford the luxury of fox hunting.

In recent years, however, the sporting potential of these predators has become more widely recognized. In its 1965 National Survey of Hunting and Fishing the U.S. Bureau of Sport Fisheries and Wildlife included for the first time a survey of participation in the sport of "varmint hunting," and came up with a surprising estimate of 2,573,000 participants—more even than had hunted migratory game birds that year. The term "varmint" is loosely used; in the sporting literature it includes many species of commonly unprotected wildlife such as crows, magpies, marmots, and jack rabbits as well as predators, but coyotes and foxes are favored on the long list of "varmints."

The inconsistencies even in adjacent states indicate clearly how our traditions relating to these predators are changing. The mountain lion, for example, is a game animal in Colorado and hunting it requires a special license. In Arizona and South Dakota a bounty is paid on it, and in seven western states it is unprotected. In 1967, Oregon declared the cougar a game animal and provided a year-round closed season pending study to determine if its population was sufficient to merit a hunting season. The previous year eight counties in Oregon had offered a bounty on the cougar.

Although the coyote is a prime target of state and federal predator control programs, it is increasingly a favorite of sportsmen, who have a variety of hunting methods from which to select. "Calling" coyotes is remarkably successful, permitting even close-up photography at times. The use of trained hounds, particularly greyhounds, is not uncommon in the western plains states.

The growing popularity of coyote hunting for sport is indicated in western states by the existence of such groups as the Arizona Varmint Callers Association, which reports seven clubs with a paid membership of 550. California, Colorado, Nevada, and New Mexico report similar clubs and a growing interest in this sport.

In New York State in 1964 and 1965 an attempt was made to coordinate predator hunting with control when the statewide raccoon hunters' organization, as part of its effort to keep the raccoon a legally protected game animal, offered the services of its members in the control of any raccoons causing damage to corn or garden crops. Properly organized, this type of cooperation could accomplish needed control where animals are doing damage, and at the same time provide recreation.

As the recreational value of hunting certain predators becomes more widely recognized, this sport might well replace some of the expensive control efforts. It should be emphasized, however, that the hunting of what are not ordinarily considered to be game animals should be done only when such animals are sufficiently abundant to sustain an annual kill without hazard to their populations or ecological values. Examples of such abundant and successful species, in much of their range, are the woodchuck, crow, coyote, and raccoon. In states where it is still to be found, the status of the cougar should be guarded to make certain that is not overhunted.

Federal Predator and Rodent Control

Control of predators and rodents by the federal government, in response to state and local requests, is a well-established activity that had its beginnings in the Bureau of Biological Survey, U.S. Department of Agriculture. The Bureau began conducting experiments in control methods for predators in 1909, and for range rodents in 1914. In 1915 Congress appropriated funds to control predatory animals that were killing livestock and transmitting rabies. Since then the activity has grown until in 1964-65 the cost of these programs was nearly $7 million, of which about a third was federal funds. This federal activity was invariably in response to requests by states, lesser divisions of government, and in some cases private organizations; these private organizations provided substantial contributions to the work.

In some areas efforts have been made to provide educational programs on the control of rodents and predators, particularly through established extension agencies. In eastern states the Fish and Wildlife Service developed extension for landowners and others who needed rodent control, and some of the states employed extension specialists who had as one of their duties the development of educational programs relating to rodent control. In the fruit-growing areas of several eastern states, particularly New York and Virginia, mice and rabbits are a considerable threat to fruit trees; here the states have been active in both research and extension to prevent losses to the orchards.

The concept of having either the state or federal government provide the landowner with information on methods he himself can use to protect his crops, instead of furnishing actual control services, is similar to policies and practices related to disease and insect control. In Kansas and Missouri, state extension specialists in predator control have been operating since before 1950.

There are compelling reasons for continuing the federal control program in some areas. In western states federal land is intermingled with private holdings, and ranchers graze their stock under permit on public lands. Thus animal damage control traditionally has been regarded as a federal responsibility. The lands on which control is practiced are extensive, and the methods used often are potentially dangerous to other animals and man. Given these conditions it is argued that control by professionals is more likely to meet acceptable standards of safety and effectiveness than that by the owners of livestock or other property. The fact that animal control left to nonfederal agencies has often employed the outmoded and inefficient bounty system is a case in point.

The administration of control programs and the setting of control policies face inherent difficulties. Until recently the Fish and Wildlife Service carried on predator and rodent abatement operations where field workers and supervisors judged them to be needed. Criteria for deciding when and where operations were desirable or necessary were not clearly established, and decisions too often reflected the personal ideas and biases of individuals. Under these conditions, and with two thirds of the funds coming from stockmen's associations and local levies, a steadily expanding and not highly discriminating program against predators and range rodents was carried on. The Service was under long-standing demand from both scientists and laymen to increase the objectivity of its methods for determining control needs and to adjust field activities accordingly.

Predator control problems and policies have been reviewed by a number of writers. A few recent representative publications include those of Allen (1963), Balser (1964), Berryman (1966), Hall (1966), U.S. Congress (1966), and Gottschalk (1967).

As a result of the concern at highest levels of government that public programs involving wildlife damage and control be in tune with modern thinking, an important study was conducted dealing specifically with these problems.

The Leopold Report

The so-called Leopold report (Leopold, 1964) on predator and rodent control in the United States was written at the request of then Secretary of the Interior Stewart L. Udall. The board of five that produced this report after a period of intensive study has an impressive record of experience in the biological sciences and in public service in wildlife management, and their conclusions and recommendations have been widely accepted.

Two basic assumptions adopted by the board were that:

1. All native animals are resources of inherent interest and value to the people of the United States. Basic government policy therefore should be one of husbandry of all forms of wildlife.

2. At the same time, local population control is an essential part of a management policy, where a species is causing significant damage to other resources or crops, or where it endangers human health or safety. Control should be limited strictly to the troublesome species, preferably to the troublesome individuals, and in any event to the localities where substantial damage or danger exists.

After its appraisal the board concluded:

It is the unanimous opinion of this Board that control as actually practiced today is considerably in excess of the amount that can be justified in terms of total public interest. As a consequence many animals which have never offended private property owners or public resource values are being killed unnecessarily. The issue is how to sharpen the tools of control so that they hew only where cuts are fully justified.

The board included in its report six recommendations:

1. Appointment of a continuing advisory board of predator and rodent control which should be widely representative of the livestock and agricultural interests, conservation organizations, and technical organizations. The Leopold board recognized the controversial nature of animal control programs and the need for a "forum for the wide spectrum of opinions" regarding control.

2. Reassessment of its own goals by the Branch of Predator and Rodent Control of the Fish and Wildlife Service, and a break with the tradition that it ". . . is primarily responsible to livestock and agricultural interests. . . ."

3. Some specific suggestions for the control program:

a. Continuation in the West of the system of trained professional hunters as being most effective.

b. Continuation of the cooperative arrangement under which at least half of the costs are borne by nonfederal sources.

c. Requirement of more proof and documentation of the need for any local control program, including statistics on the "true extent of the damage."

d. Encouragement of extension educational programs wherever feasible (generally the eastern half of the country).

e. Replacement of bounty systems with extension programs.

f. Use, in the eastern United States, of "flying squads of federal control agents" where rabies outbreaks or similar temporary situations occur.

4. An amplified research program, particularly to develop more specific controls, so that innocent animals are not so often the victims, and also to develop repellents and other protective devices that do not involve killing.

5. Selection of a new name for the Branch of Predator and Rodent Control—one that suggests a broader management function.

6. Adoption of stricter legal control over the use of poisons, particularly over 1080, which the report states has resulted in much secondary poisoning. Mentioned specifically were the need to guard against the "ecological abuses" of secondary poisoning of nontarget species, and the need to prohibit export to foreign countries where the danger of misuse is high.

Official Acceptance of the Leopold Report

The Leopold report, released to the public on March 9, 1964, at the North American Wildlife and Natural Resources Conference, was accepted officially by Secretary Udall on June 22, 1965, after 15 months of study, as a "general guidepost for Department policy," but ". . . not as a policy mandate." However, several tangible results of the report's recommendations have been evident:

On July 1, 1965, the Branch of Predator and Rodent Control became the Division of Wildlife Services, and new leadership and direction were provided. As the name suggests, the Division has far broader responsibilities than did its predecessor. In addition to control activities the Division has responsibility for surveillance and monitoring of pesticides in the environment, and for "wildlife resource enhancement work," with emphasis upon migratory species; initial efforts are to be concentrated upon Indian, military, and Interior lands (Berryman, 1966).

In May 1967 the Bureau of Sport Fisheries and Wildlife issued a statement of policy for animal damage control (Gottschalk, 1967). In announcing it, Director Gottschalk explained that drafts of the statement had been reviewed by "over 30 conservation organizations and agencies, including representative user groups. . . . The finished product is in accord with the majority of the suggestions made and incorporates much of the basic philosophy . . . of the Leopold Report."

This official document begins with a significant statement of philosophy that recognizes the esthetic value of wildlife resources. In addition, the statement indicates that the Bureau must cooperate with state game and fish agencies in the conservation of fish and wildlife resources for the use and enjoyment of the entire public, that control measures must remain flexible, that when control is needed it shall recognize fully the ecological relationships involved and must emphasize removal of specific offending individuals wherever and whenever possible.

The statement of policy emphasizes demonstrated need for control, selective control, cooperation with state and federal agencies, advance planning, the use of educational techniques where possible, avoidance of hazard to endangered species of wildlife, and a strong program of research "to find new, improved, selective, and humane methods."

This official policy is evidence that the Leopold report has been adopted to a very considerable extent. Only two recommendations of the report are not mentioned: the one calling for appointment of a continuing advisory board on predator and rodent control, and the final one urging far stricter legal controls governing the use of poisons, over which the Department of the Interior does not have sole jurisdiction.

Need for Damage Control Research

The variety and magnitude of wildlife damage to man's crops and property are sufficient to demand more effective controls than are available at present, and research is urgently needed to develop them. Changes in agriculture and land use, and changes in wildlife populations and their behavior repeatedly bring about new situations where damage by wildlife occurs. Furthermore, public attitudes toward wildlife have changed so much that it is more essential than ever that nonlethal types of control be used wherever feasible.

Federal research on wildlife damage control is being conducted in several key points in the country and many effective methods have been developed. But an accelerated program is needed for the important new problems that regularly arise; also all potential avenues to control must be explored. There is need to maintain close contact with work done on control methods in Europe, where some of the same situations have been faced far longer than in the United States.

Methods of controlling or alleviating damage fall into at least four broad categories, and studies should continue to explore all of them—biological or cultural, mechanical and electronic, chemical, and payment for damages. For each of these categories there are examples of successes in particular situations. All deserve additional study.

The biological or cultural category includes some cases, in California, where waterfowl have been lured from rice fields to areas of food planted especially for them. It also covers situations around airports, where habitats have been modified to reduce their attractiveness to birds. And it might well include the development of crop varieties that are resistant to birds, though little has been accomplished so far with this approach.

The electronic and mechanical category includes various types of scaring devices, the herding or harassing of birds, shooting, and various electronic devices, of which the most successful to date have used recorded alarm or distress calls of gregarious birds. This last technique has been used with considerable success against starlings in vineyards in Germany and France.

Chemical methods have been and are being given much attention. Several classes of chemicals offer possibilities—toxicants, repellents, soporifics or stupifacients and the antifertility agents that are being considered as a way of holding some animal populations in check.

Payment for damages, as exemplified by the waterfowl depredation crop insurance plan used in Canada, may have applicability to some conditions in the United States. From the summary by Boyd (1963), it appears that state game agencies have had experience with this method, since 10 states were paying landowners for game damage to crops, although the programs in most cases were very limited.

Looking Into the Future

Wildlife damage and nuisance situations may be expected to continue and probably to increase. The development of successful methods of controlling or mitigating damage already offers a challenge to the natural scientist or social scientist who is interested in tackling it. In the past it has been difficult to interest capable young scientists in these problems, because of the somewhat unfavorable public image of the traditional predator and rodent control programs. Those interested in wildlife management usually preferred the role of producing, rather than destroying or controlling, wildlife.

As research in bird and mammal control becomes more sophisticated, and it is more widely recognized that it draws upon many basic sciences—ecology, physiology, behavior, biochemistry, electronics—the art of controlling wildlife damage may be expected to achieve greater stature, attract more research attention, and be more frequently successful.

An example of the attention paid to bird damage and its control in Europe is provided by the discussion at a symposium held in London in 1967 (Murton and Wright, 1968). Sir Landsborough Thomson and Professor V. C. Wynne Edwards, Department of Zoology, University of Aberdeen, two of the most distinguished zoologists in the United Kingdom, acted as chairmen of sessions that reviewed bird problems on a worldwide scale. The latter concluded with remarks that are as valid in the United States as in the United Kingdom:

Given enough knowledge, rational decisions can be taken. But if people blindly take sides on questions of bird control as a matter of principle and insist on forcing the issue one way or the other by trial of strength, the decisions reached must necessarily be political decisions; and they may do quite unnecessary harm or injustice to the least appreciated interests on the other side.

Sir Landsborough Thomson's opening remarks to the session for which he acted as chairman are also pertinent:

It is to be hoped that the title, "Problems of Birds and Pests", will not lead anyone to think that this symposium has been conceived in a spirit of hostility to bird-life. Most of those taking part are in fact ornithologists or conservationists, or both. The perspective in which the topic should be viewed is that control is an aspect of conservation, requiring study like any other. In an environment where the balance of nature has been greatly disturbed, mankind has a responsibility for wildlife management; this properly includes reasonable defense of human material interests.

Birds are to a large extent economically beneficial; they are also, of course, scientifically interesting and aesthetically delightful. Yet some species tend to be harmful, and others become pests when present in excessive numbers or in the wrong places. The task is, dispassionately and objectively, to determine the facts and consider what to do.

The extent of interest in Europe in these problems also is exemplified by the organization of an international society of economic ornithologists and the appearance of its technical journal *Angewandte Ornithologie,* which deals with the positive as well as the negative economic impact of birds. It appears that in western Europe the attitudes of the public and of scientists toward wildlife damage and control have matured to a point where constructive discussion and research on the problems proceed more objectively than in the United States. The chief goal, of course, should be alleviation of the damage, rather than destruction of animals.

REFERENCES

ALLEN, D. L. 1963. The costly and needless war on predators. Audubon Mag. 65(2):85-89, 120-121.

BALSER, D. S. 1964. Management of predator populations with antifertility agents. J. Wildl. Manage. 28(2):352-358.

BERRYMAN, J. H. 1966. Trans. N. Amer. Wildl. and Natur. Resour. Conf. 31:246-258.

BOYD, R.J. 1963. A brief summary of game damage data and forage requirements in the United States. A report to the Colorado Game, Fish and Parks Commission. 14 p. (mimeo.)

FARMES, R. E. 1969. Crop insurance for waterfowl depredation. Trans. N. Amer. Wildl. and Natur. Resour. Conf. 34:332-337.

FITCH, H. S., and J. R. BENTLEY. 1949. Use of California annual-plant forage by range rodents. Ecology 30(3):306-321.

GOTTSCHALK, J. S. 1967. Man and wildlife (a policy for animal damage control). U.S. Department of the Interior, Washington, D.C. 12p.

HALL, E.R. 1966. Carnivores, sheep, and public lands. Trans. N. Amer. Widl. Conf., 31: 239-245.

JAHN, L. R. 1969. Migratory bird crop depredations: A naturalist's views of the problem. Presented at the Migratory Bird Crop Depredation Workshop, University of Maryland, July 15-16, 1969, 32p. (mimeo.)

JAMESON, E. W. 1958. Consumption of alfalfa and wild oats by *Microtus californicus.* J. Wildl. Manage. 22:433-434.

KVERNO, N. B. 1964. Forest animal damage control. Proc. 2nd Vert. Pest Contr. Conf., Anaheim, Calif. 81-89.

LEOPOLD, A. S. (Chr.) 1964. Predator and rodent control in the United States. Trans. N. Amer. Wildl. and Natur. Resour. Conf. 29:27-49.

MURTON, R. K., and E. N. WRIGHT (ed.). 1968. The problems of birds as pests. Academic Press, New York. 240p.

NEFF, J. A., and B. MEANLEY. 1957. Blackbirds and the Arkansas rice crop. Agricultural Experiment Station Bulletin 584, University of Arkansas, Fayetteville, Arkansas, February 1957, 89p.

PAYNTER, E. L. 1966. Crop insurance. The Saskatchewan Government Insurance Office, Regina. 4p. (mimeo.)

SEUBERT, J. L. 1966. Biological control of birds in airport environments. Interim report, Proj. Agreement FA65WAI-77, Proj. No. 430-011-01E, SRDS Report No. RO-66-8, U.S. Department of the Interior, Bureau of Sport Fisheries and Wildlife, Washington, D.C. 41p.

SMITH, C. F., and S. E. ALDOUS. 1947. The influence of mammals and birds in retarding artificial and natural reseeding of coniferous forests in the United States. J. Forest. 45(5):361-369.

SOLMAN, V. E. F. 1968. Bird control and air safety. Trans. N. Amer. Wildl. and Natur. Resour. Conf., 33:328-336.

U.S. Air Force. 1966. Bird/aircraft collisions. Air Force Office of Scientific Research, Office of Aerospace Research, Arlington, Va. 15p.

U.S. Congress. 1966. House Committee on Merchant Marine and Fisheries. Predatory mammals. Hearings before the Subcommittee on Fisheries and Wildlife Conservation, 89th Cong., 2nd sess. U.S. Government Printing Office. Washington, D.C. 255p.

OPERATIONS SINCE 1963 UNDER MONTANA'S STREAM PRESERVATION LAW (1970)

John C. Peters

Problems of maintaining wildlife habitat are becoming increasingly important as human populations grow. These problems can be solved when (1) effects of land development upon wildlife are well documented; (2) public awareness of these effects is transmitted into demand for saving wildlife habitat; and (3) state and federal wildlife agencies work with developers and planners to produce the best possible combination of public benefits. Peters describes successful activities of Montana's Fish and Game Department following these three steps toward saving wildlife habitat.

A day seldom passes without some mention in newspapers, on the radio, in the weekly magazines, or over television of the destruction of the environment. The public is aware that serious environmental problems exist. Their attitude today is that they want to live in a high-quality environment, relatively free of any kind of pollution, even if it means paying higher taxes or a higher price for products. This attitude could only be held in an affluent society such as ours where the more basic needs of food and shelter are adequate for most people.

Protection of trout streams from the bulldozer and dragline is only one small part of the struggle for the maintenance of a quality environment. However, such protection is a milestone because the people of Montana have achieved some success in the preservation of this important part of the landscape. A law called the Stream Preservation Law is the reason for our success. Years of disappointing efforts showed that moral indignation or social alarm will not save a meandering stream from a bulldozer. Only the legal process with delegated responsibility will do the job.

Before Montana had its law, the road builders listened to alternate proposals, but the final plans included only incidental considerations for the preservation of the trout stream environment. The Instructional Memorandums of the Bureau of Public Roads were not adequate because there were no provisions to settle differences. Legally, the road builders had no responsibility to consider requests aimed at stream protection. Only after passage of the Stream Preservation Law were we able to work out compromises that allowed the building of roads without the needless destruction of streams and the surrounding valley floors. The compromises came relatively easy once the legal framework was provided by the Montana Legislature.

History

In 1960, there was major conflict with the road builders concerning the harmful effects of road construction on trout streams. After a history of attempting to get adequate consideration for preserving the stream environment, it became painfully clear that they would listen, but could not implement major proposals for minimizing damage. We had no recourse

Reprinted from: Trans. N. Amer. Wildl. and Natural Resources Conf. 35:276-283.

but to ask the legislature to give us the legal framework to protect our stream resources from the bulldozers. Faced with that task, it was obvious that facts were needed before we could adequately support our case.

So, in 1961, a pilot study was initiated on the Little Bighorn River to develop methods for measuring channel alterations and their impact on fish populations. Using the techniques developed on this pilot study, each of seven fisheries districts measured at least one stream in 1962. We completed inventories on 13 streams and rivers located throughout the state and the results showed that far more of the trout stream environment had been tampered with than we had suspected (Peters, 1964). Two other states, North Carolina (Bayless and Smith, 1964) and Idaho (Irizarri, 1969) have completed statewide channel inventories that show the same trend. All of these studies conclude that altered channels carry far fewer game fish than natural channels. Also, a study of channelization in the Little Sioux River in Iowa revealed that the channeled portions carried far fewer game fish than the natural channel (Welker, 1967).

As we presented the results of the stream channel inventory to various civic organizations, we gained the strong support of the Montana Junior Chamber of Commerce. Later, they received a National Conservation Award for their part in obtaining passage of Montana's first Stream Preservation Law. The Montana Wildlife Federation also pitched in with the Western Association of that Federation providing noteworthy leadership. Together these groups supported by the data convinced a rather reluctant legislature that Montana needed a Stream Preservation Law. One was passed which became effective on July 1, 1963, but only for a two-year trial period. Thus we had to repeat our efforts in 1965. Armed then with facts from channel inventories on 16 streams, and the record of not having stopped the entire road building program in Montana during the previous two years, we enlisted the support of several groups. These efforts were successful because a permanent law was passed in 1965.

The following facts based on the channel inventory were presented at the 1965 legislative committee hearings:

1. That 354 of 987 miles (36%) of channels surveyed had been altered from their natural condition.
2. There were 2,401 alterations counted, nearly three per stream mile.
3. Altered channels produced only one-fifth the number of game fish and one-seventh the weight of game fish as natural channels.

These facts played an important part in convincing the legislature that protective legislation was necessary to maintain a valuable natural resource, Montana's trout stream fishery.

Examining the voting record of the Montana legislature on this issue will give some insight into the desirable effects of a well-planned implementation of a good law. In 1963, the first law narrowly passed the legislature (with the House voting 53-33 and the Senate voting 32-21) and became law for a two-year trial period. The bill was killed twice in committee, only to be pulled out and passed after some interesting political maneuvering. In contrast, the 1965 legislature enacted a permanent law with only *one* dissenting vote from a possible 146, which was cast by a road contractor. I believe the change in the voting between 1963 and 1965 is excellent testimony in favor of exerting every effort to make a good law work.

The Stream Preservation Law covers only agencies of the state and subdivisions of state government, *i.e.,* cities and counties. The State Water Conservation Board is exempt. The law gave no jurisdiction over private landowners, corporations or federal government agencies.

There were two important changes made to the original law by the 1965 legislature. Most important the law became permanent in 1965 and no longer had to be renewed at each subsequent session of the legislature. The arbitration committee under the 1963 law was made up of a member designated by the Fish and Game Commission, a member designated by the agency involved, and a third member who had no connection with either agency, selected by these two members. Under the 1965 law the three-man committee is appointed by the district court.

The Law Itself and How It Works

Both the 1963 law (Chapter 258, Montana Laws of 1963) and the 1965 law (Chapter 10, Montana Laws of 1965) have identical preambles: "An act to establish the policy of the State of Montana on protection of fishing streams, providing for submission of plans for construction and hydraulic projects affecting such streams to the Montana Fish and Game commission and for review of such plans; and providing for arbitration of disagreements between the Fish and Game Commission and the Agency proposing such acts." The following is a brief summary of the sections of the act itself and describes the mechanical operation under the current law:

1. The Fish and Game Commission is notified of a project affecting a stream on a special form accompanied by detailed plans and specifications. These documents must be provided not less than 60 days prior to the start of construction.
2. The Commission examines these plans. If they are inadequate, they so notify the applicant and may aid him in preparing better ones.
3. Within 30 days after the receipt of such plans, the Commission notifies the applicant whether or not the project affects any fish and game habitat. If the project is harmful to habitat, the Commission recommends alternatives which diminish or eliminate such effect.
4. If these alternatives or recommendations are unacceptable to the construction agency, they must notify the Commission within 15 days after receiving such alternatives and the disagreement is arbitrated. A special arbitration procedure is spelled out in the law which is binding on both parties.

However, we have learned that a much more practical operation exists with construction agencies than that formally spelled out by the law. Somewhere between 10 and 15 percent of the total cost of a highway construction project lies in its design. Once an alignment has been selected and the plans are completed, there is little opportunity for change without great cost to the construction agency. Considerable delay occurs while the project is being redesigned, too. Therefore, the conservation agency must be notified by a construction agency and be allowed to participate as a partner before such design plans are developed. In the jargon of the road-building agencies, this means notification to participate on the P-line (preliminary alignment) or L-line (location alignment) inspections. At this stage, changes are relatively easy to make. This allows the conservation agency sufficient time to make the necessary studies to collect data supporting a recommendation as may be required to justify changes by the construction agency. It is the practical way to carry out each agency's responsibility on a day-to-day, routine basis.

The Stream Preservation Law has been tested by legal decision three different times. One of the counties in the state did not believe the Fish and Game Commission had the jurisdiction to require them to abide by the law. The Attorney General ruled that the Commission did in fact have such authority and required the county to submit a notice of construction of their project influencing a stream.

As a mitigative measure in another case, we asked that a meander be built to replace one that was cut off. A landowner contested the necessity of selling his land for the new meander. After we provided testimony at a court hearing, the landowner amended his complaint, admitting the necessity for the taking of his land for the meander. He did not feel he was offered just compensation for his land from the road-building agency and continued the case in this regard. The meander has since been built, with the total cost, including right-of-way, estimated at $80,000.00.

In the third case the law was used to prevent the purchase of gravel from a site within the perimeter of a meander loop. We felt the river could erode its way into the borrow pit area and possibly upset the river's hydraulic regimen in the entire project area. The court ruled that the construction agency had the ministerial authority to make such a decision when requested to do so in accordance with the Stream Preservation Law.

What Has Been Accomplished

Two reports (Whitney, 1964 and Peters, 1966) discuss specific accomplishments of the law during 1963 and 1965 respectively. From July 1, 1963 when the first law became effective, until June 30, 1969 we have reviewed legal notices for 259 projects. Of these, we asked for special considerations on 88 projects, roughly one of every three.

Following are the highlights of what has been accomplished during the first six years with the law. Proposed road alignments were moved to avoid encroaching upon the Madison, Big Hole, Missouri and Blackfoot Rivers. Meanders were designed and built in Prickly Pear Creek, the St. Regis River and the Clark Fork River so that the channel was as long after construction as before. Extra bridges to preserve natural meanders were built in the Beaverhead and Missouri Rivers and are planned for the Blackfoot River. Brushy floodplain vegetation, removed to facilitate construction, has been replaced. Channel excavation has been limited to those times of the year when trout are not spawning and eggs are not in redds. An elevated and independent alignment has been proposed and been designed to preserve the St. Regis River and its scenic canyon. All of these fishery-saving accomplishments have been made by working with the State Highway Department with the concurrence of the Bureau of Public Roads, through the effective medium of a good law, which established the framework.

Fringe Benefits

By asking them to follow the intent of the Stream Preservation Law, we now have written agreements with the following federal agencies:

Forest Service, Bureau of Public Roads, Bureau of Reclamation, Fish and Wildlife Service, Soil Conservation Service, and the Bureau of Indian Affairs. The agreement with the Soil Conservation Service allows the Fish and Game Department to review each project under the Agricultural Conservation Program that involves work in a stream or river. No federal cost-sharing is allowed on channel work under ACP unless it meets with our written approval. Since channel stabilization work has increased in recent years to the fifth largest expenditure of funds under ACP, this has become an important part of our stream preservation program.

The Bureau of Public Roads has also followed the intent of the law. We have established liaison with the BPR that allows us to review all Forest Highway Projects from the preliminary alignment to the final construction phase.

Depending on individual forests in the region, we have established fair to excellent cooperation with the U.S. Forest Service. There are few problems with high-design forest roads as a rule. It is the smaller logging roads designed within the Forest Supervisors' offices that are often troublesome.

In 1969 the Montana Legislature appropriated $100,000.00 to the Department for the construction of recreational lakes. Involved in this program is the utilization of highway fills to impound water. The Fish and Game Department pays the difference in cost between a fill designed for a roadway and a fill designed for a dam embankment. The department has hired an engineering consulting firm to provide the design and right-of-way investigation work necessary for the development of plans and specifications. The State Highway Department provides us at cost with core log data necessary for material and foundation evaluation and with aerial photography necessary for site mapping. This is an example of an extremely efficient use of public money and illustrates what agencies can do when they are really willing to cooperate with each other.

Recently, we obtained a Memorandum of Understanding with the State Highway Department dealing with land isolated by road construction activities. It allows us to have the highway right-of-way personnel act in our behalf to purchase this isolated land for fish and game purposes. In this way, everyone can benefit, including the landowner with the isolated land. For example, some fairly large tracts of land will be isolated between the Clark Fork River and Interstate 90. It would be economically impractical to provide frontage road access to these lands, according to the highway department. Therefore, we are developing a plan to use these lands for a major waterfowl development. Since borrow will be needed to build the road, we will specify where it can come from and the size and shape of the borrow pits. These pits will become duck ponds rather than the traditional eye sores. This agreement will also be used to purchase land needed for fishing access, habitat protection for birds and fish, game checking stations, etc. It is not limited to interstate highways but can be used along new primary and secondary roads as well.

The Stream Preservation Law has been indirectly responsible for developing a more rational basis for our stream management program. Often we are asked by the construction agencies to justify our request for mitigative measures. This means measuring fish populations and providing reports describing the fishery for such justification. We have allocated time and manpower to do this in our fishery districts. Special jobs have been set up and work carried out over a long period of time to gather data for the stream preservation program. Because of this, the whole fisheries staff has increased its capabilities and practical know-how in accurately measuring stream and river fish populations.

What Is Left To Be Done

Almost all of our effort in preserving the stream environment has been devoted to the preconstruction phase of road building. This phase allows us (1) to review and adjust alignments, and (2) to work out measures for fishery mitigation. However, this effort does not do the entire job for maximum protection of the environment. Our effort up to now only enables us to keep between two-thirds and three-fourths of the stream environmental problems in our management grasp. However, to improve our ability to preserve the entire stream environment, we must get involved on a day-to-day basis during the construction phase of road building. This will involve a great improvement in our understanding of just what can be done and what cannot be done when the contractor is building the road. We may have to change or refine certain measures for habitat mitigation once this knowledge gap is closed. Trained biologists must be hired to work with the construction engineer in this important problem area.

Under our D-J fisheries program, we have evaluated a few of the channel mitigative measures to determine their value for fish. But we do not have the money or manpower to begin to evaluate all the important measures that have been designed and constructed for aquatic life. We need more money and people to do this work. Until such a program is operating we are proceeding under the belief that channels that behave well hydraulically also provide the best environment for fish. With or without a more adequate evaluation program, we must work closely with the engineering community to better understand flow in natural channels as it relates to fish.

LITERATURE CITED

BAYLESS, J. and W. B. SMITH. 1964. The effects of channelization upon the fish populations of lotic waters in eastern North Carolina. Misc. Publ. Division of Inland Fisheries, North Carolina Wildlife Resources Commission. 14 p.

IRIZARRI, R. A. 1969. The effect of stream alterations in Idaho. D.J. Project F-55-R-2, Job No. 1, 2, & 3. 26 p.

PETERS, J. C. and W. ALVORD. 1964. Man-made channel alterations in thirteen Montana streams and rivers. 29th No. Am. Wildl. Conf. 29:93-102.

PETERS, J. C. 1966. Operation under Montana's stream preservation law of 1965. Proc. 46th West. Assoc. State Game & Fish Commissioners. 46:313-315.

WELKER, B. D. 1967. Comparisons of channel catfish populations in channeled and un-channeled sections of the Little Sioux River, Iowa. Iowa Acad. Sci. 74:99-104.

WHITNEY, A. N. 1964. Montana's first year with a stream preservation act. Proc. 44th West. Assoc. State Game & Fish Commissioners. 44:229-232.

POSITION STATEMENTS OF THE WILDLIFE SOCIETY ON ENVIRONMENTAL ISSUES

The Problem—The Solution

Human Population. Many do not recognize that Earth's burgeoning human population imperils not only the intelligent management and preservation of the world's wildlife and other natural resources but also man's future. All organisms are interdependent. Our knowledge of wild animal populations makes it clear that human populations also must be adjusted to the Earth's variable capacity to sustain the total needs of man in order to achieve those physical, moral, mental and social values that provide quality living, variety of experience, and maximum opportunity for self-expression.

The production of aquatic or terrestrial, vertebrate or invertebrate wildlife may be, in many places, the most effective beneficial use of land and water areas to fulfill man's needs. An awareness of this fact needs to be created among the decision makers of the world.

The myriad wildlife species perform important roles affecting man, for they provide food and clothing, as well as esthetic or recreational pleasure to the individual, and they may be economically beneficial or detrimental.

Therefore, The Wildlife Society will carry out its own program related to human population problems and will actively support other programs which seek to:

1. Encourage man's understanding of human ecology and the realization that man shares with all other organisms a dependence upon the environment, this dependence being as real and complete for humans as it is for other organisms.

2. Develop knowledge and an ethic that will permit man to value, enjoy and conserve plant and animal communities as integral parts of his environment.

3. Minimize, within the context of human needs, all types of contamination and mass alteration of the environment by human populations.

4. Foster the concept that the human population *can* and *must* be maintained, by all civilized and peaceful means, within the flexible limits of Earth's resource base in order to fulfill man's spiritual as well as physical needs.

5. Allocate space of sufficient quality and quantity to sustain wildlife populations that will satisfy the basic needs of significant segments of the human population and enrich the world.

ENCROACHMENTS

Environmental Degradation. Changes in our environment are normal and continuing phenomena. Each life form contributes to these processes and has natural mechanisms to help it adjust to the normal changes in its environment.

Environmental degradation is one of today's critical problems. It has become possible for man to bring about rapid major changes to much of the Earth's environment. Changes in chemical and physical factors in aquatic and terrestrial systems have resulted not only in drastic reduction or extinction of many life forms, but have jeopardized the very environment upon which man's survival depends.

More needs to be known about the ecological consequences of man's decisions that affect the environment. Although it is obvious that humans can survive in some drastically altered environments, there is a need to go far beyond considerations for mere survival, and to provide for esthetics and ecological principles in environmental planning.

Therefore, It is The Policy of The Wildlife Society To:
1. Encourage appreciation of the importance to man of an environment that is esthetically and ecologically in his highest interest.
2. Encourage the search for comprehension of the environmental requirements and interspecific relations of all organisms and biological communities on the Earth and of man's dependent relationships within these communities.
3. Encourage the search for ways of controlling environmental deterioration and reclaiming our degraded resources.
4. Encourage the adoption by society of programs which seek to remove, reduce, minimize, and prevent environmental degradation of all kinds.
5. Encourage in the planning of man's activities the utilization of all available knowledge of the Earth, its organisms and biological communities, and of man, his societies and technologies, so that his environment may be not only biologically sufficient but rich in conceptual, social, biological, and physical diversity and beauty.
6. Encourage the development of social systems and technologies that tend to maintain and develop the diversity and beauty of man's environment and to refine and stabilize his adaptation within the eco-systems of the Earth.
7. Encourage, and provide leadership in, the dissemination of information pertinent to the dangers and adverse effects of all forms of environmental degradation.

Estuaries. Estuaries are dynamic ecological systems which constitute a thin boundary between the vastness of our land and the broad expanse of the sea. The complex and productive biological environments of estuaries are essential to the well-being of many species of terrestrial and aquatic life forms including shellfishes, marine and anadromous fishes important to commerce and sport. Estuaries also provide esthetic enjoyment and exciting exploration, as well as recreational sites and principal routes to the sea.

Estuaries constitute one of our most priceless natural assets, but they are being rapidly destroyed as productive natural systems. Past abuses have shown them to be extremely vulnerable to pollution and narrowly conceived human developments such as channelization, dredging, filling, and water diversion.

Sound planning and management are already long overdue if the unique natural values of our estuaries are to be conserved, restored, and enhanced for this and future generations.

Therefore, it is the policy of The Wildlife Society to:
1. Seek solutions to the major problems that impair effective management of estuaries for wildlife resources.
2. Encourage research designed to further our understanding of the ecology of estuaries.
3. Promote sound management of our estuarine wildlife resources.
4. Encourage restoration of estuaries where important wildlife values have been destroyed or damaged.
5. Foster public educational programs stressing the vital role of estuaries in the life-web of many forms of wildlife and to gain adequate support for estuarine research and management.

Stream Alteration Programs. Publicly subsidized stream alteration programs for such purposes as flood control, drainage, and power generation often result in direct loss of fishery habitat. These programs may also result in substantial losses of wildlife habitat, particularly through wetland drainage and clearing of riparian vegetation adjacent to stream channels. Further, these programs often make possible additional habitat alterations detrimental to wildlife on adjacent land.

Mitigation measures, if any, for fish and wildlife are often inadequate, resulting in loss of irreplaceable resources.

Therefore, it is the policy of The Wildlife Society to:
1. Oppose publicly funded stream alteration programs under both new and existing authorizations, until all resource values are thoroughly considered and until replacement in kind of fish and wildlife habitat is included in project cost calculations and authorization requests.
2. Support enactment of legislation to protect and enhance fish and wildlife resource values or provide for their replacement in kind, in all stream alteration programs.

LAW ENFORCEMENT

Enforcement of laws regulating harvest of game was the first wildlife management tool, preceding refuge establishment, predator control, stocking and habitat manipulation. However, wildlife law enforcement has in many ways been a neglected aspect of wildlife conservation. Most universities and research agencies have all but ignored problems of wildlife law enforcement. State conservation agencies have not produced precise goals for enforcement personnel. Communication among enforcement, management and research branches has often been inadequate.

Yet all admit the importance of enforcement personnel, particularly as conservation department employees having the most public contact. The trend is to upgrade the conservation officer position and to better integrate officers into overall state programs for conserving wildlife and habitats.

These two papers emphasize the many important roles of the conservation officer of today and particularly of the future.

LAW ENFORCEMENT–A TOOL OF MANAGEMENT (1971)

William B. Morse

Law enforcement is not only a tool of management, it is the basic tool of management. Fish and wildlife management had its beginning in control of the harvest; control of the harvest always involves some form of law enforcement.

Aldo Leopold defined game management as "the art of making land produce sustained annual crops of wildlife for recreational use." To produce that sustained annual crop for recreational use involves protection, regulation, and thus law enforcement. Without adequate law enforcement, the finest research and management programs would have little meaning. Illegal kill would reduce or exterminate most wildlife; the nation's limited wildlife population at the turn of the century showed this.

Law enforcement has come far since the old days of the country game warden. The conservation officer is no longer a politically hired "woods cop." He is a well trained generalist, charged with multiple duties, and often has a bachelor's degree in wildlife management. He spends only 60 percent of his time on law enforcement; the rest of it is spent in some phase of management (Table 1).

Law enforcement affects all other management programs. Look at the chapter headings in this manual. Law enforcement is and should be involved in nearly every one of them if they are to function well. After all, laws form the very foundation of resource management.

The modern conservation officer is uniformed, drives a marked car, and is responsible for most of the activities of his fish and game department in his area. His basic task is to enforce all state laws and regulations affecting wildlife. In some states, he may be required to enforce other laws such as those pertaining to water pollution, litter, forestry, parks, and boating. He is a peace officer in 12 states, authorized to enforce all state laws. There is no typical day for the conservation officer. It varies with the locality, the season, and particular wildlife problems.

Policy and Administration

Law enforcement personnel are vitally concerned with policy and administration. Both set the tone and scope of the enforcement effort, giving it guidance and furnishing necessary funds. Nationwide, enforcement personnel comprise over 30 percent of fish and game employees and use about a third of the budget. Conservation officers are the main contact that many citizens have with the resource agency. These daily efforts, small individually, serve to establish a valuable, acceptable image of the department statewide. The conservation officer's routine educational activities are a big factor in the general public's acceptance of laws and regulations and management programs. The conservation officer is often the first to locate areas of significant wildlife value for acquisition or easement by his department. In many states, he functions as the initial negotiator on acquisition projects.

Reprinted from: pp 120-123 in A Manual of Wildlife Conservation, R. D. Teague, Editor. The Wildlife Society, Washington, D.C. 206 pp.

The main source of revenue for department support is derived from the sale of hunting and fishing licenses. In the early days of law enforcement, the greatest enforcement effort was devoted to checking licenses. This is still important. Without general enforcement of the licensing laws, funds for all fish and game agencies would be seriously curtailed and programs would be reduced. If there were only one overriding reason that enforcement is a tool of management, license enforcement could be that one.

Analysis of any state system of laws and regulations will show that about half are not directly related to conservation of wildlife. Rather, they are to allow each hunter an equitable chance to share in the harvest. Such sociological regulation is necessary—but it adds obvious complications to the life and duties of the conservation officer. He is, in effect, a referee of the hunt and must adjust his attitudes and public contacts accordingly.

Wildlife Management

Conservation officers obtain much of the basic population data necessary for management by doing assigned wildlife census work. They also furnish extra protection for newly introduced species and usually participate in follow-up of success or failure of these animals.

The officer is usually responsible for managing special hunting seasons and operating checking stations to measure the harvest. He locates areas for wildlife habitat improvement; he sometimes helps with the physical work in improvement of the habitat. He frequently gives the landowner advice on how to improve his own property for fish and wildlife. He protects songbirds and other nonhunted wildlife. The State of Washington estimates that $200,000 a year of enforcement effort is devoted to nongame species and that much more effort is needed.

Some states give the conservation officer an active role in predator control. In others, it is only on his recommendation that predator control is undertaken.

Perhaps the most common wildlife management activity of the officer is handling wildlife damage problems. In most states, all but the largest chronic damage problems are routinely handled by the conservation officer. He may issue permits to the landowner to remove offending animals, trap them himself, or drive them away from areas where they are doing damage. He may furnish the landowner with repellents or panels to fence haystacks. Such activities are conducted within the scope of state laws, policy, and procedure.

Most conflicts between enforcement officers and wildlife managers have been due to poor internal communications. For example, the manager may not have convinced the officer of the value and necessity for a new program before it was presented to the public. It is essential to do this if the conservation officer's participation in management is to be effective and result in maximum public relations value.

Fisheries Management

Most activities by enforcement officers in fisheries management are related to measuring the catch and liberating hatchery-raised fish. A good share of creel census work, to find out how many fish are caught and thus determine fish numbers, is conducted by conservation officers. Exact methods are prescribed by the biologist and by the forms provided for reporting the information. The officer sometimes participates in stream improvement projects and often informs landowners about construction and management of farm ponds. In areas where trout fishing is a major activity, the conservation officer sometimes recommends allocations of hatchery-reared fish and usually participates in fish planting efforts.

The conservation officer is a front-line fighter in the war against pollution. Reports of fish kills and water pollution are usually received or discovered by the enforcement officer before any of the technical staff hears of it. In states or areas where pollution is a large problem, he may receive special training and work with highly trained pollution control biologists. Enforcement in this area is the most difficult, yet can be some of the most effective work the officer does.

Conservation Education

The conservation officer must be a Jack-of-all-trades, and particularly capable in conservation education. He is engaged in education every time he talks to somebody. Worth repeating is the fact that the conservation officer is the only member of the department that most hunters, fishermen, or the general public will ever see. As a result, the impressions he leaves and the information he gives them are of vital importance to public acceptance of the department's long-range programs. In addition to the individual contacts, the conservation officer is expected to attend sportsmen's meetings in his district, talk to school classes or assemblies about wildlife, and participate in summer camps for youth groups.

The conservation officer is the liaison officer between the landowner and the sportsman. Most cooperative small game hunting projects on private land are developed and patrolled by conservation officers. He usually teaches hunter safety classes and supervises volunteer hunter safety teachers.

As the officer becomes acquainted with business leaders, sportsmen, and others, he functions as an important citizen in his community. He belongs to, or at least attends meetings of, various civic organizations. Within two or three years, his advice will be sought in matters far afield from wildlife or conservation. Several conservation officers have assumed leadership in civic organizations; a number have been elected to such local offices as the school board. With such community trust and respect, the conservation officer can function at a high professional level as the conservation agency's local representative.

Supervision and Training

The conservation officer is the man who makes enforcement a tool of management. We have discussed some of the things he does that are directly related to management. Remember, however, that law enforcement itself is management, because without enforcement there would be no supplies of fish or wildlife to manage.

Law enforcement officers are usually well supervised, with from five to ten men reporting to a district supervisor. Effective enforcement efforts are closely related to this supervision and the attendant discipline. The best state programs usually have the best discipline—not an arrogant, authoritative discipline, but one where each man knows where he stands and what he can do.

The officer deals with three distinct kinds of violators:

1. the accidental violator, who has no intent to violate the law and has made a human mistake.
2. the opportunist violator, who leaves home with no intent to violate a law—but the fishing is so good, or the birds are so abundant in the adjacent closed area that he is carried away and goes after them.
3. the criminal, who leaves home with full intent to violate the law.

Each of these classes must be handled in a different manner. The officer must ask, "Will my handling of this case aid conservation and stimulate interest of this individual and his respect for law and the department?"

Administrators and biologists sometimes disagree with attitudes of conservation officers. They must remember that there are differences in how field problems can be solved. The biologist can make his study, go back to the office, search the literature, consult with experts and colleagues, and in a week or a month or more, reach a decision. The conservation officer, on the other hand, must make on-the-spot decisions, such as "Will I arrest or warn this man?" He then has to live with that decision. It may even involve him in a suit for false arrest or even be appealed to the Supreme Court. As Gilbert and Sullivan said, "A policeman's lot is not a happy one."

The conservation officer is in much the same position as a traffic enforcement officer. He deals with average citizens, not criminals. Most average citizens do not like to be told what to do, or be apprehended for what they consider minor infractions. Even though the conservation officer is respected in his community, he is often resented when performing his duty. Some of this may be due to actions of old-time wardens with a "manhunting" complex; some may stem from the present views of police by some young people. At any rate, the conservation officer, like a good policeman, has many acquaintances but few intimate friends.

The Idaho Fish and Game Commission recently adopted an official creed for its conservation officers that stresses the human relations of law enforcement:

"To assist the public in their compliance with regulations: to save unfortunate offenders from unnecessary humiliation, inconvenience, and distress; to have no compromise for crime and to resolutely seek the violator but with judgment charitable toward the minor offender; never to arrest if a citation will suffice; never to cite if a warning would be better; never to scold or reprimand, but rather to respect and inform."

Long-range effectiveness of the enforcement staff is closely related to the selection of new officers, their initial training, and their continuing education. Careful selection is a must. Initial training should be a formal mixture of classroom and field experience covering enforcement and all other field activities of the department. The best states spend at least three months on this phase.

Most states have an inadequate continuing or in-service training program. The usual three or four day personnel meeting each year accomplishes little training. It is essential, as it gives employees in a lonely job a feeling of belonging, and it brings them up-to-date on new laws and policies. It is not a substitute for frequent, short, intensive training periods conducted by specialists at the district and regional level.

There is a discernible trend to broaden the basic laws enforced by conservation officers. If this trend continues at its present rate, the conservation officer may soon become a recreation policeman, charged with enforcing all management and human conduct laws in an even smaller district. Enforcement programs must then have a broader financial base. Present funds will need to be supplemented by appropriations from general tax revenues and other agency appropriations.

Law enforcement is a tool of management—even more, law enforcement is the basis of management. Without a good, adequate enforcement program, other management tools are limited or nonexistent. It behooves administrator, biologist, educator, and sportsman alike to appreciate the values, contributions and needs of law enforcement and the law enforcement staff.

TABLE 1. How the Conservation Officer Spends his Time (Morse, 1968).

Section of the Country	Percent of Time						
	Enforce-ment	Game Mgt.	Fishery Mgt.	Hunter Safety	Youth Educ.	Public Relations	Misc.
West	57	12	7	3	2	9	13
Midwest	51	10	10	3	4	11	11
Northeast	65	7	7	2	3	9	7
Southeast	62	8	6	2	4	12	6
Nationwide	60	9	7.5	2.5	3	10	9

TABLE 2. Scope of the Conservation Officer's Job (Morse, 1968).

Item	West	Mid-west	North-east	South-east	Nation-wide
Arrests/C.O. (does not include super.)	43.9	38.2	28.6	42.6	39.3
Arrests/1000 Hunters and Fishermen	5.7	3.7	4.6	7.9	5.5
Arrests/1000 Square Miles	38.7	64.6	129.3	101.5	68.9
Average Fine Collected	$29.06	20.61	30.88	16.03	22.73
Percent of Convictions	98.8	97.3	97.7	93.7	95.8
No. Hunters and Fishermen/C.O.	7,871	10,090	6,043	5,540	7,160
No. C.O.'s with a Wildlife Degree	199	36	6	7	248
No. States Req. Wildlife Degree	7	2	0	0	9
No. States with no Residence Req.	6	2	4	2	14
Average Patrol Dist. in Square Miles	1,319	610	215	421	581

LITERATURE CITED

MORSE, W. B. 1968. Wildlife law enforcement, 1968. Proc. Western Assn. State Fish and Game Comm. pp. 683-694.

WILDLIFE LAW ENFORCEMENT AND RESEARCH NEEDS (1971)

Robert H. Giles, Jr.

Since the scientific revolution has permeated every aspect of modern life and since every wildlife agency has many scientifically trained men on its staff, it is an enigma that science seems scarcely to have touched that group of activities called wildlife law enforcement. It is true that the results of science are used by enforcement personnel. Radios, firearms, laboratory analyses of meats, and hair or bone identification are all a part of the daily routine. Nevertheless, there are few studies to determine effectiveness of enforcement activities, nature of the enforcement process or its consequences, characteristics of either violators or enforcement personnel, cost-benefit ratios, or significant differences resulting from different enforcement tactics or strategies.

Mr. W. B. Morse, of the Wildlife Management Institute, has sketched the magnitude of the enforcement program in the U.S. (1969). One hundred and fifty federal agents and over 5,500 rangers, wardens, conservation officers, and their supervisors (hereinafter called *agents*) patrol the states. These men represent 31 percent of the personnel of the state agencies and expend up to 38 percent of the total wildlife agency budget. Nationwide, agents perform many diverse tasks, but 60 percent of their time is spent on law enforcement.

Perhaps one reason for little research effort is that there has never appeared to be any "spare" money. All available money went into new positions, salary increases, or improved equipment. Each agent, on the average, is assigned 581 square miles, and has about 7,160 licensed hunters and fishermen and 3,000 to 5,000 non-sportsmen with which to work.

Another reason for lack of funds may be that appropriations through the Federal Aid to Wildlife Restoration program (Pittman-Robertson and Dingell-Johnson) specifically exclude law enforcement activities or education. There is ample justification, however, for expenditures of PR and DJ funds on carefully controlled wildlife law enforcement research (K. M. Shriner, personal communication). Such research is now in progress.

There is no strong tradition of research on law enforcement in general, so it is natural that wildlife law enforcement research should have been neglected. Its lack of status as a "profession" has probably been another factor (in 1969 only 9 of the states required a college degree of their conservation officers).

J. B. McCormick (1969), California enforcement agent, said that law enforcement personnel resist evaluation, possibly "because of an inherent resistance to close examination of our own activities for fear of what may be revealed. Whatever the reasons it has been passed over with the excuse that 'we just cannot measure the effects of law enforcement; we can't even say how many violations of the law occur, or the number that we prevent.' "

The major objectives of wildlife law enforcement have been (1) preventing law violation, (2) protecting "beneficial" species throughout their

Reprinted from: pp 131-133 in A Manual of Wildlife Conservation, R. D. Teague, Editor. The Wildlife Society, Washington, D.C. 206 pp.

breeding season, (3) rationing or assuring the sporting public a "fair share" of available game, and (4) requiring that those who enjoy or use the resource pay the bills.

The influence of the hunt (and thus game laws) on wildlife populations is recognized by many as one of the most important factors influencing game mortality and thus population dynamics and structure. Within wildlife agencies, the question of research priority is difficult. But law enforcement is so important to the wildlife resource, laws and regulations such a major technique for accomplishing wildlife management, and the number of people, capital investments, and proportionate expenditures for law enforcement activities are so large, that research on wildlife laws and their enforcement will become a future activity of research branches of game agencies or an essential part of ongoing enforcement group staffs. Research can become the corrective feedback essential for keeping such groups healthy and vigorous.

. . . .

I have outlined the major need, not to present a complete list, but to suggest appropriate avenues for investigators. All of the ideas seem feasible and require no major technological breakthroughs. Needed results can be produced by research contractors, those on special assignments within enforcement agencies, universities and wildlife graduate student programs, and interested individuals. By investing 2 to 5 percent of their annual budget, enforcement agencies could make significant inroads in the following problems within a few years.

The Violation
- Comparative studies of the psychological and socio-economic characteristics of the average sportsman and the convicted violator.
- Personal interviews with convicted poachers to determine their socio-economic level, education, reasons for poaching, attitudes toward agents, wildlife laws, and the courts as well as to appraise the influence of conviction and fines on their future action.
- Evaluation of wildlife crime rates among socio-economic strata of society and residents and non-residents.
- Descriptions of the psychology of the occasional and repetitive violator and poacher and how national trends in values, ethics, etc., may influence the incidence of illegal wildlife resource use.
- Studies of the causes of inadvertent wildlife law violation.

The Agent
- A comparative study of the psychology of and wildlife resource values held by the wildlife law enforcement agent in relation to other law enforcement agents, to wildlife managers, other wildlife agency personnel, and to socio-economic strata of the sporting and non-sporting public. Such studies could provide a guide for weighting the influence of each group on decisions about laws and regulations.
- A nationwide inventory of the agents wounded or killed while engaged in any aspect of wildlife law enforcement.

558

- Descriptions and evaluations of higher education opportunities for agents.

The Impact of Violations
- Comparisons of known deer (and other game) kills with sportsman-questionnaire reported kills, and the probabilities of reporting related to the number of contacts (i.e., a contact would be the act of an agent recording the license number on the animal check card). These studies have been conducted in New York by Hesselton and Maguire (1965) and provide the coefficients for rationally accounting for bias in reported kill.
- Questionnaire studies of observations by area managers on illegal species kills (like that by Barick, 1969, in which he reported that 20 percent of deer mortality is illegal).
- Studies of hunter submissions of waterfowl and game bird wings to obtain minimum estimates of kill of illegal species (such as during experimental teal seasons. Martinson et al., 1967).
- Expanded uses of the "spy blind" technique for evaluating crippling losses and illegal kill. The spy blind is a technique employed by an agent who watches, unknown to a hunter, the hunter's performance, records it, and later checks the actual performance with that reported in check stations or mail questionnaires. Data on rounds fired, time of shooting, cripples, and species-specific hunting can be obtained.
- Evaluations of poacher and spot-lighter activity using dummy deer and eye reflectors. (Entrapment is avoided; data are sought on characteristics of people in certain areas, on changes in behavior over time, or with factors like work layoffs.) Dummy ring-necked pheasants have also been used.
- Surveys (statewide and national) of illegal purchases of resident hunting and fishing licenses by non-residents. An indication of the scope of this problem can be obtained from returns of undeliverable post-season sportsmen questionnaires.
- Studies of simulated kills by poachers and the probability that they are detected. These studies can be used as a guide to the probability of agents detecting actual kills (Vilkitis, 1968) and for calculating within broad limits the illegal kill within a large area.

The Influence of Enforcement
- Comparisons of total effects of enforcement activities expended on "gangs" and market hunter type activities with expenditures on minor hunting regulation infractions.
- Appraisals of the ecological consequences of major wildlife laws and regulations, including application of the techniques of computer simulation.
- Literature studies and theoretical development of the concepts of "deterrence" and "prevention" as they relate to wildlife law and its enforcement. Evaluations of the punitive nature of wildlife convictions and fines and identification of the levels at which such fines inhibit violation. Comparative studies of the law and its enforcement under a preservation management philosophy (such as for rare or endangered species) and under alternate philosophies, such as multiple-use.

Improving Enforcement
- Model wildlife codes and criteria for judging such codes.
- Selection of design criteria for optimum law enforcement intelligence and information systems, including uniform reporting systems for states.
- Studies of game theory (e.g., war games) to increase the probability of the wildlife agency "winning" over the long run in "games" against poachers.
- Development of operations research for deploying agents, optimizing enforcement region size, and improving search strategies (e.g., applications of the methods of submarine warfare and search strategies to the apprehension of wildlife law violators).
- Optimizing radio networks for law wildlife enforcement.
- Applications of aerial photography to wildlife law enforcement, including infrared photography.
- Feasibility studies for regional (inter-state) wildlife law enforcement laboratories.
- Advances in techniques and methods useful in wildlife law violation detection and apprehension (e.g., the precipitin test for meat and blood identification, Brohn and Korschgen, 1950; paper chromatography for meat identification, Jackson, 1962).
- Time-motion-cost studies of the type done by efficiency experts in industries.

Effectiveness
- Studies of costs of enforcement by apprehensions, convictions, levels of activity, fines collected, estimated deterrence effects, violations detected, game population changes, and public resource use satisfactions: Walter Crissey provided the suggestion for this in 1965 when he said that "what some people fail to realize is that many of the solutions they think are possible only through habitat acquisition and management can be accomplished easier and far cheaper through regulations."
- Studies of the rates of increase in apprehensions and convictions with successive additions of agents to work areas.
- Studies of the influence of new ecological knowledge on laws, regulations, and their enforcement (e.g., Price, 1964).
- Studies of the reliability of agent diaries and reports by the use of electronic automobile "bugs" or "bumper beepers" attached to agent vehicles.
- Studies of the changes in big game populations with and without enforcement protection (currently underway in Oklahoma).

LITERATURE CITED
BARICK, F. B. 1969. Deer predation in North Carolina and other southeastern states. Southeastern deer symp., Nacogdoches, Texas, March 25.
BROHN, A. and L. J. KORSCHGEN. 1950. Precipitin test—a useful tool in game-law enforcement. Trans. N. Amer. Wildl. Conf. 15:467-478.
HESSELTON, W. T. and H. F. MAGUIRE. 1965. Report on percentage of hunters reporting the deer they take—1964. A separate report PR Project W-89-R-9, Job VII-C, Albany, New York. 4 p. (mimeo).

JACKSON, C. F. 1962. Use of paper chromatography in identifying meat of game animals. New Hampshire Fish and Game Dept., Tech. Circ. 19. 13 p.

MARTINSON, R. K., E. M. MARTIN, C. F. KACZYNSKI, and M. G. SMART. 1967. 1966 experimental September hunting season on teal. Admin. Rept. No. 127, Migratory Bird Population Station, Laurel, Maryland.

MCCORMICK, J. B. 1969. Trends in wildlife law enforcement: program management, a "systems" concept. Assoc. of Game, Fish and Conserv. Comm., New Orleans. 9 p. (mimeo).

MORSE, W. B. 1969. Law enforcement. The Wildl. Soc. News, No. 119. p. 51.

PRICE, J. L. 1964. Use of new knowledge in organizations. Human Organization 23:3, 224-234.

VILKITIS, J. R. 1968. Characteristics of big game violators and extent of their activity in Idaho. Unpub. M.S. Thesis, Univ. Idaho, Moscow. 202 p.

MANAGEMENT

The essence of management is decision-making. Wildlife management consists of a selection of goals and a series of decisions: whether to have a long or a short hunting season; whether to plant food patches or to manipulate vegetation with fire or herbicides; whether to spend money on a game-check station or on a forage survey; whether to compromise optimum-yield goals with the prevailing opinions of an inadequately informed public or to begin a public education program.

Just as there are many ways to manage a farm or a forest, there are many ways to manage a quail population, a deer herd or a songbird habitat. Public or private policy may elect to emphasize some wildlife values and not others. Thus management objectives vary, and there may be several ways to reach the same set of objectives. Each population and each habitat is in some way unique. Therefore each management opportunity is a separate challenge, requiring new decision-making. These papers illustrate the variety of problems confronting wildlife managers.

The first three papers in this section concern the selection of management goals, the gathering of information as a basis for management, and the decision-making process. These are followed by six papers primarily on habitat management, four primarily on population management, and a management case study.

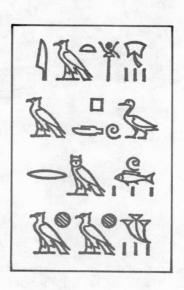

CHANGING CONCEPTS AND NEEDS IN WILDLIFE MANAGEMENT (1962)

Harold E. Alexander

Wildlife management is the art of producing sustained populations of wild vertebrates for man's convenience, pleasure and use. Which wild vertebrates? Which combination of uses? Who will enjoy and use the wildlife? These are important questions regarding goals of management. Goals must be reconsidered from time to time, especially goals for a public wildlife resource. This paper expresses concern that perhaps the profession of wildlife management is seeking outmoded goals. What of the future? Will recreation hunting remain an important value? Will we return to wildlife as an important source of food? Will nonconsumptive uses of wildlife be pre-eminent? (Perhaps they now are!)

In a little more than a half century we have seen tremendous changes in our surrounding world. Within that time our population has more than doubled, vast acreages of land and water have been altered from their original condition, and we have developed the tools and techniques to change the total environment of men and animals radically and permanently. The majority of our people have become urbanized and transient. Each day we move mountains, cut down whole forests, drain more marshes and wetlands, and engineer vast alterations in the world about us; and we have developed the means and techniques to effect even greater changes in the future to the extent that we may live in a man made world. From an agrarian "horse and buggy" way of life, we have emerged into a high speed, mechanized and specialized society. Like travelers speeding along a highway, we have lost sight of many of our goals and objectives, while concentrating on the dangers of momentary and sudden oblivion. To avoid losing our way, it is essential that we stop occasionally to determine our position and re-establish our destination. Without reappraisal, we tend to become lost in a maze of single objectives, each of which leads to a dead end or a blind alley.

In making such a reappraisal, we need to determine, first, just what we are after; whether we simply want to produce more game, fish or fowl, or whether we want to fuse all the single objectives we have, as a people, into that fundamental goal directed at preservation of an adequate environment for man. In achieving single purposes, which limit our vision, we often lose sight of the road ahead and in so doing, fail to give attention to that destination which is concerned with human welfare. The goal of those of us in the wildlife field is, fundamentally, to save and perpetuate many things for many people. This has been defined as making "the world safe for its diversity" (Anon 1962). We must keep our eyes fixed ahead on this purpose even though we wander and diversify our efforts in arriving at that end.

All this is very high sounding and may seem unrelated to what we do. If we look back at the record, however, I think we will see that we

Reprinted from: Proc. Ann. Conf. S.E. Assoc. Game and Fish Comm. 16:161-167.

have often nullified our efforts in following leads which took us into those blind alleys to which I have referred.

Looking Backward

The idea of conserving resources of any kind goes back only a short time. Theodore Roosevelt, as we all know, was among the first dynamic proponents of saving natural resources, including wildlife, in this country. Before that time, it was largely assumed that all resources were either inexhaustible or that each man had the right to take of those resources as freely as he saw fit. The development of a "high standard" of living, in a material sense, called for accelerating resource use, and constant production and use of goods to satisfy new desires and create profits. The conservation idea did, however, "catch on". We did begin to realize that some resources would disappear if we didn't act to save them.

The conservation idea first was applied to those things we needed for material development—minerals, soil, plants, water, and animals. Pengelly (1962) points out that resource conservation problems are of two types, "Survival" and "Enjoyment", and he refers to the "enjoyment" type as "the qualities that enrich our lives . . . space to live in and space to play in, wild scenery to enjoy and wild animals to observe, hunt or photograph". He comments further that textbooks deal with the "stand-ard subjects" leaving out ". . . the conservation of human resources . . ." referred to as "social capital."

The application of the "survival" resources principle to wildlife management has resulted in our attempts to calculate wildlife values and benefits in terms of numbers, or pounds or dollars worth, and this system has left us in the position of accepting "fringe benefits", after all other postulated economic and monetary desires were satisfied, which in many cases has left us holding an empty sack, and ignoring basic human needs.

Leopold was among the first to concern himself with the preserva-tion of environments in which wildlife forms could live. Prior to his monumental work "Game Management" (1933), the efforts of conserva-tion-minded scientists were largely directed at classifying living forms and at preserving dried specimens for future generations to compare and classify. Wildlife was either looked upon as inexhaustible or doomed to extinction. In his book, Leopold reviewed the history of game manage-ment, or rather attempts at preservation. He took us, chronologically, through the formulation of restrictions and laws limiting wildlife use, through the development of refuges, game farms, efforts to preserve wildlife through elimination of predators, and up to the earliest efforts at area management; and he ended his observations by concluding that man must develop an "ecological consciousness" and awareness of his relation to all living things if he was to save these resources and himself.

Wildlife management, as we interpret it, really began about the time of the establishment of the wildlife research units some 25 years ago. There were, of course, numerous practitioners before that time, but wildlife management as a profession developed with the establishment of a positive system of education to train biologists and managers. Since then, we have in some respects come a long way. In others, we have failed or floundered about, without accomplishing our purposes.

Let us look at some of our failures and accomplishments. Some of both have been due to forces over which we have had no control; others were undoubtedly due to mis-directed efforts or motivations or both.

We can take credit for doing away with many practices which were useless or even detrimental. Such misdirected efforts as large scale stocking, indiscriminate killing of carnivores, "Buck" laws, and undue restrictions on hunting have given or are gradually giving way to the knowledge that these practices are ineffectual or even detrimental. Improvements have come about as a result of the applications of knowledge and research to action. We have some shining examples of the applications of research findings carried on by wildlife biologists. We have, for example, the work done by State and Federal agencies who became concerned with the effects of pesticides on wildlife. It is largely due to these investigations that there has come about a concern over the use of poisons to control what we believe to be noxious organisms. Although the use of poisons which contaminate our environment continues, the growing public awareness of the problem is the first step toward control. This has been and is a most important contribution to knowledge and its use, and we can take much credit for what has been learned.

We can also look at increases in some of the more desirable (from our viewpoint) species with assurance that we may have them with us for a long time. The white tailed deer is one example. We can assume credit for getting them "restored" to huntable numbers, but I think we must realize at the same time that after we gave them a "boost" through protection and stocking, they came back largely under their own "steam", and because environments resulting from the uses of land fitted their particular needs. With proper management, we should have and be able to hunt deer for a long time to come.

Much of our recently acquired knowledge has, in a sense, been used to limit or prevent unwise courses of action; which have changed with new circumstances. This is demonstrated by the buck law, once valid, but now a detriment to good practices. In general, one of our most pertinent contributions is the use of knowledge to educate, to create a better understanding of goals, needs and purposes, and public recognition and acceptance of what is better or best. This education in understanding is possibly our most difficult task.

On the other hand, we have not even begun to solve some of the major problems confronting us, and in some directions we seem to be progressing backward. Each day we are confronted with the accelerated impact of increasing human use of resources and particularly land use, for "practical" profit motives, which serve single objectives or the interests of a few; or are dedicated to "multiple use" purposes, meaning their dedication to the interests of a particular group or interest. Some uses cancel out other uses. You cannot, for example, pollute a river and have it serve quality recreational purposes at the same time. Carver (1961) in discussing the proposed dedication of lands to wilderness, observed that "you can't put a mule, a miner, and a picnicker on the same ground at the same time", which observation pretty well describes the fallacy of any consistent application of this concept.

Too, we have not been able to evaluate or instill the concept of quality considerations, ignoring the obvious tenet that enjoyment, happiness, and cultural betterments are benefits to be derived from resources, individually and collectively, and that these considerations are of great importance.

One of our greatest needs is the proper orientation of our efforts to needs and purposes. Looking back, I think we can see much misdirected effort and much concern with matters having relatively little relation to the compelling problems we face. In an effort to determine the scope of our interests and professional concerns, two major abstracting journals *"Wildlife Review"* and the *"Biological Abstracts"* were periodically examined for evidence of interests and trends as indicated by papers published on wildlife, ecological and conservation subjects. No effort was made to conduct a complete review of these abstracts, since this entailed efforts beyond the scope of this paper. Rather, this review can best be described as a "spot check", spaced at random over the past 15 years. Too, in a cursory survey of this type, it was not possible to classify every paper or study under a precise category. Many titles do not lend themselves to accurate classification, or their direct relation to the categories encompassing our interests was tenuous or indefinite. This "check" did, however, demonstrate one thing. There was vastly more concern with and effort given to particularized studies aimed at obtaining data on segments of the larger categories of interest, than with evaluation of purpose or concern with the solution of problems which dominate patterns of resource use, and which prevent or inhibit the perpetuation of wildlife and resources referred to as "enjoyment" resources. The papers covering the fundamental concepts of conservation, its purposes or philosophy, in other words, its basic objectives, were few and far between. Likewise, concern with research methods or education was apparently of far less significance to the professional worker than his preoccupation with techniques of management, wildlife control, food habits, life histories or disease. Indications are that his primary interests and efforts were given to compiling data on various limited segments of his special field of endeavor. Now we can assume that this is the way science works, piece by piece, but somewhere there must be an effort to tie these pieces into a comprehensive whole, or relate them to the problems of conservation, and these efforts were minor and few in number.

It was also apparent that major problems affecting wildlife were given comparatively little attention by authors contributing to the professional journals. These abstracts do not represent the sum total of professional work, but they are, I believe, representative of his dominant interests, and demonstrate allocations of time and effort to what professionals believed to be the proper application of their knowledge.

Another discrepancy appears in evaluating the relation of efforts to purposes, if we can assume that our purpose is resource conservation. This is exemplified by the relatively limited amount of work done to establish criteria for the determination of intangible or quality values, or balance scarcity and diminishing supplies to increased worth and sentimental values. We have, it seems, become so "intimidated by (a)

. . . hard boiled approach to life" that we feel "sheepish about acknowledging the existence inside of (us) of that which distinguishes us most from the ape" (Anon 1962). Admittedly, the creation or delineation of standards of this kind is difficult in the extreme. But we must acknowledge that we are certain to lose many of those things we cherish unless we evaluate and establish standards of measurement for sentimental and esthetic values, and educate people to recognize these standards.

Looking back at the things we have written about and published, we note that abstracts presented in Wildlife Review fifteen years ago (1946 and 1947) were mainly concerned with such subjects as management techniques, wildlife control, food habits, diseases, and life history data. During those years (in 7 volumes), there were only two references to philosophy or purposes, 16 on education, and 13 topics concerned with research evaluation and technique. It is notable that, although the preservation of ducks was then as now a problem of major concern, only two papers discussed wetlands and drainage, while there were 62 titles on such subjects as food habits, specification and movements. Even then, we were painfully aware that the preservation of wetlands was the key to the perpetuation of waterfowl. With this consideration in view, why didn't we do more work to demonstrate and prove the absolute necessity of breeding grounds to ducks?

Further along, in 1954 and 1955 (6 volumes), we find 7 references to wetlands in this abstracting Journal, and 153 have reference to ducks in general. Again, in 1960 and 1961 (6 volumes), we find 13 references to wetlands, and 153 references on waterfowl food habits, or other life history details. Our increased interest in waterfowl and awareness of their critical situation is apparent, but what about the problem of saving ducks?

We have already noted that we recognize the significance of basic data, but what could be more basic to waterfowl conservation, our declared objective, than the preservation of habitats essential to their existence? We must also admit that the forces of destruction, dedicated to other purposes, are stronger and better entrenched, but at least we might give more of our time and efforts to the basic problems, unless, like the early systematists, we are mainly interested in saving a few museum specimens. It is axiomatic that without information to substantiate our arguments, we cannot make a case for the preservation of wildlife or anything else.

Today, as evidenced by the subjects of our published papers, we note that a large part of our concern still seems to be with particularized investigations of foods, habits, movements, life histories and other detailed and limited, single objective "studies". We have, I believe, avoided or failed to give the larger part of our professional efforts in solving basic problems in conservation. As I have observed there are some notable exceptions. Our concern with pesticides is one example, and another is the increasing concern with water problems and such nebulous considerations as wilderness and open space. The pressures about us are directing awareness to these intangible needs.

To make our point, we need more research of the right kind, and directed at crucial problems. Nace (1957) has observed that ". . . knowledge is costly, but it is cheap compared to the cost of ignorances', and further, "The important need is not for massive accumulations of data, but for *understanding.*"

There is the suspicion, and some evidence that too many professional scientists of all types are mainly concerned with establishment of their reputations by multitudious if "minuscule" writings, and their progress has been compared with "that of the squid, which moves rapidly backward, at the same time emitting large quantities of ink." (Kopac 1961).

Sears (1961) has stated that "One may mine a cul-de-sac with thoroughness, but unless he knows why he is doing it, and has facilities for getting his product out in some sensible relation to the (problem) . . . his efforts are likely to be wasted." More attention to acquiring data directed at the key problems in resource use and preservation and their purposes, and less "ink" emitted while progressing. backward might help in the conservation of wildlife, and the preservation of an environment of "quality" for man. Most of our problems are due to the impact of mechanized man on environment. To create "understanding" of the biological relationship of wildlife and man to environment, and feeling or desire to preserve "diversity" in a changing world—these are our purposes. We must have hindsight and foresight, which add up to knowledge, to work toward these ends.

Looking Ahead

Udall (quoting Leopold) stated that ". . . all history consists of successive excursions from a single starting point to which men return, again and again, to organize, to start another search for a durable set of values". In this discussion of needs and concepts, we have taken a brief look backward. We have noted progress and shortcomings. We have reached a point both in time and in our professions where we need to take stock and reorganize our purposes to meet changing circumstances and the needs of the future which bear down upon us. The horizon of the future is immense. Sears comments that ". . . biological science is not only expanding into realms of the infinitely small, but broadening into the baffling and difficult realm of the intangible". We have large responsibilities, and meager tools to accomplish what needs to be done. Our problems include ecological, social, political and economic considerations. In these respects, they are no different from the problems confronting other men in our time.

Looking back we can see our mistakes, and looking forward we can see, if we look closely, some of the things that need to be done. Among these things is the need for "generalization" of our efforts if we are to "put our jigsaw pieces of information into meaningful patterns". (Bates 1960). In discussing our past efforts, we have noted the multiplicity of our interests and our apparent preoccupation with a "piecemeal" approach to conservation. With reference to the enormous number of scientific papers written and published, it has been stated that if "placed end to end they will reach to utter confusion" (Zirkle 1961). To avoid this "utter confusion" we must concentrate our efforts, in the future, on the more critical issues. If we don't, some of the things we want to save will no longer be objects for concern. They simply won't exist.

We need intensified efforts to gather information on basic issues affecting resources. This is particularly needed in the field of water resources. With our present system of developments, with single or limited objectives, we are, to quote Voigt (N.D.) "freezing water into inflexible patterns of use". Water developments are "terribly" permanent. Clawson and Fox (1961) have observed that "if we build a dam that floods out a beautiful river valley, we have foreclosed its use for recreation (and scenic appreciation) . . . forever". This points up the need for protecting the intangibles which are part of our heritage and contribute to our physical, emotional and spiritual welfare. In the light of population pressures, even the problem of "space" conservation has become a matter of immediate concern.

We can, if we wish, ignore this reference to quality preservation and stick closely to the task of producing more game. We can do this expediently on game farms, but artificiality reduces quality and the product becomes "commonplace". Shooting tame ducks cast from a ramp can never equal the rewards in body and spirit that comes to the man who takes his birds over a misty wild marsh at dawn.

In the future, we need to heed that admonishment to become "generalists." We must have sufficient understanding of other sciences so that the efforts of all scientists can be merged towards the common goals of human betterment. Overspecialization warps our vision, and we lose sight of that goal we should keep in view—the preservation of "diversity" to meet the needs of men. We must, somehow, arrive at better systems for using all we know.

We should look upon "preservation" of natural resources as having equal importance with what we term management. There are some things we can't improve. In support of this concept Pengelly (1962) said, "There are some resources, however, that cannot be purchased or created, and these are the immediate cause of concern. Space is such a resource and quality is its attribute. The . . . headlong trend toward mass use or mass abuse of every square foot of the globe poses serious threats both to our standard of living and to our survival as a people . . ., blind development may degrade our society rather than enhance it".

We need to be more concerned with education in resource appreciation and use. In a sense, all of us must be educators, since our integral relationship with the earth and its resources must, to some degree, become generally understood, or we face the degradation of our environment and ourselves.

Problems needing immediate and concerted attention include more intensive studies of pesticides, of water resources, of social factors in resource use, establishment of standards for evaluating "quality" values, and immediate action to preserve natural environments for wildlife and men. Our singleminded objectiveness is leading us into fixed courses of actions which, once taken, are irreversible. We need refreshment of "spirit and mind" as well as clothing, food and shelter. Good habitat for wildlife has qualities that are also necessary to our well being.

571

Nace (1959) commented that (resources) "must be managed with the understanding that there will be a tomorrow—and a very long one—we hope", and Udall, speaking before the White House Conference on Conservation (1962) commented, that the piecemeal approach of the past toward resource problems will not suffice for the 1960's. We are in a period of last chances—the overriding need of man "for an environment that will renew the human spirit and sustain unborn generations . . . requires sacrifices of short term profits".

There are straws in the wind that suggest that we have, at least, heard these admonitions. We have a job to do, and we must keep our attention on a broadening horizon and try to meet the challenges of the future. The path ahead is strewn with difficulties for all men living in these times.

References Cited

ANON. "A Community of Hope and Responsibility", Sat. Rev. June 16, 1962, pp. 12-14.

BATES, MARSTON. "The Forest and the Sea", The New American Library, 1960.

CARVER, JOHN A., JR., "Miners Get Dutch Uncle Talk For Opposing Wilderness Bill", Nat. Wildlands News, Nov. 1961, p. 4.

CLAWSON, M. and IRVING FOX. "Your Investments in Land and Water", American Forests, 67(1): 5-10 and 53-56.

KOPAC, MILAN, JR. "Cellular Biology", Bio. Abst. 36(8): XII-XIII, Apr. 1961.

NACE, R.L. "Address Before the Texas Water Conservation Ass." Dallas, Texas, Oct. 19, 1959, pp. 1-9.

PENGELLY, W. LESLIE. "The Art of Social Conservation", paper presented at Ann. Conf. of Central Mts. and Plains States, Section, Wildlife Society, Aug. 17, 1962.

UDALL, STEWART L. "Proceedings, White House Conference on Conservation", Washington D.C. May 24-25, 1962.

VOIGT, WILLIAM, JR. "Water Policy Problems East and West", Paper, available from U.S.F. and W. Ser., n.d.

ZIRKLE, O. CONWAY. "Genetic Biology", Bio. Absts. 36(8): XVI—XVII, Apr. 1961.

THE WILDLIFE MANAGEMENT PLAN (1938)
R. T. King

King's five-step plan was evolved from Aldo Leopold's outline in his text, Game Management, and provides a logical approach to decision-making in wildlife management. The first four steps are information-gathering and analysis, emphasizing the importance of data as a basis for management decisions. Selecting the population and/or habitat parameters to be measured and used as a basis for management is one of the most important decisions of the wildlife manager.

If, for the sake of brevity, we conceive of a wildlife management program as consisting of five steps, namely: inventory, census, yield determination, diagnosis and control, it is not difficult to show that each of these steps must deal as much with environments as with the wildlife. In fact certain of the steps deal almost entirely with the environment and are concerned with the wildlife only indirectly. This is not to be interpreted as meaning that the wildlife is of secondary importance in the management program. On the contrary the primary aim of management is the maintenance of a satisfactory wildlife population, and we must always in final analysis reason from environment to wildlife. It is, however, essential that a proper and satisfactory environment be provided and maintained if an annual wildlife crop is to be produced.

Hasty analysis of the five fundamental steps of the management program will adequately illustrate the extent to which management must concern itself with environments.

First, the inventory determines what species of animals are present on the area in question and their distribution over the area. This, however, is only half of the inventory and is usually the less difficult half to accomplish. A complete inventory must determine in addition what species of food and cover plants occur on the area, their distribution, the distances separating them, their seasonal availability to the various animal species present, their accessibility to enemies, their exposure to the elements, and their trend as indicated by local cultural developments or natural succession or both.

Second, censusing is conducted in order to ascertain how much wildlife is present on the area. Unfortunately we usually think of censusing as having to do only with the wildlife of an area, this, however, is not true, or, at least, should not be true. It is equally important that we know how much habitable and productive, actual and potential, wildlife environment occurs on the area. It is not sufficient in this connection to measure the acreages of the various food and cover-producing species. The measurements must be carried to the point where they indicate not only acreages but show also the extent of interspersion of the various types, the degree of juxtaposition existing between the types, and the

Excerpted from: The essentials of a wildlife range. J. Forestry 36(5):457-464, by permission from the Society of American Foresters. The accompanying figure is from: Forest Zoology and its relation to a wildlife program as applied on the Huntington Forest. Roosevelt Wildlife Bull. 7(4):461-505.

amount and distribution of the peripheral types present. The existence of cruising radii and saturation points makes interspersion and juxtaposition the two most important considerations in any wildlife environment where there is present any food and cover at all. These ideas were first clearly expressed by Leopold (1931).

Third, yield determination as applied to the wildlife of an area measures the annual productivity; as applied to the environment, it is concerned with the quality, condition and availability of the various cover types; and the palatability, availability, dependability, yield, persistence, and location with reference to cover of the various food species. Yield determination, as far as the environment is concerned, is not simply a measure of the number of acres of the various food and cover species. It is, instead, a determination of the amount of habitable cover and available foods and an evaluation of the annual productivity of this combined food and cover. It is often the case that a measure of the annual increment of the wildlife on an area affords a means of determining environmental productivity, but this is an indirect method and frequently very difficult to accomplish. Furthermore, it is always necessary to make a complete yield determination of an environment before any proper diagnosis can be made. It is, therefore, only sound logic to complete the yield determination before attempting either diagnosis or control.

Fourth, diagnosis has almost entirely to do with the environment. After completion of the inventory, censusing and yield determination one must conclude either that the wildlife populations are all that they should be or that they are something other than they should be. If they are something other than they should be the explanation must be sought in the environment. The three steps in diagnosis are: (1) recognition of the factors operating against the various species (2) evaluation of the effects of these factors, and (3) choosing the limiting factor. It is obvious that the first step is almost entirely concerned with the environment for the factors operating against the various species are in nearly every instance environmental factors. Evaluation of the effects of these individual environmental factors is usually a matter of further censusing unless accurate life equation tables for the species in question on the area under consideration are already available (this is rarely the case in our present state of management knowledge). To successfully choose the limiting factor necessitates not only a thorough knowledge of each of the environmental factors and a keen appreciation of their relative values but involves in addition a clear understanding of the past history of the environments, their present trend, and their future probabilities.

Fifth, control measures are indicated by the results of the diagnosis and consist for the most part of modifications of the environment. Here again a thorough knowledge of the environment is of primary importance. Environmental manipulations are the basis of all control. In only exceptional cases are control measures applied directly to animal populations and in those rare instances when this does occur it is simply a preliminary step to environmental control.

574

REFERENCE

LEOPOLD, A. 1931. Game range. J. Forestry 29:932-938.

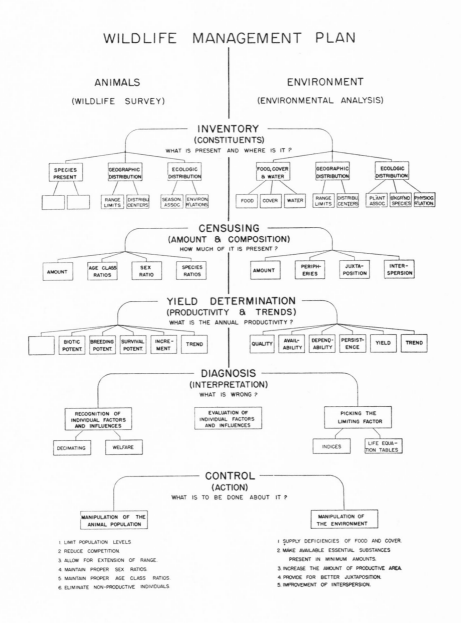

Figure 62-1.—Wildlife Management Plan.

THE SCIENCE OF "MUDDLING THROUGH" (1959)
Charles E. Lindblom

In this paper Lindblom addresses pragmatic aspects of managing a complex, publicly-owned resource. While his examples are from the fields of economics and sociology, his conclusions apply equally to wildlife management. College training of wildlife biologists often emphasizes theory and the rational-comprehensive method of decision-making. Yet practicing wildlife managers rely heavily on local experience providing empirical knowledge of habitats and populations. Often only limited or slow changes in management practices are possible under political or economic restraints. Most, if not all, wildlife managers, having limited information and faced with these restraints, practice Lindblom's method of successive limited comparisons in their management decision-making.

Suppose an administrator is given responsibility for formulating policy with respect to inflation. He might start by trying to list all related values in order of importance, e.g., full employment, reasonable business profit, protection of small savings, prevention of a stock market crash. Then all possible policy outcomes could be rated as more or less efficient in attaining a maximum of these values. This would of course require a prodigious inquiry into values held by members of society and an equally prodigious set of calculations on how much of each value is equal to how much of each other value. He could then proceed to outline all possible policy alternatives. In a third step, he would undertake systematic comparison of his multitude of alternatives to determine which attains the greatest amount of values.

In comparing policies, he would take advantage of any theory available that generalized about classes of policies. In considering inflation, for example, he would compare all policies in the light of the theory of prices. Since no alternatives are beyond his investigation, he would consider strict central control and the abolition of all prices and markets on the one hand and elimination of all public controls with reliance completely on the free market on the other, both in the light of whatever theoretical generalizations he could find on such hypothetical economies.

Finally, he would try to make the choice that would in fact maximize his values.

An alternative line of attack would be to set as his principal objective, either explicitly or without conscious thought, the relatively simple goal of keeping prices level. This objective might be compromised or complicated by only a few other goals, such as full employment. He would in fact disregard most other social values as beyond his present interest, and he would for the moment not even attempt to rank the few values that he regarded as immediately relevant. Were he pressed, he would quickly admit that he was ignoring many related values and many possible important consequences of his policies.

Reprinted from: Public Administration Review 19(2): 79-88.

As a second step, he would outline those relatively few policy alternatives that occurred to him. He would then compare them. In comparing his limited number of alternatives, most of them familiar from past controversies, he would not ordinarily find a body of theory precise enough to carry him through a comparison of their respective consequences. Instead he would rely heavily on the record of past experience with small policy steps to predict the consequences of similar steps extended into the future.

Moreover, he would find that the policy alternatives combined objectives or values in different ways. For example, one policy might offer price level stability at the cost of some risk of unemployment; another might offer less price stability but also less risk of unemployment. Hence, the next step in his approach—the final selection—would combine into one the choice among values and the choice among instruments for reaching values. It would not, as in the first method of policy-making, approximate a more mechanical process of choosing the means that best satisfied goals that were previously clarified and ranked. Because practitioners of the second approach expect to achieve their goals only partially, they would expect to repeat endlessly the sequence just described, as conditions and aspirations changed and as accuracy of prediction improved.

By Root or by Branch

For complex problems, the first of these two approaches is of course impossible. Although such an approach can be described, it cannot be practiced except for relatively simple problems and even then only in a somewhat modified form. It assumes intellectual capacities and sources of information that men simply do not possess, and it is even more absurd as an approach to policy when the time and money that can be allocated to a policy problem is limited, as is always the case. Of particular importance to public administrators is the fact that public agencies are in effect usually instructed not to practice the first method. That is to say, their prescribed functions and constraints—the politically or legally possible—restrict their attention to relatively few values and relatively few alternative policies among the countless alternatives that might be imagined. It is the second method that is practiced.

Curiously, however, the literatures of decision-making, policy formulation, planning, and public administration formalize the first approach rather than the second, leaving public administrators who handle complex decisions in the position of practicing what few preach. For emphasis I run some risk of overstatement. True enough, the literature is well aware of limits on man's capacities and of the inevitability that policies will be approached in some such style as the second. But attempts to formalize rational policy formulation—to lay out explicitly the necessary steps in the process—usually describe the first approach and not the second.[1]

The common tendency to describe policy formulation even for complex problems as though it followed the first approach has been strengthened by the attention given to, and successes enjoyed by, operations research, statistical decision theory, and systems analysis. The hallmarks of these procedures, typical of the first approach, are clarity of objective, explicitness of evaluation, a high degree of comprehensiveness of overview, and, wherever possible, quantification of values for mathematical analysis. But these advanced procedures remain largely the appropriate techniques of relatively small-scale problem-solving where the total number of variables to be considered is small and value problems restricted. Charles Hitch, head of the Economics Division of RAND Corporation, one of the leading centers for application of these techniques, has written:

> I would make the empirical generalization from my experience at RAND and elsewhere that operations research is the art of sub-optimizing, i.e., of solving some lower-level problems, and that difficulties increase and our special competence diminishes by an order of magnitude with every level of decision making we attempt to ascend. The sort of simple explicit model which operations researchers are so proficient in using can certainly reflect most of the significant factors influencing traffic control on the George Washington Bridge, but the proportion of the relevant reality which we can represent by any such model or models in studying, say, a major foreign-policy decision, appears to be almost trivial.[2]

Accordingly, I propose in this paper to clarify and formalize the second method, much neglected in the literature. This might be described as the method of *successive limited comparisons.* I will contrast it with the first approach, which might be called the rational-comprehensive method.[3] More impressionistically and briefly—and therefore generally used in this article—they could be characterized as the branch method and root method, the former continually building out from the current situation, step-by-step and by small degrees; the latter starting from fundamentals anew each time, building on the past only as experience is embodied in a theory, and always prepared to start completely from the ground up.

Let us put the characteristics of the two methods side by side in simplest terms.

Rational-Comprehensive (Root)

1a. Clarification of values or objectives distinct from and usually prerequisite to empirical analysis of alternative policies.

2a. Policy-formulation is therefore approached through means-end analysis: First the ends are isolated, then the means to achieve them are sought.

3a. The test of a "good" policy is that it can be shown to be the most appropriate means to desired ends.

4a. Analysis is comprehensive; every important relevant factor is taken into account.

5a. Theory is often heavily relied upon.

Assuming that the root method is familiar and understandable, we proceed directly to clarification of its alternative by contrast. In explaining the second, we shall be describing how most administrators do in fact approach complex questions, for the root method, the "best" way as a blueprint or model, is in fact not workable for complex policy questions, and administrators are forced to use the method of successive limited comparisons.

Successive Limited Comparisons (Branch)

1b. Selection of value goals and empirical analysis of the needed action are not distinct from one another but are closely intertwined.
2b. Since means and ends are not distinct, means-end analysis is often inappropriate or limited.
3b. The test of a "good" policy is typically that various analysts find themselves directly agreeing on a policy (without their agreeing that it is the most appropriate means to an agreed objective).
4b. Analysis is drastically limited:
  i) Important possible outcomes are neglected.
  ii) Important alternative potential policies are neglected.
  iii) Important affected values are neglected.
5b. A succession of comparisons greatly reduces or eliminates reliance on theory.

Intertwining Evaluation and Empirical Analysis (1b)
The quickest way to understand how values are handled in the method of successive limited comparisons is to see how the root method often breaks down in *its* handling of values or objectives. The idea that values should be clarified, and in advance of the examination of alternative policies, is appealing. But what happens when we attempt it for complex social problems? The first difficulty is that on many critical values or objectives, citizens disagree, congressmen disagree, and public administrators disagree. Even where a fairly specific objective is prescribed for the administrator, there remains considerable room for disagreement on sub-objectives. Consider, for example, the conflict with respect to locating public housing, described in Meyerson and Banfield's study of the Chicago Housing Authority[4]—disagreement which occurred despite the clear objective of providing a certain number of public housing units in the city. Similarly conflicting are objectives in highway location, traffic control, minimum wage administration, development of tourist facilities in national parks, or insect control.

Administrators cannot escape these conflicts by ascertaining the majority's preference, for preferences have not been registered on most issues; indeed, there often *are* no preferences in the absence of public discussion sufficient to bring an issue to the attention of the electorate. Furthermore, there is a question of whether intensity of feeling should be considered as well as the number of persons preferring each alternative. By the impossibility of doing otherwise, administrators often are reduced to deciding policy without clarifying objectives first.

Even when an administrator resolves to follow his own values as a criterion for decisions, he often will not know how to rank them when they conflict with one another, as they usually do. Suppose, for example, that an administrator must relocate tenants living in tenements scheduled for destruction. One objective is to empty the buildings fairly promptly, another is to find suitable accommodation for persons displaced, another is to avoid friction with residents in other areas in which a large influx would be unwelcome, another is to deal with all concerned through persuasion if possible, and so on.

How does one state even to himself the relative importance of these partially conflicting values? A simple ranking of them is not enough; one needs ideally to know how much of one value is worth sacrificing for some of another value. The answer is that typically the administrator chooses—and must choose—directly among policies in which these values are combined in different ways. He cannot first clarify his values and then choose among policies.

A more subtle third point underlies both the first two. Social objectives do not always have the same relative values. One objective may be highly prized in one circumstance, another in another circumstance. If, for example, an administrator values highly both the dispatch with which his agency can carry through its projects *and* good public relations, it matters little which of the two possibly conflicting values he favors in some abstract or general sense. Policy questions arise in forms which put to administrators such a question as: Given the degree to which we are or are not already achieving the values of dispatch and the values of good public relations, is it worth sacrificing a little speed for a happier clientele, or is it better to risk offending the clientele so that we can get on with our work? The answer to such a question varies with circumstances.

The value problem is, as the example shows, always a problem of adjustments at a margin. But there is no practicable way to state marginal objectives or values except in terms of particular policies. That one value is preferred to another in one decision situation does not mean that it will be preferred in another decision situation in which it can be had only at great sacrifice of another value. Attempts to rank or order values in general and abstract terms so that they do not shift from decision to decision end up by ignoring the relevant marginal preferences. The significance of this third point thus goes very far. Even if all administrators had at hand an agreed set of values, objectives, and constraints, and an agreed ranking of these values, objectives, and constraints, their marginal values in actual choice situations would be impossible to formulate.

Unable consequently to formulate the relevant values first and then choose among policies to achieve them, administrators must choose directly among alternative policies that offer different marginal combinations of values. Somewhat paradoxically, the only practicable way to disclose one's relevant marginal values even to oneself is to describe the policy one chooses to achieve them. Except roughly and vaguely, I know of no way to describe—or even to understand—what my relative evaluations are for, say, freedom and security, speed and accuracy in governmental decisions, or low taxes and better schools than to describe my preferences among specific policy choices that might be made between the alternatives in each of the pairs.

In summary, two aspects of the process by which values are actually handled can be distinguished. The first is clear: evaluation and empirical analysis are intertwined; that is, one chooses among values and among policies at one and the same time. Put a little more elaborately, one simultaneously chooses a policy to attain certain objectives and chooses the objectives themselves. The second aspect is related but distinct: the administrator focuses his attention on marginal or incremental values. Whether he is aware of it or not, he does not find general formulations of objectives very helpful and in fact makes specific marginal or incremental comparisons. Two policies, X and Y, confront him. Both promise the same degree of attainment of objectives *a, b, c, d,* and *e.* But X promises him somewhat more of *f* than does Y, while Y promises him somewhat more of *g* than does X. In choosing between them, he is in fact offered the alternative of a marginal or incremental amount of *f* at the expense of a marginal or incremental amount of *g.* The only values that are relevant to his choice are these increments by which the two policies differ; and, when he finally chooses between the two marginal values, he does so by making a choice between policies.[5]

As to whether the attempt to clarify objectives in advance of policy selection is more or less rational than the close intertwining of marginal evaluation and empirical analysis, the principal difference established is that for complex problems the first is impossible and irrelevant, and the second is both possible and relevant. The second is possible because the administrator need not try to analyze any values except the values by which alternative policies differ and need not be concerned with them except as they differ marginally. His need for information on values or objectives is drastically reduced as compared with the root method; and his capacity for grasping, comprehending, and relating values to one another is not strained beyond the breaking point.

Relations Between Means and Ends (2b)

Decision-making is ordinarily formalized as a means-ends relationship: means are conceived to be evaluated and chosen in the light of ends finally selected independently of and prior to the choice of means. This is the means-ends relationship of the root method. But it follows from all that has just been said that such a means-ends relationship is possible only to the extent that values are agreed upon, are reconcilable, and are stable at the margin. Typically, therefore, such a means-ends relationship is absent from the branch method, where means and ends are simultaneously chosen.

Yet any departure from the means-ends relationship of the root method will strike some readers as inconceivable. For it will appear to them that only in such a relationship is it possible to determine whether one policy choice is better or worse than another. How can an administrator know whether he has made a wise or foolish decision if he is without prior values or objectives by which to judge his decisions? The answer to this question calls up the third distinctive difference between root and branch methods: how to decide the best policy.

The Test of "Good" Policy (3b)

In the root method, a decision is "correct," "good," or "rational" if it can be shown to attain some specified objective, where the objective can be specified without simply describing the decision itself. Where objectives are defined only through the marginal or incremental approach to values described above, it is still sometimes possible to test whether a policy does in fact attain the desired objectives; but a precise statement of the objectives takes the form of a description of the policy chosen or some alternative to it. To show that a policy is mistaken one cannot offer an abstract argument that important objectives are not achieved; one must instead argue that another policy is more to be preferred.

So far, the departure from customary ways of looking at problem-solving is not troublesome, for many administrators will be quick to agree that the most effective discussion of the correctness of policy does take the form of comparison with other policies that might have been chosen. But what of the situation in which administrators cannot agree on values or objectives, either abstractly or in marginal terms? What then is the test of "good" policy? For the root method, there is no test. Agreement on objectives failing, there is no standard of "correctness." For the method of successive limited comparisons, the test is agreement on policy itself, which remains possible even when agreement on values is not.

It has been suggested that continuing agreement in Congress on the desirability of extending old age insurance stems from liberal desires to strengthen the welfare programs of the federal government and from conservative desires to reduce union demands for private pension plans. If so, this is an excellent demonstration of the ease with which individuals of different ideologies often can agree on concrete policy. Labor mediators report a similar phenomenon: the contestants cannot agree on criteria for settling their disputes but can agree on specific proposals. Similarly, when one administrator's objective turns out to be another's means, they often can agree on policy.

Agreement on policy thus becomes the only practicable test of the policy's correctness. And for one administrator to seek to win the other over to agreement on ends as well would accomplish nothing and create quite unnecessary controversy.

If agreement directly on policy as a test for "best" policy seems a poor substitute for testing the policy against its objectives, it ought to be remembered that objectives themselves have no ultimate validity other than they are agreed upon. Hence agreement is the test of "best" policy in both methods. But where the root method requires agreement on what elements in the decision constitute objectives and on which of these objectives should be sought, the branch method falls back on agreement wherever it can be found.

In an important sense, therefore, it is not irrational for an administrator to defend a policy as good without being able to specify what it is good for.

Non-Comprehensive Analysis (4b)

Ideally, rational-comprehensive analysis leaves out nothing important. But it is impossible to take everything important into consideration unless "important" is so narrowly defined that analysis is in fact quite limited. Limits on human intellectual capacities and on available information set definite limits to man's capacity to be comprehensive. In actual fact, therefore, no one can practice the rational-comprehensive method for really complex problems, and every administrator faced with a sufficiently complex problem must find ways drastically to simplify.

An administrator assisting in the formulation of agricultural economic policy cannot in the first place be competent on all possible policies. He cannot even comprehend one policy entirely. In planning a soil bank program, he cannot successfully anticipate the impact of higher or lower farm income on, say, urbanization—the possible consequent loosening of family ties, possible consequent eventual need for revisions in social security and further implications for tax problems arising out of new federal responsibilities for social security and municipal responsibilities for urban services. Nor, to follow another line of repercussions, can he work through the soil bank program's effects on prices for agricultural products in foreign markets and consequent implications for foreign relations, including those arising out of economic rivalry between the United States and the U.S.S.R.

In the method of successive limited comparisons, simplification is systematically achieved in two principal ways. First, it is achieved through limitation of policy comparisons to those policies that differ in relatively small degree from policies presently in effect. Such a limitation immediately reduces the number of alternatives to be investigated and also drastically simplifies the character of the investigation of each. For it is not necessary to undertake fundamental inquiry into an alternative and its consequences; it is necessary only to study those respects in which the proposed alternative and its consequences differ from the status quo. The empirical comparison of marginal differences among alternative policies that differ only marginally is, of course, a counterpart to the incremental or marginal comparison of values discussed above.[6]

Relevance as Well as Realism

It is a matter of common observation that in Western democracies public administrators and policy analysts in general do largely limit their analyses to incremental or marginal differences in policies that are chosen to differ only incrementally. They do not do so, however, solely because they desperately need some way to simplify their problems; they also do so in order to be relevant. Democracies change their policies almost entirely through incremental adjustments. Policy does not move in leaps and bounds.

The incremental character of political change in the United States has often been remarked. The two major political parties agree on fundamentals; they offer alternative policies to the voters only on relatively small points of difference. Both parties favor full employment, but they define it somewhat differently; both favor the development of water power resources, but in slightly different ways; and both favor unemployment compensation, but not the same level of benefits. Similarly, shifts of policy within a party take place largely through a series of relatively small changes, as can be seen in their only gradual acceptance of the idea of governmental responsibility for support of the unemployed, a change in party positions beginning in the early 30's and culminating in a sense in the Employment Act of 1946.

Party behavior is in turn rooted in public attitudes, and political theorists cannot conceive of democracy's surviving in the United States in the absence of fundamental agreement on potentially disruptive issues, with consequent limitation of policy debates to relatively small differences in policy.

Since the policies ignored by the administrator are politically impossible and so irrelevant, the simplification of analysis achieved by concentrating on policies that differ only incrementally is not a capricious kind of simplification. In addition, it can be argued that, given the limits on knowledge within which policy-makers are confined, simplifying by limiting the focus to small variations from present policy makes the most of available knowledge. Because policies being considered are like present and past policies, the administrator can obtain information and claim some insight. Non-incremental policy proposals are therefore typically not only politically irrelevant but also unpredictable in their consequences.

The second method of simplification of analysis is the practice of ignoring important possible consequences of possible policies, as well as the values attached to the neglected consequences. If this appears to disclose a shocking shortcoming of successive limited comparisons, it can be replied that, even if the exclusions are random, policies may nevertheless be more intelligently formulated than through futile attempts to achieve a comprehensiveness beyond human capacity. Actually, however, the exclusions, seeming arbitrary or random from one point of view, need be neither.

Achieving a Degree of Comprehensiveness

Suppose that each value neglected by one policy-making agency were a major concern of at least one other agency. In that case, a helpful division of labor would be achieved, and no agency need find its task beyond its capacities. The shortcomings of such a system would be that one agency might destroy a value either before another agency could be activated to safeguard it or in spite of another agency's efforts. But the possibility that important values may be lost is present in any form of organization, even where agencies attempt to comprehend in planning more than is humanly possible.

The virtue of such a hypothetical division of labor is that every important interest or value has its watchdog. And these watchdogs can protect the interests in their jurisdiction in two quite different ways: first, by redressing damages done by other agencies; and, second, by anticipating and heading off injury before it occurs.

In a society like that of the United States in which individuals are free to combine to pursue almost any possible common interest they might have and in which government agencies are sensitive to the pressures of these groups, the system described is approximated. Almost every interest has its watchdog. Without claiming that every interest has a sufficiently powerful watchdog, it can be argued that our system often can assure a more comprehensive regard for the values of the whole society than any attempt at intellectual comprehensiveness.

In the United States, for example, no part of government attempts a comprehensive overview of policy on income distribution. A policy nevertheless evolves, and one responding to a wide variety of interests. A process of mutual adjustment among farm groups, labor unions, municipalities and school boards, tax authorities, and government agencies with responsibilities in the fields of housing, health, highways, national parks, fire, and police accomplishes a distribution of income in which particular income problems neglected at one point in the decision processes become central at another point.

Mutual adjustment is more pervasive than the explicit forms it takes in negotiation between groups; it persists through the mutual impacts of groups upon each other even where they are not in communication. For all the imperfections and latent dangers in this ubiquitous process of mutual adjustment, it will often accomplish an adaptation of policies to a wider range of interests than could be done by one group centrally.

Note, too, how the incremental pattern of policy-making fits with the multiple pressure pattern. For when decisions are only incremental—closely related to known policies, it is easier for one group to anticipate the kind of moves another might make and easier too for it to make correction for injury already accomplished.[7]

Even partisanship and narrowness, to use pejorative terms, will sometimes be assets to rational decision-making, for they can doubly insure that what one agency neglects, another will not; they specialize personnel to distinct points of view. The claim is valid that effective rational coordination of the federal administration, if possible to achieve at all, would require an agreed set of values[8]—if "rational" is defined as the practice of the root method of decision-making. But a high degree of administrative coordination occurs as each agency adjusts its policies to the concerns of the other agencies in the process of fragmented decision-making I have just described.

For all the apparent shortcomings of the incremental approach to policy alternatives with its arbitrary exclusion coupled with fragmentation, when compared to the root method, the branch method often looks far superior. In the root method, the inevitable exclusion of factors is accidental, unsystematic, and not defensible by any argument so far developed, while in the branch method the exclusions are deliberate, systematic, and defensible. Ideally, of course, the root method does not exclude; in practice it must.

Nor does the branch method necessarily neglect long-run considerations and objectives. It is clear that important values must be omitted in considering policy, and sometimes the only way long-run objectives can be given adequate attention is through the neglect of short-run considerations. But the values omitted can be either long-run or short-run.

Succession of Comparisons (5b)

The final distinctive element in the branch method is that the comparisons, together with the policy choice, proceed in a chronological series. Policy is not made once and for all; it is made and re-made endlessly. Policy-making is a process of successive approximation to some desired objectives in which what is desired itself continues to change under reconsideration.

Making policy is at best a very rough process. Neither social scientists, nor politicians, nor public administrators yet know enough about the social world to avoid repeated error in predicting the consequences of policy moves. A wise policy-maker consequently expects that his policies will achieve only part of what he hopes and at the same time will produce unanticipated consequences he would have preferred to avoid. If he proceeds through a *succession* of incremental changes, he avoids serious lasting mistakes in several ways.

In the first place, past sequences of policy steps have given him knowledge about the probable consequences of further similar steps. Second, he need not attempt big jumps toward his goals that would require predictions beyond his or anyone else's knowledge, because he never expects his policy to be a final resolution of a problem. His decision is only one step, one that if successful can quickly be followed by another. Third, he is in effect able to test his previous predictions as he moves on to each further step. Lastly, he often can remedy a past error fairly quickly—more quickly than if policy proceeded through more distinct steps widely spaced in time.

Compare this comparative analysis of incremental changes with the aspiration to employ theory in the root method. Man cannot think without classifying, without subsuming one experience under a more general category of experiences. The attempt to push categorization as far as possible and to find general propositions which can be applied to specific situations is what I refer to with the word "theory." Where root analysis often leans heavily on theory in this sense, the branch method does not.

The assumption of root analysts is that theory is the most systematic and economical way to bring relevant knowledge to bear on a specific problem. Granting the assumption, an unhappy fact is that we do not have adequate theory to apply to problems in any policy area, although theory is more adequate in some areas—monetary policy, for example—than in others. Comparative analysis, as in the branch method, is sometimes a systematic alternative to theory.

Suppose an administrator must choose among a small group of policies that differ only incrementally from each other and from present policy. He might aspire to "understand" each of the alternatives—for example, to know all the consequences of each aspect of each policy. If so, he would indeed require theory. In fact, however, he would usually decide that, *for policy-making purposes,* he need know, as explained above, only the consequences of each of those aspects of the policies in which they differed from one another. For this much more modest aspiration, he requires no theory (although it might be helpful, if available), for he can proceed to isolate probable differences by examining the differences in consequences associated with past differences in policies, a feasible program because he can take his observations from a long sequence of incremental changes.

For example, without a more comprehensive social theory about juvenile delinquency than scholars have yet produced, one cannot possibly understand the ways in which a variety of public policies—say on education, housing, recreation, employment, race relations, and policing—might encourage or discourage delinquency. And one needs such an understanding if he undertakes the comprehensive overview of the problem prescribed in the models of the root method. If, however, one merely wants to mobilize knowledge sufficient to assist in a choice among a small group of similar policies—alternative policies on juvenile court procedures, for example—he can do so by comparative analysis of the results of similar past policy moves.

Theorists and Practitioners

This difference explains—in some cases at least—why the administrator often feels that the outside expert or academic problem-solver is sometimes not helpful and why they in turn often urge more theory on him. And it explains why an administrator often feels more confident when "flying by the seat of his pants" than when following the advice of theorists. Theorists often ask the administrator to go the long way round to the solution of his problems, in effect ask him to follow the best canons of the scientific method, when the administrator knows that the best available theory will work less well than more modest incremental comparisons. Theorists do not realize that the administrator is often in fact practicing a systematic method. It would be foolish to push this explanation too far, for sometimes practical decision-makers are pursuing neither a theoretical approach nor successive comparisons, nor any other systematic method.

It may be worth emphasizing that theory is sometimes of extremely limited helpfulness in policy-making for at least two rather different reasons. It is greedy for facts; it can be constructed only through a great collection of observations. And it is typically insufficiently precise for application to a policy process that moves through small changes. In contrast, the comparative method both economizes on the need for facts and directs the analyst's attention to just those facts that are relevant to the fine choices faced by the decision-maker.

With respect to precision of theory, economic theory serves as an example. It predicts that an economy without money or prices would in certain specified ways misallocate resources, but this finding pertains to an alternative far removed from the kind of policies on which administrators need help. On the other hand, it is not precise enough to predict the consequences of policies restricting business mergers, and this is the kind of issue on which the administrators need help. Only in relatively restricted areas does economic theory achieve sufficient precision to go far in resolving policy questions; its helpfulness in policy-making is always so limited that it requires supplementation through comparative analysis.

Successive Comparison as a System

Successive limited comparisons is, then, indeed a method or system; it is not a failure of method for which administrators ought to apologize. None the less, its imperfections, which have not been explored in this paper, are many. For example, the method is without a built-in safeguard for all relevant values, and it also may lead the decision-maker to overlook excellent policies for no other reason than that they are not suggested by the chain of successive policy steps leading up to the present. Hence, it ought to be said that under this method, as well as under some of the most sophisticated variants of the root method—operations research, for example—policies will continue to be as foolish as they are wise.

Why then bother to describe the method in all the above detail? Because it is in fact a common method of policy formulation, and is, for complex problems, the principal reliance of administrators as well as of other policy analysts.[9] And because it will be superior to any other decision-making method available for complex problems in many circumstances, certainly superior to a futile attempt at superhuman comprehensiveness. The reaction of the public administrator to the exposition of method doubtless will be less a discovery of a new method than a better acquaintance with an old. But by becoming more conscious of their practice of this method, administrators might practice it with more skill and know when to extend or constrict its use. (That they sometimes practice it effectively and sometimes not may explain the extremes of opinion on "muddling through," which is both praised as a highly sophisticated form of problem-solving and denounced as no method at all. For I suspect that insofar as there is a system in what is known as "muddling through," this method is it.)

One of the noteworthy incidental consequences of clarification of the method is the light it throws on the suspicion an administrator sometimes entertains that a consultant or adviser is not speaking relevantly and responsibly when in fact by all ordinary objective evidence he is. The trouble lies in the fact that most of us approach policy problems within a framework given by our view of a chain of successive policy choices made up to the present. One's thinking about appropriate policies with respect, say, to urban traffic control is greatly influenced by one's knowledge of the incremental steps taken up to the present. An administrator enjoys an intimate knowledge of his past sequences that "outsiders" do not share, and his thinking and that of the "outsider" will consequently be different in ways that may puzzle both. Both may appear to be talking intelligently, yet each may find the other unsatisfactory. The relevance of the policy chain of succession is even more clear when an American tries to discuss, say, antitrust policy with a Swiss, for the chains of policy in the two countries are strikingly different and the two individuals consequently have organized their knowledge in quite different ways.

If this phenomenon is a barrier to communication, an understanding of it promises an enrichment of intellectual interaction in policy formulation. Once the source of difference is understood, it will sometimes be stimulating for an administrator to seek out a policy analyst whose recent experience is with a policy chain different from his own.

This raises again a question only briefly discussed above on the merits of like-mindedness among government administrators. While much of organization theory argues the virtues of common values and agreed organizational objectives, for complex problems in which the root method is inapplicable, agencies will want among their own personnel two types of diversification: administrators whose thinking is organized by reference to policy chains other than those familiar to most members of the organization and, even more commonly, administrators whose professional or personal values or interests create diversity of view (perhaps coming from different specialties, social classes, geographical areas) so that, even within a single agency, decision-making can be fragmented and parts of the agency can serve as watchdogs for other parts.

1. JAMES G. MARCH and HERBERT A. SIMON similarly characterize the literature. They also take some important steps, as have Simon's recent articles, to describe a less heroic model of policy-making. See *Organizations* (John Wiley and Sons, 1958), p. 137.

2. "Operations Research and National Planning—A Dissent," *5 Operations Research* 718 (October, 1957). Hitch's dissent is from particular points made in the article to which his paper is a reply; his claim that operations research is for low-level problems is widely accepted.

   For examples of the kind of problems to which operations research is applied, see C. W. CHURCHMAN, R. L. ACKOFF and E. L. ARNOFF, *Introduction to Operations Research* (John Wiley and Sons, 1957); and J. F. MCCLOSKEY and J. M. COPPINGER (eds.), *Operations Research for Management,* Vol. II, (The Johns Hopkins Press, 1956).

3. I am assuming that administrators often make policy and advise in the making of policy and am treating decision-making and policy-making as synonymous for purposes of this paper.

4. MARTIN MEYERSON and EDWARD C. BANFIELD, *Politics, Planning and the Public Interest* (The Free Press, 1955).

5. The line of argument is, of course, an extension of the theory of market choice, especially the theory of consumer choice, to public policy choices.

6. A more precise definition of incremental policies and a discussion of whether a change that appears "small" to one observer might be seen differently by another is to be found in my "Policy Analysis," 48 *American Economic Review* 298 (June, 1958).

7. The link between the practice of the method of successive limited comparisons and mutual adjustment of interests in a highly fragmented decision-making process adds a new facet to pluralist theories of government and administration.

8. HERBERT SIMON, DONALD W. SMITHBURG, and VICTOR A. THOMPSON, *Public Administration* (Alfred A. Knopf, 1950), p. 434.

9. Elsewhere I have explored this same method of policy formulation as practiced by academic analysts of policy ("Policy Analysis," 48 *American Economic Review* 298 [June, 1958]). Although it has been here presented as a method for public administrators, it is no less necessary to analysts more removed from immediate policy questions, despite their tendencies to describe their own analytical efforts as though they were the rational-comprehensive method with an especially heavy use of theory. Similarly, this same method is inevitably resorted to in personal problem-solving, where means and ends are sometimes impossible to separate, where aspirations or objectives undergo constant development, and where drastic simplification of the complexity of the real world is urgent if problems are to be solved in the time that can be given to them. To an economist accustomed to dealing with the marginal or incremental concept in market processes, the central idea in the method is that both evaluation and empirical analysis are incremental. Accordingly I have referred to the method elsewhere as "the incremental method."

WILDLIFE HABITAT MANAGEMENT FOR THE CITIZEN (1967)
Frank E. Egler

It is easy but foolhardy to ignore one's critics. Their chiding need not be entirely justified nor wholly accurate to be of value. They may provide a point of view or objectivity difficult to attain within the system. They keep us on our toes and out of ruts.

Plant ecologist Frank Egler, reviewing a guidebook on wildlife habitat improvement, wrote more than a review. He censured the profession of wildlife management. Republication of Egler's comments here is not intended to support one side of an argument nor to add censure to the guidebook he reviewed. Egler says we are in a rut and has charted its dimensions. The reader may compare these dimensions with those of well-worn trails and judge for himself.

A guidebook on *Wildlife Habitat Improvement,* addressed to Mr. Citizen for his own land and for the lands of his local community, is surely urgently needed. The term wildlife is in flux in our language. By custom it has been restricted to the larger birds and mammals of interest to the hunter. With increasing numbers of camera-shooters, rather than firearm shooters, as well as watchers and observers, the connotation is changing. As one recent example of this change (*Outdoor News Bulletin* 21 (11):5. June 9, 1967), "Not more than one person in 40 using Pennsylvania's Pymatuning Waterfowl Area last year was a hunter."

The Nature Centers Division of the National Audubon Society should be eminently suited to publish such a manual, for this Division has become a leader in the nation in planning community nature centers and the use of outdoor areas in education. The more important this Division becomes, the graver its responsibility to communicate the soundest information to the citizen.

· · · · · · · · · · · · · · · · ·

Regretfully, I must report that this publication falls far short of my expectations. It says little more than I was taught in college almost four decades ago. Not that the information of that bygone era has all been superseded by an expanding science; the best of it has not yet been commonly accepted, and some of it is even forgotten. But, in brief, this bulletin (1) embraces all that is mediocre and unimaginative in the wildlife profession. (2) It is technology, rather than science. (3) It is wildlife for the hunter, rather than wildlife for the appreciative and intelligent land owner and manager. (4) Insofar as wildlife habitat management is vegetation management, it contains nothing. These points will be elaborated below.

(1) Wildlife professionals in this country are largely coordinated through membership in the Wildlife Society, and in the pages of their *Journal of Wildlife Management.* Rising head and shoulders above other

Reprinted from: Atlantic Naturalist 22(3): 166-169, Copyright by Audubon Naturalist Society of the Central Atlantic States, Inc. The guidebook reviewed by Egler is *Wildlife Habitat Improvement,* Nat. Audubon Society, 1966. 96 pp.

professionals is the figure of the late Aldo Leopold, whose books reveal a breadth of ecosystem understanding that the profession he sired has yet to acquire. The profession recognizes some of its problems, as indicated in the pages of *Wildlife Society News*. But too many of the professionals are simply hunters at heart, trying to be scientists, but not rising above the level of technicians.

Wildlife management centers around four major problems: management of food, of cover, of water, and of space. The space problem generally takes care of itself if man leaves any of it. The reproductive potential—as with human beings—normally suffices to fill available space quickly, after which populations oscillate, through natural cycles or from environmental fouling or other external pressures, even as wars, famines, climate changes and overpopulation pressures affect man, too. Food and cover are largely vegetation problems either directly or indirectly, and this is where the wildlife profession has been notoriously weak; the men are in the field because they like animals, not plants. In short, the limitations of the profession show up all the more clearly in the simplified presentation of this bulletin.

(2) There has been much criticism in recent years that technology has forged ahead of science, to the detriment of the quality of our environment. An excellent expression of this dilemma was written by Barry Commoner in *Science and Survival* (Viking 1966).

What is not so well recognized is that within the ranks of science itself, much of what passes for professional activity is routine undirected 'things to do', often with no comprehension of why one is doing them, or what is the ultimate result, or whether one should do it at all. Shomon's bulletin epitomizes this sort of 'do it' philosophy: bird houses, shelters, forestry operations, and planting, planting, and more planting. One wonders how there was any wildlife at all before man came on the scene.

I can hardly avoid the feeling that the bulletin is a plodding compilation from an assortment of 'how to' government leaflets. The suggestions, furthermore, as to 'what to do' left me feeling frustrated with almost every page. Even if sound, there are sweeping statements that would baffle a Roman emperor to put into effect. For example, for mourning doves alone, the recommended management practices are: "Establish windbreaks and Christmas-tree plantations for nesting sites. Develop water supplies through springs, water holes and ponds. Establish or maintain hedgerows. Favor borders and clumps of coniferous trees. Develop small sand and gravel beds where none exist. Use cone during orchard spraying to prevent destruction of eggs and young." At other places, one is blandly advised to "keep fires out", "clear out all brush and undesirable growth that will obstruct improvements", "water holes are constructed by digging pits to provide at least 200 square feet of water surface", "the construction of a dike is usually necessary", "dynamite may be used to create open pits", "control fire in the woodlands and fields", "provide an adequate water supply", "create and maintain openings in woods", "the water levels should be regulated to enhance the production of natural food plants and to encourage a desired ratio of cover to open water," "a gradual flooding of areas in late summer . . .

[is desirable]", "loafing islands and nesting platforms should be provided in and around semi-remote water areas", "Protection from land and air predators is essential", "leasing or encouraging privately-sponsored refuge areas near feeding grounds will be helpful", "this can be done by raising and lowering the water table", "manage forests according to accepted forest management principles", "plow in early spring when the soil is workable and not too wet. Lime, if needed. Harrow and seed one bushel of oats per acre with one of the above mixtures, using sufficient fertilizer", "avoidance of overgrazing", "keep canals, streams, ponds and lakes partially open", "control air and water pollution on own lands." Sounds easy, doesn't it?

As one would expect from the above, the food patch philosophy is recommended. This is one of the favorite games of the wildlife manager. It is essentially an agricultural operation, involving bulldozing, stoning, plowing, fertilizing, and seeding a crop of grain or other wildlife food. In two or three years, the whole process is repeated. Of course, this same food is used by blackbirds, mice, and other 'varmints'. I have yet to see any cost-benefit study of this wildlife smorgasbord, in terms of the extra wildlife actually put in the hunter's bag. The few figures informally presented to me by wildlifers have been so astronomically unbalanced that I cannot even repeat them here.

(3) Although the authors have very carefully eschewed any mention of hunting, and of 'harvesting a crop' of 'excess' game animals—which is the contemporary conventional wisdom in wildlife management—the deletions stand out too obviously. After all, many of our citizens *are* hunters. Why delete *them*? The Foreword to this bulletin is by the President of the Wildlife Management Institute (a hunter-oriented organization). The only review of this bulletin that has come to my attention was in the Journal of Soil and Water Conservation, and this was by the Vice President of the Wildlife Management Institute. As one scans the bulletin, the art work is distinctly hunter-oriented: wood duck, bobwhite, deer, rabbit, squirrel, pheasant, goose, rail, turkey, grouse, dove, coon, mink, quail, mountain lion, antelope. Only two song birds appear, and one gull illustration. Why not pictures of beaver, chipmunk, fox, coyote, cardinal, or titmouse? The fish world, presumably by definition, is unmentioned. To which audience, hunters or those with broader wildlife interests, is the bulletin aimed? Why not both?

(4) Food and cover are the two most 'manageable' aspects of the wildlife environment, and both pose problems involving plants. Yet I find no awareness at all of the idea that vegetation, the natural and semi-natural plant communities, can be manipulated to the advantage of wildlife. The authors think only in terms of planting, or of cutting out what is not wanted. There is no sophistication whatever in their awareness of this subject. In short, discussion of the most important single facet of wildlife habitat management—vegetation management—is conspicuous by its absence.

• • • • • • • • • • • • • • • • • • •

There are other omissions which are highly significant. In fact, I got the feeling that the authors purposely avoided all controversial issues, for fear of arousing antagonism or of offending anyone at all. Although *Silent Spring* is quoted in the list of references, one would not know from the text that persistent insecticides, actually biocides, have affected the very wildlife they talk about; and that these chemicals are too easily used by the local home owner or even by those involved with Nature Centers. National Audubon itself has done worthy things in this field, and its own conclusions could have been mentioned. The subject of coyotes and 1080 seems to have been rigidly deleted, as has the entire hot and alive issue of predator control. There are few mentions of fire, mainly for keeping it out. Smokey Bear (as an ecologist there are times I could ring his neck) has caused such an utterly unreasonable accumulation of inflammable junk in our forests that the fire insurance companies should sue him. The Nature Centers Division should get acquainted with the Tall Timbers Fire Ecology Conference Proceedings. In the 1966 issue an article by Roy Komarek offers a readable and enlightened piece, *A Discussion of Wildlife Management, Fire, and the Wildlife Landscape.* The subject of herbicide use is another conspicuous omission. In careful hands, herbicides can be an extraordinarily useful tool for the long-term low-cost management of semi-natural vegetation. The authors seem equally unaware that over 50 million acres of right-of-way lands exist in this country that could be producing far more wildlife if the private owners would simply demand of the public utility companies that herbicides be used wisely, not indiscriminately. Natural areas (those kept as free as possible from human interference) and their wildlife problems are most inadequately treated.

There is also no discussion of wildlife populations as such, a scientific field bursting at the seams these years. If nothing else, there should be discussion of normally fluctuating populations. One may go to considerable effort to improve grouse habitat, but if the grouse are at a low point in their cycle, even habitat improvement will not work a miracle.

And lastly, I notice a striking absence of broad ecosystem thinking. The text contains nothing like the fox-man ecosystem story recently described by Daniel Smiley (*Ecosystem Sketches No. 2. Foxes and Rabies,* published in the bulletin of the John Burroughs Natural History Society, 14(6):2-3. June 1967.) Writing for the same audience to which Nature Centers bulletins are directed, he makes a complex situation clear in terms his public can understand. Considering the considerable degree of intellectual sophistication that does lie within the National Audubon Society itself in this field, and the extent to which *Audubon Magazine* has recently played an active role in discussing such subjects, one is tempted to suggest that the authors read their own magazine more thoughtfully. One would never know from this bulletin that biologists everywhere are talking of an ecological crisis, that concern for Restoring the Quality of our Environment has seeped into the highest industrial and governmental circles, even to the White House. Wildlife is but one facet of this totality. We must have genuine understanding of it all, not just busy fussing with the landscape in a domineering way.

Let me reiterate in conclusion that the faults of this bulletin are largely a reflection of the inadequacies of wildlife professionalism today, recognized by many in the field. All the less reason why a leading natural-resource organization should be guilty of distilling those faults and of communicating them to a sizeable segment of the citizenry. I trust that when the Nature Centers Division puts out a revised bulletin, it will incorporate some of the intellectual sophistication of its parent organization, and that it will be written with verve in a style to inspire the citizen to love wildlife, whether a frog chorus or the howl of a coyote in a silent starry night; to teach how to manage to let the coyote live, even if it means to learn to manage man.

It is not the wildlife that is in need of management, so much as man himself.

RESPONSES OF BOBWHITES TO MANAGEMENT IN ILLINOIS (1969)

Jack A. Ellis, William R. Edwards and Keith P. Thomas

This paper describes a successful program of wildlife habitat manipulation. It is based upon providing the niche requirements of the target species; it shows concern for efficient use of public funds; it includes a measure of population response for monitoring program effectiveness.

One purpose of this paper is to describe management programs and the population responses by quail on two public hunting areas in Illinois. The management programs included: (1) establishment of annual food patches, and mowing to control weeds and brush; (2) prescribed burning; and (3) a combination of sharecropping and prescribed burning. A second purpose is to discuss and review the ecologic and economic bases of the three programs.

In the Midwest, much habitat management for upland game is based on planting food and cover (that is, cereal grains, forage crops, and exotic woody ornamentals) and controlling undesirable vegetation by mowing. To us, such programs appear unnecessarily expensive to establish and to maintain, and—more important—fail to recognize a game species as part of a biotic community and its evolutionary niche in that community. Too little attention has been given to manipulating natural and semi-natural vegetation.

We discovered that our findings were not new, only unappreciated and inadequately applied. We became increasingly aware of the vision and the contribution of three pioneers in game management, Herbert L. Stoddard, Sr., Wallace B. Grange, and E. V. Komarek, Sr. These men long ago recognized the significance of the evolutionary adaptation of wildlife to successional environments and repeatedly pointed out the advantages of using fire as a modifier of succession to benefit virtually every species of game in North America. This lesson, 40 years later, is still little appreciated and rarely applied except in the longleaf pine (*Pinus palustris*) savannas of Southeastern United States.

This study could not have been conducted without the cooperation of numerous fieldmen and administrators of the Illinois Department of Conservation's Divisions of Parks, Forestry, and Game. We would like to acknowledge the administrative support given us by G. C. Sanderson and T. R. Evans, and the editorial assistance given by G. C. Sanderson and Helen C. Schultz in the preparation of this manuscript.

METHODS

Study Areas

This investigation of management programs was conducted on two state-owned, multiple-use recreational areas in south-central Illinois: Stephen A. Forbes State Park (2,885 acres) in Marion County, and Sam Dale Lake Conservation Area (1,300 acres) in Wayne County. These

Reprinted from: J. Wildl. Mgmt. 33(4): 749-762.

areas are administered by the Illinois Department of Conservation for public recreation; upland game hunting, primarily for quail and cottontails (*Sylvilagus floridanus*), is considered a major recreational use. Approximately 75 percent of each area is open to hunting.

The Dale and Forbes areas are 13.5 miles apart and have many environmental similarities. This general area has an average of 180-190 frost-free days; precipitation averages 40-42 inches annually, most of which occurs from March through July; annual snowfall averages 10-15 inches (Page 1949). Soils are light colored, fine textured, with slowly permeable subsoils, and originally supported timber vegetation of the oak-hickory forest type (Vestal 1930:214). Hardwoods occupy approximately 15 percent of the Dale area and 50 percent of the Forbes area. Topography on both areas varies from flat to steeply gullied slopes along streams.

A centrally located lake and an airstrip characterize each area. The lakes occupy 585 acres on Forbes and 200 acres on Dale. The airstrips cover 6 acres on Forbes and 5 acres on Dale. Road development includes 8.4 miles on Forbes and 3.7 miles on Dale. Roadsides, airstrips, picnic and camping areas are frequently mowed from midspring to fall on both areas.

Prior to acquisition by the State in the early 1960s, these areas were privately owned farmland, with corn (*Zea mays*), soybeans (*Glycine max*), wheat (*Tricticum* spp.), hay, and pastures the chief agricultural crops. Similar cropping practices are continued on land adjacent to the areas.

Management Programs

Habitat manipulation for upland game began on the Dale area in 1961 and on the Forbes area in 1963. Initially, this development included planting multiflora rose *(Rosa multiflora)* and pines *(Pinus* spp.) on Dale and pines on Forbes. These plantings were made to subdivide the large non-timbered fields into smaller units of usually 2-10 acres. Sericea (*Lespedeza cuneata*) was seeded along the rows of multiflora and timber borders on the Dale area and along timber borders on the Forbes area. Also, on the Dale area 125 acres of open ground were seeded to redtop (*Agrostis alba*) and timothy (*Phleum pratense*). Timothy, redtop, and fescue (*Festuca* spp.) were seeded adjacent to rows of pines on both areas.

Food-Patch Program.—From 1963 through 1965, establishment of annual food patches was the principal management practice employed on both areas (Tables 1 and 2). Since 1966, the food-patch program has been continued on a major portion of both areas. Initially, this program included spring and summer seedings of corn, milo (*Sorghum vulgare*), buckwheat (*Fagopyrum esculentum*), and several varieties of millets: proso (*Panicum miliaceum*), pearl (*Pennisetum glaucum*), and German (*Setaria italica*). One or more of these crops were planted in strips from < 0.1 to 5.0 acres. Winter wheat was included in this program in 1964 and was seeded in strips similar to those planted in spring and summer. Establishment of these food patches entailed plowing, disking, fertilizing, and seeding, with no cultivation or use of herbicides to control weeds. The location of the food patches has been rotated periodically, primarily to control succession, but some sites were replanted every year.

TABLE 1. Summary of food-patch management program on the Forbes area, 1963-67.

	1963	1964	1965	1966	1967
Food plots—Spring					
Number	26	221	147	67	55
Acres	8	64	45	13	11
Food plots (wheat)—Fall					
Number	0	86	30	36	61
Acres	0	50	9	8	17
Total food plots					
Number	26	307	177	103	116
Acres	8	114	54	21	28
Acres of open land	281	526	526	339[a]	339[a]
Percent of open land	3	22	10	6	8

[a] 250 acres diverted to sharecrop-burn management program.

TABLE 2. Summary of food-patch management program on the Dale area, 1963-67.

	1963	1964	1965	1966	1967
Food plots—Spring					
Number	28	38	44	44	39
Acres	40	36	38	14	10
Food plots (wheat)—Fall					
Number	0	7	7	20	30
Acres	0	51	16	10	19
Total food plots					
Number	28	45	51	64	69
Acres	40	87	54	24	29
Acres of open land	344	536	576	337[a]	337[a]
Percent of open land	12	16	9	7	9

[a] 250 acres diverted to burn management program.

Prescribed Burning and Sharecropping.—A 250-acre tract (Zone I) located in the northeast quarter of the Dale area was designated as an area on which to study the effects of periodic burning on bobwhite populations. Prescribed burning has been the only management practice used in this zone since 1965. A 141-acre segment of the zone was divided into 21 plots ranging in size from 1.4 to 19.0 acres. Ten of the plots were burned in 1966 and 1968; the remaining 11 in 1967. This 2-year rotation is being continued. The remaining 109 acres were not burned, in compliance with an order from the Illinois Department of Conservation that stands of hardwood timber, pine plantings, and rows of multiflora be excluded from fire.

The plots on the Dale area were burned in late winter or early spring when weather conditions were favorable. Firebreaks, 8-10 ft. wide, were plowed in the fall around the plots scheduled for burning the following spring. Backfires were set to complement the existing plowed firebreaks. When the firebreaks were considered adequate and conditions favorable to contain a fire within a particular plot, forefires were started. The plots were burned using 2-3 project personnel, 2-3 park personnel, and the district fire warden.

A management program incorporating sharecropping and prescribed burning was established on a 250-acre tract (Zone I) on the Forbes area. From 1963 through 1965, this zone was under the food-patch management program and by 1966 vegetation was rank. Cropland in this zone was then divided into 14 plots from 5.3 to 10.8 acres in size. (Note: An additional plot of 35.9 acres was seeded to grass as nesting cover for a small local flock of prairie chickens, *Tympanuchus cupido*.)

In 1966, seven of the plots on the Forbes area were planted to row crops. Under the terms of the sharecropping agreement, the sharecropper planted the State's ¼ of each of the seven plots to corn and the remaining ¾ to his choice of corn or soybeans. The sharecropper harvested his portion of each plot; the corn on the State's ¼ was unharvested. After the harvest, the sharecropper planted the harvested portions of the plots to a small grain, either wheat or oats (*Avena sativa*). The following spring, ⅓ of each small-grain field was seeded to redtop and ⅓ to red clover (*Trifolium pratense*).

In 1966, three noncropped plots, comprising 22.3 acres scheduled for row crops in 1967, were burned. A total of 10 acres in 11 noncropped spots were burned in late winter and early spring on this zone in 1967. These burns were made primarily on abandoned pastureland characterized by grasses, weeds, shrubs, and scattered young trees such as persimmon (*Diospyros virginiana*), sassafras (*Sassafras albidum*), hawthorn (*Crataegus* spp.), and shingle oak *(Quercus imbricaria)*. In 1968, burning on this zone on Forbes was limited to 11.4 acres in 2nd-year oat and corn stubble.

Vegetative Analyses.—The vegetation on the plots in Zones I on Forbes and Dale was studied to determine the effects of burning and cropping on plant composition of the early successional stages. The vegetation was sampled by taking 1/16-m^2 quadrats in July and August; species were identified, and the relative abundance of each species recorded along with the amount of bare ground. From 1966 through

1968, 2,090 quadrat samples were taken in Zones I on the Dale and Forbes areas.

Food Habits—Crops were removed from quail harvested on the Dale and Forbes areas at check stations located on each area. Food items in the crops were removed and identified. Our sample represented 1,531 crops for the years 1963-66.

Roosting Studies.—Nightlighting (Labisky 1968) was used to locate night-roosting groups of quail in the open, nontimbered fields on the Forbes area in 1964. We found 23 night roosts while cruising 1,070 acres. This acreage figure included repeated searches in some fields. Vegetation at the roost sites was measured to determine the characteristics of night-roosting cover. Our observations were made in the fields that could be driven with a 4-wheel-drive vehicle. Roosting sometimes occurs in locations inaccessible to nightlighting, such as honeysuckle (*Lonicera japonica*) thickets and woods (Klimstra and Ziccardi 1963: 208, 209).

TABLE 3. Numbers of quail per 100 acres on management zones in early November at the Forbes and Dale areas. (Included is a whistling-quail index of quail abundance, W. L. Preno, unpublished data.)

YEAR	FORBES		DALE		REGION-WIDE QUAIL INDEX[e]
	Zone I[a]	Zone II[b]	Zone I[c]	Zone II[d]	
1963	40	28	35	43	2.9
1964	41	42	38	24	3.0
1965	23	28	23	17	2.4
1966	57	18	23	32	3.2
1967	95	27	52	32	3.0
1968	96	44	67	37	3.8

[a] Management 1963-65 based on annual food and cover plantings; management 1966-68 based on a combination of prescribed burning and sharecropping.
[b] Management 1963-67 based on annual food and cover plantings; management in 1968 modified to include some sharecropping.
[c] Management 1963-65 based on annual food and cover plantings; management 1966-68 based only on prescribed burning.
[d] Management 1963-68 based on annual food and cover plantings.
[e] The average number of whistling quail per stop over 20-stop routes in representative quail range in southern Illinois.

Quail Censuses.—The evaluation of the management efforts on the Forbes and Dale areas was based on the abundance of quail available to the hunter. The abundance of quail in early November was determined by censusing the areas with bird dogs, on days with good scenting conditions. Estimates were based on the locations and sizes of individual coveys in the various zones of the two areas.

The experimental design consisted of measuring the abundance of bobwhites on the study areas before and after the initiation of experimental management programs and comparing these data with the levels of quail populations on the control units. Census data were obtained during 1963-68. Where burning and sharecropping were initiated in 1966, data for the years 1963-65 represent responses to food-patch programs; data for the years 1966-68 demonstrate population levels after initiation of the experimental programs.

FINDINGS

Quail abundance on study zones on the Forbes and Dale areas evidenced pronounced declines from 1963 through 1965 (Table 3), when all zones were being managed under a food-patch system. These declines appeared relatively greater than expected on the basis of the regionwide index to quail abundance obtained from audio counts made annually by biologists of the Illinois Department of Conservation in early summer.

Regionwide quail population indices showed a pattern of general increase over the years 1966-68, with abundance higher in 1968 than at the start of our study in 1963. On Zone II at Dale, where management was based on the food-patch system all 6 years, quail numbers increased from 1966 to 1968, but the increase was not as great as anticipated on the basis of regional trends. Quail numbers on this zone are interpreted to reflect a negative response to a deteriorating habitat which was offset by favorable weather conditions or by other factors generally conducive to higher quail populations in southern Illinois during the years 1966-68.

Quail populations on Zone II at Forbes showed a general pattern of decline from 1964 to 1966, with increases in 1967 and in 1968. While managed primarily under the food-patch system, activities related to construction of a new access road through this zone in 1967 resulted in considerable disturbance and initiation of new successions; in 1968 several fields were planted to soybeans and wheat by sharecroppers. On the basis of covey distribution we believe that some of the population increase in 1967 and 1968 was the result of the road construction and sharecropping, the remainder to the general regionwide increase.

Responses of the quail population on Zone I at Forbes to a program based on sharecropping and burning initiated in 1966 were spectacular, immediate, and greatly exceeded the response expected on the basis of regional trends. The population was essentially one bird per acre on Zone I in both 1967 and 1968. Quail numbers in 1967 and 1968 were 250 percent greater than in 1963, and 400 percent more than in 1965. Trends in quail numbers on Zone I at Forbes were in marked contrast with those in Zone II on that area and on Zone II at Dale. These data indicate that effective programs of habitat management for quail in the Midwest, as in the Southeast, can be developed using only a combination of controlled burning and a proper program of sharecropping. Densities of one quail per acre must be regarded as high.

On Zone I at Dale the responses of quail to a program based only on prescribed burning were not as immediately striking as those observed on Zone I at Forbes, where both burning and sharecropping were used. However, by 1967 and 1968, quail were responding better to burning alone than they had to the intensive program based on food patches.

604

Our observations have convinced us that on areas or parts of areas in the Midwest where sharecropping is not feasible, an effective program of quail management can be conducted using only prescribed burning.

Our analysis of the vegetation resulting from the prescribed burning and sharecropping was confined to open, nontimbered fields used by quail for nesting, feeding, and perhaps most important—roosting. The plants most frequently occurring after the burning or sharecropping were: goldenrod (*Solidago* spp.), rough buttonweed (*Diodia teres*), fall white aster (*Aster pilosus*), common ticklegrass (*Agrostis hyemalis*), Korean lespedeza (*Lespedeza stipulacea*), lesser and lance-leaf ragweed (*Ambrosia artemisiifolia* and *A. bidentata*), rushes (*Juncus* spp.), and beggar-ticks (*Bidens* spp.). These plants represent the early seral stages of secondary successions in this general area. Their abundance varied according to site location and soil fertility. Within this group of plants are annuals and perennials, and, except for Korean lespedeza, all are native to the area. Korean lespedeza and common ragweed are basic quail foods. The amount of bare ground in this early seral stage (6-18 months after share-cropping) ranged from 15 to 36 percent. Thus, the life-forms of these plants created a habitat that was open underneath, with some canopy cover. In these seral stages, quail could move freely, find food, and have a limited amount of protective cover. The amount of bare ground tended to decrease after disturbance, as the age of the plant community increased.

The food items most frequently found in the crops of quail on the Dale and Forbes areas were similar to those items frequently found in the crops of quail in a more extensive study in southern Illinois (Larimer 1960). The most frequently occurring seeds in our samples were those of agricultural crops, for example, corn, wheat, soybeans, milo, buck-wheat, and the millets, and those weeds associated with agriculture (common ragweed, crabgrass (*Digitaria Ischaemum*), etc.). In 1964 and 1965, acorns (*Quercus* spp.), sassafras, and ash (*Fraxinus* spp.) samaras were important items in the diets, and these seeds occurred frequently in the crops of quail throughout this study.

The bobwhite relies on foods associated with the early and near climax successional stages as a staple diet. A stage between the early and near climax stages contributed some items to the quails' diets. Plants in this intermediate stage that are important quail foods are partridge-pea (*Cassia fasciculata* spp.), wild bean (*Strophostyles* spp.), and beggarweed (*Desmodium* spp.), but our data, as well as Larimer's (1960), indicated that plants associated with the early and near-climax stages were the most important food sources.

Night-roosting coveys located on Forbes in 1964 were in cover more than 25 cm high. The ideal height appeared to be between 30 cm and 60 cm. A relative sparseness of vegetation at the roost site seemed to be equally characteristic. Most of the roost sites were on bare ground or on a light layer of duff; five roosts were on matted grasses and low forbs. The roosts tended to be located away from edges of the fields. Only five of the 23 roosts were within 15 m of field borders. Our findings on the cover types used by night-roosting quail are in general agreement with those of Klimstra and Ziccardi (1963) and Bartholomew (1967).

As plant succession progresses, the density of vegetation rapidly increases, the percent of bare ground decreases, a "rough" develops, and the incidence of the desirable shade-intolerant quail food plants such as the ragweeds and beggar-ticks is greatly reduced. The necessity for moderately open stands dominated by seed-producing weedy forbs cannot be overemphasized in quail management. Apparently, lesser ragweed is an important indicator species of the early successional stage so critical in quail management.

DISCUSSION

Quail abundance on Zone II at Dale and Zone II at Forbes was consistent with the general population trends of quail observed on other Illinois public hunting areas intensively developed and managed under the food-patch system. These trends exhibited a pattern of rapid increase of quail the first year or two after acquisition of the areas and the discontinuation of farming, followed by a fluctuating long-term decline which partially reflected regional trends.

Management under the food-patch system did not maintain quail abundance relative to the regionwide population, or at the level present when such management was initiated. The trends are considered to reflect the rapid development of rough under a program which induced new successions on too small a fraction of the land during any 1 year. Although the densities obtained using sharecropping and burning were gratifying, they did not approach saturation. Further adjustment can be made in the sharecropping program, and woody coverts adjacent to private land are needed on some portions of Zone I at Forbes.

Densities in excess of one quail per acre are possible on Zone I at Dale using only prescribed burning. As reported, we protected extensive tracts of low-grade oak-hickory timber and plantations of pine and multiflora rose from even cool fires. As a result, even after the 2nd year, 44 percent of the potential quail range had not been treated and presented a rough condition. Protection of these tracts was costly in money and loss of potential habitat. With a shift from spot burning to extensive burning where fire control can utilize natural topographic features, we should be able to effectively treat more acreage and achieve higher quail populations at less cost than we have thus far.

We recognize the evolutionary significance of periodic disturbance in initiating those stages of plant succession to which quail are adapted. We recognize that plant succession is inevitable, and that habitats favorable today will be less favorable tomorrow. We must devise systematic economical programs of disturbing game ranges so that the necessary successional stages continue to be adequately represented and properly distributed.

Economic Considerations

Any estimate of the value of a wild animal must be considered arbitrary. However, the amount spent in management annually should bear some economic relationship to the game resource it maintains and to the recreation it provides. On our study areas, population densities of quail ranged from less than 20 to almost 100 birds per 100 acres (Table 3); this is typical of the range of densities found on many public hunting grounds in our general area. More than 100 quail per 100 acres is unusual, although densities lower than 10 per 100 acres are not uncommon on larger areas in an advanced stage of succession. We do not know what maximum densities are possible. Perhaps they can exceed two quail per acre, but at present, a density of one per acre must be considered a desirable long-term objective in quail management.

Data obtained at hunter check stations revealed that hunters remove about 40-60 percent of the fall quail populations, the extent of harvest depending on a variety of factors including quail abundance, cover conditions, weather, and hunting pressure. At the quail densities reported in this study, a 50-percent harvest represents approximately one quail bagged per 2 acres on the zone managed under the program of sharecropping and burning; one bird bagged per 3 acres under the program based only on burning; and one quail per 5 acres where management was based on food and cover plantings. Management costs must be evaluated on the basis of quail densities and expected harvest rates.

Costs of managing public hunting areas involve more than the cost of habitat management. They include such expenses as maintenance of access roads, parking lots, sanitary facilities, directional signs, fences, drainage systems, hunter control, and public relations. These costs, although not readily predictable, cut deeply into any budget that we must justify on the basis of game abundance or harvest.

No detailed account was readily available on the cost of managing quail range under a system of annual food patches and cover plantings in Illinois. We have, however, applied available data on average per-acre crop production costs and current custom rates to three hypothetical management programs applied to one of our study areas. The significance of the estimated annual operating costs under the three hypothetical management systems lies not so much in the accuracy of the estimates as in the relative differences among the three systems.

Figures compiled by Hinton (1966) and Hinton and Peverly (1966) for 1960-65 show the following average per-acre production costs: corn—$46.13, wheat—$23.18, and meadow seedlings made in small grain—$6.36. The most frequent custom rates were: brush cutting with rotary cutter—$5.00 per hour; bulldozing with 10-ft. blade—$15.00 per hour; mowing weeds—$5.00 per hour. (Note: In using Hinton's and Peverly's findings we omitted some cost inapplicable to our situation.)

Burning can be cheap or expensive, depending on how it is done. Roy Komarek (Personal discussion, March 1967) indicated that the cost of burning is about $0.10 per acre on plantations in the Southeast. Because extensive tracts in that area are burned and the art of burning is well understood, a degree of economy is achieved that will not be easy to duplicate in the Midwest. Yet, with experience, we see no reason why burning for quail in most areas of the Midwest cannot be done for no more than $0.50 per acre burned—probably half that figure. In this analysis, however, we used $1.00 per acre as the cost for spot burning in programs based on a combination of sharecropping and burning, and

$0.50 per acre for programs based solely on burning applied to extensive tracts.

The area used in our hypothetical cost analysis was the 250-acre Zone I on the Forbes area. This tract consists of 140 acres of cropped upland, 48 acres of old brushy pastureland, and 68 acres of closed-canopy oak woodland with most trees 25-50 years of age.

The hypothetical food-patch program involved the mowing of brush and some bulldozing to control succession on old brushy pastureland, the planting of a 1-acre food patch in the spring, and making a 1-acre meadow seeding of wheat in the fall per 10 acres of open land, but no management of woodland. This program is generally equivalent to management carried out on the Zone II portions of the Dale and Forbes areas since 1963, but does not account for substantial costs of initial development for items such as lime, fertilizer, planting trees and shrubs, and extensive seeding of grasses and legumes. The estimated annual cost of operating a food-patch program is conservative, because managing small, scattered tracts is less efficient than the agricultural operations from which the costs of production were borrowed.

The economic advantages of programs based on sharecropping and burning become evident when the estimated costs of the three systems are compared (Table 4). Compared with the conservative figure of $4.57 for food-patch management (Table 4), both the estimate of $0.16 per acre per year for a program based on a combination of sharecropping and burning, and $0.22 for a program based only on burning, are realistic.

TABLE 4. Estimated costs of managing a 250-acre tract on the Forbes area for bobwhites under three systems of habitat management.

Management System	Food Patch		Sharecrop and Burn		Burn Only	
	Acres	Total Cost	Acres	Total Cost	Acres	Total Cost
Timberland (62 a)						
Burning			15	$15.00	15	$7.50
Brushy pastureland (48 a)						
Burning			24	24.00	24	12.00
Bulldozing	1	$15.00				
Brush mowing	12	60.00				
Cropland (140 a)						
Burning					70	35.00
Sharecropping			61	0.00		
Food patches—Rowcrops	14	645.92				
Wheat	14	323.52				
Grass and legume	(14)[a]	99.04				
Totals	41	$1,143.48	100	$39.00	109	$54.50
Cost/acre for entire area		$4.57		$0.16		$0.22
Percent of area treated		16		40		44

[a] Planted in wheat.

The relative costs of habitat management cannot be fully appreciated until they are related to the cost required to produce a quail in the bag (Table 5). Although the estimates for producing quail under the food-patch system seem high, $22.85 per bird and $182.80 for an 8-bird limit, we consider them conservative. All estimates are low because they do not account for the routine maintenance and overhead costs mentioned previously.

TABLE 5. Approximate costs of producing harvested quail under three systems of management employed on the Forbes and Dale areas.

MANAGEMENT SYSTEM	FOOD PATCH	SHARECROP AND BURN	BURN ONLY
Quail/100 acres	37	96	67
Harvest/100 acres	20	50	33
Acres/quail bagged	5	2	3
Mgmt. cost/acre	$4.57	$0.16	$0.22
Cost/quail	$22.85	$0.32	$0.66
Acres/limit (8)	40	16	24
Cost/limit (8)	$182.80	$2.56	$5.28

Fortunately, species such as cottontails and squirrels (*Sciurus niger* and *S. carolinensis*), plus a few mourning doves (*Zenaidura macroura*) and furbearers, are produced on upland game areas and help defray the cost of management. Seasonal movements of quail from private to public lands increase harvest somewhat and thus help offset cost, but this is a relatively small factor.

While our hypothetical area and management programs are arbitrary, and our data on operating costs fragmentary, it is apparent (1) that programs based on using area managers or roving field crews, salaried and equipped by public funds, to manage land for upland game hunting by planting cereal grain and forage crops, are difficult to justify on the basis of economics; and (2) that a combination of sharecropping and burning offers an economically sound basis for managing public lands.

Fire Ecology

Grange (1949) outlined the relationship between game range and community succession, which is basic to game management. He pointed out that many animals can occupy land only so long as appropriate successional patterns persist. Many successional stages are short-lived, and therefore the tenure of game species associated with them is equally short-lived. Successional patterns must be determined for key species in the community and for the land. The major task of game management is to obtain patterns of succession appropriate to the species to be managed. The repeatedly demonstrated habitat preferences of quail indicate that the bobwhite evolved in successional environments—those subject to periodic disturbance.

Foresters and plant ecologists have become increasingly aware of the role of fire in the ecology of a variety of grassland, savanna, and transitional communities in which the bobwhite is found (Shelford 1963). It is now generally accepted that these associations represent subclimax communities created and maintained by periodic burning over long periods of geologic time (Ahlgren and Ahlgren 1960). While no clear picture is available as to the frequency and intensity of burning in the various fire types in North America prior to the coming of European Man, our present knowledge of plant ecology, plus descriptions of vegetation and of the use of fire by Indians as reported in the diaries of the early explorers, indicate that extensive areas of this continent burned with relatively high frequency (Arnold 1964, Komarek 1964, 1965, 1966, 1967).

In the absence of burning, vegetative debris accumulates rapidly. The role of fire is not so much to kill as to prune away the old, the dead, and the undesirable so that the new and the vigorous may prevail. The importance of periodic controlled burning of brushland and woodland-edge quail habitats is that it creates a relatively open mosaic of bare ground and seed-producing plants interspersed with perennial forbs, grasses, shrubs, and trees typical of the later successional stages. Food abundance and cover conditions of the necessary successional stages are combined in a pattern conducive to high-density quail populations. The effect is to minimize the necessary size of home ranges or territories so that more individuals, pairs, or coveys may occupy a unit of range.

We have stressed the dependency of bobwhites on disturbed environments and particularly on the open-forb stage occurring the first year or two after disturbance, but we do not consider the bobwhite to be a single-stage species. Food-habits studies and field observations showed that relatively open brushland and woodland stages are important in the ecology of the bobwhite in Illinois. It appears that mast-producing oaks and hickories (*Carya* spp.) in groves and forest edges, and sassafras and persimmon in combination with the oaks and hickories in fence-rows, are particularly significant. However, these woody stages, too, require some disturbance if they are to be maintained in an optimum state for quail. Thus, in quail management, burning does not just happen to work—there is a definite ecologic and evolutionary basis for its working, and for any other activity such as sharecropping which initiates "bare ground" succession. This fact is as valid in the Midwest today as it was in the Southeast 40 years ago (Stoddard 1931).

Sharecropping

The abundance of many upland game species in North America coincided with the opening of new frontiers to agriculture. The key to the game abundance of those times was man's initiation of a checkerboard of new successions as a result of logging, clearing, frequent burning, moderate grazing, and the planting of small fields of grain. The effect of the grain crops was undoubtedly in part due to the food they provided and in part to the weedy forbs that grew and competed with them. This is the pattern we are endeavoring to produce through the use of a combination of sharecropping and burning.

Cash-grain crops provided the incentive for the program. We operated on a basis whereby the lessee received ¾ of the row crop and had the option of planting either corn or soybeans for his share; the remaining ¼ had to be in corn which was not harvested. The lessee agreed to cultivate and provide all necessary seed and fertilizer. The use of chemicals to control weeds was not encouraged, because plants such as the foxtails (*Setaria* spp.) and the ragweeds are desirable game foods.

Our practice was to allow the sharecropper to seed a small grain, usually oats, in the harvested ¾ of a field seeded previously to row crops, because an unclipped small grain stubble with its volunteer weeds provides a cover type much used by quail. We usually had 50-75 percent of the small grain seeded to legumes. We are now attempting to determine whether this procedure is desirable or whether we should sow legumes in all of the small grain. Legumes may make the stubble more attractive to rabbits and less so to quail. The stubble should definitely not be clipped.

To obtain a stand of legumes, a small grain cover or nurse crop is not needed. If the legumes are seeded early enough in the spring, an adequate germination and establishment occurs on bare ground in undisturbed corn or soybean stubble. However, the cost of buying and sowing clover seed can be avoided if a legume seeding is specified as part of a sharecrop-lease agreement that includes seeding a small grain after a row crop.

While it was possible to harvest the ¼ of each plot in corn which is allowed to remain unharvested, we were reluctant to do so. We observed that the plant community that developed in old patches of standing corn, and the corn itself, provided a cover heavily used by quail and cottontails for a period of 3-4 years. This cover condition appeared enhanced by a light broadcast seeding of a legume mixture, red and Ladino (*T. repens*) clovers, in the standing corn during late February or March of the 2nd year. The vegetation that resulted was relatively open, moderately tall, and produced a variety of quail and rabbit foods in addition to the corn; some of the corn persisted at least through the 3rd year. The key legume was Ladino clover, because it is a perennial that stays green to some extent year-round.

It is our observation that, contrary to many recommendations, *seeding of domestic grasses is undesirable* because they compete with more desirable volunteer species and rapidly form dense, matted sods that do not produce the desired diversity of food plants and are not conducive to easy movement by game animals. We agree with Kilmstra and Ziccardi (1963:212) that "Systems designed for intensive and improved grassland farming . . . are entirely detrimental to quail. . . ." Of definite ecological significance was their observation that quail roosts were characteristically located in relatively low, sparse vegetation. This vegetational life-form develops on soils of moderate fertility, primarily after abandonment following cropping and as a result of burning. It represents an important aspect of the community to which quail are adapted. However, this stage persisted only 1-4 years, depending on soil fertility.

We now believe that the basic crop rotation in the Midwest should be corn, or corn and soybeans, which may or may not be followed by small grain, then 1-2 years of legumes and volunteer forbs. All old pastures and brushlands not suited to cropping should be burned regularly, probably at least every other year in February or March. While our experience in burning groves and wooded edges is limited, under the right conditions it is highly desirable. Our observations on the responses of quail and cottontails to light-to-moderately grazed pastures has convinced us that limited grazing can also be used effectively in quail and cottontail management.

Initial Development

It has become common for game managers to "develop wildlife habitat" on newly acquired public lands. The initial treatment in many midwestern states typically consists of the subdivision of large fields with rows of pine and multiflora rose, block planting of pines in "strategic" spots, seeding sericea in strips along woodland edges, and seeding former cropland to some grass—legume combination.

Initial development is expensive. Using the Dale area as an example, we estimate that about $20.39 per acre, minimum, was spent on the initial treatment of that area (Table 6). This estimate does not include the cost of applications of lime and rock phosphate. (Agronomists routinely recommend application of 4-6 tons of lime and 1,000-1,200 lbs P_2O_5 at a combined cost of about $32 per acre on soils of comparable fertility in southern Illinois.)

TABLE 6. Summary of the costs of initial habitat development on 425 acres of previously cropped or pastured land on the Sam Dale conservation area, Wayne Co., Illinois.[a]

| PLANTING AND SEEDING | MILES | ACRES | MATERIALS | | | LABOR | | TOTAL |
			Number	Cost/ 1,000	Total Cost	Cost	Total Cost	
Multiflora rose	23.50		94,000	$16	$1,504	$16/1,000	$1,504	$3,008
Pines' (Row)	21.75		15,000	18	270	22/1,000	330	600
(Block)		23	16,000	18	288	22/1,000	352	640
Sericea		20				29.60/acre[b]	592	592
Grass and legumes		125				30.60/acre[b]	3,825	3,825
Totals	45.25	168	125,000		$2,062		$6,603	$8,665

Average per acre cost of initial development = $20.39

[a] Does not include costs for lime or P_2O_5 or for annual planting of food patches.
[b] From Burger and Linduska (1967:5).

We have observed that too-high levels of fertility rather than too-low levels are frequently the greater problem in upland game management in Illinois, because on fertile soils succession is accelerated and rough develops in a brief time, frequently after only 1 year, 2 at the most. We feel that use of commercial fertilizer should be limited to the amount a sharecropper will apply to assure a corn or soybean crop. One exception might be to lime and add rock phosphate to highly impoverished fields where three-awned grass *(Aristida* spp.) occurs as a long-persisting dominant, thereby encouraging a more diverse community.

We see little advantage in planting pines or other ornamental evergreens in areas where they do not occur naturally, unless for the specific purpose of creating nesting and roosting cover for mourning doves, or to make an area pleasing to the visitor's eye. In such instances, planting sites should be selected for their ease of protection from burning. We see little value in planting any exotic woody perennial that is not fire resistant, or in extensive plantings of multiflora rose, particularly when planted in long, unbroken rows. Multiflora spreads rapidly and, unless controlled, makes hunting difficult.

If the manager is convinced that woody vegetation representing later seral stages is inadequate, we suggest allowing natural succession to develop woody coverts on selected sites. On most Illinois quail areas, for example, such woody species as persimmon, dogwoods (*Cornus* spp.), black locust (*Robinia Pseudo-Acacia*), wild cherry (*Prunus* spp.), sassafras, oaks, and hickories will invade and provide excellent food and cover in a relatively few years. Several of the oaks, particularly some of the white oaks, are tolerant of so-called "cool" burns. Less hardy, short-lived species such as persimmon, locust, and sassafras sprout rapidly from their bases when aboveground parts are injured by burning. Where it is deemed desirable to short-cut succession by planting trees, we suggest using only native species that tend to be fire hardy and are known to produce food and provide a life-form of value to the species being managed.

Game management is, after all, applied ecology. Training managers in *successional* ecology, both plant and animal, must be stressed. The emphasis should be on the community rather than the species. We are opposed to the connotations of "habitat development." We believe that upland game management should be based on manipulation of natural succession. If upland game management is to be successful, managers must return to, and concentrate on, the concept of managing natural vegetation and must develop economical ways of doing so.

LITERATURE CITED

AHLGREN, I. F., AND C. E. AHLGREN. 1960. Ecological effects of forest fires. Botan. Rev. 26(4):483-533.

ARNOLD, K. 1964. Project skyfire lightning research. Proc. Annual Tall Timbers Fire Ecology Conf. 3:121-130.

BARTHOLOMEW, R. M. 1967. A study of the winter activity of bobwhites through the use of radio telemetry. C. C. Adams Center for Ecol. Studies, Occasional Papers 17. 25pp.

BURGER, G. V., AND J. P. LINDUSKA. 1967. Habitat management related to bobwhite populations at Remington Farms. J. Wildl. Mgmt. 31(1):1-12.

GRANGE, W. B. 1949. The way to game abundance. Charles Scribner's Sons, New York and Charles Scribner's Sons, Ltd., London. 365pp.

HINTON, R. A. 1966. Crop costs and returns on highly productive soils of western and west-central Illinois. Farm management facts and opinions to help you. Univ. Illinois Coll. Agr., Cooperative Ext. Serv. 66-5. [2pp.]

_____, AND H. R. PEVERLY. 1966. Custom rates and machine rental rates used on Illinois farms, 1966. Univ. Illinois Coll. Agr., Cooperative Ext. Serv. Circ. 956. [8pp.]

KENDEIGH, S. C. 1961. Animal ecology. Prentice-Hall, Inc. Englewood Cliffs, New Jersey. 468pp.

KLIMSTRA, W. D., AND V. C. ZICCARDI. 1963. Night-roosting habitat of bobwhites. J. Wildl. Mgmt. 27(2):202-214.

KOMAREK, E. V., SR. 1964. The natural history of lightning. Proc. Annual Tall Timbers Fire Ecol. Conf. 3:139-183.

———— 1965. Fire ecology—grasslands and man. Proc. Annual Tall Timbers Fire Ecol. Conf. 4:169-220.

———— 1966. The meteorological basis for fire ecology. Proc. Annual Tall Timbers Fire Ecol. Conf. 5:85-125.

———— 1967. Fire—and the ecology of man. Proc. Annual Tall Timbers Fire Ecol. Conf. 6:143-170.

LABISKY, R. F. 1968. Nightlighting: its use in capturing pheasants, prairie chickens, bobwhites, and cottontails. Illinois Nat. Hist. Survey Biol. Notes 62. 12pp.

LARIMER, E. J. 1960. Winter foods of the bobwhite in southern Illinois. Illinois Nat. Hist. Survey Biol. Biol. Notes 42. 35pp.

PAGE, J. L. 1949. Climate of Illinois: summary and analysis of long-time weather records. Univ. Illinois Agr. Expt. Sta., Bull. 532:96-354.

SHELFORD, V.E. 1963. The ecology of North America. University of Illinois Press, Urbana. 610pp.

STODDARD, H. L. 1932. The bobwhite quail, its habits, preservation and increase. Charles Scribner's Sons, New York. 559pp.

VESTAL, A. G. 1930. A preliminary vegetation map of Illinois. Trans. Illinois State Acad. Sci. 23(3):204-217.

PRINCIPLES AND PROCEDURES OF SUCCESSFUL RANGE RESTORATION (1968)

A. Perry Plummer, Donald R. Christensen and Stephen B. Monsen

Management of wildlife habitat is primarily manipulation of vegetation. Success usually requires extensive practical knowledge of plants and their autecology. This knowledge, seldom found in textbooks, is mostly learned in the field, often by trial and error. This chapter, based on more than a decade of research, provides a basis for making management decisions related to restoration of western big game ranges. Above all, this paper illustrates the practical nature of day-to-day employment in wildlife management.

Successful planting of range areas depends upon recognizing certain principles and following tested procedures. This has been demonstrated forcefully and conclusively on many areas in Utah. Ten cardinal principles for successful range restoration are presented here with some explanation and with recommendations for procedure. Since recommendations necessarily must be made for extensive areas, they frequently must be modified somewhat in accord with local conditions, availability of seed, and facilities for doing the actual work. However, such modifications will be satisfactory if they meet the conditions discussed below under each of the ten principles.

1. *Change in plant cover must be determined, by rational criteria, to be necessary and desirable.*

The goal of game range restoration is the development of a productive stand of desirable shrubs and herbs. Where some important forage plants are present, reduction of competition by appropriate methods may be all that is necessary to achieve the desired restoration. Perhaps some change in management to lessen grazing pressure would result in an adequate stand of desired species (fig. 1). Occasionally, spraying with a selective herbicide may be sufficient. To accomplish satisfactory improvement without seeding, at least one desirable shrub and 10 desirable herbs per 100 square feet should be present.

A good balance of browse and herbaceous plants is always desirable. Even with ample browse, an area may not have enough grasses and forbs to provide succulent forage in the critical periods of late winter and early spring. Lack of such plants causes game to seek farmlands where green forage is available. Consequently, seeding herbs that grow early in the spring (*e.g.*, alfalfa, arrowleaf balsamroot, small burnet, Utah sweetvetch, Russian wildrye, crested wheatgrass, bulbous bluegrass, and intermediate wheatgrass) can prevent much game depredation on croplands. Seeding these herbs should be done in the same year that unwanted vegetation is reduced, so that seedlings will have a minimum of competition.

Many areas now support vegetation that does not provide satisfactory forage or watershed protection. Such areas include juniper-pinyon communities with little or no understory vegetation, dense sagebrush supporting

Reprinted from: Restoring Big Game Range in Utah. Publ. No. 68-3, Utah Division of Fish and Game. 183 pp.

Figure 66-1.—Desirable native grasses in this encroaching stand of juniper increased markedly after livestock grazing was reduced.

few perennial grasses and forbs, cheatgrass in fairly pure stands, and impenetrable thickets of Gambel oak, black chokecherry, and other brush. On such areas, undesirable vegetation must be destroyed or greatly reduced to allow establishment of desirable species.

2.   *Terrain and soil type must be suitable to making the change selected.*

After palatable forage becomes established on good sites with deep soil, game animals generally move there. Then, less favorable areas can improve naturally. Shallow, infertile soils generally produce too little forage to justify use of expensive restoration programs. Soil that contains more than 1 percent of soluble salts—particularly sodium—is not suitable for use of restoration measures. Some improvement may be possible and justifiable on severe sites, but similar effort expended on favorable tracts would be preferable because it would improve the stand of forage more quickly.

Of course, some poor sites may require restoration treatment because they need more vegetal cover to control erosion. Here the demand for forage is only a secondary consideration. The combined demand for soil protection and forage may give some steeper land higher priority for treatment than some level areas. A game range manager must look closely at the soil and terrain on all depleted areas to determine where appropriate treatment would produce the most forage for the game.

New chaining techniques have made it possible to restore to high productivity sites that formerly were regarded as unsuitable. This has

616

occurred many times in the juniper-pinyon type, where steep slopes (as much 50 percent) are common. Many damaging floods originate in such areas; they cut and widen destructive channels through the desert shrub type. Adequate treatment of slopes is more costly than treatment of flat areas, but it is often necessary to treat hillsides to stabilize soil so that the sloping ground can hold water deposited by sudden storms. Slopes up to 50 percent have been successfully chained and stabilized in the juniper-pinyon type.

3. *Precipitation must be adequate to assure establishment and survival of planted species.*

Water is often the critical factor determining what vegetation will grow in a given area. Therefore, the manager of a big-game range area should check closely on the average annual precipitation received by an area before planning any restoration program that includes planting. Average annual precipitation usually should be more than 9 inches where artificial seeding is part of the restoration program. However, good improvement has resulted from some seedings made where precipitation has been slightly less than this amount.

The amount of precipitation, coupled with occurrence of indicator plants, is the most important guide to what species may be seeded successfully. Where precipitation is near the minimum limit, species that may be seeded successfully are usually limited to Russian wildrye, Fairway crested wheatgrass, Standard crested wheatgrass, bluestem wheatgrass, and range-type alfalfa. As precipitation increases, a greater variety of species may be successfully established.

From the foregoing, it is apparent that indicator plants are important. Presence of juniper and pinyon trees indicates availability of adequate moisture for several commonly used species. Again, if seepweed (pickle-weed) and iodine bush are prevalent, the soil contains a high concentration of soluble salts. Presence of appreciable amounts of shrubs that grow in the mountain brush zone (including Gambel oak, true mountain-mahogany, big sagebrush, and mountain snowberry, especially on south or west exposures) indicates favorable moisture, where several species can be profitably planted. Complete absence of mountain brush species or of thrifty big sagebrush, plus a high prevalence of dwarfed salt-desert shrubs (*e.g.,* shadscale saltbush or Gardner saltbush) indicates a site too dry to justify use of artificial restoration measures.

4. *Competition must be low enough to assure that the desired species can become firmly established.*

This principle must be effectively applied for successful restoration of most ranges dominated by a prevailing competitive vegetation, particularly where seeding is necessary. Dense stands of juniper and pinyon trees, thick stands of big sagebrush, and some early-spring-growing annuals (*e.g.,* cheatgrass brome and cluster tarweed) must be considerably reduced to assure seedling establishment of desirable plants. The method used need not completely eliminate the competing plants, but should thin them enough to minimize direct competition for moisture.

Following are descriptions and evaluations of several reliable methods for removing unwanted vegetation.

Anchor chaining.—Anchor chaining is an effective, economical, and widely applicable method for eliminating competition from juniper, pinyon, and other conifers that have no commercial value. Anchor chaining is also useful for opening thicket growth of such shrubs as big sagebrush, Gambel oak, black chokeberry, blackbrush, and black greasewood. Two-hundred-foot chains with links weighing 25 to 90 pounds each, pulled between a pair of 45-horsepower crawler tractors, have been used. Chains with links heavier than 70 pounds eliminate the young flexible trees better than lighter chains, but the lighter chains do less damage to understory shrubs. . . . . the chaining treatment covers the seed and allows debris to remain on the ground as a protective mulch for both soil and seedlings.

Chaining efficiently thins and opens dense stands of big sagebrush, and it covers seed well. This allows establishment of perennial herbs or permits development of suppressed understory herbs, yet retains sufficient big sagebrush for use as a satisfactory browse component.

Cabling.—Steel cables 1½ inches in diameter and 200 to 600 feet long may be pulled by tractors in the same manner as anchor chains. Cabling is less effective than chaining for eliminating young, flexible juniper and pinyon trees, but is a reasonably satisfactory method and is more rapid. Cabling has the advantage of doing essentially no damage to the existing shrub understory; so it is a better procedure where it is desirable to retain some trees as cover for game and to keep the understory intact. Cabling is valueless for thinning or opening brush thickets.

Bulldozing.—Bulldozing is an efficient but slower method than chaining or cabling for clearing ranges of juniper and pinyon trees. The method excels in eliminating scattered patches of trees, or in thinning tree stands without damaging associated species of shrubs such as cliffrose. Bulldozing is valuable for opening conifer stands. The hula dozer, a modification of the standard blade to allow tilting, makes this operation more effective.

Harrowing.—A self-cleaning pipe harrow is a much smaller but more effective implement than anchor chains for thinning big sagebrush or opening thickets of other brush. It is simply a series of spiked iron pipes, usually 4 inches in diameter, trailing behind a spreader bar. The swiveling pipes readily rotate and thus clear themselves of debris.

The pipe harrow is especially useful on areas too small for using two crawler tractors and an anchor chain. The pipe harrow is well adapted for treating rocky areas, but it is not so well suited as the anchor chain for treating steep slopes. A 40- to 45-horsepower tractor and a 14-foot pipe harrow make a convenient unit. . . . .

Disking.—Treatment with heavy disks effectively eliminates brushy competition where soil is comparatively free of rocks. The brushland plow is particularly effective for reducing competition in rocky land. This plow can be regulated to eliminate as much or as little competing brush as may be desired (fig. 2). Like the pipe harrow, the brushland plow is useful on areas too small to justify transporting heavy crawler tractors and anchor chains to the sites. These heavy disks and plows are particularly effective for eliminating such herbaceous competition as saltgrass, Baltic rush, and

Figure 62-2.—The brushland plow, designed for use on rocky or uneven ground, can be regulated to eliminate the desired amount of sagebrush.

other low-value herbs on meadows. Where sod is especially tough, moldboard plowing may be necessary to eliminate competition effectively.

Undercutting.—Several types of undercutters or root cutters (also called planes, blades, and grubbers) are available in varied sizes. Such cutters have been widely used for clearing brushland and eliminating undesirable herbs. Usually, blades can be raised or lowered by a lever on a hydraulic lift and set to cut at fairly uniform depth. Undercutting sometimes gives nearly a complete kill of the competing vegetation. A light undercutter eliminates annual and perennial weeds in the subalpine zone, and has performed well in eliminating cluster tarweed and mountain sagebrush.

Undercutters are most useful on comparatively level, rock-free areas that have deep soils and where there is a heavy clay subsoil. They loosen the surface soil but do not turn up the heavy subsoil as plowing and disking sometimes do.

Burning.—Burning is highly successful for reducing competition of woody vegetation where fire can be appropriately used and satisfactorily controlled. Except in dense growth, presence of a dry understory fuel is required to carry the fire. Igniting the foliage of trees with flame throwers and weed burners has proved useful for eliminating scattered trees, particularly those with small crowns. Burning is especially effective where cheatgrass brome is a competitive understory in big sagebrush and grows

619

as nearly a pure type. Burning effectively controls reproduction of cheatgrass or big sagebrush if done before the seeds drop. Fire must be confined to the area to be seeded or improved. Accidental burns are excellent areas on which to gain improvement at minimum cost, and game range managers should take advantage of them. Accidental burns should be treated immediately, not only to restore soil stability but to return wild lands to high productivity by seeding desired plants while competition is low.

Chemical treatments.—Application of Dybar or Fenuron granules (3-phenyl-1, 1 dimethyurea) at one-tenth pound per tree, where the trees averaged 7 feet in diameter, completely killed the trees within 2 years. The granules were scattered beneath the crown. Poisoning is useful for eliminating scattered trees, and it leaves a better cover for game than burning or knocking trees down; but extreme care must be exercised in dispersing poisons. Dybar did not damage the more shallowly rooted perennial grasses such as bottlebrush squirrel-tail, and Indian ricegrass. Such chemicals as 2,4-D or 2,4,5-T can also be used effectively to control big sagebrush and numerous other shrubs and forbs. One or 2 pounds acid equivalent per acre effectively kills most species. Current and up to date information can be obtained from county agricultural agents.

Interseeding.—Interseeding (seeding directly into established vegetation usually with only partial reduction of competition) is a widely successful means of improving vegetal cover for game and livestock. Using drills provided with 6- to 24-inch-wide scalpers that effectively eliminate cheatgrass and cluster tarweed is a satisfactory means of seeding shrubs and perennial herbs in competitive annual types. Interseeding is also effective in establishing shrubs and forbs in perennial grass stands. Wider scalping (12 to 24 inches) is preferred when seeding shrubs, but spacings of 6 to 12 inches are satisfactory for herbaceous perennials. Planting shrub seeds in three or four spots on 2½-foot-square surfaces from which ½ to 1 inch of topsoil has been scraped away has sufficiently reduced competition to allow shrub seedlings to become established. These scalps also provide desirable spots for transplanting seedlings, nursery stock, and wildings. Interseeding is especially useful on steep slopes where it is desirable to establish shrubs in predominantly herbaceous cover.

Some stands of woody plants also can be successfully interseeded with desirable forage species. Seeds of adapted plants can be drilled into stands of salt-desert shrubs, particularly black grease-wood and shadscale saltbush, if the annual precipitation is adequate and if salt concentration in the soil is not excessive. However, before interseeding in black greasewood, one must first break down the tops by disking, pipe harrowing, or cabling. On foothill ranges, seeds of adapted herbs can be successfully planted among established plants of rubber rabbitbrush without material reduction of its stands. In fact, production of established crested wheatgrass and smooth brome has increased when growing in association with this shrub.

Stands of adapted herbs have often become established from broadcasting seeds into depleted Gambel oak, black chokecherry, and aspen before leaf fall. Many herbs consistently produce more forage in association with Gambel oak and aspen than without this association; but the association notably reduces production of the woody overstory species. We believe that new plants can be established in these long-standing associations because there is so little competition for surface moisture at the time seedlings are becoming established.

5. *Only species and strains of plants adapted to the area should be planted.*—Species to be used for seeding must be able to establish and maintain themselves on the proposed sites. . . . .

Besides selecting appropriate species, one must make sure that only adapted sources or strains are used. Ordinarily, seed from sources having greatly different soils or very different climate is much less likely to produce good stands than seed from sites similar to those where it will be planted (fig. 3). Species from cooler climates can adapt themselves to warmer climates more successfully than the reverse. Whenever possible, one should plant seed from sources whose environments approximate conditions where it is to be established.

Adaptability is especially important for shrubs. Upper branches are exposed to air temperatures throughout the year and therefore are affected much more by extremes of climate than herbs. Herbs usually are dormant in winter, and their meristematic bases are insulated by snow. Even though herbs may be less affected by extremes of climate than shrubs or trees, it is important that their seeds come from sources that have environment similar to that of the sites on which they are to be used.

Figure 66-3.—Winterfat seedlings from salt-desert shrub type (left) are short, as contrasted with much taller seedlings from the juniper-pinyon type (right).

Differences between strains of several species have been observed. For example, seed of antelope bitterbrush collected from acid, granitic soils has produced chlorotic, unhealthy plants in basic soils originating from limestone or shale. Seedlings from fourwing saltbush seed collected in the warmer blackbrush type in southwestern Utah failed to survive when moved only 50 miles into a higher mountain brush type. Good stands of Indian ricegrass from salt-desert shrubland have completely died out in the climates of nearby mountain brush and upper juniper-pinyon. This native grass has particular localization of strains. Plants from seed of Indian ricegrass from cool, moist areas can survive in warmer areas, but not the reverse. Fourwing saltbush, antelope bitterbrush, big sagebrush, rubber rabbitbrush, and winterfat vary greatly in the characteristics noted above.

Results of our studies show that much can be done to improve the amplitude of adaptation, establishment, productivity, and palatability of shrubs through selection and breeding. This work will be emphasized increasingly.

6. *Mixtures of plant types rather than single species should be planted.*— In any comprehensive project of game range restoration that includes seeding—and most restoration treatments do—it is advantageous to seed mixtures rather than single species. Mixtures provide four major advantages.

First, they are better suited to the extremely varied terrain and climatic conditions that occur typically on foothill and mountain rangelands. In these areas, site characteristics change radically, often within a few feet. Seeding several species in mixture takes advantage of this diversity, and eventually the best adapted species excel.

Second, mixtures provide variety in nourishment that is desirable for both game animals and livestock. Nutritional needs must be considered on a year-round basis. Browse is essential on winter game range to sustain game while the ground is covered by snow. In such areas, shrubs that retain some green leaves (*e.g.,* fourwing saltbush, Stansbury cliffrose, and big sagebrush) are especially desirable and should be included in mixtures where the plants are adapted.

A third, and related, advantage of seeding mixtures is that they considerably prolong the season when succulent forage is available. This is assured when shrubs, forbs, and grasses having different periods of maximum succulence are established.

A fourth major advantage in use of mixtures is that they produce better overall ground cover than single species, especially where shrubs and herbs grow together. In one 21-year-old planting at the lower edge of the juniper-pinyon type, pure crested wheatgrass was providing 50-percent ground cover; a mixed half-and-half crested and intermediate wheatgrass stand was providing ground cover of 72 percent; but with the presence of rubber rabbitbrush, the ground cover increased to 95 percent. On these experimental areas, there was no appreciable difference in production of herbaceous cover (about 900 pounds per acre) for only two species. But when production of the rabbitbrush overstory was included, the yield increased by more than one-third to about 1,300 pounds per acre.

A few unusual circumstances dictate certain cautions in using plant mixtures. Occasionally we encounter an area where the environment is suitable for establishing only a single species. Also, some shrubs grow more slowly than herbs and consequently are vulnerable to natural competition for moisture. Whenever possible, seeds of slow-growing shrubs should be segregated from seeds of herbs in order to reduce competition. This can be accomplished by drilling shrubs and herbaceous species in alternate rows.

Broadcasting seeds of shrubs and certain forbs, which are in short supply, into pits or other more favorable areas left after chaining juniper and pinyon trees permits better establishment than including them in the mixture that is broadcast over the whole range.

When some species (*e.g.,* smooth brome and orchardgrass) are known to be suited only to north slopes of an extensive area, they should be seeded only on these sites. However, the feasibility of separating species for localized areas to which they are known to be best suited depends on the size of the area and type of equipment available. Helicopters and drills are more versatile for seeding small areas than fixed-wing aircraft, but often do not justify incurring the added costs.

7. *Sufficient seed of acceptable purity and viability should be planted to insure getting a stand.*—Too heavy seeding makes range restoration needlessly expensive. On the other hand, skimpy seeding may jeopardize establishment of good stands, and this is not economy when considerable money has been spent to prepare the site. Usually 8 to 20 pounds per acre of a total mixture is suggested for seeding game ranges; actual volume depends on the individual sites and on whether seeds are drilled or broadcast. When drilling, usually 8 to 10 pounds per acre is adequate; for broadcasting, 12 to 20 pounds is advised. The rate of seeding depends on the species being planted and on the quality of the seeds. The nearly uniform placement of seed by drilling usually permits lighter seeding rates than are required for broadcasting. However, because of rough terrain and obstacles to drilling, such as fallen trees and large boulders, broadcasting must be used extensively. Where costly seeds of certain shrubs are being used, they should be planted only where they have the best opportunity to grow. This may require a separate seeding operation.

Special attention should be given to assuring that seeds are of quality good enough to make plantings worthwhile. Information can usually be obtained by submitting representative samples to a seed laboratory for determinations of viability and purity. However, seeds of several shrubs, forbs, and certain grasses have a dormancy that makes germination difficult. Also, laboratories may not be able to make the analyses when needed. Consequently, to make fairly certain of the value of seeds from recent harvests, their fill and purity should be ascertained.

Good fill of recently collected seed is a fairly adequate criterion of good seed and can be substituted for percent germination in the formula for determining pure live seed (pls).[5] Fill is readily observed by cutting through a representative sample of seeds. Seed of many species can be cut with a sharp pocketknife, heavy scissors, or good fingernail clippers; the

---

[5] Pure live seed index is determined by multiplying the purity by germination and dividing by 100. For example, if purity of a given sample is 95 percent and germination is 80 percent, pure live seed index would be 76 percent, by the formula: $\dfrac{95 \times 80}{100} = 76$.

clippers are the best and quickest instrument for determining fill of many species. Seeds with especially hard or stony seedcoats, such as black choke-cherry, can be cracked with a hammer or similar tool.

Seeding rates should be increased when a source of seed shows low germination and purity. Viability of seed older than 3 years should always be checked. Seed of herbaceous species and most shrubs should usually have a purity of at least 90 percent and a germination of 85 percent, with a pure live seed index (pls) of not less than 75 percent. Because of the difficulty and expense of cleaning, seed of several shrubs and some forbs must be accepted at much lower standards of purity than others. Important among these are big sagebrush, rubber rabbitbrush, yellowbrush, black sagebrush and winterfat. Purities of 8 to 10 percent of the first four are regarded as satisfactory. Purity of filled utricles of winterfat is usually acceptable when it attains 25 to 50 percent. Collections of utricles of winterfat are accepted as received, but stems and larger inert materials must be extracted.

.   .   .   .

Dormancy of most seeds is broken by stratification—subjecting them to temperatures between 32° and 40°F. for a period of 6 to 20 weeks in moist sand, peat moss, or moist newspaper. Subjecting seeds to outside wintertime temperatures for similar periods also overcomes dormancy. Of course, fall and winter plantings take advantage of the cool temperatures and thus break dormancy naturally. Treatment of seeds of antelope bitterbrush for 3 to 15 minutes with a 3-percent solution of thiourea breaks dormancy, so that good sprouting can be obtained from spring planting. Thiourea has also helped in breaking seed dormancy of several closely related shrubs.

For many species, scarification by sulphuric acid treatment or mechanical rubbing helps overcome dormancy for determining germination and for preparing seeds for planting. Approximate intensity of these treatments varies with species and seed source, and depends largely on the thickness and hardness of the seedcoat. Seeds of some species require both scarification and stratification, especially when both a seedcoat and an embryo dormancy are involved.

8. *Seed must be covered sufficiently.*—Seeds must have a light covering of soil—usually one-fourth to one-half inch. Very small seeds (*e.g.,* rubber rabbitbrush, big sagebrush, and sand dropseed) need no more than one-fourth inch of cover. Chaining and pipe harrowing are not likely to cover broadcast seed too deeply, and bolting depth rings to the disks prevents too deep covering in drilling. Covering seeds by more than one-half inch of soil generally reduces emergence. Deep planting is seldom desirable. Likewise, leaving seed uncovered after broadcasting is unsatisfactory except when moisture at planting time is unusually abundant.

When slopes are too steep for use of heavy machinery, planting must be done by hand. On such areas, corn planters or specially built Schussler[6] bitterbrush planters can be used advantageously to gage the depth and number of seeds planted of most species. Other similarly designed planters are available and can speed up hand-seeding on slopes.

---

[6] This bitterbrush seed planter was designed by Mr. Howard Schussler of Caldwell, Idaho.

Some compaction helps to improve stands, especially when seeds are planted in the spring. Packer wheels that follow the planting units on drills are particularly useful. Culti-packing or compaction by similar implements improves stands on soils that dry rapidly. The area where soil-packing equipment can be used to advantage is small, but it is worthwhile to use it when needed.

Large disturbed areas left by crawler tractors are favorable for planting shrub seeds of browse species. The compressed cleat marks left by tractor treads are exceptionally good places for dropping seeds. A newly designed deck-mounted "seed dribbler" drops seeds into these cleat marks.[7] This device is especially useful for placing scarce seeds of shrubs and herbs in spots favorable for establishment. From such places plants can spread to other parts of the range.

9. *Planting should be done in a season that gives promise of optimum conditions for establishment.*—Planting for range restoration may be either seeding or transplanting. Seeding is the usual means of establishing grasses, forbs, and a few shrubs; some shrubs can be propagated more satisfactorily by transplanting, and best success has come from transplanting in the spring.

Direct seeding in late fall and throughout the winter (mid-October through mid-February) gives good stands of most species. Although spring seeding of a few species (notably alfalfa, small burnet, fourwing saltbush, and winterfat) has sometimes been successful, it cannot be generally recommended. Winter seeding (late January and early February) on 5,000 acres of Daggett and Duchesne Counties successfully established alfalfa and fourwing saltbush. Wherever climate permits, winter seeding is preferred because it avoids the inherent dangers of precocious germination resulting from unseasonably warm temperatures for short periods in the fall.

Four major advantages of fall or winter seeding over spring seeding are:

1. It overcomes inherent dormancy.
2. Cold winter temperatures stimulate seedlings into more rapid growth.
3. The longer period of available adequate moisture produces larger seedlings, which can better withstand heat and drought in summer.
4. Loss of seed to seed-collecting animals is reduced because many of these animals hibernate.

When shrubs that have dormant seed must be seeded directly in the spring, seeds should be treated with a 3-percent solution of thiourea for 3 to 15 minutes to overcome some of this dormancy and to improve both emergence and establishment. This is particularly true for antelope bitterbrush. Planting of stratified seed is generally more successful for a greater number of species. However, care must be taken that stratified seeds do not dry out. Spring planting should be done as soon as the soil is dry enough to get necessary equipment on the land. This is usually before April 15 on Utah ranges. In the warmer blackbrush type in southwestern Utah, spring seeding should be completed March 1. The suitable period for successful spring seeding (2 to 6 weeks) is short, contrasted with the 4-month suitable period through late fall and winter.

---

[7] "Seed dribbler" is manufactured by the Walter Hansen Machine Company, Ephraim, Utah.

Transplanting of nursery stock, seedlings, and wildings is usually most successful when completed while the ground is still moist from snowmelt. Spring transplanting should be done as soon as it is possible to get equipment on the land. Fall transplanting frequently fails because the ground has become so dry that the roots dry out and die. Bud sagebrush and common iris can be planted either in the spring or in the fall; both grow well after fall transplanting despite dry soil. Late fall planting of wildings of these two plants, even into dry soil, survived nearly 100 percent; whereas a similar planting of big sagebrush and rubber rabbitbrush failed completely.

10. *The planted area must not be overgrazed.*—Young plants and seedlings do not develop well when grazed or severely trampled by livestock, big game, rabbits, or small rodents. Until seeded stands have become established and suppressed plants have had opportunity to recover, livestock grazing should be light, if permitted at all; and after range restoration has been accomplished, grazing should be conservative. The practice of "taking half and leaving half" is always good.

Where big-game pressure is heavy, the number of excess animals should be appropriately reduced, preferably by harvesting a greater number during hunting seasons. However, much overgrazing by game can be avoided if treated areas are large enough to prevent damaging concentrations. In Utah, 500-acre areas have usually been satisfactory. Of course, larger units can further reduce this concentration and damage.

DAMMED WATERS IN A MOOSE RANGE (1957)

R. Y. Edwards

Usually control of wildlife habitat is in the hands, not of wildlife biologists, but of farmers, foresters, ranchers, engineers and "developers". Habitat improvement for wildlife may be integrated with many land uses— up to a point determined by the intensity of development. Land development may also irretrievably destroy habitat for many species. The choices between hydroelectric power and moose, between a ship canal and an Everglades fauna, between urban development and a goose flock are not professional choices. They are public decisions, sometimes rooted in public apathy due to unawareness of potential habitat destruction. It is an obligation of our profession to predict—as best we can—the effects of development upon wildlife habitat and to promote public awareness of what is at stake.

Western Canada is witnessing a boom in power hungry industrial development. Among the more widely publicized of these developments has been that to provide hydro-electric power for a large aluminum smelter at Kitimat, on the coast of British Columbia. Water from a major tributary of the Fraser River has been diverted to generators on the coast by means of a tunnel through the Coast Mountains. As in most such engineering projects, the gain in industrial strength has been accompanied by losses to other resources. This paper examines briefly the damage to one resource, the moose population, in the vicinity of the flooded reservoir. As necessary background, some broad ecological aspects of the terrain about the reservoir are given and some changes which resulted from the rising water are noted.

The area of major interest centers upon a chain of seven lakes (Ootsa, Natalkuz, Euchu, Tetachuck, Eutsuk, Whitesail and Chelaslie) until recently in Tweedsmuir Provincial Park. These are long and narrow, forming with their connecting rivers a unique oval of waterways some seventy miles across. This chain lies in an area of topographic transition. The eastern extreme is in relatively flat plateau. Westward the country becomes progressively more precipitous, while the most westerly waters penetrate the rugged and broken topography of the Coast Range.

Most lakes in the chain lie with their long axes east and west, and most surrounding lands rise in long slopes from the water. This topographic pattern contributes to a marked vegetational contrast between slopes north and south of most waters. Slopes to the north, facing south across the lakes, grow aspen parklands, variously open, with willows common in the understory and with grasses forming dense cover on the ground. Above south shores, on the other hand, the vegetation is mainly coniferous, lodgepole pine with Engelmann spruce. This pattern is characteristic along all but the most westerly fifty miles of the two hundred mile long chain. There the influence of mountains creates subalpine conditions resulting in dense coniferous forests of spruce, true firs, and hemlock.

Reprinted from: Murrelet, Jan.–April 1957, pp. 1-3.

627

The warm parkland slopes are winter ranges for moose, by far the most common large mammal in the region. Before water levels rose, migrations involving hundreds of moose were undertaken annually across the lakes between the warm slopes and the coniferous areas to the south. The coniferous summer range has extensive poorly drained areas lying among the foothills.

A dam three hundred feet high on the Nechako River has flooded the shores of all but one of these lakes. Eutsuk Lake was spared for its waters are above the level of the reservoir. Flooding was to various depths, on one lake only five feet while four were raised over one hundred feet. In all, 170,000 acres of forest and range lands are flooded. The reservoir now has a surface area of 335 square miles and is fed by a drainage basin of about 3000 square miles.

Clearing forest from lands to be flooded was given some consideration, but was declared too expensive. Only a few key boat harbours and landings have been cleared. Because of the steep slope of most lands bordering the original lakes, most flooded stands of trees have been completely submerged. Trees have remained rooted, and will probably remain so until waterlogged. All shores, however, are fringed to various widths with a tangle of partially submerged trees and floating logs. This floating debris is composed mainly of windfalls and fire killed trees which formerly lay in the forest.

The rising water has affected the moose population in three ways. Moose trapped on hills and ridges have drowned; flooded range is a direct loss of living space and of food producing lands; debris about the shores forms an effective barrier to migration.

Moose trapped by the rising water were a common sight by the reservoir as it filled. Low hills and ridges destined to be completely submerged became islands in the process of their inundation. Moose on these were trapped by floating debris, for swimming moose are unable to pass over floating trees.

The loss of range was considerable. All but subalpine areas near the mountains supported moose in winter. Of the 170,000 flooded acres in the reservoir, half are about the lake chain considered here. Of this acreage about two-fifths supported deciduous vegetation and hence was winter range of prime importance. Most of the remainder was coniferous winter range of poorer quality. The loss of range necessary for survival in winter was about 80,000 acres, with about 30,000 of these supporting dense winter populations. Since warm, deciduous slopes are undoubtedly the key to the abundance of moose in this region, this 30,000 acre loss is the most serious. The decreased ability of the region to support moose in winter is greater than the proportion of range lost, however, since lost acreages are those at lowest elevations. In mountainous terrain it is the lowest winter ranges which are usually the most valuable. To date the full impact of this loss of range has yet to be fully reflected in the moose population. British Columbia is currently experiencing a series of relatively snowless winters, and ungulates are surviving in good condition on relatively high ranges. A return of severe winters with deep snow will bring into effect the full impact of this range lost from low elevations.

Perhaps the most important influence of the new reservoir on moose numbers is that of the barriers which floating debris has thrown across traditional migration routes. Formerly, moose in hundreds crossed the lakes on the ice in early winter to reach the slopes with shallow snow and abundant browse. Their return in the spring was in the water. In spring, 1955, moose in numbers were observed on the new shores near the former crossings. They appeared to be animals thwarted in migration. The waters of the reservoir had not frozen well in the winter 1954-55 with the result that some moose were unable to cross on the ice. Results were evident from sign near the shores. While deciduous areas were lightly browsed for the first time in many years, browse among the conifers near south shores was thoroughly utilized and aspen bark was eaten from large trees on a scale far greater than in previous years. Numbers of moose, unable to cross the lakes, had wintered on inferior range. Those that did cross were unable to return to summer range in the spring.

Local reports indicate that swimming moose were drowned. The lakes always took a small toll from moose falling through the ice, but under present conditions there is no hope for swimming animals. The extent of this mortality would be difficult to assess accurately. Most drowned animals have remained in the debris near shore where a boat can gain access only after considerable effort aided by poles, axes and power saws.

An experiment is in progress near several of the crossings used heavily prior to flooding. Small areas have been cleared of trees and debris on opposite shores in the hope that they will aid migration. Results could be good, bad, or indifferent. These new crossings may be used with success, they may encourage the animals to enter the water with little chance of their being able to find the opposite clearing and so gain the opposite shore, or they may be more or less ignored.

The dammed waters have not created an immediately serious situation in wildlife management. To date hunting in this area has been light and quite unable to hold moose populations at a level sufficiently low to prevent mortality during severe winters. It is the long range picture that is serious. The loss of living space is permanent and the barrier to migration will last for decades. Both lower the carrying capacity of the region for moose. It will be the inevitably increased number of moose hunters in the future that will experience, as they hunt, the results of this change.

While farmers and ranchers suffered immediate loss of some of their best lands, and the region was changed abruptly from an attractive recreational area to a wilderness slum, it will be some years before the hunting public can report a tangible loss.

AMID BRICK AND ASPHALT (1966)

Irston R. Barnes

Most Americans live in cities. Soon eighty-or-more percent of our children will be growing up in cities. What will happen to their instinctive curiosity for wild living things? Where will they learn to enjoy nature? Perhaps they will not. They certainly will have little opportunity to gain an appreciation for nature if their city offers only house sparrows and starlings. Lacking this appreciation, they may never care if eagles are being poisoned, if wild rivers are being dammed, or if deer herds are being poorly managed. Wise use of public wildlife resources requires a public that is interested and involved in the social process that determines each generation's definition of wise use. There will be little progress in wildlife conservation if we have a public apathy toward wildlife. Our only hope for maintaining all wildlife values lies in exposing wildlife to people who live in cities.

Birds in cities? Yes, indeed. Glover-Archbold Park, which is 4.75 miles from the White House in Washington as the starling flies, is a natural, untended woodland. The ground is deep in humus and leaves. Fruit-bearing shrubs and understory trees provide nesting sites and food for birds.

It has an abundance of wildlife: Red-shouldered hawks and barred owls, pileated woodpeckers and four of their cousins, bobwhites, chickadees and titmice, house and Carolina wrens, wood thrushes and veeries, Acadian flycatchers and wood pewees, and a dozen varieties of vireos and warblers.

It supports one of the most varied and dense nesting populations of any woodland area in the country for which population studies have been made.

European ornithologists who visited the park en route to an International Ornithological Congress expressed envy of such an area in the middle of a city. Their parks, they said, are too artificial and manicured.

Another example: A different kind of park is the Wissahickon in Philadelphia. I have visited it early in the morning and late in the afternoon and, particularly when birds are migrating, learned some significant facts with respect to migrants, the length of stopovers for individual birds, and the weather patterns that seemed to influence their flights.

Any city park set amid brick and concrete may be an oasis for a small bird caught at dawn over an extensive city. Then all kinds of unusual visitors may be seen—woodcock and sapsuckers, thrushes and warblers, sparrows and kinglets. Central Park in the middle of New York City is such an over-sized migration trap. Bird observers have enjoyed it for years.

Since rivers often are migration highways for night flyers, birding in the early morning along river banks frequently is rewarding. I have found that the narrow strip of neglected trees and grass between River-

Excerpted from: Birds in Our Lives, A. Stefferud, Editor. U.S. Dept. Interior, Bur. Sport Fisheries and Wildl., Washington, D.C. 561 pp.

side Drive and the West Side Expressway, between 96th and 125th Streets in New York City, is an excellent place to make a quick appraisal of what migratory movements have occurred on fall nights.

Still another example, but of a different kind—a city park so planted and landscaped as to leave suitable habitats for few birds and so thoroughly sprayed with chemicals that even those few birds may be missing. A biologist recently returned from a tour of duty in the West was walking with me along the Mall in Washington. As we looked over the expanse of grass and shade trees, he asked, "Where are the robins and chipping sparrows? When I was stationed in Washington, there was a robin's nest in every second or third tree."

I had to tell him that for several years we had not found a robin's nest between the Capitol and the Washington Monument and that many of the migrant robins attracted to the area died in convulsions characteristic of insecticide poisoning.

. . . .

If you are taken with status symbols (a new car, a large house, stylish clothes, a fine lawn), there is one status symbol that is not in the advertisements but may mean more than all the rest in terms of an enjoyable, liveable community—the birds that choose to reside with you.

Ecologists recognize various plants and animals, singly or in combination, as indicators of the character of a forest, field, farm, or other natural or man-altered area. Birds are among the most useful indicators. They are among the best of Nature's status symbols. Have you considered what your present bird neighbors indicate about the status of your community? Are you privileged or under-privileged, congested or spacious, urban or suburban?

To illustrate the avian status scale, we might consider the summer residents available to an eastern city:

If your only birds are chimney swifts circling in the sky by day and nighthawks zooming down at dusk, then you are a cliffdweller in the center of town. Chimney swifts are satisfied with old chimneys, which provide sites for their nests. The nighthawks find that flat gravel roofs of apartments are secure places in which to raise their young.

The house sparrow, as the sole or dominant nesting bird, is indicative of crowded houses and pavements, little or no open space, and few or no grassy areas or shrubs.

A song sparrow or a chipping sparrow would represent an improvement in the environment—pleasant lawns of some size and at least a sprinkling of small shrubs to provide nesting cover.

A cardinal or a mocking bird would be a higher status symbol for a city or urban neighborhood. Either would indicate more spacious lawns and more landscaping. The cardinal would be satisfied with a few trees and some dense shrubs. The mockingbird would insist on small trees as well, such as dogwoods or hawthorns, for they like to nest higher than the cardinal.

Young robins surviving to feed on the lawn in summer would advertise a neighborhood of grassy lawns and shade trees. Their survival would signify that the neighbors had not doused their grounds with lethal sprays and that lawns had not been poisoned with massive applications of chlorinated hydrocarbons. Robins and bluebirds are reminiscent of old-fashioned orchards. The bluebird would be the higher status symbol, for it requires not only trees and open areas but also the presence of old woodpecker holes or nesting boxes.

Chickadees and titmice would similarly reflect a community where older trees provide natural nesting cavities or where people are providing nest boxes.

The presence of red-eyed vireos and yellow-throated vireos would proclaim a fine old neighborhood with fully grown shade trees lining the streets or scattered through the yards.

The scarlet tanager is a rather special symbol, indicative of the presence of a substantial number of mature oak trees.

The top status symbols for a suburban neighborhood would be wood thrushes, catbirds, or brown thrashers. All require an area of gracious shade trees, naturalistic plantings of smaller trees (dogwoods, thorns, and the like), and many shrubs, preferably with a mulch or litter around them. Such a neighborhood would enjoy the finest of bird songs, a vocal advertisement of a place for pleasant living.

The birdlife of a neighborhood can be transformed by wise planting.

How much can be accomplished in residential areas was demonstrated to me when I found 15 species nesting in one season in a single residential yard in the Chevy Chase section of Washington. Sixteen bird families included mourning dove, downy woodpecker, wood pewee, blue jay, whitebreasted nuthatch, house wren, mocking bird, catbird, brown thrasher, robin, wood thrush (two pairs), red-eyed vireo, scarlet tanager, cardinal, and song sparrow. And the yard was visited throughout the year by a variety of other birds.

What kind of residential area could produce such abundance and variety of birds? The area had once been wooded, and mature trees were left standing when the houses were built. Not all of the neighbors had planted trees and shrubs that were specifically attractive to birds, but none of them at that time was using highly toxic insecticides or herbicides.

Few of the neighbors operated feeding stations or birdbaths, and there were a number of cats. If proper cover is provided for birds, cats are unlikely to affect seriously the bird population. Birds have many more young than the habitat can support, having become adjusted to the normal high incidence of nestling mortality in the wild.

The successful attraction of birds depends upon meeting their minimum requirements for food, water, and cover. Cover is most important during the nesting season to provide protection from weather and enemies and to afford nesting sites.

The residence to which I refer was well planted, with the general objectives of shade, foundation planting, border planting, and screening accomplished through the use of trees and shrubs attractive to birds. The canopy trees consisted of red oak, tulip tree, silver maple, American elm, apple, eastern white pine, and eastern hemlock. These trees were planted around the borders of the yard. The oaks were between the sidewalk and the street. Between the larger trees, there was an understory of smaller trees, of which flowering dogwood was the most numerous, and all around the yard was a border of low shrubs, including various azaleas, rhododendrons, and bush honeysuckles. This pattern of planting duplicates the woodland-edge effect that is so attractive to birds and provides suitable niches for canopy, understory, and ground species.

Planting may be adapted to the characteristics of the residential lot and to the other interests of the homeowner.

The basic requirements of cover and food can be provided in many ways. If the yard is small, the emphasis should be on cover, depending on natural foods to supply the few birds that can be attracted. If the yard is large, it may be possible to indulge in the luxury of a jungle of briers and vines in a back corner.

• •

Urban and suburban residents who are interested in birds and Nature generally should have an opportunity to enjoy their recreations more frequently than is possible only by making long trips.

Those who have made any progress with birding have discovered that birds are associated with particular kinds of habitats, each species having its special niche in the economy of Nature. Birding then takes on a new fascination, for birds become the keys to different types of habitats and the best fun in birding comes with observing the bird in its natural environment. The fuller, more significant experience of birding with an ecological insight requires facilities, just as baseball, golf, and other recreations require suitable facilities.

Every city, I think, should have within easy distance a variety of natural areas that collectively represent all the different types of natural areas and wildlife communities that are indigenous to the region. These natural areas should be extensive enough to support reasonable populations of the kinds of wildlife that are associated with the habitat.

Thus, there might be a marsh, a woodland lake, a bottomland forest and swamp, an upland pine woods growing up on an abandoned field, a bog that is perhaps a relict of glaciation, and as many more as the diversity of the surroundings of a city permit.

These natural areas should be living museums, preserved in their natural state, altered only to provide access for people under conditions which would not disturb the wildlife. They could serve also as outdoor study areas for children who are studying biology and for college students engaged in research.

The natural areas, or living museums, would replace the natural areas that earlier generations found within walking distance of city limits. They could be established as private sanctuaries, as public areas administered by natural history societies under a trust arrangement, or as special-status parks. They should not be "developed," but should be left in a natural state and administered only to the extent necessary to prevent abuse.

City dwellers also should have access to country places where they may observe at first hand the significance of different patterns of land use and the meaning of conservation practices as applied to our basic resources of soil and water, of farm land and forest.

Sound public policies in the management of our renewable resources depend upon a realization by our citizens that people are a part of the world of Nature.

This realization can hardly come as an abstract intellectual exercise. It can come through increasing opportunities for individuals to experience Nature.

In terms of these larger goals of making the individual a citizen of the universal natural world, as well as a citizen of his city and nation, birding and natural history studies are of more than private concern. They should be encouraged by preserving many unspoiled examples of natural areas for the enjoyment and the self-education of urban and suburban residents.

SIMULATION TECHNIQUES IN
WILDLIFE HABITAT MANAGEMENT (1970)

Robert H. Giles, Jr. and Nathan Snyder

*All management decisions are based upon information from past ex-
perience. This information may include a knowledge of biological principles; ideas from the literature on species, environments, or their interactions;
or field data obtained by the wildlife manager. The quality of a management
decision is determined by the quantity and quality of pertinent information
and by the ability to integrate information into accurate predictions.*

*The complexity of wildlife ecology is well known. The more information
available as a basis for management, the more difficult is the job of integration. The task of integrating data on several interacting factors can become
a horrendous bookkeeping problem. This paper illustrates the potential of
simulation modeling for handling a large volume of data and for predicting
results of potential management programs.*

Balancing the dynamics of habitats with the dynamics of wild animal
populations at desired densities for both is a major task of wildlife management. Perhaps it is the major task. To achieve the balance, a six-fold solution must be obtained, namely, (1) population goals rationally established
by the state conservation agency in cooperation with landowners, (2) suitable big game population estimates or indices, (3) inventories of existing
quantities and qualities of big game forage, (4) predictions of future
amounts of available forage, and (5) manipulation of habitats to achieve
the population, and (6) manipulation of the population by hunting and
other means to achieve the population goal. The state agencies (with the
help of land managers) have the responsibility for achieving the first,
second, and sixth parts of the solution. Parts 3, 4, and 5 are within the
purview of the land managers aided by various researchers.

We have concluded from the literature and our observations that total
pounds of available forage (F) on an area used by animals during the stress-
ful periods of the year (usually winter range) is the chief factor determining the annual potential big game population density (P). We see "cover"
as a concept of alternate sites within which populations can achieve desirable energy balances. We recognize many other factors influencing
density but make the basic assumption that food is most significant. By
"significant" we mean here a factor that accounts for a higher proportion
of the size of and accounts for more variability in the prediction of a value
(such as density) than any other factor contributing to such variability.
We conclude that of all environmental factors influencing populations,
food is the only one currently feasible to manipulate in any significant way
(i.e., with any reasonable expenditure of time or money to have a measure-
able influence on more than 85% of the population being managed).
Mathematically speaking, the "potential game population" is a function
of "available forage." If, for example, 33 lb. of air-dried forage per day

Excerpted from: Modelling and Systems Analysis in Range Science, D. A. Jameson, Ed. Sci.
Series 5, Range Sci. Dept., Colo. St. Univ., Ft. Collins 134 pp.

will support 11 animal units, then if there are 330,000 lb. of forage available, 110,000 animal units could be supported.

A forage function F can be defined such that given a positive number t, where t = 0 is the present and t = 5 is five years into the future, then the number F(t) is the available forage in a given area t years from the present.

A potential game population function, P, can be defined such that if x is the number of pounds of available forage, then P(x) is the number of animals that can potentially be supported by x pounds of forage. If the function, F, described above is known, by composing the functions P and F, the number P(F(t)) is the number of animals that can potentially be supported t years from now.

There is no guarantee that the number P(F(t)) is the *actual* animal population. Populations usually vary from the potential and may temporarily exceed their food supply or they may not achieve complete consumption of the available supply. There is a lag in population during food increase and when food decreases for a time, the population levels exceed it until a drastic collapse occurs. A new function, p, is desirable so that if t is greater than zero, p(t) is the actual number of animals present. There is no way to determine the number p(t) at present, without additional assumptions. We have accepted the premise that "nature abhors a vacuum" and that within a lag period of a few years (less than four), most big game populations can increase to the limit of available forage. The balance of habitat and populations is dynamic, the population or habitat responding to increases or decreases of the other. With such a premise, the main assumption that available forage determines potential populations, and one other, that there are no major habitat changes in those few years, then p(t) = P(F(t)).

Certain animal densities are more desirable than others, for example, as they may increase hunter success, reduce tree seedling losses, reduce range damage, or reduce time between sightings of animals by recreationists. Since population density can be regulated, actual density is most properly viewed as the result of human decisions made (or not made) and limited by available forage. Thus, there is a new function (D) a desired population density such that D(t) is the desired population at any time. D(t) is only realistic if $D(t) \leqq P(F(t))$. The management objective is to cause (p(t) - D(t)) to approach zero.

The decisions on desired wildlife population densities are largely the responsibility of the state wildlife agencies. Thus, the Forest Service has concentrated its efforts to understanding, quantifying, and predicting the amounts of available forage (the values of F(t)) as they influence the potential population. (The assistance of Dr. Donald Cook in the formulation of the above ideas is gratefully acknowledged.)

Achieving a capability to do the above on 2.9 million acres of key winter range in Region 1 (Montana and Idaho) is extremely difficult and complex. The vegetation for big game, for example, occurs in different types and sites, slopes, soils, and has a variety of ages. Vegetation grows to a height which animals cannot reach and on lands which conifers often invade. Food supplies (largely from shrubs; see center curve, Fig. 1) wax

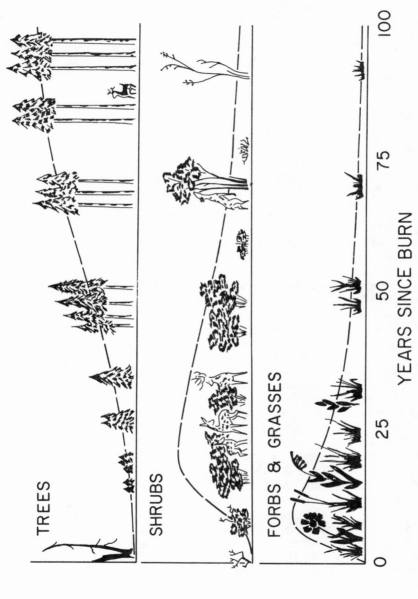

TREES

SHRUBS

FORBS & GRASSES

YEARS SINCE BURN

0   25   50   75   100

Figure 69-1.—Vegetational succession after fire, logging, or other disturbances favor for a period shrub production critical for big game forage (Figure from L. Jack Lyon).

and wane following well established concepts of plant succession. Thus, the amount and quality of big game food on any area is quite different from that on any other area.

The complexity of the problem is suggested in the early work of Daubenmire (1952) and continuing study by other researchers. Food production in various habitats is being studied by a number of agencies and individuals in the Northwest. The Intermountain Forest and Range Experiment Station (Lyon 1966) is studying succession following fire and logging. The Idaho Fish and Game Department (Leege and Hickey 1968) is studying the effects of burning on elk winter range in forest types. The Pacific Northwest Experiment Station is studying ecological change in forest types. Brown (1961) of the Washington State Game Department, related deer production to forest management, particularly clearcuts in western Washington. Pengelly (1966) related white-tailed deer habitat productivity to logging on the Coeur d'Alene National Forest in north Idaho. Gates (1969) studied deer food production in west coast forests. Special forage inventories are now underway.

A specific example of the complexity and magnitude of the problem is the Clearwater elk range. The so-called Clearwater elk herd has a fair amount of fame in the West. The herd resides in north Idaho within the drainage basin of the Lochsa, Selway, and Clearwater Rivers. There have always been elk on the Clearwater, but the herd multiplied as a result of fire and logging in the forepart of this century. Elk numbers are believed to have peaked sometime in the 1950's at about 31,000 head (Norberg and Trout 1957).

Large fires occurred on the elk winter ranges in 1931, 1934, 1936, and 1938. A large acreage was burned more than once, resulting in prolonged seral brushfield successions. There has been large-scale logging activity from the 1940's to the present. Fire and logging stimulated forage production which peaked sometime in the 1940's. Since that time, forage production has diminished as conifers have invaded the seral brushfields, and forage has grown out of reach. Fires have been largely eliminated, and timber cutting activity is not adequate to offset forage loss due to successional advances in the old burned and logged areas.

The Clearwater range is not unique. Similar land-use changes throughout the country change the successional rates of various vegetative types. It has been well established that the forage available at any time is dependent upon the stage of plant succession.

These problems and relationships are the basic causes and rationale for developing a computer-based simulation of the forage production on the Clearwater and for developing a generalized method for explaining and predicting big game forage. The simulations enable managers to gain alternatives for making more objective decisions on habitat manipulation practices. The method enables a clearer view of the influence which practices may have on game or livestock populations and allows more rational allocation of limited manpower and funds to the big game management problem.

The problem was quite real on the Clearwater. The Idaho Fish and Game Department, which is responsible for the game population on the area, and the Forest Service, which is responsible for the habitat, have been mutually concerned about the future of the Clearwater elk ranges. In 1962 Dr. Lyon (previously cited) inaugurated research on the effects of fire and logging on wildlife habitat. The ecology of seral shrub communities in the subject area was previously studied extensively by Walter F. Mueggler, Intermountain Forest and Range Experiment Station (Mueggler 1965). In 1966 the Idaho State Fish and Game Department began Pittman-Robertson fund-supported research on a project entitled "Range Rehabilitation by Spring Burn" as a phase of the Lochsa Elk Study.

In the meantime, National Forest administrators, concerned that the range resource would slip away before proper remedial measures were taken, began some prescribed burning of brushfields and some timber cutting designed to arrest the obvious trend. There was no way to decide how much rehabilitation should be done because no one had decided how many elk should be supported. A meager budget precluded much being done. The Forest Rangers had to proceed on the basis of "horseback opinion."

In 1967 the senior author, then at the University of Idaho, was developing a Browse Field and Range Growth Simulation Program as a phase of a McIntire-Stennis Project. He offered the U.S. Forest Service and Idaho State Fish and Game Department his ideas since they promised a feasible approach to the problems of digesting the habitat inventories and producing meaningful habitat manipulation plans. Howard Foulger, Chief of Range and Wildlife Management in the Northern Region, with the encouragement and cooperation of the Idaho Fish and Game Department, decided to proceed with development of the simulation program.

The program is based on the previously described relations and on the simple concept that the total food present in any large Forest Service area is the sum of the food available on each forage area throughout the Region, Forest, District, or Management Unit (Fig. 2). (All Forest Service administrative land units are hereinafter designated by the word "unit.") That is, the forage available over time is the sum of the areas under all successional curves that are descriptive of the unit. Each unit, because of its size, characteristics, and treatments has hundreds of such curves, all of different shape, amplitude, and origin (Fig. 2). The average Ranger District of Region 1 has about 29,000 acres of key big game winter range. Within this area there are 300 or more distinct habitats each lending themselves to manipulation with one overall unit-specific treatment. These are areas with reasonably uniform vegetation and topographically situated so that logging or burning is a practical treatment. The objective of the program was to assist in the explicit problem of expediting and allowing more accurate decisions to be made for achieving a habitat-dependent big game population goal (e.g., to increase the population at a rate of 0.05 per year for 10 years and then stabilize the rate at 0.0).

The conceptual model outlined herein has been used to enable computer calculations of the complex relations of area, succession, food needs, and population objectives. We define simulation as the act of building a model and then performing experiments on it by asking questions of the "What if I did this?" variety. The general approach we have used is not unlike those described by or used by Gould and O'Regan (1965), O'Regan and Palley (1965), Arvanitis and O'Regan (1967), Garfinkle (1962), Watt (1968), Newnham (1966), King and Paulik (1967), and Kelly et al. (1969).

The simulation is accomplished by five major activities: (1) determining the area and year of origin of all forage areas, (2) judging the model or curve that best describes the successional trends, (3) summing the areas under all curves, (4) generating outputs that describe forage available throughout the unit both historically and for the future, assuming no further habitat changes, and (5) generating schedules of cutting, burning, or other land treatment on specified acres that will achieve a previously decided objective function (a line representing a desired rate of wildlife population change).

The simulation was programmed in FORTRAN IV for a CDC-3100 computer.

INVENTORY SYSTEM

The inventory developed for the simulation is designed for up to 9999 habitat units. The main items used in the simulation are:

1. Acres
2. Elevation
3. Percent in winter range
4. Year of origin (succession)
5. Quality factor
6. Successional curve
7. Recommended treatment (if any)
8. Exposure

. . . .

The first inventory was conducted on the Lochsa District of the Clearwater National Forest. This was taken from aerial photos and field checked by Ranger District personnel (over a period of 5 years) and required about 60 man days. A sample of the inventory printout is shown in Fig. 3. The column headings are largely self-explanatory but a few need comment. The successional curves (col. 5) will be outlined in the next section. "Elev Code" is elevation of area coded to nearest 1,000-ft elevation. "Rec. Treat." means recommended treatment such as planting or burning. Forage equivalents is a multiple of forage per acre and the quality factor. A quality factor "Qual" has been interjected to account for nutritional and other differences. Forage from different areas has different nutritional quality; multiplication by this quality factor "standardizes" areas. Obviously, the quality factor can be used to modify forage value for influences other than nutritional quality. Table 1 illustrates how a quality factor table might look. More research will be required to enable improved use of this part of the system.

The "estimated animal unit days supported per acre on all areas" is the forage equivalents divided by 3.0. The "animal unit days supported per year on winter range" is a multiple of the proportion of the area in winter range, animal-unit days supported per acre, and the number of acres. The printout shows "animal units" which can be supported. The animal unit is 100 lb. of deer or elk support of one day. It was assumed that 3 lb. of air-dry usable forage will support each 100 lb. of animal.

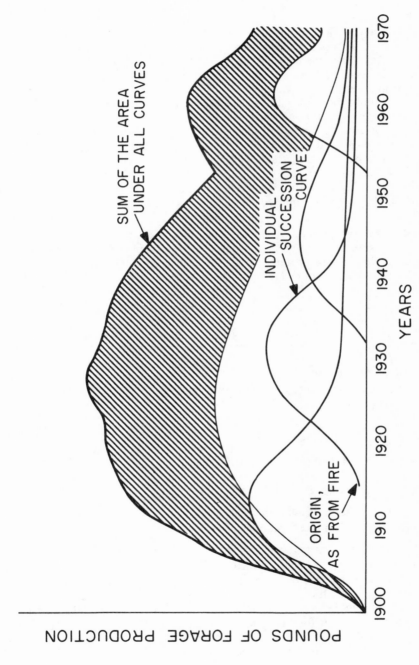

POUNDS OF FORAGE PRODUCTION

YEARS

SUM OF THE AREA
UNDER ALL CURVES

INDIVIDUAL
SUCCESSION
CURVE

ORIGIN,
AS FROM FIRE

1900   1910   1920   1930   1940   1950   1960   1970

Figure 69-2.—The sum of the areas under all curves on a unit is the total amount of forage available in any period.

643

The calculated animal units supported may be converted to elk or deer days at the user's discretion and in accordance with local population mixes. The following adjustments are necessary:

1. *Allowance for actual or proper use.* The total forage available for use may be more than double what is actually used or what should be used. Practicing range managers often consider 50% to be the proper maximum use of available forage on key big game habitat.
2. *Conversion from an animal unit to deer or elk units.* For example, an average elk in Region 1 is considered to weigh 430 lb.; thus 4.3 animal units may be converted to an elk day.
3. *Adjustment for the difference between 3 lb. and the actual intake for 100 lb. of deer or elk.* $3 \div 3.3 = 0.91$. Thus, 0.91 (animal units) = 100-lb. deer units. This illustration would be applicable for a locality where the actual intake per 100 lb. of deer averages 3.3 lb. of air-dry forage.

Once the inventory table is generated, the work does not have to be repeated; data can be updated as often as desired.

Table 1. Three methods used for assigning a quality factor to forage to standardize quantities measured or estimated. To illustrate, 1000 lb. of low protein forage located over 3000 ft elevation, would have a quality factor of (0.40×0.66) and be equivalent to 264 lb. of forage of high protein on winter range (below 3000 ft).

Classification Criteria	Quality Factor
Protein	
Average winter protein content high	1.00
Average winter protein content intermediate	0.70
Average winter protein content low	0.40
Elevation	
Under 3000 ft elevation	1.00
Over 3000 ft elevation	0.66
Cover	
Within 1/8 mile of suitable cover	1.00
1/8 to 1/4 mile of suitable cover	0.70
Over 1/4 mile to suitable cover	0.25

SUCCESSIONAL CURVES

A successional curve is a function that yields the total pounds of air-dried forage available to animals during the winter on an area of a specific size and of generally uniform topography and vegetation. Within a large area, the vegetation for big game may occur in many different ecological types, sites, slopes, and soils. They follow the gross pattern of Fig. 2. All of these variables can be described by six curves or functions. These are

FOREST 17 NEZPERCE RANGER DISTRICT 07 SELWAY STATE 11 IDAHO

HABITAT UNIT NUMBER	ELEV CODE	PORTION IN WINTER RANGE	YEAR OF ORIGIN	TYPE OF SUCCESSIONAL CURVE	REC. TREAT ACRES	ACRES	POUNDS OF FORAGE PER ACRE	POUNDS OF FORAGE EQUIVALENTS PER ACRE	ESTIMATED PER ACRE ON ALL AREAS	ANIMAL-UNIT DAYS SUPPORTED PER YEAR ON WINTER RANGE
2580	32	1.00	1934	4	0	545	193.5	.66	42.6	23202
2590	35	1.00	1934	4	0	430	193.5	.66	42.6	18207
2600	32	1.00	1934	4	0	390	193.5	.66	42.6	16604
2610	31	1.00	1934	4	0	420	193.5	.66	42.6	17881
2620	38	1.00	1934	4	0	570	193.5	.33	21.3	12134
2630	31	1.00	1934	4	0	660	193.5	.66	42.6	28099
2640	29	1.00	1934	4	0	565	193.5	.60	38.7	21868
2650	31	1.00	1934	4	0	380	193.5	.66	42.6	16178
2660	29	1.00	1920	3	0	320	168.4	1.00	56.1	17962
2670	33	1.00	1800	4	0	470	50.0	1.00	16.7	7833
2680	33	1.00	1800	4	0	230	50.0	.66	11.0	2530
2690	34	1.00	1800	4	0	550	50.0	.66	11.0	6050
2700	34	1.00	1800	4	0	540	50.0	.66	11.0	5940
2710	32	1.00	1800	3	0	535	50.0	.50	8.3	4458
NUMBER OF HABITAT UNITS = 203						TOTAL	WTD. AVG.	WTD. AVG.	WTD. AVG.	TOTAL
						55174	133.5	91.6	30.5	1681064

Figure 69-3.—Sample printout of Table 1, the basic tabulation of unit inventory and preliminary calculations.

645

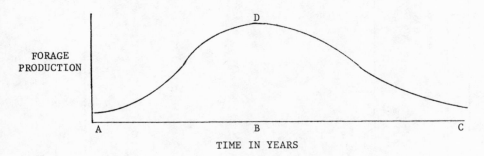

FORAGE
PRODUCTION

D

A   B   C

TIME IN YEARS

Curve Code	AB Time from Origin to Peak	BC Time from Peak to Minimum Stability	BD Peak Production
01	12 years	28 years	500 pounds
02	None	28 years	500 pounds
03	12 years	55 years	500 pounds
04	None	55 years	500 pounds
05	12 years	12 years	500 pounds
07	12 years	28 years	250 pounds

	North Slope	South Slope
Fire, less than 300 acres (includes clearcut and burn)	01	01
Fire in curve 01 or 07 between 6 and 30 years	02	02
Fire, over 300 acres	01	03
Fire, more than 300 acres in curve 03 area between 12 and 60 years	*	04
Fire, less than 300 acres in curve 03 area between 30 and 60 years	*	02
Fire, less than 300 acres in curve 03 area between 12 and 30 years	*	04
Clearcut, burn, plant 11' x 11' (or closer spacing)	05	05
Clearcut, burn, plant 12' x 12' (or wider spacing)	01	01
Existing brushfield with over 300 seedlings and saplings per acre	02	02
Clearcut, no burn	07	07

*No curve 03 on north slope

Figure 69-4.—Classification (code number) and characteristics of types of successional curves for browse fields on the Clearwater, Nezperce, and St. Joe National Forests (from Wildlife Surveys Handbook, Table 5, 190-5).

646

FOREST 17 NEZPERCE   RANGER DISTRICT 07 SELWAY   STATE 11 IDAHO

YEAR	ANNUAL FORAGE PRODUCTION IN TOTAL POUNDS	ANNUAL FORAGE PRODUCTION IN POUNDS OF FORAGE EQUIVALENTS	ANIMAL-UNITS SUPPORTED EACH YEAR ON WINTER RANGE
1964	6594864	5110459	1696362
1965	6280577	4870216	1617760
1966	5966776	4630122	1539148
1967	5655881	4391996	1461029
1968	6013683	4440483	1477191
BASE YEAR 1969	6905043	4924018	1638369
1970	7072902	4828559	1606550
1971	6779139	4606620	1532570
1972	6492349	4393133	1461408
1973	6293926	4258868	1416653
1974	6090516	4122706	1371265

Figure 69-5.—Sample of an 11-year estimate of forage production.

found in Table 5 - 190, Wildlife Survey Handbook, FSH 2609.21, R. I. A rough description of these curves is found in Fig. 5 and they are mathematically of the form (e.g., for curve type 01):

$$Y = 0.04 \, x^3 - 3.41 \, x^2 + 80.35 \, x - 68.02$$

Pengelly (1961) stated that the peak of forage production on Douglas-fir sites in north Idaho was reached in 10 to 15 years after logging. He studied both burned and unburned logging sites. He noted: "After burning, the site is dominated for two to five years by herbaceous growth. A mixed variety of shrub species then invades and may flourish for 30 to 60 years before the timber species effectively compete." And ". . . At 30 to 40 years following logging, conifers are making their greatest increase and tend to crowd out understory shrubs."

Brown (1961) indicated a somewhat shorter period of increased productivity following logging in virgin west coast coniferous forests where natural forest regeneration is rapid.

Production was deduced from fecal pellet group survey data. A weight value was established by assuming a defecation rate of 13 daily groups for deer and elk and a mean food consumption rate (air dry) of 4.5 and 12 lb. daily for deer and elk, respectively.

In constructing the production curves in Fig. 4, total forage produced was considered to be double that of calculated total forage used. There is much to be said for basing production goals and production curves on actual use rather than weight of several kinds of forage assumed to be useful to animals in varying degrees. Taber and Dasmann (1958) recognized this when they said, "It is evident that carrying capacity must be based on what deer actually will eat rather than on what they could get if they actually went after it."

The curves are based on average production for a large number of units. The production indicated would be misleading except that equally large numbers of treatments will occur often enough under planned management to achieve average results. With improved habitat manipulation techniques, constant adjustment of predicted production will be needed to avoid overshooting goals.

The vegetation on each unit may be of a different age. To properly use the functions, it is necessary to know the year of origin of the vegetation in the area. If the year of origin is t_o, then for any positive number t, the multiple of the curve function (coded) and $(t - t_o)$ is the pounds of air-dried forage produced per acre per year (e.g. $01(t-t_o)$, $02(t-t_o)$ . . . $07(t-t_o)$).

If a habitat unit can be described by exactly one succession curve (by definition), then the following additional information is needed: the year of origin, the number of acres, the area quality factor, and the proportion of the area in winter range. Suppose an area to have curve type 04, year of origin 1934, with 545 acres, a quality factor of 0.66 and to be entirely (1.0) within winter range. Then in the present year if $04(1970-1934)=04(36)$ = 193.5, that area will produce $(193.5) \times 545 \times 0.66 \times 1.0 = 69{,}596.5$ pounds of air-dried forage per year.

FOREST 05 CLEARWATER RANGER DISTRICT 05 LOCHSA STATE 11 IDAHO

YEAR	TOTAL ACRES - 32741 POUNDS OF FORAGE EQUIVALENTS PER ACRE - WTD. AVG. -	ANIMAL-UNIT DAYS SUPPORTED PER YEAR ON WINTER RANGE ONLY UPPER LIMIT	MEAN	LOWER LIMIT
1940	248.2		2708682	
1944	287.2		3134373	
1952	309.1		3373871	
1956	297.8		3250071	
1960	275.6		3007939	
1964	248.0		2706515	
1968	250.9		2738015	
1972	213.3		2327959	
1976	178.0		1942199	
1980	141.6		1545265	
1984	106.5		1162190	
1988	77.1		841364	
1992	53.1		579253	
1996	50.0		545403	

Figure 69-6.–Sample of estimates of forage production for selected years.

The available forage for any unit is obtained by (1) dividing the unit into habitat management units, A_i, each A_i with a unique successional curve; (2) determine the available forage on the unit that is

$$F(t) = \Sigma \; A_i \; (t)$$

where $A_i(t)$ is the annual forage on each habitat unit.

Calculations

Fig. 5 shows the computer printout of a summation of runs for 11 years, five years before and five years after the current year. Fig. 6 shows a run for only those years selected by the manager. Such selection is useful for checking against historical records or for predictions to be included in special reports or budgetary planning.

The final table generated, and the one of greatest management usefulness, is shown in Fig. 7. With awareness of the previous three tables, the forest wildlife manager can see what must be done to manipulate the successful changes in his unit to support desired game populations. The information is now available also to more objectively counterattack public pressures for hunting season closures, massive winter feeding efforts, and socio-political setbacks in their programs. Fig. 8 shows how a series of habitat successional curves could be initiated through time to produce a constantly increasing food supply and thus an increasing big game population. The value of "r" seen in Fig. 8 or the rate of population change is a value decided by the game agency in cooperation with landowners and managers. The large population over a broad area responds to the total food available. The objective line can be achieved by studying the minimum number of what type curves, of what acreage each, that will produce a total amount of food approximating the objective line. (Subsequent studies and development will be directed toward mathematically minimizing the distance between the *summation* line which represents the existing forage fields plus those to be created, and the *objective* line.) Put another way, the management objective is to achieve a minimum cost fit close to the objective line.

The steps used to achieve the results shown in Fig. 7 are as follows:

The originating administrative unit requests a run of Table 4 (Fig. 7), specifying habitat units for which some habitat manipulation is already planned. Prior to submitting their inventory, the originating unit has reviewed each recommended treatment for compliance with multiple use guidelines. Three examples are: (1) manipulations are not recommended for Wilderness or Natural Areas, (2) recommended treatments for campground areas are confined to those included in campground development plans, and (3) units for which silvicultural treatment is planned are recommended for that particular treatment.

The inventory deck is sorted to select units for which treatment is recommended. From these units, we select the units for which a scheduled treatment was specified by the originating unit. These treatments are then simulated and the previous summation curve is adjusted accordingly for 20 years (assuming a 20-year plan for (Fig. 7).

For the initial year, the forage deficit, if any, is calculated. (The deficit is the difference between the new summation line and the goal line.)

FOREST   05   CLEARWATER   RANGER DISTRICT   05 LOCHSA   STATE 11   IDAHO

OBJECTIVE— INCREASE PRODUCTION IN 1989 BY 50% TO SUPPORT 1001952 ANIMAL UNITS

| YEAR TO TREAT | ACRES TO BE TREATED BY CURVE TYPE | | | | | | | | | | | | ANIMAL UNITS SUPPORTED |
| | TREATING ONLY ONE CURVE TYPE | | | | | | TREATING OPTIMUM MIX OF ALL CURVE TYPES | | | | | | |
	01	02	03	04	05	07	01	02	03	04	05	07	
1971	0	0	3000	270	0	0	0	0	0	270	0	0	2187164
1972	0	0	0	415	0	0	0	0	0	415	0	0	2134205
1973	0	0	0	420	0	0	0	0	0	420	0	0	2092166
1975	0	0	0	60	0	0	0	0	0	60	0	0	1924639
1976	0	0	0	185	0	0	0	0	0	185	0	0	1855448
1977	0	0	0	206	0	0	0	0	0	206	0	0	1793414
1978	0	0	0	241	0	0	0	0	0	241	0	0	1730159
1979	0	0	0	222	0	0	0	0	0	222	0	0	1666200
1980	0	0	0	164	0	0	0	0	0	164	0	0	1599430
1981	0	0	0	207	0	0	0	0	0	207	0	0	1540263
1982	0	0	0	122	0	0	0	0	0	122	0	0	1462194
1983	0	0	0	256	0	0	0	0	0	256	0	0	1411887
1984	0	0	0	130	0	0	0	0	0	130	0	0	1342669
1985	0	0	0	140	0	0	0	0	0	140	0	0	1276115
1986	0	0	0	170	0	0	0	0	0	170	0	0	1213686
1989	0	0	0	186	0	0	0	0	0	186	0	0	1016980
TOTAL	0	0	3000	3394	0	0	0	0	0	3394	0	0	1015937

GOAL IS IMPOSSIBLE FOR CURVE TYPE 01
GOAL IS IMPOSSIBLE FOR CURVE TYPE 02

Figure. 69-7.—Sample computer printout of Table 4, the acres of various types of treatment needed to achieve stated objectives.

If a deficit exists, the next step is to select units in curve 1 within age limits suitable for treatment (as imposed by constraints). Then initiation of curve 2 is simulated beginning with the oldest unit and continuing with the next to the oldest and so on until the deficit is made up. The units and acreage needed are stored in memory.

The foregoing process is next repeated with curve 2, 3, and 4 units, in that order, always beginning with the oldest unit in each curve class because the oldest unit is assumed to have the most potential for increasing production.

In the next step, from memory are selected the unit treatments which involve least acreage to achieve the goal. These are listed with previously planned treatments as the optimum mix.

The whole process is repeated for each successive year in the plan period. Each year the summation curve is adjusted for work planned that year.

A number of constraints were imposed in order to restrict any possible treatment of acreages to reasonable and productive operations. These constraints were:

1. Total treatment shall not cause reduced productivity of more than 10% in any one year, nor more than 7% in any 5-year period.
2. A fluctuation of plus or minus 10% around a stated objective line will be considered as meeting the objective.
3. Do not simulate fires larger than 300 acres.
4. In areas of curve 01, do not simulate treatment until the 20th year after the curve origin.
5. In areas of curve 02, do not simulate treatment until the 8th year after the curve origin.
6. In areas of curve 03, do not simulate treatment until the 30th year after the curve origin.
7. In areas of curve 04, do not simulate treatment until the 18th year after the curve origin.

General Observations and Conclusions

A model has been developed for the rational manipulation of habitat to achieve predetermined objectives. The model is robust, and employs broad-brush techniques well justified in the midst of the inherent variabilities in the natural environment, shifting values and statements of population management objectives, inadequately researched relations of forage quantity and quality to big game in the wild, and the vagaries of sampling both habitats and populations.

Computer manipulation of real and projected data has allowed field *data* to be transformed into usable management *information*. Management decisions, always made under conditions of risk, are dependent upon relevant information if they are to become more objective and to improve. The results of these manipulations of data are not answers; they are inputs for the decision systems of well-educated wildland managers. Their willingness to test and improve the model, to collect more accurate data in just the right quantity, and to do research both in increasing the precision of the vegetation succession curves and the forage quality concept will make the

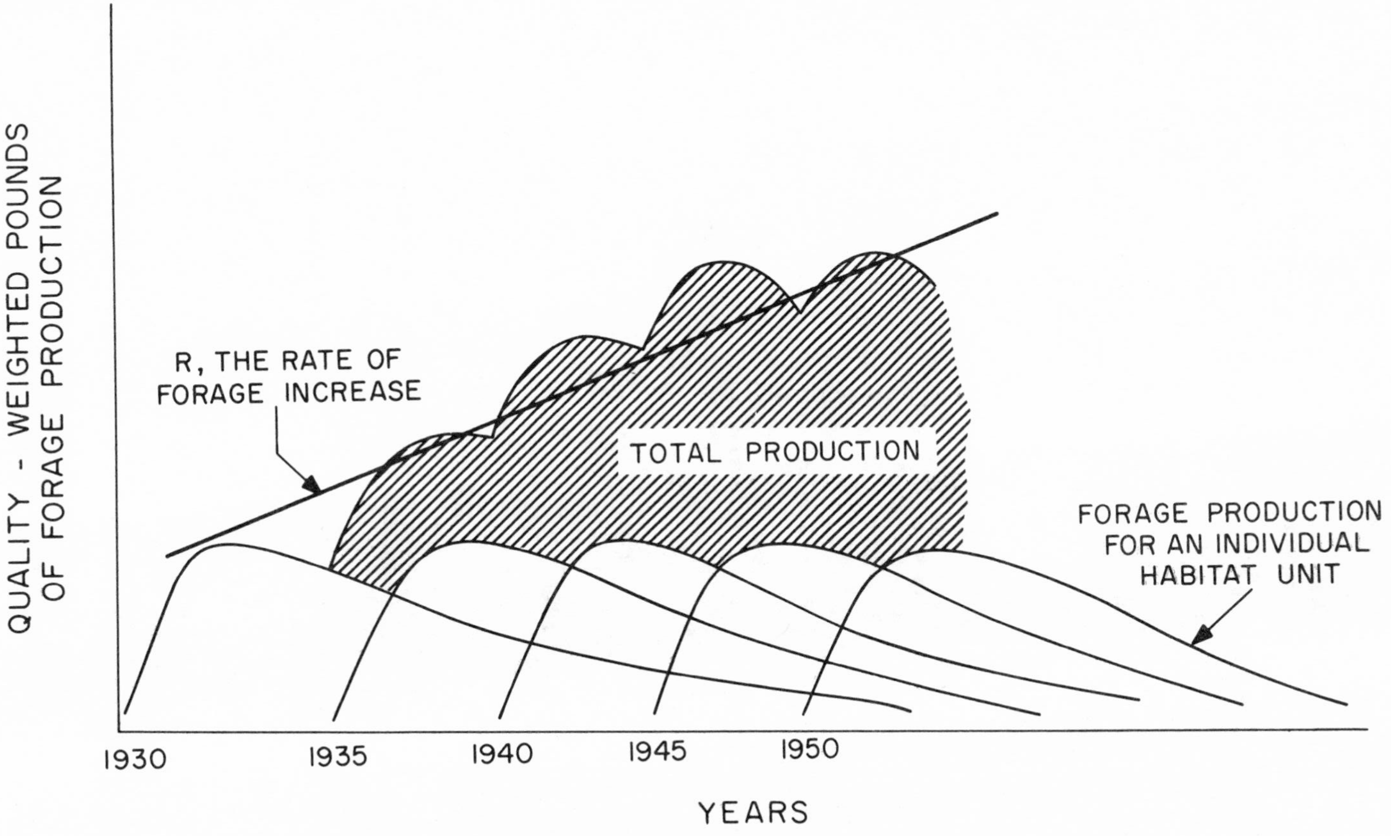

Figure 69-8.—Series of habitat successional curves initiated through time to produce a constantly increasing food supply.

simulator reported here of increasing usefulness. We, however, wish to warn against efforts toward gaining greater precision in the model that cannot be justified within the limits imposed by probability. For example, it would seem unwise for managers in-the-large to expend $20,000 to increase the precision of forage quality measurements by 5% when the normal expected variability of the end calculations may exceed 10%. Control of data and improvement of the program, however, can and should be continuous with time; efforts have been made in the design of the program to expedite such desirable feedback. The efforts at simulation have already provided new insights into the land and its ecology and the nature of the wildlife decision process. Hopefully, by its use and improvement, the simulation can become a powerful tool in the hands of the wildland manager for making decisions to secure increased resource benefits for man.

ARVANITIS, L. G. AND W. G. O'REGAN. 1967. Computer simulation and economic efficiency in forest sampling. Hilgardia 38(2): 133-135.

BROWN, E. R. 1961. The black-tailed deer of western Washington. Biol. Bull. No. 13., Washington State Game Dep. 123 p.

DAUBENMIRE, R. 1952. Forest vegetation of northern Idaho and adjacent Washington, and its bearing on concepts of vegetation classification. Ecol. Monogr. 22:325-326.

GARFINKLE, D. 1962. Digital computer simulation of ecological systems. Nature 194: 856-857.

GATES, B. R. 1969. Deer food production in certain seral stages of the Coast forest. Annu. Meeting, N.W. Section of the Wildlife Society, Vancouver, B. C. Mimeo.

GOULD, E. M. AND W. G. O'REGAN. 1965. Simulation: A step toward better forest planning. Harvard Forest Papers No. 13, Petersham, Mass. 86 p.

KELLY, J. M., P. A. OPSTRUP, J. S. OLSON, S. I. AUERBACH, AND G. M. VAN DYNE. 1969. Models of seasonal primary productivity in eastern Tennessee *Festuca* and *Andropogon* ecosystems. ORNL-4310, UC-48, Biology and Medicine, Oak Ridge, Tenn. 305 p.

KING, C. E. AND G. J. PAULIK. 1967. Dynamic models and the simulation of ecological systems. J. Theoretical Biol. 16:251-267.

LEEGE, T. A. AND W. O. HICKEY. 1968. Lochsa elk study. Idaho Fish and Game Dep., Federal Aid in Wildlife Restoration W85-R-19, Job No. 8.

LYON, L. J. 1966. Initial vegetal development following prescribed burning of Douglas-fir in Idaho. U. S. Dep. Agr. Forest Service, Intermountain Forest Range Exp. Sta. 17 p.

MUEGGLER, W. F. 1965. Ecology of seral shrub communities in the cedar-hemlock zone of northern Idaho. Ecol. Monogr. 35:165-185.

NEWNHAM, R. M. 1966. A simulation model for studying the effect of stand structure on harvesting pattern. Forest Chron. 42:39-44.

NORBERG, E. R. AND L. TROUT. 1957. Clearwater game and range study. Idaho Fish and Game Dep. Completion Rep., Proj. W112-R.

O'REGAN, W. G. AND N. M. PALLEY, 1965. Computer technique for the study of forest sampling methods. Forest Sci. 11:99-114.

PENGELLY, L. W. 1961. Factors influencing production of white-tailed deer on the Coeur d'Alene National Forest, Idaho. Unpub. Ph.D. Thesis, Utah State University, Logan.

PENGELLY, L. W. 1966. Ecological effects of slash-disposal fires on the Coeur d'Alene National Forest, Idaho, U. S. Forest Service (mimeo. pamphlet).

TABER, R. D. AND R. R. DASMANN. 1958. The black-tailed deer of the chaparral. California Dep. Fish and Game, Bull. No. 8. 163 p.

WATT, K. E. F. 1968. Ecology and resource management: a quantitative approach. McGraw-Hill Book Co., N. Y. 450 p.

THE CURRENT STATE OF THE ART (1969)

F. G. Cooch

An art is the application of knowledge to achieve goals. Wildlife managers must use the knowledge at hand while recognizing its shortcomings and seeking new and improved sources of knowledge. This paper illustrates the uncertainties that often pervade the data-bases of wildlife management.

A more appropriate title for this brief paper might be "The Current State of the Art of Waterfowl Management in Canada". This is a review of where we are as of July 1969, not where we will be in 1970, although limited reference will be made to pious hopes for the future. The first goal of this paper is thus to define where we are.

There is a tremendous need for research data in order to manage effectively migratory game birds. No one agency—provincial, state, or federal—has the resources to go it alone. In North America, several hundred biologists have been working at many locations over the past 25 years. The results of their labour are pooled and are available to all.

One problem to date has been that most of the raw data and analyses have been done at one location. To distribute this information, a plethora of conferences and technical committees, involving personnel from many agencies with a variety of interests, has arisen. To keep up with the flow of pertinent unpublished information one could spend as much as half one's time attending meetings.

Because the problem is vast and intricate, because decisions made in one area may have a direct bearing on persons living thousands of miles away, a co-operative program involving the entire continent is required. Such programs can, of course, succeed only if the need for each job is clearly understood by those co-operating.

The second goal of this paper, therefore, is to explain what we do, why we do it, and what limitations we place on decisions based on our data collection and analysis. Perhaps it's best to clarify the objectives of our management program. To my knowledge, although the federal governments of the United States and Canada have agreed on these objectives, the Canadian Wildlife Service and provincial agencies have not.

Briefly, our objectives as stated by the International Migratory Bird Committee are as follows:

1. To maintain a total population of waterfowl at levels not less than those which existed during the period 1956-62.

2. To manage migratory waterfowl for the benefit and enjoyment of people—meeting recreational, aesthetic, and scientific needs for this resource as equitably as location of habitat and requirements for preservation of this resource permit.

Reprinted from: Proc. Fed.-Prov. Wildl. Conf. Canadian Wildlife Serv., Edmonton, Alta. 33: 39-50.

These terms are extremely broad, but they do provide some recognizable guidelines.

Let us first examine that part of our objectives dealing with population levels. In this instance I propose to use a hypothetical model based on the mallard. I know that many of you would prefer use of another species, but I have chosen the mallard because it is the most common species in the bag, more data are available for discussion, and its life equation is relatively simple.

There are three ways of managing populations of migratory game birds in order to meet our stated objectives: regulations; habitat control and development; and replenishment by means of releases from hatcheries.

The key to managing waterfowl populations does not rest solely with regulations and population analysis. It is obvious that if we lose the habitat, we can never hope to attain our specified population levels, in spite of regulations. I do not propose to discuss the Canadian Wildlife Service easement program nor our program of land acquisition. These and provincial and private schemes are, however, vital to any long-range management program. The development of refuges and managed areas usually leads to increases in hunting pressure, especially in those areas where marshes have been created or restored near areas of high human occupancy.

The kinds of lands which we preserve will largely dictate the kinds of ducks that we will shoot because presumably the unprotected habitat will continue to be "civilized." If we save teal habitat, we will end up with teal; if mallard habitat, then mallards; and so on.

Broadly speaking, regulations, and all that goes into them, have an immediate effect on the harvest and its distribution; whereas habitat in the long term determines the distribution of birds, the species which can be harvested, and the upper limits of production.

The concept of "put and take" hunting may not be too palatable to Canadians, yet we must consider this procedure in the long haul. We know how to raise birds, but we do not really know how to release them successfully.

This paper is restricted to a consideration of the basis for regulations. On the Canadian prairies, we are basically interested in maintaining a population in harmony with the ability of the breeding habitat to support it. In periods when the amount of habitat is increasing we attempt to return more birds to the breeding areas each year until the quantity and quality of the habitat starts to decrease, or until some magical time when we simply have too many birds.

One indication that a species is becoming too abundant is when there is an average of more than two birds of that species per water area. Above that point a density-dependent effect becomes evident and reproductive success drops. Once that occurs, the rate of increase is checked or birds in excess of the carrying capability are harvested. In theory, this procedure of reducing kill as habitat expands and increasing kill as habitat dwindles will produce the maximum sustained harvest. No one, to my knowledge, has ever tested this hypothesis mathematically. However, it is what we try or, at least, would like to do.

The most logical alternative is the "take'em while you've got'em" school. Or rephrased—take them now because we may not have habitat next year. Under normal circumstances, conditions of habitat tend to change relatively slowly from year to year. There are exceptions, of course, and 1968 was one of them, but more about that later.

Our first task is to decide what the size of the fall flight is likely to be; second, to determine the desired level of harvest that can be safely taken; and third, to guess the probable carrying capacity for the next year, in order that population levels can be set for the next May.

The product of our labours looks like this:

Hypothetical population forecast based on the mallard

May 1969 breeding population	8,000,000
Less five % summer mortality	400,000
Number of potential breeders	7,600,000
Production ratio (IMM/AD)	1:1
Fall population (as of Sept. 1)	15,200,000
Predicted Canadian harvest	1,500,000
Predicted U.S. harvest	3,000,000
Total hunting continental kill including crippling loss	6,000,000
Other losses (natural mortality)	1,200,000
Predicted population level May 1970	8,000,000

This is one of the models which we use, and it is the simplest. The input into this model is based on many types of activities and these are briefly discussed in order of their appearance in the model.

The May population levels are based on co-operative breeding ground surveys. . . . .
I will not completely describe the survey method except to state that it is essentially based on the distribution of mallards as of the mid-1950's. The basic design has been to divide the breeding grounds into large geographical areas, called strata, which have been established on the following bases:

1. Similarity in species composition of the birds found there and their numbers.

2. The number and types of wetland depressions per square mile.

3. Ecological associations, including soil, plant cover and visibility factors.

Each stratum is sampled by means of transects, flown at a speed of 90-110 miles per hour on an east-west or west-east basis and at an elevation of 100 to 150 feet above ground level. The width of the transect is one-eighth of a mile on each side of the aircraft. Thus for every four linear miles flown, one square mile of habitat is observed. The transects are divided into 18-mile segments and completion of a segment means that

4.5 square miles of a stratum is surveyed. Depending on such factors as weather, phenology, population size, number of water areas per square mile, size of stratum, and homogeneity of habitat a maximum of a five per cent sample is flown. The results obtained are reduced to a common denominator, i.e., ducks and ponds per square mile, which is then multiplied by the total area of the stratum to give a stratum index figure.

The key to the breeding ground survey program is the 31 air-ground comparison transects made from the results of the aerial survey. This portion of the survey and some of its limitations are outlined in Anon. (1969) and Martinson (1967). The aerial portion of the survey gives by large areas, total birds seen (by species) and the number of water bodies. The air-ground portion provides adjustment factors which permit data obtained by the aerial crew to be re-evaluated on the basis of what has been seen on the ground. This is the so-called "visibility factor" and is a measure of the efficiency of the aerial crew, and differing visibilities of the various species.

Basic assumptions are made:

1. The ground crew is running a complete census.

2. The selected air-ground transects represent all habitats in the stratum.

3. The performance of the aerial crew is identical with its performance elsewhere, while over the comparison route and at varying times during the entire flight.

Probably none of these assumptions are correct, but despite these and other criticisms of the scheme, no workable alternative has been available and the scheme seems to work reasonably well.

A habitat survey (number of water areas) is being carried out in late June and early July. A third survey of prairie waterfowl habitat is being made in early July. This is known as the production survey (brood). Data on water areas, broods seen by age class, estimates of numbers of broods seen, and the late nesting index (based on lone males and pairs of mallards, pintails, and canvasbacks) are collected.

Because of difficulties associated with analysis and interpretation of the results of the brood surveys, and difficulties associated with the ground portion of the air-ground comparison study, the air-ground portion of the brood survey has been temporarily discontinued.

Those three surveys (the breeding pair, production, and habitat) give data on number of water areas in May and late June; number of ducks by species; unadjusted and unidentified brood averages; and a late-nesting index.

Their value is three-fold. They permit a check on the population model developed the previous year when, for example, the forecast May population level is checked against the actual May survey population level. They permit development of a production forecast. They give trend data from which educated guesses can be made on events, such as habitat conditions likely to occur in the following year.

The next element in the model is the production ratio of young birds to adults. This is essential when deciding how many birds may be harvested in the year of record. Crissey (1969), Anderson (1968), and Cooch (1969) have developed means of forecasting the probable production ratio in one year. The U.S. approach has been developed on a continental basis; the Canadian has been related to the production strata. Essential elements in these forecast systems have been adjusted May duck counts, unadjusted May and July water counts, and the late-nesting index.

Based on experience and an examination of the historical record of production ratios, a range from 0.5:1 to 1.6:1 immatures to adults can be anticipated. Experience has shown that when regulations and other conditions are not changed markedly, if the production ratio is 1.1:1, the population will tend to remain constant; if it falls below 1.1:1, population will decrease; if it rises above 1.1:1, population will increase. The development of the production ratio forecast is probably the major contribution to waterfowl population manipulation of this decade (1960-69).

On the basis of data from the previous surveys, it is now possible to estimate the size of the fall flight. If a breeding population of 8,000,000 is assumed after natural summer mortality, then a ratio of 1.1:1 will mean that there will be a total fall flight of 8,000,000 + (8,000,000 x 1.1) or 16,800,000. In the case of the mallard and other dabbling ducks we do not need to consider problems such as minimum breeding age.

Once we have estimated the size of the fall flight, we must quickly decide on the size of the population that we want to return to the breeding grounds in the next year. Here the system falls down because when we set regulations (mid-July in Canada, mid-August in the United States) we do not know how much habitat there will be in the next breeding season. Therefore, we do not really know how many birds we should permit to survive for return to the breeding grounds. We do, however, have a minimum population size for each species which we try to maintain.

However, I stated earlier that trends in habitat develop rather slowly. As a rule of thumb, if the trend has been swinging downward for a year or two, we will estimate a further deterioration of 10 per cent; if upward, an increase of 10 per cent. At the same time, we allow for minimum population targets agreed to by the International Migratory Bird Committee.

The regulations then are initially set on the basis of the estimated size of the Canadian and continental fall flight, and our minimum population target. At this point we subtract "natural" or non-hunting mortalities, and estimate the number of birds that can be killed by hunters.

Estimates of non-hunting mortality are based on the so-called Hickey Triangle—developed by Hickey (1952) further refined by Geis, Martinson, and Anderson (1969)—which shows that non-hunting mortality is partially replaced by hunting mortality; or conversely, that non-hunting mortality increases as hunting mortality decreases (Figure 1). This analysis was based primarily on adult mallards banded in mid-winter in the southern United States. There has been much debate about the validity of the Hickey Triangle. Here is an example of how it is used:

If 1969 hunting regulations were set with the objective of sending back 15 per cent more birds to the breeding grounds in 1970 than were there in 1969, the calculations would be 8,000,000 x 1.15 = 9,200,000 (1970 breeding population). In mid-July, the forecast fall flight is estimated to be 7,600,000 + 7,600,000 x 1.25 = 17,100,000.

Therefore, 54 per cent of the 1969 fall population must survive until spring 1970 (9,200,000 ÷ 17,100,000); and 51 per cent must survive for the entire fall-to-fall year (9,200,000 − 5 per cent mortality ÷ 17,100, 000). Thus the total, annual, allowable mortality would be 49 per cent.

Using the Hickey Triangle we can determine the rate of hunting kill that would result in a total rate of annual mortality of 49 per cent. From this approach, the allowable kill rate is 32 per cent.

Kill rate x fall population = permissible kill. That is, .32 × 17,100,000 = 5,472,000 (continental kill and crippling loss).

Before proceeding, I should state that non-hunting mortality is a poor choice of words. It could be more aptly called "mortality not otherwise accounted for" (poor syntax perhaps, but more meaningful). Included in this category are birds that die from natural causes, birds shot during crop depredation operations, birds killed illegally, birds killed by Indians and Eskimos, and self-compensating errors in survey techniques.

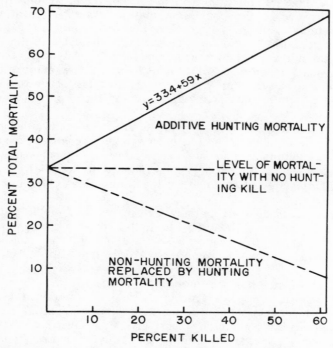

Figure 70-1.—Relation between total annual mortality and rate of hunting kill of mallards (based on the regression of mortality rate on band recovery rate of winter-banded mallards).

To digress for a moment, the kill on the breeding grounds by persons requiring birds for food is not likely to vary too greatly from year to year; crop depredation is more a problem of weather than population size (for example the autumn of 1968); the error in breeding ground surveys is greater in years when birds concentrate on available water than when they are dispersed. In short, we need to test the validity or shortcomings, or both, of the Hickey Triangle and, should it prove valid, to be able to apply it to species other than mallards.

Once the Hickey Triangle analysis has been applied to the fall flight we arrive at a figure which can be called the permissible continental (Canada and the U.S.) kill.

The procedures discussed are summarized in the following model. The fall flight is developed as follows:

May breeding population (less five per cent) times estimated production ratio equals size of fall flight population as of August 30 (fall flight)	17,100,000
Less "non-hunting mortality" (Hickey Triangle) which varies from 12-29 per cent depending on population size and proportion of populations to be removed by hunting. In this example use 15 percent.	2,500,000
Net fall flight available for hunting	14,600,000
Less desired population for next year (based on International Migratory Bird Committee targets and estimates, or guesses, of the amount of habitat which will be available)	9,200,000
Number of birds that may be removed from the population by hunting in Canada and the United States. This total includes birds hit but unretrieved.	5,400,000

It is normal practice to consider at this time the consequence of several types of regulations, i.e., those regulations which may be expected to produce kills of 4,000,000, 4,500,000 and 5,000,000, etc., and relate these to our population objective.

We know little at present about the effect of regulations on Canadian kill. Because many of our hunters hunt on the breeding grounds, or on the first pre-migration staging areas, it is not entirely safe to extrapolate from experience gained in the United States (part of the data pool referred to earlier).

There are a number of techniques available which should result in desired regulation of the size and distribution of the kill. The two obvious courses of action are to reduce the daily bag limit or the number of days available for hunting, or both. In some species, closing or opening key areas is the most effective way to regulate kill. Species restrictions, half-day hunting, season bag limits, area or species-specific quota systems, tagging, etc., are all techniques of varying effectiveness.

A major difficulty in setting regulations is unpredictable weather during the hunting season. An attempt to liberalize the regulations may fail because of "blue bird" weather. Conversely, delayed openings and restrictive daily bag limits may not be effective because the ratio of success per hunter will markedly increase during favourable hunting conditions. In 1968 for example, the combination of wheat and rainy, but not frigid, weather shortstopped mallards and white-fronted geese for weeks in Alberta and Saskatchewan.

We know that as much as 40 per cent of a season's kill and hunter-day activity occur on the opening weekend. If weather conditions are favourable for hunting, the per hunter success average can increase from 1.5 birds to 2.5 or higher. In a single weekend the effectiveness of many restrictive regulations can be lost. On the other hand, liberalized regulations may not deliver the birds to the hunter if the weather is poor.

If we want to reduce the kill in Canada, the season is delayed, or opened on Monday, or both. Bag limits are manipulated, but in all honesty, most daily bag limits in Canada are now too high to be effective. A decrease from five to four ducks a day may have a psychological effect and cause some hunters to hang up their guns, but the number of hunters that would normally be expected to get that fifth duck is very small. Consequently the kill cannot be markedly reduced until bag limits approach the daily average kill, but more about this later. At present, regulations are set to permit a kill of a certain specified size. This will permit a return of a projected number of birds in the next season to the continental breeding grounds. We cannot now ensure reaching a target for an area smaller than a continent, or for a discrete population.

This is then, the basic model for most regulations in North America. We have checks on the validity of this model, but unfortunately they are made a year after the fact. And there are some things which we cannot check, e.g., our basic assumption that a five per cent mortality of adults occurs between the May surveys and the start of the hunting season. We do, however, check on the production ratio forecast by analysing wings received during the species composition survey. Once the wings have been broken down into species, the ratio of immatures to adults is derived for each sample in excess of 20 birds. This unadjusted data is further treated to arrive at a production ratio. To use Alberta as an example, the first step is to analyse the results of the same season banding program where the ratio of immatures to banded adults, and the ratio of banded immatures to adults reported are known. The relative vulnerability of immatures and adults is then applied to the wing receipts for that province. The results are then weighted by species for each province and state, summed, and a continental production ratio produced.

The formula used to correct for the known higher vulnerability of immatures is (immatures per adult in the harvest) ÷ (immature adult relative recovery rate) = production ratio.

For an example of how the formula functions, let us take a case where the pre-hunting season population age ratio is two immatures per adult, and immatures are twice as vulnerable to hunting as adults. Since immatures in the example are twice as vulnerable to hunting, the band recovery rate for immatures would be twice that of adults, resulting in an immature-adult relative recovery rate of two. Since there are twice as many immatures as adults, and immatures are doubly vulnerable, we would then expect four immatures harvested per adult, resulting in a 4:1 ratio in the species composition survey. Dividing the 4:1 harvest ratio by the 2:1 relative recovery rate would give us the actual pre-hunting season age ratio of 2:1. Since immatures are more vulnerable to hunting than adults, the population age ratio would decrease as the hunting season progressed. However, this would be compensated for, automatically, by a corresponding decrease in the relative recovery rate, since there would also be relatively fewer banded immatures than banded adults as the season progressed.

Table 1 gives relative recovery rates, harvest age ratios, and resulting pre-hunting season age ratio estimates for 1967 mallards in Quebec, Ontario, Manitoba, Saskatchewan, and Alberta. We do not have sufficient banding data to make estimates for British Columbia.

Table 1
Relative recovery rate, harvest age ratio, and adjusted population age ratio for mallards in 1967

Province	Relative recovery rate (banding)	Harvest age ratio (wing survey)	Adjusted population age ratio
Alberta	2.22	3.60	1.62
Saskatchewan	2.38	1.79	.75
Manitoba	2.45	2.29	.93
Ontario	1.60	5.71	3.57
Quebec	2.62	12.88	4.92

Weighting each province's population age ratio by the 1967 breeding population index for that province gives a weighted age ratio of 1.08 for the prairie provinces combined.

The accuracy of the population age ratio estimates, by province, depends on several conditions:

1. The banded sample represents the provincial mallard population, as a whole, with respect to differential vulnerability.

2. Foreign mallards differing in age composition or relative vulnerability from the banded population do not migrate in large numbers into the province.

3. Large numbers of adults do not move out of the resident province into other provinces while immatures remain behind, or vice-versa.

4. If large numbers of mallards move from their home province into other provinces, immature-adult relative vulnerability remains unchanged.

This use of banding has, perhaps, not been clearly understood. It is important that usable samples be obtained from widely dispersed areas in a province and not from a single geographic location. It is equally important that overbanding does not occur. This would result in a marked depression in the rate of reporting (Martinson 1968). It would also make comparison and interpretation of mortality rates even more difficult.

The harvest survey yields data on the size of the total retrieved kill, it is not a species composition survey. Likewise, the species composition survey cannot be used as a kill survey. However, the harvest and the species composition surveys, combined, do give reasonable estimates of the size of the kill by province; and the species composition, age, and sex—at least for numerically important species. To this kill figure we add a 25 per cent unretrieved component—summed for Canada and the United States. This represents our best estimate as to the number of birds legally killed. By returning to our original model and plugging in data from the harvest and species composition surveys, pre-season banding and a new production ratio, plus the current May breeding ground survey, we can, in effect, compare the predicted and actual production ratios, the predicted and estimated hunting kill, the non-hunting mortality, and finally, the size of the breeding ground population with our own previously set target. We are also able to check our forecast of the number of water areas on which we based our derived population level for a given species.

At this point I should say if only we could do this for all of North America. In theory we should build this type of model for each species, and thus develop a provincial, national, and continental model for all species combined. We are taking hesitant steps in that direction, but at present we are restricted to one or two species. Furthermore, these are continental models, and we must make decisions on small geographical units, such as parts of provinces, and on population segments. There is little cause for self-congratulation if we reach a 6,000,000 continental mallard population objective, then discover that they are all in Alberta. Yet this is basically what we are doing.

I would like to list a few obvious deficiencies in what we do. This is not offered as an apology but there is no sense in deluding ourselves.

1. The present model is not applicable to all of North America, nor to all species for a variety of reasons, e.g., lack of roads for establishing air-ground comparison routes, and behavioural problems.

2. No air-ground adjustment factors have yet been devised for such species as canvasbacks, redheads, and scaup.

3. An arbitrary five per cent breeding ground mortality is applied to all species.

4. An arbitrary 25 per cent crippling loss factor is applied to all species in all parts of the country, although crippling losses in excess of 50 per cent have been observed for some species and in some localities.

5. The adequacy of the pre-season banding program is suspect.

6. The Hickey Triangle has not been proved valid.

7. We know that there are biases in the harvest and species composition surveys, etc.

8. Bonus seasons have been set on species, i.e., scaup and golden-eye, that cannot be counted.

9. Arbitrary air-ground visibility adjustments for forested areas are used.

The second generalized type of approach is used for those species that cannot be counted by "normal" breeding ground survey techniques. Classic examples are wood ducks and black ducks. Here the procedure is to back into the solution; i.e., to use those things that we know such as sex ratio, age ratio, size of the retrieved kill, differential vulnerability, banding analysis, and production ratio to derive an estimate of the population which must have existed in order to produce a kill of a certain magnitude. Unfortunately this means that population data are available a year after regulations are set.

It has been claimed that regulations for all of North America are based on a relatively few species, i.e., the prairie mallard, and the prairie mallard, and of course the prairie mallard, with some attention given to canvasback and redheads. By and large this is true on a continental basis because we can see and count the mallard, and in terms of numbers in the bag it is most important to hunters. Over 50 per cent of the birds harvested in the three prairie provinces, 40 per cent in British Columbia, and 25 per cent in Ontario are mallards.

Harvest of the redhead and canvasback can be controlled by restricting hunting at certain key areas.

The first population model and production ratio forecast were developed exclusively for the mallard. Although we have tried other species such as pintail, gadwall, and blue-winged teal, they do not fit our model. I personally wonder if it is because the survey system and regulations are based on mallards. Yet the survey system apparently samples habitat per stratum in almost precisely the same ratio as waterfowl capability maps prepared by the Canada Land Inventory would show in that stratum, and the production ratios are meaningful when we band enough of those minor species.

While we are able to manage in a gross way we have difficulty in restricted areas, e.g., a province. Waterfowl are mobile. They do not always return to their place of origin. Their vulnerability to hunting varies from year to year and from place to place. Hunting conditions and success vary according to the weather. For these reasons regulations that succeed often do so by chance.

The setting of regulations in Canada is probably more difficult than in the United States. In the case of mallards and black ducks, any regulations designed to protect them and increase population levels inevitably mean that Canadians are deprived of hunting other early-migrating species. A late-season opening results in the infinitesimal kill of early-migrating pintail and blue-wings.

Attempts to open the season early and still apply species management have failed. Frankly, we do not know how to harvest each species as a crop without damaging another species. In fact, we do not know the permissible harvest for most species nor do we have adequate population targets.

While I am in the process of answering unstated criticisms, perhaps we should deal with another *canard* (with apologies to all *Canadiens* present). Canadian regulations are not dictated by the Bureau of Sport Fisheries and Wildlife, although they are influenced by what the United States might do. We should all keep in mind that there are 2,000,000 U.S. duck-stamp holders and only 390,000 Canadian permit holders, that 1,200,000 of those duck-stamp holders are enjoying two or three ducks and 30- or 35-day seasons with some other restriction added. If the Bureau of Sport Fisheries and Wildlife is forced to increase bag limits by one duck, and the season in states like Minnesota, Illinois or Arkansas by five days (as happened in 1963 vs 1962) a 100 per cent increase in kill of mallards can occur in the Mississippi and central flyways.

We know that a 1968 reduction of one mallard and three ducks per bag on the prairies, plus a delay in opening the season, resulted in a 19 per cent decrease in the kill of mallards here. The 1968 U.S. regulations in the Mississippi flyway reduced the kill there by over 50 per cent. The credit for the U.S. success is due partly to the states and the bureau, and partly to Canada. If we had not reduced our bag limits and delayed our seasons, the bureau and certain states might not have been able to institute restrictions more severe than existed in 1967.

If they had merely held the line in 1968, we would have had fewer than 5,000,000 mallards on the breeding grounds today. Mallard-rich provinces like Saskatchewan and Alberta might not have noticed the difference immediately, because of their wealth and the lesser vulnerability of *their* mallards while in the United States. However, Manitoba's, southeastern Saskatchewan's, and Ontario's number one species would quickly have been in dire straits. Southern Manitoba and adjacent Saskatchewan already have as their number one breeding bird, the early-migrating blue-winged teal. To the extent described, and for the reasons listed, Canadian regulations are influenced by Washington. U.S. hunters can hurt the resource more than we can.

In the next few years our ability to make more complex analyses of population data, and to understand how to use regulations to manipulate those populations will be increased. For the first time we have Canadian data on species composition, size, and distribution of the annual harvest. We are actively investigating the present survey designs and developing means of assessing the significance of the results which we have been obtaining. Within a year, edited, up-dated tapes containing all banding records will be available at the computer in Ottawa.

What has been presented earlier in this paper relates to our present day-to-day ability to understand and manage populations of waterfowl. Where we will be in two or three years depends on the number of trained biologists which all of us can hire, the amount of additional data that will accrue, and above all, on our ability to obtain raw data and work on it. We now have data from two years of harvest and species composition surveys—work for at least 10 biologists. We have four. We annually commit 25 man-years of effort in the collection of waterfowl population data, not to mention our commitment in the Canada Land Inventory, and in habitat and enforcement programs.

At the outset it was stated that the problem was so complex that no one agency could go it alone. The recently initiated technical committees are an important vehicle by which information and views can be exchanged. However, until the provinces are able to provide well-trained waterfowl biologists, progress will be excruciatingly slow. There is so much to do that priorities will be with us for years to come.

Perhaps the statement by Churchill made after El Alamein sums up the present state of the art—I misquote "We have won a great victory (because we still have ducks) but I must advise you that we are not at the beginning of the end, (because although we are now getting the data, we have not yet begun to do the necessary analyses) but rather at the end of the beginning" (because we are only now getting the data required to manage effectively).

LITERATURE CITED

ANDERSON, D.R. 1968. Prediction of continental mallard production using multiple regression analyses. Migratory Bird Populations Sta., Maryland. Typed report, 5 p.

ANONYMOUS. 1969. The Prairies. Standard procedures for waterfowl population and habitat surveys. U.S. Bur. of Sport Fisheries and Wildlife, 68 p.

COOCH, F.G. 1969. Saskatchewan seminar. Can. Wildlife Service Rep. Ser. No. 6.

CRISSEY, W. 1969. Saskatchewan seminar. Can. Wildlife Service Rep. Ser. No. 6.

GEIS, A., K. MARTINSON, AND D.R. ANDERSON. 1969. Mallard management J. of Wildlife Mgmt. (in press).

HICKEY, J.J. 1952. Survival studies of banded birds. U.S. Fish and Wildlife Service Spec. Sci. Rep., Wildlife No. 15, 177 pp.

MARTINSON, R.K. AND C.F. KACZYNSKI. 1967. Factors influencing waterfowl counts on aerial surveys. 1961-66 U.S. Fish and Wildlife Service Spec. Sci. Rep., Wildlife No. 105, 78 pp.

OPTIMUM YIELD IN DEER
AND ELK POPULATIONS (1969)

Jack E. Gross

In a sustained-yield management regime, maximum yield requires that peak numbers of new individuals be produced as replacements for harvested animals. This paper demonstrates that for deer and elk and probably other big game, maximum yields are not obtained when year-round population densities are maximum. Nor are they necessarily obtained when fecundity rates are maximum.

This paper has three objectives: (1) to describe fecundity-rate changes that occur with density changes in deer and elk populations, (2) to show how these fecundity rates can produce dome-shaped yield curves, and (3) to show how dome-shaped yield curves may be used for producing maximum sustained annual harvests and maintaining a healthy balance between deer and elk populations and their food supply.

Leopold (1933) defined game management as "the art of making land produce sustained annual crops of wild game for recreational use." In this paper, annual crop is defined as annual harvest, and optimum yield is defined as the sustained, maximum number of animals that can be harvested annually. Leopold's sustained-annual crop principle has for 35 years been a cornerstone of wildlife management philosophy. The principle has not diminished in importance, but wildlife managers have perhaps failed to develop a full understanding and appreciation for wildlife production dynamics and yield relations. Such appreciation would enhance our understanding of population manipulation and perhaps would solve some chronic management problems. As Scott (1954) pointed out: "There seems to be an unfortunate and growing lag between the significant advances in knowledge of population phenomena, and their practical application in the field of game management." The intent of this paper is to offer a perspective of population phenomena that may shorten the lag.

The fecundity-rate patterns observed in the deer and elk populations used as examples in this paper may not apply to all deer and elk populations. Some populations occupy habitats which have been drastically altered by man, and some populations, particularly white-tailed deer in the Midwest, have adapted to artificial habitats resulting from man's cultural practices. Their fecundity-rate response to density changes may not follow the model described. However, the examples presented in this paper fit a common pattern which may give insight for a unifying biological concept. With modifications for regional peculiarities, the concept may be adaptable as an applied management tool.

Optimum Yield in Fishery Theory

The concept of obtaining optimum yield from animal populations by manipulation of population size was first stated explicitly about 50 years ago by the Russian biologist Theodore Baranov (1918, 1926). The sub-

Reprinted from: Trans. N. Amer. Wildl. and Natural Resources Conf. 34: 372-385.

stance of Baranov's theory is shown schematically in Fig. 1. Baranov commented on this theory as follows:

As we see, a picture is obtained which diverges radically from the hypothesis which has been favored almost down to the present time, namely that the natural reserve of fish is an inviolable capital, of which the fishing industry must use only the interest, not touching the capital at all. Our theory says, on the contrary, that a fishery and a natural reserve of fish are incompatible, and that the exploitable stock of fish is a changeable quantity, which depends on the intensity of the fishery. The more fish we take from a body of water, the smaller is the basic stock remaining in it; and the less fish we take, the greater is the basic stock, approximating to the natural stock when the fishery approaches zero.

Now the question is, how far can we go in the direction of increased catch, to the right of the figure shown? Here we must notice that a progressive increase in intensity of fishing, resulting in an ever smaller and smaller increase in catch, becomes, sooner or later, simply inefficient. Hence, the farther we move to the right in the figure, the smaller becomes the average age and weight of the fish caught.

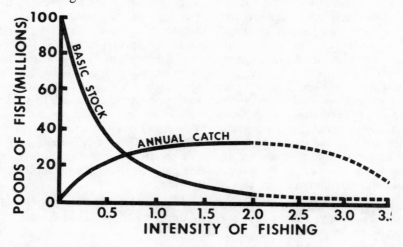

Figure 71-1.—Schematic representation of relation between size of basic stock, size of annual catch, and intensity of fishing. One pood equals 36 lb avoirdupois (solid lines from Baranov, 1918).

Modern studies in the theory of fishing have shown in general that as the intensity of fishing increases, the size of the annual catch at first increases as breeding stock declines, but eventually decreases toward the baseline as breeding-stock numbers become small (Fig. 1). The extended relation between breeding-stock size and catch size indicated in Fig. 1 permits some elaboration on Baranov's ideas. First, only one value on the breeding-stock curve corresponds to the maximum annual catch that can be obtained from a population. That value lies between the minimum and

670

maximum breeding-stock sizes that can be maintained by varying intensity of harvest. Second, catch size declines with harvest rates that adjust breeding-stock size to levels above or below the size where the maximum catch is obtained. Hence, if breeding-stock size is changed from some value where a certain size harvest is being obtained, the size of the harvest can either increase or decrease, depending on which way the breeding-stock size is adjusted. In this manner, identical annual catches can be obtained from two different breeding-stock levels.

Some deer and elk populations apparently conform, in terms of the net number of animals produced by the population per breeding period, to the basic optimum-yield concept in fisheries. Thus, maintenance of maximum annual harvest and maximum annual breeding stock are incompatible biologically, and therefore are incompatible management practices if optimum yield is the management goal.

Optimum Yield in Deer and Elk

Discussions of population-growth phenomena are usually introduced with an explanation of sigmoid-growth theory. Other demographic features may then be deduced from the existence of sigmoid growth. The opposite approach is taken in this paper by starting with the two basic components of population change, births and deaths, and inductively developing the mechanisms leading to optimum yield and sigmoid growth.

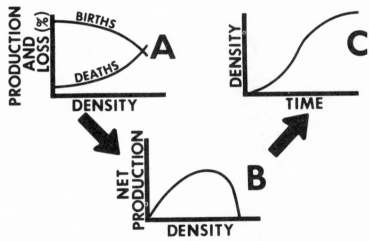

Figure 71-2.—Schematic representations of interactions between birth rates, death rates, net population production, and population growth (part A from Leopold 1955).

A conceptual model illustrating the effects of deer population densities on birth rates and death rates is shown in Fig. 2A. At lowest densities, births per unit of breeding stock are maximum and deaths per unit of breeding stock are minimum. As density increases due to positive net differences between birth rates and death rates, influences associated with increased density cause birth rates to slowly decrease and death rates to slowly increase. As population density further increases, the birth- and death-rate curves continue to converge and eventually meet. When births and deaths per unit of breeding stock are equal, the population ceases to grow.

The interaction of population size, births per unit of breeding stock, and deaths per unit of breeding stock will produce a dome-shaped net-population-production or yield curve (Fig. 2B). At lowest densities, net production per unit of breeding stock is maximum, but the net number of animals produced by the population is small because population size is small. As population size increases through lower densities, only small changes occur in the birth- and death-rate curves, and only small changes occur in net production per unit of breeding stock. Thus, the net number of young produced by the population (the product of net individual production times number of individuals producing) increases almost in direct proportion to breeding-stock size (Fig. 2B). As breeding-stock size increases and net production per unit of breeding stock simultaneously decreases (due to the increasingly rapid convergence of the birth- and death-rate curves), a certain combination of breeding-stock size and net number of young produced per unit of breeding stock will produce the maximum net number of young that can be obtained from the population. As the population density continues to increase and net production per unit of breeding stock continues to decrease, the net number of young produced by the population declines from the maximum value, and the dome-shaped yield curve is formed (Fig. 2B).

An S-shaped population growth curve is produced by the dome-shaped yield curve (Fig. 2C). The accumulation of yield values on the left side of the dome-shaped yield curve will produce the lower, concave portion of the population growth curve. The accumulation of yield values on the right side of the curve will produce the upper convex portion of the population growth curve. Conversely, if population growth follows an S-shaped form, the population must have an associated dome-shaped yield curve.

The shape of the birth- and death-rate curves need not conform precisely to those in Fig. 2A to produce the yield curve of Fig. 2B or the S-shaped growth form of Fig. 2C. The criterion for the existence of a dome-shaped yield curve and an S-shaped growth curve is: either birth rates or death rates, or both, must decrease or increase, respectively, with increasing density so that the curves eventually meet. A dome-shaped yield curve would not exist if either birth rates or death rates, or both, converged instantaneously at densities where net population production was increasing.

Thus, Fig. 2 presents a conceptual framework that numerically and functionally integrates death rates, birth rates, yield, and population density. It remains to be shown that this conceptual framework exists in wild populations of deer and elk.

Fecundity-rate Patterns:

Dome-shaped yield curves probably occur in deer and elk populations because of the tendency for the number of young produced per female (and thus net production per female) to decrease with increasing population densities in a form similar to the birth-rate curve in Fig. 2A. Fecundity-rate patterns and the dome-shaped yield curve (net population production of young) will be demonstrated in deer and elk populations by combining information on population growth form with information on population fecundity rates. In this paper, fecundity is the production of ova, full-term fetuses or live young (Cheatum *et al.* 1950).

Fecundity rates (other than young-adult ratios) can be estimated for wild populations only by sacrificing animals. Such data are seldom obtained from populations too small to permit the removal of representative samples. Thus, fecundity-rate information for lower densities must be estimated from birth-rate and death-rate values that cause a population simulation model to generate growth forms and population sizes similar to those observed in wild populations. Fecundity rates for three elk and two deer populations are obtained in this manner. Population growth was simulated with a FORTRAN coded, computer population generation model recently developed at Colorado State University (Walters and Gross, unpubl. ms.).

Interpopulation differences in fecundity rates for populations at higher densities are commonly reported in deer and elk. These differences are generally associated with nutritional differences and thus may be associated indirectly with differences in population densities. Interpopulation comparisons of *differences* in fecundity rates that occur with *differences* in densities may support the thesis of this paper, but they do not show *changes* in fecundity rates that occur with *changes* in densities. As Scott (1954) suggested, the interplay between density, fecundity rates, and mortality rates develops different patterns between populations due to racial and local environmental characteristics. Thus, density-dependent effects are difficult to isolate in intrapopulation data. Few studies have been reported where densities and fecundity rates have been simultaneously measured on one population for a sufficient period of time to show patterns of change in fecundity rates with change in population density. Five examples (four deer populations and one elk population) showing changes in fecundity rates with change in density are described.

Low-density Fecundity Rates and Production Changes:
The George Reserve white-tailed deer *(Odocoileus virginianus)* herd was established from a plant of six animals (four does and two bucks) in a fenced enclosure of about 1,800 acres (O'Roke and Hamerstrom 1948). In six breeding seasons, from 1928 through 1938, the population grew from six to 160 animals (Fig. 3A). The average annual rate of population increase was about 60 percent per year. O'Roke and Hamerstrom (1948) suggested several fecundity-rate patterns which could have resulted in the 1933 density. The population could have reached its observed density in the six breeding seasons: (1) if 100 percent of 2-year-old or older does produced two fawns each, or (2) if less than 100 percent of the 2-year-old or older does produced fawns and a portion of the 1-year-old does produced fawns. These pregnancy rates were based on the assumption of no mortality. But since mortality probably occurred during the 6 years, the actual pregnancy rates must have been somewhat higher than those calculated by O'Roke and Hamerstrom. Since the adult fecundity rate was as its maximum, 1-year-old does undoubtedly contributed to the population growth. Although several combinations and values of age-specific fecundity rates could have produced the 1933 population, production of fawns during

each of the six breeding seasons must have been at or near the maximum potential for the species. Thus, net population production must have increased almost linearly with population density.

The Seneca Army Depot white-tailed deer herd was created in 1942 when an estimated 20-40 deer were fenced within an enclosure of about 9,832 acres (Hesselton, 1965). Nothing is known of the deer densities from 1942 until 1947 when the first census accounted for 50 deer. If the original population-size estimate was correct, the population growth rate was relatively low during the first 5 years. During seven breeding seasons from 1948 through 1953, the herd increased from 50 to at least 1,121 (Fig. 3A). The average population increase rate was 56 percent per year compared to 60 percent per year in the George Reserve herd. Thus the fecundity rate per female required to produce the observed herd increase was similar to that in the George Reserve herd. The rate of increase and population size could have occurred only if near-maximum fecundity rates were maintained for most of the growth period after 1947.

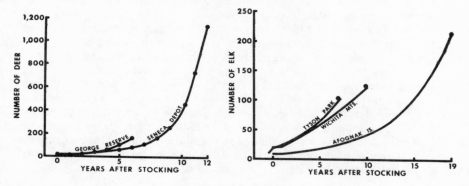

Figure 71-3.—Patterns and magnitudes of population growth in two deer and three elk herds following establishment of small herds (George Reserve from O'Roke *et al.*, 1948; Seneca Depot from Hesselton *et al.* 1965: Tyson Park from Murphy 1963; Wichita Mts. from Halloran 1962; Afognak Is. from Troyer 1960).

The Tyson Park elk *(Cervus canadensis)* herd in Missouri was established in February, 1951, with a transplant of two adult bulls and eight adult cows (Murphy, 1963). By October 1958, after eight reproductive periods, the herd had increased to 103 head (Fig. 3B). If no mortality occurred during the period of population growth, the herd could have reached its observed size with an annual adult cow pregnancy rate of about 80 percent. But Murphy concluded by inspection of the final age and sex ratio that mortality had occurred. The population fecundity rate must therefore have been higher than that provided by an 80 percent pregnancy rate in adult cows. Murphy calculated a theoretical population size of 142 at the end of eight reproductive periods, based on the following assumptions: (1) the original eight cows were pregnant, (2) only adult cows reproduce, (3) each adult cow produced a single calf, and (4) the sex ratio of the calves was even.

The computer model for this herd predicted that the assumption that only adult cows reproduced is not valid. If the herd was subjected to annual mortality rates of 10 percent for calves and 5 percent for older age classes, the herd could have grown to its observed size with annual pregnancy rates of 95 percent in adult cows and 60 percent in yearling cows. Even if the mortality-rate estimates are only approximate, the population must have increased at or near its maximum potential rate due to near maximum fecundity rates. Net population production must have increased almost linearly with population density.

The Wichita National Wildlife Refuge in the Wichita Mountains of Oklahoma was stocked in 1908, 1911, and 1912 with five bull and 16 cow elk (Halloran, 1962). The first reproduction occurred in 1913, and by 1922, the herd had increased to an estimated 125 head (Fig. 3B). By assuming the average annual adult mortality rate of 12 percent actually observed from 1925 to 1956 also applied to the earlier years of population growth, and by assuming an annual calf mortality rate of 10 percent as in the Tyson Park simulation, the Wichita herd could have increased to its observed population size with an annual pregnancy rate of 95 percent in adult cows and 30 percent in yearling cows. Thus, the Wichita Mountains elk herd also apparently grew near its maximum potential growth rate due to near maximum and constant fecundity rates. Net population production must have been similar to that of the Tyson Park elk herd.

In the spring of 1928, three bull and five cow elk calves were released on Afognak Island, Alaska (Troyer 1960). By December 1948, after 19 calving seasons, the herd had increased to an estimated 212 animals (Fig. 3B). By assuming the same annual adult and calf mortality rates as the Tyson Park herd and similar to the Wichita Mountains herd, the population could have grown to its observed size with annual pregnancy rates of 95 percent in adults and 30 percent in yearlings. The annual fecundity rates, net population production, and population growth rate of the Afognak Island elk herd were similar to the fecundity, production, and growth rates of the Tyson Park and Wichita Mountains elk herds.

Several conclusions follow from the five examples of deer and elk growth curves at low densities. First, although the assigned mortality rates for adults and young and thus the calculated pregnancy rates were approximate, all five populations apparently attained near maximum growth rates for the species and thus must have annually attained near maximum fecundity rates. Since constant fecundity rates were apparently maintained through increasing population sizes, the net number of young produced by the populations at any population size must have been directly proportional to that population size. Thus, as population sizes increased (lower part of the sigmoid curve in Fig. 2C), net population production of young increased in a manner similar to the left portion of the net-population-production curve (Fig. 2B).

High-density Fecundity Rates and Production Changes:

The effect of density on fecundity rates at higher densities has been determined in several instances by measuring fecundity rates during population-density changes. Examples below are restricted to populations in which density and fecundity rates were measured consecutively over a period of years, thereby permitting comparison of consecutive changes in fecundity rates with consecutive changes in population density.

Teer *et al.* (1965) measured ovulation rates on a white-tailed deer herd that declined to a density of nine deer per 100 acres and subsequently increased to a density of 18 deer per 100 acres. Ovulation rates were about 1.90 ova per adult doe and 1.60 ova per yearling doe at the lowest population density, and decreased to about 1.35 ova per adult doe and about 1.15 ova per yearling doe at the highest population density (Fig. 4A).

The Seneca Army Depot deer herd (see above) was opened to hunting in 1957, after the herd had increased to its highest density of 2,498 deer. Litter sizes were measured in 1,441 females harvested during five hunting seasons from 1957-1961. As the population decreased from 2,498 deer in 1957 to 263 deer in 1961, average litter sizes increased about 0.4 fetus in yearlings and adults, and about 0.2 fetus in fawns (Fig. 4B).

O'Roke and Hamerstrom (1948) calculated fawn crops as the George Reserve deer herd grew from 6 to 210 and subsequently declined to 74 head. A regression of fawn-crop sizes on preceding early-winter population densities indicates an inverse relation between fecundity rates and population size (Fig. 4C). They concluded average reproductive rates were highest (about 60 percent) when the herd was first starting to increase from a small nucleus. The average reproductive rate was lowest (about 38 percent) during a 6-year period in which they considered deer to be over-abundant. During a 7-year period after the over-population was reduced, the average reproductive rate was intermediate at about 54 percent.

O'Roke and Hamerstrom (op cit.) made several suggestions that are of particular interest to the thesis of this paper: "Our findings suggest that the George Reserve herd, in the absence of natural predation and with inadequate hunting pressure—in both of which it is comparable to many wild herds—tended to become to some extent self-limiting after it developed an overpopulation." The trend of their thinking is further indicated: "Is there here a population mechanism which may forestall the final rise to an irruptive peak, and is the significant thing about deer irruptions not that they sometimes happen but that they happen so seldom? Does such a mechanism plus predation, rather than predation alone, hold wilderness deer in check? Is reproductive capacity violently upset by nutritional deficiencies shortly before wholesale deaths by starvation begin? Does the lesser degree of variation in rate of reproduction at the lower level of population indicate that psychological, rather than nutritional, causes are involved?"

The Kaibab North mule deer *(Odocoileus hemionus)* herd in part exhibited a density-dependent reproductive pattern somewhat similar to that described above for white-tailed deer populations. The population increased from an estimated 16,869 head in 1951 to an estimated 27,456 head in 1954 (Swank 1958). During this density increase, the corpora lutea rate decreased in yearling does from 1.55 in 1951 to 1.33 in 1955 (Fig. 4D). The adult corpora lutea rate did not appear to respond to increasing density as it did in the white-tailed deer populations. However, in Swank's original data some corpora lutea rates for adults exceeded an average of three per pregnant doe, which seems abnormally high.

Fecundity rates have apparently decreased with population density in the White River elk herd (Colorado) in a pattern similar to that described above for deer herds (Boyd, in press). The White River elk herd has steadily increased from an index density of about 2,100 in 1958 to about 3,800 in 1967. During this 10-year period of population increase, the calf-cow ratio has steadily declined from 71:100 to about 59:100 (Fig. 5).

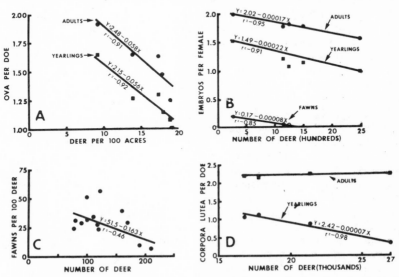

Figure 71-4.—Regressions of fecundity rates on population sizes in four deer herds (A from Teer et al. 1965; B from Hesselton et al. 1965; C from O'Roke et al. 1948; D from Swank 1958).

The above five examples clearly suggest an inverse relation between fecundity rates and densities in deer and elk at higher densities. As a response to this inverse relation, the linear relation between population size and net population production of young at lower densities must become a pronounced curvilinear relation at higher densities. Also, as population densities increase and net production of young per individual declines, densities will be reached where the maximum net number of young will be produced by the populations. Beyond this point, net population production will decrease. Thus, the examples of changing population size and changing fecundity rates provide empirical support for the optimum-yield mechanism shown in Figs. 2A and 2B.

Discussion

The principal management implication of the optimum-yield concept is that maximum annual production of young in most deer and elk herds can be obtained by keeping population densities below those which other management policies might dictate. If maximum annual harvest is the management goal, manipulation of the population to achieve maximum turnover rate should take precedence over manipulation of the population

677

to achieve maximum size. Management efficiency is thus measured in terms of achieving maximum annual net production.

The optimum-yield concept also has a significant management implication for the management of deer and elk range. Perhaps the foremost deer and elk management problem is the maintenance of a healthy balance between populations and their food supply. Much has been written about the concept and problem of carrying capacity, but the concept continues to be vague and elusive for application in wildlife populations. Considerable time, effort and money have been expended on attempts to measure changes in range conditions and browse production, which could be correlated with changes in population densities, with the objective to determine densities which the habitat could support. These efforts, however well directed, have been unsuccessful primarily because of the extreme complexity of the interactions between the population's food demand and the habitat's food supply.

Deer and elk management based on optimum-yield principles would not depend directly on population and food-supply measurements for fixing herd sizes. Population sizes which produce optimum yields are below densities where birth rates and death rates are normally balanced. If this natural balance point is at the population size that the range could support without inflicting adverse effects either on the range or on the population, then populations held at optimum-yield sizes cannot overbrowse or otherwise by direct use adversely affect the vegetation. Thus, if populations were maintained at or near optimum-yield densities, vegetative and density studies designed to relate food supply and demand would not be necessary for efficient management of deer and elk populations.

Another management implication in the optimum-yield concept is associated with the response of fecundity rates to density changes. As Scott (1954), Cheatum *et al.* (1950), Robinette *et al.* (1955), and many others have suggested, fecundity rates are readily modified by habitat conditions, and particularly by nutritional conditions. The nutritional changes are caused partially by the population's impact on the habitat and partially by factors external to the population. Thus, fecundity rates may be sensitive monitors of the total environmental impact on a herd's welfare as are measurements of body-fat, starvation rates, etc. But the latter are terminal symptoms of critical environmental conditions, while fecundity-rate changes are initial symptoms of the onset of potentially critical environmental conditions. Thus, fecundity rates of deer and elk populations may provide an indirect but objective measure of the relation between population density and food supply which direct measurements of population density and food supply have not provided.

Finally, the optimum-yield mechanism may provide an objective reference point for the adjustment of population densities. The relative position of a population's density in its higher range of densities can be estimated by comparing the fecundity rate for a population at a given density to the fecundity rate for the density which would produce optimum yield. Thus, regardless of whether a manager wanted to adjust a population to its optimum-yield density, he would have a method and an objective reference point for gauging herd-density changes and subsequent changes in the welfare conditions of the herd. Should habitat conditions change either from the effects of population density, or from the effects of extrinsic factors, either of which might not be detected with other techniques, changes in fecundity rates should provide an early warning of changes occurring in the balance between the herd and its habitat.

The experimental White River elk herd in Colorado provides an example of how the foregoing concepts might be applied. The regression of calf-cow ratios on population-index values (Fig. 5) indicates that some factor associated with increasing density is causing a constant decline in annual calving rates. If a partial cause of this decline is nutritional deficiency, then the growing population is exerting a progressively greater influence on its food supply and may ultimately produce the classical over-populated and over-browsed range. Studies of the habitat's food supply and the population's food demand probably would not demonstrate the progressive intra-specific competition indicated by the fecundity-rate pattern.

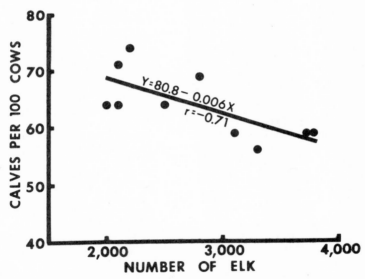

Figure 71-5.—Regression of fecundity rates on population size in the White River elk herd, Colorado (from Boyd, in press).

Production data from Fig. 5 and mortality data not presented in this paper (Boyd, in press) were used to develop a population simulation model for the White River elk herd. The model predicts that the population, at an index size of about 4,000 in 1967, will, under present harvest rates, reach an optimum-yield index size of about 6,000 in approximately 12 years. Projection of the regression in Fig. 5 indicates the annual fecundity rates will have decreased to about 44 calves per 100 cows at the optimum-yield index density. Thus, attainment of the population size that will produce the maximum annual yield and maintain a safe balance between food supply and demand can be identified from fecundity-rate measurements. Should a change in range conditions occur when the population is at a given size, the change in the balance of food supply and demand should be monitored and thus measurable by changes in fecundity rates.

LITERATURE CITED

BARANOV, F. I. 1918. On the question of the biological basis of fisheries. Nauchny: issledovatelskii iktiologicheskii Institut, Izvestiia 1(1) :81-128.

BARANOV, F. I. 1926. On the question of the dynamics of the fishery industry. Biull. Rybnovo Khoziaistra for 1925.

BOYD, RAYMOND J. The elk of the White River Plateau. In press.

CHEATUM, E. L. AND C. W. SEVERINGHAUS 1950. Variations in fertility of white-tailed deer related to range conditions. Trans. No. Am. Wildl. Conf. 15:170-190.

HALLORAN, ARTHUS F. 1962. History of the Wichita Mountains Wildlife Refuge elk herd. Proc. of the Okla. Acad. of Sci. p. 229-231.

HESSELTON, WILLIAM T., C. W. SEVERINGHAUS, AND JOHN E. TANCK 1965. Population dynamics of deer at the Seneca Army Depot. N. Y. Fish and Game Jour. 12(1) :17-30.

LEOPOLD, A. 1933. Game management. Charles Scribner's Sons, N. Y. 481 p.

LEOPOLD, A. 1955. Too many deer. Scientific American 139(1) :101-108.

MURPHY, DEAN A. 1963. A captive elk herd in Missouri. Jour. Wildl. Mgt. 27(3) :411-414.

O'ROKE, E. C. AND F. N. HAMERSTROM, JR. 1948. Productivity and yield of the George Reserve deer herd. Jour. Wildl. Mgt. 12(1) :78-86.

ROBINETTE, W. LESLIE, JAY S. GASHWILER, DALE A. JONES, AND HAROLD S. CRANE 1955. Fertility of mule deer in Utah. Jour. Wildl. Mgt. 19(1) :115-136.

SCOTT, ROBERT F. 1954. Population growth and game management. Trans. No. Am. Wildl. Conf. 19 :480-504.

SWANK, WENDELL G. 1958. The mule deer in Arizona chaparral. Wildl. Bull. No. 3, Arizona Game and Fish Dept. 109 p.

TEER, JAMES G., JACK W. THOMAS, AND EUGENE A. WALKER 1965. Ecology and management of white-tailed deer in the Llano Basin of Texas. Wildl. Mono. No. 15. 62 p.

TROYER, WILLARD A. 1960. The Roosevelt elk on Afognak Island, Alaska. Jour. Wildl. Mgt. 24(1) :15-21.

WALTERS, CARL J., AND JACK E. GROSS Determination of optimum yield in wildlife populations. Unpubl. Ms., Colorado State University.

AFRICAN GAME RANCHING:
A NEW APPROACH (1964)
Raymond F. Dasmann

Americans tend to think of harvesting wildlife only by sport hunting. However there is the possibility of intensive wildlife management aimed primarily at production of meat for human use.

While man has centuries of experience and decades of scientific study as a basis for producing crops of domestic animals, he has only recently begun to apply principles of ecology and population dynamics to the problem of producing game commercially. This paper reviews some of these recent efforts, concluding that game management can be more profitable than husbandry of domestic stock.

During the 1950s biologists from Europe and America were brought to Africa in increasing numbers. As a result of this renewed interest in African game, a new approach to conservation in Africa was developed. It is difficult to discover with whom these new ideas originated, but they have been advanced by various British ecologists, notably W. H. Pearsall, F. Fraser Darling, Harrison Matthews, and E. B. Worthington. All these men and many others participated in studies and surveys of the problem of conserving African wildlife. All of them noted that there was a basic lack of interest on the part of the African people when it came to talk about game conservation. They recognized that one of the chief problems in Africa was a shortage of food. Most of the African people were not getting enough to eat of the right kinds of food. In particular their diets were short of protein.

Most of the soils in Africa are not suited to cultivation and the growing of protein-rich farm crops. In places social customs forbade the use of cattle for meat. In other places the number of useful domestic animals was too low. Many people, particularly children, suffer from diseases caused by a protein deficiency. A hunger for meat was thought to be a principal reason for the continued poaching of game. It constituted a serious threat to the future of game, once the African nations became independent. It is difficult for anyone to enjoy beauty when his stomach is empty or he is harassed by disease. It is not unreasonable that people who have never had enough of the material needs of life, are going to lack interest in fine discussions of spiritual values.

In considering how best to meet the African's need for more protein, these ecologists were impressed by the great numbers of wild animals that were supported, year after year, in the national parks or other still wild places. In most of these places the animals were supported without damage to the veld, without destruction of the grass cover, and without serious damage from soil erosion. By contrast, those areas cleared of game and turned over to domestic animals seemed not only to support fewer animals, but did so at the cost of serious damage to vegetation and soil. W. H. Pear-

Excerpted with permission from: African Game ranching by R.F. Dasmann, Pergamon Press, Ltd., Oxford. 75 pp.

sall made a comparison for Masailand, around the Serengeti National Park. Here the best areas have been taken over by the Masai for their livestock. The game use mostly areas that are considered inferior in their production of forage. Nevertheless, in the Masai pastoral lands where supplies of water and grass were supposed to be superior there were eighty cattle and 133 sheep or goats supported per square mile. In the game area there were according to Pearsall one hundred large and ninety small wild herbivores per square mile. Pearsall concluded that the total weight, or biomass, of game on the lower quality land was about equal to the weight of domestic animals on the better quality land. More recently, however, an aerial survey carried out by the R.A.F. and by Lee Talbot and D. R. B. Stewart indicates that Pearsall's estimate of the numbers of game was conservative. In place of the hundred thousand wildebeest estimated by Pearsall, Stewart and Talbot found over 200,000. In place of the 175,000 Thomson Gazelle, the more recent survey found between 500,000 and 800,000. Thus the lower quality grazing land supports a much greater biomass of animals than the area which has been turned over to domestic livestock.

These figures are baffling to anyone who has grown up with the idea that domestic animals are much better producers of meat than are the wild. In fact, most of those people who have worked with domestic animals are often inclined to think that there must be some mistake in the figures, and simply refuse to admit the possibility that wild game can seriously compete with domestic stock. Yet the figures cannot be refuted. One must explain, therefore, the reasons why wild game should be more efficient than domestic beasts. Here the various ecologists agree that an important reason is the different ways in which wild game animals make use of the veld; differences in their food habits, the distances which they will travel, and in their need for water.

If an area of savanna or open woodland is turned over to cattle use, the cows will feed mostly upon grass, selecting some grasses which they prefer, and leaving other kinds of grass, which they find less palatable, unused. With increased numbers of cattle and heavy grazing the cattle may well be forced to eat everything available. Under these conditions, however, they will not thrive. Since they are not animals that travel long distances through choice, they will tend to concentrate their foraging in limited areas until those have been seriously overgrazed. When this happens the area is not only eroded, it is also invaded by plants of various kinds that cattle will not eat, and then becomes useless as cattle pasture.

Under natural populations of big game, however, the pressure on plants will be distributed in a different way. Giraffes will feed high on the trees, whereas eland, a cow-sized antelope, will browse at a lower level. Both however will use forage which is not available to cattle. Impala, a smaller antelope, will browse at a lower level; the smaller steenbuck will operate even closer to the ground. An elephant may feed on dry, coarse grass, avoided by cattle, or overturn trees and feed on their bark and roots. Different kinds of grasses and weeds will be used by different species of game. Each seems to have its own niche, its own place in the environment, and does not compete directly for food with another species. The whole complex of grazers and browsers will distribute their feeding over all kinds of plants and all parts of the plants, instead of being concentrated at one level, or on one group of plants. It seems reasonable to suppose, therefore, that wild game will make more efficient use of the total plant production in any area of mixed vegetation. If this were so, the game could be expected to produce more meat per acre than could the domestic animals. Studies in Uganda by A. M. Harthoorn, of Makerere College showed that the African buffalo would feed and gain weight on certain kinds of natural grasses. Even the hardy native cattle of the region would lose weight on the same diet.

It has also been noted by the various ecologists that game moves about more freely and travels farther than domestic livestock. They thus avoid grazing too heavily in any one place, but distribute their use widely, and thus cut down the likelihood of damaging the veld. When the water requirements of game and cattle are compared, it is found that some species of game, the gemsbok and oryx are examples, do not drink water at all. All their needs for water are met by the food which they eat, which of course contains varying amounts of water. Other kinds of game drink water, but drink much less often than cattle. Zebra, for example, perhaps drink once in every three days during the dry season. This allows them to travel to grazing lands far from water, only swinging back to the water hole on the third day. Thus the game makes use of many waterless areas that are completely avoided by cattle. With their higher water needs, cattle prefer to remain closer to a water source.

All this information provided a new approach to the management of African game that would perhaps make more sense to hungry people. If an annual crop can be taken from the game herds, in the same way that one markets part of a cattle herd each year, without reducing the breeding stock, then the game populations could be used as a regular meat supply. Game would produce more meat and thus yield more protein for the people of the area. This could serve as an incentive for conservation. If the Africans in rural areas could be taught to think of their game animals in the same way that they would regard their sheep or goats, then they might become convinced of the need for saving breeding herds of game.

Studies and Trials

It remained to be seen whether this theory, which seemed reasonable to an ecologist, could actually work in practice. It was true that it had been successful in America. There the game herds are regularly cropped in some areas, and the numbers that the hunters are allowed to kill are balanced against the annual gain from the production of young. In the Soviet Union also the use of game for a sustained source of meat had proved to be both feasible and economically justified. In the steppe region of the U.S.S.R. the peculiar saiga antelope finds a home. Persistent market-hunting and poaching, however, had reduced its numbers to some hundreds of survivors in a region where millions had once roamed. After the Russian revolution, laws protecting the saiga were put into effect. These were followed by careful studies of its biology, which revealed much about its life history and the factors that were causing loss. With the necessary care provided, the saiga had increased once more to about 2,000,000 animals in 1960 and had become the most numerous wild ungulate in the Soviet Union. The biological studies revealed, moreover, that it would be safe to take a crop from the saiga herds. Now in the region west of the Volga River alone hunters remove from 120,000 to 150,000 antelope each year without reducing the breeding stock. The saiga now contributes 6000 metric tons of first-class meat to the Soviet economy each year along with great amounts of leather, industrial oils, raw material for medicines and other by-products. It has been firmly established as an important economic resource.

Despite this evidence, however, there were fears that African game might be more vulnerable and unable to stand up to annual cropping. To start with there were few measurements of the actual numbers or weights of wild animals that were supported by the African veld. It was difficult to make comparisons with domestic stock. There was also little evidence to show the number of animals that could be removed from a game herd without reducing the breeding stock. It was not known how many young were produced, nor what percentage of these lived to reach adult age. There was also the serious question about how to crop game. You can't round up wild buffalo and herd them into trucks the way you do with cattle. Impala can't be driven to market. Then there was the question of whether or not people would actually buy and eat the meat from hippo or giraffe, zebra or rhino.

In further support of the idea, however, it was found that many farmers in the Transvaal of South Africa had long ago discovered that it was more profitable to raise game than sheep. Without any publicity they had given up sheep-farming and had turned to the production of springbuck and blesbuck antelope which are relatively easy to handle. On some farms these animals were allowed to run in fenced paddocks and killed for market by shooting. The meat and other products from them were sold in Pretoria or Johannesburg at a better profit than could be obtained from wool or mutton. However, these farms did not answer the basic question. Essentially they took one or two species of wild animals and treated them much the same as if they were domestic beasts. The potential of the great variety of game on natural veld was still to be explored.

In Uganda the idea of cropping game as a source of meat was given another test. Here in Queen Elizabeth National Park a plague of hippopotamus had developed. Long protected from hunting by the park regulations, and with few natural enemies, the hippos had become so numerous that they were threatening to destroy their own habitat through overgrazing. The park officials were faced therefore with the necessity of reducing the numbers of hippos, for the good of both the hippos and the park. At this point an American wildlife biologist, W. L. Longhurst undertook the job of organizing the shooting and marketing of surplus hippos. The animals were sold for meat to African dealers at an average price of 150 shillings per carcass. Between May and September in 1958, the National Parks realized nearly 38,000 shillings from hippo sales. The meat was eventually sold to the African people in the area, who were eager to obtain it. The programme went off without difficulty and led to the discovery of much valuable information on the biology of the hippo, as well as a testing of the idea of game cropping. In addition, it solved for a time, the problem of a surplus of hippos.

The results of some of this early work led the government of Kenya to institute a trial programme, known as the Galana River scheme. This was an attempt to solve a problem involving both game and people. The people concerned were the Waliangulu, a tribe whose normal way of life was hunting. In recent years however they had taken to illegal poaching on a large scale, selling ivory and rhino horn to various Asian dealers. The Africans received little income for their unlawful activities and were in danger of wiping out the elephant and rhino. Consequently it was decided to give the tribe the right to take the annual surplus produced by the game and market it, legally, through government channels. The organization, planning and supervision of the scheme was supported by a grant from the Nuffield Foundation in England. The expert skill of the Waliangulu poacher was to be put to work in cropping several hundred elephants each year for sale at a legal price of about $\sqrt{}$ 100 per animal.

Thus it is that after almost a full circle market hunting returned to the African scene. Originally, in its uncontrolled form, market hunting had brought extermination of game and as a practice it was suppressed with great vigour by wardens and game rangers. It was now being re-introduced as a method of game conservation. The difference depended on the way in which it was handled. If the cropping of game were held at a level which the game herds could tolerate, balanced by the annual increase of young, market hunting could provide meat while still encouraging the preservation of game.

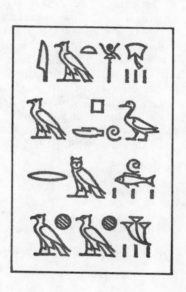

ECOSYSTEM CONCEPTS IN FISH AND GAME MANAGEMENT (1969)

Frederic H. Wagner

An ecosystem approach to wildlife management endorses a holistic philosophy and the management of natural communities rather than single species. Wagner compares the application of ecosystem concepts in fishery and wildlife biology and outlines the relevance of exploitation theory to considerations of population and community dynamics.

There are essentially two aspects to the practice of fish and game management. (The term "wildlife" is used herein to embrace both aquatic and terrestrial wild animals; the terms "fish and game" are used to distinguish, respectively, the fish and the birds and mammals.) The first aspect is the direct manipulation of wildlife populations. Most commonly such manipulation involves exploitation or harvest for economic or sporting purposes. (Exploitation is used here roughly synonymous with use . . . .) Population manipulation may also include the protection of endangered species for esthetic, educational, and scientific purposes; and it may involve the control of noxious or economically undesirable species.

The second aspect of fish and game management is manipulation of the environment to enhance or reduce the species in question according to the need. More often than not, the wildlife we utilize is produced in ecosystems not specifically manipulated by man for its production although such ecosystems may be substantially altered by or for other human activities. In some cases, however, our wildlife harvests are derived from systems managed with varying degrees of intensity for wildlife production.

Both of these applied aspects have rested heavily upon the population level of ecological theory for their base. Proper exploitive practices require knowledge of demographic patterns, of responses to exploitation, and in general of the regulatory patterns employed by wild animal populations. Environmental manipulation for wildlife, too, presupposes a knowledge of ways in which various environmental factors operate on species of interest, and again of the general principles of population regulation.

Hence, both fish and game management have been heavily population-ecology oriented, often with the individual species focused upon and only those parts of the remainder of the ecosystem considered that may impinge upon the target species. Indeed much of wildlife management has been applied population ecology, and its research along with that of economic entomology has been among the major contributors (Southern, 1965) to what probably has been the most active of the integration levels of ecology.

A. Past Usage of Ecosystem Concepts: Fishery versus Wildlife Biology

Paralleling this trend of population emphasis, fish management has also been strongly based in ecosystem theory to a degree unknown in game management. This dichotomy seems to have developed for several rea-

Excerpted from: The Ecosystem Concept in Natural Resource Management, (G. M. Van Dyne, Ed.). Copyright by Academic Press, Inc., N. Y. 383 pp.

sons. First, much of fishery theory has been developed from work on commercially important species, particularly marine and the salmonids. In these species, weight is generally a more important parameter economically than numbers. With the emphasis thus on biomass, the concept of production in the ecological sense (the rate at which energy-bearing tissue is produced) has naturally assumed great importance. This focus on production has been sharpened further by a need to take into account the indeterminate body-growth pattern of fish and the variability of growth rates and adult size in different environments. Much thought has been given to the relative merits of different growth models. Consequently, formulas for fish production exist (cf. Ricker, 1946) and empirical values are available for a variety of species.

The game biologists' concept of production or productivity has not been as explicit in terms of contemporary ecosystem theory. A. Leopold's early definition (1933)—". . . the rate at which mature breeding stock produces other mature stock, or mature removable crop . . ."—with some additional consideration for growth, and for biomass or energy would have approached the mark. While this definition is occasionally quoted, the emphasis in game has been more with numbers than with biomass—apparently for two reasons: (1) Birds and mammals have more nearly deterministic growth patterns and adult size than do fish, and therefore vary less with nutrition or age once adulthood is reached. (2) The game technician is more commonly managing a resource for sport. It is more often the number of animals than the weight which determines the number of hunters whose sporting desires can be gratified.

A second probable reason for the greater emphasis on ecosystem theory in the fishery field lies in the different trophic status of most commercial and sport fish, on the one hand, and most sporting game species, on the other. Most of the fish species are carnivorous, are near or at the top of the aquatic pyramid, and hence are the recipients of the energy flow through most of the food chains in a system. In some cases, one or two species of top carnivores may constitute the convergence point for energy flow from nearly all of the pathways present. On the other hand, most game species are herbivores and share their trophic level with many other species of animals, both invertebrate and vertebrate. Much of the energy flow may pass them by, and their production is therefore not so clearly a function of the primary production of their systems.

A third reason for the greater use of ecosystem theory in the fishery field is closely related to the last, and derives from the difference between the producers of the aquatic and the terrestrial systems. In the aquatic, particularly under pelagic conditions, phytoplankton of course represent the producer level. As such, the entire trophic level is available for utilization; and potentially, all of the energy fixed in primary production can be moved up the food chains of the system each year toward the top carnivores. This near-complete annual utilization of the primary production does in fact commonly occur, as shown in a number of studies reviewed by Raymont (1966). In the terrestrial situation, on the other hand, much of the production may go into root tissue or woody stems where it is not available even to browsing or grazing ungulates, much less to the more

688

specialized seed, mast, and bud feeders in which category most upland gamebirds and many waterfowl fall. Here again, fish production is more clearly a function of the primary production of a system than is game production.

A fourth reason may lie in possible differences in the pattern of population regulation between fish, on the one hand, and birds and mammals on the other. This will be discussed at greater length later; suffice it to say at this point that one could probably come nearer gaining a concensus among ecologists for the view that fish numbers or biomass are limited by food (and therefore energy) than one could get for the same generalization about birds and mammals.

These are the reasons underlying the more complete embrace of ecosystem concepts by fishery biologists. The most productive fisheries do tend to coincide with areas of higher primary production. The latter tend to occur in areas of higher inorganic nutrient concentrations due to seasonal thermal overturn at high latitudes, to upwelling wherever it occurs and to the higher concentrations near the continental margins provided by the emptying of nutrient-laden rivers. Accordingly, fishery biology has been very absorbed with matters of trophic structure, production and nutrient cycling. And the fishery manager has experimented with fertilizing ponds, lakes, and even portions of the ocean with the objective of increasing primary production and the amount of energy which can be transmitted up the food chains to the desired fish species.

The game biologist, on the other hand, may find that forested areas although having higher primary production than grassland or savannah (Ovington *et al.*, 1963), produce lesser game crops than the latter (Bourlière, 1963) where more of the production is usable and available. Or he may find that it is the structure of the vegetation in terms of cover, interspersion, and other habitat elements which is a more important limiting influence than the amount of energy-bearing food. These are the reasons why game biologists have thought largely in terms of populations and specific limiting factors (often not food) which restrain the number of individuals (not biomass) in their resource.

B. Recent Increasing Attention to Ecosystem Concepts

In recent years a number of developments in game management are demanding interpretation and application in terms of more comprehensive ecosystem principles. The growing prevalence of environmental pollutants, which cycle through the community food webs and converge and concentrate in carnivores, is demanding more complete understanding of nutrient cycling patterns. We are clearly in need of broader perspectives because of the diverse ways in which man's activities can attack game resources. As Holling (1966, p. 197) has stated: "We are in a moment of history when a bomb exploded in one part of the world affects the food of Arctic caribou and when insecticides broadcast in the northern hemisphere appear as residues in Antarctic penguins."

A second reason for the increasing recourse to ecosystem perspectives in wildlife management lies in a need to understand and predict long-range effects of exploiting natural systems. A considerable part of the world's food supply comes from largely wild, undomesticated systems.

Most notable, of course, is the ocean which undoubtedly will be exploited to an increasing degree in the future. In game biology there is growing interest in producing meat with wild animals in parts of the world where production by game is greater than that of livestock. Natural systems tend toward equilibria in their bioenergetic, biogeochemical, and interspecific (particularly competitive and predatory) processes. When major components are removed from such steady-state systems, some form of adjustment in pattern and process will inevitably occur. Some systems seem to absorb perturbation with a minimum of change, as Darling (1964) has stated of western Europe. But others react violently, as we shall observe later in this review. If we are to maintain the productivity of the world's ecosystems and derive a sustained yield, we must understand and be able to predict the effects of perturbation, exploit judiciously, and take counteractions to prevent violent change.

Finally, the growing interest in systems analysis in ecology and resource management (cf. Watt, 1966, 1968) suggests that this approach might become a means for unifying these fields. Watt (1968) envisions all the fields of natural resource management as potentially being unified by a common body of theory and methods, and having a common body of processes and mathematical properties. In this perspective, game population problems not only have a common theoretical base with fishery problems, but also become part of the broader subject of managing whole systems.

C. Objectives of the Review

The objectives of this chapter are twofold. The first is to consider several aspects of wildlife management, particularly but not exclusively game, in terms of ecosystem concepts. The emphasis here is on game because less ecosystem attention has been given this group. To attempt a general review of ecosystem concepts in fishery management would involve the assimilation of an already mountainous aquatic literature. The result could not be contained in a one-chapter review such as this. Many excellent review works and symposia already exist in various aspects of this field.

The second objective is to explore the bases for several divergences of view and concepts between the fish and game areas. Several points of disunity exist between these two fields, and one cannot avoid wondering whether the principles underlying the population processes of these two groups may not be more similar than present concepts imply. One such divergence is the greater consideration of ecosystem principles in fish than in game management.

A second dichotomy is in exploitation theory. With fishery population theory dating back at least a half century to Baranov (1918), and the greater mathematical rigor which has pervaded fishery work, this field seems to have taken on more theoretical precision and depth. Critical review of game exploitation theory and evidence vis-à-vis fishery theory might disclose more similarities to the latter than now seem to exist. According to Watt (1968), the various fields of resource management often have not familiarized themselves with each others' theory and techniques. This has tended to be true even in such closely related fields as fish and game exploitation. A detailed review of exploitation theory would be somewhat

690

tangential to the present subject, but is touched upon briefly here as it relates to ecosystem implications of single-species exploitation.

A final area of disunity, both in basic and applied ecology, is in population regulation theory. Since the regulation and equilibria of entire trophic levels and ecosystems constitute the collective regulation of the constituent species, and since the principles involved are germane to proper wildlife population manipulation and environmental management, a consideration of this subject seems appropriate here.

Hence, the pattern of this review is a consideration of several aspects of wildlife management in an ecosystem perspective, and an attempt at confrontations where dichotomies exist.

II. IMPLICATIONS OF SINGLE-SPECIES EXPLOITATION

In the short fish and game management history of less than a century, most research on the exploitation aspect has understandably concentrated on the responses of individual species to exploitation. A great deal still remains to be learned on this subject, and undoubtedly much research emphasis will continue. However, investigations more and more are looking beyond the species in question to broader effects of exploitation on other facets of the ecosystem, biotic and physical. While concentrating their efforts on single-species problems in their classic work, Beverton and Holt (1957, p. 24) stated in their opening section that this is ". . . now perhaps the central problem of fisheries research: the investigation not merely of the reaction of particular populations to fishing, but also of the interactions between them and of the response of each marine community to man's activity." Several developments of recent years in this general topic merit attention here.

A. Population Responses to Exploitation

Before considering some of the side effects on the ecosystem of exploiting individual species within the system, it may be well to review briefly the effects of exploitation on fish and game populations. The two fields have traveled rather different paths on this subject, and one wonders whether more interchange between the two disciplines might not turn up a common set of principles underlying the two.

1. SIGMOID THEORY IN FISHERIES

Beverton and Holt (1957) have traced two separate, though related, lines of development in fishery population theory. One, which they termed "the analytical," dates back to Baranov (1918) and is based on estimating separate population parameters of recruitment, growth, natural mortality, and fishing mortality. These are integrated into mathematical models which express the response of a fish population to varying levels of exploitation, and which hopefully predict the maximum sustained yield. The analytical method has received a great deal of emphasis, with models varying in detail according to the assumptions different authors make about the nature of the relationship between breeding population size and recruitment, body-growth patterns, survival characteristics, and other parameters.

The second line of development, actually convergent with the first, is based, as a first and simplest approximation, on the well-known logistic population-growth curve of Verhulst (1838) and Pearl and Reed (1920). It assumes that any given species has a characteristic, potential rate constant of increase in a specified physical environment. Termed by Lotka (1956) "the instantaneous rate of increase" and by Andrewartha and Birch (1954) "the innate capacity for increase," we shall use the notation r_n for this parameter. (A subscript is used with this parameter to avoid confusion with r, the actual rate of population increase which will also be used.)

In an unlimited environment a species would increase exponentially according to this rate. No environment is unlimited however, and every population presumably stops its growth when it reaches some equilibrium density, K. The pattern of growth which a population thus undergoes is described by the logistic formula:

$$\frac{dN}{dt} = r_n N \frac{(K - N)}{K}$$

A population growing according to this formula describes a symmetrical sigmoid curve (Fig. 1A) in which the inflection point is at the midpoint of density between zero and K.

Two important implications of this formula derive (1) when the rate of increase per individual in the population, $dN/N\,dt$, and hereinafter designated by the notation r, is plotted as a function of density, N, (Fig. 1B); and (2) when the increment of growth, dN/dt, is plotted as a function of density (Fig. 1C). The first implication follows from the parenthetical term of the equation and implies that the actual growth rate per individual declines as a straight-line function of the density (Fig. 1B).

The second implication (Fig. 1C) is the important one for our discussion at this point. If the time intervals, t, are taken as years in species which reproduce seasonally, then the increments of growth could be taken as the annual recruitment of individuals into the population from reproduction. These increments represent the excess of births over deaths at different densities of a population.

The parabola in Fig. 1C thus indicates that the birth rate is equal to the death rate at K, and no excess exists—the obvious condition of equilibrium. As a population is progressively reduced, however, births numerically exceed deaths to an increasing degree up to the midpoint between zero and K. Below this density the increase increments decline, even though the increase per individual is higher (Fig. 1B), because the breeding population or capitol upon which the interest rate operates is too small.

The exploitation implication here is that at equilibrium the population has no margin which it can yield to exploitation. Any removal reduces the population by raising the decrement of natural mortality and harvest above the reproductive increment. At any density below equilibrium, an excess does exist and the population can be stabilized by the removal of exactly that excess. The parabola in Fig. 1C indicates the number of animals which could be removed on a sustained-yield basis at any given standing-crop level of the population. The highest sustained yield obviously could be removed from the density between zero and the natural equilibrium untampered by human exploitation.

The concept is used in a somewhat specialized sense in fishery problems. The additional dimension of weight is added so that the curve actually represents the biomass production of a population. Furthermore, as generally used in commercial fisheries, the model applies only to that segment of the population which has reached sufficient age to be taken by the fishing gear.

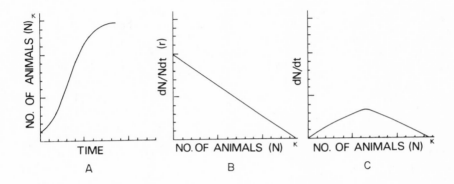

Figure 73-1.—Logistic population growth (A) with its implied relationship between r, the instantaneous rate of growth per individual, and population density (B), and between dN/dt, the increments of growth per unit of time, and population density (C).

The validity of this model as a generalization about population behavior has been widely questioned (cf. F. E. Smith, 1952; Andrewartha and Birch, 1954; Slobodkin, 1954). Although these criticisms have all been well taken, the model and its implications are sufficiently close to population behavior to be useful conceptual tools and first approximations. Hutchinson (1957) pointed to ". . . the almost universal practice of animal demographers to start thinking by making some suitable, if almost unconscious, modification of this much abused function." Allee *et al.* (1949) and Dasmann (1964a) have reviewed several cases of approximate logistic fit to vertebrate populations. Tanner (1966) reviewed evidence from studies on 71 species reported in the literature and calculated r-density regressions. Of these, 47 were significant (negative) while 15 more were negative but short of significance suggesting the general existence in animal populations of a relationship similar to that in Fig. 1B and some type of sigmoid pattern.

In actuality, symmetrical sigmoid curves (logistics) may not be general. The more common curve applicable to the fisheries biomass situation may be a right-skewed curve with the inflection point to the left of mid-density (Gulland, 1962). Wagner *et al.* (1965) found the r-density regression in several pheasant populations to be curvilinear and approach a negative exponential, also implying a right-skewed growth curve. Similar curves may be inferred for a number of species in plots of reproductive rate on density (Kluijver, 1951), percentage spring-fall increase on density

(Errington, 1945) and r on density in some laboratory populations (F.E. Smith, 1963). Such right-skewed sigmoids would imply a maximum, sustained-yield density somewhat less than half the unexploited, equilibrium density.

Beverton and Holt (1957) point out that the analytical and sigmoid approaches are actually convergent, leading to a similar general concept of population behavior. This concept basically holds that in a population at equilibrium, its productive processes (growth and reproduction) are equaled by dissipative processes (predation, respiration, and decomposition). There is no net excess of production over dissipation which could be taken as yield without altering the standing crop.

At densities below the equilibrium point, there is an excess of production over dissipation, the obvious condition underlying population growth. The excess per individual is highest at the very low densities, but because the producing population is small, the total production is small. At high densities near equilibrium, the producing population is large, but the production per individual and total production are small. In the intermediate ranges, production per individual is not at its maximum, but it is large enough that it can, with a moderate-sized, standing crop effect the largest total production.

The important point for our consideration here is that the imposition of a fishery on a balanced population temporarily increases the mortality rate above the reproductive rate and induces population decline. As it declines, reproductive and/or survival rates (the components of r) increase and eventually stabilize the population at some lower density, provided the level of exploitation does not exceed the density-dependent leeway present in the r-density relationship. The harvest thus reduces the population standing crop, the maximum sustained yield coming from no more than half, and quite possibly less than half, the pristine equilibrium level. In the process, a component of an interrelated system with homeostatic tendencies has been reduced, and one would expect some adjustment in the system.

2. EXPLOITATION THEORY IN GAME

With a decade or two less time to pursue what is in any event a young field, with a variety of species ranging from large ungulates with low reproductive rates to highly fecund upland game, and to migratory species which spend half the year away from their nesting range, and with generally less mathematical rigor, game management has not had the unifying benefit of a single, explicit theory or population model. The nearest thing to such a theory has been a general philosophy based on the work of Paul L. Errington. This philosophy, derived largely from his work with bobwhite quail *(Colinus virginianus)* and muskrat *(Ondatra zibetheca)* and with predation on these species, has two major facets which are generally assumed to operate, one or both, in most small-game species.

The first facet, here termed the winter threshold effect, visualizes game populations occupying environments with limited and generally well-fixed capacity to protect animals during the winter season. Each year the reproductive season produces a number of animals in excess of the winter threshold. This annual surplus inevitably disappears through predation, weather, or emigration because of the animals' intolerance to crowding into the limited habitat niches. The animals living within the security threshold experience little if any losses, barring catastrophic weather incidents. If pitched so as to remove no more than a number equivalent to the annual surplus, hunting can take a portion of animals without increasing the fall-spring mortality rate or affecting the population level (cf. Lauckhart and McKean, 1956; Uhlig, 1956).

The second facet, here termed the inversity principle, is based on spring and fall censuses in a number of populations which have shown higher rates of spring-fall increase in years when breeding densities were low than when high. Sufficient flexibility exists in this phenomenon that something approaching a summer or fall threshold level exists, and varying numbers of breeding adults are capable of producing the same crop of young by summer or fall. The implication here again is that even if the winter threshold effect does not operate, the population can be shot in fall and the reduced breeding population which results can produce virtually as large a crop of young as more breeders would have (Allen, 1956, 1966; Linder et al., 1960).

The important point here is that hunting is assumed not to affect the standing-crop density of populations. Small-game hunting philosophy is based on this premise, two eminent spokesmen for the profession (Allen, 1947; Hickey, 1955) having stated that hunting is justifiable only as it does not affect standing-crop levels of harvested species. Sigmoid population-growth patterns have occasionally been alluded to in small-game publications, but it seems fair to say that the sigmoid model and its implications in terms of exploitation effects on standing-crop levels have neither served as a general conceptual base nor been fully perceived or embraced in small-game management.

Although critical review and resolution of this problem are needed, such an analysis is beyond the scope of this review. At this stage the evidence is conflicting. Several studies seem to show complete compensation for hunting loss with no effect on density (cf. numerous examples cited by Allen, 1954; Uhlig, 1956; Peterle and Fouch, 1959). Subjectively it does appear that many game populations can exist under heavy hunting pressure without obvious effects on their density. Yet Wagner et al. (1965) and Wagner and Stokes (1968) have pointed out certain population implications of Erringtonian theory and the fact that these do not hold in pheasant (Phasianus colchicus) populations. I have (Wagner, unpublished data) found a similar failure in bobwhite and ruffed grouse (Bonasa umbellus) data published respectively by Kozicky and Hendrickson (1952) and Edminster (1938).

Even less of a formal theory or population model exists in migratory waterfowl. Although migration largely obviates any assumption of a winter threshold effect, there has been at least some tendency in the field to apply approximate Erringtonian philosophy, perhaps dependent on the inversity phenomenon; and some workers (cf. Hickey, 1955) have been inclined to hold that hunting could not be justified if population levels were affected. However, since Hickey (1952) first showed that annual mortality rates in mallards (Anas platyrhynchos) are a straight-line function of the level of hunting kill, this relationship has been shown in a variety of species including the black duck *(Anas rubripes)* by Geis and Taber (1963), the green-winged teal *(Anas carolinensis)* by Moisan *et al.* (1967), and pheasant hen (Wagner *et al.,* 1965). As Wagner *et al.* pointed out, such a correlation violates one implication that follows from a strict security-threshold phenomenon.

Although waterfowl populations clearly fluctuate with precipitation and the amount of habitat, Hochbaum (1947) some time ago signaled a concern for the possible effects of hunting on population levels. Today (1969) there is a wide, though by no means universal, suspicion that the shotgun is a significant depressant on waterfowl numbers.

The general exploitation philosophy in many large ungulates has been quite different from that in upland game and waterfowl. Some species, primarily those of climax communities, such as big-horned sheep *(Ovis* spp.) and barren-ground caribou *(Rangifer tarrandus)* in North America, have not fared well and restrictive exploitation philosophy is in order. However, the more common situation has been one of population increases occasioned by the elimination of large predators, improvement of habitat, and earlier restrictive hunting regulations (cf. A. Leopold *et al.,* 1947). The need has often been to reduce populations and there has been little doubt of the additiveness of natural mortality and hunting kill. In some populations, there may be virtually no other source of mortality, beside firearms once adulthood is reached (cf. Eberhart, 1960).

In summary, then, there is little doubt of the reduction effect of hunting on ungulate populations, the general goal being to reduce them to and hold them at levels where they maximize the energy flow from the vegetation without harming that vegetation. A. S. Leopold (1949) and Dasmann (1964a) have advocated an actual sigmoid management philosophy in big game. In waterfowl and upland game the picture is somewhat ambiguous. The suspicion persists that hunting influences waterfowl levels and perhaps upland game more often than we suspect. Perhaps a sigmoid view would be realistic in these species along with a goal to harvest at maximum sustained-yield densities rather than hope for a yield without depressing standing crops. Both Scott (1954) and Darling (1964) have advocated a sigmoid philosophy as a general approach to the management of wildlife.

As stated above, however, the manner in which populations respond to exploitation is relevant in this review to the effects on entire ecosystems which result from the exploitation-induced change in numbers of important species. Several responses of this kind have been documented.

．　．　．　．　．　．　．　．　．　．　．　．　．

Conclusion
Our knowledge of the patterns and processes of ecological systems, while still in the early stages of development, is beginning to disclose some of the underlying principles on which these systems operate. Since the resources of any ecosystem are limited and the reproductive and growth tendencies of the biota constantly press it toward the limits of resources,

we expect competitive interactions between organisms. The long-range, approximate stability of ecosystems suggests that the component species have achieved a degree of homeostatic coexistence. One would predict that alteration of the pattern of an ecosystem, as with exploitation for food or sport, would elicit adjustments of various types. We have examined a few examples of such adjustments.

The results of these exploitation-induced changes in the outcome of competitive situations point to a need for looking beyond single-species responses to the broader impact on other ecosystem components. Traditionally, we have weighed the values of predator control for wildlife management and livestock husbandry against the possibility that it could release incipient pest species. Now an entirely new consideration enters the picture: the possibility, as Paine suggests, that predation may promote community complexity. If this suggestion is correct—and it may yet not be past the hypothesis stage—then we must evaluate reduction of predatory species against the ecological, conservation, and esthetic values of community complexity. Parenthetically, one may wonder what the sale of dried starfish in the curio stores and tourist shops of coastal cities portends for the intertidal fauna of these regions.

Similarly, we need in exploitative situations to be aware of competitive species which could displace those exploited, and perhaps apply pressure to these competitors. Larkin suggests, as one implication of his work, that fishermen may need to guard against the use of highly selective gear which only takes a single, desired species. Murphy advocates applying "judicious" pressure to all of the ecologically similar species within a trophic level. In fact, he concludes more broadly: ". . . the intelligent use of living resources by man must be based on a thorough understanding of the total ecology of the communities involved, and it is unlikely that this would be dominated by any single environmental factor."

One could examine the effects of exploitation on other ecosystem processes beside the competitive. Foresters, for example, have devoted considerable attention to the effect of removing timber crops on the biogeochemical equilibrium of a forest system. Removal of an animal crop could also alter nutrient budgets and affect long-range productivity. For example, the annual removal of between a half million and a million cutthroat trout (*Salmo clarkii*), mostly 12-16 inches in length, by tourists in Yellowstone National Park must effect a substantial nutrient transport. That transport might as easily be beneficial as inimical to the perpetuation of the pristine condition. With several million persons visiting the area each year, there may well be a long-range trend toward enrichment as is occurring in many lakes of western United States that are frequented by numbers of tourists. The fish removal could conceivably be retarding such a trend.

Our long-range goal should be to perpetuate the productivity and integrity of the world's ecosystems while utilizing them for human use. The goal of our ecological research is to understand these systems so that we can predict the effects of perturbation and avoid irrevocable changes.

REFERENCES

ALLEE, W. C., E. EMERSON, O. PARK, T. PARK, AND K. P. SCHMIDT. 1949. Principles of Animal Ecology. Saunders, Philadelphia. 837 pp.

ALLEN, D. L. 1947. Hunting as a limitation to Michigan pheasants. J. Wildl. Mgmt. 11: 232-243.

——————. 1954. Our Wildlife Legacy. Funk and Wagnalls Co., N. Y. 422 pp.

——————. 1956. The management outlook. pp. 431-466 in Pheasants in North America (D. L. Allen, Ed). The Stackpole Co. Harrisburg, Pa., and the Wildlife Mgmt. Institute, Washington, D. C.

ANDREWARTHA, H. G. AND L. C. BIRCH. 1954. The Distribution and Abundance of Animals. Univ. of Chicago Press, Chicago. 782 pp.

BARANOV, T. I. 1918. On the question of the biological basis of fisheries. Izv. Nauchn. Issled. Ikliol. Inst. No. 1, 71-128. (English translation by W. E. Ricker with assistance of Natasha Artin. 53 pp. mimeo).

BEVERTON, R. J. H. AND S. J. HOLT. 1957. On the dynamics of exploited fish populations. Vol. XIX. Min. Agr., Fisheries Food, Fishery Invest., Ser. II. H. M. Stationery Office. London, 533 pp.

DARLING, F. F. 1964. Conservation and ecological theory. Brit. Ecol. Soc. Jubilee Symp., London. Blackwell, Oxford.

DASMANN, R. F. 1964. Wildlife Biology. Wiley, N. Y. 231 pp.

EBERHARDT, L. 1960. Estimation of Vital Characteristics of Michigan Deer Herds. Mich. Dept. Cons., Game Div. Rpt. No. 2282. 192 pp.

EDMINSTER, F. C. 1938. Productivity of the ruffed grouse in New York. N. Amer. Wildl. Conf. Trans. 3:825-833.

ERRINGTON, P. L. 1945. Some contributions of a fifteen-year local study of the northern bobwhite to a knowledge of population phenomena. Ecol. Monographs. 15:1-34.

GEIS, A. D. AND R. D. TABER. 1963. Measuring hunting and other mortality. pp. 284-298 in Wildlife Investigational Techniques (H. S. Mosby, Ed.) 2nd ed. Edwards, Ann Arbor, Mich.

GULLAND, J. A. 1962. The application of mathematical models to fish populations. pp. 204-217 in The Exploitation of Natural Animal Populations (E. D. LeCren and M. W. Holdgate, eds.) Wiley, N. Y.

HICKEY, J. J. 1952. Survival Studies of Banded Birds. U. S. Fish and Wildl. Service, Spec. Sci. Rept.: Wildl. No. 15, 177 pp.

——————. 1955. Is there a scientific basis for flyway management? N. Amer. Wildl. Conf. Trans. 20:126-150.

HOCHBAUM, H. A. 1947. The effect of concentrated hunting pressure on waterfowl breeding stock. N. Amer. Wildl. Conf. Trans. 12:53-62.

HOLLING, C. S. 1966. The strategy of building models of complex ecological systems. pp. 195-214 in Systems Analysis in Ecology (K.E.F. Watt, Ed.). Academic Press, N. Y.

HUTCHINSON, G. E. 1957. Concluding Remarks. Cold Spring Harbor Symp. Quant. Biol. 22:415-427.

KLUIJVER, H. N. 1951. The population ecology of the great tit, *Parus m. major* L. Ardea 39:1-135.

KOZICKY, E. L. AND G. O. HENDRICKSON, 1952. Fluctuations in bob-white populations, Decatur County, Iowa. Iowa St. Coll. J. Sci. 26:483-489.

LAUCKHART, J. B. AND J. W. McKEAN. 1956. Chinese pheasants in the Northwest. pp. 43-89 in Pheasants in North America (D. L. Allen, ed.). The Stackpole Co., Harrisburg, Pa. and the Wildl. Mgmt. Inst., Washington, D. C.

LEOPOLD, A. 1933. Game Management. Charles Scribner's Sons. N. Y. 481 pp.

LINDER, R. L., D. L. LYON AND C. P. AGEE. 1960. An analysis of pheasant nesting in south-central Nebraska. N. Amer. Wildl. Conf. Trans. 25:214-230.

LOTKA, A. J. 1956. Elements of Mathematical Biology. Dover, N. Y. 465 pp.

MOISAN, G., R. I. SMITH AND R. K. MARTINSON. 1967. The Green-winged Teal: Its Distribution, Migration, and Population Dynamics. U. S. Fish and Wildl. Serv., Spec. Sci. Rept.: Wildl. No. 100, 248 pp.

OVINGTON, J. D., D. HEITKAMP AND D. B. LAWRENCE. 1963. Plant biomass and productivity of prairie, savanna, oakwood and maize field ecosystems in central Minnesota. Ecology 44: 52-63.

PEARL, R. AND L. J. REED. 1920. On the rate of growth of the population of the United States since 1790 and its mathematical representation. Proc. Natl. Acad. Sci. U. S. 6: 275-288.

PETERLE, T. J., AND W. R. FOUCH. 1959. Exploitation of a Fox Squirrel Population on a Public Shooting Area. Mich. Dept. Conserv., Game Div. Rept. No. 2251, 4 pp. (mimeo).

RAYMONT, J. E. G. 1966. The production of marine plankton. Adv. Ecol. Res. 3:177-205.

RICKER, W. E. 1946. Production and utilization of fish populations. Ecol. Monographs 16:373-391.

SCOTT, R. F. 1954. Population growth and game management. N. Amer. Wildl. Conf. Trans. 19:480-503.

SLOBODKIN. L. B. 1954. Population dynamics in *Daphnia obtusa* Kurz. Ecol. Monographs 24:69-88.

SMITH, F. E. 1952. Experimental methods in population dynamics: A critique. Ecology 33:441-450.

_____,1963. Population dynamics in *Daphnia magna* and a new model for population growth. Ecology 44:651-663.

SOUTHERN, H. N. 1965. The place of ecology in science and affairs. New Zealand Ecol-Soc. Proc. 12:1-10.

TANNER, J. T. 1966. Effects of population density on growth rates of animal populations. Ecology 47:733-745.

UHLIG, H. G. 1956. The Gray Squirrel in West Virginia. West Va. Conserv. Comm., Charleston. 83 pp.

VERHULST, P. F. 1838. Notice sur la loi que la population suit dans son accroisement! Corresp. Math. Phys. 10:113-121.

WAGNER, F. H. AND A. W. STOKES. 1968. Indices to overwinter survival and productivity with implications for population regulation in pheasants. J. Wildl. Mgmt. 32:32-36.

_____, C. D. BESADNY AND C. KABAT. 1965. Population Ecology and Management of Wisconsin Pheasants. Wis. Conserv. Dept. Tech. Bull. No. 34. 168 pp.

WATT, K. E. F., ED. 1966. Systems Analysis in Ecology. Academic Press, N. Y. 276 pp.

_____. 1968. Ecology and Resource Management—A Quantitative Approach McGraw-Hill, N.Y. 450 pp.

A CASE STUDY IN CANADA GOOSE MANAGEMENT:
THE MISSISSIPPI VALLEY POPULATION (1968)

Henry M. Reeves, Herbert H. Dill and Arthur S. Hawkins

Management is a dynamic process. Habitats and land-uses change. People's desires and management goals change. Our knowledge of wild species changes and hopefully improves. Mistakes are made, admitted and new programs begun. Managing the public wildlife may be a hectic profession, but it will not be dull. The management biologist must be prepared for and should anticipate change. He anticipates change by keeping an active, inquisitive mind. His education in wildlife-management doesn't end in college. It begins there as preparation for continued seeking after new ideas throughout life. This paper illustrates the challenges presented in managing Canada geese of the Mississippi Valley during 38 years.

Seldom, if ever, has wildlife been subjected to a greater variety of management efforts than have geese of the Mississippi Valley Population. Various management techniques and special regulations have been tried. Some have proven successful; others have failed. The basic principles in Canada goose management are involved in this case history; therefore, the story of these geese is told in the following pages.

For over three decades, problems associated with the Mississippi Valley Population have plagued management biologists and administrators in the central corridor of the Mississippi Flyway. In fact, if judged by volume of newsprint, correspondence with legislators, and the hours spent by game managers in meetings relating to hunting regulations, the perplexities posed by these geese seem unequalled by any other species of game!

The traffic jams every nice Sunday during the fall or spring on Highway 49 where it transects Horicon National Wildlife Refuge attest to the great popularity of the honker among nonhunters. But most of the problems which we shall discuss are related directly or indirectly to harvesting these birds, which are the most highly prized of all the waterfowl of the flyway.

With the decline in numbers of ducks in the Mississippi Flyway from 1956 through the following decade, the sale of waterfowl hunting stamps declined about 26 percent (Table 65). But in Wisconsin, duck stamp sales declined only 17 percent. In Illinois during this period, sales fell off 47 percent! Because both states are favored with large numbers of ducks and geese in the fall, this suggests that more people in Wisconsin actively participated in goose hunting than in Illinois. This statement is further supported by the fact that more than 45,000 applications for Canada goose hunting permits were received by the Bureau in 1967 from Wisconsin hunters. In both cases, it appears that most duck stamp buyers are potential goose hunters and that the Canada goose is of major interest to all wildfowlers.

The following account of the Mississippi Valley Population of Canada geese has been placed in chronological order, but with greater emphasis on more recent years as management problems intensified.

Reprinted from: Canada Goose Management, Ruth L. Hine and Clay Schoenfeld, Eds. Dembar Educational Research Services, Madison, Wis. 195 pp.

Original Status

Our knowledge of the original size and distribution of the Canada geese now referred to as the Mississippi Valley Population is incomplete. Hankla and Rudolph (1967) attempted to consolidate early records of Canada geese in southern states, especially along the lower Mississippi River and the adjacent Gulf Coast. Their studies, and reports of others (Hanson and Smith, 1950; Crider, 1967), substantiate the fact that scattered wintering populations of Canada geese, totaling tens of thousands, existed over wide areas in the south as late as the turn of the century. Since this period predates the development of flyway concepts, integrated censuses, and most important, banding or marking programs, it is impossible to identify migration routes of these overwintering geese in the south. It is agreed, however, that most of these wintering concentrations dwindled, and larger midflyway wintering flocks have appeared.

Two theories seek to explain these changes. One asserts that these shifts in wintering areas occurred simply because the southern population was over-harvested. The northern populations had mortality rates lower than productive rates; therefore, they increased. The second postulates that improved habitat in the north, created by the production and harvest of corn and other grain, simply intercepted geese migrating farther south to traditional wintering areas. It seems reasonable that both explanations, when combined, account for the shifts in overwintering populations. Generally speaking, we did not recognize manageable goose populations until the flyway management concept evolved, goose banding was initiated, and national and state wildlife refuges were established in the 1930's.

Through the pioneering efforts of Hanson and Smith (1950), the results of early banding were analyzed. This included bandings by Jack Miner near Kingsville, Ontario. The theory of managing definable populations of Canada geese resulted from this work. This study showed that the Mississippi Valley Population nested in the Hudson Bay Lowlands of Ontario from the south end of James Bay north and west to about the Manitoba border (Fig. 1). The migration route extended southward to central Iowa and northwestern Ohio, narrowing to the junction of the Mississippi and Ohio Rivers, and continued southward along the Mississippi River to its delta and a short distance westward along the Gulf Coast. Another population of Canada geese to the west was termed the Eastern Prairie Population. Canada geese to the east were named the Southeast and South Atlantic Populations; in recent years, much of the Southeast Population has been included in the Tennessee Valley Population. Band recovery data indicate varying degrees of overlap between these management populations.

Geese of the Mississippi Valley Population typically consist of the Todd's or interior Canada goose, *Branta canadensis interior,* although geese of other subspecies are intermixed. Within the migration and wintering areas described are scattered populations of giant Canada geese, *Branta canadensis maxima*; however, these usually do not mix with those of the interior subspecies.

Exploitation

Regulations during the early period of Canada goose abundance were lenient, or nonexistent, and countless birds were transported to markets for sale. Hawkins (1941, unpubl.) relates the following information concerning early distribution and commercialization of Canada geese in southern Illinois:

> It is possible to partially reconstruct the status of the "honker" in Alexander County during the nineties due to the recollections of old goose hunters.
>
> Mr. Emil Lieb, a market hunter, found it profitable to hunt along the sand bars between Chester, Illinois, and Wolf Island, Missouri, a river distance of about 75 miles. The bars between McClure and Cairo, however, offered the best shooting. In marked contrast to their highly concentrated range today, the range of the geese in the nineties was widely dispersed.
>
> Some idea of former goose numbers can be obtained from the statement of Mr. Lieb that he and two partners in the market hunting business during 1895 killed 2,280 geese, as high as 50 geese a day. Mr. Edwin Halliday had this to say concerning goose numbers in 1895, "Wild geese were hanging in front of every market and even in front of restaurants along and near 8th Street in Cairo. As the weather was turning warm, the storekeepers were trying to dispose of the geese. I recall one price tag said forty cents. All the hotels had geese too." The old timers agree that there were more wintering geese then, than now.

TABLE 65. Statistics on the Principal Canada Goose Areas of Illinois and Wisconsin

County	Area (Sq. Miles)	Human Population		Cropland Acreage — 1965			Duck Stamp Sales	
		1950	1960	Corn	Soybeans	Total Cropland	1956	1967
Wisconsin								
Dodge	892	57,611	63,170				131,101	108,833
Fond du Lac	724	67,829	75,085					
Totals	1,616	125,440	138,255	124,100	4,200	1,034,000	Percent Change: -17%	
Illinois								
Alexander	224	20,316	16,061	13,300	22,900		125,185	66,180
Union	414	20,500	17,645	25,800	10,700			
Jackson	603	38,124	42,151	44,700	35,400			
Williamson	427	48,621	46,117	12,300	13,000			
Totals	1,668	127,561	121,974	96,100	82,000	1,067,200	Percent Change: -47%	
Mississippi Flyway							1,019,145	756,768
							Percent Change: -26%	

Even after the passage of the Migratory Bird Treaty Act in 1918, the goose season extended 107 days, from September 16 to December 31, in the central portion of the Mississippi Flyway, and in the southern portion, from November 1 to January 31. The allowable daily bag of 8 and no possession limit, did little to restrict the kill although commercialization for the market was prohibited. Baiting and the use of live decoys was permissible, and these practices were widely used. Lenient regulations remained in effect until 1929 when the daily bag was reduced to 4 and an 8-bird possession limit was imposed. This seems to be the first federal regulation toward restricting the harvest. In 1935 and 1936, the seasons were shortened to 30 days and baiting and decoys banned. No doubt this was because of the shortage of ducks more than for any special concern for geese. In 1935, the Canada goose bag and possession limit was reduced to 4; the season was shortened to 30 days.

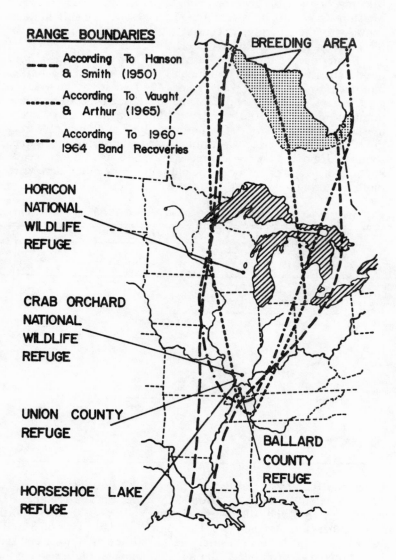

Figure 74-1.—Range of the Mississippi Valley Population of Canada Geese.

In 1936, the first attempt to census the wintering population of Canada geese was made in what is now the Mississippi Flyway. The total recorded was 47,510 (Fig. 2). It seems likely that this and subsequent early censuses represented minimum populations because of incomplete coverage. This seems reasonable since the 175,000 censused in 1939, just 4 years later, is biologically unlikely if the 1936 count was indeed correct. The early populations and kills shown are questionable since wide-area census and harvest methods had not yet been developed. Nevertheless, they do represent the best information available, and for that reason have historical significance.

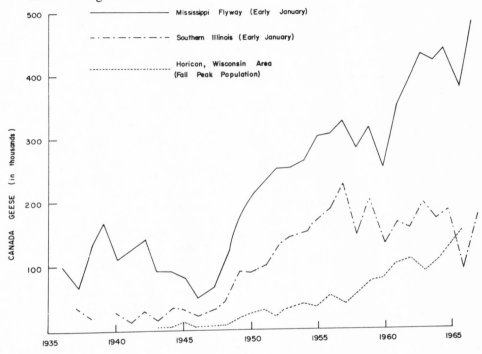

Figure 74-2.—Numbers of Canada Geese in the Mississippi Flyway, and the Number of Canada Geese of the Mississippi Valley Population in Southern Illinois and at Horicon, Wisconsin.

In the early 1940's, it became evident that the number of Canada geese that traditionally wintered in the lower Mississippi Valley and central Gulf coastal area was decreasing. Also, it became apparent that Canada geese that traditionally wintered on the sandbars of the Mississippi River required more habitat. Increasing hunting pressure, channelization of the Mississippi, the discontinuance of floods which scoured the sandbars keeping them clear of brush and trees except willow sprouts which apparently were an important browse item, and changes in cropping from corn to soybeans were important factors in making the area south of St. Louis less attractive to geese (Davis, 1954).

The first deliberate expansion of goose range was in 1927, when the Illinois Department of Conservation purchased 3,500 acres, including Horseshoe Lake, an oxbow of the Mississippi River northwest of Cairo. Previously, only an occasional goose had stopped on the area and its major value was for duck hunting and fishing. Additional land was added and an agricultural program started to produce goose food. Geese were quickly attracted to the area and Horseshoe Lake had its beginning.

While the Horseshoe Lake Refuge served to concentrate geese, it also attracted hunters to its boundaries. Publicity, good accommodations, and high success rates resulted in exceptionally high hunting pressure with resulting heavy kills and crippling losses. The kill mounted as Horseshoe Lake became less capable of providing food and sanctuary for large numbers of geese. Its carrying capacity was soon exceeded and geese became dependent on private lands where selling hunting rights became more profitable than raising crops.

The Horseshoe Lake situation in 1941 was evaluated by Hawkins (unpubl.) as follows:

According to Pirnie (1935), "The primary function of refuges is to save game for breeding stock, not to make it easier to kill more." Horseshoe Lake cannot qualify as a refuge under this definition. However, let us not sit back and point an accusing finger at those who originated the refuge. Their idea was a good one, and they should be commended for it. The present critical situation has resulted from a lack of information on how to maintain a true goose refuge, among waterfowl authorities as well as among government administrators. Nor is there any reason why the present so-called "refuge" cannot become a true refuge in the future.

The foregoing shows that the unfortunate goose situation in Alexander County is a problem of concentration. In the first place, it is an hereditary trait for geese to concentrate in or near Alexander County; the establishment of a refuge has intensified this gregarious habit. Secondly, hunters concentrate there because the geese do. The inevitable result is overshooting.

In commenting on quality hunting and increasing hunting pressure in southern Illinois, Hawkins continues:

One answer to increased hunting pressure was the formation of goose hunting clubs, but since the time of the Egyptian Hunting and Fishing Club, organized in 1904, goose clubs have changed considerably in Alexander County. Present-day clubs, with one or two exceptions, have one function—to make money. In contrast, this first club, which had annual dues of five dollars, was organized to have fun. At one time, it boasted a membership of 50, all local sportsmen. There are at least two dozen clubs in Alexander County today that kill more geese annually than did the Egyptian Club, according to a direct comparison of kill records. The reason appears to be that these early hunters concentrated more on having an enjoyable outing than in bagging a limit with all possible haste, as is the modern philosophy of goose hunting in this area.

706

Goose hunting first took on a commercial aspect when in 1913 an organization known locally as the "Chicago Millionaires Club" began to lease the sandbars most frequently used by the geese. By 1916 most of these bars were no longer open to public hunting. Up to that time field shooting had been scorned by most real goose hunters. Now that river shooting was largely under the control of a few wealthy men, it was field shooting or nothing.

The purchase of Horseshoe Lake for a refuge in 1927 created a boom in commercialization of goose shooting. Mediocre farm lands located near the refuge suddenly commanded fancy prices. In almost every field located along the goose flight line between the refuge and the river, pits were dug to make "blinds" for hunters. Some farmers even altered their cropping system to make their farms more attractive to geese. The goose hunting flourished until 1935 when the Federal government drastically curtailed hunting privileges as a measure to conserve our waterfowl resource which as the result of drought and other influences had declined to an alarmingly low point.

Horseshoe Lake became notorious for the goose slaughters that occurred in its vicinity. Public sentiment ran high but the kill continued as commercial interests resisted needed change. A severe population decline was inevitable.

In 1944, the situation became so serious that the Secretary of the Interior closed the goose season in Alexander County after only 21 days of shooting. In 1946, for the first time in history, the entire Mississippi Flyway was closed to Canada goose hunting. These were the first of numerous closures in Illinois and later in Wisconsin. In 1945, a similar closure was effected after only five 4½-hour shooting days, or a total of 22½ hours of shooting. In January 1946, the population of Canada geese numbered but 53,000 of which only 22,000 were located in Illinois. This marked the lowest level for this population ever recorded.

The seriousness of the Mississippi Flyway Canada goose situation is best described by a Department of the Interior news release dated April 4, 1946:

"The flock of Canada geese which winters at the Horseshoe Lake Refuge presents one of the most serious and difficult problems in wildlife conservation at the present time," stated Mr. Day. "The only way to maintain this flock of geese in numbers approximating its present size is to give it absolute protection from shooting for an indefinite period.

"In 1945, when the Fish and Wildlife Service was advised that 2,100 geese were killed during the first two days of shooting, the agency moved promptly to stop the organized slaughter by having the Secretary of the Interior issue a closing order, effective at 4:30 p.m. on November 28, in accordance with the provisions of the Migratory Bird Treaty Act. . . .

"Had the shooting been permitted to continue at that rate," Mr. Day declared, "the entire flock of some 26,000 honkers might have been completely wiped out in a single season. Approximately

275 birds an hour—five a minute—fell to the hunters' guns in the 22½ hour 1945 season, spread over five half days of 4½ hours, from noon to 4:30 p.m. We discovered that on the opening day, from noon to 4:30 p.m., the total kill in that time equalled the total season's kill for 1938, and every day's kill in 1945 exceeded the top in any previous year.

"Since the controls instituted by this Service and the Illinois Conservation Department have failed to achieve the desired results, the prohibition of shooting for an indefinite period is our only recourse if this flight of Canada geese is to be saved from serious damage or extinction."

Recovery

Public indignation finally resulted in the realization that harvests and management practices must be geared to habitat requirements and reproductive capabilities, even if it required subjugation of powerful economic and political interests not conducive to the welfare of the goose resource (Elder, 1946).

Presidential Proclamation No. 2748, dated October 1, 1947, (12 FR 6521) established an area of approximately 20,000 acres in Alexander County which was closed to goose hunting. Within the area closed were located privately owned hunting clubs which had previously accounted for many of the geese that were shot.

An interesting sidelight to the Presidential Proclamation was a damage suit of $3,000 brought against the government by a group of hunters for loss of shooting rights. On appeal, the 7th U.S. Circuit Court of Appeals, on February 13, 1950, affirmed a lower court's decision by holding that the Presidential Proclamation was constitutional, and that no one had property rights in migratory birds. Furthermore, it declared that the hunting of migratory game birds is illegal except as made legal by Presidential Proclamation; inasmuch as these lands were excluded by Presidential Proclamation, then the plaintiff suffered no loss of property rights (Landsen vs. Hart, 180 Fed. (2nd) 679).

In an attempt to relieve the situation at Horseshoe Lake, the Crab Orchard National Wildlife Refuge was also established in 1947 about 50 miles north of Horseshoe Lake in Jackson and Williamson Counties, Illinois. The large 44,000-acre area contained about 3,500 acres of cropland where food for geese and ducks could be raised. It was hoped that this new area, the first "satellite," would provide additional habitat for geese at Horseshoe Lake. Theoretically, by splitting the Horseshoe Lake concentration, problems of overharvests, poor kill distribution, and crop depredation threat could be resolved. In the winter of 1947, the refuge wintered 2,000 geese. Goose-use steadily increased in the years following.

Along with increasing Horseshoe Lake to about 7,000 acres, the Illinois Department of Conservation acquired the 6,500-acre Union County Refuge located approximately 25 miles north of Horseshoe Lake. The purchase of the Union County Refuge and the enlargement of Horseshoe Lake were made possible by a $375,000 special legislative appropriation. The Union County Refuge included 3,150 acres of cropland, 1,600 acres of water, and 1,500 acres of timber. Theoretically, this new refuge could provide each goose overwintering with 500 to 600 square feet of pasture and 14-16 pounds of corn. In addition, large amounts of waste grain were available on the private farmlands near the refuge.

In 1947, the closed area, plus a season shortened to 30 days, a bag and possession limit of but 1 Canada goose reduced the kill. In January, 1948, 63,000 geese were censused; the number in southern Illinois had increased 9,000 from the previous year.

Besides land acquisition and management, a dispersal program was initiated at Horseshoe Lake and was continued in 1949. Hazing was conducted by the state and the Bureau between October 4 and 29 using aircraft, rifle-launched rockets and flares, and parachute-type flares; the crews operated on land and water. Altogether, 183 hours of flying time were logged by two pilots, and 202 cases of flares and exploding rockets were expended. The peak goose population on October 7, just after operations commenced, totaled 12,000; this number was sharply reduced as the geese were driven to islands in the Mississippi and into Missouri. By October 11, only 300 geese remained on the state refuge; continued hazing prevented a build-up from recurring. Despite a protest meeting held on October 17 at the Cairo courthouse, the hazing continued. The widely scattered geese provided excellent hunting but there were few reports of excess killing, large-scale commercialization, or crop depredations. An estimated 30,000 geese lingered throughout the winter in Mississippi and Scott Counties, Missouri, but there was no indication that geese had been forced farther south.

The area closed by Presidential Proclamation was reduced in size to 9,000 acres prior to the 1953 season. Hunters quickly responded and an unprecedented harvest estimated at 56,000 geese occurred. Aroused conservationists across the nation demanded action to prevent another slaughter of this magnitude (Schendel, 1954; East, 1954).

The high kill of 1953 was removed from a population which had increased three-fold since the low year, 1946. It caused a temporary set-back in population growth which was offset by greatly reduced kills the following two hunting seasons. By that time, three major goose management areas in southern Illinois were operating smoothly, apparently with sufficient control over the goose harvest to prevent further slaughters. But in 1957 the kill rate again erupted reaching the highest level ever recorded in southern Illinois. This coupled with a sharply increased kill at Horicon in 1958, set the stage for the quota system inaugurated in 1960. The southern Illinois harvest, brought under control in 1959, has remained so to date. However, to the north on the newly created Horicon National Wildlife Refuge, another problem associated with Canada geese of the Mississippi Valley was beginning.

Stabilization

The Horicon National Wildlife Refuge was established primarily for ducks, more specifically for redhead ducks. Even though it was situated directly astride the migration route for Canada geese, at the outset no one thought that it might eventually attract tens of thousands of Canada geese.

In 1940, the federal refuge was established on the northern two-thirds of Horicon marsh which had been drained but later reclaimed. The state acquired the southern third bringing the total area to 31,653 acres. Small, scattered tracts of cropland were added on the periphery to provide grasslands and to straighten out the boundary.

Geese did not immediately stop at Horicon. Refuge manager Jerome Stoudt commented in his 1942 Refuge Narrative Report as follows:

There seems to be quite a flight of geese through this part of Wisconsin, but few, if any, appeared to stop over on the Horicon Marsh. Only one Canada goose was observed actually resting on the marsh itself, and that may have been a cripple. Many flocks were observed flying southward from the first day of the hunting season and several flocks were within easy gunshot but none of these were seen to actually alight on the area.

Between 1946 and 1949, a breeding flock of Canadas was established on the state's end of the marsh which had produced nearly 500 goslings by 1957 (Hunt and Jahn, 1966), but when wild Canada geese finally began to stop at Horicon, it was in relatively small numbers. Everyone was delighted to see them. In 1951, the last major water control structure was completed and the marsh reflooded. In that year, the Canada goose peak population reached 24,000. By 1957, the Mississippi Valley Population had stabilized (fig. 2). While year-to-year estimates have varied since then, the median number has remained about the same. Even though the fall population at Horicon continued to grow, it was not until the carrying capacity of the refuge had been exceeded that real concern developed.

The geese were encouraged to move out from the refuge onto private lands through the establishment of zones where shooting was permitted only part of each day. This type of management increased vulnerability to the gun. The geese became less wary. As wariness decreased, the bird lost some of its trophy value. Goose hunting had become goose shooting!

Behavioral Changes

No case history of the Mississippi Valley goose population would be complete without noting how these birds responded to certain forced changes in their mode of living. Before Horseshoe Lake became a refuge, these geese wintered in widely scattered flocks along the sandbars of the Mississippi River between Chester, Illinois, and the Gulf of Mexico. Enroute to their wintering grounds the birds migrated through the flyway in small flocks, stopping to feed briefly until hunters discovered them and drove them out. When sanctuaries were established along these flightlanes, the birds soon discovered them and gradually built a tradition of returning to these areas bringing other members of their flock with them.

Most authors, lyricists, and wildfowlers of the past have lauded the honker as the symbol of wildness. But those who have observed the Canadas at Horseshoe Lake or Horicon Marsh have a different idea. At both places, these great birds often appear stupid. They readily fly over conspicuous blinds—even those containing poorly concealed hunters. At Horicon Marsh, we have observed several carloads of hunters in a parking lot slamming car doors, loading guns, and boisterously talking with several hundred geese feeding noisily around the nearest blinds scarcely a gunshot away. This was after the season had been open several days.

Yet these same birds elsewhere in the flyway may do honor to the best traditions of the species. Apparently the sheer weight of large numbers and freedom from harassment lulls these birds into complacency. This coupled with the great competition for food, especially on the sanctuary area, causes the type of behavior illustrated above, a pattern which apparently does not exist until concentrations build up to several thousand individuals.

The birds have adjusted to their new-found existence in other ways. Formerly, they shied away from standing corn, although this grain has long been a preferred food. An interesting account of a changing feeding behavior at Horicon has been provided by Jahn (unpubl.):

Changes in feeding behavior of Canada geese using Horicon Marsh have, in certain respects, been rather spectacular over the past 20 years. On my first trip to Horicon in the spring of 1947, Canadas refused to feed into the edges of large fields or strips of standing corn. By the fall of 1950, geese in the Federal refuge fed under the husks on ears hanging down on upright stalks on the edges of strips or block-type fields of corn. Art Hughlett's thesis shows that kernels were consumed on ears up to about 38 inches from the ground.

Our first boom nets were placed along the juncture of corn and hay fields to trap Canada geese in the fall of 1950. The birds landed in the hay field and walked toward and finally into edges of the standing corn. Our bait and traps intercepted these movements of the birds.

In the early 1950's, feeding Canada geese worked through 100-foot strips of standing corn that were relatively weed-free. But only edges (a few rows) of strips of corn having heavy stands of weeds (i.e., foxtail, pigweed, lambs quarters, dock, smartweeds, bindweed, etc.) were used. Later on weed control became more efficient and the open stands of corn encouraged greater use by Canada geese. In the 1960's, geese would alight directly in strips and blocks of standing corn where they had fed previously.

Behavior of the geese at a particular cornfield seems to be conditioned by prior experience. When the field is first approached, the birds commonly land nearby, walk into the edges, and, if undisturbed, ultimately feed throughout it. This pattern of use was evident in refuge corn fields in the 1950's and may now be observed in refuge fields and lightly shot or unshot private fields experiencing crop depredations.

Over the past two decades (1947-1967) Canada geese have adapted and perfected their habits for feeding in standing corn. Twenty years ago the birds rarely fed in standing corn. Today they readily feed there. A combination of factors seems involved in this behavioral change. Geese naturally prefer corn as food. Fields on the Horicon National Wildlife Refuge provided an opportunity for geese to feed in standing corn with only minor and infrequent disturbance. Improved weed control now provides relatively open standing cornfields that are more attractive to feeding Canada geese than the weed-choked fields commonly encountered twenty years ago. These factors interacted to permit repeated satisfying experiences from which evolved the feeding patterns now demonstrated by Canada geese using the Horicon National Wildlife Refuge.

Hanson and Smith (1950) speculated that "wariness is related to the total size of an aggregation and its size in proportion to the area it uses." They advised "insofar as possible, reduce contact between human beings (both the public and refuge personnel) and the geese." Part of the problem in managing the Mississippi Valley Population of geese may stem from failure to recognize the importance of this advice and to follow it.

From this, it is clear that goose behavior may change somewhat in adjusting to changing conditions. The flexibility of the species should be an asset to management if it is understood and used properly.

Gradually, the duration of the fall stay of geese at Horicon has increased with some variations due to weather. In 1961 and in 1966, over 12,000 geese were still present in January in the Horicon vicinity. Despite limitations pointed out by LeFebvre and Raveling (1967) Horicon, during these two mild winters, with low snowfall, became a wintering area. In 1965, approximately 65,000 geese remained at Horicon until mid-December and equal numbers were still present at the time of this writing (December 3, 1967).

In addition to the major concentration at Horicon, geese gathered on the numerous marshes and lakes of the rolling glacial terrain of eastern Wisconsin. Because of the wide area in Wisconsin and Illinois over which geese were being hunted, the problem of overharvest during the 70-day season was not immediately recognized. However, after 1957, the population failed to increase as had some other Canada goose populations in the flyway (fig. 2).

Management Objectives and Guidelines

The Mississippi Valley Canada goose population includes nearly half the members of this species wintering in the Mississippi Flyway. So that the various agencies of the flyway involved in the research and management of Canada geese would work cooperatively toward common goals, the Flyway Council has included in its Management Plan a statement of objectives and guidelines for fulfilling them. According to Section 221.11 of the management Guide as revised July 8, 1965, the objective is to "distribute Canada geese throughout the Flyway in order to supply as many portions as possible with reasonable recreational opportunity of the highest possible quality."

To accomplish this end the following facets of management must be considered:

1. Improving distribution, and utilizing recreational opportunity by providing a wider choice of stopping places.
2. Managing by sub-units and even individual flocks.
3. Setting quotas in line with production.
4. More fully utilizing potential nesting grounds.

712

5. Reducing waste from various causes.

6. Improving the quality of the recreation provided by these birds.

The plan states that "the ideal pattern (of distribution) would include numerous stopping places between northern nesting grounds and southern wintering grounds. Through proper management the geese would be encouraged to proceed slowly but steadily down the Flyway spreading their benefits more or less evenly both enroute and at the terminals. The geese themselves determine their distributional pattern to a large extent because each population has its traditional range."

This arrangement is recognized as somewhat idealistic because the plan adds that "flocks firmly attached to a wintering area must be managed where they have chosen to remain. Methods of dispersion of such concentrations should be a research endeavor of high priority."

To date, efforts to move a substantial portion of this population farther south in the flyway have met with failure. Methods tried included the establishment of major refuges south of the Ohio River managed specifically for geese; trapping and transporting to these southern areas large numbers of geese hoping that they would return in future years; and dispersal tactics on wintering areas including food reduction in managed areas. There may be no other alternative left than to manage the geese on the areas of their choice even though the winter terminals are farther north than desirable or than originally existed.

Management objectives and guidelines should be reviewed from time to time in the light of new knowledge and experience. One of the Council's most active technical subcommittees spends long hours annually on this never-ending task.

Quota System

The principle of the quota system was not new in that it had been applied in the past to individual areas as a guide for terminating the season. For example, local allowable harvests were sometimes geared to a predetermined percentage of the peak population. As early as 1949, Hawkins (unpubl.) stated:

> It looks to me like the best procedure is going to be (a) determine how much shooting the goose population can stand, (b) set a kill quota each year for the Horseshoe Lake area based on estimated breeding success, and (c) keep close tabs on the take and close the season when the quota is reached.

It was not until 1960 that a quota system involving the two major harvest states, Illinois and Wisconsin, came into being. This action was deemed necessary because of the 37 percent reduction in the 1960 winter inventory from the previous year (Green, Nelson, and Lemke, 1963).

Basic principles in the quota system followed those stated earlier by Hawkins. Because summer inventories were not being conducted on the breeding grounds of the Mississippi Valley Population of Canada geese, the estimate of the previous wintering population served as a base from which an expected fall flight was projected. Factors considered in these calculations included the proportion of potential breeding females, average gosling production per female of breeding age, natural mortality, kill by

Indians, other Canadian harvest, and crippling loss, leaving an estimated number of geese that could safely be harvested in the United States. From the latter figure, a crippling loss was deducted and a kill set aside for states other than Illinois and Wisconsin. The respective Illinois and Wisconsin quotas were mutually agreed upon or set with the assistance of the Mississippi Flyway Council, or on rare occasions, set by the Bureau. While quotas determined in this manner are useful, they fail to reflect variations in the fall flight due to annual changes in nesting success. Furthermore, in retrospect it seems that biologists used several estimates made at different times during December and January for determining the winter population upon which the projection was based. This estimate was corrected for geese "known to be present but not actually observed." While the result represented a concensus based on the best data available, the population figure used was invariably the highest estimate made (Tables 66 and 67).

TABLE 66. Canada Goose Quotas in Wisconsin and Illinois.

WISCONSIN			
Year	Horicon Zone*	Statewide	Total
1960	7,000	None	
1961	12,000	None	
1962	8,000	None	
1963	12,000	None	
1964	11,000	None	
1965	11,000	None	
1966	8,000	6,000	14,000
1967	15,000	5,000	20,000
ILLINOIS			
Year	4-County Zone**	Statewide	Total
1960	14,000	None	
1961	20,000	None	
1962	10,000	None	
1963	20,000	None	
1964	15,000	None	
1965	15,000	None	
1966	18,000	2,000	20,000
1967	18,000	2,000	20,000

* Portions of Dodge, Fond du Lac, Juneau, Monroe and Wood Counties.
** Union, Jackson, Alexander and Williamson Counties.

Two conditions must be met if the quota system is to function as a true control of harvest in a given area such as a state or portion of a state: (1) at least 75 percent of the kill must occur within the quota area (selected), and (2) a relatively accurate method must be available for measuring the kill.

In Illinois, the quota area comprised four counties totaling approximately 1,600 square miles (Table 65). The kill was recorded at goose hunting clubs licensed by the state within the quota area.

TABLE 67. Estimated Harvest of Canada Geese in Wisconsin and Illinois

		WISCONSIN		
Year	Quota Zone*	Season Length (Days)	Statewide Harvest	Season Length
1960	10,900	9½	Unknown	70
1961	11,141	10½	Unknown	60
1962	7,093	7½	Unknown	60
1963	12,746	35½	20,300	70
1964	13,066	11½	25,400	70
1965	13,354	12½	31,800	70
1966	9,617	2½	31,193	70
1967		58		70

		ILLINOIS		
Year	Quota Zone**	Season Length (Days)	Statewide Harvest	Season Length
1960	14,900	42	Unknown	45
1961	18,500	40	Unknown	40
1962	10,717	44	Unknown	44
1963	9,635	45	Unknown	45
1964	16,159	29	Unknown	58
1965	15,079	45	Unknown	45
1966	18,724	40	21,990	47
1967				

* Portions of Dodge, Fond du Lac, Juneau, Monroe and Wood Counties.
** Union, Jackson, Alexander and Williamson Counties

In Wisconsin, the quota area used in most years was much smaller than in Illinois. Actually, banding data reveal that Dodge and Fond du Lac Counties, which totaled about 1,600 square miles (Table 65) comprised the area in which most of the goose harvest occurred. The Horicon quota zone from 1963 through 1965 was approximately 238 square miles (fig. 3). A number of methods for recording the kill in Wisconsin have been tried annually through 1966. These included spot checking at farms, mail questionnaires, and mandatory registration at manned and unmanned checking stations.

While the quota provides an equitable means on paper for distributing the allowable harvest, it does not plug certain "leaks" which result in an overharvest. The failure of this population to increase, despite the setting of quotas designed to insure for substantial increases, proves that a significant fraction of the kill went undetected. The key points of the quota system in Illinois and Wisconsin since 1960 are summarized in Table 68.

TABLE 68. Synopsis of Special Management Practices Applied to the Mississippi Valley Population of Canada Geese *

Year	Location	Practice
1927	Horseshoe Lake, Illinois	Refuge established for geese (state)
1941	Alexander Co., Illinois	Weekly bag limit of geese imposed: 3 geese in any 7 consecutive day period (federal)
1941	Illinois	Licensed hunting club established (state)
1942	Alexander Co., Illinois	Restricted shooting hours, sunrise to noon (federal)
1944 and later years	Alexander Co., Illinois and later in Wisconsin	Emergency closure of goose hunting season (federal, state or both)
1946	Entire Mississippi Flyway	No goose hunting season proclaimed (federal)
1947	Portion (20,000 acres) of Alexander Co., Illinois	Limited area completely closed to goose hunting (federal and state)
1947	Crab Orchard National Wildlife Refuge, Illinois, Union County, Illinois	Dispersal of population by satellite management areas (federal and state)
1948-49	Horseshoe Lake, Illinois area	Population dispersal attempt by hazing (federal and state)
1954	Portion of Horicon National Wildlife Refuge, Wisconsin	State managed goose hunt allowed on federal lands (federal and state)
1957	Horicon area	Goose season opening delayed to allow geese to develop off-the-refuge feeding flights (federal and state)
1957	Horicon area	Goose shooting stopped at 2:00 p.m. to allow geese to develop off-the-refuge feeding flights (state)
1959 and later	Horicon area	Intensive field surveys undertaken to measure extent of goose kill
1960	Four counties in Illinois and areas surrounding Horicon and Necedah National Wildlife Refuges, Wisconsin	Kill quota system inaugurated (federal and state)
1963	Wisconsin	Goose registration system established (state)
1963	Wisconsin	Calculation of goose harvest by tail fan and registration compliance checks (federal)
1965	Horicon National Wildlife Refuge, Wisconsin	Massive feeding program (federal and state)
1965	Horicon area, Wisconsin	Early season opening in advance of regular statewide goose hunting season (federal and state)
1965	Wisconsin	Law enacted for payment of crop damages resulting from waterfowl (state)
1965	Horicon area, Wisconsin	Alternate day shooting initiated in effort to reduce rate of kill (state)
1966	Horicon Marsh, Wisconsin	Population dispersal attempt by hazing
1967	Portion of Horicon National Wildlife Refuge, Wisconsin	Closed to state-managed goose hunting
1967	Wisconsin	Statewide goose tagging system inaugurated (federal and state)

* Also, see Nelson, 1962 and Hunt, Bell and Jahn, 1962.

Feeding Shelled Corn

Frost limited the production of corn at Horicon in 1965. Because goose food was in short supply on the refuge, concern was felt for (1) the high rate of kill of geese flying off the refuge in search of food, and (2) the threat of depredations to corn on private lands. Wisconsin authorities pressed for a feeding program on the refuge to relieve these imminent threats. The feeding program was started September 29. A total of 467.5 tons of shelled corn was hauled and spread on the refuge dikes. Feeding continued until November 12. Although up to 50,000-60,000 geese at a time accepted this "bread line", a new record for daily kill was set on October 7 when 2,367 geese were registered, indicating strong off-refuge flights. The threat of serious depredations failed to materialize, however, because scaring devices, hazing with aircraft, and other control measures proved effective in protecting unharvested corn on private lands.

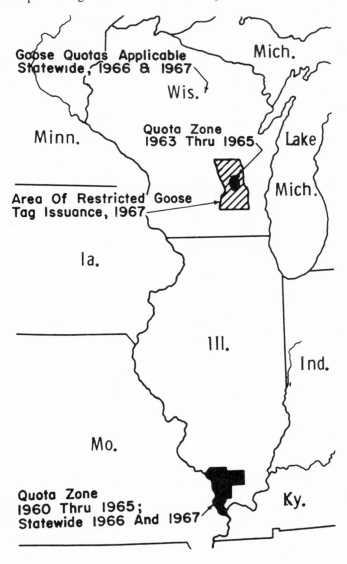

Figure 74-3.—Canada Goose Quota Zones.

Conclusion: The feeding program, expensive though it was, failed to hold the majority of the geese on the refuge. At the time the total estimated goose population using Horicon was 120,000.

Hunting Pressure Used to Induce Migration

With larger and larger autumn concentrations of geese, more emphasis was placed on retarding, or even reversing this trend. In 1965 at the request of Wisconsin administrators, the Bureau agreed to try an earlier opening date in the quota zone. The season for Canada geese was opened September 25. The theory was that if the first geese arriving met shooting pressure, they might migrate. This in turn would reduce the rate of build-up on the area.

The result was that the regulation seemed to have no appreciable effect on the rate of kill. The season in 1965 was closed within the quota area (Horicon Zone), October 7, with the kill quota filled, plus some overrun (Table 67).

Hazing

Early in 1966, federal and state officials agreed that an attempt to haze geese from Horicon Refuge should be made during the ensuing fall. The objective would be to reduce the refuge population to about 50,000 geese. The plans for goose management, including hazing, were reviewed at a number of public meetings by state and federal personnel. The plans were also reviewed with members of the Mississippi Flyway Council in St. Louis, Missouri in February, 1966. While there was some concern in Wisconsin over the proposed hazing, no alternate plan was offered.

Planning for the cooperative experiment continued until suddenly, on September 9, a member of the Wisconsin Conservation Commission publicly threatened the arrest of federal agents participating in the experiment. In view of the reaction that these threats created, the hazing plan was modified so as to restrict federal aircraft and personnel engaged in hazing to federal lands. The hazing program got underway on September 20 under threat of legal action by the state. The Horicon hazing experiment became the subject of widespread publicity in the press, on nationwide television and radio, and in national magazines.

Wisconsin implemented its threatened action by a civil complaint filed in State Court on September 23 seeking to enjoin six named Bureau employees from engaging in hazing operations on the refuge proper or anywhere else in Wisconsin. The action was subsequently moved to U.S. District Court in Milwaukee. There it remained until October 2, 1967, when the state withdrew its complaint.

The experiment was pursued with vigor by the Bureau. At the peak of activity the week prior to the season's opening, this involved use of a helicopter, 2 fixed wing aircraft, 2 airboats, 2 marsh vehicles, 6 conventional boats, 15 floating platforms mounted with crop depredation exploders, 16 land-based exploders, and other frightening devices such as shot-shells and firecrackers. Thirty-nine individuals were directly involved in field work. Hazing was discontinued the morning of October 7, 24 hours before the season opened. Results of the experiment may be summarized as follows:

718

1. Hazing efforts were successful in removing most of the geese from the refuge during daylight hours; however, they returned to the refuge at dusk.

2. Predictions of wholesale crop damages failed to materialize; the damage that did occur was local and relatively small.

3. An unprecedented kill occurred in the 2½ days of shooting allowed in a 7-county area before a closing order was issued. The remainder of the state stayed open to hunting for an additional 20 days. Distribution of the harvest in the 7-county area was to individual hunters over a relatively large geographical area.

4. There was no evidence that the hazing operations as conducted resulted directly in migration of geese to areas farther south.

5. Compliance with the state's goose registration system was poor; it deteriorated further as the season progressed.

6. There was some evidence that the hazing broke up some family groups, making them more vulnerable to shooting.

7. Nearby state-owned areas failed to attract significant numbers of geese. The Thornton Area, under private control, doubled its usual population. On October 3, an estimated 15,000 geese were present on the 19-acre pond that is the nucleus of the management area.

Information from the goose tail-fan collection survey, plus registration compliance records, indicated that the statewide kill approximated 31,000 geese, more than twice the desired number.

The events of 1966 re-emphasized the need for cooperative federal-state management, oriented to the welfare of the goose resource and the public who is privileged to use it.

Estimating Canada Goose Kills

In 1963, a mandatory system of registration was initiated in Wisconsin. Goose hunters were required to fill out cards showing their name and address, species of goose killed, date and location of kill and the license number of the motor vehicle used during the hunt. This system was continued through 1966. Registration cards were made available at manned and unmanned checking stations. Registration cards were gathered and tallied daily which provided a crude estimate of the kill.

Compliance with the regulation requiring goose registration was checked by observing from a distance geese being loaded into automobiles. The auto license number was later checked against goose registration cards to see if the geese loaded into the car had actually been registered. The results of this comparison provided an index to compliance with the regulation requiring registration.

In order to better determine the statewide Wisconsin kill, the parts collection survey carried on by the Migratory Bird Populations Station was enlarged and improved. In this survey, a sample of waterfowl hunters are supplied with franked, addressed envelopes prior to the season. They are asked to insert into the envelopes tail feathers from each goose they killed during the season. On the face of the envelope, they entered their name, address, and location, date and time of kill. Envelopes were mailed to a central location.

The survey indicated that a significant portion of the total number of geese so reported were being killed outside the registration zone (Geis, Carney, and Hunt, 1965). It substantiated the fact that some geese being killed in the zone were not being registered. Results of the surveys revealed a total statewide kill well above the desired level of harvest (Geis and Carney, 1966):

Year	Quota for Horicon Zone	Calculated State-wide Kill
1963	12,000	20,300
1964	11,000	25,400
1965	11,000	31,800

These figures would be larger if associated crippling loss were included.

The tail-fan-registration systems analysis was intensified in 1966 to permit daily processing of all records (Carney and Geis, 1966). This enabled the Bureau to terminate, with justification, the season in the 7-county area after 2½ days of shooting, even though only 9,617 geese had been registered, and the quota for the state was 14,000. By 1966, field observations indicated that hunter compliance with goose registration had declined to about 59 percent. Clearly, another method of controlling the Wisconsin kill was urgently needed.

In 1966, preliminary examinations of the illinois kill by R. C. Hanson and H. M. Reeves through the tail-fan collection survey and band recovery analysis suggested that the statewide Illinois quota was also being exceeded but not to the extent occurring in Wisconsin. In 1967, the Illinois quota was converted from the 4-county area to a statewide basis; 10 percent of the kill has been allotted to the portion of Illinois outside the 4-county area. Probably, the deduction should be larger.

Tagging System

Many western states have used tagging as a management technique to distribute harvest of big game by time, distribution, and extent. Game managers in Colorado, Utah, and Wyoming have used tags on Canada geese to curtail excessive harvests by individual hunters. The Federal government first used tags to control harvest of migratory waterfowl in 1962 to limit the harvest of whistling swans in Utah.

Jahn (1953) suggested the use of tags at Horicon in his penetrating analysis of the Canada goose problem there. He suggested issuing 4 tags to each hunter and thereby limit their individual bag. The advantage here would be to improve the distribution of the harvest among hunters, discourage land leasing, and possibly eliminate the need for expensive public hunting areas. He recognized that this action probably would not improve the quality of the hunt because landowners would continue to attract as many hunters to their property as possible. Jahn also questioned whether a tag system could be enforced. He did not propose the issuance of a predetermined number of tags to limit the total number of geese taken.

A special meeting of the Mississippi Flyway Council was held in St. Louis, Missouri, in February, 1967, to develop management plans for the Mississippi Valley Population of Canada geese. At this meeting, the Wisconsin Conservation Department proposed a tagging system for their state. Although having much merit, the plan met with considerable opposition from landowners near Horicon and enabling legislation was not passed. Since the tagging system could not be implemented under state auspices, the Bureau of Sport Fisheries and Wildlife, acting for the Federal government, executed the Wisconsin plan with slight modifications, through a private electronic data processing firm. Major points in the plan were:

1. Only persons possessing permits and tags could hunt Canada geese.
2. Applications for the free permits were submitted during a specific time period.
3. Permits and tags were nontransferrable.
4. Three-fourths of the state's quota was allocated to the Horicon Zone. A 90 percent success rate was anticipated, so an additional 10 percent of the number of permits were allowed. Thus, 16,500 permits and tags were issued for the Horicon Zone.
5. "Party" applications for 2 hunters were authorized to encourage father and son hunting.
6. Permits for the Horicon Zone were randomly selected by computers.
7. Persons requesting permits outside the Horicon Zone would receive 2 tags valid for the entire season.
8. If they so requested, unsuccessful applicants for Horicon Zone permits would receive permits valid outside the zone.
9. Persons killing Canada geese were required to immediately lock the tag on the leg of the bird before transporting it in any way.
10. All persons issued permits were required to report tag use or nonuse in franked envelopes provided them. Successful hunters were required to report within 12 hours after killing a goose, and unsuccessful hunters were required to report within 12 hours after the close of their hunting period.
11. Each nonrespondent to the reporting requirement would receive one reminder. Following this, persons still not responding would be investigated by law enforcement officers. If warranted, prosecutions would be made.

Permits were issued in the Horicon Zone in 6 periods. Opening weekend was considered period 1. Each of the remaining periods were 7 days in length. In Period 1, 1,650 tags were issued; 2,970 tags were issued for each of the remaining periods.

The tagging system has not yet been completely evaluated, but indications are that it has achieved the desired objectives of controlling the magnitude of the kill and distributing the harvest among the maximum number of persons over an acceptable time span. It has opened to hunting lands formerly closed to the general public by lease or other arrangements, and has markedly improved the quality of the hunting experience. But it has not been well received by some local landowners, or lessees of hunting rights who have been restricted to a single goose per season.

Unusually heavy crop depredations in October and early November 1967, triggered by an extremely wet fall which delayed the harvest, has been blamed by some farmers on the light hunting pressure resulting from the tagging system. To alleviate this criticism and perhaps reduce the problem, some rearrangement in the distribution of tags may be in order, concentrating more of the hunting pressure during the time when crops are most vulnerable to depredations.

This has been a case history, and as such, does not require conclusions. However, one seems obvious: the final chapter in this story has yet to be written even though most of the problems in goose management have been encountered. Surely, much has been gained from these experiences and a sound management program is that much closer to realization.

LITERATURE CITED

CARNEY, S. M. AND A. D. GEIS, 1966. A preliminary estimate of the Canada goose kill during the first three days of the 1966 Wisconsin goose season. U.S. Fish and Wildl. Service, Admin. Rep. No. 124. 3 pp.

CRIDER, E. DALE, 1967. Canada goose interceptions in the Southeastern United States with special reference to the Florida flock. Paper presented at 21st Annu. Conf. of the Southeastern Assoc. of Game and Fish Comm. 26 pp.

DAVIS, F. H., 1954. The Horseshoe Lake flock of Canada geese and some of its management problems. Rep. filed U.S. Fish and Wildl. Serv., Minneapolis, Minn. 9 pp.

EAST, BEN, 1954. The truth about Cairo. Outdoor Life 113(3):33-35, 118-122.

ELDER, WILLIAM H. 1946. Implications of a goose concentration. Trans. N. Amer. Wildl. Conf. 11:441-446.

GEIS, AELRED D. AND S. M. CARNEY. 1966. Effectiveness of the quota system in controlling the harvest of the Mississippi Valley Canada goose flock. U.S. Fish and Wildl. Service, Admin. Rep. No. 123. 5 pp.

GEIS, AELRED D., S. M. CARNEY AND RICHARD A. HUNT. 1965. Distribution and degree of registration of the Canada goose kill in Wisconsin and Illinois, 1963 and 1964. U.S. Fish and Wildl. Service, Admin. Rep. No. 76. 9 pp.

GREEN, W. E., HARVEY K. NELSON AND CHARLES W. LEMKE. 1963. Methods for determining cumulative goose kill on special areas. U.S. Dept. Int., Spec. Sci. Rep. Wildl. 72. 43 pp.

HANKLA, D. J. AND R. R. RUDOLPH. 1967. Changes in the migration and wintering habits of Canada geese in the lower portion of the Atlantic and Mississippi Flyways with special reference to National Wildlife Refuges. Paper presented at 21st Ann. Conf. Southeastern Assoc. of Game and Fish Comm. 25 pp.

HANSON, HAROLD C. AND ROBERT H. SMITH. 1950. Canada geese of the Mississippi Flyway with special reference to an Illinois flock. Bull. Ill. Nat. History Survey 25(3): 67-210.

HUNT, RICHARD A. AND LAURENCE R. JAHN. 1966. Canada goose breeding populations in Wisconsin. Wis. Conserv. Dept., Tech. Bull. No. 38, 67 pp.

HUNT, RICHARD A., J. G. BELL AND L. R. JAHN. 1962. Managed goose hunting at Horicon Marsh. Trans. N. Amer. Wildl. and Nat. Resources Conf. 27:91-106.

JAHN, LAURENCE R. 1953. Aspects of a Canada goose management plan for Wisconsin, Part I. Wis. Conserv. Dept. 19 pp.

LEFEBVRE, EUGENE A. AND DENNIS G. RAVELING. 1967. Distribution of Canada geese in winter as related to heat loss at varying environmental temperatures. J. Wildl. Mgmt. 31:538-545.

NELSON, HARVEY K. 1962. Recent approaches to Canada geese management. U.S. Fish and Wildl. Service Spec. Sci. Rep., Wildlife 66. 25 pp.

SCHENDEL, GORDON. 1954. They call it "sport". Argosy 338(1):32-33, 73-77.